RAJASTHAN
STATE GUIDE

First Edition 2007
Copyright © Outlook Publishing (India) Private Limited, New Delhi. All Rights Reserved
Price: Rs 295
ISBN 81-89449-05-2

outlooktraveller.com
For updates, packages, news and new destinations, log on to our website
www.outlooktraveller.com

OTHER TITLES FROM OUTLOOK TRAVELLER GETAWAYS

Introducing CITY GUIDES

INTERNATIONAL TITLES FROM OUTLOOK TRAVELLER

www.outlooktraveller.com

Editorial
EDITOR-IN-CHIEF Vinod Mehta
PRESIDENT & PUBLISHER
Maheshwer Peri
DEPUTY EDITOR Manju Rastogi
ASSOCIATE EDITOR Lesley A. Esteves
ASSISTANT EDITOR Deepa A
CONSULTING EDITORS Ranee Sahaney,
Nagraj Adve

Research
INFO AND RESEARCH COORDINATORS
Mridula Bhalla, Rani G. Kalra, Julia Dutta,
A. Prabhavati
RESEARCHER-WRITER Prerna Singh
RESEARCHERS Geeta Tuteja,
Rajini Vasanth

Design
CONSULTANT ART DIRECTOR
Runu Saxena
DESIGNERS Deepak Suri, Rahul Sharma,
Ashish Rozario, Ronald Joseph
DTP COORDINATORS Rajesh K.G.,
Ganesh Shah

Graphics
Suraj Wadhwa

Photography
PHOTO EDITOR Sanjay Sharma
PHOTO COORDINATORS Kanupriya
Sisodia, Raman Pruthi, Priyam Dhar,
Kuldeep Kalia

Production
GENERAL MANAGER Anup Dwivedi
REGIONAL MANAGER Rakesh Mishra
ASSOCIATE MANAGERS Shashank Dixit,
Shekhar Pandey

Business Office
NATIONAL MANAGER Anand Dutt
NORTH Hiramoni Sarma, Arti Marwah,
Niraj Dubey
CIRCULATION Sudipto Mookherjee

Printed and published by
MAHESHWER PERI
on behalf of Outlook Publishing (India)
Private Limited from AB-10, Safdarjung
Enclave, New Delhi-110029

Printed at Infomedia India Ltd
A Wing, Ruby House, JK Sawant Marg
Dadar (West) Mumbai-400028

Dear Reader,

As a state that has captured the hearts and wallets of tourists both in India and abroad, Rajasthan has the unenviable task of constantly living up to its exotic image. Its sand dunes have to be impeccably silky, its camels content, its forts magnificent, and its palaces opulent, sumptuous or such other adjective that a travel agent decides is apt for the occasion. But, as *Outlook Traveller Getaways* discovered in the course of putting together this state guide, Rajasthan rather charmingly and effortlessly weaves together all clichés and adjectives into its colourful tapestry.

Indeed, it is this burst of colours that's most unusual for an arid landscape that once went under the decidedly lustreless name of Marusthali, or the Region of Death. Almost as if to defy that uncharitable description, Rajasthanis coloured their towns pink, green or blue; dressed in striking reds and yellows; and painted their walls with frescoes in many hues. This patchwork of distinctive colours, in such sharp contrast to the muted homogeneity of the desert, is a celebration of life in many ways. As you will discover in the pages of this book, it's a testimony to the extraordinary fortitude of ordinary people, who created towns and cities and civilisations in this most inhospitable of terrains. It's an enduring symbol of resilience, of impertinence even, intended to challenge the odds the people face everyday, be it in the form of parched earth or pouring rain. It's also what makes Rajasthan such a unique destination. Etched in its sands, along with the stories of brave warriors and beautiful queens, is a timeless ode to the indomitable human spirit that helped life blossom in a desert.

VINOD MEHTA
Editor-in-Chief

CONTENTS

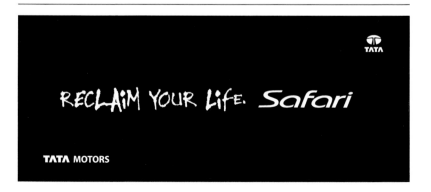

One of India's youn
has India's

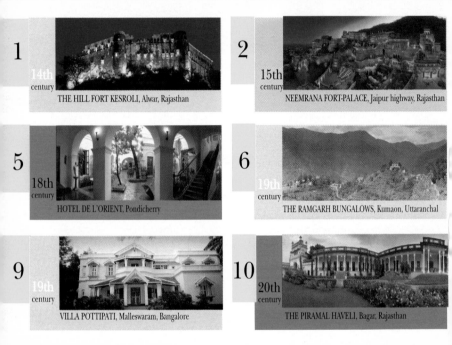

1 — 14th century — THE HILL FORT KESROLI, Alwar, Rajasthan

2 — 15th century — NEEMRANA FORT-PALACE, Jaipur highway, Rajasthan

5 — 18th century — HOTEL DE L'ORIENT, Pondicherry

6 — 19th century — THE RAMGARH BUNGALOWS, Kumaon, Uttaranchal

9 — 19th century — VILLA POTTIPATI, Malleswaram, Bangalore

10 — 20th century — THE PIRAMAL HAVELI, Bagar, Rajasthan

We don't let history become just a bygone.
Neemrana Fort-Palace, originally designed in 1464
to keep people out, was restored and refurbished in 1991
to welcome people in! Today twelve historic Neemrana properties
welcome you all over India. Each unique & ncredible!
They make the marks of exclamation stand on their head!

Be a traveller, not just a tourist in !ndia.

gest hotel chains
oldest properties !

3 **16th** century
LE COLONIAL, Cochin, Kerala

4 **17th** century
THE BUNGALOW on the BEACH, Tranquebar

7 **19th** century
VERANDAH in the FOREST, Matheran, near Mumbai

8 **19th** century
WALLWOOD GARDEN, Coonoor, Tamil Nadu

11 **20th** century
THE PATAUDI PALACE, Village Pataudi, Haryana

12 **21st** century
GLASSHOUSE on the GANGES, above Rishikesh, Uttaranchal

Re-live history: from 14th to the 21st centuries -
a panorama of 700 years !

NEEMRANA
non-hotel
HOTELS

A-58, Nizamuddin East, New Delhi-110 013, India
Tel: +91-11-41825001, 24356145, Fax: +91-11-2435 1112
e-mail: sales@neemranahotels.com, website: www.neemranahotels.com

HOW TO USE THIS BOOK

How the book is organised

The book opens with a photo feature on Rajasthan, followed by a piece on the history of the state. The destinations are arranged geographically, divided into **North**, **East**, **South-East**, **South**, **Central** and **West** sections of Rajasthan. This is followed by a section on **Wildlife**, featuring the state's wildlife sanctuaries and national parks. The **Experience** section provides an introduction to the state's culture and heritage while the **Specials** section offers interesting insights into the Rajasthani mind and ethos

Route Guide

Each of the six sections, which are arranged geographically, opens with a route guide showing the recommended routes with distances from the closest metros and, wherever applicable, from state capital Jaipur. Also highlights national and state highways

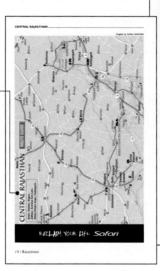

Info Box

Each destination opens with this box, which has useful information about the place's geographical location. Also highlights the distances, journey time and routes from the closest metros

Tourist Guide

Many of the destinations have their own tourist guides, showing the important roads and tourist attractions in the place, besides shopping areas and hotels

Orientation

This section has information on the layout of the destination, featuring key details such as the topographical spread of the tourist attractions, location of the airport/ railway station/ bus stand, and the most convenient modes of transport with average fares

Fast Facts
Indicates the best time to visit with reference to the climate/ season. Also lists the tourist offices at the destination or in the nearest town, with icons indicating whether only information is provided or if booking is also possible. The STD code is appended too

Shopping
Highlights the unique buys in each destination, be it a wooden toy or a lac bangle, plus the main shopping areas, popular shops and, sometimes, the average prices of items

Getting There
Provides details of air, rail and road connections, with nearest airports and railheads, and taxi fares to the destinations. Info on convenient train and bus connections as well as road conditions are given in certain cases

Where to Stay
A representative listing of the accommodation options in each destination, with details such as phone numbers and tariffs (only the lowest and highest rates are given) and the writer's comments on the pros and cons of the stay option

Where to Eat
This section highlights the culinary experience in each destination. It mentions known and little-known restaurants along with their specialities, must-try dishes and even places to pick up savouries and mithais

Around the Destination
This section lists the tourist attractions close to the destination, usually within a 50-km radius, which tourists can visit as a side-trip during their holiday

---

BUNDI — SHOPPING
Copies of the famous Bundi murals of Garh Palace on silk or paper (starting at Rs 20) are ideal souvenirs. These are available at **Bundi Art**, just inside the Garh Palace, and at other shops in Nahar ka Chotta. Bundi ladoos are said to have originated here and you can pick these up from any of the sweetshops in the bazaars for Rs 80-100 for a kilo.

For traditional Kota-Bundi School of Art miniatures, you can get in touch with artist Soni Gopal at **Mayur Art** (Tel: 0747-2447297), which is located at Nahar ka Chotta in Bundi. Gopal has been trained in the traditional style of Kota-Bundi painting which features hunting scenes, animal fights and landscapes, and makes use of red as the predominant background colour. He paints on paper, silk and marble, and can also paint as per the Jaipur School of Art. Gopal, who can be commissioned to do paintings, was chosen to do the cover illustration for a travel guide brought out by New Zealand-based travel company Indian Motorcycle Adventures (*see pix*), which arranges mobike tours in Rajasthan.

WHERE TO STAY
Bundi is a new star on the tourism horizon, and the hotel industry is keenly catching up, heritage hotel being in catch phrase. As of now, you can land up in Bundi even without reservation and find a decent place to stay.

Heritage
The best area to stay is just below the palace in the Balchand Para, with homely guest houses in havelis and old houses, some with obviously spurious claims about their age. The **Haveli Braj Bhushanjee** (Tel: 0747-2442322; Tariff: Rs 950-2,450) is a 250-year-old building that has been converted into a hotel with beautiful effect. Living in the immaculately clean, well-kept premises is like

An old painting style gets a mood look

GETTING THERE
Air Nearest airport: Sanganer, Jaipur (200 km/4 hrs). Taxi from Jaipur to Bundi costs Rs 2,000 approx
Rail Nearest railhead: Kota Junction (35 km/45 mins), on the Delhi-Mumbai rail route. Taxi to Bundi costs Rs 400
Road Bundi is located 36 km between Jaipur and Kota. The road conditions vary with rains and disrepair. There are frequent buses from Kota to Bundi and the journey by bus takes about an hour. A few buses run daily from Jaipur too and the trip takes 7-8 hrs

RAJASTHAN | 121

AJMER
Sufi's passion, which makes him forget attributes of the self. **Dargah Office** Tel: 0145-2429095, 2623948. You have to park your vehicle else Rs 20 outside Delhi Gate and walk for 5 mins down the bazaar for it.

Other sights
Walk 5 mins down a congested alley to the left of the dargah entrance and see the exquisitely carved 12th century **Adhai-Din-ka-Jhonpra**, built by Qutubuddin Aibak and completed by Iltutmish. Its name literally translates as the two-and-a-half-day-shed, and it is a relic of the largest mosque in the country, ordered by the invader Muhammad Ghori to be readied in this short time. A later example of Mughal architecture is the white structure of **Abdullah Khan's Tomb**.

There are also charming picnic spots in the vicinity. These include **Ana Sagar** (open 8 am-5 pm), an artificial lake; **Ajaipal**, where the founder of Ajmer retired after his reign; and **Foy Sagar**, another artificial lake under Nasirabad town. Visitors are allowed to see the museum on the premises of **Mayo College**, on request.

Also on the tourist's itinerary is the unbelievably ornate Golden Hall of **Jain Nasiyan Temple**, located near Ana Sagar. It is replete with gold models of the life of Tirthankara Adinath. The **Taragarh Fort** (open all day) is 5 km from town.

SHOPPING
Ajmer's specialities deal with religion, so you will find interesting **metal ware** in the form of pitchers and urns. Visitors from the region always make sure they have room to carry back with them the **cane chairs** and **moodas** that are part of the essential furniture in any verandah. Naturally, you can hardly return without a concentrate of *attar*, amply found in the Dargah Bazaar for Rs 50 upwards. Also available are **chaadars** for the dargah (between Rs 500 and 5,000), and cheap CDs of qawwalis and dargah tours.

FAST FACTS
When to go The winter season is best, but Kishangarh can be charming during the rains. Summer is best avoided
Tourist office
» *Rajasthan Tourism* @
Tourist Reception Centre
Hotel Khadim (RTDC), Ajmer
Tel: 0145-2627426
STD code 0145

WHERE TO STAY
Ajmer can claim to have the best hotels in the region, and their advantage is that they operate round the year. **Hotel Mansingh Palace** (Tel: 0145-2425702/ 855/ 857; Tariff: Rs 3,000-7,500), near the lake in Vaishali Nagar, is Ajmer's finest hotel. Boasting its own shopping arcade, the hotel also arranges folk dances, fireworks and sightseeing tours. **Hotel Embassy** (Tel: 2623859, 4100775; Tariff: Rs 850-2,500), opposite the Power House on NH8 (Jaipur Road), is another fine hotel offering rooms with all the important facilities, including complimentary transfers from the railway station. RTDC's **Hotel Khadim** (Tel: 2627490/ 536; Tariff: Rs 400-2,000), adjoining the bus stand, has a wide variety of rooms accommodating all budgets. The added advantage is the travel desk and tourist information centre here. **Hotel Ambassador** (Tel: 2420595, 2428479; Tariff: Rs 600-2,950) on Ashok Marg in Nagina Bagh is a good option. **Hotel Regency** (Tel: 2620296, 2622439; Tariff: Rs 450-1,500), near Delhi Gate, is a simple set-up, but well-located at walking distance from the Dargah Sharif, and 1 km from the bus stand and railway station. **Hotel Sahil** (Tel: 2632994/95; Tariff: Rs 500-2,000) nearby is a budget option with

RAJASTHAN | 185

WEST RAJASTHAN — DUNGARPUR
shops selling handicrafts. Their prices seem to have a margin for bargaining.

WHERE TO STAY
Jaisalmer has many staying options inside and outside the fort. While staying inside the fort can be romantic, the accommodation here is more basic. Besides, vehicles go only till the main courtyard of the fort, and the luggage needs to be carried manually till the hotel. Staying inside the fort also increases the pressure on the infrastructure of the fort and contributes to its degradation. Visitors are therefore being urged to make the ethical choice of staying outside the fort. Also, do remember that in high season, most good hotels are booked much in advance.

Heritage
The hotels and guest houses in the fort are small establishments, and are mostly converted old houses and havelis. **Hotel Killa Bhawan** (Tel: 02992-251204; Tariff: Rs 2,700-5,500) is a small place with beautiful *d cor* and a great location. **Hotel Jaisal Castle** (Tel: 252362; Tariff: Rs 1,500-2,000) is situated high on the ramparts with spacious but rundown rooms. **Desert Boys Guest House** (Tel: 253091; Tariff: Rs 450-1,500) is a family-run place and some of their rooms are later additions to an older residence. There are good views and clean rooms but some of the rooms are not very well ventilated.

Narayan Niwas Palace (Tel: 251901-04; Tariff: Rs 3,500-5,500) in Malka Prol, near Jain Bhawan, is a 19th-century ancestral property converted and restored into a luxurious heritage hotel. It is within walking distance of most of the major sights in the citadel. A meal at their rooftop restaurant is among the most special you can have, with views of the golden city and the sand dunes beyond.

Others
Fort Rajwada (Tel: 253233; Tariff: Rs 4,100-12,000) is a lavish place with ornate architecture and interiors, situated about 3 km from the Jaisalmer Fort. The yellow sandstone **Hotel Himmatgarh Palace** (Tel: 252002-04; Tariff: Rs 2,500-3,500), located on the Ramgarh Road opposite Dessaur Ground, has very interesting cottages shaped like the huts of rural Kutch. Inside, the rooms are spacious and well

Priceless buys: Patwon-ki-Haveli has a shop that stocks textiles

24 | RAJASTHAN

DUNGARPUR

Good food and a great view at the Udai Bilas Palace (above). A painted spot (left)

For more details see Dungarpur Accommodation Listings on page 462

WHERE TO EAT
The **Udai Bilas Palace** is the obvious place to eat. Non-resident guests are also welcome. They mainly have buffets, which are predominantly Indian. You can have a variety of sumptuous meat dishes and such vegetable preparations. Charges for meals are: breakfast Rs 250, lunch Rs 400 and dinner Rs 450. Some Continental, Chinese and Indian dishes feature in the *la carte* menu. The meals can be served either in the banquet hall or the more intimate dining hall. Weather permitting, the outdoor restaurant next to the pool is ideal for a drink or an unhurried meal. The town centre has some small restaurants and dhabas.

AROUND DUNGARPUR
Rishabdeo (41 km N)
An important pilgrimage site just off NH8, Rishabdeo is a captivating place.

The origins of the temple here are unknown but there is evidence of some repairs having been done in the 15th century. The temple is built of grey *pareva* stone with beautiful white marble carvings. The multi-pillared hall has an extraordinary intensity about it. In the centre is a big idol of black marble. Interestingly, Jains, Hindus and Bhils worship the deity in their own ways. For Jains the deity is Rishabdeo, also called Adinath, their first Tirthankara. For Hindus the deity is Kesariyaji, a reincarnation of Vishnu. Bhils worship the icon as their Kala Deo, the Black Lord. The temple is also famous as Kesariya Temple because *kesar* (saffron) is the chief offering made to the deity here. Taxi fare will be Rs 800 for a return-trip. **Timings** 6 am-9.30 pm.

Deo Somnath Temple (26 km NE)
When you reach Deo Gaon, a small village famous for its Shiva temple, the first thing you notice is not the temple but an incredible banyan tree. The huge tree seems as old as the temple and its canopy is spacious enough to function as a village

RAJASTHAN | 195

EAST RAJASTHAN

Curse cure

Fauna
A box appended to the destinations in the Wildlife section, listing the mammals, birds, insects and reptiles in the park, with emphasis on the rare or endangered species

Park Guide
Sketches of parks indicate their entry points, road routes within and around the park, directions to closest towns, location of Forest Rest Houses and private properties

USP Box
A short feature that either highlights a unique attraction in the destination, such as a temple known for ridding evil spirits in Kalakho, or presents an interesting insight, such as the opium trade that was the source of Bundi's riches

Specials
Interesting reads that will enhance the reader's understanding of Rajasthan, dwelling on unique facets such as the state's nomadic tribes and folk tale and puppetry traditions

Experience
This section introduces the reader to the rich culture and heritage of Rajasthan, and presents ways in which the tourist can experience its richness: by staying at a palace turned into a hotel, watching a folk music or dance performance, or stepping into the state's painted havelis

The camel ride guide

ABHILASH GAUR goes on a camel safari and lives to tell the tale

Till death do us part

Where Romeo and Juliet ride into the sunset on camelback

BY KISHORE SINGH

An artist's rendition of Dhola-Maru, Rajasthan's most beloved folk tale

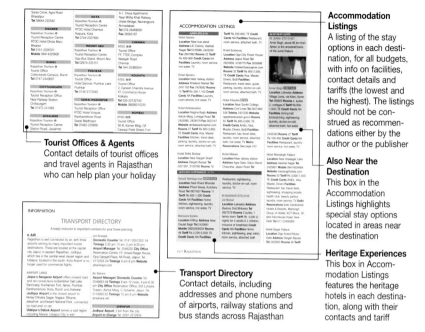

Accommodation Listings
A listing of the stay options in each destination, for all budgets, with info on facilities, contact details and tariffs (the lowest and the highest). The listings should not be construed as recommendations either by the author or the publisher

Also Near the Destination
This box in the Accommodation Listings highlights special stay options located in areas near the destination

Heritage Experiences
This box in Accommodation Listings features the heritage hotels in each destination, along with their contacts and tariff

Tourist Offices & Agents
Contact details of tourist offices and travel agents in Rajasthan who can help plan your holiday

Transport Directory
Contact details, including addresses and phone numbers of airports, railway stations and bus stands across Rajasthan

Go there for...
Lists the state's main attractions under broad heads such as Wildlife, Forts and Palaces, among others

Feedback
We hope you find this book useful. We welcome your comments and suggestions as to how we can make it even more user-friendly. Please do fill in the Feedback Form at the back of the book so that we can incorporate the best suggestions in the next edition. You will also receive email updates on special offers, travel features and news from our website outlooktraveller.com

→ Route/ Tourist Guide Legend

⌄	Distance in km	⊙	Arounds	⋈	Bridge		Dargah
65	NH Number	◎	Other Places		Gate/ Pol		Temple
=	National Highway	▣	District Capital		Water Body		Church
—	Road		Hotel/ FRH		Clock Tower		Masjid/ Mosque
▭	District Boundary		Camping	✉	Post Office		National Park/ WLS
····	State Boundary	▣	Restaurant		Bank		Palace
┼┼┼	International Boundary	✈	Airport	⊕	Hospital		Cave
▫▫▫	Train Route		Railway Station	⚠	Tourist/ Info Centre		Camel Safari
⊙	Destination		Bus Station	ℝ	Range Office		
☀	Tourist Places		Petrol Pump		Fort		

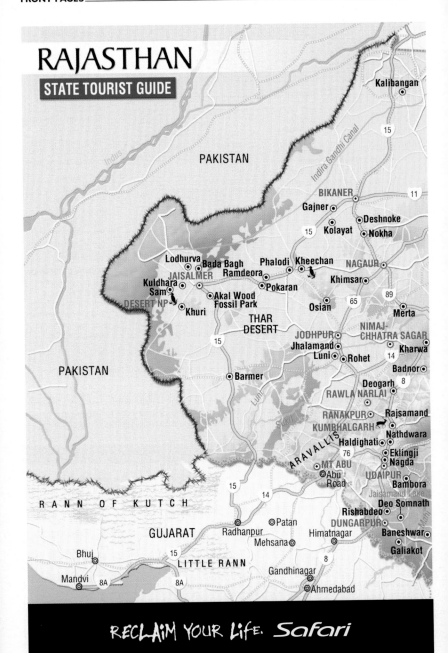

RAJASTHAN
STATE TOURIST GUIDE

RECLAIM YOUR Life. Safari

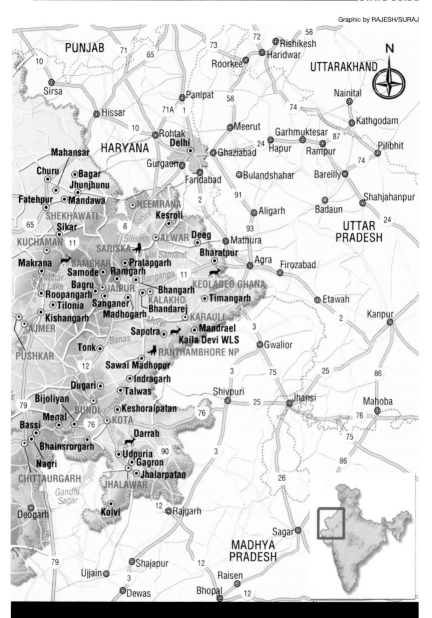

Graphic by RAJESH/SURAJ

RECLAiM YOUR Life. *Safari*

When the battlelines are drawn: A miniature painting seen in a fort

The idea of Rajasthan

How history defied geography to create the state that we see today

■ BY DILBAGH SINGH

We are so used to the image of 'Rajasthan' as the land of the Rajputs (Rajputana), the land of the kings (Raethan or Rajasthan), or the region of death (Marusthali) that we tend to forget that it does not make for a natural geographical region — the Aravallis forming its middle rib separate two absolutely distinct geographical zones. On the west and north-west of the Aravallis is the Thar or the greater Marwar, the desert where it is mostly level country. Here rainfall does not exceed 254 mm; vegetation is stunted and thorny and open scrub; and sand and sand dunes abound. To the south and south-east of the Aravallis, hill-spurs slope down towards tablelands scarred by valleys; the rainfall rises to 508 mm and above; tree clusters merge into true jungle; and rock and alluvium alternate.

South-eastern and eastern Rajasthan was prominent in ancient Indian history. It appears in references to Maccha or Matsya, one of the 16 *mahajanapadas* or kingdoms; in Ashoka's rock inscription at Bairat; and in the Gupta gold-coin hoard at

AMIT PASRICHA

Bayana. The Thar on the other hand appears more as a geographical expression; it's 'Maru' in ruler Rudradaman's inscription at Junagadh while the desert's two outposts of Abu and Pushkar are mentioned in pre-Gupta inscriptions. For the rest, if epigraphic sources are to be believed, the land was terra-incognita, with little to contribute to economic or political history. With the seventh century, however, the Thar sprung to historical life. Yuan Chwang, journeying through it in 643 CE, describes the Gurjara kingdom.

Beyond the Rajput connection

Historians of all hues associate medieval Rajasthan with the Rajputs. This image is so deep-rooted that one tends to overlook the history of Rajasthan's pre-Rajput ruling tribes. Dungar Bhil, Bansia Bhil and Kotia Bhil tribes dominated parts of south-eastern Rajasthan at one time. The Meenas, also one of the major aboriginal tribes of Rajasthan, had their settlements in south-west and north-eastern Rajasthan.

Subjugating the Meenas was an essential stage in the emergence of Rajput polity in various parts of Rajasthan. One of the earliest recorded encounters was at Mandore in the 12th century, where Prithviraj Chauhan fought against them in order to capture the place. Muhta Nainsi, a mid-17th century historian of Marwar, implied that the Meenas did not accept the norms laid down by the victorious Rajputs and continued to create trouble in various ways. The Rathores, Kachhwahas and the Hada Chauhans later on succeeded the earlier tribal chiefdoms of the Bhil, Med and Meena.

With the decline of the Gupta period, a newer political apparatus and a newer ruling class — namely the Rajputs — emerged. From the seventh century onwards, Rajput ruling families dominated the history of Rajasthan. The origin of Rajputs is a red herring that has taken up much space in historical writings on early medieval and medieval India. The writings reveal an extreme polarity of opinions. Some attempt to trace the Rajputs to foreign immigrant stock of the post-Gupta period, explaining in the process a legendary myth about their origin. As the Rajputs are called the Agnikula (clans which originated from a sacrificial fire), some claim the fire association came from a purification rite performed for those with immigrant blood. Others offer contrived justifications for viewing the Rajputs as of pure Kshatriya origin.

Much more convincing is an approach that treats the emergence of the Rajputs as an inter-connected political, economic and social process.

The argument is that the Rajputs had a miscellaneous origin (from mixed castes); the criterion for a group to be included in the list of Rajput clans came from the status of the clan, this being the case at least in the early stages of the crystallisation of Rajput power. These clans, in turn, qualified for the prized Rajput status by either of the following means: through their role in colonising land with potentially subordinate peasantry, or by the acquisition of political power by force or through upward mobility.

The Gurjara-Pratihara Rajputs were the first to make their presence felt in the political field of Rajasthan during the early medieval period. They rapidly extended their political control over much of northern and western India. Under Bhoja (836-885 CE), the Gurjara-Pratihara empire extended from the Sind to the lower Ganges Valley, and from the Himalayan foothills to the Narmada River. Although rival clans such as the Chauhan, Parihara and Guhila rose to prominence

We are neglecting the history of the state's ruling tribes by associating medieval Rajasthan solely with the Rajputs

in Rajasthan following the disintegration of the Gurjara-Pratihara empire towards the end of the 10th century, major centres of Rajput power continued to exist throughout North India. Yet it is Rajasthan that is identified with Rajputs and the Rajput ethos.

The rise and fall of powers
The decline of the Gurjara-Pratihara empire paved the way for the rise of the Chauhans. They dominated south-eastern and central Rajasthan. The area near Sapadlaksha or Shakambhri (Sambhar) became the epi-

centre of the Chauhans. The events towards the end of the 12th century, however, drastically altered the power of the Chauhans. The Muslim conquest of India following Prithviraj Chauhan's defeat at the hands of Muhammad Ghori, during the second battle of Tarain in 1192, led to the end of Chauhan power in Rajasthan. The land of the conquered Chauhans was incorporated into the Delhi Sultanate, and from this base, Qutubuddin Aibak, who succeeded Muhammad Ghori in 1206, made repeated attempts to subdue the Rajput clans of Rajasthan.

Yet, Prithviraj Chauhan's defeat did not mean the extinction of Chauhan rule. Various branches of the Chauhan clan continued to rule over Ranthambhore, Nadol, Jalor and Sirohi. When Qutubuddin Aibak occupied Nadol, the Chauhans were forced to migrate to Sanchor and Jalor. Allauddin Khalji captured both Ranthambhore and Jalor. A branch of the Nadol Chauhans migrated to the south-eastern part of Mewar and, under Mankik Raj II, founded a new principality with Bambavada as its capital. One of Mankik Raj's descendants was Harraj or Hadarao, whose descendants in turn came to be known as Hada Chauhan. Rao Deva granted Bambavada to his son Harraj and proceeded to Bundo Nal (Bundi). Deva, with the help of the Rana of Mewar (Rana Arsi), destroyed the Meenas and occupied Bundo Nal. The territories of Bambavada were also merged into the newly carved-out Bundi state. Subsequently, the Hadas subjugated the Bhil chief Kotia and extended the boundaries of Bundi up to the Bhil-dominated area of Kota. In between, the Ranas of Mewar controlled this region. Ultimately Rao Surjan accepted the overlordship of the Mughal Emperor Akbar and surrendered the fort of Ranthambhore to the Mughals. During the Mughal Emperor Shahjahan's reign, the principality of Kota was separated from Bundi and Rao Madho Singh was appointed as the ruler of Kota.

Mewar, earlier known as Medpat, was dominated by the Med tribe. The Guhilas subjugated them in the 7th century. Guhil, the founder of Mewar state, assumed sovereignty with the help of the Bhils of Ider. All traditional accounts pertaining to Mewar indicate that the rulers of Mewar utilised the services of the Bhils for territorial expansion. In 1326, Rana Hamir succeeded in recapturing Chittaur — it had been taken over by Allauddin Khalji. Mewar became the most powerful state of Rajasthan during the reign of Maharana Kumbha, who also fought with the Sultans of Gujarat and Malwa.

The Kachhwahas of Amber claim to have descended from Kusha, the son of Lord Ram. Dhola Rai, son of Sodhdeo, the prince of Narwar, laid the foundation of the state of Dhundhar, or Amber, in 966 CE. He acquired Dausa from the Badgujars and expelled the Meenas from Machi and Khoh. His son Kakil, who ascended the *gaddi* in 1036, wrested Amber from the Meenas. The place remained the Kachhwaha capital for about 700 years. In 1562, Amber ruler Bharmal accepted the overlordship of Akbar.

The Rathore kingdom of Marwar came into existence towards the end of the 13th century through the adventurous moves of Rao Asthan, son of Rao Siha of Kannauj, who decided to migrate to western India to seek his fortune. He set off towards Gujarat with two of his brothers. While encamping near Pali, he protected the Brahman traders of Pali and the Chaudharis of nearby villages from the depredation of Kanha Med,

Painting of Rajput ruler Rana Pratap

AMIT PASRICHA

who had rights as thakurs over Pali. Asthan gradually built up a band of Rajput followers and acquired the resources necessary for ruling Pali. Thereafter began the process of further conquest and colonisation, which continued under Asthan's successors at an uneven pace. The Rathores are credited with having acquired fresh territories at the cost of Guhils of Khed and Panwars of Barmer. Their capital Mandore was ultimately moved to Jodhpur (the last shift was by Rao Jodha).

Rao Bika, Rao Jodha's son, founded the Rathore principality of Bikaner. Rao Jodha persuaded Bika to carve out an independent kingdom for himself and in the long process of state formation, he fought Mohils, Johyas, Bhattis and Sankhla Rajputs, among others.

Devraj was the founder of the ruling dynasty of the Bhattis in the 11th century. He made Lodhurva the capital but Rao Jaisal shifted the capital to Jaisalmer. The Bhattis clashed often with the neighbouring states of Sind, Multan, Marwar and Bikaner. Jaisalmer was also invaded by the Khaljis. Rao Bhim accepted the Mughal imperial service during Akbar's reign.

The initial stage

It is evident that the several new states were relatively unstable in their initial

DINESH SHUKLA

phase of formation. Environmental constraints inhibited the growth of a large population in Rajasthan and as a result, the economic base was not strong enough to sustain these states. Not only were there continuous attempts to expand their dominions, they even shifted to newer places for better prospects. The Guhilots, who were initially based at Nagda, shifted to Valabh and finally settled in the more fertile region of Mewar. The Rathores shifted from Pali to Khed and later on to Mandore. The Bhattis initially inhabited Lodhurva and later on moved to Jaisalmer.

Initially, there was not much legal recognition of the power of the new rulers. In order to consolidate power at the local level, Rajputs, traders and peasants belonging to the middling castes were induced to migrate to territories conquered by Rajput chiefs. Brahmans, Charans and Bhats were patronised and they glorified the ruling clan. A code of conduct and a value system was evolved for the Rajputs to differentiate them from the other castes.

For some four centuries, in addition to the internecine conflicts within Rajasthan, there were also clashes between the Sultans of Delhi and the Rajputs in Rajasthan. The popular perception of Rajputs as chivalrous warriors arises from this time. In bardic accounts, the Rajput's authority is connected to the fact that he is a special king, a soldier more effective than other soldiers. One must remember that in all bardic traditions, the Rajput was always a horseman; the bull-and-horseman coinage of Rajput dynasties also reflects this equestrian ideal.

The use of horses by the Rajputs in the context of their conflicts with tribal chiefs is significant. Harraj Panwar is portrayed as a single mounted horseman and yet able to savage the

SANJAY SHARMA

Chittaurgarh Fort (above); **A fresco of a ruler at Dungarpur** (left)

land of Meenas of Bundi at will. The failure of the Meenas to check his onslaught depicted the power that a mounted horseman could exercise against a whole group of people unfamiliar with the use of horse or a war machine. The revival of the military reputation of the Rajputs under Rana Kumbha, Rao Maldeo and Rana Sanga doubtless lay in the fact that the Rajputs fully realised the effectiveness of mounted horsemen in the battlefield. One could almost argue that just when the Rajputs had mastered this form of warfare, they were undone by a new element, artillery, of which they had as yet no inkling.

The Mughal influence

Prior to the Mughal conquest, political organisation in Rajput states centred on the little kingdoms of the important members of the clan and their followers. The inherent rights of the clan members in their miniature states formed the basis of political authority as well as distribution of resources. In this structure of polity, the Rajput clan state could hardly be viewed as a cohesive territory with a centralised authority and it was bound to generate intra-clan conflicts that would considerably weaken the Rajput states. Two pillars of the Mughal-Rajput alliance, the rulers of Amber and Bikaner, faced numerous problems from the members of their own clan. Intra-clan tussles in Marwar during Maldeo's reign and his successor Chandrasen's reign led to the intervention of the Mughals. Akbar grasped the problems arising from the clannish structure and took advantage of its weakness while formulating his Rajput policy.

Through a combination of military action and diplomacy, Akbar succeeded in enlisting many of the prominent Rajput chiefs into his service, cementing alliances through marriage with ruling Rajput families. Mughal troops still faced Rajputs in the battlefield, as at Chittaur and Ranthambhore and in Marwar, but by 1572, with the exception of Mewar, all the Rajput rulers accepted the overlordship of Akbar. Following the death of Rana Udai Singh, Akbar made a concerted effort to bring his son and successor, Rana Pratap Singh, into the Mughal imperial system. Rana Pratap did not agree and by 1576 he embarked on a lifelong course of armed resistance to Mughal hegemony. Ultimately Jehangir succeeded in securing the submission of Rana Amar Singh, Rana Pratap's son and successor.

Indeed, much of the success and stability of the Mughals depended on the willing cooperation of the Rajputs, who served the empire with distinction as military commanders, provincial governors and advisors. The Mughal imperial service enhanced the prestige of the Rajput rulers. The imperial umbrella helped them in overcoming intra and inter-clan disunity, by more or less transferring the rivalries from the battlefield to the imperial court. The quantitative aspect of Rajput participation in the Mughal empire is revealed by the fact that in 1595 they constituted about 17 per cent of the total number of higher Mughal nobles and in 1656-57 about 19 per cent.

In spite of the 1679-81 Rajput rebellion during Aurangzeb's reign and the Rajput princes' support for Prince Azam Shah in the war of succession of 1707-08, the attachment of the Rajput principalities to the Mughal empire remained fairly firm until 1739, when Nadir Shah's invasion shattered all illusions about the empire. However, it may be noted that even after their integration into the Mughal empire, the Rajput states had managed to maintain a discreet, albeit subordinate political existence. In doing so, they preserved much of their Rajput heritage in terms of cultural tradition, elements of which survived relatively unaltered until the middle of the 20th century.

The idea of Rajasthan

The Mughals can be credited with having been the first ones to draw a boundary around the region approximating the modern state of Rajasthan. In 1594, they grouped together all the Rajput states subdued by Akbar to form the *subah* (province) of Ajmer. Although it is doubtful that the Rajputs or any other inhabitants of the area at that time shared any sense of belonging to a regional entity, the *subah* of Ajmer was created as a political space and represented the first formal delineation of Rajasthan encompassing the Rajput states.

The *subah* of Ajmer reappeared under a different guise during the British period. Though the Rajput states of Rajasthan remained outside direct British rule, they were eventually brought under British hegemony in the aftermath of the Maratha wars.

The Maratha intervention itself happened at a time when in the face of the waning Mughal imperial authority in Rajasthan, there was a revival of the pre-Mughal Rajput polity marked by inter and intra-clan feuds. The Maratha chiefs, especially Sindhia and Holkar as well as the Pindaris, squeezed Rajput states and created a feeling of helplessness. Taking advantage of the situation, the English stepped forward in 1818 as the protectors of the Rajput states. The princely states of Rajasthan were grouped under the Rajputana Agency, which was later renamed the Rajputana Province.

From retelling this story, it's clear that the formal outlines of a political Rajasthan were established under Emperor Akbar but it was reaffirmed by an independent India in the middle of the 20th century. This persistence of Rajasthan as a discrete political space, over almost four centuries, suggests an underlying unity that originates in the shared history and common traditions of the Rajput states in the region. ■

a window
to
Rajasthan

Towns and streets dress up in pinks and blues, turbans and skirts sport the brightest hues, and a desert land comes to life

RAHUL SHARMA/INDIAPICTURE

The face that holds a million dreams: A boy peeps out of a makeshift window

Turbanator tales (above); **Murals enliven the walls of the Morarka Haveli, Shekhawati** (right)

AMIT PASRICHA

GIREESH GV

Rainbows on earth: Women at a village (above) **and the colours of the Karni Fort, Bambora** (left)

SARVESH

Powerpuff lady enjoys a smoke

Men add colour to their lives and garb

NANDAN SAXENA

The ship of the desert on NH8 (above); **Knives out for a worthy cause** (right)

DINODIA PHOTO LIBRARY

A blue Bundi reflects the sky (above); **Holy smoke envelops Pushkar** (left)

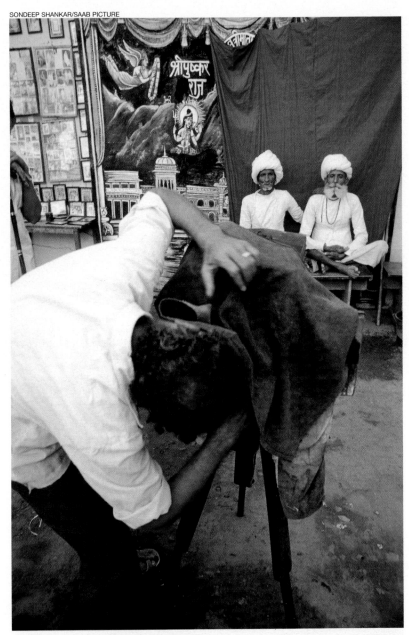

Say cheese: A shot from the Pushkar Fair

SELECT CIRCUITS IN RAJASTHAN

A few itineraries to help you plan your holiday better plus four offbeat circuits for those interested in Rajasthan's arts and crafts

9 HOT CIRCUITS

- **Golden Triangle**
  Delhi-Agra-Jaipur
  2N/ 3D
- **Desert Circuit**
  Bikaner-Jodhpur-Jaisalmer-Barmer
  4N/ 5D
- **Mewar Circuit**
  Udaipur-Rajsamand-Chittaurgarh
  4N/ 5D
- **Hadoti Circuit**
  Bundi-Kota-Jhalawar
  3N/ 4D
- **Mewat-Brij Circuit**
  Alwar-Bharatpur-Sawai Madhopur-Tonk
  3N/ 4D
- **Merwara Circuit**
  Ajmer-Pushkar-Merta-Nagaur 3N/ 4D
- **Vagad Circuit**
  Dungarpur-Banswara 2N/ 3D
- **Dhundar Circuit**
  Jaipur-Dausa 2N/ 3D
- **Shekhawati Circuit**
  Jaipur-Sikar-Jhunjhunu-Churu
  (havelis and palaces) 5N/ 6D

4 SPECIAL CIRCUITS

Jewellery Circuits
- Udaipur-Nathdwara-Pratapgarh
- Jaipur-Bikaner-Jodhpur-Jaisalmer

Jaipur is known for meenakari and kundan jewellery and semi-precious stones while Pratapgarh is famous for delicate thewa work (gold filigree on glass). Nathdwara and Udaipur are known for silver enamel and kundan work, Bikaner for meenakari, Jodhpur for kundan, lac, beaded and old silver jewellery, and Jaisalmer for silver jewellery.

Textile Circuits
- Alwar-Jaipur-Sanganer-Bagru-Sikar-Jhunjhunu
- Jodhpur-Bikaner-Barmer
- Udaipur-Nathdwara

Sanganer is known for block printing and khari work; Bagru for printed textiles made using vegetable dyes; Barmer for geometric Ajrak prints; Nathdwara for pichhwai-style designs in quilt covers, scarves and saris. Bandhani (tie and dye)

OTG ITINERARIES

Alwar-Sariska-Bhangarh
Neemrana-Delhi 2N/ 3D
- Siliserh-Sariska-Bhangarh-
  Ajaibgarh-Pratapgarh-
  Delhi 2N/ 3D
- Alwar-Sariska-Bharatpur-
  Deeg-Dholpur 2N/ 3D

Kalakho-Bhandarej-Delhi
1N/ 2D

Ajmer-Kishangarh-Roopan-
garh Fort-Badnor-Tilonia
2N/ 3D

Karauli-Sawai Madhopur-
Ranthambhore NP-Tonk
3N/ 4D

Jaipur-Amber-Jaigarh
Nahargarh-Sanganer-Bagru-
Ramgarh Lake-Samode
Abhaneri-Sambhar Lake
Kuchaman Fort 4N/ 5D
- Jaipur-Abhaneri-Sambhar
  Lake-Kuchaman Fort
  2N/ 3D

Nagaur-Khimsar-Nokha
2N/ 3D

DINODIA PHOTO LIBRARY

Kota-Bundi-Menal 2N/ 3D
- Kota-Bundi-Jhalawar 2N/ 3D
- Kota-Bardoli-Bhainsrorgarh -
  Darrah Wildlife Sanctuary-
  Baran 3N/ 4D

Shekhawati-Jaipur-Mandawa
Mukundgarh-Dundlod-
Nawalgarh-Bagar-Bissau-
Mehansar 4N/ 5D

Udaipur-Eklingji-Nagda-Devi
Garh-Haldighati-Nathdwara-
Rajsamand 2N/ 3D
- Udaipur-Kumbhalgarh-
  Jaisamand Lake-Ranakpur
  3N/ 4D
- Udaipur-Chittaurgarh-
  Kumbhalgarh-Rawla Narlai
  3N/ 4D

Chittaurgarh-Bassi-Bijaipur-
Menal 2N/ 3D

Kumbhalgarh-Ranakpur-
Rajsamand Lake 2N/ 3D

Mount Abu-Udaipur-
Chittaurgarh 4N/ 5D

Dungarpur-Baneshwar-
Bhuvaneshwar 2N/ 3D

Bikaner-Deshnoke-Gajner-
Kolayat-Kalibangan 3N/ 4D

Jodhpur-Balsamand Lake-
Mandore-Kailana Lake-Osian-
Nagaur-Rohetgarh-Luni Fort
6N/ 7D
- Jodhpur-Osian-Mandore-
  Khejarli-Luni-Sardar
  Samand-Kheechan 3N/ 4D
- Jodhpur-Osian-Pokaran-
  Jaisalmer-Barmer 4N/ 5D

Jaisalmer-Lodhurva-Akal-
Sam-Desert NP 3N/ 4D

work in leheriyas (diagonal stripes), mothda
(checks), ekdali (small circles and squares) and
shikari (human and animal motifs) are seen in
Sikar, Jaipur, Jodhpur, Bikaner, Barmer, Udaipur
and Nathdwara. Kota is famed for its ancient
tradition of delicate mahsuria muslin (Kota doria)
saris and fabrics. Mirror work on fabric can be
found in Sikar and Jhunjhunu, Alwar (chain-stitch
motifs of flora and fauna, the Mandala and Tree of
Life) and in Barmer, where they use geometric
designs in herringbone and satin stitch.

NANDAN SAXENA

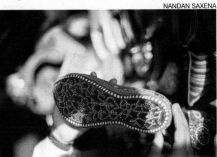

Crafts Circuits
- Alwar-Jaipur-Bikaner-Jodhpur-Jaisalmer-
  Pokaran
- Shekhawati Region
- Udaipur-Nathdwara-Kishangarh-Bassi-Tilonia

Alwar is known for Kagzi (paper-thin) pottery,
Jaipur for blue pottery, Pokaran for white and red
items with geometric designs, and Bikaner for
painted pottery. Jodhpur and Barmer are known
for carved doors and windows. The painted furniture of Jodhpur, Kishangarh, Tilonia, Ramgarh,
Shekhawati and Bikaner are also prized buys.
Mojris can be bought from Jaipur, Jodhpur,
Jaisalmer and Bikaner. Jaipur is famous for enam-
elled brassware and sculptures; Alwar and Jaipur
also have koftagari, which is damascening work
done on swords. Jaipur is also known for white
marble sculptures, and Dungarpur for soft pink
sandstone and soft chlorite craft. The best places
to pick up toys are Jaipur, Bassi and Merta.
Jaisalmer is known for its puppets.

Painting Circuits
- Jaipur-Bhilwara-Udaipur-Nathdwara-
  Kishangarh
- Shekhawati Region ■

HIDDEN GEMS OF RURAL
RAJASTHAN

TODA RAI SINGH
BEAUTIFUL BAOLIS

Founded in the 4th century and called by several names, including Takshakpur, Todapattan and Ishtikapur, Toda Rai Singh received its current name in honour of the Rajput Toda Rai Singh, who was a Mughal mansabdar during the time of Mughal Emperor Shahjahan. Its historical past is still evidenced in the town, which boasts a number of fascinating sights.

There are many sights to see here such as Raja Rai Singh's palace and several beautiful temples. The palace is a grand, yet eloquent, affair. The temples are from ancient times, when the Nagas, Guhilas of Chatsu and Chauhans of Ajmer used to rule the area. The ancient Usha Temple, or temple of the dawn, is especially beautiful.

However, the most unusual sights are the baolis: the Hadi Rani ki Baoli, the Isar Baoli, and the Bhopat Baoli. These step-wells were designed to collect rain water and were essential in dry desert areas like Rajasthan.

Toda Rai Singh is 94 km from RTDC's Hotel Khadim (Tel: 0145-2627490; Rates Rs 400-2,000) at Ajmer.

SHRI MAHAVIRJI
CALLING THE FAITHFUL

A beautiful red sandstone and white marble Jain temple, dedicated to Shri Mahavir, graces this town. The origins of the temple have to do with a cowherd whose cow would return home every evening with its udders empty. Curious, the cowherd followed his cow, only to discover that it voluntarily gave up its milk at particular spot. Upon digging that spot, the cowherd discovered an idol of Mahavir. Thus was the temple born. Pilgrims throng to a fair held here every March, when scores of handicraft stalls spring up.

Shri Mahavirji is 85 km from RTDC's Hotel Saras (Tel: 05644-223700; Rates: Rs 350-900) in Bharatpur.

BAYANA
DUAL HERITAGE

A curious mixture of Hindu and Muslim relics and ruins characterises Bayana, which rose to prominence in the Mughal era, situated as it is near the two Mughal capitals of Agra and Delhi. Ancient temples sit side-by-side with medieval Muslim architecture.

An ancient fort , Bijaigarh, crowns Bayana. The fort contains several temples and a pillar that indicates that Bayana used to belong to the kingdom of Samudragupta. Babur called it India's most formidable fort. Though the fort is now in ruins, one can still see why.

Bayana is 45 km from RTDC's Hotel Saras (Tel: 05644-223700; Rates: Rs 350-900) in Bharatpur.

HIDDEN GEMS OF RURAL RAJASTHAN

BAIRAT

MAHABHARAT-ERA TOWN

Bairat, earlier known as Viratnagar, has been an important town from ancient times, though today it is among the quieter parts of Jaipur District. Remains of a Buddhist monastery, Asokan inscriptions, and a beautiful Jain temple speak of antiquity in this deserted place. The Pandavas, of the Mahabharata, are fabled to have spent a year of their exile in Viratnagar.

Various places of interest proliferate Bairat. Bhima, one of the Pandavas, is said to have made his home in cave on a hill near Bairat. Known as Pandu Hill, this hill is popular with the locals and is called Bhim-ki-Dungri in the local language. Bairat also houses the ruins of two Buddhist monasteries built between 3rd and 1st century A.D. Inscriptions on the ruins indicate that the monasteries were built by Kind Asoka. These monasteries were well known in their time — Huen Tsang, the great traveller from China, praised them in his book on India. Nearby is the beautiful Jain temple, Parsvanath. The pillared porticos complete the temple's beauty.

Bairat is 76 km east of RTDC's Hotel Gangaur (Tel: 0141-2371642; Rates: Rs 1,200) and RTDC's Teej Hotel (Tel: 0141-2203199; Rates: Rs 700-1,000) in Jaipur, on the Jaipur-Shahpur-Alwar highway.

BAGHERA
LORD VISHNU'S REALM
Baghera is famous for its ruined temples. The remains of a Vishnu temple, uncovered through excavations, are part of the Varaha Avatar temple and depict Vishnu in the form of a boar. Excavations have also uncovered Jain images that indicate the erstwhile presence of a Jain temple. A little farther away a torana and the remnants of several ancient residences have also been excavated.

The Vishnu idol is now housed in a fairly new building near a sacred tank called the Varaha Sagar.

Baghera is 95 km from RTDC's Hotel Khadim (Tel: 0145-2627490; Rates Rs 400-2,000) at Ajmer.

SITABARI
STORY FROM THE RAMAYANA
Sitabari is fabled to be the place where Sita was left by Lakshman, when Ram exiled her. Lakshman shot an arrow into the ground here in order to create a stream of drinking water for Sita. This stream, which still exists, is called the 'Lakshman Babhuka'.

There are seven tanks and two temples in the locality: to Sita and to Laxman. The biggest water tank, the 'Lakshman Kund', has a gate called the 'Lakshman Darwaza', with an unusual idol of Hanuman.

Before Dussehra every year, a fair is held in Sitabari. Local artisans from nearby districts come to here to sell their handmade crafts.

Sitabari is in Baran District, located 107 km from RTDC's Hotel Chandrawati (Tel: 07432-234023; Rates: Rs 500-700) in Jhalawar.

HIDDEN GEMS OF RURAL RAJASTHAN

SITA MATA
SQUIRREL SANCTUARY

Spread across the Aravalli and Vindhy ranges, the Sita Mata wildlife sanctuary is a forest of bamboo and deciduous vegetation. Three rivers flow through the forest and sustain the wildlife that inhabits this area.

Tree varieties grow in abundance: teak, salar, tendu, amla, bamboo and bel are the most common. Valuable teak trees that can be used for building grow in especial abundance.

Several varieties of deer including the chousingha, wild boars, pangolin and leopards make the sanctuary their home. Hyenas, jackals, foxes, jungle cats, porcupines, spotted deer, wild bears, four-horned antelopes and nilgais, revered by the Bishnoi tribe, are also easily spotted in Sita Mata. The sanctuary is also rich with bird life. The flying squirrel, however, is the most unusual and exciting animal found here. These squirrels glide from tree to tree, usually after sunset.

The best time to visit Sita Mata is in the winter months, when the bird life is swelled by many species of birds from across Asia on their winter migration. The flying squirrel is best seen between February and March when most of the trees have shed their leaves, and the branches are bare.

Sita Mata is 88 km from RTDC's Hotel Panna (Tel: 01472-241238; Rates Rs 200-700) at Chittaurgarh.

JALORE
STRENGTH AND HONOUR

Jalore lies on the left bank of the Sukri River. As a river town, it flourished in the middle of the 8th century, and was ruled by Pratihar Kings. It boasts of many temples, as well as the mandatory fort. Two great poetic works — the *Kuvalayamala* and the *Kanhad Dev Praband* — were composed in Jalore.

Today Jalore is known for this fort. Built in the 10th century, it is the simplest of forts without much embellishment. A work of elegance, it speaks of strength. The fort is unusually spacious. It houses the mosque of the great saint Malik Singh.

Another structure within the fort is the cannon foundry, known as the Topekhana. Its ruined architecture is indicative of its past majesty. A spacious forecourt and an intricate, beautifully carved façade make the structure unusual and imposing.

Both the Topekhana and the mosque are said to have been built by Alauddin Khilji. Jalore also boasts Jain temples dating back to the eighth century. It has a shrine dedicated to Saint Jallindernath Maharaj.

Jalore is the headquarters of Jalore District, easily accessed by road and train. It is 95 km from RTDC's Hotel Panicharin (Tel: 02932-231839; Rates Rs 75-1,100) at Pali.

HIDDEN GEMS OF RURAL RAJASTHAN

ARTHUNA
JEWEL OF VAGAD

Clusters of other ruined Hindu and Jain temples from the 11th through the 15th century can be found all over Arthuna. An unusual carving of Lord Hanuman, inside one of these temples, is a remarkable sight.

Arthuna is also a pilgrimage destination for Jains. The Digamber Jain Nasiyaji Atishaya Kshetra, atop a hill close to Arthuna, is a must-see. This kshetra houses 49 idols in yogic Padmasana and Khadgasana postures. There is also an ancient Digambar Jain temple within Arthuna Village.

Arthuna is located 55 km from Banswara, on the Udaipur-Anandpuri railway line, in south Rajasthan's Vagad circuit.

Gaily decorated jeeps — which can carry up to 15 or 20 people with a tight squeeze — are among the most common mode of transport across rural Rajasthan

But in the desert regions, the most popular transport remains the camel cart — today Rajasthan's unique form of sightseeing

TODGARH FORT
CAPTAIN TOD'S LEGACY

In the midst of the Aravalli Hills, Todgarh fort is an unusual reminder of colonial times. Unlike all the other forts in Rajasthan, it was built by the famous Englishman Captain Tod, who spent much of his career documenting the architectural heritage of Rajasthan.

About 3,300 feet high, Todagarh is cool in summer too. Surrounded by hills and set between two rivers, Todgarh has a sense of peace. It seems set to be the next Mt. Abu. Todagarh is 80 km from RTDC's Hotel Panicharin (Tel: 02932-231839; Rates Rs 75-1,100) at Pali.

TIJARA

SITE OF MIRACLES

Tijara, earlier known as Trigatpur, has always been an important pilgrimage site for Jains. In ancient India, Tijara was a prosperous city, populated mostly with Jains. The city was subsequently sacked by invaders, during the course of medieval wars. Recently however, Tijara is seeing a resurgence of its ancient prosperity. Many attribute this to two Jain idols that mysteriously appeared from below the ground in late 20th century. Legend says that in 1956 a devout Jain dreamt that the idol of Chandra Prabhu was underground. Upon digging on the site, such an idol was indeed found. Subsequently, a second idol was similarly found in 1970. Jain pilgrims now flock to Tijara, to visit the Shri 1008 Chandra Prabhu Digambar Jain Atishaya Kshetra Dehra Tijara temple.

An attractive fort stands forth on the crest of Tijara hill. It represents the time when Tijara was the capital of the Mewat area, and it is associated with a wondrous history of bravery and sacrifice.

The city is just 2.5 hours drive from Delhi and is located 52 km north-east of RTDC's Hotel Meenal (Tel: 0144-2347352; Rs 400-700) at Alwar. It lies within the Mewat Circuit. While here, make a visit to the famous halwai shops of Alwar as well.

HIDDEN GEMS OF RURAL RAJASTHAN

SOJAT
RICH WITH SIGHTS

In ancient times, Sojat was well known for its manufacture of cutlery, daggers, swords, bridles and saddlery. Today, it is well known as a tourist destination — for its big reservoir, dargah, old temples, and the magnificent Sojat Fort.

Located on the left bank of the Sukri River, Sojat is picturesque. Although a small town, it houses many interesting sites nearby. The fort is atop a hill named Nani Sirari and is surrounded by high walls.

During the time of Urs, the town fills up with pilgrims who come to visit the dargah of Pir Mastan. Several temples such as Sejal Mata and Chaturbhuj also make this an attractive place to visit. The old temple of Chamunda Mata, located atop a hill, is especially remarkable. One of the most popular times to visit this town is during the season when mehendi trees are planted.

Places of interest nearby are the temple of Ramdeoji near village Biratiya and the fort of Desuri. Kurki, the birthplace of the Krishna devotee Mirabai is also nearby.

Not far away is the impressive fort of Rawla Jojawar, which has been converted into a heritage hotel.

Sojat is located in the district of Pali. It is 38 km from RTDC's Hotel Panicharin (Tel: 02932-231839; Rates Rs 75-1,100) at Pali, and can also be visited from Jodhpur.

पधारो सा ....

फोन नं:

North Rajasthan

Step into a world where the walls speak of another era, where the tales of yesteryear remain etched in the shifting sands of the Thar

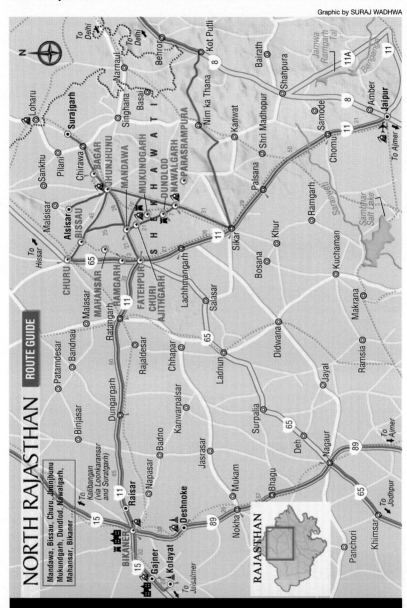

Graphic by SURAJ WADHWA

Nadine le Prince Haveli, where fading art has been given a fresh lease of life

SHEKHAWATI
WHERE WALLS HAVE MOUSTACHES

Districts Sikar, Churu and Jhunjhunu
Location The desert villages of the Shekhawati region are spread across the districts of Churu, Jhunjhunu and Sikar in north-eastern Rajasthan, on the border with Haryana. Mandawa, the most convenient base to explore the region, is 26 km south-west of Jhunjhunu, the most important town in Shekhawati
Distances Mandawa is 169 km NW of Jaipur and 275 km SW of Delhi
Journey time *By road* 3½ hrs from Jaipur, 6 hrs from Delhi
Route from Jaipur NH11 to S ikar via Chomu and Palsana; state highway to Nawalgarh; district road to Mandawa via Mukundgarh and Churi Ajitgarh (*see route guide on facing page*)

■ **BY RAKESH KALSHIAN**

In every human settlement, there will be men who tell stories. And they will tell them their way. Even in one corner of the hostile desert sands, where nothing grows but evening shadows, scattered in a cluster of impoverished human hubs where life's preoccupation is with living, they will rise to say something everyday. This is the story of some such men, anonymous forever, who lived long ago in the Thar Desert in a region that's loosely called Shekhawati.

Here those men painted on the walls of houses and told the simple tales of their times. That's how seven princes stand today, stuck forever on a wall. They hold identical swords at their groins and look grim, perhaps because they have been standing for over 60 years. Their moustaches are curled up in the high fashion of those times, arousing an unreasonable urge in the spectator to straighten them out in keeping with contemporary standards.

On another wall, a steam engine is heaving into a station, belching black smoke. In another scene, a ship is still in harbour. On its hull is 'Made in Germany' written upside down, because the artist who copied the lines of the English letters from some imported paint tin was holding the can the wrong way up!

Must you cross the desert sands, journey into an ocean of nothingness just to catch a glimpse of ancient scenes on older walls? You must. As soon as possible. Shekhawati might be frozen in time, but there is a slow, invisible dance of destruction going on in the background. Often, owners of these ancient havelis are in multiples of ten, making it very difficult for any one person to either sell or restore them. So they lie neglected. Some murals suddenly get random whitewashes, while other havelis are collapsing because the woodwork has been pulled down for antique shops. Piece by piece, the murals of Shekhawati are sadly but surely disappearing.

Bharat Petroleum

→ **FAST FACTS**

When to go The Shekhawati region has very hot summers and cold winters, which should make the travelling seasons obvious. While winter nights are bone chilling, the days are crisply pleasant
Tourist office
● RTDC Central Reservation Office ❶❻
Hotel Swagatham Complex
Near Railway Station, Jaipur
Tel: 0141-2315714, 2202586
STD codes Mandawa, Bagar and Jhunjhunu 01592; Mahansar 01595; Nawalgarh, Mukundgarh and Dundlod 01594; Jaipur 0141

THINGS TO SEE AND DO

The village of **Mandawa**, with its cluster of hotels, is the most suitable base for exploring the region. The best of the painted towns are within a 50-km radius from here. Plus, this is as equipped as a town gets in these parts for fulfilling the unfamiliar needs that tourists bring with them. However, do keep in mind that Mandawa is not connected by train. You'll be getting off either at Jhunjhunu, Dundlod or Nawalgarh, about a half-hour ride from Mandawa. Once there, you can hire a car to take you to the surrounding towns but don't forget to carry two essentials. First, get schematic maps of at least the major towns — such as those of Mandawa, Nawalgarh and Churu provided in *The painted towns of Shekhawati* by Ilay Cooper (*also see page 420*). Without these, it's impossible to locate the havelis amidst modern constructions and a maze of lanes. Second, a pair of binoculars will come in handy for close-up views of paintings high up on the walls, especially the erotica!

TIP It's not always possible to locate the haveli you plan to visit as you travel through different towns, so don't hesitate to ask for directions a couple of times to make sure you're on the right track

Local hotels organise horse rides/ safaris, camel rides and village visits on request. Rates vary according to the duration of these activities, especially during the high season. There's not much by way of shopping here (at best you can pick up Rajasthani handicrafts at the hotel gift shops) except around Castle Mandawa where you can also watch local craftsmen at work.

TIP You may be asked to pay a nominal Rs 10 per head to enter some havelis. Since these are private properties, it is advisable to observe decorum — particularly if a haveli you wish to see is locked, or the caretaker denies you permission to enter

Driving is the most convenient way to explore the Shekhawati region. If you

AMIT PASRICHA

Streetside story: Boys on their way home in Shekhawati

don't have your own car, hire a taxi from Jaipur and create your own itinerary. Taxis (Indica/ Ambassador) cost about Rs 1,500 per day (200 km minimum). The charges depend on the number of overnight stays and the type of vehicle you choose. Rates shoot up during the high season. Contact DD Sharma at Travel Plan (1 Anand Bhavan, Jacob Road, Civil Lines, Jaipur; Tel: 0141-2222332/ 517; Mobile: 09829053632; Email: ddsharma@ travelplanraj.com) for details. *Also see Jaipur and Metro Travel Agents Listings on pages 448 and 450-453.*

Bissau (25 km NW of Mandawa)
Bissau is a quaint little oasis. I chose Bissau as my doorway to the frescoes of the region purely for reasons of convenience and economy of time. If you are camping in Mandawa, then Bissau is a good starting point, being the northernmost end of the western arc connecting the four towns of Fatehpur, Ramgarh, Mahansar and Bissau. There is absolutely no reason why you can't enter this world through any of the other doors, though.

Till recently, Bissau was — at least for me, I must confess — the capital of Guinea Bissau, a small country on the western coast of Africa. That it had a namesake right in my backyard was a revelation of how our worldview is shaped by what lens we view it through — and that it is more often than not, not our own, but that of the Western anthropologist. The Bissau of Shekhawati — like most small towns in the postcolonial world — seems trapped in a triple time warp. The 250-year-old **Keshargarh Fort** here was built in 1746 by Keshri Singh, one of the five sons of the legendary Sardul Singh, who ended three centuries of Muslim ascendancy over large parts of Shekhawati. It proclaims its medieval origins with impressive bastions; the stylised caricatures of Europeans on haveli walls betray its brush with colonialism; the bazaar, with shops selling Coke and electronic goods, advertises its chaotic leap into modernity.

One can amble through the bazaar and drink in the town's distinctly provincial ambience — low-key, unhurried and

A painted entrance to a haveli

fatalistic. By now, I hope I have provoked the locals' curiosity, not least because of my capris and red Reebok sandals. An old Muslim gentleman emerges from a barber shop, caressing his well-trimmed white beard and looking meaningfully at my notebook, asks if I'm a government representative come to survey the town's civic services. I tell him the motive of my visit. He seems at a loss, unable to understand why anyone would be interested in the havelis. And how could my writing about the murals contribute to improving the quality of their lives?

The origin of the havelis
Ironically, until the latter half of the 19th century, Bissau — along with the other towns of Shekhawati — was a flourishing and prosperous town. It was on the corridor which caravans and trading traffic took between Delhi and the various ports of Gujarat. It was also an important link

on the Southern Silk Route, which connected West Asia with China. The Thakurs and the business community enjoyed a symbiotic relationship — the Thakurs protected the trade from brigands, in lieu of which the merchants paid a 'security fee'. Little wonder, then, that the entrepreneurs of this region (wrongly clubbed with the Marwaris of Marwar, the erstwhile Jodhpur Estate) amassed great fortunes until the rise of the British Empire and the dominance of its imported goods destroyed this trade.

Gradually, most of the merchant families — the Goenkas, Poddars, Singhanias, Ruias and Birlas — migrated to the port towns of Kolkata and Mumbai, slowly establishing a stranglehold over commerce between India and Britain. The tradition in those days was that whoever made it good would come back and build four things: a haveli, a *baoli*, a mandir and a dharamshala. With their multiplying wealth, they went on erecting colleges, cenotaphs, grander and grander havelis and — finally, when nothing else could be thought of — ordered that the havelis be painted. This competitive grandeur was also a way of spoiling the families they had to leave back at home for long periods.

But with the dissolution of the princely states after Independence, the intricate social network that radiated from royalty and had held people to this region withered away, consigning Shekhawati to the dustbin of history.

The frescoes
I leave the bazaar behind and turn into one of the narrow lanes leading deep into the bowels of the town, where most of the havelis sit. Welcome to **Motiram Jasraj Sigthia Haveli**, my introduction to the world of Shekhawati frescoes.

I enter, bent over in half, through a small opening in a high wooden gate with exquisitely carved motifs in brass. Indeed, these feature in all the havelis. The façade is an impressive riot of rich colours, with blue dominating. Not a single inch of the wall has been left unpainted. Indian gods and goddesses dominate the canvas, but some royals can also be seen, rubbing shoulders with divinity. One of the royals looks like Lord Shiva, despite beard and turban. A woman is massaging the king's legs. Krishna is riding an elephant with gopis inside it. I don't know what it all means.

There are more paintings inside the haveli. On the first floor, a man is shown wearing his turban before a mirror; another is working out. In yet another panel, a royal is watching a 'nautch-girl' perform. In a room on the first floor, now used as a children's classroom, one can see stylised portraits of women.

The technique

What is remarkable about these frescoes is that many of them have endured for over 100 to 200 years. The technique employed by the Shekhawati fresco painters was similar to the one developed in Italy around the 14th century. In the *fresco buono* (true fresco) method, which refers to painting on wet plaster, the mortar for the walls (of brick or stone) was prepared from a very fine clay, often collected from anthills. This is known in Rajasthan as *ala gila* or *arayish*. After three such layers, three more layers of plaster were applied, using such diverse raw materials as marble dust, lime, sour buttermilk and jaggery. In between, each layer of plaster was burnished with agate or white stone. Crucially, the painting was done before the wall lost its wetness. As the wall dried, a chemical reaction between the plaster and pigments fused the painting with the plaster. Finally, the painting was smeared with coconut oil, which covered the fresco with a diaphanous patina that did not yield to the onslaught of the elements.

Mahansar (28 km NW of Mandawa)

Ten kilometres away from Bissau, Mahansar is a charming, laidback little town.

AMIT PASRICHA

Shekhawati has an old-world charm

The layout is geometric and one can explore it in less than half an hour. Mahansar is also known as the traditional business bastion of the Poddar family, which moved its flourishing business in chintz and opium to this town in the early 19th century. Ironically, the opium trade turned out to be their nemesis when two shiploads of the intoxicant capsized in the late 1840s.

However, while the going was good, they commissioned some of the most accomplished murals in Shekhawati. Among them, the **Sone-ki-Dukan** (Golden Shop), which was the head office of the Poddars and was so called because of the lavish use of gold in the murals inside, is the *piece de resistance*. Whoever painted the murals was not only a consummate illustrator but also possessed a great sense of colour and composition. In particular, check out the elaborately depicted war between the armies of

Rama and Ravana, Rama's wedding, Vishnu's incarnations and a schematic representation of Dwarka. Also worth contemplating is a portrait of Krishna, in which he is a composite of many creatures — snake's tail, tiger's torso, elephant-horse-snake as neck, horse's limbs.

TOTAL CONTROL

→ GETTING THERE

Air Nearest airport: Sanganer, Jaipur (184 km/ 3$^1/_2$ hrs), connected daily to Delhi, Mumbai, Kolkata, Chennai and Bangalore. Expect to pay about Rs 2,000 (if not more) for a taxi ride to Mandawa

Rail The Shekhawati region is served by several stations. Jhunjhunu (26 km), Dundlod-Mukundgarh (14 km) and Nawalgarh (26 km) are the best railheads for Mandawa and its surrounds. The Shekhawati Express from Delhi has been discontinued as the track is being converted to broad gauge. Instead drive or take any train (hourly) to Rewari from Delhi to catch the Loharu-Jaipur Express, which serves Mukundgarh Station in Shekhawati as well as Jaipur. However, train journeys are not recommended as arrival and departure hours are pretty outlandish. Driving is the most convenient and enjoyable way to explore Shekhawati

TIP If you still prefer to go by train, transport is available at the stations, but it is best to ask your hotel for a pick-up

Road Shekhawati lies within the angle formed by NH8 and NH11, which connect Delhi to Jaipur and Jaipur to Bikaner respectively. Right-turns from Rewari on NH8 and from Sikar on NH11 lead to Jhunjhunu and on to Mandawa. From here, a series of smaller, and poorer, roads connect the haveli towns

Where to stay

About five minutes walk from Sone-ki-Dukan is the Mahansar Fort, founded by Thakur Nahar Singh in 1768. Like many forts in Rajasthan, a portion of it has been turned into a heritage hotel called **Narayan Niwas Palace** (Tel: 01595-264322; Tariff: Rs 800-1,200). It is owned and run by Thakur Sahib Tejpal Singh and his family.

Mahansar Fort

Thakur Sahib's younger brother Kunwar Maheshwar Singh offers to take me on a guided tour of the fort. He ushers me into Room No. 1, which is airy and spacious with interiors that are elegant and romantic. Perched a notch below the pinnacle of the fort, it affords a romantic view of the town and the sprawling countryside in the distance. For its fairytale atmospherics, the room is reasonably priced at Rs 900. "An old English painter makes this his room for two months every year," he boasts.

The view from atop the fort, which offers a complete 360^0 view of the horizon, is quite picturesque. The present thakur is also well-known for his special home-brewed wines, of such exotic flavours as orange, saffron, mint and anise. Not being a connoisseur, I am not able to appreciate the fine distinctions of taste and flavour. Nevertheless, I ask him to pack a few bottles for friends. Prices vary between Rs 100 and 450 per bottle.

Ramgarh (34 km W of Mandawa)

About 6 km south-west of Mahansar, Ramgarh was one of the wealthiest towns of Shekhawati in its prime. Indeed, it is still referred to as **Sethon-ka-Ramgarh** (Ramgarh of the Merchants) to distinguish it from its namesakes. Founded in 1791 by the Poddars, who were fleeing Churu after the thakur there had levied heavy taxes on their wool business, Ramgarh boasts the largest number of murals in the whole of Shekhawati. By now, my head is swimming in a sea of

AGP PHOTOBANK/RAJEEV RASTOGI

Livestock and livelihoods: Women tend to their four-legged flock

frescoes. Unless you are an art student, it is hard to sustain enthusiasm for the numerous murals with their repetitive themes of gods, royals and Europeans. Besides, the quality of the art varies considerably, from very amateurish to the exceptionally good murals of Sone-ki-Dukan which constitute a small minority. Therefore, if tedium grips you, drop your mural fetish and take a random walk through the town, making conversation with the locals as you go along.

Fatehpur (21 km SW of Mandawa)
About 15 km south of Ramgarh, Fatehpur is one of the oldest towns in Shekhawati. Established in 1451 by Fateh Khan of the Muslim clan Kayamkhanis, the town has a rich and interesting history. It is said that, in 1799, the Irish freebooter George Thomas marched on the city with the help of the Marathas, but his designs were thwarted by the military intervention of the Maharaja of Jaipur.

Because of its long history, Fatehpur boasts some impressive feats of engineering in its *baolis*, wells and *joharas* (reservoirs). The town was also home to such

well-known Marwari business families as the Singhanias, Poddars, Devras, Saraogis and Choudharys, who built some of the most opulently decorated havelis here.

At least one haveli here offers a 'different' experience — not because of its painted walls, but because of the inspiring endeavour of a Frenchwoman to give these fading works of art a fresh lease of life. A painter herself, Nadine le Prince bought the **Nand Lal Devra Haveli** in 1998 for the grand sum of Rs 3 million; now it is known as the **Nadine le Prince Haveli**. I am not able to meet her as she is away in France, but the caretaker tells me that she has already spent another Rs 6 million on restoration work, a sum gainfully used to create a charming garden, a luxurious sitting room and courtyards. The entry fee of Rs 50 is an excellent bargain (though the Rs 30 to Rs 60 postcards of her own paintings are not).

At Fatehpur, also watch out for the **Singhania Haveli** with its huge painting of four elephants cradling goddess Lakshmi with their trunks and exquisitely painted dancing gopis. The **Choudhary Ki Haveli** is said to be one of the most richly painted in Shekhawati but is unfortunately shut. The outer left wall has some interesting erotica and other amusing paintings.

Where to stay
If you wish to spend a day here, the only comfortable stay option is **Hotel Haveli** (Tel: 01571-230293; Tariff: Rs 400-700), an RTDC property on NH11. It has a restaurant and arranges sightseeing.

Nawalgarh (28 km SE of Mandawa)
Nawalgarh is one of the biggest and busiest towns of Shekhawati. Founded in 1737 by Nawal Singh, a son of Shardul Singh, Nawalgarh saw a series of rulers who managed, by dint of their sharp political acumen, to keep the state together even as many of their neighbours gradually came apart. Therefore, it was able to attract a number of rich Marwari merchants who built many richly painted havelis here.

Most of these now are in a state of disrepair, the only exception being the **Poddar Haveli**, which has been turned into a museum. Although the haveli is not very old — it was built around the 1920s — the murals have been carefully restored to their original glory. The museum also exhibits **wedding costumes** of different communities of Rajasthan. As for the other murals, it seems the Nawalgarh artists had much greater freedom in choosing their themes. For instance, there are pirated editions of Ravi Varma's works and imaginative illustrations of a whole range of early 20th century technologies such as the air balloon, the Wright brothers' attempt at flight, motorcars, modern railways and sewing machines.

But in terms of artistic brilliance, the painted ceiling of a small room in the fort called **Bala Qila** stands out. The room, studded profusely with mirrors, is circular, about 8 ft in diameter and almost as high. The murals, lustrous and colourful, depict an artist's impression of the cities

A ceiling to rival a starlit sky at Ramgarh

and armies of Jaipur and Nawalgarh in the 1850s. It's now owned by a family that charges Rs 10 as entry fee.

Aath Haveli here is where you can see a long train with one passenger per compartment, a woman feeding a child and at the same time doing her make-up and a couple making love.

Morarka Haveli is right across the back street from Aath Haveli, and it has one of the most elegantly and finely sketched paintings. Two prominent frames show the celebration of traditional festivals like the Teej and Gangaur. **Saraogi Haveli** has amusing reproductions of Ravi Varma's paintings. The seduction of Vishwamitra by Menaka is erotic. Check out the front wall at **Sheksaria Haveli**, whose murals have been all but whitewashed. Portraits of gods have of course been spared! **Chaucharia Haveli** has women angels alongside Europeans going up in air balloons.

Where to stay
Of the two good options here, **Hotel Roop Niwas Kothi** (Tel: 01594-224152;

Ray·Ban

GENUINE SINCE 1937

WWW.RAY-BAN.COM

CHANGE YOUR VIEW

EXPERIENCE THE RAY-BAN 2006 COLLECTION.

RB 3239 Sidestreet Semi Rimless
MRP Rs.4990/-

RB 4039 Predator Sport Nylor II Square
MRP Rs.3690/-

RB 4062 Sidestreet Plastic
MRP Rs.3690/-

Choose from over 250 styles at your nearest authorized Ray-Ban dealer.

Tariff: Rs 1,700-3,000) is a sprawling mansion inspired by Italian originals. This **heritage hotel** has well-kept gardens, verandahs and courtyards which are ideal for those looking for a quiet refuge from the town's hustle and bustle. It also arranges horse safaris. Another excellent option here is **Apani Dhani** (Tel: 222239; Tariff: Rs 600-995), an eco lodge, 20 mins drive from Nawalgarh, which has eight huts. Apani Dhani arranges camel cart excursions and guided tours of havelis.

Parasrampura (46 km SE of Mandawa) About 18 km from Nawalgarh, this little village has some of the finest and earliest murals in Shekhawati. The murals decorate the **chhatri of Shardul Singh**, who spent his last days in this village. Built in 1750, the cenotaph depicts scenes from the Ramayana and other themes from Hindu mythology. It also shows Shardul Singh presiding over his court along with his five sons.

Mandawa (26 km SW of Jhunjhunu) Mandawa came into being in 1756, when Nawal Singh built the fort that has now been turned into the hotel called Castle Mandawa. But it became a full-fledged town only after Nawal Singh's two grandsons decided to make it their home at the close of the 18th century.

Like Nawalgarh, Mandawa too remained undivided, thus luring many merchants to set up shop here. In particular, the murals of **Gulab Rai Ladia Haveli** are exceptional, especially in the variety of their themes. It is quite a mixed basket — scenes from the life of the owner with the fort in the background; a curly-headed Greek 'portrait'; a woman giving birth; mirror images of a tiger and a horse; a bird tending her eggs; a couple making out in a train compartment and another on a chair.

It's difficult to say if this 'eroticism' was at the owner's request or an artist's rebellion against an oppressive society.

Whatever the reason, these bold strokes provide a refreshing counterpoint to the sometimes tediously ubiquitous portrayals — gods, royals and colonialists.

The **Bansidhar Nevatia Haveli** shows the Wright brothers' maiden flight and a European making a telephone call — presumably reproduced from magazines. A rather nationalistic tug-of-war between a strongman called Prof Ramamurti and a motorcar driven by an Englishman is also portrayed in a painting.

The *baithak* or sitting room of the **Sneh Ram Ladia Haveli** has a rather amateurish though amusing group portrait of rulers of various princely states. On the other hand, consider the almost photographic portraits of the merchants who owned the haveli. These were done by a man called Babu Lal who, in a rare exception, signed his works.

Bad imitations of European artworks can be seen at **Murmuria Haveli**. Check out the artist's amusing attempt to set Indian themes against a European background — Krishna shepherding cows in a typically English countryside, for instance. The **Double Goenka Haveli** has amusing erotica painted on the outer left wall such as a *melange a trois*, a woman having sex with two men, and Krishna making love to a gopi. Access to this wall is through a narrow passage from inside the haveli.

If you start getting 'muralitis' from craning up to see the details, especially the bits of the *Kama Sutra* (which are often tucked away in obscure corners), consider spending some tranquil moments atop one of the bastions of **Castle Mandawa**. The view from this vantage point, particularly during sunrise or sunset, is most therapeutic.

Where to stay
Castle Mandawa (Tel: 01592-223124/ 480; Tariff: Rs 2,500-12,000) is the most famous hotel in these parts. This **heritage hotel** is popular with Europeans, mostly the French and the Spanish, who arrive

Castle Mandawa, a popular heritage hotel, is a vision of light at night

here in droves. The rooms have period furniture and a colourful local touch. No two of the 70 rooms at the castle are alike. The verandah, which houses the bar, is a favourite with travellers. Horse rides/safaris and camel safaris (Rs 400-1,000 per day) are available at the castle on request. Though the gift shop in the hotel is good for souvenirs, locally made lac bangles, *bandhej* (tie-and-dye) textiles, soft leather *jootis* (plain and embroidered) and pottery items can be easily picked up in the shops behind the castle area.

The **Desert Resort** (Tel: 223245/ 514; Tariff: Rs 2,500-12,000), associated with Castle Mandawa, has a pool. **Hotel Mandawa Haveli** (Tel: 223088; Tariff: Rs 1,550-2,700), located near the Sonthaliya Gate in Mandawa, offers comfort at down-to-earth prices.

Hotel Shekhawati (Tel: 223036; Tariff: Rs 300-800) on the Mukundgarh Road from Subhash Chowk has even lower prices, offering 20 rooms to the budget traveller.

Churi Ajithgarh (10 km SE of Mandawa)

En route to Nawalgarh, the twin towns of Churi and Ajithgarh were founded in the late 19th century and were home to the well-known Marwari families of the Kejariwals and the Nemanis.

The **Sheonarayan Haveli** has some interesting murals — portraits of Bengali women, a moustachioed Shiva posing with his entire family, an unusually morose-looking Krishna and Vishwamitra looking lustfully at a seductive Menaka. It is said that one room, mostly kept locked, has one of the most explicit samples of erotica in Shekhawati. I try to persuade the caretaker to open the room for us, but in vain. The haveli behind Sheonarayan's has an interesting mural of Indian nobles looking at a model locomotive.

Mukundgarh (14 km SE of Mandawa via Churi Jodhan)

You'll find good frescoes at the **Gopinath** and **Venugopal** temples in Mukundgarh,

AMIT PASRICHA

A haveli in Sikar looks out at the splendour outside

and at **Ganeriwal Haveli**. Look out particularly for the erotic frescoes, though you may need help spotting them.

Where to stay
The heritage **Mukundgarh Fort Hotel** (Tel: 01594-252397-98; Tariff: Rs 1,500-2,500) on the Dundlod Road offers 49 rooms, a swimming pool and camel cart rides to the sand dunes around.

Dundlod (21 km SE of Mandawa)
About 7 km from Mukundgarh on the road to Nawalgarh, Dundlod is a small and relatively tidy town, which was founded in 1750 by Keshri Singh, also the founder of Bissau. The **Dera Dundlod Fort**, founded in 1750, has been converted into a hotel. Nothing much to write home about, except that it has a very opulent hall, called the **Diwan-i-Khana**. The Goenkas were the ruling business clan here and most of their havelis are worth a visit. Horse riding/safaris can be arranged by the Dundlod Fort hotel whose stables boast of the famous Marwari horse. For shopping, the

hotel's gift shop is the only real option. You can also pick up wooden toys made by the village craftsmen. At the cluster of **Goenka havelis**, you can see two white men with a giraffe and a rhino and a man grooming himself. The **Jagathia Haveli's** outer wall has one of the most detailed scenes of a railway station. Apart from the havelis, the **cenotaph of Shiv Bux Goenka** is worth a visit.

Where to stay
Dera Dundlod Fort (Tel: 01594-252199; Tariff: Rs 2,000-3,850) in Dundlod looks more like a big mansion with pretensions to fort-hood. The **Diwan-i-Khana** of this heritage hotel is worth a dekko, though, as its aristocratic character has been well preserved. Ask here for the 5-day horse safari (Tariff: Rs 7,500 per person per day) covering the Shekhawati region, including stay at heritage hotels and meals.

Jhunjhunu (26 km NE of Mandawa)
Among the many sights here are the **Khetri Mahal**, near Nehru Bazaar, and

the many havelis near it. The Khetri Mahal is a run-down palace dating to 1770, and offers good views of the town. The **Modi Havelis** nearby have some exquisite murals, though some have been lost to modern paint, while the **Kaniram Narsinghdas Tibrewala Haveli** has two painted trains. The **Mohanlal Ishwardas Modi Haveli** also boasts of a train mural, among several others.

Where to stay
Jhunjhunu has a low-budget **RTDC Tourist Bungalow** (Tel: 01592-238266; Tariff: Rs 300-400), with four AC rooms and two ordinary and a restaurant.

Bagar (41 km NE of Mandawa)
The haveli here boasts of colonial frescoes, including some of flying angels and gods in motor cars.

Where to stay
The **Piramal Haveli** (Tel: 01592-221220; Tariff: Rs 1,500-2,000), run by Neemrana Hotels, is another heritage property. It used to be the haveli of Seth Piramal Chaturbhuj Makharia, who made his fortune in trading in Mumbai.
TIP The choice of places offering decent boarding and lodging is limited in Shekhawati. So, especially in the tourist season, (that is, the winter months beginning October to February), go only after you make bookings

Churu (60 km NW of Mandawa)
The painted havelis here are worth a visit. Do check out the **Malji ka Kamra**, near the bus stand, which has statues of women with wings and angels. Nearby is the **Surana Double Haveli**, known for its many windows.

From Churu, you can also travel to the **Tal Chhapar Wildlife Sanctuary** (90 km SW), a 71-sq km park that's home to the blackbuck, chinkara, desert fox, desert cat, partridge and sandgrouse. The sanctuary is close to Churu, and is best visited at morning or dusk. For more information, contact the Forest Office in Churu (Tel: 01562-250938; Assistant Conservator of Forests, Mobile: 09414466103; Deputy Forest Officer, Mobile: 09414681079).

Where to stay
The RTDC **Chirmi-Churu Hotel** (Tel: 01562-256272; Tariff: Rs 300-400) offers four basic rooms and a dining hall.

For details of all hotels in this region, see *Shekhawati Accommodation Listings on* *pages 489-491*

For details of all hotels in this region, see Shekhawati Accommodation Listings on pages 489-491

WHERE TO EAT

Do not expect great restaurants or food in Shekhawati. Most restaurants serve banal Mughalised fare. If you are looking for authentic Rajasthani cuisine, you will have to make a special request to the cook. You can dine at most of the hotels in Shekhawati after making reservations. At **Castle Mandawa**, the Indian, Continental and Rajasthani food is nothing to write home about, except that dinners are often served on the well-groomed lawns. The **Desert Resort** serves more of the same, and both hotels have bars.

The speciality of the restaurant at Piramal Haveli in Bagar is vegetarian Marwari food. Visitors can place an order, look around the haveli and then settle down to a sumptuous thali.

Mukundgarh Fort has a multi-cuisine restaurant. They don't have a bar but serve liquor on demand. **Roop Niwas Palace** at Nawalgarh offers Rajasthani, Indian and a few Continental dishes at its restaurant. It also has a bar. While here, do try the traditional vegetarian Shekhawati dishes made from farm-fresh organic vegetables grown at **Apani Dhani** hotel's own farm. Host Ramesh Jangid needs just an hour's notice that you're coming. Again, just an hour's notice and you can sample Rajasthani food at **Dera Dundlod Fort**. But keep in mind that there's just a 2-hr window for meals here. ■

Just picture-perfect: The red sandstone Junagarh Fort in Bikaner

BIKANER

THE OUTPOST OF CIVILISATION

District Bikaner
Location Bikaner, a sandy trough in the deserts of northern Rajasthan, forms the apex of a triangle with the desert cities of Jaisalmer and Jodhpur, not far from India's western border with Pakistan
Distances 317 km NW of Jaipur, 544 km SW of Delhi
Journey time *By road* 5 hrs from Jaipur, 9 hrs from Delhi
Route from Delhi NH8 to Kot Putli via Behror; state highway to Sikar via Nim ka Thana; NH11 to Bikaner via Fatehpur, Ratangarh and Dungargarh **Route from Jaipur** NH11 to Bikaner via Chomu and Sikar; rest as above **Route from Ajmer** NH89 to Bikaner via Merta, Nagaur and Deshnoke **Route from Jodhpur** NH65 to Nagaur via Khimsar; rest as above (*see route guide on page 34*)

■ BY KISHORE SINGH

Sandstorms lash the town in summer and a golden haze hides even the tallest buildings. Fierce winds effort-lessly and persistently bend trees. A land more hostile is difficult to imagine and yet, a full five centuries ago, a band of warriors rode into this very desert to lay the foundations of a kingdom that would bring prosperity to the region.

Most of what was built by those warriors, the Rathores, scions of the royal house of Jodhpur, still stands, a testimony as much to the quality of the construction as to the arid conditions that retard decay. They speak of the colourful legends that blend into their walls, narrating among others, the tale of a certain Rao Jodha of Jodhpur, who once reprimanded his brother and his son Bika for whispering in court, asking in jest whether the two were plotting to build their own kingdom. They took the remark to heart and set out on their own. For 30 years, Bika led a band of marauding freebooters all over Rajasthan till he finally settled down here.

But all that is history now. Even though the titans of this kingdom once wielded tremendous influence over the Mughal Court and the British Raj, Bikaner passed into near oblivion with Independence. With almost no industry and poor connectivity, it remained lost, a sandstone jewel hidden in the desert, till its resurrection by the tourism industry some years ago. Even so, Bikaner has been largely ignored by the average traveller, despite its splendid havelis and palaces. It could be one of your finest finds if you like your destination less trodden.

ORIENTATION

The old part of town lies to the south-west of Bikaner while both the **Junagarh Fort** and the **railway station** are located to the centre of town. The **main bus stand** is about 3 km from the centre of town, to the north. Hotels are scattered all across the town as are the shopping areas. Autos are the preferred mode of transport but don't run on meter, hence bargaining is the norm. Locals say the fares vary between Rs 10 and 20 for distances up to 5 km.

THINGS TO SEE AND DO

On the face of it, Bikaner is dusty, ill-kempt at the edges, vestiges of its erstwhile grandeur shining through but not quite managing to obliterate the haphazard growth of tacky modernity. But then it's a town known less for its architectural splendours — though these

Graphic by SURAJ WADHWA

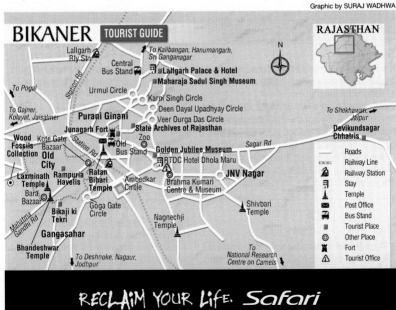

are truly marvellous — than for its savouries. Bikaneri bhujia may have become an exportable commodity in recent years; but once Bikaner's greatest export was its international diplomacy, raised to a fine art in the course of the sandgrouse shoots arranged by Maharaja Ganga Singh, remembered as the founder of modern Bikaner. Keep aside at least two days to do justice to Bikaner's older heritage, plus at least two days for Gajner and other arounds.

From fort to fort

Bikaner's history is inextricably linked with that of its ruling family and their seat of power, the **Junagarh Fort**. This red sandstone fort lies at the centre of Bikaner. At first glance, it appears to be a low mass of buildings, which, though impressive, does not exactly have a majestic mien. But in an almost flat country surrounded by shifting sands, the royals could not find a naturally imposing site. So Raja Rai Singh commenced the building of Junagarh a full century after Bikaner had been founded at **Rati Ghati** (now on the outskirts of the city) by Rao Bika.

The original fort at Rati Ghati soon outlived its purpose, and only fragments of its original walls survive. In 1589, Rai Singh ordered the more spacious and strategically superior fortification of Junagarh, which was completed in five years. Added on to gradually over three centuries, Junagarh looks today much as it probably did under the monarchic dispensations. Enter through its stone elephant-flanked gates, go past the hand-prints of the ranis whose lives were forced to culminate in sati, and you come to the impressive ceremonial courtyard, where you get the first glimpse of the architectural treasures of Junagarh.

When Maharaja Rai Singh laid the foundations of Junagarh in 1586, he had already sworn fealty to the Mughal Emperor Akbar. As a result, he could concentrate on consolidating his kingdom

→ **FAST FACTS**

When to go Definitely avoid in summer. October to March is excellent
Tourist office
● Rajasthan Tourism Reception Centre ❶ Hotel Dhola Maru Campus, Bikaner
Tel: 0151-2226701
STD code 0151

and building a self-contained fort-capital undistracted by territorial fears. Surrounded by a moat for defence, with public and private buildings added by succeeding maharajas, the whole effect is that of a series of buildings that seemingly blend on the outside but are vastly different within. The oldest parts are constructed in yellow sandstone (the famous 'golden stone' of Jaisalmer) while the rest are mostly in red sandstone.

◆**Location** Centre of town **Entry fee** Indians Rs 20, foreigners Rs 100 **Cameras** Still Rs 30, video Rs 100 **Timings** 10 am-4.30 pm, open all days (fees and timings applicable for museum as well)

The most opulent of the palaces within the fort is **Anup Mahal**, which includes the **Raj Tilak Mahal** (or Coronation Hall) with embossed lacquerwork of striking lavishness. **Badal Mahal**, painted with large blue clouds (perhaps aspirational in this desert state), gives pride of place to a large portrait of Maharaja Sardar Singh, painted by a visiting Italian artist. Open courtyards, interspersing the fort, lead into different apartments. In one of these, durbars were held with the maharaja seated on a marble platform rising from a pool of water. The courtyards house the family temple of Joramal, as well as **Har Mandir**, where weddings took place. The **Karan Mahal** courtyard leads to **Dungar**

Niwas, with its fine inlays reminiscent of *pietra dura*. The **Chandra Mahal** is beautifully painted and was built by Gaj Singh, along with **Phul Mahal**, which boasts the small bed of Rao Bika.

Maharaja Ganga Singh, the last of the royals to inhabit Junagarh, gifted it a pair of grand sandstone staircases as well as its stately **Durbar Hall**, which has — somewhat unusual for a Rajput monument — a floor as well as ceiling made entirely of wood. The hall is now a museum filled with an eclectic collection of family and clan memorabilia. The entrance courtyard of the fort now also houses **Prachin**, a storehouse of vintage textiles and costumes, as well as a few souvenir shops. Notable among these is **Urmul**, a cooperative that has put together an important 'community milk scheme' (Bikaner District exports most of its produce), showcasing handwoven and handprinted textiles as well as readymades.

→ GETTING THERE

Air Nearest airport: Jodhpur (243 km/ 5 hrs), connected by daily flights to Jaipur, Delhi, Udaipur and Mumbai. Indica taxi transfer will cost Rs 1,000 approx
Rail Bikaner Junction, well-connected to Delhi by the Bikaner Mail, to Mumbai by the Jammu Tawi and to Kolkata by the Howrah-Jodhpur Express. The Jaipur-Bikaner Intercity and Jaipur-Bikaner express trains are the best options to Jaipur. Both taxis and autos are easily available at the station
Road Bikaner is at the western end of NH11 that links Agra to Jaipur. Travellers from Delhi should turn off NH8 at Kot Putli and take the road to Sikar via Nim ka Thana and Khandela. From here, take NH11 to Bikaner

◆**Prachin entry fee** Indians Rs 10, foreigners Rs 25 **Timings** 9 am-5 pm

Bikaner new and old

The greatest symbol of Bikaner's aspiration to be one of the world's modern kingdoms was the building of **Lallgarh Palace** (named after Maharaja Lall Singh, who insisted on the two *ll*s). On the one hand, it served to advertise Ganga Singh's endeavour to make Bikaner more robust economically (to which end he developed the state railways so as to exploit local coal deposits and commissioned the Ganga Canal waterworks to overcome drought). On the other, it also served as a link with the continuing traditions of the past. And all this was achieved through an architectural plan drafted by Sir Swinton Jacob, the foremost architect of the early 20th century.

A huge but compact palace, Lallgarh is built — appropriately — entirely of red sandstone. Said to be the best exemplar of a Rajput palace, its façade is composed of the pierced stone screens called jaalis. A prominent feature of Rajasthani architecture, the jaalis keep most of the sun out as they let even the tiniest whiff of breeze in. Inside, the palace wings combine Western en suite living with the need for zenana privacy and concealed corridors.

Today, the palace is the sum of many confusing parts. The main building consists of the personal living quarters of several members of the royal family, some of which have been recently renovated while others still retain their past grandeur. There is, for instance, the section where the Rajmata or Queen Mother resides, which is never photographed because of the large number of shikar trophies that line its walls. Though Lallgarh has several small courtyards, the two main ones now belong to two separate hotel complexes — one managed by the Maharaja Ganga Singhji Trust, the other by a private hotelier (to whom it was sold by the maharaja, causing no small confusion about ownership

DINODIA PHOTO LIBRARY

Anup Mahal, the most opulent of the palaces within Junagarh Fort

and propriety). Since part of the palace is also the **Maharaja Sadul Singh Museum** (*see below*), visitors can enjoy looking around the handsome corridors and impressive stonecraft.

♦**Lallgarh location** Near Central Bus Stand on Sriganaganagar Road **Entry fee** Indians Rs 10, foreigners Rs 20 **Cameras** Still Rs 30, video Rs 100 **Timings** 10 am-5 pm (includes entry to museum)

Museums

For its modest size, Bikaner has quite a few museums. Several of these are managed by trusts and foundations associated with members of the former royal family. The **Junagarh Fort Museum** is entirely taken up by clan memorabilia and consists of everything from a World War I fighter aircraft to more personal artefacts and insignia of the Rathores (including their original sandalwood throne). The **Sadul Singh Museum** within Lallgarh is almost bare in comparison, with only some utensils and miniature paintings of note. However, it does serve as an archive of all correspondence (which was

considerable) and publications by Bikaner's First Family.

♦**Junagarh Fort Museum info** *See Junagarh Fort on page 51* **Sadul Singh Museum info** *See Lallgarh Palace info at left*

At the government-managed **Golden Jubilee Museum**, or the Ganga Singh Government Museum as it is generally referred to, Bikaner's history is more neatly packaged under one roof. Here are large oils by the German artist Mueller, sculptures from the Gupta and Kushan periods (a Saraswati, in particular, is of sterling worth), remnants from pre-Harappan archaeological finds in Kalibangan as well as armour, coins, pottery and carpets of more recent vintage.

♦**Location** Near Circuit House **Entry fee** Rs 3 **Timings** 10 am-5 pm, open all days

Anup Sanskrit Library at Lallgarh is one of the largest private collections of manuscripts in India — many are originals, and a number of these in Sanskrit. The initial collection was put together by Maharaja Anup Singh, who ruled from 1669 to 1698, during his Golconda campaign (on behalf of Aurangzeb) to

MANU ANAND

It's time for a break at Bikaner

save them from possible destruction by the Mughals. It is, however, no longer open to the public.

Interestingly, the **State Archives of Rajasthan** too are housed in Bikaner and consist of all records centrally housed in one building, making it a fulfilling retreat for the scholar. Apply to the Director, State Archives (Tel: 0151-2545354), to use its facilities.
♦**Location** Near MN Hospital **Timings** 10 am-5 pm, Sundays closed

Temples and memorials
The ruling family still visits the temples in Junagarh and Lallgarh for private ceremonies, but the most popular temple for the masses is **Shivbari**, set within its own fortified walls and dedicated to Shiva, on the Camel Farm Road. However, for the visitor driven less by faith and more by curiosity, visits are recommended to the temples of **Ratan Bihari** and **Rasik Shiromani**, located within Ratan Bihari Park, in the heart of town. These mansion-style structures have handsome façades of sandstone and

marble. Also noteworthy is the 16th century **Bhandeshwar Jain Temple** (in the old town), particularly its mirrors and gold-leafed paintings. The **Laxminath Temple** next door is also worth seeing.
♦**Timings** Open all day

Those more inclined to lay their faith in history may find the picturesque **Devi-kundsagar Chhatris** worth a visit. Made of lime-based plaster and marble, these are memorials to members of the royal family. The cenotaphs with footprints beneath the images of mounted kings depict the women who committed sati, following their royal consorts to the funeral pyre. For those interested in symbolism, memorials carved with suns and lotuses mark the final resting places of princes and princesses respectively.
♦**Location** On Jaipur Road

Havelis
Bikaner's mercantile community built themselves impressive homes — once again in red sandstone. Unfortunately, unlike the more visible havelis of Jaisalmer or even Shekhawati, those in Bikaner are tucked away from the public eye in narrow lanes, by open drains overflowing with refuse. As a result, they do not attract many visitors. Also, since most of the families who own them do not stay here any longer, it is almost impossible to view the interiors. However, a visit is recommended if only to see them from the outside. In particular, go see the **Rampuria havelis**, famed for the beautiful stonework of their facades in the Old City, near Kote Gate.

Shipyard of the desert
Bikaner's **camel breeding farm** (National Research Centre on Camels) is a unique institution devoted to improving indigenous species by crossbreeding. As a result, it is not unusual to find breeds of camel from as far as West Asia here. For rides into the dunes outside the farm, get in touch with local tour operators, who also arrange camel safaris into the desert

either as day-trips or longer excursions. But be warned: though camel safaris sound glamorous, they can prove a boring, bumpy tramp for many of us. **Camel Man** (Mobile: 09829217331), run by Vijay Singh, is a good option as is **Vino Desert Safari** (Tel: 2270445, 09414139245).

◆**Farm location** Shivbari Temple Road **Entry fee** Rs 10 **Cameras** Still Rs 20, video Rs 30 **Timings** 3-5 pm, open all days

Camel Festival

This mid-January festival, held in conjunction with the full moon, is a celebration of the Ship of the Desert, the predecessor of the motorcar and the key to survival for our ancestors in the inaccessible city of Bikaner. The camels of this region are famous for their endurance and strength.

The festival begins with a colourful procession against the scenic backdrop of Junagarh Fort. The camels, resplendent in regalia, respond obediently to their trainers with synchronised footwork and dance. As the evening draws to an end, one gets the opportunity of attending performances by renowned Rajasthani folk artistes (*also see below*).

A ride through the sands of time

DINODIA PHOTO LIBRARY

Though Rajasthan has roads now, the camel has remained the cheapest mode of transport as well as the most enduring and fuel-efficient. To add to its eco-friendliness, most camel carts today come fitted with tyres rejected by the aviation industry.

Naturally, the camel was an important component of medieval trading caravans. But it also played an important part in defence strategies. Bikaner's 18th Maharaja, Ratan Singh, won over the British with his gesture of sending across 200 camels to serve in the First Afghan War.

Again, it was the progressive Maharaja Ganga Singh who founded the world's first camel corps when he raised the Ganga Risalla. By the time World War I commenced, the Bikaner camels had a well-established reputation and were called into service in Egypt. And after India got its Independence, the Risalla went on to become an army battalion. Although it was later disbanded, the Border Security Force uses camels for patrolling its long desert border with Pakistan even today.

It is not surprising that the **National Research Centre on Camels** is located in Bikaner, 8 km from the city centre. Close to 300 camels live in the pens and open stables here. Among the Indian breeds, the Bikaneri

(distinguished by its tawny colour) and Jaisalmeri (lighter of colour and slimmer of build) are considered superior. The Bikaneri camel is known for its strength and the Jaisalmeri for its speed. Understandably, the Bikaneri camel was used on the battlefield and the Jaisalmeri for patrolling, though both have been employed equally for the less glorious purpose of carrying loads over long distances. The third most popular Indian breed is the Gujarati camel. Darker and smaller than the other two, it's said to yield the highest quantity of milk.

SHOPPING

If you're among those who prefer the contemporary shopping experience, then Bikaner is not for you. The diligent, however, can discover a whole maze of treasures that would, perhaps, astound even Bikanerwallas. The main shopping area is the market running the length of **Mahatma Gandhi Road**. This is Bikaner's most happening place, though what you need is right at the end of the street. **Katla** at Kote Gate has good *jootis* that can be made to order in 24 hrs (though they aren't as comfortable as those of Jodhpur). Other typical buys include **handprinted cotton textiles** and **tie-dyed saris, light quilts** and **kundan jewellery**. Though the textiles are easier to locate, it is more difficult to find jewellery shops. Locals still operate on the feudal system of summoning jewellers home to place orders.

If you want to see some examples of the **Bikaner school of miniature paintings**, a good option is **Swami Art** at Kirti Stambh, Lallgarh Palace Road. They also do paintings on order. Another art peculiar to Bikaner, that of **gesso work** (on buffed camel-hide), went into decline since it was only able to produce poor examples of lamps and frames and the like. More recently, this has been rescued and adapted to painting with 24-carat gold on wood. Opulent, if expensive. You're most likely to find examples of these at stores on MG Road or your hotel showrooms. But it is best to ask to meet with the artisan directly should you wish to splurge good money on good art (a wooden mirror frame would cost anywhere between Rs 3,500 and 10,000).

However, it is the **bhujia** and related savouries industries that could well be the most fascinating for the visitor. While Bikaner's namkeens remain incomparable and are well packaged, visitors will find the whole range of papads and *baris* and Rajasthani uncooked meals tremendous buys. Among the favourites are **Bikaner**

Bhujia Bhandar, Haldiram's (yes, the original!) and **Chotu Motu Joshi**, as well as a host of small shops on **Station Road**.

WHERE TO STAY

There is now no dearth of accommodation in Bikaner, though there is usually a dearth of tourists. Even so, getting rooms can sometimes be a problem as Bikaner and its palaces are often used as locations for shooting films.

Heritage

Lallgarh Palace (Tel: 0151-2540202-07; Tariff: Rs 3,000-4,800) is run by the trust under which it is managed. Within the same complex is **Laxmi Niwas Palace** (Tel: 2521189; Tariff: Rs 5,000-9,000), perhaps the most beautiful wing of Lallgarh Palace. There are a large number of hunting trophies in the bar and conference rooms. The ownership represents new money, so don't expect old-world courtesies and you won't be disappointed. Next door, adjoining the Zenana Bagh of Lallgarh Palace is Maharaja Ganga Singh's sandstone **Basant Vihar Palace** (Tel: 2250675; Tariff: Rs 1,200-2,150), converted into a heritage hotel in 1993 by the House of Bikaji of namkeen fame. The glitzy **Rajvilas Palace** (Tel: 2525901-3; Tariff: Rs 1,950-5,000) is one of Bikaner's newer heritage hotels. It once housed the Resident and Agent to the Governor General of India. **Bhanwar Niwas** (Tel: 2529323; Tariff: Rs 2,400-3,300) is one of the city's heritage havelis, built by the Rampuria family in 1927 and now converted into a hotel. Guests who have stayed here swear by its charm and excellent vegetarian cuisine. **Karni Bhawan** (Tel: 2524701-06; Tariff: Rs 2,000-4,000) is an art deco bungalow with a pleasing old-fashioned ambience.

Others

Among the cheaper options, there is **Hotel Maru Udyan** (Tel: 2400735; Tariff: Rs 1,000-1,200) on NH11, which has a

Laxmi Niwas Palace was the personal residence of Maharaja Ganga Singhji of Bikaner and now converted into a luxurious Heritage Hotel. Most of the rooms are decorated lavishly using pure gold wall paintings and have painted or curved wood ceilings. The rooms of Laxmi Niwas Palace have witnessed history being made and till today they retain their unique flavour and provide guests with an unforgettable experience.

Facilities available are:
• Conference Rooms • Cultural programs • Business Centre • Money Exchange
• Shopping Arcade • Desert Trekking • Wedding • Games and Entertainment
• Recreation • Dinner in Sand Dunes • Lounge & Bar etc.

For reservation, please contact:
The Laxmi Niwas Palace
(A unit of Golden Triangle Fort and Palace Pvt. Ltd.)
Dr. Karni Singhji Road, Bikaner – 334001 (India)
Tel: +91-151-2202777, 2521188, Telefax: +91-151-2521487
E-mail: reservation@laxminiwaspalace.com;
Website: www.laxminiwaspalace.com

pool, while **Hotel City Palace** (Tel: 2526320-21; Tariff: Rs 400-1,100) on MG Road and RTDC's **Dhola Maru** (Tel: 2529621; Tariff: Rs 400-700) in Sadul Ganj offer bare and strictly okay rooms.

For more hotels and details, see Bikaner Accommodation Listings on pages 458-460

WHERE TO EAT

In the absence of a local clientele, there are no stand-alone restaurants in Bikaner. Your best bet, therefore, are the hotel dining rooms. While some provide excellent vegetarian cuisine (**Bhanwar Niwas** in particular), the dining halls at the **Laxmi Niwas** are so well appointed that it doesn't matter what you order — it is the atmosphere that remains queen. Most of the hotel restaurants serve a pan-Indian meal at best, but they can rustle up Rajasthani specialities on request (worth the effort). If you're into snacking, Bikaner can offer you a vast choice. **Station Road** is best for its spicy samosas, crisp kachoris and hot mirchi-vadas, followed by some soothing ras malai.

AROUND BIKANER

Gajner (32 km SW)

The private hunting preserve of the royal family of Bikaner, Gajner was developed under Maharaja Ganga Singh into the finest sandgrouse shooting reserve in the country. The palace, built to front an artificial lake, attracted sufficient wintering birds from distant Siberia, as well as a variety of deer. Shooting is, of course, prohibited now. The ownership of Gajner no longer lies with the Rathores either. It was bought some while back by the Maharana of Udaipur. Run as a heritage hotel, **Gajner Palace** (Tel: 01534-275061; Tariff: Rs 2,900-3,600) is perfect for a quiet holiday in truly regal surroundings. Photographic shoots are not only permitted but also encouraged. You will no doubt be inspired by the views of

AMIT PASRICHA

The many colours of Junagarh Fort

spectacular sunrises and sunsets from the deck of the former hunting lodge, while the solar-powered boat on the lake can get you within a few feet of water birds.
◆**Entry fee** Rs 100 per person for those just wanting a 'dekko' of the palace

For more hotels and details, see Bikaner Accommodation Listings on page 459

Attempts are on to link Gajner and Bikaner by the old railway saloon service, which might be an experience worth waiting for in itself. Until then, drive down NH15 (Bikaner-Jaisalmer Highway) to Gajner. Or hire a taxi for Rs 400-450.

Deshnoke (30 km S)

In surprising Bikaner District, it should not be extraordinary to find a temple dedicated almost entirely to rats. The **Karni Mata Temple** at Deshnoke is known by the sobriquet of 'Temple of Rats'. Since it was Karni Mata who had bestowed her blessings on Rao Bika, the

GIREESH GV

Gajner Palace, today a heritage hotel, overlooks an artificial lake

royal family has always held the saint-goddess in especially high regard. She is said to protect the city even today against everything from war to disease. It's not exactly clear how the rodents became an integral part of this temple, but thousands of them overrun the place today. Apparently the temple has a budget to feed them, and they are protected from cats and other predators by the staff. If you step on one and kill it (not a very unlikely prospect considering their numbers), you will be struck by grave misfortunes — unless, of course, you choose to make up for it by presenting the temple a rat made of gold! These saintly rats are of a breed called *kaba*. If you manage to get over your fear of trampling the goddess' own creatures long enough to look up from the floor, notice the beautifully carved marble façade and silver doors of the temple.

◆**Temple timings** 6 am-9.30 pm

There are no hotels in Deshnoke, only a few dharamshalas for backpackers, so your best bet is to visit on a day-trip. Deshnoke is a short drive away on the Nokha Road. Taxi from town should cost about Rs 450-500 approx (return).

Kolayat (52 km SW)

This is where the **Kolayat Fair** is held, the sacred site where sage Kapil Muni is supposed to have meditated centuries ago. The fair lasts for 10 days in November. **The Kolayat Lake** has 52 ghats, shaded by banyan trees.

◆**Location** On the Jaisalmer Road **Temple timings** 6 am-9 pm

Kalibangan (205 km NE)

This is an early settlement thought to have been part of the Indus Valley Civilisation. Excavations yielded evidence that town-planning measures were followed here. Remains dating to both the Harappan and pre-Harappan periods have been found at Kalibangan. An **archaeological museum** near the site houses the remnants found here, such as pottery, bricks, bangles and terracotta figures. Kalibangan can be reached from Bikaner by taxi, the charges being calculated at the rate of Rs 3.50 per km (approx fare Rs 700).

◆**Location** About 25 km from Hanumangarh, on the Hanumangarh-Pilibanga Road **Entry fee** Rs 2 **Timings** 9.30 am-5 pm, Fridays closed ■

East Rajasthan

Cradled by the mighty Aravallis, sparkling with hidden and known gems, this region offers a wealth of history and culture

HOLIDAY

Twenty-nine awards worldwide. Car of th

Are you ready to party wit

CAR OF THE YEAR 2006

Call 1800-1800-180 (toll free) or (0) 9811801515 for a test drive

1.3 LITRE · 87 BHP · 6 ON-BOARD COMPUTERS · AUTOMATIC CLIMATE CONTRO

 MARUTI SUZUKI

www.marutiswift.com

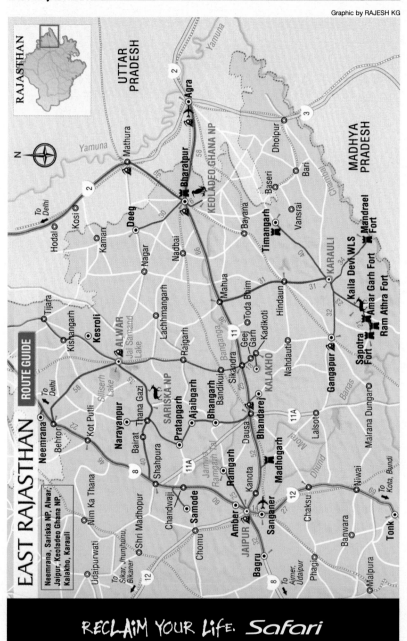

Graphic by RAJESH KG

RECLAiM YOUR Life. Safari

Untouched by winds of change, the Hawa Mahal continues to be Jaipur's icon

AMIT PASRICHA

JAIPUR

A NEW SHADE OF PINK

District Jaipur **Region** Dhundhar
Location Cradled by the Aravallis, state capital Jaipur lies on the edge of the Thar Desert in East Rajasthan
Distances 143 km NW of Ajmer, 243 km SW of Agra, 256 km SW of Delhi
Journey time *By road* 4¹/₂ hrs from Delhi, 5 hrs from Agra
Route from Delhi NH8 to Jaipur via Dharuhera, Behror, Shahpura, Kot Putli, Chandwaji and Amber (*see route guide on facing page*)

■ BY DHARMENDAR KANWAR

In 1743, 16 years after Jaipur was founded, Jesuit Father Jose Tieffenthalar visited the city and was charmed by what he saw. He wrote: "The city, while it is new, is assuredly the most beautiful among the ancient cities of India, because in the latter everything is old, the streets are unequal and narrow. This on the contrary has the splendour of the modern, with equal wide and long streets."

Three centuries later, its reputation as a beautiful, well-planned city is something that Jaipur, Sawai Jai Singh II's beloved creation, has to constantly live up to. Rajasthan's capital does this without difficulty for the most part: its enchanting bazaars wear 200 years on their sleeves with pride, its perfectly laid-out streets are easily navigated and the uniform pink that the city sports inspires and enthrals visitors in equal measure. But — and there is bound to be a but — having lived here for 30 years, I often feel that today's Jaipur doesn't wish to be left behind in the race towards modernity. It seeks a combination of the modern and the ancient, of kings and software czars, of

gleaming malls and resplendent palaces. Indeed, it's this often heady and sometimes puzzling mix that the visitor to Jaipur will today discover. There is not one Jaipur, but two cities that reflect the vivacious blend of the new and the old. Behind the city walls, you will find the original, planned heritage city that dates to the 18th century. Outside those walls is 21st century Jaipur, with spanking new multi-storeyed buildings, shopping malls, call centres and fast-moving traffic. The two Jaipurs make for an intriguing contrast: one that many books have lauded in superlatives already, and the other that you discover as you go along.

ORIENTATION

Pick up a city map (Rs 20-30) from any bookshop or from your hotel, where it's likely to be distributed free. The **railway station** and the **bus stand** are both located to the north-west and lie within a kilometre of the centre of the city. The **airport** is 14 km south of the city. Hotels are spread all over and transport, in the form of scooters, cycle rickshaws and pre-paid taxis, are readily available. It's advisable to fix the fare for both rickshaws and scooters before you hire one as they do not always run on meter. Expect to pay a minimum fare of Rs 25 from the station to **Bani Park** (a kilometre-and-a-half); keep in mind that the entire city lies between **Amber** and **Sanganer** and the distance between the two is 26 km. The main shopping areas are located within the walled city. For sightseeing, it's best to arrange a taxi through your hotel. Average taxi fare for a full day (8 hrs or 60 km) is between Rs 1,200 and 1,500. All trips out of Jaipur are charged at the rate of Rs 6-8 per km, depending on the type of car and usage of AC. A minimum fare for 250 km has to be paid regardless of how many kilometres are covered. One of the oldest and most dependable travel agencies in Jaipur is **Rajasthan Tours** (Tel: 0141-2385141/ 486).

→ FAST FACTS

When to go October to March and in the monsoons
Tourist offices
● Tourist Reception Centre ❶
Rajasthan Tourism
Government Hostel Campus, MI Road
Tel: 0141-5110598, Fax: 5110591
● RTDC Central Reservation Office ❶❶
Hotel Swagatham Complex
Near Railway Station, Jaipur
Tel: 2315714, 2202586
STD code 0141

Graphic by RAJESH KG

JAIPUR CITY TOURIST GUIDE

To Amber, Delhi

To Sikar

N

Man Sagar Lake

Dargah Amani Shah

**Jal Mahal
Jaigarh Fort**

Gaitore

**Maharani
ki Chhatri**

Jotwara Rd

Nahargarh

Walled City

Ganga Pol

Samode Haveli

Chand Pol

Bissau Palace

Bani Park

**Purani
Basti**

**Chowkri
Ramchandraji**

Ram Temple

St.Andrew's
Church

**Chowkri
Modikhana
Vishveshwarji**

Cantt

Hotel
Rajputana

**Topkhana
Desh**

Jaipur City
Rly Stn

Kishan Pol

**Ghat
Darwaza**

**Topkhana
Hazuri**

Suraj Pol

Khatipura Rd

**Chomu
House**

Mirza Ismail Rd

Ram Pol

Galta

Jai Mahal Palace

Man Pol

Sardar
Patel Marg

Statue Circle

**Albert Hall
Museum**

Jamnalal
Bajaj Marg

Civil Lines

Rajmahal
Palace

Rajasthan
Polo Club

Rambagh Palace

Ram Mandir

**Sisodia Rani
ka Bagh**

To
Ajmer,
Udaipur

Bais Godam
Rly Stn

Narayan
Niwas

To
Agra

Ajmer Rd

Bhawani
Singh Rd

Rambagh Circle

Industrial Area

Indira Circle

Ram Niwas Garden

Shanti Path

Gurudwara

Shanti Path

Indian Airlines

Gandhi Marg

**Rajasthan
University**

Jawahar
Kala Kendra

Gandhinagar
Rly Stn

**Arjun
Nagar**

Geological
Survey of Inida

Walled City

1 Nehru Bazaar
2 Bapu Bazaar
3 Johari Bazaar
4 Ramganj Bazaar
5 Tripolia Bazaar
6 Chandpol Bazaar
7 Kishanpol Bazaar
8 Gangauri Bazaar
9 LMB
10 Sireh Deori Bazaar
11 Hawa Mahal
12 Jantar Mantar
13 City Palace

8 Durgapura
Rly Stn

Birla Institute of
Scientific Research

Ayyappa Temple

Tonk Rd

To
Tonk, Bundi,
Kota

Clark's Amer

To
Sanganer Airport

To
Sawai Madhopur

— —	Main Road
····	Train Route
▪	Tourist attractions
◎	Other Place
⚎	Gate
♜	Fort
🏨	Hotel
🍴	Restaurant
⚲	Temple
⚱	Church
⚰	Masjid
🚉	Railway Station
🚌	Bus Stand
✉	Post Office
~	Water body

RECLAiM YOUR Life. Safari

You can also opt for a **bus tour** organised by the RTDC (Tel: 2202586, 2203531; full-day tour/ 9 am-6 pm, Rs 175; half-day tour/ 1.30-6 pm, Rs 80). **Siyaram City Cabs** (Tel: 6451234, Siyaram Street, Tonk Road, Durgapura) runs **Pink Pepper**, a pink double-decker bus whose upper deck doubles as a restaurant. The bus takes you around historic sights, and you can go in for a breakfast tour (8.30 am-12.30 pm), snack tours (1.30-3 pm, 4-5.30 pm, 6.30-8 pm) or a dinner tour (9-10.30 pm). Fares range from Rs 175 to 325. **Camel cart tours** of Rajasthani villages are arranged by the **Hotel Bissau Palace** (Tel: 2304371) at Rs 950 per head (Rs 750 per head for a group of seven; charges inclusive of lunch).

THINGS TO SEE AND DO

Sightseeing in Jaipur is like the city itself — neat and well-planned. This is because most of what Sawai Jai Singh, a king who

An elephant ride to Amber Fort

SANJAY SHARMA

was also an astronomer, built in 1727 still stands in a very good condition. Apart from the major monuments that are located within the walled city of Jaipur, the forts of Amber, Jaigarh and Nahargarh are must-visits for tourists. The last three will require an entire day. Keep at least four days for Jaipur.

Walled City

When Jai Singh felt the need to move his capital from Amber (*see page 71*) to a bigger place, he called upon the best available talent. The Bengali architect Vidhyadhar Chakravorty formalised the new city's plans according to a grid system. After dividing the city into nine blocks, or **chowkries**, and laying down wide and straight streets, he encircled it by a formidable wall.

As Jai Singh had the city map before him, it was an easy task for him to allot a different area for each trade. Two of the *chowkries*, taking up about one seventh of the total area, were used to locate the palace complex. The other seven blocks were given equal attention, with beautiful buildings lining the wide streets.

When you set out to explore the city, keep this pattern in mind for a better understanding of the location of the more interesting areas. **Chowkri Sarhad** was the palace block with temples, gardens and other royal buildings; **Purani Basti** was earmarked for courtiers' residences; **Topkhana Desh** was for the *thikanedars*, or the chiefs of the state's divisions; **Chowkri Modikhana-Vishveshwarji** was for Jain and Hindu businessmen and other officials; **Ghat Darwaza** was for merchants, though artistes occupied certain parts; and **Chowkri Ramchandraji** had temples and havelis built by royalty. These *chowkries* were further divided into smaller wards and sub-wards.

The least developed were **Topkhana Hazuri** and **Chowkri Gangapol** as these were later additions. The city had seven (considered an auspicious number) major gates, similar in design, with a large

SANJAY SHARMA

A bird's eye-view: Jaipur spreads out under the Amber Fort

central opening flanked by two smaller ones on either side. The gates are **Suraj Pol, Chand Pol, Ram Pol, Shiv Pol, Kishan Pol, Ganga Pol** and **Dhruv Pol. Man Pol** was a later addition.

Bazaars

The main bazaars are located within the walled city. The area opposite Hawa Mahal (*see page 69*) forms the **Sireh Deori Bazaar**, which has shops selling colourful textiles, light quilts, puppets, leather footwear, jewellery and other handicraft items. All the markets are located around the two main city blocks, or **chaupars**. Just after Hawa Mahal is the main square called **Badi Chaupar**, which leads to some interesting bazaars such as the **Ramganj Bazaar** to the east, where you can see leather shoe-makers at work. To the west is the **Tripolia Bazaar**, known for its steel and brass utensils.

Johari Bazaar, south of Badi Chaupar, is famous for **bandhani** and **block-printed textiles**. Some of the city's most well-known jewellers have their showrooms here. To see the famed *meenakari*

artisans, gem-cutters and polishers at work, head to **Gopalji ka Raasta** and **Haldiyon ka Raasta**, just off Johari Bazaar. The other important square is **Chotti Chaupar**, with very many bazaars surrounding it. To the north is **Gangauri Bazaar**, which may not have too many touristy things but is still an interesting place to explore, mainly because there has been minimum modernistic intervention here.

Towards the east is the other end of Tripolia Bazaar (it starts from Badi Chaupar), with its metal shops. At a small lane called **Maniharon ka Raasta**, off Tripolia Bazaar, you can watch lac bangle-makers at work. To the south is **Kishan-pol Bazaar**, which has wood cots, jute strings and silver items. To the east is **Chandpol Bazaar**; and Jaipur's marble workers and painters are to be found at the **Khazane Walon ka Raasta** here. The other two important markets within the walled city are **Bapu Bazaar** and **Nehru Bazaar**. The upmarket shopping area **Mirza Ismail Road** (MI Road) lies just outside the city wall.

City Palace

Palace architecture in Rajasthan is simple in design, elaborate in execution and magnificent in appearance. The City Palace complex, an integral part of the Walled City, is a fine example of this pattern. It is a sprawling enclosure with many courtyards, gateways and gardens.

Today, the former maharaja and his family occupy a part of the City Palace. Enter from **Atish Pol**, and go on to **Mubarak Mahal**, which has an exquisitely decorated marble and sandstone exterior. Designed by Sir Swinton Jacob, it was originally a royal guest house that was later turned into the **Mahakama Khas** or the Royal Secretariat. It is now the **Maharaja Sawai Man Singh II Museum**, one of the finest museums in the city, with a display of costumes, weapons, miniature paintings, rare manuscripts and other royal and historical memorabilia. One part houses the **toshakhana** or the royal wardrobe section. The other part is the **pothikhana** or the

Seller of turbans at Johari Bazaar

GIREESH GV

manuscript section. North of the Mubarak Mahal is the **Sileh Khana**, once part of the old *gunijankhana*, or the Department of Music and Dance. It now houses an armoury.

Located on a raised platform in the inner courtyard is the **Diwan-i-Khas**, a simple structure where an impression of intricate design has been created by the clever use of pink and white colour on its walls. It was used during ceremonies and is a large, pillared hall with rows of elegant marble pillars and arches. The highlights here are the two **silver water containers**, the largest in the world, mentioned in the *Guinness Book of World Records*. Sawai Madho Singh II took along these containers, after filling them with Ganga water, on a trip abroad to avoid having to use 'foreign water'.

Diwan-i-Aam, the hall of public audience, is an enclosed area where court durbars and ceremonies were held. Built by Sawai Pratap Singh, this huge hall has painted walls, cut-glass chandeliers and massive marble pillars. It houses the king's collection of miniature paintings, manuscripts and carpets.

The **Pritam Niwas Chowk** is an enclosed courtyard where dance performances were once held. Built by Pratap Singh, it has four beautifully painted gateways that represent different seasons. Beyond this lies the seven-storeyed **Chandra Mahal**, the oldest structure of the City Palace complex where the royal family still lives. North-east of it is the famous **Govind Devji Temple**, built so that the king could view it from his apartments.
◆**Palace entry fee** Adults: Indians Rs 35, foreigners Rs 180 (inclusive of entry to Jaigarh); children: Indians Rs 20, foreigners Rs 75 **Timings** 9.30 am-4.45 pm daily **Still camera** (included in ticket) Indians Rs 20, foreigners Rs 50 **Video** Rs 200 **Guides** English Rs 200, Hindi Rs 100 (1 hr)

Jantar Mantar

Located just outside the City Palace, the Jantar Mantar, or the Observatory of

SANJAY SHARMA

Looking for signs: Jantar Mantar has a collection of astronomical instruments

Sawai Jai Singh II, has an extraordinary collection of complex astronomical instruments. This one is the largest and the best preserved of the five he built in different parts of the country, the others being Delhi, Ujjain, Mathura (which no longer exists) and Varanasi. Fascinating architectural innovations were designed and built to measure the altitudes and eclipses of the sun, moon and other planets at different times of the year.

◆**Entry fee** Rs 10 **Still camera** Indians Rs 20, foreigners Rs 50 **Video** Indians Rs 50, foreigners Rs 100 **Timings** 9 am-4.30 pm

Hawa Mahal

Also called the Palace of Winds, Hawa Mahal is Jaipur's most famous monument. All ornamentation is confined to the rear portion of this five-storey structure. The façade has semi-octagonal overhanging windows with perforated screens, curvilinear roofs, domes and finials. Sawai Pratap Singh built this rather unusual palace in 1799 for the royal women to watch processions and other activities on the streets below.

◆**Entry fee** Rs 5 **Still camera** Indians Rs 10, foreigners Rs 30 **Video** Indians Rs 20, foreigners Rs 70 **Timings** 9 am-4.30 pm

Havelis

The havelis in Jaipur stand out for their architectural features such as arched entrances, carved balconies with coloured glass windows and painted inner chambers. Topping the list is the huge **Nattani ki Haveli**, also known as the Saat Chowk ki Haveli because of its seven courtyards, which overlooks Chhoti Chaupar. The **Nattanis** were important officers in Sawai Jai Singh's court. Today, half of this haveli houses the local police station while the other is being used for a girls' school.

Located a short distance from the Tripolia Gate is the well-maintained 18th century **Nawab Saheb ki Haveli**. Though named after Nawab Faiz Ali Khan, a prime minister at the time of Maharaja Madho Singh, this haveli had several illustrious occupants with Ali being the last one. The terrace of this haveli is open to tourists and presents some spectacular views of Jaipur's main streets.

Further down, when you get to Ramganj Chaupar, to the right is the **Rajputana Haveli**. The family is quite open to having visitors dropping in. Interestingly enough, many temples, such as the **Ramchandraji Temple** at **Sireh Deori Bazaar**, are also built like havelis.

Albert Hall Museum

This impressive museum, now called the Central Government Museum, is located in **Ram Niwas Garden**. Sir Swinton Jacob modelled this structure on the Victoria and Albert Museum in London. The museum has displays of Indian arts and crafts, including metal ware, ivory and woodcarvings, jewellery, textiles, pottery, sculptures and paintings. The garden here has a greenhouse, a herbarium and several sports grounds.

♦**Entry fee** Indians Rs 5, foreigners Rs 30 **Timings** 10 am-4.30 pm, open all days **Cameras** No photography allowed inside

Raj Mandir

Whether you want to watch movies or not, it's a good idea to drop in at the kitschy Raj Mandir Cinema, located on Bhawani Singh Marg in Panch Bhatti, purely for its unique architecture. Built in 1976, the structure has chandeliers, domes and an impressive foyer, not to forget 1,200 seats. All in all, an effect to rival the most colourful Hindi film sets!

Of gardens and cenotaphs

On the way to Galta and Sisodia Rani ka Bagh is the area called **Ghat ki Guni**, or **Purana Ghat**, around 6 km from the centre of the city, to its east. There are gardens and small temples here, which have been left undisturbed for years. Located 6 km to the east of Jaipur is the **Sisodia Rani ka Bagh**, the garden built for the second wife of Maharaja Jai Singh II, a Sisodia princess from Udaipur. The double-storeyed palace comprises open halls and multi-level terrace gardens with bathing tanks and pavilions. Some beautiful murals, now in a damaged state, can be seen on the palace walls.

♦**Garden entry fee** Indians and foreigners Rs 5 **Timings** 8 am-6 pm

Galta, 10 km to the east of Jaipur, was home to sage Rishi Galav. The drive to Galta, on the road behind Sisodia Rani ka Bagh, passes through one of the most beautiful areas surrounding Jaipur, verdant and untouched by urbanisation. On the ridge is the 18th century **Sun Temple**.

Gaitore is nestled in the valley between Nahargarh (*see alongside*) and Ganeshgarh, about 6 km on the Amber Road. This is a walled complex which houses the cenotaphs erected in the memory of the deceased rulers of Jaipur.

The cenotaph built for Sawai Jai Singh is the oldest. Ram Singh II's cenotaph, like that of Jai Singh, is well-decorated with carved stone pillars and panels on the domes.

Just as the rulers had separate chambers for women in their palaces, there was also a separate cremation ground for them. The **Maharani ki Chhatri** or the Maji ki Chhatri was one such. It's located on Amber Road.

JK TYRE

TOTAL CONTROL

→ **GETTING THERE**

Air Jaipur's Sanganer Airport is just south of the city (14 km/ 1/2 hr). Taxi to the city centre charges Rs 200
Rail Jaipur Station, well connected to Delhi by Ajmer Shatabdi and Delhi-Jaipur Express, to Mumbai by the Bombay Central-Jaipur and Aravalli expresses, and to Kolkata by the Howrah-Jaipur Express
Road NH8 links Jaipur to Delhi (256 km) via Shahpura and Dharuhera, and to Mumbai (1,202 km) via Ajmer, Udaipur, Ahmedabad, Baroda, Bharuch, Pardi, Talasari and Manor. RSRTC operates deluxe coaches from Bikaner House (Tel: 011-23383469) in Delhi near Pandara Road. Bus fares: Volvo Rs 460 (AC), Silverline Rs 270 (non-AC). Excellent bus connections are also available from Jaipur's Sindhi Camp Central Bus Terminal (Tel: 0141-5116031) to other destinations in Rajasthan and beyond

SANJAY SHARMA

The Albert Hall Museum has a steady stream of winged visitors

Amber

Amber, also known as Amer, was the capital of the Kachhwaha Rajputs for over 700 years. The fort here was established in 1592 by Maharaja Man Singh and successive rulers added to the majestic structure until the early 18th century when Sawai Jai Singh decided to build a new capital and shift base there. The Amber Fort straddles the hillside overlooking the small **Maota Lake**. You can walk up, if you're fit, or, if you're feeling adventurous, take an elephant ride up to the fort. It is also possible to drive up from the rear portion of the fort. Of interest here are the stunning **Diwan-i-Aam**, built of sandstone, the magnificent **Ganesh Pol**, **Sukh Niwas**, **Jai Mahal**, **Jas Mandir** and **Sheesh Mahal**.

Next to the entrance is the **Shila Devi Temple** (the kul-devi of Jaipur's rulers). The temple has fixed timings for darshan, usually 6-8 am and 4-8 pm.

◆**Location** 10 km north of Jaipur; taxis cost Rs 600 to and fro **Entry fee** Indians Rs 10, foreigners Rs 50 **Still camera** Indians Rs 50 (inclusive of entry), foreigners Rs 75 **Video** Indian Rs 100 (inclusive of entry and camera fee), foreigners Rs 150

Elephant ride (drop to fort) Rs 550 for 2 **Timings** 8 am-6 pm **Guide** Rs 100-400 (1 hr; price depends on group size)

Jaigarh

This lovely fort is within walking distance of Amber and was once the royal treasury. Of interest here is the **Jai Vana**, a huge cannon on wheels, and the gorgeous view of Jaipur the fort's ramparts offer.

◆**Entry fee** Indians Rs 20, foreigners Rs 50 **Cameras** Still Rs 40, video Rs 150 **Vehicle entry fee** Rs 50 **Timings** 9 am-4.30 pm

Nahargarh

Also known as Tiger Fort, Nahargarh was built in 1734 by Jai Singh II as a defence post. There is an RTDC restaurant here.

◆**Location** 2 km to the south of Jaigarh **Entry fee** Rs 5 **Fort timings** 10 am-10 pm **Museum timings** 10 am-5 pm **Vehicle entry fee** Rs 5

Jal Mahal

Located in the middle of Man Sagar Lake, this palace was built by Madho Singh I in the 18th century as a convenient place to conduct duck shoots from.

◆**Location** Off Amber Road

GIREESH GV

Wide open: The Nahargarh Fort

Block-printed and tie-and-dye textiles, quilts, ethnic silver and traditional gold jewellery will top your list of buys here (*also see Bazaars on page 67*). **Gopalji ka Raasta** in Johari Bazaar is a good place for jewellery; quilts are available opposite Hawa Mahal. Go to Sanganer (*see page 74*) for hand block-printed fabric.

For more expensive clothing, try **Soma** (Indian and Western clothes, and furnishings), **Cottons** (for kurtis), **Killol** (saris and kurtas), **Suvasa** (kurtis and skirts) and **Anokhi** (clothes, furnishings and quilts). **Ratan Textiles** (clothing, furnishings) is slightly cheaper and has excellent prints. All these stores are conveniently located in C Scheme and are close to each other. Prices range from Rs 350-1,500 for kurtis/ kurtas and Rs 250-1,200 for long skirts. You can buy blue pottery from Padmashri Kripal Singh Shekhawat's studio **Kripal Kumbh** (Tel: 0141-2201127) on Shiv Marg in Bani

Park. **Neerja International** in C Scheme is best for utility items in blue pottery. For traditional jewellery or *meenakari* work, try **Amrapali** at Paanch Batti. You can pick up silver bracelets, earrings, rings and necklaces from **Tholia's Kuber, Silver Mines** and **Jeypore Jewellers** on MI Road. If you're looking for *meenakari* and kundan jewellery, head to **Gem Palace** and **Rajmal Bhuramal Surana**, also on MI Road. Prices vary from a few thousand rupees to lakhs depending on the purchase. Both Irshad (Tel: 2632757) and Ramesh Chand Sharma (Tel: 2630149), **miniature painters** located on Amber Road, take orders. For customised idols, contact marble carvers **Pandey Murti Kala Kendra** (Tel: 2318834) at Narain Bhawan, Kheje ka Raasta.

Jaipur offers something for everyone, from 7-star super-deluxe hotels to inexpensive homestays.

Heritage

The city has well-run heritage hotels and havelis, the latter being somewhat more affordable. The newly renovated **Rambagh Palace** (Tel: 0141-2211919; Tariff: Rs 20,300-1,76,000), on Bhawani Singh Road, has a popular pub, beautiful lawns and plenty of old-world charm. The Polo Bar here is a great place to hang out. **Jai Mahal Palace** (Tel: 2223636; Tariff: Rs 13,000-18,500), near Civil Lines, is tucked away from the crowded areas and is popular with those looking for a peaceful stay. **Rajmahal Palace** (Tel: 5105665; Tariff: Rs 2,500-4,000), located in C Scheme, is one of the palaces of the Jaipur royal family that was turned into a hotel. It has huge palatial rooms, friendly staff, and is surrounded by huge gardens. However, it can sometimes get a little noisy as it is a popular venue for music shows and other events.

Other heritage options include: **Narayan Niwas** (Tel: 2561291; Tariff:

SIMPLY SAMODE

SANGANER Paper mill

Raja Man Singh and Mahatma Gandhi have little in common apart from the fact that they both took the Kagzis — papermakers since the days of Sultan Firoz Shah Tughlaq — under their wing. In the 16th century, Man Singh brought them to Sanganer, an ancient town that existed long before Jaipur. A few hundred years later, in the 1930s, when bereft of state patronage and undone by machine-made paper from Europe, the Kagzis were teetering on the verge of ruin, Gandhiji played saviour to them by ordering a bulk consignment of handmade paper for his ashram. Allah Bux Kagzi, a veteran papermaker from Sanganer, even made history by demonstrating papermaking at the Congress' 1938 session in Haripura.

Just 14 km from Jaipur's busy Narayan Singh Circle, Sanganer today is a busy centre of paper manufacture. The main change that has come over the years is that papermaking has evolved from being a household industry to a more organised activity. There are half-a-dozen large factories now, all strongly export-oriented. The other major change that has come about is in the equipment used and the varieties of paper produced.

The Kagzis use three types of raw material to produce paper: cotton rags, silk and banana trunk fibre. Cotton-based paper makes up 90 per cent of their produce, but despite the humble raw material, the final product comes in myriad attractive finishes.

There's metalised paper, glazed to look like foil, and leatherised paper, deliberately creased to resemble leather. Then there's paper infused with flower petals and leaves, or decorated with tinsel or even block-printed just like cloth.

While the price of paper varies from Rs 4 to Rs 35 per sheet, products made out of it are much more steeply priced. A simple photo frame, for instance, costs upward of Rs 75. Then there are lamps and boxes, trays and plates, but diaries and greeting cards far outnumber the rest. If you wish to buy some handmade paper, or paper products, just visit any of the big factories, for shops in Sanganer don't stock these things. Also, while in Sanganer, don't forget to visit the beautiful 10th century **Digamber Jain Temple**, just a stone's throw away from the papermakers, which is decorated all over with carved figures.

Some major **handmade paper units** include: **Kagzi Handmade Paper** (Tel: 0141-2730019/ 76; Email: kagzi@datainfosys.net), Gramodyog Road; **Kalpana Handmade Paper** (Tel: 2732115; Email: kalpanah@satyam.net.in), Bawadi ka Bas; **Kohinoor Paper** (Tel: 5171048; Email: info@kohinoorpaper.com) on Malpura Road; **AL Paper House** (Tel: 2731706), near Tempo Stand; and **Century Papers** (Tel: 2730766), located on Jain Hostel Road.

Abhilash Gaur

Rs 2,365-4,500), at Narayan Singh Road; **Alsisar Haveli** (Tel: 2368290; Tariff: Rs 2,400-3,650), just off Chandpol Bazaar; **Mandawa Haveli** (Tel: 2374130; Tariff: Rs 2,000-3,000) opposite Alsisar Haveli; **Shahpura House** (Tel: 2202293; Tariff: Rs 2,500-3,500) at Bani Park; and **Hari Mahal Palace** (Tel: 2221399; Tariff: Rs 2,800-4,000) at Civil Lines. These are all palatial havelis that have been converted into lovely heritage hotels complete with restaurants, swimming pools and Internet facilities. Most have fairly large gardens and an excellent ambience.

The **Diggi Palace** (Tel: 2373091; Tariff: Rs 600-1,800) on SMS Hospital Road is a pretty haveli that has been turned into a hotel. It is set in a green lawn, and has fresco-painted rooms.

Others

Oberoi's **Rajvilas** (Tel: 2680101; Tariff: Rs 22,500-1,27,000) on Goner Road is 8 km from the city centre and is a little world

Snehdeep

First stop for all cars and buses entering Jaipur Either from Delhi or Agra Highway

- Proximity to the historical walled city of Jaipur
- Well furnished air-conditioned / air cooled rooms
- Roof top restaurant, ' Bird's Eye View' serving Indian and Continental cuisines
- Room tariff ranging from Rs. 550/- to Rs. 1200/- per night
- Sightseeing packages available for Rs. 850/- per pax including pick-up and breakfast

Contact:
Dr. Smita
B-33, Sethi Colony
Govind Marg, Jaipur – 302004
Ph: 0141 – 2604570
Cell: 09351793444, 09314880887
E-mail: snehdeep_jp1@sancharnet.in,
wildbrook@gmail.com
Website: www.snehdeep.com

Check-out 12 Noon

TRIBHUVAN TIWARI

Diggi Palace, a pretty haveli that has been turned into a hotel

in itself. One of the country's leading spas, it's the first choice for visiting Presidents and is listed among the top 10 hotels in the world.

Amongst the many 5-star hotels are **Trident Hilton** (Tel: 2670101; Tariff: Rs 5,000-7,000) on Amber Road, with some rooms offering views of the Jal Mahal; **Rajputana Palace** (Tel: 5100100; Tariff: Rs 8,000-50,000), with a restaurant serving sumptuous non-vegetarian food; and **Clarks Amer** (Tel: 2550616; Tariff: Rs 5,000-17,500), close to the airport. Many of the better-known residential houses converted into family-run hotels are located in Bani Park. These excellent stay options include: **Jas Vilas** (Tel: 2204638; Tariff: Rs 2,000-4,000); **Megh Niwas** (Tel: 2202034-36; Tariff: Rs 1,400-2,600); **Tara Niwas** (Tel: 2206823; Tariff: Rs 750-950); **Arya Niwas** (Tel: 2372456; Tariff: Rs 500-990); and **Jaipur Inn** (Tel: 2201121, 098290 13660; Tariff: Rs 750-1,250).

If you're looking for a rural ambience, a good option is **Chokhi Dhani** (Tel: 2225001; Tariff: Rs 5,000-8,000). Located 6 km from the airport, and 12 km from Jaipur, on Tonk Road, this hotel has recently been given 5-star status and is an unusual place with a rural museum, camels, bullock carts and an excellent restaurant (*also see Where to Eat on page 78*). The rooms here have all the modern facilities imaginable. Be prepared for a mela atmosphere here, however.

Homestays

Clarks Amer (*see alongside*) has started a homestay project by the name of **Jaipur Pride**. Bookings can be done through the hotel and the rates vary between Rs 600 and Rs 6,000. A list of homestay options is available with Clarks Amer or you can book directly through their website jaipurprideproject.com.

Each of the homes on the list has been selected by Clarks and some training has been provided to the owners. The rates vary according to the facilities available. You can expect clean, comfortable rooms with or without ACs. However, be warned that there are no swimming pools or restaurants in these places. The families usually provide simple meals.

For more hotels and details, see Jaipur Accommodation Listings on pages 462-469

WHERE TO EAT

Over the years, Jaipur has emerged as a fine dining destination. Fast food outlets are on MI Road, and there are numerous places that serve the local speciality of dal-baati-choorma. Some places to check out are: **Niro's** on MI Road for excellent Indian, Continental and Chinese — do try their chicken *á la kiev* and chicken stroganoff; **Natraj**, also on MI Road, for good Indian food and a tasty Rajasthani thali; **Skylark**, off Rambagh Circle, for consistently good Indian and Thai food; **Copper Chimney** on MI Road for lal maas as well as excellent vegetarian dishes; and **Annapurna** just off MI Road for its Gujarati thali. **The Royal Treat**, a multi-cuisine restaurant at Ramgarh Modh on Amber Road, is popular with tour groups as they organise Rajasthani cultural programmes in the evenings.

Spice Court in Civil Lines has traditional Rajasthani food such as keema baatis (mince stuffed wheat balls), safed maas (white mutton) and sulas (barbecued mutton); **Four Seasons** in C Scheme has good masala dosa and channa bhatura while **Garden Café**, also in C Scheme, has scrumptious paneer tikkas, pindi channa and kulcha. Try **LMB** in the Old City and **Kanji** on Station Road for alu tikki, dahi bara, chaat and a wide variety of mithai. **Surabhi** on Amber Road serves authentic Rajasthani non-vegetarian food — try their lal maas, garlic naan and chicken tikka butter masala. An added attraction here is the interesting **Turban Museum** for guests. For coffee, there is **Barista** at Paanch Batti, **Café Coffee Day** at Gaurav Towers, **Mr Beans** and **The Rock** on Sardar Patel Marg and **Café Kooba** on Jamnalal Bajaj Marg.

At **Chokhi Dhani** (*see Where to Stay on page 76*), food is served in the traditional style, with seating on the floor, and an array of delicious Rajasthani dishes such

GIREESH GV

Delicious spread: A Rajasthani thali

as gatta, ker sangri, bajra roti and lahsun mirch ki chutney will leave you asking for more. The rural ambience is also to be found at **Sharma Dhaba**, which has the best butter naan, chutney and paneer masala in town and **Apno Rajasthan**, which serves delicious Rajasthani dishes such as khaata, ker sangri and rabdi. Both are on Sikar Road.

For savouries, a few places include: **Rawat Mishthan Bhandar**, near Polo Victory, for mirchi vada and mawa ki kachori; **Shankar Namkeen Bhandar**, off Chaura Raasta, for mixed namkeen; **Bhagat Mishthan Bhandar** at Kishanpole Bazaar for the best laddoos in town; **Pandit Kulfi** at Sireh Deorhi Bazaar for kulfis; and **Narayanji Gajjak Wale** at Johari Bazar for excellent gajjak.

AROUND JAIPUR

Bagru (32 km SW)
Bagru is known for its block-printed textiles. It's a small village, and as there are only a few families who do block-printing, it's easy to locate them. Most work on orders from exporters but it's possible to pick up surplus fabric from them. Taxi costs Rs 500 approx for a return-trip from Jaipur.

Hotel Connections India is one of the most prominent & professional delhi based Hotel Marketing company. **HCI** provides Marketing services to the Member hotels only . Established just 4 years ago in Delhi, the company now markets over 19 Hotels of different kinds across 14 destinations in India. The company offers Quality service and instant confirmations with full of comforts and very efficient service & a warm friendly welcome under one roof at **HCI**.

Presently we have 14 destinations into three parts, in the first sector we have chosen prime locations of the "Royal Rajasthan" which includes (Pink city Jaipur, Pushkar, Jodhpur, Jaisalmer, Ranthambhore & the city of lakes Udaipur).

Apex International, Jodhpur

Hotel Goyal Inn, Pushkar

Las Vegas, Jaipur

Hotel Neelam, Jaipur

Vishnupriya, Udaipur

Tiger Villa, Ranthambhore

Dhola Maru, Jaisalmer

DINESH SHUKLA

Making history: The Samode Palace, a heritage hotel that's the last statement in luxury

Samode (42 km N)
Samode should be visited for its palace-hotel, showcasing a fine blend of Rajput-Mughal architecture styles, which has been well restored today. Rawal Sheo Singh, who was the prime minister of Jaipur during the mid-19th century, gave the palace its most fabulous addition — the extravagantly hand-painted Darbar Hall and the overlooking gallery, which forms the breathtaking Sheesh Mahal. **Samode Palace** (Tel: 01423-240014; Tariff: Rs 7,700-19,350) was transformed into one of the country's premium palace hotels in 1987. Tourists not staying here are required to pay Rs 250 as entry fee. The palace runs a restaurant, so you can even spend a full day here. Taxi from Jaipur costs Rs 1,400 for a return-trip.

Ramgarh (25 km NE)
The manmade lake in Ramgarh is the main source of water supply to Jaipur. On its banks is the Taj Group-managed **Ramgarh Lodge** (Tel: 01426-252217; Tariff: Rs 4,400-7,000), a one-time hunting lodge of the Jaipur royal family. The lodge is open to tourists for a fee of Rs 200; if you would like to have a meal here, do inform the staff in advance. The

Jamwa Mata Temple is located 2 km from the lodge on a small hillock and attracts hundreds of devotees throughout the year. The area around Ramgarh is lush green and an ideal getaway. It's best to avoid visiting on weekends and other holidays as it can get crowded. It is half an hour's drive by car from Jaipur. Taxi costs Rs 1,500 approx for a return-trip.

Tonk (110 km S)
This 17th century town lies en route to Ranthambhore. You will find a colourful medley of mansions and colonial buildings here. Of special interest here is the **Sunheri Kothi** (Timings: 10 am-5 pm; Sundays closed) in the heart of town. Though not a very impressive building from the outside, every square inch of the inner chamber of the building is studded with tiny mirrors and painted in bright hues. Permission to explore the haveli has to be taken from the MAKA Arabic and Persian Research Institute (Tel: 01432-247389) near the new bus stand. Tonk is also known for its *namdah* (woollen rugs) industry; the designs are either embroidered or appliquéd. Taxi fare from Jaipur would be Rs 1,500 approx for a return-trip. ∎

The **Ultra** Edition 12.9

SAMSUNG SGH D-900

① Albert Hall   ② Amber Fort   ③ Elephants at Amber Fort

④ Raj Mandir Cinema Hall   ⑤ City Palace

imagine doing more with less.
The Ultra Life.

Imagine always being in two places at once, doing two things at once. No office. No boundaries. No restrictions. With Samsung's new Ultra Edition it's not that hard to imagine.   www.samsung.com

Features: 3 Mega Pixel Camera with Auto-Focus • MP3 Player • Intelligent Display • Large 262K QVGA TFT Screen • Direct TV Out

Free accessories: *Bluetooth™ Headset • 256 MB T Flash Memory Card • TV Out Cable • Battery Charger • Travel Adapter • Car Adapter • Straight Headset • Battery (2 Nos.) • Data Kit*

The **Ultra** Edition 12.9

SAMSUNG SGH D-900

Leo Burnett D SMSCHLB-00013H

SAMSUNG

ABHILASH GAUR

The walls of the Bala Qila spread over the green hills like tentacles

ALWAR

A SECRET OUT IN THE OPEN

District Alwar **Region** Mewat
Location In north-eastern Rajasthan, Alwar is set amidst the Aravalli Hills, not far south of Delhi
Distances 148 km NE of Jaipur, 156 km SW of Delhi
Journey time By road 3 hrs from Jaipur, $3^1/_2$ hrs from Delhi
Route from Jaipur NH8 to Shahpura via Amber; state highway to Alwar via Bairat, Thana Gazi and Sariska **Route from Delhi** NH8 to Dharuhera via Manesar; state highway to Alwar via Tijara (*see route guide on page 62*)

■ BY ABHILASH GAUR

Most Rajasthan Roadways' buses racing down to Alwar have 'Matsyanagar Aagar (depot)' painted on their rear panels. But the last time Alwar was referred to by that name was immediately after Independence, when the kingdoms of Alwar, Bharatpur, Dholpur and Karauli were merged to form the short-lived 'United Kingdom of Matsya'.

But the name itself is older than recorded history, its antecedents hailing from mythology. The Matsya kingdom, for instance, figures in the Mahabharata.

Historians are divided on the origin of the modern name Alwar. Some say it is a corruption of Salwapur, Salwa being the name of a tribe that lived here. Others say it is a corruption of Aravalpur, Aravallis being the hill range running through the district. Still others see it as a corruption of Alpur, the name of the city founded by Maharaja Alaghraj in 1049.

Legends apart, the oldest extant thing in the city today is the Bala Qila, built by the Nikumbha Rajputs in the 10th century. The fort spreads over the surrounding hills, which, along with the nearby lakes, are Alwar's most alluring assets. If you come in the rains, they are bright green; if you come in the dry season, they are ruddy and rocky.

All that rock has been put to good use in and around Alwar. Forts, tombs and palaces abound. It is said that as Alwar was the youngest kingdom in Rajputana — it came into existence in 1775 — its rulers never tired of pomp and pageantry to make their mark amidst the older kingdoms. This should explain why they built 52 forts and innumerable palaces in the 175-odd years that they ruled.

Modern Alwar is a repository of much of that heritage. Unfortunately, it does not seem to get any returns on its investment, as tourists bypass Alwar for places like Sariska. Wandering around the town's old streets, one realises how much there is to cherish in Alwar, and how little the outside world knows about it.

Alwar Town does not have public transport, but cycle rickshaws are cheap and easily available along most roads. The city stretches west from the railway line to the hills crowned by the 10th century **Bala Qila**. Most of the sightseeing and buildings such as the **City Palace** and **Moosi Maharani ki Chhatri** are concentrated on this far side, under the fort's watchful eye. The **Alwar Inter-State Bus Terminus** is also nearby, within walking distance of the **Prem Pavitra Bhojanalaya**, the best place to lunch at after a long journey. North-east of the bhojanalaya is **Hope Circle**, a busy traffic intersection surrounded by markets like **Churi Bazaar** and **Kalakand Market**. While cycle rickshaws charge at least Rs 10, the fare varies

according to not only the distance but also the gradient of the roads traversed. The usual fare from the bus terminus to the railway station is Rs 15. While there are diesel autos that run both inside and outside the town, they are expensive to hire solo and run like shared cabs. The cycle rickshaw is a more eco-friendly option for short distances.

THINGS TO SEE AND DO

You can do all the sightseeing in Alwar in a day, but don't take this to mean that there is little of note in the town. The city is dotted with heritage buildings, though it hasn't learnt to showcase them yet. Therefore, one finds that the City Palace, a sprawling complex, is consumed by government offices, with only a rooftop museum there for consolation; the Vijai Mandir Palace is locked up owing to a legal dispute; the Bala Qila is with the police; and the guard at Fateh Jung ka

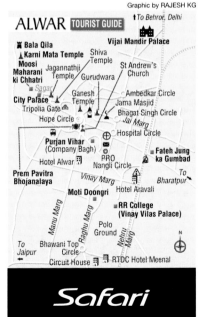

ABHILASH GAUR

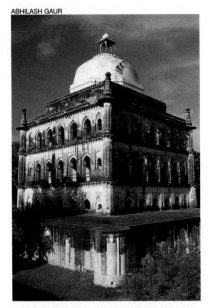

Fateh Jung ka Gumbad, a medieval tomb

Gumbad may or may not turn up, and the tomb may remain locked during your visit. That one manages to enjoy one's stay in Alwar, despite these hurdles, is an indication of its charms.

A tomb and a palace that wasn't

A five-storey medieval tomb, **Fateh Jung ka Gumbad** outclasses all its contemporaries in Delhi, barring the tomb of Emperor Humayun. It is the easternmost of Alwar's monuments, lying just across the railway line by a pedestrian overbridge, close to the Bharatpur Road. The tomb stands amidst a walled garden, which houses a school. The guard who unbars the steps leading up to the mausoleum seldom turns up before 9 am.

After Fateh Jung ka Gumbad, cross the railway line back into the city, and take a rickshaw to **Moti Doongri**, the grand palace that couldn't be. Built in 1882, Moti Doongri was the main residence of the Alwar royals till 1928, when Maharaja Jai Singh decided to raze the palace and

build a more magnificent one in its place. However, the ship carrying materials from Europe for the new palace sank, and with it ended the grand project. Nonetheless, climbing up the wide ramp to the top of the old rock has its reward: an unhindered view of the city.

Purjan Vihar

A short walk away from Moti Doongri, towards the railway line, stands **RR College**, once known as the **Vinay Vilas Palace**. The building is worth a look from up close, and from here, you can head to Purjan Vihar, or **Company Bagh**, as it is called. This is a beautiful garden with a large, domed summer house, called **Shimla**, set in a trough amidst the rich verdure. Maharaja Sheodan Singh laid out the garden in 1868, and Maharaja Mangal Singh built Shimla in 1885. Locals take great pride in Shimla, which has walkways and fountains.

♦**Company Bagh timings** Always open **Summer House timings** 9 am-5 pm **Entry** Free

From Company Bagh, head up the Church Road, past the stone-built St Andrew's Church, which is usually locked. By evening, Church Road is a busy market, but in the morning you can

→ **FAST FACTS**

When to go Winter (October to March) is the official season, but monsoon is magical
Tourist office
● Tourist Information Centre ❶
RTDC, Opp Alwar Railway Station
Tel: 0144-2347348
TIP Ask for the very useful, free Alwar city tourist map here
STD code 0144

Photographs by GIREESH GV

A haveli in Alwar welcomes visitors by blowing its own trumpet

stop and admire the old havelis here. At the end of the road lies Hope Circus, a traffic island with shops on the street level and a temple above. Seven streets radiate outwards from the circle. The fifth from Church Road leads to the **Clock Tower** and has the **Kalakand Market** (*see Where to Eat on page 92*) strung along it. The fourth street from Church Road leads to the Tripolia Gateway and on to the City Palace complex. From outside, **Tripolia** looks like an unremarkable gateway, but small shrines have been built into its corners. On either side of the gate, while going towards City Palace, are old markets, called **Sarafa Bazaar** and **Bajaja Bazaar**. Both are famous for the gold ornaments sold at the shops. You will also find beautiful havelis along the way.

City Palace

The City Palace complex is accessed through a gateway with projecting balconies on either side. Beyond the gate lies an open ground with Krishna temples on all four sides. The City Palace, **Sagar**, a tank, and **Moosi Rani ki Chhatri** are located just behind these temples.

Morning is the best time to visit City Palace as the sun shines directly on its façade. The building has been completely taken over by state government offices, the Alwar Collectorate and the police superintendent's office. Still, apart from admiring the architecture and ornamentation of this late 18th century palace built in 1793 by Raja Bakhtawar Singh, visitors can climb up to the **museum** at the top. It has three sections: the first hall has royal robes and clay toys, an interesting exhibit here being the bicycle of Maharaja Jai Singh with three hub gears and brakes built into its pedals. The second hall is a storehouse of paintings, including large canvases of notable Central Asian conquerers, right from Timur to Aurangzeb. The third has a display of weapons, and placed without obvious distinction among other weapons are the swords of Akbar and Jehangir.

◆**Entry fee** Rs 3 **Timings** 10 am-5 pm, Fridays closed

Just behind the palace lies the large tank called **Sagar**, which has beautiful, two-tiered, domed pavilions set around it. Steps go down to the water, which was used for ritual bathing in the old days. Feeding pigeons is a tradition at the tank. Across the water is a string of temples, and on the right, the beautiful marble and **Karauli sandstone cenotaph** of Raja Bakhtawar Singh. But it is named after his mistress, Rani Moosi, who performed sati on his funeral pyre.

Vijai Mandir Lake Palace

This beautiful palace, built in the year 1918, was the royal residence of Maharaja Jai Singh. It is a sprawling building with a beautiful Ram Temple inside, but it lies locked up because of family disputes. The palace cannot be seen from the front but you can get a good view of it from the shore of the lake behind it. The road past the lake leads up to the Bala Qila (*see below*). Diesel autos charge about Rs 200 for the 40-km Alwar-Vijai Mandir-Bala Qila-Alwar trip.

TIP The palace is off-limits to tourists

Bala Qila

The City Palace complex forms the eastern extremity of Alwar, and beyond it run the Aravallis, with Bala Qila standing guard atop them. The fort's walls spread out over the hills like tentacles, piercing the green cover in wild sweeps. The name Bala Qila (Young Fort) is ironic, as it is the oldest extant structure in town, dated to 928 CE, when the Nikumbha Rajputs were

TOTAL CONTROL

→ GETTING THERE

Air Nearest airport: Sanganer Airport, Jaipur (162 km/ 3½ hrs). Taxi costs Rs 700-800 to Alwar

Rail Alwar Station is well-connected to Delhi and Jaipur by the Ajmer Shatabdi and the Jammu-Delhi and Delhi-Jaisalmer express trains. Taxis are available at the station, but there is often a shortage of vehicles. So ask your hotel for a pick-up or hire one at the station for the length of your stay

Road Alwar is well-connected to the capital by the Bhiwadi-Alwar toll road. Turn left off NH8 at Dharuhera and drive down straight to Bhiwadi, the origin of the toll road. Though not an expressway, the two-lane road is well-maintained and bypasses towns like Tijara. Cars are charged Rs 35 (single way) on the toll road from Bhiwadi to Alwar

The last notes

In Alwar you can hear an unusual one-string instrument called *bhapung*. A part of Mewati music culture, its best known proponent is Zahoor Khan Mewati, whose story is fascinating. One day, years ago, when he was hawking bidis and using the *bhapung* to draw attention to himself, the film actor Dilip Kumar, who was in Alwar for a shoot, heard him. He took Khan to Bollywood, where the latter provided part of the background score to films such as *Ganga Jamuna, Naya Daur* and *Aankhen*. Khan has also performed abroad but now continues to live and teach in Alwar. Interestingly, traditionally all *bhapung* players, born Muslim, are also devotees of Shiva because they believe the instrument derives from Shiva's *dumroo*. If you are in Alwar, try calling the local *bhapung* group (Tel: 0144-2372168; Mobile: 09352204242) or locating Khan (Flat No. 2, Near Takya, Delhi Road, Mungaska, Alwar). The group also performs privately for a fee.

Madhavi Sanghamitra Bhatia

At the old Churi Bazaar, it's shopping for bangles as usual

in power. There's little of worth within the fort — the Durbar Hall at the top now houses Alwar Police's wireless room — but the 10-km drive (Rs 120 by diesel auto from ISBT Alwar; *also see Vijai Mandir Lake Palace on facing page*) is its own reward. The road is good, the tree cover dense all along, and the majestic old wall, with steps built along it, surfaces from time to time. The fort is entered through **Jai Pol**, which remains open from 6 am to 7 pm on all days but Tuesdays and Saturdays, when it closes at 9 pm for the convenience of devotees visiting the **Karni Mata Temple** down a hillside.

While entry into the inner fort at the top is free (the permission of the Superintendent of Police's office is not required now, as was the case earlier), visitors need to sign in the register kept with the sentry before they can walk around. In case of harassment by the constable there, call the SP's office at 0144-2337453.

near Hope Circle most interesting. Alwar is famous for its **shellac bangles**, and here they sell two thick *karas* for Rs 10 to Rs 250. In all, there are about 15 bangle shops in this market, such as **Rajasthan Bangle Store** and **Rajesh Bangle Store**. Shops selling Alwar's famous **milk cake** or kalakand line the main road between Hope Circus and the Clock Tower, where the sweet is sold for Rs 100 a kilo. Marble sculptors have their workshops at **Ghora Pher ka Chauraha**, on the road to **Siliserh Lake** (*see page 92*). There are about a dozen workshops with names like Shiv Murti, Jai Shri Ram Murti and Deepak Murti, and they use the stone mined within the district at Pratapgarh. While they specialise in **religious idols** and busts of national leaders, they also sculpt designs and statues on order. Prices range from Rs 2,500 for a foot-high idol of Krishna to Rs 16,000 for a half-tonne idol of Hanuman.

SHOPPING

Alwar is the major city of the district, with big markets. But the tourist would find the old bazaars such as **Churi Bazaar**

WHERE TO STAY

Alwar has many hotels, most of them inexpensive, but only a handful are suitable for families on vacation. Luxurious

The Hotel Lake Palace at Siliserh, which wins hands down for location

accommodation is, however, on offer at heritage hotels located within a few kilometres of Alwar Town.

Heritage

The most famous of the heritage properties here is 12 km away, the Neemrana-run **The Hill Fort Kesroli** (Tel: 01468-289352; Mobile: 0982981765; Tariff: Rs 2,000-5,000). The 14th-century fort has 21 rooms with names like Hindola Mahal and Sitara Mahal. Off-season discount of 20-40 per cent is available from May 1 to August 31. During the off-season, rooms can be rented for **day-trips** (between 9 am and 5 pm) at a discount of about 60 per cent on the normal tariff. The hotel arranges camel rides. The fort is said to be the "oldest heritage site in India where you can stay", standing on a high rock with ramparts rising to about 214 ft. It was built by the Yaduvanshi Rajputs, who converted to Islam during the reign of Firoz Shah Tughlaq in the mid-14th century. Hire a cab from Alwar Railway Station (Rs 350) or a diesel auto (Rs 200) for the fort.

About 7 km from Alwar is **Hotel Burja Haveli** (Tel: 0144-5131288; Mobile: 09829096285; Tariff: Rs 1,800-4,000), the 'newest' heritage hotel around Alwar. Situated in Burja Village, on the Alwar-Rajgarh Road, the 240-year-old haveli opened to guests in June 2005, and is equipped with a conference hall, pool and a restaurant serving Rajasthani, Indian, Continental and Chinese fare.

The **Circuit House** (Tel: 2700650; Tariff: Rs 300-450), formerly Maharaja Jai Singh's guest house, to the city's south, between Raghu Marg and Nehru Marg, is another heritage option. You need the district magistrate's permission to stay here (Tel: 2337565). They will ask you to fax a request (Fax: 2336101). RTDC's **Hotel Lake Palace** (*see page 92*) at Siliserh is also an option.

Others

Hotel Aravali (Tel: 2332883/ 316; Tariff: Rs 300-3,000) is by far the best bet in Alwar. It is recognised as a 2-star hotel, and offers safe, clean accommodation just opposite the railway station. **Hotel**

Experiencing the
Living Coultures of India

Dera Sand Dune Resort

World's first air-conditioned resort atop a 130 feet high sand dune in the Thar Desert. Facilities include Swimming pool, Spa, Restaurant and Bar. The range of activities include wildlife watching, camel safari and 4x4 dune and tribal jeep safari.

Dera Lake View Retreat

A village air conditioned retreat situated on the banks of the Madhosagar Lake, between Agra and Jaipur. A unique and comfortable country side rural tourism concept. Activities include hiking, camel safari, jeep safari and farming experience.

Far Horizon Tours Pvt. Ltd.
66, Charmwood Plaza, Eros Garden, near Surajkund, Faridabad–121009, India.
Tel: +91-0129-4098000, Fax: 91-0129-4098098
info@farhorizonindia.com; www.farhorizonindia.com

Still life in blue and grey: The Neemrana Fort-Palace is a pool of serenity

NEEMRANA Holding fort

BY ABHILASH GAUR

There are no turbaned and moustachioed doormen to stamp their feet and salute you as you enter, no bent-over ushers holding onto your words. At the Neemrana Fort-Palace, the service is discreet and friendly, a description that holds true for the rooms as well. Each room, or rather mahal, is tastefully done up with period furniture and antiques, without ever going over the top. Neemrana, in fact, is a study in architectural influences, showcasing styles dating as far back as the mid-15th century. From Delhi Sultanate architecture as seen in Neelam Mahal to the 19th century influence in Colonial Francisi Mahal to the contemporary Deva Mahal, you can take your pick of the era you wish to be transported to.

The fort-palace started taking shape during 1464, under the area's Chauhan overlords. The palaces became bigger with additional structures being added till about the late 19th century, when it altogether covered three

acres. Then it went into decline, and had become a ruin by 1986, when it was taken over for conversion to a heritage resort (*also see And the rest is history on page 316*).

The fort-palace is always quiet, notwithstanding the mostly occupied 46 rooms and suites. The silence of the place is conducive to relaxation, which is what most big-city dwellers turn to this laidback nook for.

Things to see and do
The nine-tiered fort-palace offers many pleasures for the tourist, beginning with its rooms that are full of surprises. Even the public spaces have their quiet charms. The **Tibari** (a room fronted with three arched gates), for instance, has a beautiful view of the palace building and the path leading inside from **Suraj Pol**, the main gate. From the swings in **Hindola Mahal** (*hindola* is a large swing with space for four), you have an uninterrupted view of the plains below the fort. The lotus pool called **Holi Kund** and the terrace beside **Aranya Mahal**

are also vantage points with unique views. For relaxation, there are options such as swimming or an Ayurvedic massage at the spa, or a workout at the gym. The reception houses a small library, and the new wing has a games room with chess, carrom and cards.

Outside the fort, hardly five minutes away by car, lies a **nine-storey deep baoli**. You can also walk or ride a camel cart to reach here. There is a small watchtower, a 500-m climb away. The village below the fort has silver-smiths, who still use *angithas* (clay furnaces), and their work is a joy to watch.

Sightseers are welcome at the fort-palace during the day (9 am-5 pm), on a payment of Rs 200 per head for 2 hrs, which entitles them to walk around the public areas and eat at the restaurants. Picnics are not allowed.

Cuisine

The cuisine at the fort-palace represents the diverse tastes of the guests as well as the management, ranging from Rajasthani to Continental, with a special mention for French. Their Rajasthani menu includes dal-baati-choorma, gatte ki subzi, kair sangri, papad mangori, panchmela dal, karhi pakodi, lal maas, chicken vindaloo, shahi tukra, halwa, balushahi, kheer, shrikhand and Alwar's famous kalakand.

The interior of the Bada Mahal

Fixed menus are offered at per head rates of Rs 250 for breakfast, Rs 500 for lunch and Rs 600 for dinner. Day visitors and other non-residents have to pay Rs 400 for breakfast and Rs 700 for lunch and must book meals in advance at the Delhi office (011-24356145). Their Rs 200 entry fee is then waived. Dinner, however, is only for residents. Beer is served to all but the bar is only for residents.

Shopping

The fort-palace has its brand shop, **The Neemrana Shop**, just after Suraj Pol. It sells merchandise ranging from table linen, clothes, candles and pottery to tea sets. Just below the fort are two shops, **Ambika Arts** and **Shyam Silver Craft**, which stock Rajasthani souvenirs. If looking for traditional jewellery, walk down the old market, which has some 35-40 shops of jewellers selling handcrafted jewellery such as heavy **newris** (anklets).

Accommodation details

At the **Neemrana Fort Palace** (Tel: 01494-246006-08; Tariff: Rs 1,500-15,000), you will find rooms in a wide price range, each with diverse architectural styles. The check-in time at the property is 2 pm, while the check-out time is 12 noon. The off-season lasts from May 1 to August 31, when 20 per cent rebate is offered on AC rooms, and 40 per cent on all others. The management allows the chartering of the entire fort-palace on a payment of Rs 20,000 as premium.

Around Neemrana

The fort-palace is ideally situated as a getaway from Delhi and as a stopover to Jaipur (120 km/ 2 hrs along NH8 from Delhi and 140 km/ $2^1/_2$ hrs from Jaipur). Alwar is even closer (90 km/ $1^1/_2$ hrs) via Behror, Sodawas and Tatarpur. The **Hill Fort Kesroli** (*see page 88*), another Neemrana property, is 90 km away via Alwar.

Getting there

The hotel arranges pick-ups from Delhi for Rs 2,700 (both ways, including taxes). From Delhi, non-AC taxis are cheaper at Rs 2,000 plus taxes (return). From Jaipur, a taxi will charge you Rs 3,000 (return). ∎

Alwar (Tel: 2700012, 3205251; Tariff: Rs 900-2,200), on Manu Marg, close to Hope Circus, has spacious rooms and is within a few minutes of most monuments. RTDC's **Hotel Meenal** (Tel: 2347352; Tariff: Rs 400-700), close to the Circuit House, lies a little out of town and you would have problems finding rickshaws to and from it. But it is a safe bet.

For more hotels and details, see Alwar Accommodation Listings on pages 457-458

WHERE TO EAT

While in Alwar, it's best to opt for local cuisine. The city does have its cafés, ice-cream parlours, pastry shops and pizzerias, but they may not suit all palates. The city has only one good restaurant, **Prem Pavitra Bhojanalaya**, which serves simple Rajasthani fare. Do try their karhi-pakori or gatte ki sabzi with missi roti. Depending on where you are staying, you can eat at the branch close to the bus terminus or the new one at Moti Doongri.

Monsoon magic

Alwar is most beautiful in the monsoon, when the hills are green, the lakes full of water, and the hills abound with cascades. Chief amongst the places you must visit during the rains is **Talvriksha**, about 45 km south-west of Alwar. A 10-km diversion from Kushalgarh on the Sariska-Alwar Road leads up to some cold and hot water springs, a Ganga temple, and abundant natural beauty. About 25 km down the Jaipur Road is the village **Natni ka Baran**, from where a 6-km trek leads to **Naldeshwar**, a breathtakingly green area with a naturally formed Shivaling. About 10 km from the Siliserh Lake is the beautiful waterfall called **Garbhaji**, while another waterfall, called **Choohar Sidh**, can be found near Dehra Village, a couple of kilometres away from Vijai Mandir Palace.

The other indulgence you must not deny yourself is Alwar's famous milk cake, or **kalakand**, as it is locally called. **Baba Thakur Das and Sons**, set up at Kalakand Market near Hope Circus post-Partition, is the most famous sweet shop.

AROUND ALWAR

Jai Samand Lake (8 km S)

Not only is Alwar blessed with green hills, it also has several beautiful lakes in its vicinity. The best time to visit them is, of course, the monsoon. The lake nearest to the city is the Jai Samand Lake, created in 1910 by Maharaja Jai Singh of Alwar as a picnic spot. He even built a large island in its midst that has lasted these 96 years. But the prettiest sight at the lake is the string of canopied pavilions lining the promenade. The Jai Samand Road is terrible and instead of testing the resilience of autos, hire a cab for a Jai Samand-Siliserh-Alwar round-trip (Rs 400) that shouldn't take more than 4-5 hrs. There is no accommodation at the lake.

Siliserh Lake (13 km SW)

The most famous and, no doubt, most beautiful of the lakes around Alwar was formed in 1845, during the reign of Maharao Raja Viney Singh, who dammed a tributary of the River Ruparel. The lake spreads over 10.5 sq km during monsoon, and is a marvellous sight with green hills around it and white clouds above.

The **Hotel Lake Palace** (Tel: 0144-2886322; Tariff: Rs 2,350-3,425) here is a government-run property built on a hillside overlooking the lake. It's not very promising, judging from the state of the rooftop terrace restaurant, and the sight of garbage dumped just behind the building. But for sheer location, this hotel is unparalleled. There is a cover charge of Rs 30 for entering the palace complex, which is fully redeemable at the terrace restaurant. You can also go boating on the lake (Rs 80 for a pedal boat/ 30 mins; Rs 400 for a motorboat/ 15 mins). ■

KALAKHO
A TOUCH OF GREEN

District Dausa **Region** Dhundhar
Location This Meena tribal village is in East Rajasthan, just off the Agra-Jaipur Highway
Distances 94 km E of Jaipur, 272 km SW of Delhi
Journey time By road 1$\frac{1}{2}$ hrs from Jaipur, 4 hrs from Delhi
Route from Jaipur NH11 to Sikandra crossing via Dausa; district road to Kalakho via Geej Garh **Route from Delhi** NH8 to Behror via Dharuhera; state roads to Sikandra crossing via Alwar, Rajgarh and Bandikui; rest as above (*see route guide on page 62*)

■ BY MEENAKSHI PANDEY

In the rains, Kalakho is a study in green. It stands across golden fields, boasting of lakes bursting at the seams with the monsoon's bounty, a picture of serene beauty. It lies amidst the Aravalli Hills, beckoning tantalisingly as you drive on a dirt road zigzagging past mustard fields, a hidden getaway in the true sense of the word. It has escaped the attention that so easily comes Rajasthan's way and makes nary an appearance in the tourist itinerary. Perhaps that's what makes it such a wonderful place for a holiday.

Kalakho lies just a few kilometres off the least-explored stretch of the Golden Triangle that connects the historic

capitals of Delhi, Jaipur and Agra. Go there on a journey of discovery and you won't be disappointed.

THINGS TO SEE AND DO

You'll rarely find names like Abhaneri, Madhogarh, Bhangarh and Bhandarej in travel guides, or even on most maps. These are all places that can be easily accessed from Kalakho, spread along NH11 between Bharatpur and Dausa. The Dera Lakeview Retreat, which is one stay option in Kalakho, lies deep in the interiors of the Aravallis, in Kalakho Ambari Village in Sikrai Tehsil (Dausa District), 12 km from Sikandra on NH11 and 90 km short of Jaipur.

There is a lot to discover around Kalakho and a number of activities are on offer, ranging from safaris to camel cart rides. The Dera Retreat offers a different experience from Umaid Lake Palace

→ FAST FACTS

When to go October to March is the best time to visit Kalakho, but it is in the monsoon that the lake becomes full. The green surroundings then are quite scenic and perfect for a romantic getaway
For information
- Far Horizon
B-209, Chittaranjan Park
New Delhi-110019
Tel: 011-46563600, 26277625/ 222
- Camps of India
75 Sant Nagar, East of Kailash
New Delhi-110065
Tel: 011-41659622
STD code 01420

(*see Where to Stay below*), which is set next to a lake, albeit closer to NH11. You could spend a night in each place to enjoy their unique charms.

Note All distances given here are from Kalakho Ambari in Sikrai Tehsil, not to be confused with the Kalakho Village on NH11 in Dausa District in the Kalakho area, 70 km short of Jaipur

Explore Kalakho

Kalakho is set amidst fields against the backdrop of hills. This woodsy part of the Aravallis is the perfect playground for birdwatchers. Let your feathered friends lead you right up the hills, to old forts and the panoramic view from the pinnacles. Those with a yen for solitude should stride forth with a packed lunch.

Monsoon oasis notwithstanding, Kalakho wouldn't be Rajasthan without the ships of the desert to ferry you to the sights. If riding atop one seems too up close and personal, try the camel cart 'safari' at Kalakho, if only to be different.

Chand Baoli

Drive straight past the busy Sikandra crossroads and on to the village of **Gular**, then take a right to **Abhaneri**. The 8th-century *baoli* (stepwell) here is enormous. Built by Raja Chand, a Nikumbha Rajput of the Chamana dynasty, it is close to 65 ft deep. To reach the water, you have to go down 3,500 narrow and steep steps, punctuated by 13 landings. Today, the stepwell is under the aegis of the Archaeological Survey of India (ASI), which has managed to make this age-old monument look like a thing of the future, with their heavy metal frames and cordons keeping people away from the carved stone idols here.

Harshata Mata Temple

Just across from the well is the Harshata Mata shrine, dedicated to Parvati. Built in the 7th-century Mahameru style, it bears a surprisingly strong resemblance to the intricate carvings and ornate arcades seen at the temples of Khajuraho.

JK TYRE
TOTAL CONTROL

→ GETTING THERE

Road Driving down from Delhi is the best option, leaving one the option of squeezing in as many excursions as desired. It's good going till Sikandra. Thereafter, it's narrow tarmac for 19 km, with a few rough patches in the monsoons. The route from Sikandra goes past Geej Garh, Kadikoti and the Madhosagar Bandh. The last stretch after the bandh, less than a kilometre from Kalakho, is a dirt path through mustard fields. If travelling from Jaipur, take the Agra Highway to get to Sikandra. Far Horizon and Camps of India (*see Fast Facts on the previous page*) arrange tours to Kalakho

WHERE TO STAY AND EAT

In Kalakho Ambari in Sikrai Tehsil, **Dera Lakeview Retreat Village** (Tel: 01420-246088; Delhi Tel: 011-46563600/ 38, Mobile: 09414035871; Tariff: Rs 3,780-6,500) offers accommodation in 12 AC *deras* (Portahuts), each with private facilities. There's an excellent chef who cooks a variety of mouth-watering meals. There's hot and cold water in the huts, an AC restaurant, a host of indoor games, local musicians to serenade guests in the evening, drives, rides and treks and many more activities to choose from. Another good option is the **Umaid Lake Palace** (Tel: 01427-283426, Mobile: 094140 35666; Tariff: Rs 2,500-4,000) at Kalakho Village in Dausa Tehsil near a lake by the Agra-Jaipur Highway. Though not a heritage property, it has a traditional Rajasthani feel to it with its architecture and interiors. It has a swimming pool, a yoga centre, and the staff arranges safaris

GIREESH GV

Over 3,500 steps lead down to the green depths of the Chand Baoli

and sightseeing. Walks by the lake at the back are a pleasant diversion. It might become a bit noisy if a wedding is on.

For details, see Kalakho Accommodation Listings on pages 476-477

For details, see Kalakho Accommodation Listings on pages 476-477

AROUND KALAKHO

A visit to Bhandarej, Bhangarh and Fort Madhopur from Jaipur via Dausa Town by an Indica or Ambassador taxi would cost about Rs 2,000. Expect rates to go up considerably in the high season.

Bhandarej (25 km W)
Bhandarej Fort is 60 km from Bhangarh. Bhandarej was founded seven centuries ago, on the banks of the Bhadrawati River, by Badgujar Rajputs and Chauhans. Kachchwaha chieftain Dhula Rao Sahib later conquered Bhandarej. The clan rose to become senior officers under Maharaja Sawai Jai Singh II (1700-1744), the founder of Jaipur. Dhula Rao's descendant, Rawal Raghubir Singh of Dhula, has converted the elegant sandstone **Bhadrawati Palace** (Tel: 01427-283351; Mobile:

09414043117; Tariff: Rs 1,500) in Bhandarej into a heritage hotel. Go on day-long horse safaris or half-day camel safaris, with lunch thrown in. On your jaunts, you'll ride past silent *ret-ka-tilas* (sand forts) in the open desert area that touches the highway. Enjoy a walk around the village to see traditional crafts being made in the potters', ironmongers' and shoemakers' colonies. Bhadrawati Palace also arranges visits to Abhaneri and Bhangarh. Coming from Kalakho via Sikandra, Bhandarej is 11 km before Dausa Town, off NH11. Turn left off NH11 and drive another 5 km till you reach Bhandarej. Taxi for a day-trip costs Rs 1,950 (min 200 km) and for a night-stay Rs 2,750 plus Rs 100 for the driver.

Bhangarh (80 km N)
At the edge of the **Sariska forests** is the ghost city of Bhangarh, with its ruins of temples and havelis, homes and markets, believed to have been cursed by a tantric sage who lost favour with Rani Roopmati, who ruled Bhangarh. The entire city is said to have been destroyed overnight because of the curse. In its time,

Curse cure

SANJOY GHOSH

The Mehendipur Balaji Mandir is known for ridding one of evil spirits and curing madness. Staunch believers claim that Balaji can cure any evil: all it takes is a wish and a donation, and Balaji dutifully obliges.

We visited him, as advised, on a Saturday evening for the weekly aarti, after which experience it is my earnest advice that you go on any other day but Saturday. At least 1,000 devotees were packed in like sardines, many of them in a state of frenzied ecstasy. We saw all this through a window as stepping in was impossible. In a quadrangle behind the temple, there were eight people lying about with their various appendages pinioned beneath huge boulders in the belief that the 'shakti' (flowing from Balaji via the boulder) would cure each limb. The hilly area around the quadrangle was dotted with little shrines — home to the 'spirits'. Visit if you must, but this is no place for the squeamish. Drive back to Sikandra, turn left on NH11 towards Agra and left again at Balaji Morh, 25 km on.

Bhangarh must have been a beautiful capital, for the Old City of Jaipur is said to have been designed along the same lines. Though it is a longish 2-hr drive from Kalakho, it's worth the visit. Bhangarh is 35 km from Dausa Town. A day-trip to Bhangarh by taxi costs approx Rs 1,500.

Fort Madhogarh (70 km W)
This small Rajasthani town, dominated by a fort set on a hill, is close to Jaipur as well. Maharaja Sawai Ram Singh of Jaipur bequeathed the Madhogarh Fort to Thakur Pratap Singh, a Rajput of the Bhati clan. However, Madhogarh features in history books only from the time Maharaja Sawai Pratap Singh made it his headquarters during his campaign against the Marathas.

A decisive battle between the Rajputs and the Marathas was fought on the plains of **Tunga**, just a kilometre from Madhogarh, in 1787. Here the Rajput armies of Jaipur and Jodhpur defeated the Scindias in a day-long battle. The remains of that day still turn up in the now silent battlefields of Tunga in the shape of bits of rusty armour or human bones.

The current owner, Thakur Shiv Pratap Singh, has turned his ancestral property into a heritage hotel. **Fort Madhogarh** (Tel: 01429-281141, Mobile: 09829056676; Tariff: Rs 1,390-1,990) counts among its guest rooms the one used by Maharaja Sawai Pratap Singh while he fought his campaign against the Marathas. Most rooms offer good views of rural Dausa. Visits to the nearby **Nai-ka-Nath Temple** and the Tunga battle-grounds, cenotaphs and *baolis*, as well as the **Patan Dam** (for birdwatching) are organised on request. The hotel also arranges camel rides and jeep safaris.

To get here from Delhi, drive to Jaipur on NH8, then turn left onto the Agra Highway towards Dausa Town. After 25 km, turn right to Bassi, just 2 km off the highway. The villages of Tunga and Madhogarh are 15 km further south-east of Bassi. A day-trip from Kalakho by taxi will cost Rs 1,500, and an overnight trip Rs 2,750 plus Rs 100. ∎

Photographs by GIREESH GV

A bicycle rests against the painted wall of a village house

KARAULI

HISTORY'S SIDESHOW

District Karauli **Region** Dhundhar
Location The erstwhile state (and, since 1997, the district) of Karauli occupies the rugged region to the north of the Chambal Valley. With Jaipur, Bharatpur and Gwalior for its neighbours, the town is situated on the banks of the River Bhadrawati
Distances 176 km SE of Jaipur, 313 km S of Delhi
Journey time *By road* 4 hrs from Jaipur, 6 hrs from Delhi
Route from Jaipur NH11 to Mahua via Kanota and Dausa; state highway to Karauli via Hindaun (*see route guide on page 62*)

■ BY AMIT MAHAJAN

At first glance, Karauli appears to have been a serene pit stop for a marauding history — a whole town that marching armies forgot to raze or hoist to power. No tempestuous rises and tragic falls here. No famous men either. Medieval Karauli, history's sideshow, was ruled by kings who believed they were descendants of Lord Krishna.

Karauli's story began in the 14th century, when one Arjun Pal founded the town. It was never a glorious empire, but at one point had considerable real estate. At its peak, the state of Karauli held the present district of Karauli, as well as parts of Alwar, Bharatpur, Dholpur and Gwalior. During the reign of Akbar, it was incorporated into the Mughal Empire. Later, it was subjugated by the Marathas and, in 1817, taken under British

protection. Then something interesting happened in 1838. Karauli's king, Harbaksha Pal, died without any progeny. A relative, Pratap Pal, was raised to the throne. At this juncture, the dead king's queen suddenly declared that she was pregnant and, a few days later, circulated reports that she had given birth to a prince and the legitimate heir to the throne. The British promptly appointed a commission to enquire into the legitimacy of this child. It's not clear how the Englishmen went about it, but the commission reported that the queen's rumours were absolutely false. She was so ashamed that she left Karauli and settled in Bharatpur nearby. In the annals of Karauli, such machinations were par for the course, though. If there is one thing this erstwhile princely state might have been famous for, it is the inability of its incumbent kings to sire descendants. In the 19th century, at least seven consecutive rajas succeeded by adoption.

Karauli won over the British rulers in India during the events of 1857. For the support he gave the Englishmen during the insurgency, King Madan Pal got the salute of honour for the Raja of Karauli raised from 15 to 17 guns.

By 1906, Karauli was being described thus by the *Imperial Gazetteer of India*: "Viewed from some points whence the palace is seen to advantage, the town [of Karauli] has a striking appearance. It is surrounded by a wall of red sandstone, and is also protected on the north and east by a network of ravines. The streets are rather narrow and irregular, but since 1884 most of them have been flagged with local stone, and they can be easily cleansed as natural drainage is excellent. Indeed, Karauli is one of the cleanest towns in Rajputana."

Even today, the walled city, with the bastioned fort looming large over the crumbling chhatris along the River Bhadrawati, does evoke a prosperous past. But, much like many small North Indian towns, the increasing neglect of Karauli's

Bharat Petroleum

→ **FAST FACTS**

When to go From early winter to spring
Tourist office
● Tourist Reception Centre ❶
Rajasthan Tourism
Government Hostel Campus
MI Road, Jaipur
Tel: 0141-5110598, Fax: 5110591
STD code 07464

poorer areas points to contemporary, unsavoury realities. Yet, even now, Karauli remains an unpolished gem in Rajasthan's map, one that a tourist will always be delighted to discover.

THINGS TO SEE AND DO

Karauli's main attraction, the City Palace, is reached via a narrow, sloping road through an extremely crowded bazaar. Though parts of the palace have been ransacked by local pillagers, it is still very beautiful. Autos are the best mode of transport in Karauli. To travel to places near Karauli, you can hire jeeps and sumos for around Rs 1,000-1,200 per day (extra charges for long hours) plus diesel costs. The Bhanwar Vilas Palace Hotel (*see Where to Stay on page 103*) also arranges horse riding and horse safaris. Rates vary from Rs 250 for a 2-hr ride to Rs 1,000 for a full-day safari (prices inclusive of snacks, mineral water and guide fee).

City Palace

Start off with the City Palace, which you'll enter from the **Ganesh Gate**. Arjun Pal built the palace, along with the town, in the 14th century. However, little or nothing of the original can now be seen. What you do see is the structure erected

A structure built using Karauli stone

by Raja Gopal Singh in the 18th century. He chose to adopt the Delhi style of architecture — the abundance of red sandstone in Karauli, similar to that used in Delhi, made this rendering easy. The more embellished additions came in the 19th century. White and off-white stones have been used very becomingly, painted upon with bright blues, reds, browns and oranges. From the terrace atop the palace, you can see the town laid out by the River Bhadrawati below, and the ravines and hills beyond. The labyrinthine pathways through the palace and the many stairways climbing up and down should afford you a happy half-day.

The **Diwan-i-Aam**, the hall where the king met his subjects, has exquisite floral patterns in bright colours on the walls and ceiling as well as painted wooden doors. The upper floor has jaali work on the walls, from behind which ranis could observe the goings-on below. The coloured glass jharokhas of the **Rang Mahal**, with their one-way visibility,

made for beautiful purdahs. The mirror theme continues from the hall to the walls and ceilings of the bedrooms. **Barahdwari**, the women's dance hall, is lined with moustachioed portraits of the kings of yore. In a move to avoid paying taxes, the palace was gifted to the Madan Mohan Temple Trust (the sole trustee of which was the Raja of Karauli) in the 1950s. After years of neglect and disfigurement, restoration work on the palace has been underway for some time now in the palace.

◆**Location** Main bazaar **Entry fee** Indians Rs 15, foreigners Rs 100 (inclusive of camera fee) **Timings** 6 am-7 pm

Shrines and cenotaph

The **Madan Mohan Temple**, adjacent to the palace, is a Vishnu temple. It is considered highly auspicious to visit the Govindji and Gopinath temples of Jaipur and the Madan Mohan Temple of Karauli on the same day. The idea is to attend the morning aarti in one city and the evening aarti in the other. Jaipur is about $3\frac{1}{2}$ hrs away. The **chhatri of Raja Gopal Singh**, outside the Nadi Gate leading out of the palace to the river below, is stunningly adorned with frescoes. Dayanand Saraswati, the 19th century reformer and founder of the Arya Samaj, is said to have given a sermon here. Unfortunately, it is a shamefully neglected relic, with both the cenotaph and riverside mired in filth.

◆**Temple timings** Summer: 4-11.30 am, 6.30-9 pm; winter: 5 am-12.30 pm, 5.30-8 pm

Karauli Cattle Fair

Every February, thousands of animals tramp into the town for a fair that coincides with the religious festival of Maha Shivaratri. Competitions provide both spectacle and a means to pick out the best of the animals. It would be well worth your while to visit Karauli and witness the fair in February. You will also get to buy many goods usually not available in Karauli, from Nagauri bead necklaces to Jodhpuri brassware and horn decorations at the stalls.

◆**Fair venue** Outside the city wall near the Mela Gate, 1 km from the Bhanwar Vilas Palace hotel **Timings** 6 am-7 pm

SHOPPING

Walk down from the City Palace Fort through the bazaar that winds all the way downhill. Look for leather *jootis* and printed chintz fabric, silver jewellery and steel utensils, clay images of gods and the local milk sweets. The small bazaar may not be very inspiring for shopaholics, but local lac and glass bangles and wooden toys make for lovely souvenirs.

WHERE TO STAY

Most of the options here are rudimentary except for the **Bhanwar Vilas Palace** (Tel: 07464-220024, Mobile: 09414054257; Tariff: Rs 1,400-3,000), a heritage property named after Raja Bhanwar Pal, who was among the more flamboyant rulers of Karauli. He left the native tigers with little choice: they could either be his pets or his trophies. The raja was thus extensively painted and photographed with his tigers, both dead and alive.

At Bhanwar Vilas, it is a pleasure to follow the example of the friendly staff and walk barefoot down the cool stone corridors. Always keeping you company will be the framed Rajput shikaris of old, posing with guns and game. In the chowk, there are sculptures recovered from the Timangarh loot. Ask to see the 'museum', which is the garage for the old Buick and other aristocratic paraphernalia. The hotel offers folk dances and camel or horse rides. You can also call ahead to get them to organise a 'royal welcome' for you (at the cost of Rs 1,100) in which, the manager shyly confesses, they blow trumpets, do an aarti and get caparisoned camels. A simple aarti and tika affair doesn't cost anything though.

For details, see Karauli Accommodation Listings on page 477

Karauli's colourful bazaar has equally colourful lac and glass bangles

At the **Bhanwar Vilas Palace**, the chef is excellent and the service amiable. They are flexible about menu options and you can choose from many Indian, Continental and Chinese dishes. Before the meal, you may even be called upon to choose where you want to eat: near your room, in the main dining hall, or outside — all very pleasant options. At Hindaun Morh, there are some dhabas that offer reasonably good vegetarian dishes and superb besan-mixed rotis. Inside the walled city, **Khana Khazana**, near Ganesh Gate, is an okay non-vegetarian

TOTAL CONTROL

→ GETTING THERE

Rail Nearest railhead: Gangapur City (32 km/ 1 hr), an hour before Sawai Madhopur (on the Delhi-Mumbai broad gauge), is well-connected to Delhi and Mumbai by the Golden Temple Mail and the Paschim Express, and to Kolkata by the Howrah-Jodhpur Express. There are few local transport options connecting Gangapur with Karauli apart from the ordinary state transport buses and three-wheelers. Bhanwar Vilas Palace will arrange jeep/ taxi pick-up for Rs 750 one way
Road Karauli is a short way off NH11, which links Agra to Jaipur. Drive till Mahua via Kanota and Dausa. When you get to the middle of Mahua before the main bus stand, turn left and carry on straight for about 30 km to Hindaun. After the Delhi-Mumbai broad gauge railway crossing, go through Hindaun Town for about 15 km when you'll come to a tri-junction. The road to the right takes you to Shri Mahabirji and the left goes to Karauli, about 18 km away

place. There are hardly any eating options outside Karauli Town. Mineral water is available only in town. If you run short of bottled water, there are some 'English wine and beer' shops. For those who would rather play it safe, they have Aristocrat whisky and McDowell's rum. But for the connoisseur of adventurous spirits, there is Karauli's favourite, **Bullet Beer**. Bhanwar Vilas is not very enthusiastic about serving alcohol.

The trips you can make from Karauli Town, primarily to see other forts of the erstwhile state, are more in the nature of excursions than pleasant picnics. It is best to move around in a hardy vehicle, for roads can be bumpy or even non-existent. Inevitably, a local guide or driver will convey to you the foolhardiness of venturing out of Karauli with tales of dacoits. Laugh these warnings off, but make sure to take someone knowledge-able along — some tracks are not easy to follow and facilities for travellers are few and far between.

Timangarh Fort (40 km NE)
A bouncy drive through ravines and villages brings you to Timangarh, but you will get your first view of the fort once you reach the 3-km-odd manmade Sagar Lake situated at the bottom of the foothills. To get there, take the Hindaun Road, turn right towards Dholpur at Hindaun Chungi and, after about 8 km, head off the highway towards Masalpur. About 10 km beyond Masalpur, a bumpy ride on a fair-weather-only road is **Sagar Lake**. Park your vehicle on the platform beside the lake and relax under the shade of the many-armed banyans as you watch the villagers take a dip or harvest water-chestnuts in small dinghies. Buy a supply of water-chestnuts (the smaller the sweeter) and walk a quarter of an hour along the lake's periphery until you come to a narrow passage between two hills.

One for the road: Karauli's idyllic landscape is punctuated by the odd vehicle

Follow its gentle incline to find your way to the fort. Today, a thick forest has made itself at home inside the extensive precincts of the fort. Occasionally, you come across a majestic gate or a forlorn pavilion. Often you walk into the remains of a lovely idol or exquisite statue. You will have the odd peacock and some other birds for company and it's easy to lose all sense of direction if you stray. It is best to start making your way back while there is some daylight left.

Timangarh was the centre of a local kingdom in the mid-12th century. In 1196, in the time of King Kunwar Pal, Muhammad Ghori and his general Qutubuddin overran the Karauli territory, including this fort. Kunwar Pal himself fled to a village in Rewa. It is believed that several valuable sculptures and idols were hidden here in the course of these campaigns. Many of these idols have been stolen over the past years. A helicopter was once used to airlift some of these sculptures. One of the biggest lifts was a 1,000-yr-old, $2^1/_2$-ft-high statue of Vishnu that weighed 50 kg. How this could happen without some form of official assistance is anyone's guess.

Fortunately, the theft was treated with the seriousness it deserved, when the matter was raised in Parliament. The art thieves were subsequently hunted down and jailed. Now a police outpost is stationed near the fort, and the guard looks askance at any vehicle venturing onto the path between the lake and the fort. A half-day taxi from Karauli costs about Rs 600-750 (return).

Mandrael Fort (34 km SE)
The origins of Mandrael are not well documented. What we do know is that Arjun Pal captured it and was based here when he founded Karauli. The relatively better laid-out road from Karauli to Mandrael runs though some interesting scenery, and the fort, perched atop a lonely hill, is visible from afar.

The fortified hill is ringed by the town of Mandrael and a few small villages. From Ganesh Gate, the fort is a demanding 10-min climb away. Though old and decaying, the fort has managed to retain its identity. The remains are lit poignantly by the setting sun; the old temple by the pond looks far removed from the everyday world and the views of the

At the Karauli Cattle Fair, when thousands of animals tramp into town

country below are captivating. A half-day taxi costs about Rs 600-750. The **Chambal River** is also nearby. You could either drive to the **Chambal Ghat** (10 km) or to the more picturesque **Rau Ghat** (13 km). If the dirt track to Rau Ghat is motorable (enquire at Mandrael before you set out), you can see the river transform itself into a waterfall here.

Kaila Devi Sanctuary (23 km SW)
The **Kaila Devi Temple** may interest the devout. The Kaila Devi Wildlife Sanctuary begins right after the temple (no entry fee or permissions required and no gates, for good measure!) and runs along both sides of the road all the way to **Karanpur** (34 km from Kaila Devi), and further on to join the Ranthambhore National Park. Chinkaras, nilgai, jackals and leopards are to be found here, as are birds such as sandpipers and kingfishers. Bhanwar Vilas arranges picnics (for a minimum of three people) to the sanctuary at a cost of Rs 600 per person.

Other forts
The forts of Sapotra, Ram Athra and Amar Garh are within a couple of kilometres of each other. Sapotra Town is 44 km southwest from Karauli via Kurgaon. The **Sapotra Fort** rests atop a hill and is approached through the town. The lonely, abandoned ruins gaze sleepy-eyed at life below, half-awakening to receive the rare visitor.

In contrast, the **Ram Athra** and **Amar Garh** forts are still lived-in and eagerly welcome visitors. They are close to the **Kali Sil Dam**, a 15-km stretch of water reaching up to Kaila Devi. On the hill adjacent to Ram Athra are ruins of what is said to be the old town of Sapotra, abandoned a couple of centuries ago. From Sapotra, the Ram Athra Fort is about 4-5 km and Amar Garh is another 5-6 km away. It's a narrow single road, which gets rutted in the rains in parts. Pack a picnic basket and make it a day-trip as there's some climbing involved. A taxi will cost about Rs 1,000-1,500. ∎

Courtesy New Holland Publishers (NZ) Ltd; Illustrator Soni Gopal

South-East Rajasthan

A fantasy world that's a few notches better than perfect, here you can amble along quiet lanes and glimpse a lost world in havelis and palaces

Graphic by RAJESH KG

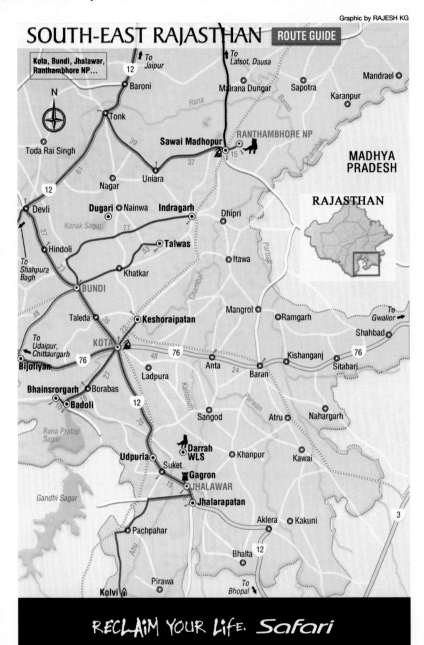

SOUTH-EAST RAJASTHAN ROUTE GUIDE

Kota, Bundi, Jhalawar, Ranthambhore NP...

RECLAiM YOUR Life. Safari

The Kota Fort, a gargantuan monument that encircles the town

KOTA

THE PRODIGAL LITTLE TOWN

District Kota **Region** Hadoti
Location In south-east Rajasthan, on the east bank of the Chambal River
Distances 35 km SW of Bundi, 249 km S of Jaipur, 505 km SW of Delhi
Journey time *By road* 45 mins from Bundi, 5 hrs from Jaipur, 9 hrs from Delhi
Route from Jaipur NH12 to Kota via Sanganer, Chaksu, Tonk, Mendwas, Devli and Bundi
(*see route guide on facing page*)

■ **BY KISHORE SINGH**

The surprising fact is that Kota has a history — industrial towns with power and atomic plants aren't supposed to, belonging as they do to the genre of sci-fi cities. Kota's broad avenues, leafy roads and its status as a divisional headquarter of the Indian Army further hide its ancient beginnings. But Kota is as much a child of fractious history as its fellow Rajput kingdoms, born of blood, gore and diplomacy.

It was in 1241 (or 1341, depending on who's telling the story) that a classic Rajput, Deva Hara of the fierce Hara clan, came to these parts, wanted what he saw and attempted to conquer. He won and the kingdom of Bundi was established. Around that time, nearby Kota was under the Bhil tribals led by their chief Koteya. He was defeated by Bundi's Jait Singh in 1264 (or 1364) and a fort's construction was started there. Koteya's severed head was buried, as tradition decreed, in its foundation. And so Kota became a *jagir,* or land grant, of Bundi, at the dispensation of the heir apparent.

However, in 1624, the Mughal Emperor Jehangir agreed to separate Kota from Bundi and award it to Rao Madho Singh, a Hara scion. Kota suddenly found itself an independent kingdom, lying on a major trade route that regularly saw marching armies and camel trains. Continuing independence in those days was often dependent on taking the right side in the frequent Mughal quarrels. Kota had to come of age quickly. Its rulers became more savvy, more open to foreign influences, willing to make expedient treaties. It soon overshadowed Bundi, which remained provincial and secretive. It's a difference that can be seen in some ways in both the cities to this day.

THINGS TO SEE AND DO

For all that, Kota has retained a certain lazy charm. Most industries here are self-contained establishments and all that is visible is a gentle prosperity. There are not too many malls, restaurants and multiplexes and despite a contemporary atmosphere, Kota is inextricably linked with its historic and architectural past. Though the town is not very big, you will need transport to get around. Unmetered autos charge about Rs 40 from the railway

→ FAST FACTS

When to go October to early March is best. But the monsoon has its own charm
Tourist office
● Rajasthan Tourism Reception Centre ❶❻ Chambal Tourist Bungalow, Bada Bagh Nayapura, Kota
Tel: 0744-2327695
STD code 0744

station to the Nayapur area and Rs 350-400 for 4 hrs of travelling within Kota. Tourist taxis charge Rs 600-800 for half-day and Rs 1,300-1,400 for a full-day trip in and around Kota. RSRTC does not run bus services here, but the tourist office can help in organising transport for tours within and beyond Kota.

City Palace and Fort complex

If you are coming from the north, your train will cross the Chambal, Rajasthan's only perennial river, and your first sight of Kota will appear to be a huddle of houses crammed on one bank. These are actually the bastions of **Kota Fort**, encircling the pristine City Palace with its wealth of treasures. The fort's construction was begun in 1264 (1364), after Koteya was slain. Each generation of rulers that came along built on, around and over what was already standing, resulting in a gargantuan monument. Along the fort's inner battlements, public and private buildings, schools and homes have come up. But you'll soon leave these behind as **Naya Darwaza**, built circa 1900, looms ahead. The oldest gate, called **Sailar Ghazi** and which dates to 1264 (1364), commemorates the spot where Koteya's head was buried in the fort's foundations.

Among the parts open to the public are **Hawa Mahal** and **Jaleb Chowk**, where parades and processions used to be held, the **Nakkarkhana Darwaza**, where kettledrums played, and **Hathia Pol**, where flanking stone elephants recreate a motif borrowed from the palace in Bundi. The apartments that can be visited include **Kunwarbade ka Mahal**, the wing where the heir apparent was traditionally in residence, **Bada Mahal**, the palace where the king resided, and **Raj Mahal**, the throne room. Private audiences were given at **Bhim Mahal** and parties at **Baradari**. Elaborate work characterises **Sooraj Gokh**, the **Chattra Mahal**, **Zenana Mahal** and **Alsi Mahal**. The richness of detail in the delicate fluted pillars, mirror inlays and murals

SANJOY GHOSH

Kota lies on the east bank of the glorious Chambal River

that wash the walls in colour is what makes Kota's City Palace exceptional. Among the murals are court scenes and portraits, but look out for the famous hunting scenes that made the Kota school of painting so well known.

The **Rao Madho Singh Museum** is another inlet into Kota's past though the atmosphere is slightly more stilted and formal. You'll see fine examples of Kota painting, sculptures, photographs, arms and armour and other regal memorabilia. Guides can be hired but you will probably enjoy exploring on your own.
♦**Entry fee** Rs 10; upper section (paintings) Rs 50 **Timings** 10 am-5 pm

Just outside the City Palace are two of Kota's better known temples — **Neelkanth Mahadeo**, dated to the 10th century, and **Mathureshji**, built in the 18th century. Both have outstanding carvings. The **Government Museum** is near the City Palace, with a collection of sculptures from the ruins of temples in the Hadoti Region, but is badly kept.
♦**Entry fee** Rs 3 **Timings** 10 am-5 pm, open all days

Lakes and gardens

There's the artificial **Kishore Sagar Lake**, close to the City Palace, also known locally as Bada Talao, built as far back as 1346 by a Bundi prince. Centuries later, in 1740, a striking palace, **Jagmandir**, was built in the centre of the lake for a Mewar princess who couldn't bear Kota's heat (*see Saris to beat the heat on page 118*). On the rare day when the paddleboats are working here, you can ride up to get a closer look at the palace. Unfortunately, visitors are not allowed to go in.

On the banks of the same lake stand the **Chhattar Bilas Gardens**, said to have been beautiful once. The location is still enchanting though, flanked on one side by **Sarbagh**, where the royal cenotaphs stand, and **Brij Bilas Palace** on the other. This palace is now a somewhat lacklustre government museum of manuscripts, weapons, paintings and photos.
♦**Entry fee** Rs 3 **Timings** 10 am-5 pm

Chambal Gardens, to the south of the fort, is along the banks of the Chambal and next to **Amar Niwas**, a former royal pleasure retreat. They are now

DINESH SHUKLA

Jagmandir, the palace built for a princess on Kishore Sagar Lake

Kota's picnic grounds. You can relax here after visiting the residents of the **alligator pool** in the centre of the garden.
♦**Entry fee** Rs 2

Chambal River cruise

Boat rides, birding tours and adventure sports activities are on offer on the Chambal River now. Contact the tourist office (*See Fast Facts on page 110*) for details. For birdwatching, contact Anil Nair (Mobile: 09828214901) of Hobby Nature Club, which is involved with sarus crane conservation, and Bombay Natural History Society conservationist and naturalist Manoj Kulshreshta (Mobile: 09314880887) of Nature Trails.
♦**Boating fee** Rs 12 per head **Chambal cruise fee** Rs 300 per person (min 6 pax) **Cruise bookings** Rajasthan Tourism office (*see Fast Facts*)

The Pathan interlude

For a brief while, two Pathan brothers, Kesar Khan and Dokhar Khan, seized Kota between 1531 and 1551. After a savage battle, Bundi's Rao Surjan won it back but the tombs of the Pathan usurpers still stand in the old city, next to the bustling Sabzi Mandi. And just to round off Kota's history, which like all its neighbouring kingdoms owed allegiance to the British, there is a **cemetery** where there are memorials to Raj officers killed during the 1857 War of Independence.

Other attractions

Claimed to be dedicated to Raja Shivgana Maurya is the 8th century **Karneshwar Mahadeo Temple**, located about 10 km from Kota. Some 6 km further is **Umed Ganj**, a lakeside pleasure pavilion built at the end of the 18th century. About 3 km further on the road is Dadh Devi, a complex of interesting temples. **Karni Mata's shrine** at Abhera, 6 km west of Kota, is a popular shrine.

WHERE TO STAY

Perhaps because it is a busy commercial town, Kota offers a reasonable choice in hotels, even though it may lack somewhat in numbers. Even then, getting a room is not a problem here. In the budget hotels, which aren't the best you'll find, keep some mosquito repellent handy.

Heritage

Umed Bhawan Palace (Tel: 0744-232526-65; Tariff: Rs 1,700-3,500), part of the WelcomHeritage chain, is Kota's best option, designed by Sir Swinton Jacob, the British architect known for his Rajput/ Indo-Saracenic palaces. Till recently it was the residence of the royal family; the queen mother still lives here. There isn't too much by way of spit and polish, though, so you end up feeling you're in a stately home on a private visit rather than in a commercial establishment. The residence of the current head of the Hara clan and formerly the British Residency, **Brijraj Bhawan Palace** (Tel: 2450529; Tariff: Rs 1,740-2,900) is located along the Chambal's banks, and has nice views of the town.

Built by the British in 1870, the family-run **Sukhdham Kothi** (Tel: 2320081, 2332661; Tariff: Rs 1,000-1,500) in Civil Lines is a delight to stay in. The owners have painstakingly restored the sandstone architecture and personalised service and food fit for a king complete the sumptuous facilities. **Palkiya Haveli** (Tel: 2387497; Mobile: 09829747316; Tariff: Rs 1,400-2,000), more than a hundred years old, is built in traditional Rajput style with carved balconies, open terraces, courtyards and gardens.

Others

Phul Plaza (Tel: 2329350; Tariff: Rs 550-1,200), in Civil Lines, is a two-star property. RTDC's **Chambal Tourist Bungalow** (Tel: 2326527; Tariff: Rs 600-700), near Kishore Sagar, has rooms with TV and its own restaurant and parking. **Navrang** (Tel: 2323294; Tariff: Rs 385-2,400), near the GPO, has rooms with room service and TV. **Hotel Menaal Residency** (Tel: 2371073-74; Tariff: Rs 750-2,500) has 40

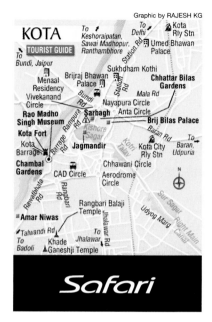

Graphic by RAJESH KG

rooms (all AC), a swimming pool and a big garden. **Col Sudhir Farm** (Tel: 0744-2481841, 09829036384; Tariff: Rs 1,100-1,800), en route to Khaithoon Village, is a unique stay option in Kota. You can learn about local farming methods and social customs while participating in some of the daily activities of the farm.

For more hotels and details, see Kota Accommodation Listings on pages 479-480

WHERE TO EAT

Here's one town where it's practically impossible to find a decent restaurant outside of hotels. **Navrang** is where you'll get the closest imitation of Chinese and Continental cuisine. The soups seem healthy and nourishing though. For homeliness and variety, **Brijraj Bhawan** is the best place but it's open only for resident guests. You'll fare better at **Umed Bhawan** where you can count on satisfying fare and a groaning board by way of choice. But the best way of getting

The Bhainsrorgarh Fort, audaciously perched on a cliff above the River Chambal

a good meal would be to order the simpler items on the menu. **Phul Plaza** has a passable veg restaurant. Almost all eateries, such as they are, can be found on **Station Road**. These are dhabas without fancy trimmings, with food that is simple but incendiary.

AROUND KOTA

Geparnath Temple (22 km SW)
Tired of maintaining its calm demeanour, the Chambal River decides to become playful and hides in a deep ravine. You go looking for her, climbing down endless steep steps cut on the stony wall of a gorge, following lakhs of seekers over many hundred years. You only get a glimpse of the river veering away into another valley, but you find a waterfall rushing down to meet the river, and an ancient shrine to Shiva, the Geparnath Mahadeo. The place has been an important pilgrimage for Shaivites since the 5th-6th century, and a temple was built here in 1569. There is an old inscription in the temple to this effect. The three-step

waterfall cascades down into this narrow gorge among trees and foliage where birds, pilgrims and picnickers wait with open hearts to drink in the beauty. A taxi to Geparnath, located off the road to Badoli, costs Rs 600.

Udpuria (25 km S)
Udpuria was a common enough village, with 100-odd households, set around a pond of unremarkable dimensions. It took only a few birds to change all that. For some reason, a group of painted storks adopted this pond more than a decade ago. Now some 200-300 birds come here sometime every August, flying around, feeding themselves, breeding their young ones next to the pond and departing when the new generation is able to fly. The villagers make sure that no harm is done to them, and have stopped fishing in the pond. But now, they are feeling threatened by the Tourism and the Wildlife Department because there are proposals to ban the use of the pond by the people and their cattle. A taxi to Udpuria costs Rs 800.

Sukhdham Kothi

C Come and explore the verdant greenery of the Hadoti Region of Rajasthan with its magnificent rivers and National Park. Stay in our family run home with its beautiful garden and treat it as a home away from home.

Built by the British in 1870 it later became the residence of Col. Prithvi Singhji and is now run by the family as a Heritage Hotel. Sukhdham Kothi offers 15 rooms with large attached bathrooms at reasonable rates, Homemade Indian cuisine, an intimate setting for parties and functions and many more.

For further queries, please contact:
Jaiwardhan / Harshvardhan Singh,
Sukhdham Kothi, Civil Lines, Kota,
Rajasthan – 324001, (India).
Ph: 91-744-2320081, 2332661;
Fax: 91-744-2327781,
mail to:sukhdham@datainfosys.net,
www.sukhdhamkothi.com

Keshoraipatan (22 km NE)

Shri Keshav Rai Ji is the presiding deity of Hadoti and its Hada rulers. And the residence of the deity is Keshoraipatan, a medieval temple with fort-like walls on the riverside. The temple stands on a promontory and overlooks a curve of the sweeping river running through a vast spread of green cultivated landscape. Occasionally, the temple fills up with people, especially during the fair in the month of Kartik (Oct-Nov), when devotees take a dip in the Chambal, seek Lord Krishna's blessings and enjoy the race between decorated boats. A taxi to Keshoraipatan costs Rs 600.

Bundi (35 km NW)

See page 119

Garadia Mahadev (20 km S)

A short drive from Kota, the small temple on the river heights has little significance in itself. However, it is worth visiting for

SANJAY SINGH BADNOR

The Chambal as a waterfall at Geparnath

the panoramic views of the Chambal gorge. A taxi to Garadia costs Rs 600.

Badoli (45 km SW)

On the road to Rawatbhata, not far away from the Chambal, there is an ASI-enclosure containing an enchanting copse of trees — kadam, mango, jamun, peepal — and underneath them a complex of temples, indicating a past Hindu religious site in a forest. The temples are dated between the 9th and the 12th centuries and the eight big and small temples show a varied degree of preservation, decay and destruction.

The main shrine is dedicated to Shiva as Ghateshwara. Outside the sanctum sanctorum, the temple extends into a sabha mandap, beautifully embellished with carvings, especially on the columns. Look for Ganga Jamuna as *dwarpalas*, the trinity of Brahma-Vishnu-Mahesh, and many images of Shiva in his different forms. The other two bigger temples are to Mahishasurmardini, with a delicately carved pagoda, and to the Trinity.

The complex has some ruins strewn around and many images show signs of defacement. Some of the sculptures from these temples are now in the Government Museum at Kota, including a celebrated image of *shesh-shahi* Vishnu

TOTAL CONTROL

→ **GETTING THERE**

Air Nearest airport: Sanganer, Jaipur (235 km/ 5 hrs), connected by daily flights to all metros. Taxi costs about Rs 1,500 to Kota

Rail Kota Junction is well-connected to Delhi by the new Nizamuddin-Udaipur Express, Mumbai August Kranti and Trivandrum Rajdhani superfast trains and to Jaipur by the Jaipur-Kota Fast Passenger and Jaipur-Bombay Central superfast trains

Road Kota is a comfortable 5-hr drive along NH12 from Jaipur via Tonk, Devli and Bundi. From Mumbai, turn right off NH8 at Udaipur onto NH76 for Kota via Chittaurgarh, Debari, Bhatewar, Bhadaura, Bichor and Bijoliyan

Palkiya Haveli

Palkiya Haveli is the house of the Rathores of Palkiya. Built in the traditional Rajput style by Thakur Deo Singhji, the Haveli has beautiful carved balconies, attractive courtyards, open terraces, lovely gardens and comfortable rooms with old design fabrics and antique furniture. Palkiya Haveli is situated in a quiet, peaceful area with lots of greenery, beautiful gardens and ample parking space. The Haveli is situated within walking distance of the City Palace of Kota.

Come and rejuvenate yourself at Palkiya Haveli, Kota

Palkiya Haveli
Mokha – Para, near Suraj Pole
Kota – 324006, Rajasthan, India
Tel: +91-744-2387497, Mobile: +91-9829747316
Fax: +91-744-2387075, Website: www.alsisar.com
Contact Person: Mrs. Indira Kumari

Saris to beat the heat

DINESH SHUKLA

This is a true story of a princess who married a prince of a tiny kingdom that stood on the edge of a desert, not far from home, but nothing like home either which was Udaipur, lauded even then as a city of lakes. Though Kota had a lake too, our princess couldn't take the heat that would rise from the ground in the hot summer. So circa 1740, a palace called **Jagmandir** was built specially for her in the middle of the **Kishore Sagar Lake**. But she found the heat stifling even then. And so, the princess decided that she needed clothes that were friendlier to the breeze that sometimes blew her way. A royal order was passed and the weavers got to work. Perhaps they took inspiration from the thin ribbon-like clouds that streak the summer skies here for the new sari was just as light and ephemeral. The number of threads in the warp and weft was reduced but to make up for this lost weight, they wove the **Kota-doria saris** in solid geometric patterns of alternating checks. And these saris were woven only in five different shades of white — the colour that would best keep out the horrible heat. These five whites were lyrically named 'conch shell', 'sea-foam', 'jasmine', 'August moon' and 'clouds after they have spent their rain'. The saris were a big hit and variations were spun quickly. In **Kota-mungia** or **Kota-masuria**, the checks are supposed to be the size of a single grain of moong or masur dal. Now these saris are available in other colours. Drive to **Khaithoon**, a village of weavers 22 km from Kota, and you will see these saris stretched out on the looms. These will cost a few hundred rupees, a little more if the gold border has used real zari.

lying on Ananta, the cobra. A taxi to Badoli costs about Rs 800.

Bhainsrorgarh (55 km SW)

A further 10 km from Badoli, on the road to Chittaur across a bridge, is the amazingly located fort called Bhainsrorgarh, audaciously perched on a cliff right above the mighty River Chambal. It's 200 years old and contains a small village inside it, and the principal building here is a private property being converted into a hotel (*see page 480 for accommodation details*). There are great views of the Chambal from the fort. A taxi to Bhainsrorgarh costs Rs 800.

Darrah Sanctuary (50 km S)

Spread across 213 sq km, the sanctuary has sloth bear, leopards and panthers. To visit, permission has to be obtained from the local forest officer or the District Forest Office in Kota (Tel: 0744-2321263). A jeep from Kota costs Rs 1,400.

♦**Entry fee** Indians Rs 10, foreigners Rs 80 **Vehicle entry fee** Rs 65 **Timings** Sunrise-sunset **Cameras** Still free, video Rs 200 ∎

with inputs from Amit Mahajan

BUNDI
A DROP OF FANTASY

District Bundi **Region** Hadoti
Location A small town of medieval origin, Bundi is set in a narrow curvaceous valley in the Aravalli Hills in south-east Rajasthan
Distances 35 km NW of Kota, 214 km S of Jaipur, 470 km SW of Delhi
Journey time By road 45 mins from Kota, 4 hrs from Jaipur, 8 hrs from Delhi
Route from Jaipur NH12 to Bundi via Niwai, Tonk and Devli **Route from Kota** NH12 to Bundi via Taleda (*see route guide on page 108*)

■ BY AMIT MAHAJAN

Wish with all your heart. Wish that one day you will go to Bundi. And wish that when that day dawns, the ingredients are just right. That the day you do go to Bundi is a day in the month of sawan, blessed by an animated south-west monsoon. That there is a heavy downpour for a couple of hours in the morning after which the weather relents, but not much, just a wee bit, so that it drizzles on and off all day.

The clouds drift from one mountain-top-lookout-tower to the next, often revealing blues you have never imagined. The breeze stirring the skies occasionally comes down to ruffle your hair, clouds roll down the mountainside and wrap all manner of things in a moist blanket, the sun is present but only just to make it day and is content to let the clouds hold sway. When you have these ingredients in place, Bundi is a few notches better than perfect. Then your options are wide open. You can amble along the lazy lanes

and bazaars, going from havelis to baoris to mosques. Or visit temples and figure out why Bundi was also called 'Chotta Kashi'. Hire a bicycle or a mobike or a car and cruise across Bundi, often coming across people packed in Sumos or tractors, cooking, bathing and playing in the numerous tanks, lakes, streams and waterfalls. Or spend the day in the royal enclave ruminating on love, romance, worship, architecture and military strategy. Look through the palace jharokhas and get enchanted by the orange-red-yellow brush strokes in the evening sky. Or just sit at a rooftop restaurant, sipping the ambience. Follow with your eyes the monkeys and langurs, travelling from the palace on their highways of walls and roofs, spread across houses and hotels, to steal clothes, find food, pick nits and play playfully. In the evening hike up to the fort to gaze at the tiny drop that is Bundi hiding in the fold of a green leaf that is the Aravallis.

Graphic by SURAJ WADHWA

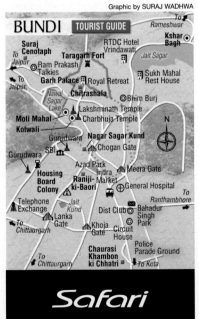

ORIENTATION

The ruins of **Taragarh Fort** are to the north of Bundi, perched on a hill. Below, on the mountain slope, is the **Garh Palace**, an ensemble of mahals. Further down and towards the south-west is the **Nawal Sagar Lake**, with **Moti Mahal** and havelis along its north and east banks. Outside the Garh Palace, to its south, is **Nahar ka Chotta**, the bazaar for tourists' daily needs — Internet, ISD, STD, car/bike hire, beverages — and it leads into the old walled town. The **bus stand** and the **tourist office** are to the south. Autos are available and the minimum fare of Rs 20 will cover any two points within the town. For visiting places just outside or beyond the town, taxis are best arranged by your hotel. Taxis are available for Rs 5 per km for a minimum of Rs 1,100 per day or Rs 700 for half a day.

THINGS TO SEE AND DO

It is not difficult to imagine that a Rajput royal in the 14th century searched high and low for a suitable hilltop in the Aravalli Range to build a fort. Imagine then that over the next eight centuries life flowed down the hill and spread in the valley below. This will give you a sense of the temporal-geographical spread of Bundi, and a couple of meandering days will give you time enough to explore it. For a relaxed schedule, give a day for any of the arounds. Talwas, Dugari and Indergarh are in the same direction and two of them could be combined in a day visit.

Garh Palace

This is a fortified complex of many palaces built by different kings between the 17th and 18th centuries. Unoccupied in the second half of the 20th century, it lay decaying till three years ago, when the potential of tourism-generated revenue inspired a clean-up and re-opening. You enter through the huge and magnificent **Hathi Pol** into a world where local stone

DINESH SHUKLA

Chitrashala or Ummed Mahal at Garh Palace, with painted walls and ceilings

has been used in typical Rajput-style architecture to create jharokhas, pillars and intricately carved brackets. The **Chhatra Mahal, Phool Mahal** and **Badal Mahal** are justly famous for their murals (*see Intoxication in art on next page*).

◆**Location** North-west of the bazaar **Entry fee** Indians Rs 10, foreigners Rs 50 **Cameras** Still Rs 50, video Rs 100 **Timings** 8 am-5 pm, open all days

Chitrashala

The Chitrashala or **Ummed Mahal** is part of the Garh Palace, with a separate entrance, and is located on a slope. Built in the 18th century, it is a set of rooms on a raised platform above a garden courtyard, and its walls and ceilings are embellished with paintings.

◆**Entry fee** Free **Timings** 8 am-5 pm, open all days

Taragarh Fort

A walk up from the Garh Palace will convince you of the fort's reputation for inaccessibility. Built on a 1,426-foot high hill, the 14th century ramshackle but impressive structure will reward you with

bewitching sunsets, immense bastions and the aroma of a disappearing past.

◆**Location** North of Garh Palace **Entry fee** Free **Timings** Sunrise to sunset, open all days

Stepwells

Baori, vav, kund, vapi, sagar — different shapes of collected water, different shades of collective lives. Bundi is famous for its 50-odd ancient wells and tanks, sources of water in a land easily dehydrated. In

Bharat Petroleum

→ **FAST FACTS**

When to go October to March is pleasant, as is July to August, when it rains

Tourist office
● Rajasthan Tourism Reception Centre ❶ Circuit House, Bundi
Tel: 0747-2443697
STD code 0747

Intoxication in art

Episodes of Krishna Lila, glimpses of courtly life, snatches of love stories and scenes of battles, in a turquoise, tan and green rendition, trapped within the white of lime plaster. These are the elements that combine together to ensure the marvellous simplicity of Bundi miniature painting (*also see A painted world on page 420*). Patronised by the Hada Rajputs, Bundi art derived from folk traditions and Mughal painting. The initial spurt of paintings came under Chhatra Sal, who established a painters' school in the **Chhatra Mahal**, within the Garh Palace, in the mid-17th century. The tradition reached its pinnacle under Ummed Singh more than a century later, when the Chitrashala paintings were done. Check out the picture of Chitrashala itself, done with loving detail. Or see the magic of Krishna doing a breathless *ras* with 16 gopis at the same time. The paintings are sometimes hauntingly reflected in the beautiful inlaid mirrors.

The Chhatra Mahal has ceilings adorned with floral patterns, and wall murals depicting Krishna lifting the Govardhan, elephants and other animals and the life at the palace. The Phool Mahal depicts a royal procession. The mythological paintings in Badal Mahal, interestingly, show Chinese influences in the faces and the flowers thus hinting at the source of Bundi's riches — from poppy, cultivated to carry on a lucrative opium trade with China.

addition to their utilitarian value, baoris were centres of religious and social existence. The rich and the powerful made building these marvels of craftsmanship and architecture a sacred act (*also see Not just a pipedream on page 416*).

Raniji-ki-Baori is the most famous because of its impressive composition with arches and pillars, and beautiful ornamentation. Commissioned by Rani Nathvatiji in 1699 (she is reputed to have built 20 other *baoris* too), this is the most well-maintained baori, but unfortunately open only to tourists, thus denying the structure and its waters any life.

♦**Location** Near Indra Market **Timings** 10 am-5 pm, Sundays and holidays closed

Dhabhai Kund (south of Raniji-ki-Baori) creates a fascinating geometry with its steps and deserves a look despite its abysmal state. A pair of matching stepwells (just outside Chogan Gate) is called **Nagar Sagar**. The 16th century **Bhoraji-ka-Kund** (north of Nawal Sagar) is impressive and attracts birdlife post-monsoon. In Bundi, you will often cross one stepwell or the other, most of them reservoirs of refuse and neglect. Is their state a reflection of the inhabitants' alienation from the heritage of the rich?

Other sights

The **Nawal Sagar** is an 18th century lake with a temple of Varuna, the god of water, presiding at the head of Bundi just below the Garh Palace. To the north-east of the town is the lake **Jait Sagar**, on which stands a small palace called **Sukh Mahal**, famous for once hosting Rudyard Kipling. On the other bank of the lake is **Kshar Bagh**, the final resting place for Bundi's royalty, with some beautiful cenotaphs built between the 16th and 19th centuries. The door is usually locked but check at the nearby houses and someone will have the key to the place.

The finest cenotaph in Bundi is to the south of the town, the **Chaurasi Khambon ki Chhatri** (the 84-pillared cenotaph). This artistic 17th-century creation is a two-storeyed structure on a high plinth and is stunning when lit up at night. **Phool Sagar** (10 km west of town on Ajmer Road) is a 17th century palace, closed to the public but worth visiting for its location, nestled as it is between hills next to a lake filled with quiet.

Shikar Burj (8 km north-west of town) was a hunting lodge next to a water tank, and is now a picnic haunt for nearby villagers.

Copies of the famous **Bundi murals** of Garh Palace on silk or paper (starting at Rs 20) are ideal souvenirs. These are available at **Bundi Art**, just inside the Garh Palace, and at other shops in Nahar ka Chotta. Bundi ladoos are said to have originated here and you can pick these up from any of the sweetshops in the bazaars for Rs 80-100 for a kilo.

For traditional **Kota-Bundi School of Art miniatures**, you can get in touch with artist Soni Gopal at **Mayur Art** (Tel: 0747-2447297), which is located at Nahar ka Chotta in Bundi. Gopal has been trained in the traditional style of Kota-Bundi painting which features hunting scenes, animal fights and landscapes, and makes use of red as the predominant background colour. He paints on paper, silk and marble, and can also paint as per the Jaipur School of Art. Gopal, who can be commissioned to do paintings, was chosen to do the cover illustration for a travel guide brought out by New Zealand-based travel company Indian Motorcycle Adventures (*see pix*), which arranges mobike tours in Rajasthan.

Bundi is a new star on the tourism horizon, and the hotel industry is keenly catching up, 'heritage hotel' being its catch phrase. As of now, you can land up in Bundi even without reservation and find a decent place to stay.

Heritage

The best area to stay is just below the palace in the Balchand Para, with homely guest houses in havelis and old houses, some with obviously spurious claims about their age. The **Haveli Braj Bhushanjee** (Tel: 0747-2442322; Tariff: Rs 950-2,450) is a 250-year-old building that has been converted into a hotel with beautiful effect. Living in the immaculately clean, well-kept premises is like

An old painting style gets a mod look

Air Nearest airport: Sanganer, Jaipur (200 km/ 4 hrs). Taxi to Bundi costs Rs 2,000 approx
Rail Nearest railhead: Kota Junction (35 km/ 45 mins), on the Delhi-Mumbai rail route. Taxi to Bundi costs Rs 400
Road Bundi is located on NH12 between Jaipur and Kota. The road conditions vary with rains and disrepair. There are frequent buses from Kota to Bundi and the journey by bus takes about an hour. A few buses run daily from Jaipur too and the trip takes 7-8 hrs

staying in a museum as the place is full of memorabilia. The **Royal Retreat** (Tel: 2444426; Tariff: Rs 750-1,250) in the Garh Palace complex has a beautiful and spacious location and pleasant rooms.

Others

Ishwari Niwas Palace (Tel: 2442414; Tariff: Rs 3,000-4,000) is clean and well-maintained, with some royal connections and memorabilia, but suffers because of its non-romantic location near the Circuit House. **RTDC Hotel Vrindawati** (Tel: 2442473; Tariff: Rs 400-800) is invitingly situated opposite Jait Sagar, just outside town, but its stale air is a dampener. **Kasera Paradise** (Tel: 2444679; Tariff: Rs 500-2,500) has a great rooftop terrace but the bathrooms aren't well-drained and the owner's bad behaviour with his overworked staff creates a bad taste. **Haveli Katkoun** (Tel: 2444311/ 679; Tariff: Rs 350-600) is homely and clean.

For more hotels and details, see Bundi Accommodation Listings on page 460

For more hotels and details, see Bundi Accommodation Listings on page 460

WHERE TO EAT

There are no stand-alone restaurants in Bundi, and many hotels cater only to their in-house guests. **Royal Retreat** and **Ishwari Niwas** have decent North Indian food and some Rajasthani dishes. Some of the dishes you can try out include malai kofta, navratan korma, mutton do pyaza and gatte ki subzi. **Haveli Braj Bhushanjee** serves breakfast and dinner only to their resident-guests. The lunch here is a Rajashani thali.

AROUND BUNDI

Rameshwar (17 km NE)
After driving through many villages, past Jait Sagar Lake, just before Rameshwar, you enter a refreshing forest of broad-leaved trees and end up near a stream. A walk up the narrow gorge-like valley leads you to a Shiva temple and a gorgeous waterfall with a pool below. You can have a bath in the pool with the horde of devotee-picnickers or climb up the mountainside to come out on top of the waterfall and enjoy the breeze and the views. A taxi would cost Rs 700-800 for a return-trip.

Talwas (53 km NE)
Close to Ramgarh Sanctuary is a beautifully situated lake flanked by low hills and decorated with lotus plants. Nearby stands a fort and also a Shiva temple called **Dhoolshwar Mahadev**, located

SHAHPURA BAGH A garden in the desert

About 82 km north-west of Bundi is what is touted as an oasis in the desert state of Rajasthan. Shahpura Bagh, once the summer home of the kings of Shahpura, is today part of Bhilwara District.

Spread across 30 acres, the land on which it stands was gifted to Rajadhirah Suraj Mal, Rana Pratap's grandson, by the Mughal Emperor Shahjahan. As elsewhere in Rajasthan, now it is a heritage property that's fortunately tucked away from the tourist circuit, with suites and double rooms, Continental, Indian and Rajasthani food on the menu, and Internet. Members of the royal family live in one of the two residences that make up the estate. The resort arranges tours to the places around, and the town itself has several attractions, such as the **Dhikola Fort**, an old palace and lots of shopping opportunities. You can also travel to the areas nearby for picnics; there are many lakes and dams that make for scenic spots here.

For more details, contact the resort (Mobile: 09828122012/ 13; Tel: 01484-222077). The tariff is Rs 5,400 for a double room and Rs 7,000 for a suite.

PRAKASH ISRANI

Bundi's motorcycle dairies: Milk vendors on the road

next to a waterfall. To get a glimpse of rural Bundi, visit Thikarda (6 km north) or Borkhandi (7 km west). Interact with the village folk chatting under a tree and potters busy with their wheels, or experience the charm of their houses. A taxi would cost Rs 800-1,000 for a return-trip.

Dugari (65 km NE)
Dugari has a huge and lovely lake called **Kanak Sagar**, home to migratory birds in the winters. On the bank of the lake is a fort famous for its Bundi-style wall paintings depicting *ras lila* and Radha-Krishna. One reaches Dugari via Talwas, on a road that's not well-levelled in parts; a taxi will take you there and back to Bundi for around Rs 1,100.

Indragarh (77 km NE)
Indrasal Singh Hada of the ruling family of Bundi, an elder son of the king, left the capital and founded the fort and the town of Indragarh in the 17th century. The fort looms over the side of a mountain and has a unique structure. Its impressive ruins command spectacular views of the countryside spread out in front. The palaces in the fort — Hawa Mahal, Janana Mahal and Supari Mahal

— are decorated with frescoes and murals typical of Bundi. The fort is approached through the pleasant and winding lanes of Indragarh. Just before the gate of the fort look out for a board on a house saying 'To visit fort contact here'. The courteous family has the keys to the fort and someone will show you around. It's best to go during the day. The road to Indragarh is via Talwas and taxi fare should be Rs 1,100 for a return-trip.

Bijoliyan (48 km SW)
The small town of Bijoliyan lies on the road to Chittaurgarh and you reach it after crossing a picturesque plateau. It has three lovely 13th century Shiva temples located around a pretty tank called **Mandakini Kund.**

The **Uddeshwar Temple**, with a sunken Shivling, is the most exquisite with some fabulous carved images on its outer walls. Ask the ASI caretaker to point out the sculptures of Ardhanareshwar, Harihar, Natraj and Surya. The other two shrines are devoted to Mahakal and Hazareshwar. The Hazareshwar Shivling consists of a thousand smaller Shivlings. Taxi fare from Bundi for a return-trip would be between Rs 900 and 1,100. ∎

JHALAWAR
OF GODS AND KINGS

District Jhalawar **Region** Hadoti
Location In south-east Rajasthan, at the edge of the Malwa Plateau that Rajasthan shares with Madhya Pradesh
Distances 85 km SE of Kota, 334 km SE of Jaipur, 590 km SW of Delhi
Journey time *By road* 2¹/₂ hrs from Kota, 8 hrs from Jaipur
Route from Jaipur NH12 to Jhalawar via Tonk, Devli, Bundi and Kota (*see route guide on page 108*)

■ BY JUHI SAKLANI AND
 RANEE SAHANEY

In an earlier life, he had danced in rage and grief carrying her dead body in his arms. In a previous birth, she had stood on one foot for 16 years, eating only dying leaves, in her passion to possess the loved one. But now they look as if their foreheads have never known nightmares. They tend towards each other in lazy serenity, Shiva and Parvati, seated on a Nandi, holding each other with more than just arms. Their passionate peace fills the sanctum sanctorum of the 7th-century remains of the Chandra Mouli Mahadev Temple, perched on the

→ FAST FACTS

When to go October to March is the most pleasant time to visit; Jhalawar can get hot in the summers and the roads can get very troublesome in and after the monsoons
Tourist office
● Tourist Information Bureau ❶
RTDC Hotel Chandrawati, Jhalawar
Tel: 07432-230081
STD code 07432

banks of the Chandrabhaga River in Jhalarpatan, the 'old town' near Jhalawar. The temple announces the once-presence of Chandravati, a city founded by the successors of Vikramaditya. It is only one of the many gems that lie scattered in the area as if a bag of treasures had burst here.

Understanding the region invoked by the word 'Jhalawar' means unpeeling layers of religious expression, commercial undercurrents and political thicknesses. When Rajasthan Tourism uses the word 'Jhalawar', they mean Jhalawar District which, along with Kota and Bundi, makes up the old cultural region of 'Hadoti'. There's the town of Jhalawar itself, the seat of the 160-year-old Jhalawar kingdom and its gorgeous palaces. Just 5 km away, there's Jhalarpatan, teeming with old temples and havelis, and with the even older ruins so gushingly described above. At a distance of 15 km, there's the Gagron Fort controlled by different dynasties over 1,300 years. And there are any number of ancient Hindu temples, Buddhist cave temples and viharas, and sculptures strewn around in forests... All this in an area called the 'Cherrapunji of Rajasthan' by locals, a green hillock-dotted terrain that bursts into huge ponds and lakes during the rains.

Strictly speaking, there was no entity called Jhalawar in earlier times. This area of south Rajasthan was part of the history and fortunes of the Malwa Plateau (ruled from Ujjain and Mandu) from the time of

Photographs by RANEE SAHANEY

the Mauryas and eventually became part of the Kota kingdom. It held the forests in which kings are shown hunting in the famous Kota-Bundi miniatures. An able Kota minister, Zalim Singh, became Kota's de facto ruler and developed good relations with the British. The state of Jhalawar was created in 1838 out of parts of Kota kingdom because of a treaty between the British and Zalim Singh's descendants. It was called Jhalawar thanks to their ancestors, who were the Jhalas, hailing from Kathiawar.

ORIENTATION

Taxis from Kota are the best option to visit Jhalawar and its arounds (Rs 1,200 a day); it's difficult to get autos in the town itself. A one-day sightseeing tour of Jhalawar and Jhalarpatan costs around Rs 200 by auto. The **bus stand** near the dharamshala in Jhalawar Town offers connections to other towns in the district and Kota. The **Garh Palace** is situated in the centre of Jhalawar Town. The **Prithvi Vilas Palace** is 2 km west of Garh Palace. The **Tourist Reception Centre**, located in **RTDC's Chandravati Hotel**, is about $1^1/_2$ km south-east of the Prithvi Vilas Palace.

THINGS TO SEE AND DO

The infrastructure of Jhalawar District hasn't yet kept pace with the richness of its offerings. The town is small enough to hardly take up a day of your time. Jhalarpatan can keep you occupied for a day, but to merely 'see the sights', half a day is sufficient as well. For every other visit described in the *Arounds* section (*see page 130*), keep a day each.

Garh Palace

The best treasures Jhalawar Town has to offer are locked up and accessible only to the persistent. The original residence of the royal family, the Garh Palace is, as its

The Chandramouli Mahadev Temple

name suggests, a grandeur-defining citadel-palace. Built by Maharaj Madan Singh during 1840-1845, it was later handed over to the government to house collectorate offices. You can walk through and see the **Sheesh Mahal** rooms partitioned into cubicles, splendid **frescoes** with electric fittings, and the inlay work on walls and ceilings covered by dust. A few locked rooms are repositories of every variety of artistic expression, from *pietra dura* to miniature styles to religious portrayal to portrait painting to English landscapes and floral studies to some rare glasswork. **TIP** If you stay at the Prithvi Vilas Palace (*see Where to Stay on page 130 and also Darbar Ki Kothi on page 132*), you have a good chance of accessing closed rooms

Within the Garh Palace enclosure stands the very interesting **Bhawani Natya Shala**, an opera-house-style theatre made by Bhawani Singh, the king

Adinath Jain Temple gets a touch-up

responsible for the creation of modern Jhalawar. Again, this is a faded and uncared-for structure, locked and forgotten except in tourist brochures. But this was once a vibrant centre for staging the works of Kalidas and Shakespeare; the proscenium is built with an underground extension, such that horses and chariots could appear on stage! At the **Government Museum**, just outside the Garh Palace, you can see abundant treasures of ancient Indian art, many dating back a millennium if not more, some of them rescued from the jungles of **Kakuni**. It houses lovely sacred sculptures, rare manuscripts, paintings, coins and interesting 5th and 7th century inscriptions.

♦**Location** Garh Palace, at the heart of Jhalawar, is its biggest and easiest to find landmark **Entry fee** Free **Museum entry fee** Rs 3; Mondays free **Camera** Free **Timings** 9 am-5.30 pm, Fridays closed **Museum timings** 10 am-5 pm

Rain Basera

Another of the royal family's former residences, the Rain Basera makes for a lovely short foray from Jhalawar, made all the more lovely for its association with a king who would not rule. Maharaja Rajendra Singh had a dream of abdicating the kingdom for his son and retiring to write poetry. He saw this timber house in an exhibition in Lucknow in 1936 and had the whole edifice transported and installed at the vast **Krishna Sagar Talab** here. But — it does break your heart to think of it — he died soon after. It is today managed by the Irrigation Department.

♦**Location** On Kota Road, about 8 km from Garh Palace

Jhalarpatan

Zalim Singh, the founder of the Jhalawar kingdom, used to camp at Jhalawar but the place he lovingly nurtured from 1796 was Jhalarpatan, translated as 'the City of Temple Bells', locally called Patan. The riverside township overlaps the city of Chandravati, said to have been founded

A few permanent effigies of Ravan on the ground where Dussehra is celebrated

by Parmar Chandra Sen, Vikramaditya's grandson. Rajasthan's chronicler James Tod counted 108 temples here. Today, innocent of Coke or Pepsi, chowmein or burgers, Maruti or any other brand of car, Patan is a walled settlement you enter through a formal doorway and are immediately gifted with the combined stillness of three banyan trees, a huge pond and quaint chhatris under which villagers rest in the afternoon. On the day of the local haat, nomadic men and women, iron-smiths by trade, bounce their red *ghagras*, silver jewellery and black moustaches off the bright yellow mounds of *poha*.

For some uncluttered moments you can always stroll or drive down to the site of the **Chandramouli Mahadev Temple**, cared for by the Archaeological Survey of India (ASI), in beautifully maintained grounds next to the Chandrabhaga River. This complex holds the remains of many 7th-14th century shrines. In early mornings or at dusk, the quiet river, the shrines and temples, the richly carved pillars, and the profusion of heart-stopping art bathe themselves in a golden glow and match the serenity that can be found, in the best traditions of classical Indian art, on the faces of the icons. While Jhalarpatan is dotted with old Jain and Hindu temples,

the 11th-century **Sun Temple** is the pride of the town. Strictly speaking, it's a temple of Padmanath, whose image was enshrined here in the 19th century. With its lofty 97-foot high shikhar and its association with the sun, the Jhalarpatan residents call it the 'Konark of Rajasthan'. The shikhar is indeed impressive, teeming with small images of gods, goddesses, ganikas, apsaras, animals, and, inevitably, some erotica.

♦**Location** In the old quarter about 5 km south of Jhalawar, along NH12 **Timings** 6 am-9 pm

SHOPPING

You would not go to Jhalawar for shopping. But the artisans in Jhalarpatan may part with their stone and marble images in the tradition of the carvings of the Sun Temple or the Chandravati temples. The rates are negotiable.

WHERE TO STAY

The few stay options in Jhalawar include a heritage property and a couple of budget hotels. If you are planning only a day-trip to Jhalawar, then the best bet would be to stay in Kota.

Heritage

The **Prithvi Vilas Palace** (Tel: 07432-231347; Tariff: Rs 1,250-3,000), in Civil Lines, is locally recognised as 'Darbar ki Kothi' and offers 16 rooms (*also see page 132*). Prithvi Vilas arranges guided tours on request. There is also an elegant **Palace Guesthouse** (Tel: 231347; Tariff: Rs 1,500-2,000), which is adjacent to the main palace, with four rooms on offer. Breakfast is included in the price.

Others

RTDC's **Hotel Chandrawati** (Tel: 234023; Tariff: Rs 500-700), on Patan Road, has six rooms with TV and attached bathrooms, a restaurant and laundry service. With the permission of the Irrigation Department at Jhalawar, you can stay at the **Rain Basera Guesthouse** (Tel: 232349, 09414310401; Tariff: Rs 250) by the lake.

→ GETTING THERE

Air Nearest airport: Jaipur (334 km/ 8 hrs). A deluxe night bus leaves from the Sindhi Camp Central Bus Stand daily for Jhalawar; there's a return service as well. Taxis charge about Rs 5-6 per km **Rail** Nearest railhead: Kota Junction, where all Delhi-Mumbai bound trains halt en route. The best options are: from Delhi, the Intercity; and from Mumbai, the Dehradun Express. From Kota, taxis take $2^{1}/_{2}$ hrs to get to Jhalawar. The price can be brought down to Rs 900 (from initial quotes of 1,200). It's not easy to get taxis from Ramganjmandi, which is the nearest railhead **Road** Express buses (Rs 44) ply regularly to Jhalawar from Kota's Central Bus Terminal near Chambal Bridge. Buses heading for Ujjain or Indore also stop here

It has four rooms with attached bathrooms. There is no arrangement for food.

For more hotels and details, see Jhalawar Accommodation Listings on page 472

WHERE TO EAT

Meals are another good reason to stay at the **Prithvi Vilas Palace**. The cooks are efficient and there's an interesting Gujarati flavour to the home-made food, since the Jhalas originally hailed from there and often married into Gujarati royal families. The road between Jhalawar and Patan has roadside restaurants of which **Rupali Dhani** has a pleasant garden setting. Try the red-hot sev ki subzi at the highway dhabas and the poha from local halwais in Patan.

AROUNDS

Gagron Fort (12 km N)
The huge and dramatic Gagron Fort is located at the junction of the Ahu and Kali Sindh rivers that protected it from three sides. In the classical categorisation of forts in India, this is a rare one because it is a *jal-durg* (water-protected fort) as well as *van-durg* (forest-protected fort). Begun in the 7th century, with additions till the 14th, it was controlled successively by Rajputs, Mandu Sultans, Khaljis, Mughals, Kota and Jhalawar. The fort provides spectacular views from many vantage points, especially from the *burj* at the very end, and unexpected treats in the form of well-preserved chambers, stunning doorways and arches and pillars.

Chandkheri (35 km NE)
The scenic road to **Adinath Jain Temple** at Chandkheri, near Khanpur, meanders past soyabean and maize fields and ponds and lakes, all punctuated by the Kali Sindh, Ahu and Ujad rivers. Held sacred by Digambar Jain devotees, the temple's tranquil sanctum sanctorum features a stunning, larger-than-life stone statue of

The huge and dramatic Gagron Fort, located at the junction of two rivers

the first Jain Tirthankara Adinath. Ghee offerings and the aromatic smoke from joss sticks have given the original red stone of this 5th-century statue a rich chocolate colour, lending it a beauty that is at once earthy and celestial. The statue was placed in this huge temple complex — where expansion work continues to this day — in the 17th century, after it was discovered in the nearby Shergarh-Barapati forests. Images of Lord Parshwanath, Chandra Prabhu and Sambhavanth adorn the upper sanctum. The temple is crowded during the birthday celebrations of Adinath (from Chaitra Shukla 7, 8 and 9), when the deity is taken in a procession around the complex.

◆**Temple timings** 6 am-10 pm

It's best to hire a taxi from Kota to explore Jhalawar, Jhalarpatan and Chandkheri together. Indicas cost about Rs 1,200 a day, but as the roads are patchy, it's best to hire a Scorpio/ Tavera (Rs 3,300 a day). The **Adinath Yatrinivas** (Tel: 07430-261616, 261358) in the temple complex has seven halls of which the halls for groups of 20 to 40 have attached baths. Bookings are on a first-come, first-served basis (except for groups) and you can check in 24/ 7. Only veg food is served (Rs 10-50 per meal).

Buddhist Caves (90 km SW)

Few visitors to Rajasthan are aware of the existence of the antique Buddhist monastic caves in the **Kolvi** and **Vinayaka hillocks** in Jhalawar District. The drive to these hillocks, en route to Dag, gives one a splendid introduction to Jhalawar's pretty countryside, which is a mosaic of fields and water bodies.

The caves date back to the post-Ashoka period of Buddhist expansion. The Hadoti group is said to share the chhatri of the Bhaja, Karla and Ajanta cave monasteries in Maharashtra. The Kolvi, Vinayaka and Hathygod Cave complexes are separated from each other by about 5-6 km, so if you want to explore all three, keep at least 2 hrs in hand. The **Kolvi Complex** (protected by the ASI and also the most approachable

Darbar ki Kothi

The royal family of Jhalawar continues to stay in what the locals call the Darbar ki Kothi, generously sharing not just their home but also their memories and traditions with the guest. For the heritage enthusiast, this palace, formally called **Prithvi Vilas Palace**, is better than an impersonal heritage hotel inasmuch as it is a lived-in home. Set in some 150 acres of land, surrounded by a delicious lotus moat, replete with intricate carving, domes, chhatris, sumptuous furniture and old portraits, it's the best place to stay in Jhalawar, but is also a site worth visiting in its own right.

The Prithvi Vilas Palace

If one went nowhere else in the Jhalawar area, one could just retreat here — relaxing with a book and some squirrels and birdsong in the grounds; having tea at the brimming *baoli*; or strolling to the Sati Temple, made of marble, and red and pink sandstone. You can discover a facsimile of a 1664 edition of *Mr William Shakespeare's Comedies, Histories and Tragedies* in the atmospheric library, and

get away from the world on the windswept rooftop. And, of course, you can hear stories from an erstwhile queen, such as that of the 'ikdanta haathi' (one-tusked elephant) that came as a gift on the occasion of a royal engagement. Some special pachydermal dentistry was done to create a twin tusk for him, which was so strong that the dancer Kukki Bai could perform on a wooden slab placed between the two!

cave) can be accessed from the Bhawani Mandi railhead; a 3-km long gravel path to the right side of the main road will lead you here. Do remember that you need to climb up by about 200 ft before you reach the cave. A steep walk up a hill will get you to both the Vinayaka and Hathyagod caves as well.

A decorative temple structure greets the visitor at the **Kolvi Cave**, which is scattered with images of meditating Buddhas set in stupa-like structures. The vaulted ceiling, the ornamental and pillared *chaityas* (prayer halls), the stupas (some of which rise from the floor to ceiling), the double-decker residential quarters and the jharokas are lovely but in dire need of conservation.

The **Gunai Cave**, a short distance away, has nine residential quarters. The **Kayavarneshwar Shiva Temple**, with a lotus pond, is a little further on, and is

quite crowded with devotees on Maha Shivaratri. The **Vinayaka Cave Complex** is full of bats and is the farthest from the main road. It has 23 residential quarters (some double-storeyed) and a stupa-like temple structure. Though the **Hathyagod Cave** is the first one from the Bhawani Mandi side, you may want to visit it on your return to Jhalawar. A tough climb up the hill will take you to the cave's rock-cut temple and 11 residential cells.

Do remember that it will help to ask the locals for directions to the caves. It is also advisable to wear a sturdy pair of walking shoes.

TIP Kota-based **Hadoti Travels** (Tel: 0744-2326221/ 24; Mobile: 09414183045) arranges tours to Jhalawar, Jhalarpatan, Chandkheri and Kolvi caves. Taxis cost between Rs 3,300 (for a Tavera) and Rs 1,000 (for an Indica) per day. The guide fee is Rs 300 per day ∎

South Rajasthan

A doorway to the world of
intrepid Rajputs, bursting
with real and imagined tales
of valour and victory, of
battles won and lost

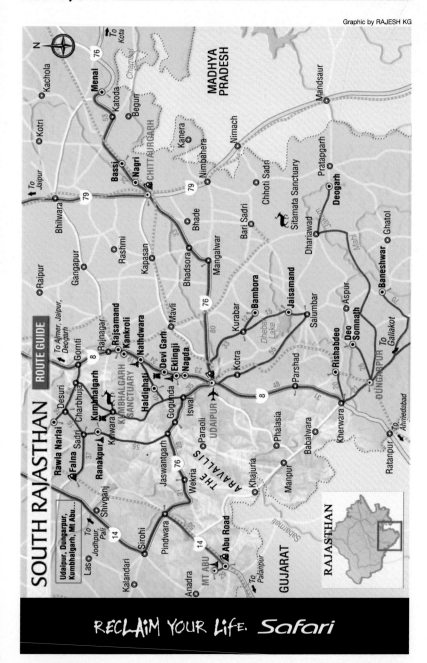

RECLAIM YOUR Life. Safari

Lake Palace Hotel, the 18th-century summer palace of erstwhile rulers

UDAIPUR

WATER KINGDOM

District Udaipur **Region** Mewar
Location In southern Rajasthan, amidst the low hills of the Aravallis, bounded by its two big lakes, Pichola and Fateh Sagar, and River Ahar
Distances 276 km SE of Jodhpur, 396 km SW of Jaipur, 652 km SW of Delhi
Journey time By road 5 hrs from Jodhpur, 9 hrs from Jaipur, 14 hrs from Delhi
Route from Jaipur NH8 to Udaipur via Ajmer, Beawar, Rajsamand and Nathdwara (*see route guide on facing page*)

■ BY AMIT MAHAJAN

Udaipur is happy again. And the stimulus of Udaipur's happiness has stirred everybody. The miniature painter at Hanuman Ghat adds strands of emotions to his creations with nonchalant ease. The white-bearded Sikh guide is childishly cute as he does a Col Tod in Gujarati. The owner of a restaurant is adamant about reciting the verses sent by his Polish love, the ones that inspired him to visualise her as a mermaid. This happiness will also imbue your being. It will make you sit by the lakeside and listen to its sounds and cherish its silences. It will make you climb up a fish-shaped hill to gently stroke age-old, crumbling walls. It will make you wander aimlessly in the *galis* and streets, or spend hours in the palaces learning about history and fate, war and misfortune.

Udaipur is happy again. After many parched years, its skies are full of water and so are its lakes. The walls are a smiling cream or a radiant white, and the caparisoned elephants and horses painted next to welcoming doors sport a splash of

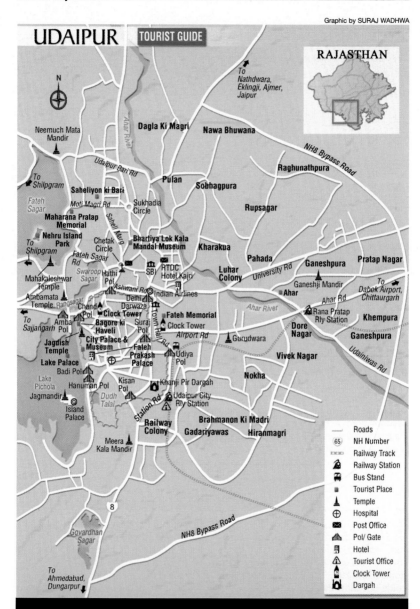

Graphic by SURAJ WADHWA

UDAIPUR TOURIST GUIDE

RAJASTHAN

To Nathdwara, Eklingji, Ajmer, Jaipur

Neemuch Mata Mandir

Dagla Ki Magri

Nawa Bhuwana

NH8 Bypass Road

To Shilpgram

Udaipur Bari Rd

Pulan

Raghunathpura

Ahar River

Saheliyon ki Bari

Sobhagpura

Fateh Sagar

Moti Magri Rd

Sukhadia Circle

Rupsagar

Maharana Pratap Memorial

Saheli Marg

Bhartiya Lok Kala Mandal Museum

Kharakua

Pahada

Ganeshpura

Pratap Nagar

Nehru Island Park

Chetak Circle

To Shilpgram

Fateh Sagar Rd

SBI

RTDC Hotel Kajri

Luhar Colony

University Rd

Ganeshji Mandir

To Dabok Airport, Chittaurgarh

Swaroop Sagar

Hathi Pol

Ashwani Rd

Indian Airlines

Ahar

Ahar Rd

Mahakaleshwar Temple

Ambamata Temple

Rangsagar

Chand Pol

Delhi Darwaza

Ahar River

Rana Pratap Rly Station

Khempura

To Amba Pol

Clock Tower

Fateh Memorial

Dore Nagar

Ganeshpura

To Sajjangarh

Bagore ki Haveli

Suraj Pol

Clock Tower

Town Hall Rd

Airport Rd

Jagdish Temple

City Palace & Museum

Fateh Prakash Palace

Udiya Pol

Gurudwara

Vivek Nagar

Udainiwas Rd

Lake Palace

Badi Pol

Lake Pichola

Hanuman Pol

Kisan Pol

Khanji Pir Dargah

Nokha

Jagmandir

Dudh Talai

Island Palace

Station Rd

Udaipur City Rly Station

Meera Kala Mandir

Railway Colony

Brahmanon Ki Madri

Gadariyawas

Hiranmagri

8

Govardhan Sagar

NH8 Bypass Road

To Ahmedabad, Dungarpur

—	Roads
65	NH Number
▭▭▭	Railway Track
🚉	Railway Station
🚌	Bus Stand
▪	Tourist Place
⚲	Temple
⊕	Hospital
✉	Post Office
⛩	Pol/ Gate
🏨	Hotel
⚐	Tourist Office
♟	Clock Tower
⚑	Dargah

RECLAIM YOUR Life. Safari

red and indigo. The mango and rayan trees are vibrant green and muted auburn, the skies a brooding grey or a tender crimson. The abandoned ruins muster up an ochre melancholy, and the lively palaces are a shower of gold. The waters provide a silvery sheen. Colours have come to life and Udaipur has become a charming, seductive miniature painting of the Mewar School, once again.

ORIENTATION

The **Old City** is to the east of **Lake Pichola**. The city wall is hardly seen, but many areas are still known by the gate names of yore: **Suraj Pol**, **Hathi Pol**, et al. The **City Palace** sits on the east bank of Lake Pichola, with its back towards it. The tourist hub is to the north of City Palace. **Fateh Sagar Lake** is further north. The **train station** and the **bus stand** are just outside the Old City, to the south-east. The **airport** is 25 km from the city centre to the east. Autos here don't run on meter and the minimum fare is Rs 20-25. An auto for the day should cost Rs 300-350. The taxi fare for the day should be Rs 1,000-1,100. There are numerous travel agents around the city centre, and it's best to compare rates or ask your hotel to arrange a taxi.

THINGS TO SEE AND DO

A tourist's itinerary in Udaipur inevitably revolves around the sites of the erstwhile rulers: the palaces they lived in, the lakes they built, the gardens they frequented and the cenotaphs built for them. All these places today dutifully echo a fictional history in which the Sisodia Rajput rulers of Mewar are famous for their virtues, victories and fierce independence. However, the splendours of Udaipur's architectural heritage belong mainly to the peaceful periods when Mewar accepted at first the sovereignty of the Mughals and later that of the British. Having done the regular tourist bit, the best thing to do

SANJAY SHARMA

At the City Palace complex

in Udaipur is to discover the quiet in the maze of streets between Jagdish Temple and Suraj Pol. You will need at least three days in Udaipur. Keep another day or two to visit nearby places of interest.

City Palace complex

The City Palace is where it all began in the 16th century when Udai Singh met a sage who advised him to establish a city here. Now the complex is a conglomeration of palaces built over 400 years. This largest palace complex in Rajasthan is a fascinating edifice. Twenty-two maharajas of Udaipur contributed to this structure and yet it maintains a graceful uniformity. Despite its huge size and the profusion of architectural elements — jharokhas, columns and towers — the elegant palace has an airy lightness about it. Perhaps that's because of its creamy hue. It also gels easily with the blue waters of Lake Pichola.

Keep aside a few hours to explore the City Palace. Walk up the hill from **Jagdish Temple**, buy your tickets at **Badi Pol**, and enter the complex. After Badi Pol, the imposing **Tripolia Gate** welcomes you, with seven arches or toranas to its left, commemorating the seven times when the maharajas were weighed against silver and gold which was then distributed among the people. On the right is a wall called **Agad**, across which elephants were made to fight each other — a royal idea of sport. Further ahead is the entrance to the palace building and above the entrance, the Mewar crest, an image of the Sun God (from whom the Mewar royalty claim to have descended), flanked by a Rajput warrior and a Bhil.

A part of the **City Palace Museum** in the complex has been made the Government Museum. **Shambhu Niwas** is the present home of the royal family. Further south are **Fateh Prakash Palace** and **Shiv Niwas Palace**, both luxury hotels today.

City Palace Museum

Ganesh Deori leads you into the City Palace Museum, and you enter a maze of narrow passages, steep staircases, terraces, patios and apartments. Just inside the entrance, where your tickets will be checked, notice the paintings of the important Krishna deities of Mewar — Srinathji, Eklingji and Charbhujaji — all

The splendid Shiv Niwas Palace

MADHU KAPPARATH

lovely examples of the Mewar School of painting. Now begins a series of mahals and chowks, with their names, dates of construction and the names of builders displayed prominently, but soon you will be lost — in a world of luxury, indulgence and comfort. Note the **Rajya Aangan**, the spot where Udai Singh met the sage. **Chandra Mahal**, with elegant columns and beautiful windows, is a great palace with stunning views of Lake Pichola, its islands and the surrounding hills. **Badi Mahal**, or Amar Vilas, was built on a rock formation and ingeniously incorporated into the complex with an enclosed garden. The **Kaanch Ki Burj** is a chamber with its walls inlaid with red and silver glass. The **Krishna Niwas** has some remarkable miniature Mewar paintings. A room is dedicated to James Tod, displaying a manuscript of his *Annals* and his portrait. The **Mor Chowk**, originally built in 1620, was decked with brilliantly coloured mosaics of three dancing peacocks in the 19th century. The **Zenana Mahal** has princesses' apartments.

♦**Location** 150m south of Jagdish Mandir **Entry fee** Adults Rs 50, children Rs 30 **Cameras** Still Rs 20, video Rs 200 **Timings** 9.30 am-4.30 pm, open all days

Government Museum

The Government Museum is also accessed from the Ganesh Deori. They have splendid acquisitions but lacklustre display and shoddy maintenance have all but killed them. There are **stone inscriptions** from the Mewar region, dating from the 2nd century BCE to the 19th century. A collection of sculptures is also seen. One gallery depicts the Mewar tradition of miniature art, and includes a series on Krishna-Rukmini. The museum also houses eclectic exhibits including a turban belonging to Khurram (later Shahjahan), who took refuge in Udaipur during a rebellion against Jehangir.

♦**Location** Within the City Palace complex **Entry fee** Rs 3 **Timings** 10 am-5 pm, Fridays closed

DINODIA PHOTO LIBRARY

LAKE PICHOLA Centre of attention

Although its name means 'the backyard', Lake Pichola is the centre of imagination in Udaipur. The town grew up on the shores of Pichola and now lives on its banks. Palaces and hills hug its contours. Havelis and houses and hotels find sustenance in its waters. When the lake is full, people bathe in it, swim and take boat rides, or simply gaze at it. The lake's waters are reflected in the life of Udaipur. When Pichola is dry, camels and buffaloes graze on its surface, and every heart sinks.

You can sit on the numerous rooftop restaurants on **Lal Ghat**, **Gangaur Ghat** and **Hanuman Ghat** and enjoy the changing colours of the lake and its environs. You can take a boat ride from the City Palace jetty on **Bansi Ghat** (adult/ child: Rs 250/ Rs 130 for 1 hr; Rs 130/ Rs 50 for $^1/_2$ hr) and enjoy wonderful views of the lake's shores and its elegant buildings. The lake has two island palaces, **Jagmandir** and **Jagniwas**. The palace on Jagmandir Island was built in the 17th century and its courtyard has a restaurant offering scenic views. The Jagniwas Island hosts the famous **Lake Palace Hotel**. The longer boat ride includes a 20-min halt at Jagmandir Island.

Crystal Gallery

The Crystal Gallery has a profligate display of wealth. In a shopping binge, Rana Sajjan Singh ordered an assortment of crystal objects from F&C Osler & Co in England in 1877. He died before the crystal chairs, beds, sofas, glasses, dinner sets and flywhisks arrived in Udaipur. Successors thought this was a bad omen and the extraordinary bequest stayed packed in boxes for 110 years before somebody thought of making money from this misadventure. The rather overpriced admission fee includes the entry charges to the grand Durbar Hall of the Fateh Prakash Palace and a drink in the Gallery Restaurant.

♦**Location** Fateh Prakash Palace **Entry fee** Adults Rs 325, children Rs 165 (includes entry fee to palace premises and a beverage) **Cameras** Not allowed **Timings** 10 am-8 pm, open all days

Vintage cars

About 2 km away from the City Palace complex is the **Vintage and Classic Car Collection**, where about two dozen vehicles are on display in garages. There's a 1934 Rolls Royce Phantom II and also a 1939 Cadillac convertible, which transported Jackie Kennedy during her visit to Udaipur. Here too the entry fee includes a free beverage, but it still seems steep.

♦**Entry fee** Rs 100 (with a beverage), Rs 130 (includes a veg thali) **Timings** 9.30 am-5.30 pm daily

Jagdish Temple

Built in 1651 in the Indo-Aryan style, the temple is located high above the streets, on a crossroad. The outer walls have carvings typical of Mewar temples, and Vishnu, as Jagannath, is the chief deity.

♦**Sanctum timings** 5 am-2 pm, 4-11 pm

Bagore ki Haveli

The residence of a former prime minister of the state, Amarchand Badwa, the haveli sits right on Lake Pichola. This 18th century haveli has been diligently restored. The 138 rooms around courtyards are set up to evoke the past and exhibit the traditional arts and crafts of the region.

→ FAST FACTS

When to go October to February is best though July to August is pleasant when it rains. Avoid summers
Tourist offices
● Rajasthan Tourism Reception Centre ❶
Fateh Memorial, Suraj Pol, Udaipur
Tel: 0294-2411535
● RTDC Tourist Reception Centre ❶
Dabok Airport, Udaipur
Tel: 2655433
STD code 0294

Impressive dance performances in the Mewari and Rajasthani traditions are held here every evening at 7 pm. The **Bharatiya Lok Kala Museum**, a couple of kilometres away, has interesting dresses, paintings and puppets on display.

♦**Location** Gangaur Ghat Haveli **Entry fee** Rs 25 **Haveli timings** 10 am-7 pm, open all days **Bharatiya Museum entry fee** Indians Rs 15, foreigners Rs 25 **Museum timings** 9 am-6 pm, open all days

Ahar

Now famous as the cremation site of the royal family of Mewar, Ahar has an array of cenotaphs of 19 Mewar rulers, built over four centuries. The first and the most striking cenotaph is that of Maharana Amar Singh, who after abdicating his throne spent his last days in a haveli here. Ahar is also an ancient site with a history going back to 2000 BCE. The Archaeological Museum here is worth visiting for those interested in history.

♦**Location** 2 km east of city centre **Museum entry fee** Rs 3 **Museum timings** 10 am-5 pm, Fridays closed

Monsoon Palace

Originally called Sajjan Garh and built by Sajjan Singh of the 'crystal collection' fame, this 19th century palace was supposed to be an astronomical centre, but became a hunting lodge. Perched atop Banswara Hill, this neglected building has a fairy-tale quality about it. A drive up here, especially around sunset, guarantees spectacular views.

♦**Location** 8 km west of city centre **Entry fee** Rs 80 per vehicle **Timings** 10 am-6 pm, open all days

Udaipur's seven sisters

Udaipur's rulers understood the importance of water, built dams and created reservoirs. You can see some of the most amazing and artistic engineering feats in Udaipur's lakes: Pichola, Dudh Talai, Govardhan Sagar, Kumaria Talav, Rangsagar, Swaroop Sagar and Fateh Sagar.

DEVI GARH

MAJESTIC

INVITING

TRANQUIL

MAGICAL

INSPIRING

ETERNAL

JOYFUL

POETIC

Devi Garh | Boutique Hotels India Ltd.
Delwara, NH-8,Near Eklingji,Nathdwara, | UCO Bank Building, III rd Floor
Dist. RajsamandRajasthan-313202, India | Parliament Street,New Delhi – 110001, India
Tel: +91-2953-289211, Fax: +91-2953-289357 | Tel: +91-11-23354554 / 23755540,Fax: +91-11-23718447
reservations@deviresorts.com | sales@deviresorts.com, www.deviresorts.com

DEVI GARH

GIREESH GV

Classic driving: The Vintage and Classic Car Collection at Udaipur

Collectively, they are called the seven sisters of Udaipur, and there are more. These water bodies have been Udaipur's lifeline over centuries. All these lakes are inter-connected, and the surplus water from one flows into the next (*also see Lake Pichola: Centre of attention on page 139*).

SHOPPING

The touristy areas near City Palace, Jagdish Temple, Lalghat and Gangaur Ghat are akin to a huge shopping plaza selling all manner of artefacts and crafts. Miniature paintings are Udaipur's most famous craft. There are many painters and scores of shops selling miniatures done on paper, cloth, stone and wood (Rs 20 upwards). Silver jewellery, handmade paper, fabrics, papier-mâché, wooden and stone statues, and block-printed clothes are on offer. Much time can be spent in the shops outside the City Palace, and the government-run **Rajasthali** showroom near the Jagdish Temple.

Inside the City Palace complex, in the big courtyard beyond Tripolia Gate, are three shops: **Anokhi** selling block-printed cottons, **Aashka** with souvenirs and **Anmol** offering gems and jewellery. **Mystique**, at 14, Lalghat, is a more upmarket shop for textiles and curios.

The wares sold at **Shilpgram**, a crafts village built about 3 km west of Fateh Sagar Lake, are not necessarily of better quality, but all the money goes into the artisan's pocket. If you are looking for *pichhwais*, pigment-painted temple hangings, **Raja Ram Sharma's Studio** near Brahm Pol (Tel: 0294-2432763) is a good place to visit. He executes new compositions using traditional pigments and has a few paintings in stock, but the bulk of his work is executed to order.

WHERE TO STAY

Udaipur has a wide range of stay options but it is advisable to come here only with a booking in the high season. As is to be expected, the most romantic, scenic and exhilarating stay options are around Lake Pichola. Some of these are also the most expensive. However, there are scores of budget and mid-range hotels around Lake Pichola and near Fateh Sagar Lake.

Heritage

The 18th century summer palace of the erstwhile rulers, **Lake Palace Hotel** (Tel: 0294-2528800; Tariff: Rs 19,500-60,000), on the Jagniwas Island in Lake Pichola, is the traditional, dream stay option. You can expect all imaginable luxuries and more here. **Shiv Niwas Palace** (Tel: 2528016-19; Tariff: Rs 12,500-45,400) and **Fateh Prakash Palace** (Tel: 2528016-19; Tariff: Rs 15,900) are famously part of the City Palace complex. Their ambience cuts through several centuries, and the service borders on the obsequious.

Jagat Niwas Palace (Tel: 2422860; Tariff: Rs 1,250-3,999), located in the Lal Ghat area, in two renovated 17th century havelis, is a good option. **Amet Haveli** (Tel: 2431085; Tariff: Rs 2,500-3,000), another restored haveli, has an enchanting location on Hanuman Ghat.

Others

Udaivilas (Tel: 2433300; Tariff: Rs 22,500-1,27,000) is a new claimant to the throne of India's best hotel and promises you the experience of staying in your own palace with your own piece of Lake Pichola (*also see page 139*). **Udai Kothi** (Tel: 2432810; Tariff: Rs 3,800-4,300) is an over-the-top replica of a haveli on Hanuman Ghat. **Hotel Wonderview Palace** (Tel: 2432494; Tariff: Rs 500-3,000) on Hanuman Ghat and **Kankarwa Haveli** (Tel: 2411457; Tariff: Rs 1,350-1,850) on Lal Ghat are worth the money.

Among the budget hotels, try RTDC's **Hotel Kajri** (Tel: 2410501-03; Tariff: Rs 500-1,200), perched on a hilltop 3 km from the lakefront. It has 63 rooms, its own restaurant and parking and is within easy reach of the railway station.

For more hotels and details, see Udaipur Accommodation Listings on pages 491-494

TOTAL CONTROL

→ GETTING THERE

Air Nearest airport: Maharana Pratap (Dabok) Airport, Udaipur (25 km/ 45 mins), connected to Jaipur, Jodhpur, Aurangabad, Delhi and Mumbai. Taxi costs Rs 300 approx to centre of town
Rail Udaipur Station has speedier connections with Delhi with the recently launched Mewar Express from Nizamuddin Station. The Lake City Express and Mewar Express are excellent options from Jaipur. Good connections from Ahmedabad as well as Mumbai
Road Udaipur is on NH8 which links Delhi to Mumbai via Jaipur and Ahmedabad. It is a 9-hr drive from Jaipur, a 14-hr drive from Delhi and a 17-hr drive from Mumbai (797 km). Halt for the night at Ajmer if driving down from Delhi, and at Ahmedabad if coming from Mumbai

WHERE TO EAT

Udaipur is bursting with beautiful, utterly romantic and dreamy eating joints — rooftop cafés, lake-view eateries, and restaurants on the lake — but it is sadly deficient in good food. Most places serve strictly passable Indian and Continental food, so it's best to enjoy the ambience and not expect much from the chef.

Ambrai, the open-air restaurant in Amet Haveli, has a unique location at water level and is a beautiful place to sit. It offers a few Rajasthani specialities, including mutton soweta, a dish that uses corn. If you want basic vegetarian Rajasthani fare, head to **Santosh Daal Baati Bhojanalaya** at Suraj Pol, where you can have dal-baati-choorma. The rooftop terrace at **Udai Kothi** is set around a pool and has good enough food including dal makhani and tandoori chicken and fish. **Café Edelweis** on Gangaur Ghat is popular for its coffee and Continental snacks. The kadhi and seasonal vegetable dishes at **Sunrise** are tasty. **Savage Garden** near

Sneh Resort

Enticing Luxury
Enchanting Culture
Engrossing Environment ...

... to make your vacation *Memorable*

Swirled in the sacred mists of time, nestled in the Aravallis is Sneh Resorts - a world class resort. The precincts invite the leisure, lifestyle and business traveller. Within a verdant heaven of well being, at an interesting place, soothe your senses with serene silences. Attain sanctuary of the mind and body, and discover the luxury of living.

Rashtriya

jain bandhu Sneh Resort Pvt. Ltd.

Sethji Ki Kundal, Udaipur-Ahmedabad Road,
National Highway No. 8, UDAIPUR - 313002, {Rajasthan} INDIA
Tel. : +91-294-3290302, 3291831 Cell : 0-9414156777, 778
website : www.snehresorts.com E-mail : helpdesk@snehresorts.com

Delhi Office :
F-14/71, Model Town -II, Delhi -110009
Tel. : 011-27120001/0002 Fax : 27120003
Cell : 9868230001, 0002

Mumbai Office :
1/14, Nirmal Niwas - 2,
August Kranti Marg, Mumbai - 400036
Cell : 0-9323105863, 9820030288

Chand Pol can be found only after much looking around but is worth the effort for its location and décor if not for its pizzas and pastas. For a cheap thali (Rs 60), go to **Garden Hotel Restaurant** on Lake Palace Road. For an expensive meal, take the boat to **Lake Palace Hotel** (Rs 1,500 for food and boat crossing).

Beware of the fact that many café owners here earnestly believe that the essence of the place is to be found in watching the Bond flick *Octopussy*, which features Udaipur, and towards this end they've been screening the film every evening for over 20 years now!

AROUND UDAIPUR

Nagda (22 km N)
Approached by a country road a little before Eklingji, the ancient town of Nagda was once the capital of Rawal Nagaditya. Now it is a quiet hamlet

Painters engrossed in their work

SANJAY SHARMA

famous for 11th century temples called *saas-bahu* temples, their names a strange distortion of Sahastrabahu (1,000-armed). The temples are small but have fine architecture and intricate carvings, including some erotic figures. The taxi fare is Rs 500 for a return-trip.
♦**Location** 2 km off NH8

Eklingji (23 km N)
The Eklingji Shrine is located in Kailash-puri Village. A form of Shiva, Eklingji is considered to be the real ruler of Mewar and the kings ruled as the deity's representatives. It is believed that Bappa Rawal originally built the shrine in the 8th century; it suffered destruction and was rebuilt. The present form is attributed to Maharana Raimal (15th century), according to a plaque on the south gate of the temple. The temple complex has 108 shrines. The main temple has a four-faced idol of Eklingji. There are hourly buses to Eklingji from town; taxi fare is Rs 500 for a return-trip.
♦**Location** On NH8 **Timings** 4-6.30 am, 10.30 am-1.30 pm and 5.30-8 pm

Haldighati (40 km N)
Haldighati got its name from the yellow-coloured soil of this rugged landscape. Its fame rests upon a short battle fought here on June 18, 1576, between Rana Pratap's forces and those of Akbar. Pratap lost his horse Chetak in a famous skirmish and was forced to flee the battle. Recently, a museum was opened in Haldighati with a model of the battlefield and a series of dioramas depicting Pratap's story. The whole affair is quite tacky. Haldighati is about 18 km from Eklingji. The taxi fare is Rs 600 for a return-trip.
♦**Museum entry fee** Rs 20 **Museum timings** 8 am-8 pm, open all days

Nathdwara (47 km N)
The temple of Srinathji at Nathdwara is among the most sacred places of worship for adherents of the Pushtimarg sect, many of whom travel from Gujarat to

The **Ultra** Edition 12.9
SAMSUNG SGH D-900

① Inside Chandra Mahal   ② Delwara Jain Temple   ③ Cadillac Saloon 1938
④ Jagdish Temple   ⑤ City Palace

imagine doing more with less.
The Ultra Life.

Imagine always being in two places at once, doing two things at once. No office. No boundaries. No restrictions. With Samsung's new Ultra Edition it's not that hard to imagine.   www.samsung.com

Features: 3 Mega Pixel Camera with Auto-Focus • MP3 Player • Intelligent Display • Large 262K QVGA TFT Screen • Direct TV Out

Free accessories: *Bluetooth™ Headset • 256 MB T Flash Memory Card • TV Out Cable • Battery Charger • Travel Adapter • Car Adapter • Straight Headset • Battery (2 Nos.) • Data Kit*

The **Ultra** Edition 12.9
SAMSUNG SGH D-900

Leo Burnett D SMSCHLB-000 13H

SAMSUNG

RANAKPUR Marble in motion

BY AMIT MAHAJAN

When you see Ranakpur from a distance, it appears as an expanse of greenery, with hills weaving in and out of one another. Far below in the valley, amidst all this green, stands a gleaming white jewel, radiant in the wilderness. The radiance is the work of the marble-carvers who made Adinath glow with spiritual bliss. They have made the white marble come to life, speak, and tell beautiful stories — the legend of Lord Rishabhadeva, who meditated under a rayan tree and left his footprint here; the account of Dharanashah, the minister to Rana Kumbha, and his vision of a celestial vehicle as a temple to the lord; the tale of Depa, the architect and his team of artists who gave life to the stones. Not to forget Rana Kumbha, who gave land for the temple and his name to this place, Ranakpur.

Orientation

Ranakpur is just a temple complex flourishing in a forest on the banks of a rivulet called Maghai, 90 km north-west of Udaipur in Rajsamand District. Three **Jain temples** to Rishabhadeva, Neminath and Parsvanath, and the **dharamshalas**, stand close to each other in a walled enclosure.

Just outside is a **Hindu temple** dedicated to the Sun God. The **bus stand** is next to the complex, and is also the place to hire jeeps. The hotels are on the road to Sadri, too long a

The interior of a Ranakpur Jain temple

AMIT PASRICHA

walk from the temple complex. From Udaipur, a taxi for a day-trip costs Rs 1,100-1,400.

Things to see and do

Most people visit Ranakpur for a day-trip, which is adequate. But, to experience the inspiring setting, an overnight stay is recommended.

Temple trail

The gloriously sculptured and enchantingly situated main temple, called the **Chaturmukha Adinath Temple**, is a 15th-century ode to Rishabhadeva, or Adinath, the first of the Jain Tirthankaras. The three-storeyed marble edifice is perched on an elevated plinth, and has an unusual four-sided plan. The unadorned exterior does not prepare you for the shower of architectural complexity and intricate ornamentation as you enter the assembly halls and shrines. Gradually, the vastness of the structure, the architectural balance and symmetry will envelope you. The minutiae and the delicacy of the carvings combine beautifully with the loftiness of the 1,444 pillars seen here, each of them engraved with unique patterns. Four huge luminous white-marble images of Adinath face the cardinal directions in the sanctum sanctorum. The pujaris of the temple will offer you guide services (pay as you wish), and they enliven the experience. Do look for the column with the carved figures of Dharanashah, the chief financier of the temple, and that of Depa, the chief architect. Marvel at the translucence given to marble, at the poise of the dancing figures, at the delicacy of the Kalpavalli (wish-fulfilling creeper) medallions, and at the immensity of the architects' imagination.

The other two temples are dedicated to the Jain Tirthankaras Parsvanath and Neminath. Though dwarfed by the main temple, they exhibit some exquisite carvings and pierced stonework. Nearby is an older temple dedicated to the Sun God. The temple has beautiful sculpture panels, embellished with carvings of warriors and solar deities riding splendid chariots. ◆**Entry fee** Free **Camera** Rs 40 **Timings** 6 am- 9 pm, open all days

TRIBHUVAN TIWARI

White marble comes to life in Ranakpur's magnificent Jain temples

If you are staying longer at Ranakpur, go for walks in the surrounding forest. The hotel you stay in will organise these for you.

Where to stay and eat
There are only a few places to stay because most people come for a day-trip. It is best to book in advance. The only restaurants here are those attached to the hotels.

The luxurious **Fateh Bagh Hotel** (Tel: 02934-286186; Tariff: Rs 5,000-6,500) is a unique hotel; a few years ago, the crumbling ruins of a 200-year-old Rajput-style palace near Jodhpur were relocated stone by stone to Ranakpur (4 km from the temple complex) and converted into a luxury retreat, with a pool, spa and a restaurant. The restaurant offers Indian and Continental food.

The **Maharani Bagh Orchard Retreat** (Tel: 285105; Tariff: Rs 3,000-3,800) is a set of comfortable cottages prettily located in a mango orchard next to Fateh Bagh. Their restaurant is open to non-guests and offers Indian (some Rajasthani dishes) and Chinese cuisine. **Shivika Lake Hotel** (Tel: 285078; Tariff: Rs 600-3,000) is a tastefully done up property set in a tranquil location, which hugs the shore of Lake

Nalwania, 2 km from the temples. **Sheth Sri Anandji Kalyanji Trust** (Tel: 285019; Tariff: Rs 100) provides accommodation in dharamshalas. The RTDC-run **Shilpi Hotel** (Tel: 285074; Tariff: Rs 300-700), located near the Jain temples, is a more modest affair. It has a vegetarian restaurant.

For more hotels and details, see Ranakpur Accommodation Listings on pages 486-487

Fast facts
When to go Most pleasant from October till February end
Tourist office
RTDC Hotel Shilpi (offers tourist information and guidance) ⓘ
Tel: 02934-285074
STD code 02934

Getting there
Udaipur is the closest airport and railway station. The $2^1/_2$- to 3-hr long journey by taxi from the airport will cost Rs 1,100 approx. The road from Udaipur through Iswal, Gogunda and Saira is usually well-maintained, but it can be a bumpy ride during the monsoon ∎

The Deogarh Mahal, a castle converted into a hotel, radiates a quiet beauty

worship the icon of Krishna. Pushtimarg, which means 'Path of Divine Grace', is a sect founded by Vallabhacharya in the 16th century, which revolves around devotion to Krishna.

The Vishnu image here, made of black stone, is said to have been brought from Mathura in 1669 to protect it from Aurangzeb. The temple opens seven times for public worship every day, but only for half-an-hour each time. The timings change often, but it's worthwhile to get there and see the interesting bazaars and streets of the fort-like temple town while waiting for the temple to open. You could either pay money to touts to get quick access or stand in a long queue like the rest. Once the gate opens, there are separate queues for men and women, and different doors, and there is plenty of jostling inside as people try to get a good peek at the idol.

Nathdwara is accessed via Eklingji. Incidentally, the place is also known for **pichhwai paintings** done on hand-spun fabric. Beware of poor imitations, however. There are regular bus services from Udaipur. Taxis cost about Rs 600 for a return-trip.

Kankroli and Rajsamand (66 km NE)
Rajsamand Lake is a huge expanse of water between Kankroli and Rajsamand towns. The lake was created in the late 17th century as an employment programme for drought-affected villagers, initiated by Maharana Rajsingh of Mewar. The lake was formed by damming the rivers Gomti, Kelwa and Tali.

Towards the Kankroli end, the lake has an immense white stone embankment called **Nauchowki**, with ornamental arches and pavilions. Large marble terraces and an intricate network of stairs lead down to the water's edge. Nearby, in Kankroli, on the banks of the lake, is the beautiful temple to **Dwarkadheesh**, the Krishna of Dwarka. From there you can go down to the lake and watch people feeding pigeons and fish. The lakes are located en route to Nathdwara via Eklingji. Regular bus services are available from Udaipur. Taxis cost about Rs 800 for a return-trip.

The original.

Maharana Bhupal Singhji (1930-1955)presiding over the Ashwa-Gaj Poojan at The Manek Chowk, The City Palace Complex, Udaipur-1939 or earlier.

At the original.

Shriji Arvind Singh Mewar presiding over the Ashwa Poojan at The Manek Chowk, The City Palace Complex, Udaipur-2006

Everything inside HRH Palaces and Retreats- the paintings, the festivals, the very air you breathe
- is a testimony to a legacy unbroken since 734AD . To experience it, check in.

HRH Group of Hotels
Experience the Original

For reservations and enquiries contact:
Central Reservations, Udaipur
Toll Free:1800 180 2933 & 1800 180 2944
crs@udaipur.hrhindia.com

HRH Winter Packages
At Grand Heritage Palaces in Udaipur Shiv Niwas Palace and
Fateh Prakash Palace: Starting from Rs 22,999*
In Gajner (near Bikaner) Gajner Palace: Starting from Rs 10,555*
At Royal Retreats in Udaipur, Kumbhalgarh, Ranakpur,
Jaisalmer, Bikaner: Starting from Rs 9,999*

* Terms and conditions apply. www.hrhindia.com

Jaisamand Lake (48 km SE)

Said to be the largest artificial lake in the country, Jaisamand's circumference measures 88 sq km. Maharana Jaisingh had the lake built in the late 17th century by damming the River Gomti. The embankment has marvellous marble cenotaphs and a Shiva temple. On either side are summer palaces built for royal entertainment. The lake has seven islands and hills surround it on all sides.

Two of the hills have palaces on top. One of these is **Hawa Mahal**, a stroll of less than a kilometre from the embankment. The other palace, curiously named **Roothi Rani ka Mahal**, is a more serious hike of about 4 km. There are wonderful views of the lake and the surrounding countryside from the palaces. Boat rides cost about Rs 30-80. The **Jaisamand Wildlife Sanctuary** in the vicinity is home to panthers, wild boars, blue bulls and spotted deer.

A devotee at the Eklingji Temple complex

GIREESH GV

◆**Sanctuary entry fee** Indians Rs 10, foreigners Rs 80 **Camera** Rs 200 **Timings** 10 am-5 pm, open all days

If you are looking for a usual hotel with the usual modern facilities in this unusual lake, **Jaisamand Island Resort** (Mobile: 09928098555; 09829044432; Tariff: Rs 2,200-6,000), situated on one of the islands of the lake, is a good bet. You can also go to the resort for a meal (breakfast Rs 150, lunch/ dinner Rs 400; buffet meals with Indian and Continental dishes are served). To and fro boat trips cost Rs 150. Taxi fare to Jaisamand via Kotra is about Rs 600 for a return-trip.

Bambora (45 km SE)

Bambora is a large village that is becoming a sleepy town. Amidst these unpretentious surroundings is a striking structure perched on top of a hill. An 18th-century edifice known as **Karni Fort** (Tel: 0294-2398283-84; Tariff: Rs 2,800-5,000), it has undergone the inevitable renovation and conversion to a hotel. The result is a superbly relaxing place, where there is nothing else to do but sit in the strong breeze or swim in the pool or go horse riding in the countryside. Taxi from Udaipur costs Rs 600 return.

Devi Garh (30 km N)

See page 410. Taxi costs Rs 1,000 for return.

Deogarh (135 km N)

Known for the quiet beauty and bliss it offers, Deogarh has a castle that's been converted into a hotel. The **Deogarh Mahal** (Tel: 02904-252777; Tariff: Rs 6,000-9,000) has 60 rooms and all modern amenities, including a jacuzzi and multi-cuisine restaurants and a bar. The royal family lives in a part of the complex. The hotel offers jeep safaris, walking tours, trekking and birdwatching opportunities, and rides in vintage cars. They also organise trips to places nearby such as forts and the **Anjana Mahadev Temple**. Taxi from Udaipur costs Rs 1,200 for a return-trip. ∎

And the battle rages: The race for victory continues on a truck in Chittaurgarh

CHITTAURGARH

WHERE THE WINNER LOST IT ALL

District Chittaurgarh **Region** Mewar
Location By the Gambhiri and Berach rivers in the shadow of the Aravallis in south-eastern Rajasthan, 38 km short of the Madhya Pradesh border
Distances 113 km NE of Udaipur, 330 km SW of Jaipur, 588 km SW of Delhi
Journey time *By road* 2¹/₂ hrs from Udaipur, 7 hrs from Jaipur, 11 hrs from Delhi
Route from Jaipur NH8 to Kishangarh via Dudu; NH8A to Nasirabad; NH79 to Chittaurgarh via Bandanwara and Bhilwara (*see route guide on page 134*)

■ BY CHRISTINE CIPRIANI

Chittaurgarh is all about the romance of history. Where a less imaginative eye can see only a mound of rock, the artistic mind can find a glorious past of 275 years etched on stone, a time when death was preferred to dishonour and swords clashed with alarming regularity. A magnificent fort watches over the town, defying the everydayness of the landscape with stories so incredible that only a thin line seems to separate fact from fiction.

Indeed, the story of Chittaur is primarily the story of its 700-acre fort. Built by the Mauryas between the 5th and the 8th centuries, it fell in 734 to the Gehlot founder Bappa Rawal and was occupied for the next eight centuries by a succession of Rajputs and Gujaratis, with intermittent Muslim assaults. Having housed 70,000 people in its heyday, the fort is today more a 500-foot high colony than a monument. As a testimony to its origins and its many rulers, it's littered with Hindu, Jain and Muslim construction, sometimes merged in one building.

Chittaur was the Sisodia capital of Mewar from the early 13th century until the Mughal Emperor Akbar's conquest of 1567, at which point Rana Udai Singh decamped to the hills. History, as warfare later comes to be glamorously known, having moved on, the beauty of this windswept swathe of eastern Mewar today lies in its quietude.

Some people visit Chittaurgarh as a day-trip from Udaipur, but this is not recommended as you then spend half the day on the road. It's best to base yourself in a resort in the countryside and then visit the fort, the villages, woodlands and temples nearby. From the city, you can drive up to the fort yourself or hire an auto in the main market. Autos cost about Rs 150-200 for 3 hrs of sightseeing and taxis about Rs 1,200. A taxi from Bassi Fort Palace Hotel (20 km/ $^1/_2$ hr)

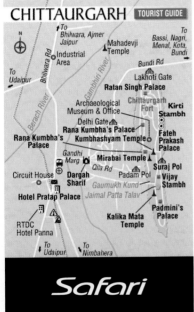

Graphic by RAJESH KG

charges Rs 800 (return) for 3 hrs of sightseeing in Chittaur.

Chittaurgarh Fort

Many battles were fought in and around this strategic bastion. The town faced three sieges, and each time, the women and children committed *jauhar*, or mass suicide, in the face of defeat. Today, the uphill road to the fort passes through various gateways, some with recognisably Gujarati elements. The tour begins with **Rana Kumbha's Palace**, one of the fort's most evocative sections and a model of Rajput architecture. Kumbha didn't establish the complex, but during his long rule (1433-68), he renovated and added to it considerably. Just inside the entrance, you can see where he sat to watch the sun rise and pray to Surya, to the tunes of musicians seated in the chhatri opposite. ◆**Entry fee** Indians Rs 5, foreigners Rs 100 **Timings** 8 am-sunset **Camera** Rs 25 **Guide fee** Rs 230 for a 3- to 4-hr tour

Memories of a queen

Within the **Zenana Mahal** of the Kumbha Palace, the upper floors were knocked out by invaders — the better to view the lovely ceiling dome today. You can even pop into the rani's toilet; with lively authenticity, it still smells like a loo. Around these chambers are an endless array of ruined maidservants' quarters, with stairways leading up to nowhere. Outside, there are faint traces of pink and blue paint on the walls and, when the sky is pure blue, you can imagine how stunning this place must have been. A guide can point out the stairway to the long underground passage, no longer accessible, through which Padmini and her ladies passed down to the bathing tank, **Gaumukh Kund**, and where eventually, under duress, Chittaur's first *jauhar* also took place. It was in 1303 that the Delhi Sultan Allauddin Khalji decided he must have Chittaur and cut off the fort's food supply for six months. Rawal Ratan Singh I of Mewar would not surrender. Legend

DINESH SHUKLA

Chittaurgarh Fort, which saw a number of pitched battles

has it that Allauddin offered to vanish if he were allowed a glimpse of Padmini, the Rana's queen and to keep the peace, Ratan Singh agreed. Afterwards, the Rana escorted Allauddin back to the gate, whereupon the former was captured and told that he would be released only if Padmini were to be handed over. No one was more appalled by this thought than Padmini, who craftily replied that she would only give herself up if the sultan sent 700 palkis for her 700 maids first. She filled these with Rajput soldiers disguised as women — no sooner had they reached the sultan's camp than they leapt out and freed Ratan Singh. Thereafter, the still courteous Rana had a phalanx of armed 'footmen' help Allauddin find his way back to Delhi.

Frustrated, the sultan regrouped, returned, killed 30,000 men who rushed out to face death and stormed the fort. Padmini and the women built a massive pyre and burned themselves and their children to death. This sack-and-suicide is known as Chittaur's first *saka*. Allauddin's army, says historian John Keay, "marvelled that principalities so agriculturally disadvantaged and forts so poorly endowed with treasure should occasion such passionate resistance".

Secular strains

Wander on to see where Mirabai spent much of her life as the widow of the young Sisodia prince Bhoj Raj. Little of this atmospheric building remains, but two green parrots greeted us from the dome and the view of the city of Chittaur, all periwinkle-blue houses with teal-green doors, is worth checking out. The **Diwan-i-Aam** (the Hall of Public Audience) is essentially a tree-dappled lawn, at the end of which stands the Rana Sangha's elephant chamber.

The fort's Jain population comprised accountants and bankers who worked for the Ranas, and they left their mark architecturally. Across the road from Rana Kumbha's palace is a 15th century Jain temple, **Shanti Nath**, built by the Rana's accountant. It now represents an astonishing duality — a neat square, elaborately carved on all sides, capped with a simple Islamic dome. Nearby, in the 19th century **Fateh Prakash Palace**, a museum houses weapons, sculptures, artefacts and some folk art.

♦**Entry fee** Rs 3 **Timings** 10 am-4.30 pm

Continuing south, the 15th century **Kumbhashyam Temple** keeps the **Mirabai Temple** company. The queen is famed for having thrown herself into a

The nine-storeyed Vijay Stambh

romantic devotion to Krishna after her marriage and soon became a young widow, after which — because she recommenced singing too soon and declined to stay in purdah — her brother-in-law tried repeatedly and creatively to poison her. This is a memorial temple, not an actual haunt of Mirabai's.

Beyond the next patch of custard-apple trees is the tower you can see from afar, the **Vijay Stambh**. Built by Rana Kumbha to celebrate his 1437 routing of the Sultan of Malwa (Mandu), it rises nine storeys and is covered head to toe with Hindu deities. In a nod to secularism, Allah's name is inscribed in Arabic on the third and eighth storeys, but that didn't stop later Muslim invaders from taking shots at this amazing structure. If you can cut through the monkeys chasing each other around the base, flash your fort ticket to climb to the top.

South of the tower is the site of the second great *saka*, in 1534, this one owed

to Bahadur Shah of Gujarat. Among the patchwork of Hindu, Jain and quasi-Muslim shrines is the enormous cremation ground where 13,000 women and their children embraced the flames after their men had ridden out to death's door.

Padmini again

On the road to Padmini's Palace, you'll pass the **Kalika Mata Temple**, dedicated to Surya in the 8th century CE, but spruced up and rededicated in the 14th.

Padmini's own portion of the palace, the **Zenana Mahal** (opposite the main building, known popularly as the 'Gents Palace'), was built in the middle of a lotus pond, the better to keep her cool in the summer. It is said that this is where Allauddin had his glimpse of her — standing perhaps in the jharokha of the Gents Palace guest room, he watched her appear in a mirror across the water. But most historians say that this was a condition the Rajputs would have never agreed to. Make your way to this vantage point in the main building, however, as the view of the floating mahal and the rugged land beyond is quite something.

In 1567, when it was clear that Mewar would not join the Mughal army as Amber had done, Akbar attacked. This

→ **FAST FACTS**

When to go To avoid the heat, go between mid-October and mid-March. The rainy season has one advantage: only then does Menal's waterfall roar

Tourist office
● RTDC Tourist Reception Centre ❶
Janta Avas Grih, Near Railway Station
Chittaurgarh
Tel: 01472-241089
STD code 01472

would be Chittaur's third and final *saka*. Under the command of the young Jaimal and Phatta, 8,000 men gallantly defended the Rajputs and gallantly lost. The Mughal Emperor killed about 30,000 more men, the ladies immolated themselves and this time the silence was permanent. Udai Singh established a new Mewar capital (called Udaipur) and his son Maharana Pratap kept the Sisodia flame alive.

Corner of the rising sun

Drive up the fort's eastern side for your last spectacular treat — a landscape of sandstone scree, wildflowers and custard-apple trees culminating in the **Suraj Pol** (gate), which faces east above a 5th century Maurya-built portion of the fort's wall. This is where the battle was often joined and it's thrilling to look straight out to the Aravallis, 10 km away, and see the crack in the hill from which Allauddin would have approached. The plains, almost 600 ft below, are simply immense. On the way back north you'll pass the **Kirti Stambh**, a 12th-century Digambar Jain tower honouring Adinath, the 1st Tirthankara.

The modern city of Chittaur, based on the cement and marble industries, does not beckon with any great attraction. The one exception is the **Dargah Sharif Hazrat Kazichalphir Shah**, a white-marble confection on the chowk in the main bazaar. Although only 85 years old, it's a beautiful space, with intimate, clean chambers and a potted garden.

PARVIN SINGH

Padmini's Palace is set on a pond

SHOPPING

The only indigenous crafts are the **painted wooden toys** of Bassi Village (*see page 160*). Enter Bassi's cheerful old quarter, known simply as Sheher (town), and wander into the workshops. Dancers, musicians, soldiers and animals are all charmingly rendered, with Parvati (Gauri) a particular favourite — especially when painted in choli and churidar, in an impressive disco-dancer avatar! The most elaborate speciality is the kavadh, a sort of miniature altar painted with scenes from the epics and hinged so that it can be folded up like a book.

WHERE TO STAY

Lodgings in Chittaur are uninspiring. To best experience the flavour and peace of this region, spend a few hundred extra bucks — or not, as tariffs are negotiable — and stay in heritage resorts in Bassi (20 km/ $^1/_2$ hr) or Bijaipur (40 km/ 1 hr), both short drives away on the Bundi Road.

Heritage

The oldest wing of the **Bassi Fort Palace** (Tel: 01472-225321/ 248; Tariff: Rs 1,500-2,000) was built in the 16th century by a cousin of Maharana Pratap, after he wrested the area from the Mughals. Every 'room' is a suite with faux-antique furniture, pretty floor tiles and jharokha, and

Castle Bijaipur is not just enchanting, it's a romantic fantasy

the bar is wonderfully old-world. The garden is divine in the evenings.

One hesitates to use the word 'enchanting' for **Castle Bijaipur** (Tel: 276222; Tariff: Rs 2,640-7,500), as it appears in the hotel's brochure, but this place is a romantic fantasy. The rooms are tiny, but with antique furniture and display niches and original stone jharokhas, you may not feel like going out anywhere at all!

Others

In Chittaur itself, try Castle Bijaipur's sister concern, **Hotel Pratap Palace** (Tel: 240099, 243563; Tariff: Rs 1,440-2,040), a quirky home kitted out with a mixture of antique, kitschy and shabby furnishings, once a guest house for the Rana of Udaipur. The AC rooms have lurid Krishna murals. There's a nice garden for meals and tea. The private balconies of the top floor rooms at **Hotel Padmini** (Telefax: 241711/ 18; Tariff: Rs 500-1,700), some at bottom-floor rates for a business hotel, offer fabulous fort views. RTDC's

Panna (Tel: 241238; Tariff: Rs 200-700) is the best of several budget options in town.

For more hotels and details, see Chittaurgarh Accommodation Listings on page 461

WHERE TO EAT

Restaurants have not caught on here, so stick to the hotels. Most of the food served is 'general Rajasthani', not Mewari, but **Castle Bijaipur** prepares elaborate spreads and the **Bassi Fort Palace** serves wonderful paranthas with excellent vegetarian food (the non-vegetarian is less thrilling). Wherever you go, enjoy the local sweets, which take various flour-based forms that may or may not have names ("It is mithai, madam") but include simple versions of patisa and besan-ki-barfi. Enjoy dal-baati-choorma, the speciality of the house at **Pratap Palace**. You will need to make reservations to eat at any of these three hotels.

You needn't call ahead to eat at the canteen at RTDC's **Panna**, which serves

The **Ultra** Edition 12.9
SAMSUNG SGH D-900

① Fateh Prakash Palace ② Samdeshwara Temple ③ Medangarh Fort
④ Meera Temple ⑤ Khumba Palace

imagine doing more with less.
The Ultra Life.

Imagine always being in two places at once, doing two things at once. No
office. No boundaries. No restrictions. With Samsung's new Ultra Edition it's
not that hard to imagine.   www.samsung.com

Features: 3 Mega Pixel Camera with Auto-Focus • MP3 Player • Intelligent Display
• Large 262K QVGA TFT Screen • Direct TV Out

Free accessories: *Bluetooth™ Headset • 256 MB T Flash Memory Card • TV Out Cable
• Battery Charger • Travel Adapter • Car Adapter • Straight Headset • Battery (2 Nos.) • Data Kit*

Leo Burnett D SASCHELB-00012-H

The **Ultra** Edition 12.9
SAMSUNG SGH D-900

SAMSUNG

regular Indian food, or at **Hotel Meera**, which serves Indian and Mughlai meals for which you can pay with plastic. For South Indian meals, stop by at **Hotel Vinayak Palace** at the Collectorate Circle. **Hotel Padmini** is a good option for pure vegetarians.

AROUND CHITTAUR

Any drive outside Chittaurgarh helps one experience a culture that combines the traits of Bhils and Banjaras. Women drape their *pallus* and *chunnis* every which way — over the left shoulder, over the right shoulder, into the waist, over the head, over the face, over the child — and, of course, favour those radioactive colours so pleasing to the jaded urban eye. To help the tourist interested in seeing the places around, most hotels arrange horse and jeep safaris in and around Chittaur.

Nagri (18 km NE)
Called Madhyamika in its prime, Nagri is now an **excavation site** where discoveries have included Hindu and Buddhist

→ GETTING THERE

Air Nearest airport: Dabok Airport, Udaipur (113 km/ 2$\frac{1}{2}$ hrs), well-connected to Delhi, Mumbai, Jodhpur and Jaipur by daily flights. Taxi fare to Chittaurgarh Rs 1,000 (one way)
Rail Chittaurgarh Station is linked to Delhi by the Nizamuddin-Udaipur Express and to Jaipur by the Mewar Express. There are some other good options between Udaipur and Chittaur
Road NH8 connects Jaipur and Delhi to NH79 at Ajmer, along which Chittaur is a 3$\frac{1}{2}$-hr drive away via Nasirabad and Bhilwara

temple remnants and earthenware from the Maurya to the Gupta periods. The coins discovered here can today be seen at the museums in Chittaurgarh and Udaipur. Nagri is connected to Chittaurgarh by bus; a taxi will cost approximately Rs 400 for return.
◆**Location** On the road (NH76) from Chittaurgarh to Kota and Bundi

Bassi (25 km NE)
The cheerful village of Bassi is a jewel. Wander through the main bazaar to the old quarter, **Sheher**, where houses lining the medieval lane are sky-blue, mint-green, purple and yellow. Down by the lake, there's a stepwell between the **Laxmi Nath Temple** and the **Shiva Temple**, the interior of the latter beautifully painted by the toy-makers.

Bassi also has a **wildlife sanctuary** with panther, wild boar, antelope, mongoose and migratory birds. A visit to the sanctuary can be arranged only through your hotel. The best way to see it is to stay in Bassi Fort Palace or Castle Bijaipur or Hotel Pratap Palace (*see Where to Stay on pages 157-158*) in Chittaurgarh. With advance notice, you can even tour the sanctuary on horseback. Alas, animals are not in evidence during or after the rainy season, as overgrown grass obscures them. Bassi is a half-hour drive down the Bundi Road from Chittaurgarh. A taxi charges Rs 350-400 for a drop.

Menal (78 km NE)
Though not at first sight the 'little Khajuraho' it's billed as, Menal is a great experience — a medieval **Shiva Temple** with erotic carvings, other poetic ruins and an enormous gorge that turns into a **waterfall** after the rains. Scrutinise the main temple for the couples in erotic poses and godheads of dubious sexuality; then scramble across the gorge to see another temple. Drive down the Bundi Road via Bassi, Parsoli and Ladpura to Menal. The best way to visit Menal is by taxi (Rs 1,200 return). ■

AGP PHOTOBANK/RAJEEV RASTOGI

It's a virtual display of bright colours at the Baneshwar Fair

DUNGARPUR

HILLSIDE STORY

District Dungarpur **Region** Vagad
Location The town occupies the rugged terrain in the southern foothills of the Aravallis in south-east Rajasthan
Distances 100 km S of Udaipur, 496 km SW of Jaipur, 752 km SW of Delhi
Journey time By road 2 hrs from Udaipur, 11 hrs from Jaipur, 16 hrs from Delhi
Route from Jaipur NH8 to Kherwara via Ajmer, Beawar, Rajsamand, Nathdwara and Udaipur; state highway to Dungarpur (*see route guide on page 134*)

■ BY AMIT MAHAJAN

The bird is black with a white crest and a red beak. The lotus leaf is its emerald island, Gaibsagar Lake its sea, and Dungarpur its preferred universe. The water ripples because of the waves created by your feet and the kikar trees on the nearby shore. The bird, still perched on the lotus leaf, avidly catches insects and eyes the small fish. The temple complex stands nicely blackened and ancient across the road from the lake, and the prayers emanating from there float imperceptibly on the water surface. The surrounding foothills are low and stooping, as if trying to imbue a sense of the countryside. The sounds of Dungarpur drift in indolently in the mild breeze — the daily grind of the autorickshaws, the rush of the local bazaar and the resonant bells of the temple.

Before that, as you approach Dungarpur, through the rocky, craggy terrain dotted with cacti bushes, mimosa trees and teak forest, the first sights will be typical of a small town. You will see jeeps heavy with men and boys hanging out from their doors, loud autos tumbling across the town and markets full of chemists and mechanics. You go past these, also past a small dam, and reach

DINESH SHUKLA

The interiors of the Udai Bilas Palace

the newer palace of erstwhile Dungarpur kings — part of which is today a hotel — and settle in their lakeside, poolside open-air restaurant. Now you notice the surroundings again, and the town is not very far but appears distant. The tract is surrounded by hills, low hills but hills all the same and the name 'Dungarpur, the City of Hills' now makes sense.

Later, with some difficulty, you will tear yourself away from the soothing waters of the lake and visit the old palace. Then the very old past of the not-so-well-known kingdom of Dungarpur will slowly emerge from the closed cupboards and the forgotten recesses, enchanting you with its colours and its stories.

The **Udai Bilas Palace** is situated right on the south bank of the lake. On the west bank is the dam that created the lake, now the notional centre of the town. Across the road from the dam is the

Srinathji Temple. The old palace, called **Juna Mahal**, is 4 km south-east of the Udai Bilas Palace, and is approached by a bumpy road. The **old fort** is located on a hill rising above the Juna Mahal. Below it is the **old Dungarpur Town**.

Your hotel is the best place to ask for a taxi; the charges are Rs 1,000-1,300 for a day for places around Dungarpur. In good weather, a taxi in good condition can manage the steep half a kilometre climb up to the fort. Autorickshaws can be found in the market next to the dam; they don't run on meter but the fares are usually Rs 25 for Udai Bilas Palace and Rs 50 for Juna Mahal.

One of the reasons for coming to Dungarpur can well be that you want to do nothing. In that case, book yourself a room in the Udai Bilas Palace (*see Where to Stay on page 164*), grab a long chair near their pool all day long and just be. On the other hand, if you are in Dungarpur to absorb all that it has to offer, it has a trick or two up its sleeve. The antiquity and the hidden treasures of the Old Palace, the surfeit of birdwatching opportunities and the multi-cultural dimensions here take you by surprise. Dungarpur can keep you interested for two or even three days.

Bharat Petroleum

When to go October to February is best, July to August is pleasant when it rains. Avoid summers
Tourist office
● Rajasthan Tourism Reception Centre ❶ Fateh Memorial, Suraj Pol, Udaipur
Tel: 0294-2411535
STD code 02964

Ek Thambia Mahal, a bluish grey stone structure with balustrades and balconies

Juna Mahal

Literally the Old Palace, the Juna Mahal is well and truly old. Some claim, with justifiable reasons, that it is the oldest existing royal palace complex in India, perhaps in the world. The construction of the palace was started sometime in the 13th century and for about 650 years it was occupied by a single royal dynasty — the Guhilot Rajputs. Throughout these centuries the palace building was growing, usually vertically. Now it is a wonderful edifice, nine storeys high, with two levels underground. The structure has suffered in the few decades of non-occupancy.

The Juna Mahal has a dominant location on a 1,476-foot high hill atop the old township of Dungarpur, and its towering chhatris and engraved balconies are eye-catching even from a distance. The palace is made of a beautiful bluish grey local stone called *pareva* stone and is an exquisite example of temple architecture being introduced into royal residences. The decorative elements include pillars, brackets

and arches; the carvings depict warriors, dancers and musicians. The interiors of the palace are a veritable museum — its various chambers are tastefully decorated with ornamental mirror work, stone inlays and glass inlays.

However, the most impressive are the paintings. There are depictions of gods, with Krishna and his playful stories being the favourite. There are court scenes and hunting expeditions. On the walls you will see Gangaur Festival being celebrated, the Bhils of Dungarpur being defeated in a battle by the Rajputs and a portrait of Queen Victoria. There is also a whimsical display wherein murals dramatising highly athletic Kama Sutra postures are concealed discreetly in a cupboard. You can spend over two hours at the palace.
♦**Location** 4 km south-east of Udai Bilas Palace **Entry fee** Rs 150 **Timings** All day **Note** Tickets have to be bought from Udai Bilas Palace, and the caretaker at the Juna Mahal will show you around. Do give him a tip

Birdwatching

Gaibsagar and the adjoining woodlands are great places to observe birdlife. November to February is the time for migratory birds and the monsoon months, from July to October, is the nesting season for local birds. Painted storks, pond herons, egrets and coots can be seen on the lake. The woods are home to the grey partridge, the paradise fly-catcher and the golden-backed woodpecker. In the marshy area between Udai Bilas Palace and the Juna Mahal, you can spot the sarus crane and the wading bird.

SHOPPING

Dungarpur is too small a town to offer much by way of shopping opportunities. In the old town in the main bazaar you will come across silver smiths who have charming silver jewellery in local designs.

WHERE TO STAY

This is again very limited. Apart from the Udai Bilas Palace described below, the

only other staying options are a few cheap hotels in the town centre.

Heritage

The **Udai Bilas Palace** (Tel: 02964-230808; Tariff: Rs 3,025-5,750) is the place to stay in Dungarpur, and in fact one of the reasons to visit the town. Though quite close to the centre of the town, Udai Bilas Palace occupies a secluded location flanked by the Gaibsagar Lake on one side and a small forest on the other. The construction of the palace was started in the mid-19th century when the **Ek Thambia Mahal** (literally, the One-Pillared Palace) was built. This bluish grey *pareva* stone structure has intricately sculptured pillars, ornate balconies and carved balustrades. A part of the palace is still the royal residence. There are 23 rooms open to guests; every room is different, but equally comfortable, spacious and lavish. The best place to be is the swimming pool and the attached restaurant, right on the lake. The pool is built in such a way that it appears to merge with the lake waters.

AMRIT P SINGH/WILDPHOTOS

→ **GETTING THERE**

Air Nearest airport: Udaipur's Maharana Pratap (Dabok) Airport (125 km/ 2 hrs), which is connected to Jaipur, Jodhpur, Aurangabad, Delhi and Mumbai. Taxi will cost Rs 1,200 approx

Rail Dungarpur Station on the Udaipur-Ahmedabad metre gauge line. But Udaipur (100 km/ 2 hrs) is a more convenient railhead as the road journey to Dungarpur is shorter by 2 hrs

Road Dungarpur lies 21 km east of NH8, which links Delhi and Mumbai via Jaipur and Ahmedabad. From Udaipur, there are frequent buses to Dungarpur

DINESH SHUKLA

Good food and a great view at the Udai Bilas Palace (above); **A painted stork** (left)

For more details see Dungarpur Accommodation Listings on page 462

For more details see Dungarpur Accommodation Listings on page 462

WHERE TO EAT

The **Udai Bilas Palace** is the obvious place to eat. Non-resident guests are also welcome. They mainly have buffets, which are predominantly Indian. You can have a variety of sumptuous meat dishes and rich vegetable preparations. Charges for meals are: breakfast Rs 250, lunch Rs 400 and dinner Rs 450. Some Continental, Chinese and Indian dishes feature in the *á la carte* menu. The meals can be served either in the banquet hall or the more intimate dining hall. Weather permitting, the outdoor restaurant next to the pool is ideal for a drink or an unhurried meal. The town centre has some small restaurants and dhabas.

AROUND DUNGARPUR

Rishabdeo (41 km N)
An important pilgrimage site just off NH8, Rishabdeo is a captivating place.

The origins of the temple here are unknown but there is evidence of some repairs having been done in the 15th century. The temple is built of grey *pareva* stone with beautiful white marble carvings. The multi-pillared hall has an extraordinary intensity about it. In the centre is a big idol of black marble. Interestingly, Jains, Hindus and Bhils worship the deity in their own ways. For Jains the deity is Rishabdeo, also called Adinath, their first Tirthankara. For Hindus the deity is Kesariyaji, a reincarnation of Vishnu. Bhils worship the icon as their Kala Deo, the Black Lord. The temple is also famous as Kesariya Temple because *kesar* (saffron) is the chief offering made to the god here. Taxi fare will be Rs 800 for a return-trip.
◆**Timings** 6 am-9.30 pm

Deo Somnath Temple (26 km NE)
When you reach Deo Gaon, a small village famous for its Shiva temple, the first thing you notice is not the temple but an incredible banyan tree. The huge tree seems as old as the temple and its canopy is spacious enough to function as a village

A scene at the Baneshwar Fair, a raucous affair with swings, singing and bonfires

square. There are people idling under its shade and small shops do their business beneath the tree. The temple occupies a scenic spot next to the River Som. The temple, said to be from the 12th century, is a three-storeyed structure. The architecture of the temple gives a very satisfying effect, not because of its delicacy but because its large constituents come together in a rare harmony. From the temple walk down to the river through a grassy patch and sit at the small but attractively made ghat on the river. The taxi fare is Rs 600 for a return-trip.

Galiakot (49 km SE)

Galiakot is an important pilgrimage site especially for Dawoodi Bohra Muslims. The small village hosts a marble dargah of Saint Fakhruddin (called Babaji Fakhruddin Moula). Dawoodi Bohra Muslims were Brahmin traders in Gujarat who converted to Islam, and now the sect is spread over South Asia. Pilgrims visit the dargah throughout the year, but the most popular pilgrimage time is during the Urs of the saint in the month of Muharram.

The white marble shrine is located on the banks of Mahi River. Galiakot was once the capital of the Parmars and also of the erstwhile Dungarpur State. A taxi will cost Rs 1,000 for a return-trip.

Baneshwar (70 km E)

The small town of Baneshwar lies on the delta formed at the confluence of the rivers Som and Mahi. The town has many Hindu temples but is famous for two important temples. The first is the temple to Baneshwar Mahadeo, meaning the 'Lord of the Delta', a form of Shiva. The other is a shrine dedicated to Mavji, worshipped as a reincarnation of Vishnu. Every January/ February, the Baneshwar fair is held here. It is a raucous affair with swings, merry-go-arounds, singing and bonfires. A taxi will cost Rs 1,000 for a return-trip.

Jaisamand Lake (70 km NE)
See page 152

Udaipur (100 km N)
See page 135 ∎

Nakki Lake, one of Mount Abu's biggest tourist attractions

MOUNT ABU

SITTING PRETTY ON A PLATEAU

District Sirohi **Region** Godwad or Godwar
Location Mount Abu, Rajasthan's only hill station, sits astride a plateau up in the Aravalli Hills near the south-western border with Gujarat, 4,000 ft above sea level
Distances 29 km NW of Abu Road, 173 km W of Udaipur, 220 km N of Ahmedabad, 520 km SW of Jaipur, 776 km SW of Delhi
Journey time By road 3$\frac{1}{2}$ hrs from Udaipur, 12 hrs from Jaipur
Route from Jaipur NH8 to Beawar via Dudu and Ajmer; NH14 to Abu Road via Pali and Sirohi; hill road to Mount Abu (*see route guide on page 134*)

■ BY JUHI SAKLANI AND KISHORE SINGH

Mount Abu's reputation as a 'honeymooners' paradise' does not do justice to the charms of this lovely hillscape. To begin with, it takes something special to be a lush hill station in a desert state. Then, there is the long history of Hindu myths that is attached to the lakes, caves, temples and ashrams tucked away in these rocky hills.

Added to this, there are the more recent layers of Rajputana palatial and British colonial architecture through which one can amble one's time away. Further, there are dense forests and trekking trails vanishing into them, not at some unapproachable distance but right in the heart of things. And most of all, there are the Jain temples of Delwara, where marble becomes rain, dew, fire, silk... leaving all but the tourist guides speechless.

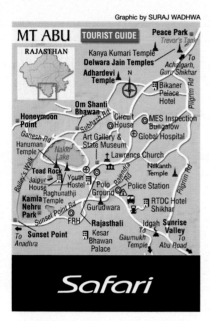

Graphic by SURAJ WADHWA

market begin. In the market, the **Chacha Museum Chowk** is where shared jeeps begin their shuttle route to Delwara. The same road goes further to the **Achalgarh Fort**; and a diversion from it leads to Mount Abu's highest point **Guru Shikhar Peak**. There are sightseeing buses that charge Rs 120 in season, Rs 80 off-season, per person for a full day. Taxi hire for half-day costs Rs 400-500.

THINGS TO SEE AND DO

Mount Abu sits around the Nakki Lake, which, according to legend, the gods scraped from the ground using their nails. The lake is also the centre for most activities in Abu, and boating on the lake is a must-do activity. Give at least three days to soak in the place and its charms.

Viewpoints

For some more sightseeing, or trekking, head towards **Toad Rock** (south-west of the Raghunathji Temple near the lake) or **Sunset Point** (2 km south-west from town on Sunset Point Road), the latter for its panoramic views. There is also an amusement park for children at Sunset Point, ideal for a family outing. At **Guru**

Legend has it that a huge yagna was conducted at Mount Abu by Sage Vashishta, who created the four *agnikuls*, or the Rajput fire-born dynasties. The rest of the clans are said to have descended from the sun and the moon. The *agnikuls* were entrusted with the task of protecting the earth from demons. The descendants of many of the princely kingdoms that governed these Rajput clans built themselves summer palaces in Mount Abu, the coolest spot in overheated Rajasthan to escape the heat of the desert. Dozens followed their lead, and continue to do so decades down the line.

ORIENTATION

Mount Abu is a hill station, the settlements in which are closely interspersed with forests, lakes and rocky terrain. All roads lead to **Nakki Lake**, the town centre around which sprawls a **market**. The **bus stand** and the **Tourist Reception Centre** across from it are among the first few landmarks as the town and the

→ FAST FACTS

When to go Summer, Holi, Diwali, Christmas and New Year are crowded and get very expensive. Visit between Diwali and Christmas or in January-February, despite the chilly nights
Tourist office
● Rajasthan Tourism ❶
Tourist Reception Centre
Opp Bus Stand, Mount Abu
Tel: 02974-235151
STD code 02974

Shikhar, the highest peak (5,650 ft) of the Aravallis, located 15 km out of town, one may combine views of the range with a visit to a temple to **Dattatreya** (Shiva). **WARNING** The forests surrounding these sites are home to wildlife, so trekking late into the evening is not recommended

A walk on the wild side

Mount Abu has a **wildlife sanctuary** that spreads over 288 sq km. The park is another summer draw, for during the hot months of March and April, the champa, jasmine, mango and khajur trees that give the animals shade and cover are weighed down with blooms and fruit. It is also a **birdwatcher's paradise**, with more than 250 species of birds. The most common among them is the grey jungle fowl; leopard, chinkara, sloth bear, wild boar and hundreds of langurs are also seen here. The Tourism Department has identified 17 **nature trails** that make for

→ GETTING THERE

Air Nearest airport: Udaipur (173 km/ 3½ hrs). Taxi to Mt Abu costs Rs 1,400. Ahmedabad (220 km/ 4½ hrs) is another option. Taxi to Mt Abu from Ahmedabad costs Rs 2,000 approx
Rail Nearest railhead: Abu Road (29 km/ 40 mins), well-connected by Western Railways to Delhi, Jaipur, Ahmedabad and Mumbai. Taxis from here cost about Rs 250. Shared taxis charge Rs 20 per head. There are frequent local buses (fare Rs 20) to Mt Abu
Road RSRTC (Tel: 011-23864470) offers a direct service (16 hrs/ Rs 384) to Abu Road from ISBT Kashmere Gate in Delhi. There are private and RSRTC connections to Mt Abu from Jaipur, Jodhpur and Udaipur in Rajasthan, as well as from Ahmedabad in Gujarat

lovely hikes. Guides for the walks can be contacted through the Tourist Reception Centre (*see Fast Facts on page 168*). ♦**Location** 8 km north of town **Entry fee** Indians Rs 10, foreigners Rs 80 **Jeep/ car fee** Rs 65 **Timings** Sunrise to sunset

Nearby is a reservoir constructed as a memorial to the British Colonel Trevor. **Trevor's Tank** is particularly a treat for birdwatchers, as the densely wooded hills around it are a haven for pigeons, peacocks and partridges. Panthers, sambar, jungle cats and wild boar are also found here, and if your timing is right, you may just spot them having a drink from the reservoir, after sunset.

Delwara Jain Temples

Originally Devalwara (home of the gods), the village called Delwara houses a complex of five Jain temples. From the outside, the complex looks whitewashed, plain and quite disappointing. But this is before you actually step into the temples. Of the five temples here, two of the earliest temples, Vimal Vasahi and Luna Vasahi, have glorious marble work.

The temples are marvels of sculpture, not architecture. Their plan — of a courtyard encompassing a circular mandap hall and a portico, all supported by pillars, leading to a sanctum — is shared by many Jain and Hindu temples of the Solanki era in western India. But it is the breathtaking sculpture and carving of the pillars, arches, doorways, and even the ceiling that give a unique feel to these temples. The exactly date-able monuments in Mount Abu are the Delwara Temples, among which the two oldest were built in 1031 and 1230. The **Achalgarh Fortress** that looms over the landscape was built in the 15th century.

Vimal Vasahi Temple

Named after minister Vimal Shah of the Gujarat Solanki court, who built it in 1031, this temple is dedicated to the first Jain Tirthankara Adinath (also called Rishabhdev). Each block of marble here — whether it makes a pillar or a ceiling

The **Ultra** Edition 12.9
SAMSUNG SGH D-900

① Jaipur House   ② Mount Abu   ③ Achalgarh Temple

④ Brahma Kumari Ashram   ⑤ Gurushikhar

imagine doing more with less.
The Ultra Life.

Imagine always being in two places at once, doing two things at once. No office. No boundaries. No restrictions. With Samsung's new Ultra Edition it's not that hard to imagine.   www.samsung.com

Features: 3 Mega Pixel Camera with Auto-Focus • MP3 Player • Intelligent Display • Large 262K QVGA TFT Screen • Direct TV Out

Free accessories: *Bluetooth™ Headset • 256 MB T Flash Memory Card • TV Out Cable • Battery Charger • Travel Adapter • Car Adapter • Straight Headset • Battery (2 Nos.) • Data Kit*

Leo Burnett D-SMSCHLB-00013-H

The **Ultra** Edition 12.9
SAMSUNG SGH D-900

SAMSUNG

All specifications, features and prices mentioned herein are subject to change without notice. *Bluetooth™ is the registered trademark of Bluetooth™ SIG Inc.

PRAKASH ISRANI

The Delwara Jain temples are marvels of sculpture, not architecture

slab — is carved with the care, precision and detail with which one puts a thread in a needle. The pillars in the entrance portico and in the corridors surrounding the shrine have figurines carved with great detail of movement, clothes and jewellery. Since the stories of Hindu mythology criss-crossed those of Jain mythology, Hindu figures such as Indra, Saraswati, Gandharvas and apsaras can be seen. Sixteen four-armed Vidyadevis preside on the pillars supporting the dome, each holding her own symbol. Fifty-two smaller shrines in the corridor hold images of the tirthankaras. Inside the finery lies a plainer hall in which Jain devotees sit in preparation for a ritual. In the sanctum is a 57-inch high icon of Lord Adinath cast in a brass-gold alloy.

Luna Vasahi Temple

Locally called the Devarani-Jethani Temple, this was built by two brothers — Vastupal and Tejpal — ministers of a Gujarati Jain king, in 1230, and is dedicated to the 22nd Tirthankara Lord Neminath. Its beauty is as simultaneously awe-inspiring and serene as the first temple. The Luna Vasahi's literal centre of attraction is the gigantic inverted lotus that 'hangs' from its dome. The lotus is made of hundreds of delicate tiny marble petals that look as if they were made of luminous crisp paper. Guides here will show you how the marble has become almost transparent in places. It's said that to encourage artisans to carve finely, they were paid according to the quantity of marble dust they generated with their carving. The idol of Neminath, seen through ornately carved doors, is an impressive basalt image.

The **Pittahara Temple** was made in the 14th century, dedicated to Lord Adinath. It contains a celebrated image of the lord, 41 inches high and made of *panchdhaatu* (an alloy of five metals), with a substantial proportion of gold. The **Chaumukha Temple** was made in the 15th century and dedicated to the 23rd Tirthankara Parshvanath. It has a tall pinnacle, which sets it apart from the flat roofs and small domes of the other temples. The **Mahavira Temple** is a small

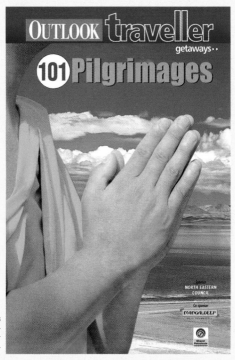

Catch the birdsong

Boating in Nakki Lake is one of the more charming attractions in Mount Abu. Nakki is a

pristine and clean lake, making a ride on its waters a must-do proposition. Your best choice is to get there first thing in the morning — most visitors seem reluctant to rise early, and boating at sunset is more popular. It's best to negotiate with someone to take you to the lake in the early morning; your hotel staff should be able to help organise this.

There are the usual rowboats at Nakki, a few motor boats, and even some kitschy stuff such as boats shaped like swans. All these are great for a photo opportunity, but you're better off with a good paddle boat and a sound oarsman who, after the mandatory rounds and view of Toad's Rock, can point out to you different birds by the shoreline (carry binoculars!) close to the forested ridges of the lake. For that alone, it's worth the effort of getting to the lake at dawn. The early bird may get the worm, but you will catch the birdsong.

18th century shrine to Lord Mahavira; on its ceilings, you can see fading frescoes.

♦**Timings for all temples** Noon-6 pm for tourists; 6 am-noon for Jain devotees **Temple Tel** 02974-238424 **Sirohi office Tel** 02974-222525

Adhardevi Temple

An atmospheric natural cave structure with a very low and narrow entrance, the temple is crowded during Navratra time. Adhardevi, also called Arbuda Devi, is seen as a form of Durga, and was the family goddess of the Parmar kings. It's a climb of some 350 steps to the goddess.

♦**Location** 1 km north of the market **Timings** Sunrise to sunset

Achalgarh Fort and temples

The ruins of this fort, built by Rana Kumbha of Mewar, preside from over a hilltop, on two temples. At the foot of the hill, the 15th century **Achaleshwar** (or **Neelkanth Mahadev**) **Temple** lays claim to a toe impression of Lord Shiva. Perched

some way up the hill (driving is not possible but *dolis*, or palanquins, are available for Rs 200) are the 16th century marble **Kantinath Jain temples**, which make a brave attempt to live up to Delwara in the quantity of marble and sculpting.

♦**Location** 8 km north-east of the Delwara Temples **Timings** 6.30 am-7.30 pm

SHOPPING

Rajasthani **handicrafts** are ubiquitous in the shops that fringe Nakki Lake. In particular, look out for **marble statuary** and **Kota cotton** saris. The shops also have tribal silver jewellery from the region. Other than these shops, pay a visit to **Rajasthali** at Chacha Chowk.

WHERE TO STAY

Mount Abu has a number of stay options. But prices vary wildly between season and off-season, so do remember to phone and check tariffs in advance.

Airtel welcomes you to the Land of Kings

Manual Network Selection Process

A step-by-step guide on how to connect to the best mobile network in Rajasthan.

Go to the menu on your mobile phone and select 'Settings' * Go to 'Phone Settings' * Click on 'Network Settings' * Select 'Manual' * Select Airtel / INA Airtel / INA 70 / Oasis

Stay with Airtel! Win exciting gifts and special roaming privileges.

Rediffusion-DY&R/Del/BCL/011

Mobile Services

Heritage

At the upper-end are heritage properties such as **Palace Hotel** (Tel: 02974-238673, 235121; Tariff: Rs 2,300-4,000), the erstwhile Bikaner House, 2 km from the market on the Delwara Road with beautiful, spacious grounds incorporating a lake. **Cama Rajputana Club Resort** (Tel: 238205-06; Tariff: Rs 3,200-4,950), near the Circuit House, is 125 years old and has landscaped grounds.

Others

The Jaipur House (Tel: 235176; Tariff: Rs 2,500-4,900), located on a cliff over Nakki Lake, has the best views of Mount Abu. Another option is the luxurious **Hotel Hillock** (Tel: 238463-65; Tariff: Rs 2,990-5,990), situated near the market.

Mid-range hotels include the pleasant RTDC **Hotel Shikhar** (Tel: 238944; Tariff: Rs 500-1,670) opposite the bus stand. **Mushkil Aasaan Guest House** (Tel: 235150, 09824022565; Tariff: Rs 650-1,000) on Delwara Road has hospitable staff, old-world charm and great vegetarian food. **Lake Palace** (Tel: 237154; Tariff: Rs 1,200-1,800) has good rooms and an uncrowded lake view. Among budget hotels, the **Shri Ganesh Hotel** (Tel: 237292, 235591; Tariff: Rs 150-500), on the way to The Jaipur House, with basic but clean rooms, is a favourite with foreign backpackers.

For more hotels and details, see Mount Abu Accommodation Listings on pages 482-483

WHERE TO EAT

Try the heritage experience at the **Palace Hotel**, serving Continental and Indian meals: breakfast (Rs 225), lunch (Rs 325) and dinner (Rs 350). For great views and food, do visit the **Jaipur House Restaurant**, with vegetarian dishes for Rs 110-150 and non-vegetarian for Rs 250.

The market is full of dhabas (and Gujarati food), among which **Kanak Dining Hall**, near the bus stand, with its Rs 50 Gujarati thali, stands out. Near Chacha Museum, there's a typical **Sher-e-Punjab**. Also nearby, under Hotel Maharaj, stands a **Café Coffee Day**. Near the lake you will find more Gujarati food, and children's favourites such as the fast food joint **Hanky-Franky** (truly!) and **Kings Food**. ∎

Catching them young: A shop selling colourful gear in Mount Abu

GIREESH GV

GIREESH GV

Central Rajasthan

Rich with faith and commerce, resounding with the fervour of prayer and celebration, an array of flavours and colours are on offer here

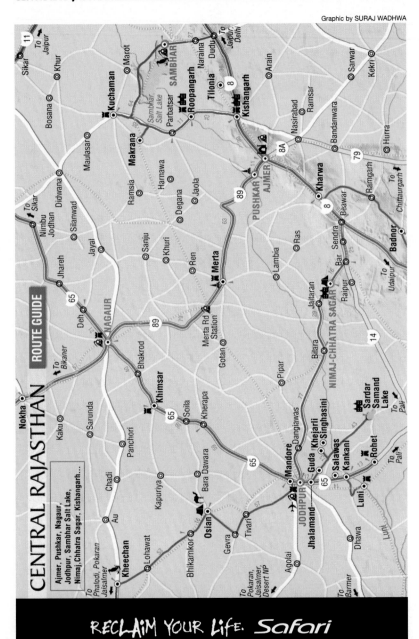

Graphic by SURAJ WADHWA

CENTRAL RAJASTHAN

ROUTE GUIDE

Ajmer, Pushkar, Nagaur,
Jodhpur, Sambhar Salt Lake,
Nimaj, Chhatra Sagar, Kishangarh...

RECLAIM YOUR Life. Safari

AMIT PASRICHA

Devotees throng the dargah of Saint Khwaja Moinuddin Chishti

AJMER
A MATTER OF FAITH

District Ajmer **Region** Merwara
Location Nestled amidst the Aravalli Range, Ajmer sprawls along Taragarh Hill in central Rajasthan. To its north-west lies the Ana Sagar Lake and beyond it the famous cattle fair town of Pushkar
Distances 11 km SE of Pushkar, 143 km SW of Jaipur, 399 km SW of Delhi
Journey time *By road* 15 mins from Pushkar, 2 hrs from Jaipur, 7 hrs from Delhi
Route from Jaipur NH8 to Ajmer via Bagru, Dudu and Kishangarh (*see route guide on facing page*)

■ BY KISHORE SINGH, JUHI SAKLANI AND SANJAY BADNOR

Faith and history inarguably define Ajmer. At the tomb chamber of Khwaja Moinuddin Chishti, the air is thick with not just the scent of roses and incense but also the fervour of prayer. Outside, even in the dingy lanes of the modest town, it's possible to glimpse the layers of the past that bestow upon Ajmer a unique charm.

Once a stronghold of the Chauhan Rajputs, the legendary Prithviraj Chauhan lost Ajmer (then called Ajayameru) when he was defeated by Muhammad Ghori in 1193. Akbar annexed it to the Mughal empire in the 16th century. It became, for the Mughals, first a centre of operations against the kingdoms of Rajasthan and Gujarat, and later, a pilgrimage site.

The Mughal empresses and princesses spent time here, and invested this region with their trademark preferences. Nur Jahan, for instance, had roses cultivated for the making of her favourite attar.

It was at Ajmer that the English ambassador Sir Thomas Roe presented his credentials to Jehangir. Roe was granted trading concessions that allowed the British to usurp power and establish themselves as a colony in India, and in the early 19th century, Ajmer came under the domain of the British empire. Like the Mughals, the British used it as a centre for exercising control over the kingdoms of the region, but they also provided it with educational institutions — including the Mayo College, initially set up for boys from India's princely families. It's with such glorious glimpses of its past, and with the promise of answered prayers, that Ajmer beckons us to drop by.

ORIENTATION

In the north-west of Ajmer lies the **Ana Sagar Lake**, adjacent to the road leading to **Pushkar** (11 km). The **railway station** is at the exact centre, the **Tourism Information Centre** right opposite it and the **Dargah of Khwaja Chishti** about a kilometre to the west. The **Adhai-Din-ka-Jhonpra** is a 5-min walk from the dargah. The **Nasiyan Jain Temple** is about a kilometre north of the railway station, down Prithviraj Marg. The **Taragarh Fort** lies to the south-west, about 5 km from town. Autos charge about Rs 200 for a 2-hr trip to the fort and back; taxis about Rs 300.

THINGS TO SEE AND DO

Ajmer's closest association is with the Dargah Sharif of Khwaja Sahib, the final resting place of the Sufi saint Khwaja Moinuddin Chishti, whose disciples included the Mughal emperors. The town is teeming with other interesting sights as well. Two days are adequate, and an active one day feasible for seeing all this.

The centre of faith

The **Ajmer Dargah** (dargah is an Islamic shrine built on the grave of a saint) is a complex bewilderingly full of many structures. The **entrance gates**, which loom 70 ft over the congested bazaar, were built by the Nizam of Hyderabad in 1915. The drums kept atop the gateway were gifted by Akbar after his successful campaign in Bengal. To the right, steps lead to the red sandstone **Akbari Masjid** (1571). Ahead lies the **Buland Darwaza**, grand and stolid, possibly built by Mahmud Khalji in the 15th century.

Next come two *degs* (cauldrons), of which the Badi Deg or big cauldron has a circumference of over 10 ft. Gifted by Akbar, it is used — as is the smaller deg gifted by Jehangir — to cook food sponsored by rich devotees for mass distribution. On the right spreads the **Mehfil Khana**, a hall opened only for the Urs, and on the left, the **Langar Khana**, where porridge is cooked for the poor.

The fervour of prayer shows itself in many ways at the dargah (left & right)

PHOTOS GIREESH GV

Straight ahead lies the compound in which various buildings stand around the tomb. The first is the **Sandali Masjid**, built by Aurangzeb, and it's here that sandalwood for the tomb is prepared. The path to the right leads to the tomb of the Khwaja's daughter, Bibi Hafiza Jamal; the **tomb of Nizam Sikka**, a water-carrier who had saved Humayun's life; and a silver **Jannati Darwaza**, rarely opened. Overlooking these is Shahjahan's **Jami Masjid** (1638), a gracious play of white marble. On the left of Sandali Masjid is the tiny **Auliya Masjid**, marking the spot where the Khwaja first stayed after arriving in Ajmer.

From here, a path leads to the **dargah chamber**. From the outside, the marble tomb is a soothing structure, with silver doors and a golden finial. The vast courtyards on both its sides are often full of qawwali gatherings. The facet on the left is called the **Begumi Dalaan**, built in 1643 by Shahjahan's daughter Jahanara.

Its walls were gilded in 1888 and the ceiling later etched with gold. In the chamber, the man who said "a faqir is one who is free of all needs" lies under a silver canopy in a world of costly velvet and silks, attar and sandal, and gold and silver zari chaadars. A silver railing, inside which only the khadims (officials of the dargah) stand, separates the tomb from devotees. Despite the crowd, the noise is hushed. The saint is asleep.

◆**Dargah inner sanctum timings** 5 am-3 pm, 4-9.30 pm **Related info** The sanctum area is closed for about an hour (3-4 pm) for cleaning but devotees can visit the outer areas anytime of day and night. The Khwaja's death anniversary, the Urs, is observed every year during the first six days of Rajaab, the seventh month of the Hijri calendar. Qawwalis are sung almost all night; these are devotional songs, the lyrics of which are suffused with 'love', 'longing', 'union' or 'surrender for the beloved', all mystical metaphors for the

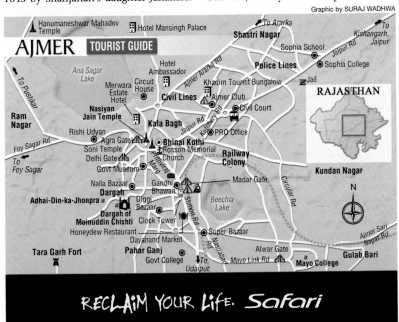

Graphic by SURAJ WADHWA

Sufi's passion, which makes him forget attributes of the self **Dargah Office Tel** 0145-2429095, 2623948

TIP You have to park your vehicle (fee Rs 20) outside Delhi Gate and walk for 5 mins down the bazaar to the dargah

Other sights

Walk 5 mins down a congested alley to the left of the dargah entrance and see the exquisitely carved 12th century **Adhai-Din-ka-Jhonpra**, built by Qutubuddin Aibak and completed by Iltutmish. Its name literally translates as the two-and-a-half-day-shed, and it is a relic of the largest mosque in the country, ordered by the invader Muhammad Ghori to be readied in this short time. A later example of Mughal architecture is the white structure of **Abdullah Khan's Tomb**.

There are also charming picnic spots in the vicinity. These include **Ana Sagar** (open 8 am-5 pm), an artificial lake; **Ajaipal**, where the founder of Ajmer retired after his reign; and **Foy Sagar**, another artificial lake outside town. Visitors are allowed to see the museum on the premises of **Mayo College**, on request.

Also on the tourist's itinerary is the unbelievably ornate Golden Hall of **Jain Nasiyan Temple**, located near Ana Sagar. It is replete with gold models of the life of Tirthankara Adinath. The **Taragarh Fort** (open all day) is 5 km from town.

Ajmer's specialities deal with religion, so you will find interesting **metal ware** in the form of pitchers and urns. Visitors from the region always make sure they have room to carry back with them the **cane chairs** and *moodahs* that are part of the essential furniture in any verandah. Naturally, you can hardly return without a concentrate of **attar**, amply found in the Dargah Bazaar for Rs 50 upwards. Also available are **chaadars** for the dargah (between Rs 500 and 5,000), and cheap CDs of qawwalis and dargah tours.

Bharat Petroleum

→ FAST FACTS

When to go The winter season is best, but Kishangarh can be charming during the rains. Summer is best avoided
Tourist office
● Rajasthan Tourism ❶
Tourist Reception Centre
Hotel Khadim (RTDC), Ajmer
Tel: 0145-2627426
STD code 0145

WHERE TO STAY

Ajmer can claim to have the best hotels in the region, and their advantage is that they operate round the year. **Hotel Mansingh Palace** (Tel: 0145-2425702/ 855/ 857; Tariff: Rs 3,000-7,500), near the lake in Vaishali Nagar, is Ajmer's finest hotel. Boasting its own shopping arcade, the hotel also arranges folk dances, fireworks and sightseeing tours. **Hotel Embassy** (Tel: 2623859, 4100775; Tariff: Rs 850-2,500), opposite the Power House on NH8 (Jaipur Road), is another fine hotel offering rooms with all the important facilities, including complimentary transfers from the railway station.

RTDC's **Hotel Khadim** (Tel: 2627490/ 536; Tariff: Rs 400-2,000), adjoining the bus stand, has a wide variety of rooms accommodating all budgets. The added advantage is the travel desk and tourist information centre here. **Hotel Ambassador** (Tel: 2425095, 2428479; Tariff: Rs 600-2,950) on Ashok Marg in Nagina Bagh is a good option. **Hotel Regency** (Tel: 2620296, 2622439; Tariff: Rs 450-1,500), near Delhi Gate, is a simple set-up, but well-located at walking distance from the Dargah Sharif, and 1 km from the bus stand and railway station. **Hotel Sahil** (Tel: 2632994-95; Tariff: Rs 500-2,000) nearby is a budget option with

GIREESH GV

On the same wavelength? Snacks and photos of film stars at a shop in Ajmer

basic facilities. **Hotel Aaram** (Tel: 5120096, 2425250; Tariff: Rs 400-900) offers similar facilities and prices as Sahil, and is located near Hotel Mansingh Palace in Vaishali Nagar.

For more hotels and details, see Ajmer Accommodation Listings on pages 456-457

For more hotels and details, see Ajmer Accommodation Listings on pages 456-457

WHERE TO EAT

During the Urs, it is expected that you partake from the consecrated food cooked in huge cauldrons that were gifted to Dargah Sharif by Emperor Akbar. The cauldrons are so large that food has to be served by people standing within the cauldrons! And there's no dearth of volunteers — no less than Akbar's son Jehangir served pilgrims with his own hands when he was the emperor.

In the lanes around the dargah, you'll find a number of roadside eateries specialising in **biryanis**. Among the city's better known restaurants is the multi-cuisine **Honeydew** on Station Road, established in 1962, which claims to be the first-ever air-conditioned restaurant in all of Rajasthan. Continental and Mughlai are on offer. **Tandoor Restaurant** on Jaipur Road is predictably famous for tandoori specialities, though Chinese and South Indian food are also served.

Gangaur Fast Food off Kutchery Road has burgers and pizzas. Another fast food option is **Mango Masala Restaurant** on Kutchery Road (Sardar Patel Marg), with pizzas, snacks, South Indian and Chinese food. Other options are **Kancha's Restaurant** on Pushkar Road and **Eat and Enjoy** on Srinagar Road. Both serve Indian and Chinese food.

For those who would prefer to dine at Ajmer's hotels, there is the choice of enjoying a Rajasthani meal facing the lake at **Sheesh Mahal**, the restaurant at Hotel Mansingh Palace, accompanied by live music. Sheesh Mahal also offers Mughlai, Chinese and Continental, and has a bar called **Sipha Salar**. Hotel Khadim's **Nemad Khana Restaurant** serves Indian, Chinese and Continental food. Opt to have your meal on the huge lawns. **Silverleaf**, the restaurant at Hotel

KISHANGARH Radha kaise na jale

The tiny kingdom of Kishangarh was founded by Kishan Singh, a prince of the pre-Independence Jodhpur state who carved out his own fiefdom from the kingdoms of Marwar, Amber and Mewar. It is famous for its marble quarries, from which the stone for the Taj Mahal was sourced. Lesser known is the fact that Kishangarh was once the centre of a fine artistic tradition. Its artists, with the patronage of the kingdom's rulers, created some of the finest miniatures the country has seen. The most famous paintings are of **Bani Thani**, the royal mistress, whom the painters used as a model for Radha — the icon of the Kishangarh School (*also see page 426*). She's the lady with the high forehead, arched eyebrows, half-open lotus eyes, sharp, pointed nose, thin, curved, sensuous lips and dainty chin, holding two lotus buds in her hand.

Founded in the 17th century, Kishangarh enjoyed little political power, and so has remained largely ignored, a medieval settlement with charming houses on both sides of the lane leading to a lake. It is here that you will find the **Kishangarh Fort**, with its

palaces. The Kishangarh family, led by Maharaja Brajraj Singh, converted the **Phool Mahal Palace** (Tel: 01463-247405, 247505; Tariff: Rs 2,000-2,500) on the Gundalao Lake into a **boutique heritage hotel** — also your only stay option in Kishangarh. Each room has a distinct character and a unique colour scheme, with high ceilings. Walls are decorated with frescoes in the Kishangarh style and furnished with period pieces in teak and hardwood. Tiny jharokha windows let in a cooling breeze.

Within Kishangarh Town, which is 30 km north-east of Ajmer on NH8, there are a large number of studios where painters continue to create miniature paintings, and these make the finest souvenirs of this place. Their quality, however, is sadly nothing like the original. Kishangarh is also known for its fabrics and red chillies. Buy some marble sculpture, ashtrays, bowls, boxes, water fountains and the like as keepsakes.

♦**Getting there** Taxi is the best option to cover the short drive to Kishangarh; charges are Rs 700 approx

Roopangarh Fort, 25 km north of Kishangarh, was built by Maharaja Roop Singh in 1648 and was the capital of Kishangarh state for a 100-year period. The Roopangarh Fort was originally a nine-turreted fort, to which several additions were made by succeeding maharajas. Roopangarh was built around the mausoleum of the 12th century Sufi saint, Sultan Pir, and was located strategically on what used to be a major trade route of the Mughal empire. It became the hub of activity in Kishangarh. Within its walls were foundries, armouries, granaries, jails and, of course, palaces.

The palace within the fort has been restored and converted by Maharaja Brajraj Singh into a **heritage hotel** (Tel: 01497-220217, 220444; Tariff: Rs 2,000-3,600). It has 22 rooms, a restaurant, a tennis court and arranges camel safaris and sightseeing. The taxi fare for the 40-min drive is Rs 700. ∎

PRAKASH ISRANI

By a lake that supplies water to Ajmer

Embassy, serves only vegetarian Indian and Chinese cuisine.

Pushkar (11 km NW)
See page 191

Fort Kharwa (38 km SW)
Located in Kharwa, this imposing 16th century fort is picturesquely situated on a hillock at the edge of the village, over-looking a lake. It was once the stronghold of the Jodha Rajputs, descendants of the Rathore rulers of Jodhpur. In 1596, Mughal Emperor Akbar bestowed the *jagir*, or principality, of Kharwa on Raja Shakti Singh, son of Mota Raja Udai Singh of Jodhpur, as a gesture of thanks-giving for saving him from drowning during an expedition against his son Jehangir, who had revolted in Allahabad.

The fort has been home to 17 gen-erations of royals. Today, the family has

opened its gates to tourists who can visit its rooms, and take a look at their collection of hunting trophies, antique weapons and sepia-toned shikar photo-graphs. The fort is constructed out of limestone and sandstone. Entering it is like stepping into a maze of rooms upon rooms, constructed over various levels.

Certain sections of the fort are used by the family, hence these are private. Among the parts that are open to tourists is the large drawing room, where you will come across hunting trophies and photos of duck and tiger shoots. You can also visit some rooms that have frescoes depicting scenes from Hindu epics.

While there was no hotel here at the time of writing, there are plans to convert it into a heritage property. As of now, you can make use of the family's offer to cater for group lunches. The cuisine at the fort is worth sampling. The recipes, originally used for cooking game meat, have been handed down generations. Today, these have been adapted to cook mutton and chicken.

There is a lake just below the fort that attracts birds and birdwatchers alike.

For inquiries and group bookings, contact the **Kharwa Fort** on 01462-265342 or 09414003189. Do remember that there are no stay options at Kharwa. ♦**Location** On the main NH8 towards Udaipur **Getting there** From Ajmer, it's a comfortable 30-min drive. Taxi costs approx Rs 700 for a return-trip from Ajmer. From Pushkar, it's about 40 km and taxi costs approx Rs 800

Tilonia (47 km NE)
This is a village that is internationally known as the address of the Social Work and Research Centre, established in 1972 by the activist duo Aruna and Bunker Roy. Now known as the **Barefoot Col-lege**, the NGO has several high-profile patrons including the Prince of Wales, Prince Charles, who has also visited this centre. While small and dusty Tilonia has little to tell it apart from other Rajasthani

The **Ultra** Edition 12.9
SAMSUNG SGH D-900

① Adhai Dinka Jhopra   ② Adhai-Din-Ka-Jhopra   ③ Ajmer Sharif

④ Ittar at shop   ⑤ Dargah Sharif

imagine doing more with less.
The Ultra Life.

Imagine always being in two places at once, doing two things at once. No office. No boundaries. No restrictions. With Samsung's new Ultra Edition it's not that hard to imagine.   www.samsung.com

Features: 3 Mega Pixel Camera with Auto-Focus • MP3 Player • Intelligent Display • Large 262K QVGA TFT Screen • Direct TV Out

Free accessories: *Bluetooth™ Headset • 256 MB T Flash Memory Card • TV Out Cable • Battery Charger • Travel Adapter • Car Adapter • Straight Headset • Battery (2 Nos.) • Data Kit*

Leo Burnett D SMSCHLB-0001H

The **Ultra** Edition 12.9
SAMSUNG SGH D-900

towns, the Barefoot College has made a name for itself by helping the locals find solutions to problems from within the community itself; thus far, it has addressed issues such as drinking water shortage, education of girls, unemployment and sanitation. Little wonder then that a visit to its campus, located just ahead of the village of Tilonia, is an uplifting experience.

Spread over 80,000 sq ft, the campus has many facilities, ranging from a library and dining room to a 10-bed referral base hospital and a teachers' training unit. It also boasts of a water testing lab, a crafts shop, an Internet café and even a 700,000 litre rainwater harvesting tank.

Visitors are welcome to learn about the college's various programmes and schemes and also encouraged to lend a helping hand. Tourists may find a visit to the **rural handicrafts shop** in the complex enjoyable. One can shop for block-printed and patchwork bed linen, kurtas, leather chairs and tables, footwear, tie and dye salwar suits and dupattas,

block-printed quilts, bags and other items, all made by the people in and around the Barefoot College. The shop is open on all days of the week from 8.30 am-5.30 pm and is closed only during festivals such as Holi and Diwali.

Yet another interesting aspect of the Barefoot College is the Children's Parliament that is organised here. Elected by children hailing from nearby villages, the parliament has a prime minister, a speaker and other members. This parliament meets once every month, on a date and time decided by the children themselves. Do look out for this when you are visiting. Tourists visiting Barefoot College can **stay at the guest house** located within the campus at a nominal cost (Rs 100); they also arrange food.

◆**Location** On the main NH8 towards Jaipur (off NH8) from Ajmer **Getting there** Tilonia is a comfortable 45-min drive; from Ajmer, cross Kishangarh and continue on the main NH8 for another 12 km till you reach a village named Patan, where you have to turn left for Tilonia. From this turn-off point, it is yet another 7 km to the centre. Taxis charge Rs 800 approx **Timings** The centre is open all days of the week from 9 am-5 pm **Tel** 01463-288210

→ GETTING THERE

Air Nearest airport: Sanganer Airport, Jaipur (143 km/ 2½ hrs). Taxi charges Rs 1,000
Rail Ajmer Junction is connected to Delhi and Jaipur by a few trains including the Ajmer Shatabdi
Road Ajmer is on NH8, connecting Delhi to Mumbai via Jaipur and Ahmedabad. Deluxe coaches (8 hrs/ Rs 339) run from Bikaner House in New Delhi to Jaipur. Numerous connections are also there from ISBT Sarai Kale Khan in Delhi. Onward options from Jaipur include buses (from the Sindhi Camp Central Bus Station) and taxis

Badnor (95 km SW)
Badnor was a former *thikhana* or feudal principality of the Rathore Thakurs of Badnor, who owed allegiance to the state of Mewar. It was one of the 16 major principalities of Mewar and its rulers joined hands with the Sisodias of Mewar to fight against the Mughals. Maharana Udai Singh, the founder of Udaipur City, granted Badnor to Rao Jaimal in 1554.

The present Badnor Thakur resides at **Jal Mahal**, a lakeside retreat that offers lovely views of the surrounding hills. Recently, a section of this property was opened to tourists. The facilities for guests include two suites with sitting rooms, a dining area and two bedrooms. Of the two suites, the main suite overlooks the

SANJAY SINGH BADNOR

Age tells on the Badnor Fort, yet it remains as impressive as ever

lake. The living room has windows opening right onto the lake and its walls are adorned with miniature paintings from the Badnor school of miniature art. The family's **Venetian glass collection** is also on display here. The second suite has huge paintings that depict the fort in all its grandeur. Within the Jal Mahal complex, there is also a **stepwell** built in 1897, with a square enclosure and steps leading down on three sides and an eight-pillared balcony on the fourth side.

Where to stay The tariff at **Jal Mahal** (bookings and enquiry Tel: 0145-2627579) is Rs 2,500 per day for one suite (two adults and two children), inclusive of breakfast. However, visitors must book for at least two nights; the package is valid from October to March. The staff at Jal Mahal organises group lunches, and the rates depend on the dishes you choose from the menu. The food at Jal Mahal is a mix of Rajasthani, Indian and Continental cuisine.

Unless you have a booking at Jal Mahal, you may not be entertained here. However, try asking the manager or the guard for permission to take a look at the gardens and the lake. There are no charges for this, and the best time to visit will be from 9 am to noon and 3 to 5 pm.

The **Badnor Fort** is now in a dilapidated state but makes for an interesting visit. It is located at the edge of the village and is flanked on two sides by the Vinod Sagar Lake, by which lies the Jal Mahal, and the Akshay Sagar Lake. In the latter, a

cluster of cenotaphs have been found on the lake bed. Some date back to the late 18th and early 19th centuries.

Other places of interest in Badnor include the **15th century temple** dedicated to Kushla Mata, said to be an incarnation of Durga. The temple is located on the edge of Vinod Sagar; one can access it by road, in which case it's about 2 km from Jal Mahal. When the lake is dry, you can walk across the lake bed from Jal Mahal to the temple in less than 30 mins.

Another interesting excursion can be to **Ojhiyana Village**, about 10 km from Badnor on Beawar Road. While ploughing, villagers stumbled on old statues here and subsequent excavations conducted by the ASI revealed a 2,000-year-old inscription on a rock. The letters engraved on the rock follow the Ashoka-Brahmi script that was used around 3 BCE and indicate that these areas were part of an ancient trade route.

Getting there Badnor is quite accessible although it is not on the main highway NH8. It is a convenient stopping point for tourists en route from Udaipur to Jaipur or Udaipur to Ajmer or vice versa. Badnor lies to the north-east of Bhim Town, connected by a district road. Taxi fare from Ajmer is Rs 1,000 (return).

While in Badnor, the tourist can also visit **Deogarh Mahal** (*for details, see Udaipur Arounds on page 152*), a heritage property. It's a 30-km drive to Bhim, from where you can take NH8 to Deogarh (45 km away). ∎

A colourful tale unfolds as the Pushkar Mela gets underway

PUSHKAR

THE FLOWER CHILD

District Ajmer **Region** Merwara
Location Nestled in the Aravalli Valley in central Rajasthan, at the foot of Nag Pahar or Snake Mountain, which forms a natural border between Pushkar and Ajmer
Distances 11 km NW of Ajmer, 154 km SW of Jaipur, 400 km SW of Delhi
Journey time *By road* 15 mins from Ajmer, 2¹/₄ hrs from Jaipur, 7¹/₂ hrs from Delhi
Route from Jaipur NH8 to Ajmer via Dudu and Kishangarh; NH89 to Pushkar (*see route guide on page 178*)

■ BY JUHI SAKLANI AND CHARU SONI

The man's skin glows in the sunset. His hair blows, his muffler flutters and he shivers in the quick chilly breeze. But there is no breeze. The surface of the lake is placid and the dust on the lake's ghats unruffled. His own private breeze has been created by some 300 pigeons that have swooped around him of their own accord. For, he has just made one of the more beautiful gestures of a devotee visiting Pushkar — he has bought a five-rupee packet of grain and scattered it around him with generosity. At this moment, it's possible to take in the wintry watercolours of this lake, the sun and the pigeons, and be grateful for their creation. And as mythology attests, Pushkar is a fitting place for this gratitude.

A very small town, seemingly just about bigger than the lake it adjoins, Pushkar attracts Hindu devotees and Hindu dilettantes in large numbers. The dilettantes consist of a colourful variety of foreigners — Israelis, Americans, Koreans, British — all of whom lend the town an unexpectedly quaint air. Pushkar is thus as much about aarti and chants as about 'Om Shanti' T-shirts, Shiva tattoos, Rastafarian hairstyles and digital cameras. Amidst all this, there are the genuine devotees: Vaishnavas in white with their eyes closed, a researcher on Hinduism who lives in her lake-facing room for six months every year, a Croatian couple who sponsor a section of the paving on a ghat. Layers of human experience, all blending together to make Pushkar as mythical as the legends warrant it to be.

ORIENTATION

Pushkar Town is divided into **Badi Basti** and **Chhoti Basti** (earlier known as Varahpura), of which the latter is considered older. The geographic, religious and emotional centre of tiny Pushkar is the **lake** (commonly called *sarovar*) surrounded by **52 ghats**, concentrated more on the eastern and northern sides. Immediately next to the ghats, hugging the buildings, runs the **main bazaar**, spreading from **Jaipur Ghat** in the south-east and curving around the ghats through the east, north and part of the west till the **Brahma Temple**. A walk from the Jaipur Ghat to the Brahma Temple can be done in a leisurely 20 mins if you don't stop to eat or buy anything. This is difficult. The Nag Pahar and other hills bound the town on almost three sides. Pushkar Town spreads out a bit only towards the north, where there are some sand dunes.

Of the three main ghats, the **Varaha Ghat** and **Gau Ghat** are to the north of the lake and the bazaar lane takes a sharp turn south to the **Brahma Ghat**. The **Savitri Temple** is on **Ratnagiri Hill**,

roughly behind the Brahma Temple, and it's a steep climb. Walking is the best way to see Pushkar, and everything can be accessed on foot. Only the Brahma Temple can be accessed by a wide road. Tented camp accommodation is set up by RTDC and the Jodhpur Royal Tents during the Pushkar Fair (*see Where to Stay on page 198*).

THINGS TO SEE AND DO

Visit the ghats and temples, offer prayers at the lake while trying to avoid *pandas* (local priests), take a dip in the Pushkar Lake, have bhang lassi, attend the Pushkar Cattle Fair, do yoga at sunrise or sunset, take an exotic camel ride that's tough on your derriere or get massaged into shape with rose-scented oils. Better still, you can go on a lazy nonchalant stroll through the bazaar circling the lake, eat local delicacies and spend time browsing through touristy bric-a-brac. Do remember that consuming non-vegetarian food and alcohol is strictly prohibited within 5 km of the town.

A holy lake and its ghats

The Pushkar Lake is the cynosure — in the town, on the religio-mythic map, and

→ FAST FACTS

When to go Best between October and March. The Pushkar Fair is usually held in November
Tourist office
• Rajasthan Tourism ❶
Tourist Reception Centre
Hotel Khadim (RTDC)
Savitri Girls College Road, Ajmer
Tel: 0145-2627426
STD code 0145

MALINI SHARMA

The whitewashed ghats of the sacred Pushkar Lake

in the visitor's itinerary. Lined by pure white ghat buildings, encrusted with pearly grey pigeons and with white ducks and geese, filled with mysterious dark green waters, with the smoky hills receding at a distance, it provides a singular monochromatic aesthetic experience. Only the devotees in their quest for purification and the Brahmins in search of a living provide splashes of colour here. Even after your holy dip is over, you would want to be near the lake, ruminating on the changing colours of life, or just of the day.

The lake, according to legend, was created by Brahma by combining the waters of the four places of pilgrimage sacrosanct to Hindus — Badrinath, Jagannath, Rameshwaram and Dwarka. According to the Padma Purana, Brahma was searching for a place to perform a yagna when the lotus he was holding fell from his hand and landed in Pushkar. He resolved to perform the yagna there and then, but when his wife Savitri failed to join him, he married a local damsel (Gayatri) and completed the formalities. When Savitri arrived, she discovered Gayatri and, enraged, ticked off Brahma

saying that Pushkar would be the only place where he'd be worshipped. Today, you will see a floating chattri in the centre of the lake, built in 1791 by the Thakur of Khimsar to commemorate Brahma's yagna spot.

The lake is hugged by 52 ghats, teeming with sadhus, devotees and enthusiastic tourists. Most of the ghats are no older than 300 years, and have innumerable small temples. The pandas hanging around the ghats have the uncanny ability of being able to spot a newcomer. Invoking ancestors both living and dead, they make an offering to the holy lake of rose petals and coconut. But it's possible that all you will be left with is a sacred thread and a hole in your pocket.

Offerings made at Brahma, Gau and Varaha ghats, which are also the oldest, are considered to be most auspicious. Some ghats bear the stamp of North and Central India's most important kingdoms. Hence there is the Jaipur Palace (called **Man Mahal**, now part of RTDC's Sarovar Hotel), the Jodhpur Palace (now **Kishangarh Palace**, also a hotel), the **Scindia Haveli**, the **Indore Haveli** and the **Bhadawar Raja's Ghat**. The last was converted into a police station by the British after 1857 as punishment to the raja for having joined the 'mutineers'.

Though the **Brahma Ghat** is the oldest and most hallowed (said to be built by the Jodhpur family in the 10th century), the **Gau Ghat** is equally venerated. It's here that the ashes of India's famous politicians, including Mahatma Gandhi, Jawaharlal Nehru and Indira Gandhi, have been immersed. Both these ghats have separate enclosures for female bathers. The enclosure on the Gau Ghat was built with money (Rs 1,000) contributed by Queen Mary in 1911.

The **Varaha Ghat**, named after Lord Vishnu, and the temple there, has little to attract even though it is one of the oldest. At **Narsimha Ghat** have a dekko at the preserved remains of a crocodile that attacked a priest on this ghat some 30 years ago! Rest assured, they say no reptiles have been seen since.

TIP Pay what you wish to the *pandas* and do not be taken in by their piety

Give yourself the gift of an hour or two at the **Kishangarh Ghat** (between hotels Sarovar and Pushkar Palace, *see Where to Stay on page 197*) at sunset time, preferably everyday! This is the only ghat at Pushkar with hardly a priest in sight, and where a lot of foreign tourists feel at home. Unlike at many other ghats, it's possible to sit here a long time, take a photograph or two, and feel at one with the lake. The sun sets with its own slow and sensuous intoxication behind the Ratnagiri Hill, imprinting its various selves on the lake for over an hour, mutating moment to orange-pink-golden moment. A number of performers from the famous Bhopa balladeers tribe of Rajasthan dot the wide, relatively clean ghat with their mellifluous ravanhatta instruments and their haunting desert voices. The **Sunset Café** (*see Where to Eat on page 198*) here provides chairs and a wide-ranging menu, and a couple of generous banyan trees give shade. What else could one need?

Temple trail

Pushkar is a microcosm of celestial and mortal society. It represents the Hindu Trinity with all its attendant gods and goddesses, but Pushkar also has shrines that have special significance for different castes. Rajputs, Rawats, Jats, Gujjars, Malis, Loharias, Kalbelias, Mochis, all have their own shrines where they

Pushkar attracts Hindu devotees and Hindu dilettantes in large numbers

PP

Magical colours: Women sell vegetables on the streets of Pushkar

worship the same gods. Another unique feature of its older temples is the embedded silver coins (circa 1900) found at the entrance to the shrines.

Among the abodes of the Trinity, the temples of Brahma, Varaha and Aptaeshwar are considered the oldest and the most sacrosanct. All three are said to have been in existence around the 10th century AD though not necessarily in their present shape or look. At **Brahma's Temple**, on the ghat of the same name, look for the four-faced icon of the lord accompanied by his shy bride, Gayatri, and the silver turtle in front of the shrine's entrance, all three probably installed in 1809 when the temple was rebuilt. At the **Varaha Temple**, while taking a round of the shrine, don't miss its different layers. The temple is said to have suffered destruction at Aurangzeb's hands. At the **Aptaeshwar Temple** is an underground shrine where a lingam has been installed. Another imposing temple in the city is the Dravidian **Rangji Temple**, first built in 1844, run by the

Tamilian Vaishnava sect founded by an 11th century saint, Ramanujacharya. No foreigners or non-Hindus are allowed within its precincts.

The intriguing story of Brahma's marital discord is reflected in the location of the temples dedicated to Brahma and Savitri, at diametrically opposite sites in the city. A million years, one would have thought, would be enough to kiss and make up. But not so with Brahma and Savitri. So while Brahma sits happy with his coy, young bride in the temple dedicated to him near the lake, Savitri frowns from atop Ratnagiri Mountain. She too got her first concrete abode in the 10th century AD, but her current quarters were built in 1687. It's a steep, 4-km climb to the top, and driving is not possible, but the views, particularly at sunrise, are worth the effort.

Pushkar Fair

On Kartik Purnima (the new moon, roughly Oct-Nov) each year, Pushkar explodes into Rajasthan's most exuberant and colourful festival, for which it is widely renowned. Cows, camels, sheep, goats and their traders flood the city. And if price is any indication — in 1940, the costliest camel went for Rs 77; in 2002, the price was nearly Rs 11,000 — the four-legged animals still call the shots in India's countryside. The fair is a weeklong fiesta with competitions and state-sponsored entertainment programmes thrown in. Storytellers, hypnotists, snake charmers, magicians and monkey trainers will all vie for your attention. Contact the Rajasthan Tourism (*see Fast Facts on page 192*) office for festival dates (*also see Festivals and Fairs on page 392*).

TIP Carry mosquito repellent cream if you plan on watching night-long festivities

Song and dance
Even if you're not going during the fair, it's difficult to get bored in Pushkar, a fact underlined by the absence of TV sets in most hotels. Like Varanasi, Pushkar has its own ways of passing time. For those wishing to do some yoga, there are a

→ GETTING THERE

Air Nearest airport: Sanganer Airport, Jaipur (154 km/ 2½ hrs). Taxi to Pushkar costs Rs 1,400. Rates can double during the Pushkar Fair
Rail Nearest railhead: Ajmer Junction (11 km/ 15 mins). The Ajmer Shatabdi from Delhi and Jaipur is the best option. Auto fare to Pushkar ranges from Rs 80-120; taxi fare Rs 250 and above (Rs 400 and above during the fair)
Road Pushkar is on NH89, 11 km off NH8, which connects Delhi to Mumbai via Jaipur, Ajmer and Ahmedabad. Private operators run daily deluxe buses to and from Jaipur via Ajmer

number of gurus, among whom Yogacharya Yogesh Bharati (Tel: 0145-2772481) is the most respected. He can be found at Gwalior Ghat. Those interested in listening to fine classical music, vocal or instrumental, can contact Brajesh Kumar Devder *aka* Birju at Badi Basti (Tel: 2773124; 09829106258), a highly accomplished young artiste. Or you can request local Lohar and **Gujjar folk performers**, who you will see all around the city, to perform for you — at a price of course.

Camel safaris
An interesting excursion from Pushkar can be made to the sand dunes on its outskirts, where the mela is held. The Sunset Café, Pushkar Palace and many other hotels can arrange camel safaris. This involves a camel-pulled cart with a mattress and bolsters to lean back and feel like royalty. A cart can accommodate four people. The charges per person range from Rs 150-200 for an hour. The package may involve just a trip for an hour or two, or could be spread out with dinner by a bonfire, and even local dance performances. Taxi charges for half-day sightseeing are about Rs 400 (Ekta Travels Tel: 0145-2772888; they also arrange customised packages and camel safaris).

SHOPPING

Many shops in Pushkar sell poor quality stuff (bead and mirror-embroidered shoulder bags, cushion covers, bangles and block-printed pyjamas and tops) lapped up with glee by backpackers. If, however, you are interested in quality work, step into **Bhagwan Barmeri Handicraft Shack**, in Badi Basti, opposite Shiva Cloth House, to pick up exquisite bed covers. For Rajasthani miniature paintings (on silk paper/ cotton with single squirrel brush!), including Kishangarh-style paintings, check out the curios at the **Sarweshwar Kala Mandir** (open 8 am-10 pm), whose master artist SN Dhabai (Tel: 0145-2772573) also

Fun and frolic: At the Pushkar Fair, where life is a merry-go-round

works in brass and wood. The prices vary from Rs 100-10,000 depending on quality and craftsmanship. A medium-sized **pichhwai** can cost anything from Rs 250-2,000. At **Dhabai's shop** on the first floor, you can also find antique pieces discarded from old havelis. At **Ethnic World**, look for cotton embroidered kurtas (Rs 1,500). Since the area is famous for growing roses, **gulkand** — a confection of rose petals and sugar, which is a major component in sweet *paans* — is a speciality here. On the street, near Lake View Hotel, you get **gulkand thandai**, for mixing in milk, for Rs 30. At the **Kamal and Co** outlet, you can buy it at Rs 40 for a kilo, and buy pure **rose water** or **rose sherbet** as well.

TIP Half the price is usually a good deal, so haggle aggressively

WHERE TO STAY

Accommodation ranges from Rs 50 per night for a hole in the wall to Rs 6,000 for a suite overlooking the holy lake. Either way, except during the cattle fair season, finding accommodation is a non-strenuous exercise as most of the hotels in Pushkar are within calling distance of each other. If you're at a loss where to go, ask RTDC's Tourist Assistance Office at Ajmer Railway Station (Timings: 10 am-5 pm), which also provides information on paying guest accommodation (*see Fast Facts on page 192*).

Heritage

A heritage property and the only luxury hotel on the lake, **Pushkar Palace's** USP (Tel: 0145-2773001-03; Tariff: Rs 2,200-6,000) is the dining area, which overlooks the lake and where in the evenings one can watch a truly bewitching sunset. Most rooms are situated around a lush green courtyard. Off-season discounts up to 30 per cent of the tariff are available.

The largest royal house in Pushkar, RTDC's **Hotel Sarovar** (Telefax: 2772040; Tariff: Rs 250-900) was built by Raja Man Singh of Jaipur and was known as Man Mahal. Today only some rooms offer a

NARENDRA BISHT

Tourists have lots of souvenir options to choose from at Pushkar

heritage experience, as the rest of the hotel is a modern construction. The property gives a clear view of the lake's banks and temples located around. But the food is below par.

Others

Jagat Palace (Tel: 2772952-54; Tariff: Rs 2,200-2,700), situated near Pushkar Lake, has a restaurant, a health club, indoor games and a swimming pool. Mostly catering to the foreign backpacker, **Hotel Sunset** (Tel: 2772725/ 382; Tariff: Rs 300-600) has a café on the ghat, a good place to relax. **Hotel White House** (Tel: 2772147; Tariff: Rs 150-450), near Marwah Bus Station, has a restaurant, hot water, and offers massage and yoga.

During the fair, the RTDC erects a **Tourist Village** that includes deluxe and super deluxe tents and cottages (Tel: 2627426; Tariff: Rs 4,000-7,000, including meals), and ordinary tents (Tariff: Rs 300 per bed). Indian toilets are standard. The Tourist Village's USP is its proximity to the mela ground where most of the festival activities are centred (to book, *see Fast Facts on page 192*). A more luxurious stay is provided by **Royal Tents** (Jodhpur

Tel: 0291-2572321-27; Tariff: Rs 9,000-11,000), situated on the fair ground. It has a restaurant, doctor-on-call, forex, room service, and arranges safaris. The camp is managed by the Delhi-based WelcomHeritage wing of ITC Hotels.

For details, see Pushkar Accommodation Listings on pages 484-486

WHERE TO EAT

Food in Pushkar is entirely vegetarian. Among a range of average restaurants and cafés, **Honey and Spice** is by far your best bet. Between the ginger cinnamon coffee, fresh uncorrupted juices, and great dishes such as spinach-pineapple noodles or tofu on toast, life is a healthy treat in relaxed surroundings. **Moondance Café**, opposite the new Rangji Temple, offers food such as a great pizza for Rs 90 or a satisfying, if oily, spinach enchilada for Rs 65, in a pleasant garden setting. For an exhaustive menu and the best possible lake-at-sunset views, patronise the **Sunset Café**, situated on the Kishangarh Ghat, between Sarovar Hotel and Pushkar Palace, with options such as pizza/

NARENDRA BISHT

Soul curry: Under the watchful eyes of gods, a tourist gets down to dinner

spaghetti/ lasagna, sandwiches, Indian dishes and cake. Open from 8 am till about midnight.

Raju in the bazaar street offers a roof-top restaurant with nice lake views and 'homesick food' for foreigners; nice baked potato with butter and cheese for Rs 50. Indian dishes here are not bad at Rs 30-60. The **Halwai-ki-Gali**, stretching serpentine-like in front of the Gau Ghat, offers a variety of snacks including kachoris and samosas with spicy, flavoured kadi plus jalebi and malpuas that make you slurp for more. For a taste of India, **RS Restaurant**, opposite Brahma Temple, is a good place. It offers many inexpensive Indian dishes and paranthas as well as the Rajasthani dal-baati-choorma. Also stop at the halwais around Gau Ghat for street food at nominal cost: jalebi, malpua, kachori-sabji and samosa.

Middle of the road, safe Indian food is available at **RTDC Hotel Sarovar**, with the usual dal, mixed veg, palak paneer kind of menu, and at the **Pushkar Palace's Prince Restaurant**, which offers buffet meals (breakfast: 6-10 am for

Rs 200; lunch: noon-3 pm for Rs 250; dinner: 6.30-9.30 pm for Rs 300).

AROUND PUSHKAR

Ajmer (11 km SE)
See page 179

Merta (63 km W)
Today known as the home of the mystic poet-princess Meera Bai, Merta was founded in 1488 by Rao Duda, the fourth son of the Marwar ruler Rao Jodha. The region witnessed struggles between the Mughals and the Rathore Rajputs, and the Merta Fort itself was the centre of their attention. In 1562, Akbar captured the Merta Fort, built by Rao Maldev of Marwar, after facing stiff resistance. However, he restored it back to the ruler of Marwar after 20 years.

Situated on the outskirts of town, 2 km south-east of the Charbhujanath Temple, it is now known as the **Malkot Fort**. Once a mighty citadel, today it has been reduced to ruins. **Dudagarh** is another fort at Merta, located to the

DINODIA PHOTO LIBRARY

Beneath a quiet sky: A horse and his owner take a break

north of the Charbhujanath Temple, which was built by Rao Duda. Although a small fortress in comparison to Malkot, Dudagarh is worth a visit to sample its late 15th century architecture.

The **temple to Charbhujanath** or the four-armed god is the main attraction of Merta. Located in the centre of town, the 400-year-old temple gained importance due to its association with Meera Bai. Charbhujanath is believed to be a manifestation of Krishna and is the tutelary deity of the Rathores of Merta. Meera Bai was a Rathore princess who was a staunch follower of Krishna and the bhajans she penned in the lord's praise are popular even now all over India. Devotees flock to this temple to pay their respects to Charbhujanath as well as to the poet princess. Apart from the idol of Krishna, there is also a life-size statue of Meera Bai at the temple; its outer galleries are painted with various scenes from her life. Each year, in July-August (or the Hindu month of Shravan), a festival known as **Meera**

Mahotsav is held in Meera Bai's honour at Merta. Other places of interest in and around Merta include the **Palace of Meera**, which is near the Bevcha Talab. This edifice, however, is in ruins; there is no entry fee to visit and no timings either. There is also an awe-inspiring mosque in the centre of town, known as the **Shahi Jama Masjid**, built by Aurangzeb.

Getting there As most hotels at Merta are basic, it's best visited as a day-trip from Pushkar. A return-trip to Merta from Pushkar would cost Rs 1,100 approx in a non-AC Indica (Rs 250 extra for an AC taxi). Merta also has a railway station that is 11 km from town on Merta Road. It has direct train connections to Jodhpur, Jaipur and Bikaner. From the station, there are buses to town at regular intervals (fare Rs 8 per person). Shared jeeps are also available for Rs 15 per head; if hiring a jeep for yourself, it will cost Rs 100.

Nimaj-Chhatra Sagar (115 km SW)
See page 203 ∎

SONENDRA SINGH

By a placid lake: Tented accommodation at Chhatra Sagar

NIMAJ-CHHATRA SAGAR

MARWAR'S FIRST DEFENCE

District Pali **Region** Marwar
Location In central Rajasthan, between Jodhpur and Ajmer, with Jaitaran and Bar as the nearest towns
Distances 95 km SW of Ajmer, 106 km SE of Jodhpur, 238 km SW of Jaipur
Journey time *By road* 2 hrs from both Ajmer and Jodhpur, 4 hrs from Jaipur
Route from Jaipur NH8 to Beawar via Dudu and Ajmer; NH14 to Bar; state highway to Nimaj **Route from Jodhpur** State highway to Nimaj via Dangiawas, Bilara and Jaitaran (*see route guide on page 178*)

■ BY ABHILASH GAUR

The dunes are gone — consumed by sweat and replaced by fields. But the sand can still be glimpsed on unclaimed land. Tufts of grass, acacia trees and thorny bushes, or leafy ones rife with burs, mark the landscape. The rocky hills and ravines are left behind in Bar. The road to Nimaj is flat and smooth, although narrow and sometimes serpentine. Henna shrubs and the last of the barley stalks remain in the fields. Come winter and the farmers will even coax a wheat crop out of this hard land, but there was a time when barley and millets were all it produced. Yet, the sultan of Delhi almost lost his all for this "handful of barley".

Little wonder then that you cannot visit Nimaj and come away without hearing the legend of Giri-Sumel. It's the proudest moment in the history of the Udawat Rathores, who have held sway here for the last 500 years. Descendants of Uda — the grandson of Jodhpur's founder, Rao Jodha, and the first cousin of its most powerful king ever, Rao Maldev — they are a proud lot, but also the most gracious hosts, as you will discover regardless of whether you choose to stay at the

Nimaj Palace or at the lakeside tents at Chhatra Sagar. But first the legend.

In 1544, the sultan of Delhi, Sher Shah Sur, launched his Marwar campaign with "the largest army he had ever deployed". In his *Annals and Antiquities of Rajasthan*, James Tod puts the Afghan host's strength at 80,000 men. Sher Shah had good reason to be wary: he was up against Rao Maldev, a man described by Ferishta as "the most potent prince in Hindustan" at the time.

Sher Shah's army was midway between Ajmer and Jodhpur, on land governed by the Udawats, when Maldev checked its advance with 50,000 men. But instead of clashing, the armies set up camp in the adjoining villages of Sumel and Giri. A month went by and Sher Shah realised that the only way to defeat the Rajputs was to sow the seed of suspicion in Maldev's mind. So he planted letters 'exposing' the infidelity of four of Maldev's lieutenants, including the Udawat chief, Rao Khinwakaran of Jaitaran. Suspicious by nature, Maldev left the battlefield with his army that night, despite protestations of loyalty by the chiefs. Next morning, to clear their name, all four, along with their 12,000 troops, ploughed into the sultan's camp. Such was the force of their attack that they almost reached Sher Shah's quarters before being cut down to a man. The battle shook Sher Shah, and though he returned victorious, he remarked, "I nearly lost the empire of Hindustan for a handful of barley." As for the Udawats of Jaitaran-Nimaj, their house is feted in Rajput lore as *Marwar ra bhad kiwad* (the first defence of Marwar).

ORIENTATION

On the road to Nimaj, you will come across a board announcing **Piplaj Village**. It might set you thinking about the origin of both names. Piplaj, because it has a lot of pipal trees? And Nimaj, because of neem trees? It's a good guess,

for the moment you turn off the Jodhpur Road, into Nimaj, the path is lined with neem. The trees grow all over the village-town: along the roads, in the fields, beside the temples and even in the backyards. And as any of the cousins who run the Nimaj Palace and Chhatra Sagar properties will confirm, the village is indeed named after the trees. In fact, its original name — and the name by which it is still known locally — is Nimbaj, short for neem, *babul* and *jal* (water), three things this oasis has never lacked.

On the town's outskirts, you will find two prominent pointers to **Nimaj Palace** and **Chhatra Sagar**. The latter lies about a kilometre away to the left, while the palace lies in the heart of the village-town, 3 km straight ahead. The road cuts Nimaj into two parts. One has the **fort palace** and most of the population, while the other has the old gardens, orchards and crumbling cenotaphs fronted by new shops and houses. Within the fort stands an ancient Shiva temple almost entirely covered by a large pipal tree. Nimaj was a fortified village and its old gates stand to this day. The gate to the fort's rear leads into the fields, while the one on its left opens onto the market.

TOTAL CONTROL

→ GETTING THERE

Air Nearest airport: Jodhpur (106 km/ 2 hrs). Taxi fare is Rs 1,500 approx. Do remember to bargain so as to get the prices down

Rail Nearest railhead: Ajmer (95 km/ 2 hrs). Taxi charges Rs 1,500 approx. Rates again need to be negotiated. Jodhpur, from where too you can hire taxis, is also a convenient option. Luxury buses ply regularly between Jodhpur and Ajmer, but they bypass Nimaj. You could come up to Bar or Jaitaran by bus, but the only vehicles you can rent from these places are jeeps. Therefore, it's best to rent a taxi in Jodhpur or Ajmer

Road From Delhi, the road is excellent till Kishangarh (via Jaipur), but traffic is heavy up to Manesar. Beyond Kishangarh, the road narrows but there's less traffic along the way. From Bikaner House in Delhi, the night bus to Jodhpur leaves at 10 pm and reaches Bar at 8.30 am. Non-AC bus fare is Rs 460 (one-way). The Jodhpur-Nimaj section is narrow but nicely surfaced, and there's not much traffic. You can request the palace or camp officials (depending on where you are staying) for a pick-up from RTDC's Midway Motel at Bar. However, if coming from Jodhpur, it is best to hire a taxi

THINGS TO SEE AND DO

In Nimaj, you can live in palatial comfort or experience camp life in the lap of nature. Neither of these experiences come cheap — tariffs start at Rs 4,600 at the palace and go up to Rs 12,000 at the camp. But such is Nimaj's hospitality that you won't feel short-changed.

NIMAJ PALACE

The old fort is Nimaj's hub. It's named **Jagram Durg** after Thakur Jagram Singh, who was given Nimaj by Maharaja Ajit Singh of Jodhpur in 1708, for his loyalty. The present thikanedar of Nimaj, Thakur Bhagwati Singh, is the 15th in the line of descent from Jagram Singh, and it was he who started the transformation of this fort-palace into a heritage hotel in the mid-1980s. The fort continued to be called Jagram Durg till a few years ago, when a cyber-squatter compelled Bhag-wati Singh to think up a new name for his website. Hence the name Nimaj Palace. With 25 rooms, the palace is a fairly large heritage property, and beautifully done up as well. The suites are so large that

Luxury speaks in colourful tones: The Rang Mahal suite at the Nimaj Palace

their bathrooms could easily qualify as bedrooms. Everything, from the furnishings to the plumbing, is excellent.

As you draw up at the whitewashed palace gate called **Loha Pol**, your eyes will rest on the three vermilion-coloured hand imprints on the wall. These are reminders of those of Nimaj's *thakurains* who performed sati. **Dalwans** or arched halls for receiving guests are part of the gateway, and beyond these is an open courtyard that the palace overlooks.

It is on the terrace ahead of the **darikhana**, or the old durbar hall, that you will find your reception party, including Bhagwati Singh or his wife Divya. The *darikhana* is now a restaurant, and its outermost arches are sealed with glass. On its walls you will find portraits of Rao Uda, Thakur Jagram Singh and Thakur Chhatra Singh. The Singhs live on the floor above the *darikhana*, and the suites lie further up.

The most striking thing about the palace's suites is the painted walls with porthole-like windows overlooking the courtyard. The rooms are air-conditioned,

and the palace has power backup, so the hottest summer day is made bearable. An enjoyable way to spend the afternoon is by chatting up the manager Thakur Harjit Singh over lunch. A proud but polite and pleasant man, he's a walking encyclopaedia of Rajput lore, and where memory fails him, he always has a tome at hand.

Nimaj Palace has a well-deserved reputation for **Rajasthani food**. Be it their gatte ki subzi or batias (rotis made out of flour kneaded in ghee), or the melt-in-the-mouth *parodis* (small sweet balls made out of wheat flour, powdered dry fruits, sugar and ghee), your stay will be peppered with many gastronomic surprises, all of them pleasant.

If you can stand the sun, check out the portions of the fort that have not yet been restored in the afternoon. The rows of stables, the old rooms locked up with equally ancient locks, and the heavy-doored garage housing the rusty carriages give an idea of life in a *thikana* (fief). As the afternoon cools off, head to the village on a camel or go on a jeep safari to observe the local way of life. For the city

ABHILASH GAUR

Hand imprint at the Nimaj Palace gate

dweller, it's usually a novelty to see farmers in their fields or goldsmiths and cobblers at work, or even cows being milked. A few kilometres away from the fort stands the **Magar Mandi Mata Temple**, which is in ruins. A Durga temple, it is dated to the 9th century, and people in the region believe that appeasing the goddess will result in bountiful rain. Till the early seventies, a buffalo was sacrificed here every year to this end. Although the temple as a whole is not a patch on the magnificent Ranakpur temples (174 km away), or even the buildings in Mandore (119 km NW), its detailed carvings might interest you.

The palace also organises trips to the battlefield of **Giri Sumel** (38 km), where some cenotaphs of Rajput heroes exist on a barren ground between the hills. It is also possible to make day-trips to **Ajmer-Pushkar** (95-106 km NE) and **Kurki**, the birthplace of Meera (55 km NE).

Contact info To stay at the palace, call Bhagwati Singh (Tel: 02939-230022, Mobile: 09414008787) or his brothers, Bharat Singh (Mobile: 094140 74546) and Bhagirath Singh (Mobile: 09414072158).

Tariffs (inclusive of break-fast) range from Rs 4,600-5,400. *Also see page 461.*

CHHATRA SAGAR

If the palace lies amidst the bustle of Nimaj, the **Chhatra Sagar Camp** is an island of quiet, perched on a dam upon a stream that once formed the town's physical boundary. Five generations ago, in 1890, Thakur Chhatra Singh got the dam built to create a lake that would irrigate Nimaj's fields, and also provide recreational activities during winter. After a good monsoon, the lakeside swells to about 10 km, and in winter it becomes the refuge of thousands of migratory birds. That's the time when the brothers Nandi and Harsh, along with their cousins Jai and Raj, set up what is one of the finest tented resorts anywhere in the world.

Unlike the palace, where you get a colourful traditional welcome with a garland and a vermilion mark, climbing up the steps to the dam, you will first meet Taurus, the little dog whose sole aim in life is to make friends. Even if Nandi and Harsh are away, their wives Vasundhara and Shrinidhi are always around, and it is under their supervision that the camp's excellent meals are prepared. Eggs on batias, or a raita of pomegranate, honey, curd and cornflakes, followed by an extra large mug of cappuccino, give you the power start to a day of camp life, while kheer, bajra rotis, *rabodi* (wafers made using a sun-dried paste of maize flour, buttermilk and spices, and then cooked in a gravy) and tomatoes cooked in cream charge you up at other times.

The tents at the camp are large and clean. As for the bathrooms, they are pucca — made out of slate tiles — with plumbing and running hot and cold water. But to preserve the camp ambience, the bathrooms have been covered with cloth. The tents are equipped with beds, chairs, tables, lights and fans. For privacy, the camp staff stays away from the tents, unless summoned. The thick poles that anchor the tents are

DHONI DRIVES ON Speed

High-flying sixes. Blazing fast fours. Quickfire innings. Speed has always been the essence of Mahendra Singh Dhoni's incredible performance on the field. And now on the road too.

Bharat
Petroleum

SONENDRA SINGH

A photo-op represents a melting pot of cultures at Nimaj

pegged almost on the edge of the dam, so guests have an unhindered view of the water and the countryside beyond it. Since the tents face east, guests can watch the sun rise above the distant Aravallis from their deckchairs.

In the early morning, it's a treat to watch herds of nilgai drinking water at the far end of the lake. Jackals, antelopes and fox are some of the other animals seen on the grassy bank. The brothers, each one of whom is an amateur ornithologist, delight in pointing out the various species of birds that abound around the lake. In all, they claim, about 250 species of birds are seen at the lake. While bar-headed geese are the most common, demoiselle cranes and black-shouldered kites are also easily spotted.

A Nikon telescope on a tripod, binoculars, hats and Richard Grimmet's *Pocket Guide to the Birds of the Indian Subcontinent* are always available in the dining tent for the guests' use. And at least one of the brothers is around to answer wildlife-related queries. In the evenings, they take guests to **Karner Village** to

introduce them to rural life. The two-hour jeep trip includes stops for birdwatching, visits to fields, farmers' houses and shepherd settlements. Tourists get to learn interesting bits about local culture, such as the significance of turban colours in Nimaj — for instance, while a red turban denotes an active farmer, a white turban denotes a life of retirement.

In its six years, Chhatra Sagar has been a successful model of eco-tourism, and to make the area more attractive, the brothers have given up farming on a large tract of land. They are letting the grass grow to attract more wildlife. So, in a few years from now, the nilgais might have the company of other species during their early morning drinking sessions.

Contact info To stay at the camp, call Harsh at 09414123118 or 02939-230118. Single occupancy tariff (inclusive of all meals and non-alcoholic beverages) is Rs 10,000, while double occupancy costs Rs 12,000. Children aged 10 or less are not charged while additional tents for adults are provided at Rs 3,000. *Also see page 460 for accommodation details.* ∎

Photographs by GIREESH GV

All wrapped up and ready to go: A proud owner at the Nagaur Cattle Fair

NAGAUR

AS HOT AS IT GETS

District Nagaur **Region** Marwar
Location In the sandy tract midway between Jodhpur and Bikaner
Distances 138 km NE of Jodhpur, 296 km NW of Jaipur, 554 km SW of Delhi
Journey time *By road* 2½ hrs from Jodhpur, 4 hrs from Jaipur, 8 hrs from Delhi (via Jaipur)
Route from Jaipur NH8 to Ajmer via Dudu; NH89 to Nagaur via Pushkar and Merta
Alternative route NH11 to Sikar via Chomu; state road to Salasar; NH65 to Nagaur via
Ladnun **Route from Jodhpur** NH65 to Nagaur via Khimsar (*see route guide on page 178*)

■ BY KISHORE SINGH

A one-street town, a haze on the highway between Jodhpur and Bikaner that has always lived by the cycle of summer sandstorms and brilliant winter sunshine, only just letting in the modern world because no force on earth can keep out Pepsi and Coke ads, Nagaur will not impress itself upon you in any extraordinary way. When you first see it, you will find the mandatory vegetable stalls and a Gandhi Chowk, poster commercials and village boys swaggering as if they do it for a living. Don't let this first impression dampen your excitement. For what Nagaur offers ranges between the hot and the incendiary. The first is its famous red chillies and the second is the story of the man who's the reason why people visit Nagaur today.

THINGS TO SEE AND DO

Nagaur's Hindu and Islamic lineage has given it architectural wealth that belies its sterile main street. Even then, it can be a challenge for those who travel by a clock and an itinerary. Big-time tourism hasn't thankfully reached here yet, so though the missing touts and guides will be a relief, chances are you'll also muddy your feet as you navigate congested lanes searching for little-known places. It's ideal if you're looking for a bit of exotica minus the frills. And except at the fort — Nagaur's star attraction — don't expect anyone at hand to fill in on the local lore and colour. Time a visit during the annual Nagaur Fair in January/ February. Even if you do not find bullocks a tempting buy, the famous Mirchi Bazaar is bound to add spice to your trip. Autos are a convenient mode of transport in Nagaur; the minimum fare is around Rs 80 per hour.

Amar Singh's Cenotaph
Before the fort should come the tale of the man who built it. Had it not been for Amar Singh Rathore's legendary temper,

Nagaur would have never blipped on the map. Amar Singh, or Umra as he was called, was the first-born prince of the House of Rathore, the Jodhpur clan. He was adored by his army because in battle there was perhaps no one more inventive than him. But in times of peace, when there was no enemy against whom to work out his tempestuousness, Amar Singh was a troublemaker of epic proportions. It's not clear what he finally did to incur his own father Gaj Singh Rathore's wrath, but in 1634, Gaj Singh organised a ceremony called *des-vatoh* so that Umra would not succeed him. The ceremony was marked as a day of mourning. That day Amar Singh lost his citizenship of Marwar and was exiled. He left the kingdom with a band of faithful companions and made his way to the Mughal court at Agra. And though the Mughals respected Gaj Singh's decision, they were smart enough to realise that Amar Singh could be very useful in war.

His high-spirited gallantry soon won him the title of Rao and he received Nagaur as his independent fief. But his irrepressible nature had him in trouble soon enough. He once kept away from the court for a fortnight without the

→ FAST FACTS

When to go October to March
Tourist offices
● Regional Tourist Office ❶❻
RTDC Hotel Ghoomar Campus
High Court Road, Jodhpur
Tel: 0291-2545083
● Tourist Reception Centre ❶
Rajasthan Tourism, Govt Hostel Campus,
MI Road, Jaipur
Tel: 0141-5110598, Fax: 5110591
STD code 01582

The Ahchitragarh Fort: More than just a strategic retreat

emperor's prior permission, to hunt boar and tiger — apparently a favourite hobby. This angered Shah Jahan who promptly fined him. An official, Sallabat Khan, was sent to Amar Singh's quarters to collect this fine. Singh refused and asked Khan to leave. Courtly etiquette-wise, this was a direct insult to the emperor and Amar Singh was asked to present himself. He appeared, and ignoring all officials, went to Sallabat Khan and stabbed him with a concealed dagger. He then drew his sword and tried to attack the emperor, hitting a pillar instead. The emperor picked up his skirts and fled into his apartments while Singh continued an impartial slaughter. Five Mughal chiefs fell before his brother-in-law Urjan Gore, another courtier, could control him. There are conflicting versions as to what followed. Either Urjan Gore killed Amar Singh there on the pretext of cajoling him or later, pretending that a peace had been brokered, killed him in a narrow doorway. Amar Singh's wife, the princess of Bundi, came personally to take away her husband's body.

Umra went on to become a Rajput folk hero, remembered as their brave prince who stood up to the Mughals. In truth he worked for them. Today, a handsome yellow sandstone cenotaph honours him, with his footsteps inscribed in the centre, next to which incense sticks are lit. There is a little floral carving on the pillars and ceiling, and surrounding it are cenotaphs in pink sandstone that honour his chief wife who died before he did, and three other ranis who committed sati on his funeral pyre, as well as later members of his clan. All are well preserved. Close to the entrance is a small Hanuman shrine where puja is regularly performed. A caretaker looks after this ASI-protected monument though you might have to wait for him to turn up.

♦**Location** Near Collectorate

Ahchitragarh Fort

Nagaur was a stop on medieval trade routes, and hence the Rajputs and Mughals keenly contested control over it. After Amar Singh's demise, the fort passed back to the Mughals with whom it remained for a long period. Thereafter, it came under British vassalage, even though it was recognised as part of the Marwar inheritance. After Independence, the fort went into decline as the government neither looked after it nor protected it from vandalism. Following a petition from Maharaja Gaj Singh II, the current head of the Rathore clan, it was restored to him as family property about a decade ago. It has been under maintenance ever since, looked after by Jodhpur's Mehrangarh Museum Trust.

For a restoration project that's won a United Nations award and could prove to be Nagaur's turning point, it's surprisingly difficult to obtain clear directions to Nagaur's most imposing sight. It's built on a slightly hilly elevation, and once you get there, you'll park by the entrance to **Hadi Rani's Palace**, and enter the section of the **Zenani Deodi** into what

was the women's wing. It becomes immediately apparent that though the battlements might have been defensive, our late lamented Rathore had actually planned a pleasure palace for himself. There is a great delicacy to the buildings, and it is clear that it was a sybaritic rather than strategic retreat that the Rathores and Mughals sought here.

Overlooking ghostly remains of gardens, water bodies and fountains — which await the next stage of funding for restoration — are buildings such as the **Hawa Mahal**, in which remnants of wall paintings reveal the hedonistic nature of pleasures once offered there. To another side is the **Diwan-i-Khas**, where an elaborate system for trapping fresh breeze, as well as channelled water through a network of shallow canals, must have added to the comfort of the apartments. Most of their floral paintings have survived. An interesting part of the chamber are the **hamams** where the ruler bathed in water tanks with piped hot and cold water. The maharaja's gaddi was positioned before a pool with a fountain, more akin to Mughal style than Rajput, bearing testimony to Amar Singh's proximity to the Mughal Court.

Nagaur was also significant to the Mughals for its proximity to Ajmer — an important site of Muslim pilgrimage (*see page 179*). And so the fort houses the **Akbari Mahal**, a Mughal guest house built surrounding a water tank with a **Sheesh Mahal** where faint traces of mirrors and frescoes provide a glimpse of what must have been a sumptuous palace. In fact, water played a major part in the planning of Ahchitragarh, and the pillared pavilion called the **Baradari** overlooks a huge pool of water that the guide referred to as "a swimming pool". If, in fact, this was a bathing section for the queens, it must have been a first for a Rajput palace, given its size and scale.

Ahchitragarh Fort's apartments may be an attraction for many, but its true charm lies in the fact that one can sit on

---

JK TYRE
TOTAL CONTROL

→ **GETTING THERE**

Air Nearest airport: Jodhpur (140 km/ 2¹/₂ hrs), connected by daily flights to Delhi, Mumbai, Jaipur and Udaipur. Qualis taxis charge Rs 3,800 plus taxes (return) and Indigo Rs 3,360 plus taxes (return) to Nagaur from Jodhpur
Rail Nagaur Station, well-connected to Jaipur by the Jaipur-Bikaner Intercity Express and to Kolkata by the Howrah-Jaipur Express. There are no direct connections to Delhi or Mumbai. Jeep and autos available for local transport
Road There are three ways to get here — from Jaipur via Sikar or via Ajmer, or from Jodhpur, as the town is within easy reach of the three Golden Triangle desert cities. The first route is shortest, the Jodhpur Highway is the smoothest

The ornate and wondrous interior of the Parsvanath Jain Temple at Nagaur

any low wall, under trees probably a century old, and gaze about the shadows of its falling ruins.

◆**Location** Dilli Gate, 2 km from main bus stand **Entry fee** Indians Rs 15, foreigners Rs 50 **Guide fee** Negotiable **Timings** 8.30 am-1 pm, 2.30-5 pm **Car parking fee** Rs 15 **Tel** 01582-242082

Places of worship

One of the labyrinthine, narrow lanes leading out from Gandhi Chowk will take your car to the Jain **Kaanch ka Mandir**. It houses large-eyed, marble Tirthankaras, their images multiplied a thousand times in the bits of coloured glass covering the walls, pillars and ceilings. The sight is even more remarkable in the evening by lamplight. **Bansiwale ka Mandir**, nearby, has a series of huge courtyards. Inside are idols of Krishna and Radha, whose attire is changed for the *jhanki* (viewing), which takes place a number of times during the day. **Khwaja Hamiduddin ka Dargah**, also known as Tarkin ka Dargah, is a mosque with an elaborately carved

entrance. Inside, you are surrounded by graves, and right in front are two domed structures that are clearly modern. It is behind them that you will find the original, domed, stone cenotaph of Hamiduddin. To one side, there is a dharamshala with one locked room. Peep in to see the broken remnants of sandstone arches, pillars and other bits and pieces. The **Bade Pir Sahib ki Dargah** was built in the memory of a saint and disciple of Ajmer's Khwaja Moinuddin Chishti. This mosque is one of the oldest in Nagaur and a major attraction.

◆**Location** All the religious sites are close to Ahchitragarh Fort **Timings** The temples are usually open from 9 am to 5 pm; the dargahs are open 24 hrs

Nagaur Cattle Fair

Nagaur is known for its fine cattle and, not surprisingly, one of the largest cattle fairs of the region is held in Nagaur sometime in January-February each year. Cattle and camel races and cockfights are also held then (*also see page 387*).

Dolled up for the tourist

◆**Location** At Manasar Circle, on the Jodhpur-Bikaner Road

At first sight, the lanes of the old town surrounding Gandhi Chowk seem straight out of some medieval souk, bustling with activity and colour. Though none of the wares are meant for tourists, you can still pick up some nice clay cooking pots for a song. The local fabrics are interesting too, and the patterns are likely to be very bright. As elsewhere, you'll need to indulge in some good-natured bargaining. **Nagauri methi** and **chillies** are popular with culinary artists. Look for shops stocking the famous soft, warm **quilts** of Nokha.

As yet, Nagaur is not equipped to handle tourists in large numbers. Most of its 'hotels' are tiny hovels. Therefore, unless you're in for the spiffy experience of camping in the 10 luxury tents (with attached baths) of **Royal Camp** (Jodhpur Tel: 0291-2572321-27; Tariff: Rs 6,000-7,200; during the Nagaur Cattle Fair, the tariffs go up to Rs 11,000-12,100, inclusive of meals and taxes) pitched on the old polo ground within Ahchitragarh Fort, it's best to stay in Khimsar (*see Around Nagaur below*) at the fort hotel or the camp at the Khimsar Sand Dunes Village. WelcomHeritage, a wing of ITC Hotels, manages all these properties. The state highways are excellent, and you can commute back and forth easily.

For details, see Nagaur Accommodation Listings on page 483

If you are staying at Ahchitragarh, food can be arranged. There are no full-fledged restaurants in this town. All you'll find are *bhojanalayas* (eating-houses) where truck drivers pull over for a meal. If you are here on a day-trip, carry a picnic hamper. The *bhojanalayas*, though, are not a bad choice if you don't mind spicy food and strictly veg fare. If you are lucky, they will serve a local speciality such as *sangri* (dried beans) or *gwarphali* (cluster beans), with piping hot rotis. The best you can do here is **Jai Gopal Chhagan-lal**, on the main road where you have a choice of samosas and kachoris (greasy), cream rolls (sweet), chaat in the evenings, and the best rasmalai I have ever tasted. The *bhojanalaya* beside it could be your ticket for a fuller meal.

Khimsar (40 km SW)
This *thikana*, or fiefdom, paid allegiance to the kingdom of Marwar, though tales are told of how it tried to establish itself separately. There is also a rumour that Aurangzeb once visited this village as a

Give me red

One thing you must take from Nagaur is its famous red chilli powder, available at any spice shop here. When still green, these chillies are cooked as a vegetable (hot but manageable), but when dried and powdered, they become a staple in all Rajasthani kitchens. This is because the Nagauri chilli has an especially lovely, deep red colour, so you need to add a lesser amount to get richly coloured gravy that does not taste too hot either. Rajasthan's famous *lal maas* or red meat curry, for example, must be cooked with chilli powder only from Nagaur to give it its beautiful red tinge. Here is the recipe:

Ingredients 1 kg lamb cut into pieces, 1¹/₂ cups or 300 ml oil, 30 gm red chilli powder, 50 gm coriander powder, 3 sliced onions, 250 gm curd, 1 tsp haldi, 2 tbsp garlic paste, 400 ml lukewarm water, 1 tbsp chopped coriander, salt to taste **Method** Mix all ingredients except garlic paste and marinate the lamb pieces for 1 hr. Heat oil in a heavy bottomed pan, add lamb pieces and cook for 45 mins on slow fire till the pieces become tender. Add garlic and cook till the oil separates. Add water and bring to boil. Garnish with green coriander and serve. Serves four to six people.

Recipe by Pushpita Singh

guest of the thakur, but there seems to be little validity in the claim, even though a part of the fortified castle is named after him. The castle or **Khimsar Fort** (Tel: 01585-262345-49; Tariff: Rs 4,000-5,000) is a heritage hotel. It has a charming ambience, and the meals and entertainment are splendid. Part of the package includes camel and jeep safaris to view blackbuck and gazelle. Another option is to stay at the **Khimsar Sand Dunes Village** (Tel: 262345-49; Tariff: Rs 4,500-5,000), 6 km from Khimsar Fort. The retreat is surrounded by sand dunes with a water body towards the centre. Many of its facilities are shared with Khimsar Fort. However, it is operational only in winter.

For details, see Nagaur Accommodation Listings on page 483

Nokha (57 km NW)

Though one of the largest wholesale markets for wool and grain, Nokha is famous for its quilts, which rival Jaipur's. It's a mystery why these quilts, despite being light, are so warm. Apparently the trick lies in the quality of *dhunai*, or the whisking of the cotton that goes in to fill a quilt. No more than a kilogramme of cotton for a large quilt is used and this is spun so fine that it traps air not just in layers but also between the fibre. The trapped air is what makes these so warm. The only difference is that Jaipur quilts are hand-stitched, whereas the ones in Nokha are made using machines. You can pick these up very cheap here. Nokha is on the Nagaur-Bikaner Road. Take any RSRTC or private bus going to Bikaner. Taxis charge Rs 1,000 (return). ∎

Heady picture: Turbans tell many a tale in colourful Rajasthan

JODHPUR
FEELING BLUE

District Jodhpur **Region** Marwar
Location At the edge of the Thar Desert, in western Rajasthan
Distances 253 km S of Bikaner, 280 km SE of Jaisalmer, 344 km SW of Jaipur, 600 km SW of Delhi
Journey time *By road* 5 hrs from Jaisalmer, 5$^1/_2$ hrs from Jaipur, 9$^1/_2$ hrs from Delhi
Route from Jaipur NH8 to Beawar via Dudu and Ajmer; NH14 to Bar via Sendra; state highway to Jodhpur via Bilara and Dangiawas (*see route guide on page 178*)

■ BY PRERNA SINGH

There is something magical about Jodhpur. I knew that when I first set foot here as a child and my most recent visit only confirmed that belief. Pink sandstone and clear blue skies greeted me once again as I stepped out of the train into the hustle and bustle of the Station Road. A lot had changed and yet, in many ways, nothing had. Jodhpur was no longer as green as it used to be, and

the winds of modernity had taken away some of its delectable small-town feel. But, like a reassuring constant, the Mehrangarh Fort loomed over the skyline, as it did in my memories.

I had lived in Jodhpur for a few years a decade ago, and on this return, waves of nostalgia swept across me. A part of me felt like a tourist, marvelling at angles and perspectives hitherto unexplored, discovering treasures amidst everything I had taken for granted when I was a resident of

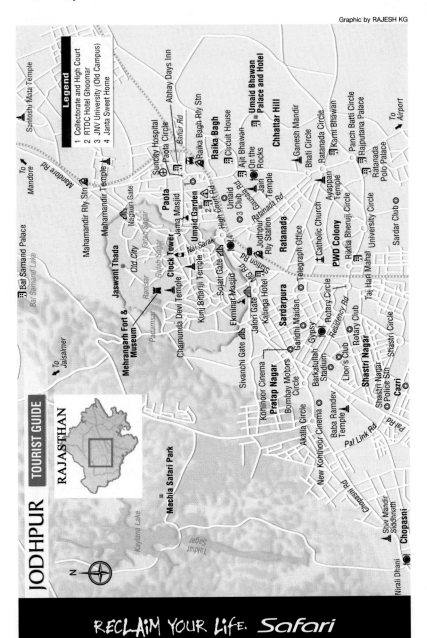

Graphic by RAJESH KG

The Blue City spreads out under the imposing Mehrangarh Fort

the Blue City. A part of me rejoiced at what I knew was indeed my homecoming and I savoured every part of the trip, exulting in the rediscovery of Jodhpur's architecture, colours and its history.

Rao Jodha of the Kanauj family founded the house of Jodhpur in Marwar, the Land of 'Maroo' or death, thus named because of the region's extremely hostile living conditions. Their first capital was at Mandore, an honour which went to Jodhpur after the Mehrangarh Fort was constructed towards the end of the 15th century. The fort was built with defence in mind, and the slopes and the sudden twists and turns in the structure were meant to hinder the movement of enemy elephants. There was good reason for this too — the state was often at war with the neighbouring Rajputs and Mughals.

Nevertheless, the Rathore clan managed to hold on to its possessions and expanded over time. It eventually rose to become one of the strongest and biggest

kingdoms of Rajasthan, along with Mewar and Amber.

It is said that at the time of Independence, Jodhpur was so prosperous that it was slated to be the capital of the new state of Rajputana in the Union of India. However, because of its distance from Delhi, and assorted political factors, it lost out to Jaipur.

ORIENTATION

Jodhpur is Rajasthan's second largest city. The **Old City** that lends it the name Blue City is to the north, around the **Mehrangarh Fort**. It opens up into what is now the main city via the **Sojati Gate** and the **Jalori Gate** in the southern walls of the fort. The original capital of **Mandore** lies to the north of the town. The **Station Road** is the hub of all activity. A good place for shopping, it has a number of budget hotels and several travel agencies. The Station Road leads on to the Sojati

Gate and **Nai Sarak** areas, which are the important commercial hubs. The **airport** is situated near **Ratanada**, 6 km from the main town.

Jodhpur has good local transport, comprising buses and autos (for some reason, more popularly known as taxis). The **main bus stand** is at **Raika Bagh** and the local buses take you almost anywhere within Jodhpur and also to Mandore and **Kaylana Lake**, on the Jodhpur-Jaisalmer Road. Autos don't run on meter and what you end up paying will mostly depend on your bargaining skills. Ideally, the fare should range between Rs 10 for a short distance and Rs 250 for a full day-trip around the city.

The most comfortable way of moving around is to hire a taxi from a travel agency or hotel. The average fare is Rs 750 (plus Rs 200 for AC) for 8 hrs or 80 km, after which they charge Rs 4-5 per km. The fare will be more if you want to travel out of the city.

THINGS TO SEE AND DO

Jodhpur Town can be covered in two to three days in a leisurely manner. About three days should be kept aside for all the arounds (*see pages 226-227, 232-234*). While Rohet and Luni don't offer much by way of sightseeing, the heritage

properties here are excellent stay options, provided their high tariffs are not a deterrent. A day could also be devoted to a visit to Osian where you can go on a camel safari or stay at a night camp. Keep aside a day for the Bishnoi village safari (*see page 226*).

Umaid Bhawan Palace

The palace is a magnificent structure that's representative of the Indo-Saracenic style of architecture, and is made of sandstone that has been put together without the use of mortar. Umaid Singh, the then Maharaja of Jodhpur, ordered the construction of the palace in order to give relief and work to the people affected by the famine of the late 1920s. The project took 15 years to complete and gave employment to 3,000 artisans. In 1977, following the abolition of the privy purses, the current royal Maharaja Gaj Singh converted a part of the palace into a hotel. Today, the palace is divided into three sections: the royal apartments, the hotel that is now run by the Taj Group, and a museum. The royal wing is closed to tourists. To enter the hotel, one has to pay a cover charge of Rs 800 per head, which is then adjusted against the expenses of eating and drinking inside the hotel.

The **museum** has a display of royal artefacts collected over the years, such as crystals, clocks, crockery and anything else that might have caught the royal fancy. The clock collection is perhaps the most interesting of all.

♦**Location** To the east of the town, adjacent to the cantonment **Hotel entry fee** Rs 800 **Museum entry fee** Indians Rs 20, foreigners Rs 50 **Cameras** Not allowed **Timings** 9 am-5 pm

Mehrangarh Fort

The most imposing structure in Jodhpur is also the biggest fort in Rajasthan. Built atop a 150-m high hill in 1459 by Rao Jodha, the fort has withstood many a battle, as is evident today from the marks

Umaid Bhawan Palace, a magnificent structure made of sandstone

of cannonballs on the fort walls. The entrance ticket has to be bought at the main entrance at **Jai Pol**, built by Maharaja Man Singh. From here you can either climb up or take the elevator service. For me, the best part of any visit to the fort is the walk up to the ramparts, and beyond that to the mandir located in one corner of the fort. The view from here, of the entire city, is simply breathtaking. To the south you can see the Umaid Bhawan Palace and closer to the fort, the Old City, famously painted blue to ward off Marwar's terrible heat.

There is a **museum** here with an exquisite collection of artefacts, including some very fascinating war booty and even more fascinating armoury (perhaps some of the deadliest looking swords one might ever get to see). The first several rooms of the museum are arranged around a courtyard called **Sangar Chowki**, where coronations were held until 1952. Inside, in the delicately worked sandstone apartments, there is a wonderful collection of palanquins and elephant

seats (*howdahs*), the outstanding one being a silver *howdah* gifted by Shahjahan. It is decorated with a relief of lions, whose faces look peculiarly like shocked Rajput warriors. Up one level is a room full of excellent **miniature paintings** in the Marwar style of the 18th and the 19th centuries. After this comes a series of apartments decorated with gilded wood, Murano glassware, Chinese tiles, murals, an opulent mix-and-match from different regions and historical periods that covers every available square inch of space. The royal splendour of the first family of Marwar is evident in the spread of costumes on display.

The **Zenana Mahal** and the **Phool Mahal** have frescoes and stained glass. If you want to pick up souvenirs, the museum gift shop has designer items as well as stalls run by local craftspersons.

When you're done with the museum, turn left and take a $1/_2$-km walk past the **Chamunda Mata Temple** to catch wonderful views of the Old City. Return to the right of the museum to exit the fort via

Loha Pol, where you can see handprints of Raja Man Singh's widows, who committed sati in 1843. On your way down you'll pass **Rao Jodha Ka Phalsa**, where folk musicians will greet you. This used to be the last point of the old fort in the times of Rao Jodha. Walk past **Fateh Pol** and turn right for **Jai Pol** to exit the fort. To get to the Old City go straight down from Fateh Pol.

♦**Entry fee** Indians Rs 20 (50 per cent concession for defence personnel, students below 18 and senior citizens), foreigners Rs 250 (this includes the charge for the audio guide) **Cameras** Still Rs 50, video Rs 200 **Timings** 9 am-5 pm **Guide fee** Rs 100-250 (depending on group size)

Jaswant Thada

This is a beautiful marble cenotaph that was built by Sardar Singhji in the

Inside the Mehrangarh Fort

GIREESH GV

memory of his father, Maharaja Jaswant Singh II, who ruled over Marwar in the latter part of the 19th century. Jaswant Singh tried to set up a welfare state and was known for his reform measures. The grounds around it became the crematoria for subsequent rulers.

♦**Location** ¹/₂ km from the Mehrangarh Fort **Entry fee** Indians Rs 10, foreigners Rs 20 **Cameras** Still Rs 25, video Rs 50 **Timings** 8.30 am-5.30 pm

Mandore

Mandore, the erstwhile capital of Marwar, lies on the outskirts of Jodhpur, about 9 km north of the main city. The **Mandore Gardens** today are better known for the cenotaphs of the former rulers, built not as chhatris but like temples. The **Hall of Heroes** and the **Shrine of the Three Hundred Million Gods** here are worth a dekko. Further on lie the ruins of the abandoned Mandore City, which today serve as the stage for a number of cultural programmes. Also at Mandore is a temple to Mirabai.

♦**Garden timings** 8 am-8 pm

Kaylana Lake

On the western outskirts of Jodhpur, about 11 km from the city, lie the Kaylana and **Takhat Sagar** lakes, adjacent to each other, separated only by a narrow strip of land through which the Jodhpur-Jaisalmer Highway passes. The Kaylana Lake is a picnic spot where visitors can go boating. Even though Kaylana is not clean, it is still popular with the locals, given the picturesque landscape.

SHOPPING

Jodhpur is a paradise for shoppers. It is well-known for its tie-and-dye fabric, *jootis* and *mojaris*, lacquer-ware, silverware, semi-precious stones, antiques, woodwork and marble souvenirs. The area around Ghanta Ghar or the Clock Tower is the best place to shop. For tie-dyed fabrics, head to **Kapra Bazaar**, and

PRAKASH ISRANI

In memoriam: The Jaswant Thada, a beautiful marble cenotaph

for silver jewellery, **Sarafa Bazaar. National Handlooms,** which has branches on Nai Sarak, near the Circuit House, Pratap Nagar and Gandhi Maidan, and **Thar Handlooms, Shyam Silk Store** and **Lucky Silk Store,** all near Sojati Gate, are good for saris, dupattas, block-printed textiles and suit pieces. Camel leatherwork and *jooti* shops are to be found all over the city, but the best place to shop for traditional Jodhpuri *mojaris* and *jootis* is **Juti Corner,** right across the railway station. Prices begin at Rs 100 and can go up as high as a few thousand rupees depending on the kind of craftsmanship you are looking for.

The area between the Palace Road and the Circuit House has a number of antique and woodwork shops. Doors, jharokhas, chowkis and Jodhpur's trademark wooden musicians may be picked up from here, although these are by no means cheap. Prices start at around Rs 250, and can go up to a lakh or even more. Some of the handicraft stores in the city that you can check out include

Lalji Handicrafts, Shekhawati Art Emporium, Rajasthan Art Emporium, Maharani, Heritage Art School and **Rama Bazaar.** Both Umaid Bhawan and Ajit Bhawan have shops that sell exclusive, boutique-style jewellery, handicrafts, accessories and souvenirs.

WHERE TO STAY

Jodhpur offers plenty of stay options if you are looking for a luxury holiday, especially in terms of a heritage hotel experience. There are also mid-range and budget options.

Heritage
The **Taj Umaid Bhawan Palace** (Tel: 0291-2510101; Tariff: Rs 14,000-1,15,000) is the most obvious option for those who can afford a royal experience. With its quiescent splendour, the hotel offers the facilities of a luxury spa, an indoor swimming pool and other sports facilities. A heritage hotel now, the **Ajit Bhawan,** near the Circuit House (Tel: 2510610/410;

The colours and sounds of Bishnoi villages

The Village Safari, better known as the **Bishnoi Safari**, serves as an introduction to the Bishnoi sect, founded by Jambheshwarji. They follow a set of 29 (*bis* and *noi*) principles, which include several norms related to the protection of animals and conservation of trees. Most hotels and tour operators organise these safaris.

Usually, the first stop is the Bishnoi village of **Khejarli** (25 km south-east of Jodhpur). Khejarli is best known as the place where the precedent for the **Chipko Movement** was established.

In 1730, the Maharaja of Jodhpur, Abhay Singh, ordered the cutting down of trees in and around Khejarli for the renovation of the Meh-rangarh Fort. In protest, about 360 people, including women, from 84 Bishnoi villages wrapped themselves around the trees, in the hope that they would be able to save them. However, the maharaja's armies ruthlessly went ahead and cut down the trees, along with the people clinging to them. Three hundred and

sixty-three people died at that time and today, 363 trees have been planted around the **Jambheshwarji Temple** in their memory.

The safari then heads to the **potters' village** of **Singhasini** (27 km). The potters here use clay and sawdust as raw material and it's interesting to watch them at work. This is followed by halts at the **shepherds' village** at **Rebari** and the Bishnoi village of **Guda**. Here you can enjoy tea and conversation with the women and the children of the village and take a peek into their mud houses whose interiors are cool even in the desert heat.

There is something to learn from here about living in harmony with one's surroundings; the villagers' lives are environment-friendly — they use every scrap of waste, be it to decorate their homes or to make cots. Not far from the Guda Bishnoi Village is the **Guda Lake**, a retreat for birds including the sarus and demoiselle cranes. Apart from blackbuck,

At a potter's house near Jodhpur (below); **A Bishnoi woman** (right)

ROHET Quiet holiday

The jagir of Rohet came into being in the 17th century, and what was then the fort of Rohet is now a heritage property. Part of it, however, is still home to the family of Rohet, a fief of the kingdom of Jodhpur. Set right next to a beautiful lotus-filled pond, and replete with bougainvillea bushes, this is the place to visit if you are looking for a quiet holiday.

The **Hotel Rohet Garh** (Tel: 02936-268231, 268531; Tariff: Rs 2,750-5,000) offers luxurious rooms with good views of the lake, the swimming pool or the splendid manicured lawns of the fort. Although the heritage hotel lacks any sense of grandeur, the well-furnished halls, the breezy verandahs and the open terrace overlooking the lake add to the charm of the place. The delicate archways and the clusters of neem trees, the drawing room with the wooden ceiling, and the breezy verandahs are all enchanting. A quiet dinner by the pool offers romance in a fairy-tale beautiful setting.

The hotel organises jeep, camel and horse safaris to the villages of Bishnois and craftsmen (charges Rs 500-550; *see alongside*). The half-day **camel safari** includes a picnic lunch, and is only conducted if there is a group of five to six people (Rs 1,700-2,500). The **horse safari** could be a 2-hr ride in the morning or evening, or a full-day ride with a picnic lunch, or even an overnight safari with a night stay in the desert (Rs 850-6,000).

The hotel also organises **birdwatching** trips for nature enthusiasts, who are taken cycling to nearby lakes. A guide will accompany you; packed breakfast is also provided (Rs 850). You can attend a regional festival if there is one or attend a cooking workshop. Bookings can also be done from Jodhpur on 0291-2431161.

Rohet is 39 km south of Jodhpur. Taxis cost about Rs 500 (one-way) and Rs 1,000 (return).

nilgai and chinkaras, one may also get to see turtles in this area. The next stop is **Kankani**, which is known for lovely **terracotta** work and **block printing**. Here you can see how the block-printed cloth that Jodhpur is so famous for is crafted.

Salawas, famous for its **dhurries**, is an obscurely located village, down a bumpy road that takes you nowhere else. The **Pukhraj Prajapat Dhurry Udyog** (Tel: 0291-2696744; Mobile: 09414720724; Email: pukhraj_dhurry@sify.com/ chhotaramprajapat@rediffmail.com) here is known for its dhurries, priced between Rs 200 and 1,500.

The Prajapats also run a **homestay** where you are put up in circular huts and served sumptuous Rajasthani meals. They can also take you on camel safaris.

You can base yourself at **Luni**, **Rohetgarh** or **Jhalamand** if you want to go on a village safari. Fort Chanwa at Luni and Hotel Rohet Garh also give you the option of doing the safari by jeep or by horse. The **Bishnoi Village Camp and Safari** (Mobile: 09414129233, 09314716401; Tariff: Rs 1,200-2,000) at Guda is also a good option. ∎

Tariff: Rs 4,500-7,000), was built to be the home of Umaid Singh's younger brother. With a rather grand ambience about it, the hotel offers luxury tents and exquisitely done up rooms. An excellent heritage-cum-homestay option is the **Ratan Vilas Haveli** (Tel: 2614418; Tariff: Rs 1,400-1,650), on Loco Shed Road, a 1920s villa set in a large garden, centred around a pretty courtyard, with exquisite antiques dotting the house. There used to be horses on the grounds, but though that isn't the case now, Brij Raj Singh and his family, who own the haveli, have a tie-up with the Jodhpur Polo Club; they also arrange horse rides on request.

Others

The **Taj Hari Mahal** (Tel: 2439700; Tariff: Rs 7,500-14,500), on Residency Road,

although not a heritage hotel, is a fine blend of tradition and modernity in terms of hospitality, ambience and service. Nai Sarak, to the south of the Clock Tower, has a number of mid-range hotels, catering to businessmen rather than tourists. **Hotel Ratnawali** (Tel: 2555698-99; Tariff: Rs 1,050-1,350) on Nai Sarak is centrally located, and close to the railway station and the commercial centre. The **Kalinga Hotel** (Tel: 2627338; Tariff: Rs 1,100-2,800) is located right opposite the railway station, in the hub of all activity. It is well-known for its restaurant that serves excellent Rajasthani, North Indian and Mughlai cuisine.

Hotel Durag Villas (Tel: 2512298; Tariff: Rs 300-1,250), close to the Circuit House, is in a comparatively quiet location, and is furnished in traditional Rajasthani style. With comfortable rooms, it offers good value for money.

Abhay Days Inn (Tel: 2542980; Tariff: Rs 2,700-5,000) is a straightforward, 3-star hotel near the bus stand, which is not in a great-looking area. The best mid-range option in town is **Devi Bhawan** (Tel: 2511067; Tariff: Rs 850-1,500), a friendly guest house set around a spacious garden. The rooms are large and clean, with antique wooden furniture. If you're in Jodhpur to relax and don't care much if the television works or not, this is the place for you. **Mandore Guest House** (Tel: 2571620; Tariff: Rs 500-950), located near Mandore Gardens, offers 14 cottages and also arranges trips to Bishnoi villages. Its restaurant is quite famous for its Rajasthani cuisine.

As uninspiring as most government-run hotels, the **RTDC Hotel Ghoomar** (Tel: 2544010; Tariff: Rs 550-1,200) is near the Umaid Gardens. The dorm beds are among the cheapest lodging options in the town. **Raman Palace Guest House** (Tel: 2513980; Tariff: Rs 350-1,500) is in a quiet part of the town and has a pleasant rooftop dining area. The premier budget hotel in the city, **Haveli Guest House** (Tel: 2614615; Tariff: Rs 300-2,000) has

→ GETTING THERE

Air Jodhpur Airport, connected by IA, which flies three times a week from Delhi, Mumbai, Jaipur and Udaipur. Jet Airways has daily flights from Mumbai and flights four days a week to Delhi

Rail Jodhpur Junction, connected by Mandore and Intercity expresses from Old Delhi; and by Rajasthan Sampark Kranti (a superfast train) from Sarai Rohilla, which runs on alternate days. Suryanagari Express from Bandra (W), Mumbai, is the best option via Ahmedabad and it runs on alternate days; also Ranakpur Express from Bandra (W) via Ahmedabad and Surat and the Howrah-Jodhpur Express

Road Travellers from Delhi should turn off NH8 on to NH14 at Beawar. At Bar, turn right onto the state highway to Jodhpur via Pilara

The **Ultra** Edition 12.9
SAMSUNG SGH D-900

① Ajit Bhawan ② Rajasthani Flutist ③ Coloured glass at Maharangarh Fort

④ Visitors to the Fort ⑤ Maharangarh Fort

imagine doing more with less.
The Ultra Life.

Imagine always being in two places at once, doing two things at once. No office. No boundaries. No restrictions. With Samsung's new Ultra Edition it's not that hard to imagine.   www.samsung.com

Features: 3 Mega Pixel Camera with Auto-Focus • MP3 Player • Intelligent Display • Large 262K QVGA TFT Screen • Direct TV Out

Free accessories: Bluetooth™ Headset • 256 MB T Flash Memory Card • TV Out Cable • Battery Charger • Travel Adapter • Car Adapter • Straight Headset • Battery (2 Nos.) • Data Kit

The **Ultra** Edition 12.9
SAMSUNG SGH D-900

Leo Burnett D SMSCHLB-0001JH

SANJAY SHARMA

Some local colour and flavour: At a vegetable market

clean rooms, some of which have a good view of the fort. **Shivam Guest House** (Tel: 2610688; Tariff: Rs 450-650) is a homely place, run by two brothers, which has recently been expanded with the addition of large new rooms.

Homestays

The **Indrashan Homestay** (Tel: 2440665; Tariff: Rs 900-1,200), located in Jodhpur's High Court Colony, has a handful of AC double rooms. The rooms are charming and spotlessly clean and the best open into a lovely courtyard in the middle of the house, but remember to carry your own toiletries. The food is exceptional.

For more hotels and details, see Jodhpur Accommodation Listings on pages 472-476

WHERE TO EAT

The **Mehran Terrace** (Tel: 0291-2555389) is an evening restaurant at the Mehrangarh Fort. The tables are laid out on the ramparts of the fort, and you can enjoy a view of the lit-up city as you enjoy a traditional Rajasthani thali (Rs 300 veg; Rs 350 non-veg). The non-vegetarian

thali is recommended. Do remember to book in advance — it's mandatory and you will not get a table otherwise.

Nirali Dhani, on Chopasani Road, is another option if you want to enjoy a traditional menu and ambience. There is a cover charge of Rs 220 per person, which includes an unlimited supply of food. You have to pay extra only for the bottled water or soft drinks that you might have. The **Gypsy** restaurant chain is also extremely popular, with two branches in Sardarpura and one in PWD Colony. The **Gypsy Dining Hall** in Sardarpura is known for its thalis. Priced at Rs 78 per person, the thali has a wide variety and makes sure you are not left asking for more. The *chhach* or buttermilk is particularly enjoyable. **On the Rocks** near Ajit Bhawan is one of the more upmarket establishments. It has a bar and a discotheque. It also boasts of a confectionery. **Kim 15AD** in Sardarpura is a good confectionery and offers a large variety of cakes, pastries and cookies. **Janta Sweet Home**, adjacent to the station, is popular for sweetmeats and ice-creams. The kachoris, samosas and mirchi vadas at Sojati Gate are not to be missed.

AROUND JODHPUR

Jhalamand (12 km S)
A small hamlet on the Jodhpur-Pali Road, there is very little of interest to the tourist in Jhalamand itself. However, **Hotel Jhalamand Garh** (Tel: 0291-2720481; Tariff: Rs 2,500-4,000), the old castle of Jhalamand, a fiefdom of Jodhpur, is a becalming retreat. The heritage hotel is run in the manner of a homestay by host RP Singh and his wife, who pay personal attention to each and every guest, and even dine with them. The rooms are plush and have an old-world grandeur. The terrace offers a beautiful view of Jodhpur. It is also breezy and ideal for the terrace parties hosted by the Singhs. Mr Singh's music collection is an attraction in itself. They arrange jeep, camel and horse safaris. Taxi from Jodhpur costs Rs 250 (return).

Osian (66 km NW)
The **Jain Mahavira Temple** here is famous for the idol of Lord Mahavira in the sanctum sanctorum, which is said to be made of cow's milk and mud, with a coat of gold. The intricate stonework on

SONDEEP SHANKAR/SAAB PICTURE

At Mandore, the erstwhile capital

the ceilings and the sculptures along the temple walls is magnificent, but time has taken its toll on these. A renovation project is underway, which is a job being done well, but doesn't quite match the standard of the original work, which can be glimpsed even now.
♦**Entry fee** Rs 10, only for foreigners
Cameras Still Rs 40, video Rs 100
    The **Sachayee Mata Mandir** is the most important of the 16 Hindu temples here. Although the temple is dedicated to

LUNI Of forts and serenity

En route to Pali, 30 km south of Jodhpur, along the banks of the River Luni, is the hamlet of Chanwa. Granted as a *jagir*, or a principality, in the late 19th century to Kaviraj Muraridanji, who built Fort Chanwa, the land reverted back to Jodhpur, only to be subsequently granted as a *jagir* to Dalip Singhji, the younger son of Maharaja Umaid Singh. Post-Independence, the fort fell into disarray. It was only in the early 1990s that extensive renovation and restoration was carried out, and Fort Chanwa became a heritage hotel.
    Fort Chanwa (Tel: 02931-284216; Tariff: Rs 2,500-4,500) is an enchanting place with a quiet splendour and a romantic air about it. The imposing stone fort surprisingly radiates

gentleness, a dreamy look that's fittingly enhanced by the stained glass and stone friezes here. The interiors are done up in traditional art deco style.
    The rooms are neat, with several thoughtful touches: the air-conditioners are hidden behind jharokhas; dhurries, not carpets, adorn the floors; and there are nice bay windows, all adding to the royal feel.
    Although Luni itself does not have much to offer, the hotel is a destination in itself. The hotel also organises village safaris (Rs 550-8,000) and sightseeing at Jodhpur.
    Bookings can be done from Jodhpur by calling 0291-2432460. Taxi from Jodhpur costs Rs 1,000 (return).

Airtel welcomes you to the Land of Kings

Manual Network Selection Process

**A step-by-step guide on how to connect
to the best mobile network in Rajasthan.**

Go to the menu on your mobile phone and select 'Settings' • Go to 'Phone Settings'
• Click on 'Network Settings' • Select 'Manual' • Select Airtel / INA Airtel / INA 70 / Oasis

Stay with Airtel! Win exciting gifts and special roaming privileges.

Rediffusion-DY&R/Del/BCL/011

Mobile Services

ABHILASH GAUR

Carvings at a temple in Osian

Sachayee Mata, the sculpture here depicts most gods of the Brahmanical pantheon. A lot of attention has been paid to detail.
◆**Aarti timings** 6 am and 8 pm

A trip to Osian is incomplete without a camel ride. Tourists can stay in a desert camp (open or tented) and also go on a camel safari. The most popular ones are **Reggie's Camel Camp** (Tel: 0291-2437023, 2610192; Mobile: 098281 42102; Tariff: Rs 9,000) and **Camp Thar** (Tel: 2573466; Mobile: 09414128574; Tariff: Rs 7,000).

Some locals have also cashed in on this trend and offer you the opportunity to go on a camel safari and spend the night at a village home where you are served delightfully traditional Rajasthani meals. For this, one option is to contact Prathviraj Ojha (more popularly known as Babloo guide) on 09413279747. Taxis from Jodhpur cost about Rs 500 (one-way) and Rs 1,200 (return).

Sardar Samand (55 km SE)
A long bumpy ride takes you to this isolated lake and palace in Pali District. Built by the Maharaja of Jodhpur as a hunting lodge, the **Sardar Samand Palace** (Tel: 02960-245001-03; Tariff: Rs 3,300-4,400) is now a heritage hotel. Its grounds are home to plenty of fauna. The lake is a winter home to many species of birds and a favourite with birdwatchers. The property is closed between April and September. The Sardar Samand offers 3D/ 2N packages. However, the rooms here are not as luxurious as those offered at several other heritage hotels. Taxis cost about Rs 1,200 for a day-trip.

Kheechan (135 km NW)
Every winter, when it becomes too cold in their native Central Asian lands, thousands of demoiselle cranes migrate to Kheechan, a village 5 km from **Phalodi**, where they are fed and protected by the villagers. Locally the cranes are known as *kurjan* because of the sound they make. They are to be found around the little ponds here, or at the **Pakshi Chugga Ghar** run by certain locals, where the cranes are fed grain. The funds come from Jains across the country.

Kheechan and Phalodi are also known for their spectacular red sandstone havelis. However, most of these havelis remain locked for a major part of the year. The haveli of the Dadhas, **Lal Niwas** (Tel: 02925-223813; Tariff: Rs 2,000-2,600) has been turned into a heritage hotel. Although not very grand, the hotel has a quaint charm. Adjacent to Lal Niwas is the **Museum of Jain and Oriental Art**, which houses artefacts and manuscripts. It has European curios, ancient manuscripts and an enviable coin collection. A day-trip by taxi costs about Rs 1,500.
◆**Museum entry fee** Rs 10 **Timings** 10.30 am-7 pm

For more hotels and details of stay options around Jodhpur, see Accommodation Listings on pages 473-476 ∎

West Rajasthan

The last outpost of the desert, where a golden fort, teeming with life and history, full of glory and memories, rises above the sands

Striking colours: A puppet seller looks customers in the eye

JAISALMER

THE GOLDEN TOWN

District Jaisalmer
Location On an ancient trade route in the Thar Desert; the border with Pakistan is a few miles to the west
Distances 280 km NW of Jodhpur, 352 km SW of Bikaner, 624 km W of Jaipur via Jodhpur and 670 km via Bikaner, 884 km SW of Delhi
Journey time *By road* 5 hrs from Jodhpur, 6$^1/_2$ hrs from Bikaner, 14 hrs from Jaipur, 18 hrs from Delhi
Route from Jaipur NH8 to Beawar via Dudu and Ajmer; NH14 to Bar via Sendra; state highway to Jodhpur via Bilara and Dangiawas; state highway to Pokaran via Agolai and Dechhu; NH15 to Jaisalmer via Odania and Chandan **Alternative Route** NH11 to Bikaner via Chomu, Sikar, Fatehpur, Ratangarh and Dungargarh; NH15 to Jaisalmer via Gajner, Phalodi, Pokaran and Chandan (*see route guide on facing page*)

■ BY AMIT MAHAJAN

Nobody can be immune to the charms of Jaisalmer. The very first glimpse of the golden Jaisalmer Fort, occupying the pride of place in the monochromatic sandy landscape, is bewitching. Inside the citadel, turbaned faces carry a smile hidden in thick moustaches, long skirts catch the brilliance of the sun in their mirror work and the cobbled streets and the painted houses promise a view of an enchanted world.

It's also a world that has managed to survive for long. The fort, whose walls chronicle the deeds of its Rawals and the riches of its traders, recently celebrated 850 years of uninterrupted vitality. Its havelis speak of the long trains of camels that trekked across deserts to reach Sindh and Afghanistan and West Asia, carrying silver, cloth and expensive goods. Its musicians sing the songs of its daily existence, of the beauty of their desires, and this music will echo in your ears for long.

Going to Jaisalmer is about learning these melodies and hearing these narratives. Going to Jaisalmer is also about visiting the desert and a far outpost therein, an outpost built out of the same sandstone that stretches all around. Here you will realise that the desert is not an endless sequence of sand dunes — but there won't be any reason for disappointment.

For, the sand dunes have an inescapable magnetism that will draw you in, just as Jaisalmer effortlessly does.

ORIENTATION

Jaisalmer is a small, walk-able town and the **fort**, built on a small hill called **Trikuta**, is its essence. The rest of the town exists to its east and north. The main entrance to the fort is from the east. The square outside the main entrance is called **Gopa Chowk**. The fort is small and its streets narrow, and therefore, vehicles are allowed only till the main courtyard outside the palace. The town outside the fort can also be covered on foot. The **railway station** is 3 km from the fort entrance to the east, and the bus stand 1¹/₂ km to the south-west (north-west). Unmetered taxis and autorickshaws are available. The minimum charge for autos is Rs 20-25. Taxis charge Rs 700 for a 3- to 4-hr long excursion and Rs 1,200 for 6-7 hrs. The

Graphic by SURAJ WADHWA

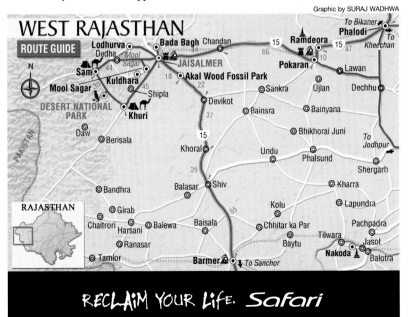

RAHUL SHARMA/INDIAPICTURE

Quiet passage: Jain temple at Jaisalmer

Jaisalmer Municipal Corporation has introduced a tax (Indians Rs 10, foreigners Rs 20) for entering Jaisalmer City.

THINGS TO SEE AND DO

The muted colours of the desertscape, the radiance of the traditional lives and the artistry embedded in stone are the highlights of Jaisalmer. Three days should be sufficient to see the place. Factor in more time if you want to go on a camel safari and camp out under the desert sky (*see Around Jaisalmer on page 248*).

Jaisalmer Fort

From the outside, the fort looks small and toy-like, a fragile castle built on a miniature hill. You enter the fort from the **First Fort Gate** at **Gopa Chowk**. Yellow stone towers all around, often becoming golden, and stone-paved passages wind through a series of massive and intricately positioned gates. All of it is teeming

with life and history. Walk about in the narrow streets of the fort soaking in the ambience; often you will lose yourself in the maze, but not for long — the fort is not big enough for that.

Rawal Jaisal, a ruler belonging to the Bhatti clan of Rajputs and who gave his name to the town, is said to have started constructing the fort in 1156. Later rulers added to the edifice, which faced attacks by armies from Delhi and Jodhpur. Throughout its history, people have been living in the fort, and this adds to the extraordinariness of the place.

The main courtyard of the fort is called **Dussehra Chowk**, below the Rajmahal, reached after passing through **Hawaprol**, the last of the gates. From here streets paved with stone and busy with touristy shops, hotels, restaurants, temples and houses lead to various parts of the fort. Enlivening these winding lanes are children coming back from school, women cleaning and washing, and milkmen with metal pots on their motorcycles. You can walk up to the ramparts and the numerous bastions, and absorb the stunning views of the town outside the fort and the rocky landscape beyond. Mornings and evenings are especially good times to do this.

Rajmahal

The palace of the former rulers is a seven-storey structure and towers above the Dussehra Chowk, the central square that was the space of interface between the rulers and the ruled. Now you can stand in the square and marvel at the intricate stonework on the façade of the palace building. This former royal residence is now being restored and parts are open to the public as the **Jaisalmer Fort Palace Museum and Heritage Centre**. The museum is unexciting.

The palace was built over many generations and the various buildings are connected by low and narrow passages, a protective measure against invaders used in most palaces of Rajasthan. The main building dates from the 19th century and it boasts of beautifully carved stone. The most spectacular views are from the rooftop, the highest point in the vicinity. ◆**Entry fee** Indians Rs 30, foreigners Rs 250 (with audio guide and one still camera) **Cameras** Still Rs 50, video Rs 100 **Timings** 8 am-6 pm (Apr-Oct), 9 am-6 pm (Nov-Mar), open all days

Jain temples

Inside the fort are seven beautiful Jain temples, delicately carved in yellow sandstone and built in the 15th and 16th centuries. The temples are well-maintained and were revamped in the 1970s. Yet, do remember that these are not spacious; some parts are quite dark. However, when not many people are inside the temple, the interiors look serene.

The **Parsvanath Temple**, dedicated to the 22nd Tirthankara, is the largest of the lot and the most impressive. The entry is through a magnificently carved torana with an image of Parsvanath at its summit. Inside the mandap, the ceiling has the sculpture of a demon-like head with five bodies. The main idol of the temple is said to have been brought here from Lodhurva, the earlier capital of the Bhatti Rajputs of Jaisalmer (*also see Around Jaisalmer on page 248*).

Nearby is the **Chandraprabhu Temple** dedicated to the eighth Tirthankara. The sanctum sanctorum has four images of Chandraprabhu, and outside it are finely sculpted statues of other Tirthankaras. There is an upper gallery with marble images of Parsvanath. The **Rishabhadeva Temple** is known for its beautiful sculptures, especially the numerous apsaras on its pillars. The **Sambhavanath Temple** is a dimly lit chamber, and steps from the temple lead down into a basement called **Gyan Bhandar** — a tiny, fascinating 16th-century library housing a number of ancient manuscripts, some of them dating to the 11th century. The

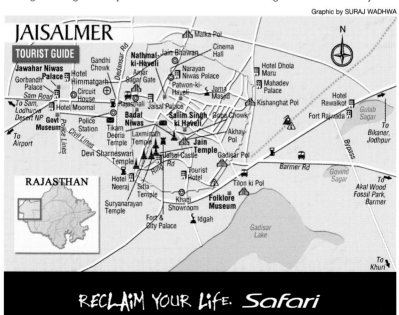

Graphic by SURAJ WADHWA

other Jain temples are **Shitalnath**, **Shantinath** and **Kunthanath**.

◆**Location** 150m south-west of Dussehra Chowk **Entry fee** Rs 10 **Cameras** Still Rs 50, video Rs 100 **Timings** 8 am-noon, open all days

There's also the Hindu temple to Laxminath nearby, not of note architecturally, but interesting because it's the oldest temple in the fort, built by Rawal Jaisal during its construction. It was damaged during Khalji's invasion and then renovated in the 15th century.

Gadisar

Just outside the town is this elegant tank, which was earlier the source of water supply to Jaisalmer. The tank was built in the 14th century by Rawal Gadsi Singh with the idea of collecting precious rainwater. Now the Indira Gandhi Canal (*also see Once there was a desert on page 440*) supplies water to the tank and it is, therefore, never dry. Many pavilions and shrines are there on the tank's banks, and there is a domed pavilion to its centre. Gadisar, also called Gadisagar, is a popular picnic spot and people come here to shoot the breeze, feed the numerous catfish in the pond and also enjoy boat rides.

◆**Location** 1 km south-east of the fort **Entry fee** Free **Boat rides** Row boat Rs 10, paddle boat Rs 50, shikara Rs 100 for 30 mins **Boating timings** 8 am-8 pm

Bharat Petroleum

→ **FAST FACTS**

When to go October to March is best. Avoid summers
Tourist office
● Rajasthan Tourism Reception Centre ❶ Near Gadisar Lake Circle, Jaisalmer
Tel: 02992-252406
STD code 02992

Havelis

The wealthy merchants of Jaisalmer chose to be remembered by posterity by commissioning some of the most ornate residences human beings ever built. These havelis were built in the 18th and the 19th centuries when trade was most lucrative, before the rise of sea trade and the Bombay (now Mumbai) harbour made land routes redundant. The havelis are made of yellow Jaisalmer sandstone and are adorned with jaalis, carved balconies and elaborate façades. The most skilful stonework is done on the outside, reminding you that the havelis are a show of wealth more than anything else. In some of the havelis, the top portions are later additions and this is clearly discernible in the quality of stonework (*also see To the mansion born on page 354*).

One of the heartening developments of the past 20 years is that many new buildings are using traditional sandstone and employing local stone carvers. The new buildings in the city don't quite match the elegance of the heritage buildings, but they bolster Jaisalmer's unique look and feel.

Patwon-ki-Haveli

The biggest and the most ornate of the havelis is the Patwon-ki-Haveli, a set of five houses adjacent to each other, built by five Jain brothers in the first half of the 19th century. The most impressive work is on the outside, and the work is so intricate that the more time you spend studying it, the more it reveals itself to you. The multi-storeyed buildings are constructed in the traditional style of rooms set around a central courtyard. There are remnants of exquisite paintings on some of the walls; many walls have lovely jharokhas opening out to the courtyard or the street below. From the terrace there are great views of the fort. One of the havelis now has a shop selling brocades and embroidered textiles to tourists.

◆**Location** Outside the fort; 1 km northeast of Gopa Chowk **Entry fee** Rs 20

Gadisagar Lake, built in the 14th century to collect rainwater

Cameras Still/ video Rs 20 **Timings** 9 am-6 pm daily
♦**Entry fee for government havelis in the complex** Rs 3 **Camera** Free

Salim Singh-ki-Haveli
Built in the early 19th century and named after a notorious prime minister of Jaisalmer, this haveli is made of stone without the use of any cement or mortar. Elephants carved out of stone welcome you into the haveli. Notice especially the upper storeys, which are replete with delicate carving and garnished with charming balconies.
♦**Location** Old town; 300m east of Gopa Chowk **Note** Entry restricted due to damage by rains

Nathmal-ki-Haveli
Built by two brothers in the late 19th century, this haveli is still partly inhabited. The exterior is beautifully carved. There is no entry fee and the family living here tries to earn money by selling paintings and artefacts to visitors.
♦**Location** Old town; $^1/_2$ km north of Gopa Chowk **Timings** 8 am-7 pm daily

Relics of a golden past
The **Jaisalmer Folklore Museum**, located near Gadisar Lake, contains a few puppets and traditional items of daily use, while its twin, the **Desert Culture Centre and Museum**, located at Gadisar Circle, displays fossils, coins and musical instruments. A ticket bought at either museum is valid for both.
♦**Folklore Museum entry fee** Rs 5 **Timings** 8 am-6 pm **Desert Culture Museum entry fee** Rs 5 **Timings** 8 am-8.30 pm
There's also a **Government Museum** next to the RTDC Hotel Moomal. The exhibits include a few fossils, a stuffed bustard and some antiquities.
♦**Entry fee** Rs 3, Mondays free **Timings** 10 am-4.30 pm, Fridays closed

SHOPPING

Inside the fort, the main road leading to the Rajmahal and also the paths to the Jain temples are lined with shops and vendors. Particularly attractive, and therefore prominently displayed, are colourful textiles with mirror work, to be used as wall hangings, bedspreads or

POKARAN Tracing the unknown

BY PRERNA SINGH

Made famous by India's nuclear tests, the small town of Pokaran lies on the highway that links Jodhpur to Jaisalmer. It's 110 km east of Jaisalmer and 171 km north of Jodhpur. While the chief attraction here is Fort Pokaran, with its museum and heritage hotel, there is a lot to be explored around Pokaran too. The museum is obscure but interesting, housing artefacts ranging from armoury to costumes to minia- tures, which have been collected by the Poka- ran family over the years. (The thakurs of Poka- ran were nobles in the darbar of Jodhpur.)

◆**Entry fee** Indians Rs 10, foreigners Rs 50
Timings 7 am-7.30 pm, open till 9.30 pm during the Ramdevra Fair

A part of **Fort Pokaran** (Mobile: 094144 69761; Tariff: Rs 1,700-4,999) was converted into a heritage hotel by the present Thakur and his wife, with the aim of promoting Pokaran as a tourist destination. The rooms are vibrant, luxu- rious and very tastefully done. The hotel also organises safaris to nearby villages (Rs 650 per head) as well as theme dinners with light and sound programmes (Rs 1,000 per head). Book- ings can also be made from Jodhpur (Telefax: 0291-2432390; Mobile: 09414409761).

Village safaris from Pokaran include visits to nearby potters' villages, where terracotta work is done, and weavers' villages, which now get help from the **Urmul Marusthali Bunkar Vikas Samiti** (Tel: 02925-22272). This NGO

was set up in 1991 with the idea of streamlining the production and marketing of textiles woven by its member villages in Jodhpur and Jai- salmer districts. These textiles are woven in the traditional 'pattu' style of weaving, with *kashida* or ornamentation on the surface of the fabric. While the original textiles were mostly wool, **Urmul Trust** has also started providing the weavers with cotton yarn to cater to urban tastes and preferences. The products range from kurtas, shawls, stoles and jackets to bags, table mats and soft furnishings. Products are retailed through exhibitions, bazaars and exports, and through the **Urmul showrooms** in Bikaner, Phalodi and Pokaran.

About 10 km east of Pokaran is **Ramdeora**, the temple built around the samadhi of Bhag- wan Ramdeoji Maharaj, revered by Muslims as Ramshahpir or Ramapir. He was a Tunvar Raj- put, believed by the Hindus to be a reincarnation of Lord Krishna. Legend has it that five pirs from Mecca came to test his miraculous powers and after being convinced of them, paid him homage. He is thus revered by both Hindus and Muslims. Ramdeoji took samadhi in 1459. A tomb was built at the spot and subsequently a temple was constructed. Every year, a fair is held around August-September, when devotees from all over throng the temple.

◆**Aarti timings** 5 am, 9 am, 7 pm and 10 pm

For more details, see Pokaran Accommodation Listings on page 484

duvet covers. Carved stone pieces, tur- bans and *ravanhattas*, musical instru- ments typical to Rajasthan, make for interesting souvenirs. **Light of the East** in the lane leading to the Jain temples has a rare collection of mineral specimens including zeolites and an interesting story of its owner who came to Jaisalmer on a visit and stayed there, entranced by its mystique. The roads leading away from the fort to its north and east also

have many shopping options. Leather goods like bags, sandals, *jootis*, especially those made of camel leather, are popular buys. The government-run **Rajasthali** at Gandhi Chowk and Amar Sagar Gate sell handicraft products such as embroidered textiles, tie-and-dye fabric, wooden deco- rations and stone items. **Khadi Gramod- yog Bhavan** in Dhibba Para has blankets, leather goods and shawls. **Nathmal-ki- Haveli** and **Patwon-ki-Haveli** both have shops selling handicrafts. Their prices seem to have a margin for bargaining.

Jaisalmer has many staying options inside and outside the fort. While staying inside the fort can be romantic, the accommodation here is more basic. Besides, vehicles go only till the main courtyard of the fort, and the luggage needs to be carried manually till the hotel. Staying inside the fort also increases the pressure on the infrastructure of the fort and contributes to its degradation. Visitors are therefore being urged to make the ethical choice of staying outside the fort. Also, do remember that in high season, most good hotels are booked much in advance.

Heritage

The hotels and guest houses in the fort are small establishments, and are mostly converted old houses and havelis. **Hotel Killa Bhawan** (Tel: 02992-251204; Tariff: Rs 2,700-5,500) is a small place with beautiful décor and a great location. **Hotel Jaisal Castle** (Tel: 252362; Tariff: Rs 1,500-2,000) is situated high on the ramparts

with spacious but rundown rooms. **Desert Boys Guest House** (Tel: 253091; Tariff: Rs 450-1,550) is a family-run place and some of their rooms are later additions to an older residence. There are good views and clean rooms but some of the rooms are not very well ventilated.

Narayan Niwas Palace (Tel: 251901-04; Tariff: Rs 3,500-5,500) in Malka Prol, near Jain Bhawan, is a 19th-century ancestral property converted and restored into a luxurious heritage hotel. It is within walking distance of most of the major sights in the citadel. A meal at their rooftop restaurant is among the most special you can have, with views of the golden city and the sand dunes beyond.

Others

Fort Rajwada (Tel: 253233; Tariff: Rs 4,100-12,000) is a lavish place with ornate architecture and interiors, situated about 3 km from the Jaisalmer Fort. The yellow sandstone **Hotel Himmatgarh Palace** (Tel: 252002-04; Tariff: Rs 2,500-3,500), located on the Ramgarh Road opposite Denasar Ground, has very interesting cottages shaped like the *burj* (tower) of a fort. Inside, the rooms are spacious and well

Priceless buys: Patwon-ki-Haveli has a shop that stocks textiles

SANJAY SHARMA

FORT RAJWADA
JAISALMER

Looking over the fortress of Jaisalmer lies a six acre legacy of royal interiors and gardens called Fort Rajwada. Original balconies with intricate carvings and jalis as old as 450 years adorn the walls of the grand lobby of Fort Rajwada, and are a true example of heritage preserved.

Complimented by some of the finest conveniences of 21st century, the princely home has an interior decor, created by the genius of renowned opera set designer Ms. Stephanie Engein. In the midst of the Thar Desert this grand fort like hotel consisting of 87 rooms and 4 royal suites welcomes you with commitment and attention to detail. Relive your life as the Rajwada Thakurs, majestic, royal and elegant.

Phone: 91-2992-253233, 253533, 254608/09, Fax: 91-2992-253733
E-mail: sales@rajwadafort.com Website: www.fortrajwada.com
Email sales@fortrajwada.com gmo@rajwadafort.com

appointed, and there's a charming star-shaped pool. **Gorbandh Palace** (Tel: 253801; Tariff: Rs 5,000-7,000) is 2 km west of the fort and is a big modern hotel. **Rang Mahal** (Tel: 250907-09; Tariff: Rs 3,000-3,500) on Sam Road offers a royal welcome, a restaurant, pool, folk dance and music and round-the-clock room service. **Mahadev Palace** (Tel: 254991-93; Tariff: Rs 2,500-3,500), located near the station, arranges folk dances and camel safaris. The hotel has a beautiful pool designed in the style of a *baoli*.

Jaisalmer also has a decent budget option in **Dhola Maru** (Tel: 252863; Tariff: Rs 2,500-3,250) on Jethwai Road, near the station. **Hotel Jaisal Palace** (Tel: 252717; Tariff: Rs 500-1,000), at Gandhi

→ **GETTING THERE**

Air Nearest airport: Jodhpur (280 km/ 5 hrs). Taxis charge about Rs 800 approx
TIP Do remember that rates fluctuate during the high season
Rail Jaisalmer Station, well-connected to Delhi by the Delhi-Jaisalmer Express (19 hrs), which starts from Old Delhi Railway Station. Mumbai offers conn-ections up to Jodhpur via Ahmedabad (Surya Mail). From Jodhpur, there's the Jodhpur-Jaisalmer Express (8 hrs)
Road Jaisalmer is at the far western end of India, tucked into the hip of Rajasthan. Though it is just a few degrees off the same latitude as Jaipur, you have to arch up to Bikaner or way down to Jodhpur to get here from the state capital. So road journeys to this desert town tend to be long. Only travellers coming in from the north should use the Bikaner route. Luxury buses connect Jaisalmer to Jodhpur, Bikaner and Jaipur

Chowk in Talaria Pada, is one of the older hotels in Jaisalmer. Its sister concern **Hotel Moonlight** (Tel: 250267; Tariff: Rs 1,050-1,250) at Hanuman Circle, near the post office, is architecturally much more appealing. Many of the large, spacious rooms here have chhatri-style windows facing the streets.

For more hotels and details, see Jaisalmer Accommodation Listings on pages 469-471

WHERE TO EAT

It's best not to expect too much in terms of excellent food even though there are quite a few options to choose from. For some reason, the fort is replete with 'Italian' restaurants and many have the same menu. Inside the fort the food is almost entirely vegetarian. **Little Italy** on the First Fort Gate has a unique location as it occupies a part of the fort gate and is ornately decorated. They serve salads, pasta and brochettes. **Ristorabte Italiano La Purezza** is a rooftop place on the fort ramparts and is best visited for the beer and views. They serve pizzas and pastas. The **8th July Restaurant** sits right above the Dussehra Chowk and is a good place to sit and watch the world go by. They serve a variety of passable Indian and other dishes.

Trio, near the Mandir Palace outside the fort, is the best restaurant outside of the big hotels. It provides excellent, if slightly pricey, Indian and Western food. **Natraj Restaurant**, next to Salim Singh Haveli, is reasonably priced, but the ser-vice is terribly slow. If you want luxury rather than a meal with a view, try the restaurant in the **Rang Mahal Hotel**, where you can get traditional Rajasthani dishes like lal maas, safed maas and ker-sangri, which are well-spiced without depending excessively on chillies. Equally luxurious are cocktails at **Paatu**, the bar at Fort Rajwada, to be followed by a pool-side barbecue. For multicuisine fare, head to the **Desert Boys Dhani** eatery within

Time stops at the sand dunes of Khuri

the Khadi Bhawan complex outside the fort. If you go ambling in the bazaars you will find Jaisalmer's local favourites. Chilli pakoras, which are not very hot, are made of long green chillies stuffed with tangy mashed potatoes. Ghottu laddoos are made of gram flour, and the flour is mixed with huge wooden ladles, and watching these made is as much fun as eating them. Try these at **Dhanraj Bhatia Sweets** in Bhatia Market. If bhang agrees with you (don't have too much in any case) you can have bhang-laced lassis, cookies and cakes from the **Bhang Shop** at Gopa Chowk.

AROUND JAISALMER

Ideally, about three days should be kept aside to see places around Jaisalmer. While Bada Bagh, Lodhurva, Amar Sagar, Mool Sagar and Kuldhara can be covered in half a day if you do not spend too much time over them, Sam and Khuri need more time. Barmer should be done as a full-day trip, and you can halt en route at the Akal Wood Fossil Park. Taxis

are the best way to travel. They are easily available at a rate of Rs 5 per km, Rs 450 for a half-day (60 km) trip, and Rs 850 (130 km) for a full-day trip. A return taxi to Barmer would cost about Rs 2,000.

Bada Bagh (6 km N)
The cenotaphs of the Bhatti rulers are at Bada Bagh. The cenotaphs come in two varieties, pyramidal and domed, with the latter being a little more impressive. There's an array of windmills close by, creating a peculiar contrast.
◆**Entry fee** Indians Rs 20, foreigners Rs 50
Timings Open 24 hrs

West from Bada Bagh is **Amar Sagar**, with a 19th-century Jain shrine whose architecture is a fascinating mix of temple and haveli. Ten kilometres west of Amar Sagar is **Lodhurva**, the former capital of the Bhatti Rajputs, destroyed by Muslim invaders in the 11th century. Lodhurva's main attraction is a **Jain temple** dedicated to the Tirthankara Parsvanath. The most impressive thing about the temple is the gateway, best viewed from the temple steps. There's also a huge sculpture of a *kalpavriksha* (the wishing tree) encased in a wire cage.

Mool Sagar (9 km W)
The small royal pleasure-garden fronting a lake is en route to Sam. The lake's usually dry, but the garden's being carefully restored. Entry was, however, restricted at the time of writing as Maharaja Gaj Singh was planning to introduce a tented camp here. Another 9 km west of Mool Sagar lies **Kuldhara**, a village complex abandoned by the Brahmins who lived there centuries ago, following a dispute with the king. You will be asked to pay Rs 10 as a Kuldhara Conservation fee and Rs 50 for getting your vehicle near the complex. The charges are apparently being used for restoration.

Akal Wood Fossil Park (18 km SE)
This is as ancient as Jaisalmer gets. At the park, you can see fossilised remains of

The **Ultra** Edition 12.9
SAMSUNG SGH D-900

① Sand Dunes ② Patwaon ki Haveli ③ Gadsisar Lake

④ Rajmahal ⑤ Haveli

imagine doing more with less.
The Ultra Life.

Imagine always being in two places at once, doing two things at once. No office. No boundaries. No restrictions. With Samsung's new Ultra Edition it's not that hard to imagine. www.samsung.com

Features: 3 Mega Pixel Camera with Auto-Focus • MP3 Player • Intelligent Display • Large 262K QVGA TFT Screen • Direct TV Out

Free accessories: *Bluetooth*™ Headset • *256 MB T Flash Memory Card* • *TV Out Cable* • *Battery Charger* • *Travel Adapter* • *Car Adapter* • *Straight Headset* • *Battery (2 Nos.)* • *Data Kit*

Leo Burnett D SMSCHLJI-00013H

The **Ultra** Edition 12.9
SAMSUNG SGH D-900

tree trunks, some of them as old as 180 million years here.

◆**Location** On the road to Barmer **Entry fee** Indians Rs 5, foreigners Rs 10 **Timings** 8 am-1 pm, 2-5 pm, open daily

Sam (42 km W)

On the road that leads to the Pakistan border, on the edge of the Desert National Park (*also see page 307*), are glorious white mounds of clean dry sand. Here you will find for yourself the picture-postcard image of the desert: camels silhouetted against a setting sun, surrounded by glistening sand. Hordes of tourists descend on the sand dunes in the evening pursued by camel drivers, but this does not in any way reduce the charms of the place. However, don't hope for a 'lone-ranger-in-the desert' experience.

During the high season (Oct-Feb), many travel companies pitch their tents here. They offer packages that include transport from Jaisalmer in the late afternoon, dinner, entertainment and night-stay, breakfast next morning and transportation back to Jaisalmer for around Rs 3,000. It's a good idea to ask around in Jaisalmer to get a good deal. Camel drivers will charge Rs 50 onwards for camel rides. Besides this, you can ride for days with only a camel driver for company and the most basic provisions. The best option for reasonably hardy travellers is a two-day **camel safari** with one night spent under the immense canopy of the desert sky. When you start on the safari, the camel driver will walk alongside the animal, guiding it when the reins in your hand don't do the job — which is often. If you tug too hard, your camel will grunt in protest. Riding on a camel for the first time strains your thighs, but that's relatively easy to cope with. The tough part is bouncing up and down in the saddle when the beast starts running, usually at the driver's prodding! **Ganesh Travels** (Tel: 02992-250138, 09414319891), near the city palace inside the fort, run by camel drivers, and **Sahara Travels** (Tel:

252609), owned by 'Mr Desert' and located outside the fort near Akhayprol, are the most popular travel agencies and offer two-day jaunts for prices starting at Rs 800 per person. The RTDC Tourist Reception Centre (*see Fast Facts on page 240*) can help you find a good agent for a safari to match your pocket.

For stay options in Sam, see Where to Stay in Desert NP on page 314 and Accommodation Listings on page 462

Khuri (40 km S)

The small village of Khuri is another option to experience the beauty of sand dunes. It's largely peaceful even though it's also a popular place with tourists. The dunes here seem a bit higher than in Sam, and also a bit more vegetated providing many solitary-tree-on-the-dune photo frames. There are many guest houses here, which are basic thatched mud huts; these are comfortable but do not expect luxury. Some offer shared bathrooms while others have private bathrooms. Facilities keep getting upgraded, so check before deciding the guest house you stay in. Some guest houses also offer packages that include camel rides and dinner with a traditional dance around a bonfire.

For stay options in Khuri, see Where to Stay in Desert NP on page 314 and Accommodation Listings on page 462

Barmer (153 km S)

Known for its woodcarvings, embroidery and other handicrafts, Barmer is a quiet village. The town's Station Road is where you can pick up crafts; Sadar Bazaar is where embroidered items are sold. From Barmer, it's possible to make a few excursions. The **Kiradu temples**, 35 km from Barmer, are constructed in the Solanki style of architecture but are in a damaged state. Amongst this group of five, the **Someshvara Temple** is relatively more intact. **Nakoda**, 125 km from Barmer, is famous as a centre for Jain pilgrimage. ■

Wildlife

Where birds of different feathers flock together, where the tiger burns bright, where life is governed by the skies and the wind

SOMETIMES, I WONDER WHY I PAY ROAD TAX. I HARDLY USE THEM.

NARAIN KARTHIKEYAN AND HIS LIFE ON JK TYRE.

— Pioneers in Steel Radials ▪ Technology perf

www.jktyre.com

When Narain Karthikeyan takes the driver's seat, he doesn't like anyone else to dictate terms. **He simply likes to stay in control.** Ask him how he manages to tame the road so effortlessly, and he won't hesitate in telling you: "JK Tyre".

JK TYRE

TOTAL CONTROL

ted at HASETRI-Asia's leading R&D Centre

Graphic by ANIS KHAN

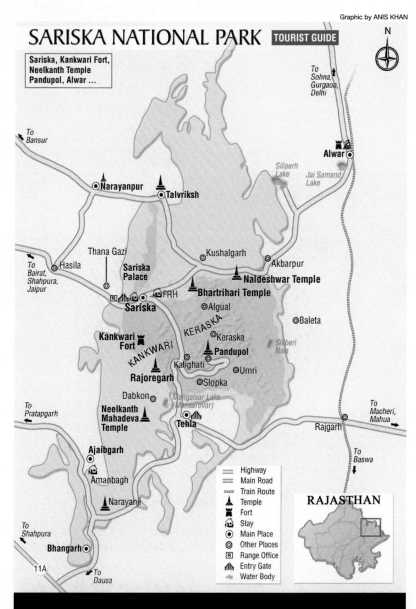

SARISKA NATIONAL PARK TOURIST GUIDE

Sariska, Kankwari Fort,
Neelkanth Temple
Pandupol, Alwar ...

N

To Sohna, Gurgaon, Delhi

To Bansur

Alwar

Siliserh Lake

Jai Samand Lake

Narayanpur

Talvriksh

Thana Gazi

To Bairat, Shahpura, Jaipur

Hasila

Kushalgarh

Akbarpur

Sariska Palace

Naldeshwar Temple

FRH

Bhartrihari Temple

Sariska

Algual

Baleta

KERASKA

Kankwari Fort

Keraska

Siliberi Nala

KANKWARI

Pandupol

Kalighati

Rajoregarh

Umri

Dabkon

Slopka

Mangalsar Lake (Mansarovar)

To Pratapgarh

Neelkanth Mahadeva Temple

Tehla

To Macheri, Mahua

Rajgarh

Ajaibgarh

To Baswa

Amanbagh

Narayanji

To Shahpura

Bhangarh

11A

To Dausa

	Highway
	Main Road
	Train Route
▲	Temple
	Fort
	Stay
⊙	Main Place
◎	Other Places
R	Range Office
⚶	Entry Gate
	Water Body

RAJASTHAN

RECLAIM YOUR Life. Safari

JAGDEEP RAJPUT

Finding their way home: Cheetal make a leap of faith

SARISKA NATIONAL PARK
THE ARAVALLI RETREAT

District Alwar **Region** Mewat
Location In the Aravalli Hills, 35 km from Alwar in north-east Rajasthan
Distances 108 km NE of Jaipur, 236 km SW of Delhi
Journey time *By road* 1 hr from Alwar, 2 hrs from Jaipur, 4 hrs from Delhi
Route from Jaipur NH8 to Shahpura via Chandwaji; state road to Sariska via Thana Gazi
Route from Delhi NH8 to Shahpura; rest as above (*see route guide on page 62*)

■ BY HIMRAJ DANG

Throughout the past century, Sariska was known for guaranteeing tiger sightings. In fact, it was thanks to its impressive tiger population that Sariska was afforded protection by the erstwhile Alwar state; these grounds were once the hunting preserve of the royals, who had goats tied to poles to attract tigers. Such tales were consigned to the past when conservation became the buzzword and Sariska was made a Project Tiger reserve. Ironically, today Sariska has come to represent much that is wrong with India's efforts to protect forests, a telling comment on the extent of neglect the reserve suffered. In early 2004, the nation awoke in disbelief to the news that rampant poaching had wiped out the entire tiger population in Sariska.

It is this unfortunate story that forms the backdrop to any visit to Sariska. Yet, its history, and its surviving wildlife, continues to be captivating in its own right. There's the sight of the first hill burnished with the rust leaves of *dhok*, or *Anogeissus pendula*, as one crosses over the hill into Kalighati Valley. There's the leaf-fringed avenue of *dhok* that greets the visitor at the old gate leading to Kankwari and the sound of the rill, overgrown on both sides with old trees of *guler* and *pilkhan*. There's the sight of an explosion of the blue-breasted quail, of the pools of the Siliberi Nala flowing down from Pandupol and of eagles watching for prey from evergreen trees. There's the enduring memory of the six porcupines we saw in the course of an early evening drive near Umri, and that of the reclusive Indian pitta at Taraunda late one evening. All these and more are what I treasure from my numerous visits to Sariska.

My last tiger sighting at Sariska, one hot April, was in the grassland beyond Kalighati. In the late morning, as we were returning past Bhaironghati from a drive to Pandupol, we stopped near the salt lick short of Kalighati Chauki. We saw langurs climb up the trees on the hillside. They soon started calling. Then it was the turn of a sambar concealed in the grass. Clearly, a predator was moving nearby. We drove down the crest of the hill so that we wouldn't miss the animal. Before long, we could hear the loud and impressive calls of a tiger, and then we saw him cross the road behind us, indifferent to our presence. It was late in the morning, and he was in a hurry to get to the water hole behind the hill. We were grateful for the unimpeded, glorious view.

That there is no chance of such a sighting anymore is disheartening. Despite this, I would urge visitors to enjoy the other sights and sounds of the Aravalli forest. I know I will return for more.

→ FAST FACTS

When to go The park is open throughout the year for pilgrims to Pandupol. But in the rains, it's closed for wildlife visits. The most comfortable time to go is November to March, though the best wildlife viewing is during the warmer months

Go there for The memory of tigers (alas!), but there's enough wildlife, and history, to interest tourists

Wildlife/ Forest Dept office
● Field Director, Project Tiger
Sariska Tiger Reserve, Sariska PO
Alwar District
Tel: 0144-2841333

Tourist office
● Rajasthan Tourism ❶
Tourist Reception Centre
Opp Railway Station, Alwar
Tel 0144-2347348

STD code 0144

ABOUT SARISKA

Sariska was established as a Tiger Reserve in 1978. Before independence, the reserve was part of the erstwhile Alwar state. In 1955, hunting, shooting, trapping or capturing wild animals was made unlawful. In 1958, the reserve was upgraded to a sanctuary, and later, areas contiguous to the sanctuary were also included.

There are 16 revenue villages and associated *guadas* or cattle camps inside its boundaries. The semi-arid Aravalli forest suffers from enormous human and livestock pressures. The poachers who killed all of Sariska tigers (according to a Project Tiger report, there were 24 tigers in the reserve in 1997) are said to have received help from the villagers, who felt the tigers were a threat to their livestock. The huge number of pilgrims visiting the temples in Sariska has also adversely affected the forest. Afforded protection, these semi-arid forests can support high ungulate (camels, horses, hippos and

The ruins of ninth century Shiva temples at Rajoregarh

other herbivorous mammals) populations and exhibit rich predator diversity.

ORIENTATION

Visitors enter through the **Sariska Gate**, to the centre of Sariska (north-west of the reserve's core area) after paying their fee at the office nearby. The standard itinerary includes taking the main road to **Pandupol**, which passes by Karnakabas Lake, Brahmnath, Kalighati Chauki and Bhaironghati. Those with more time and varied interests can turn off at **Kalighati** to visit **Kankwari Fort** (to the west of the core area) or **Neelkanth Mahadeva** via the exit at **Tehla Gate** (to the south).

Almost all of Sariska is hilly terrain dominated by the **Aravallis**, which run north-south along the park. The Aravalli Mountains at Sariska are topped by two vast plateaus, each 5 km wide: **Kankwari** and **Keraska**. The park itself varies in altitude from 270-360m.

There are three large lakes within the boundary of the park: **Mangalsar** (also known as Mansarovar), **Siliserh** (to the north-east), and **Somasagar**. To counter the scarcity of water sources at Sariska, the administration makes arrangements

for providing water to animals in summer and this has helped in sustaining high numbers of ungulate populations.

◆**Entry fee** Indians Rs 25, foreigners Rs 200 **Vehicle fee** Rs 125 **Video camera** Rs 200 **Park timings** 6-10 am, 3-6 pm **Guides** Enquire with your hotel

TIP Diesel vehicles are allowed to ply only on the tarmac routes in the jungle

THINGS TO SEE AND DO

Sariska gives you a chance to see langur and nilgai and birds such as the white-breasted kingfisher. The locality also has places of historic interest.

Aravalli drive

There are no government vehicles, so you'll need to rent a jeep (Gypsy) from a lodge or a travel agency if you don't have your own. Gypsies are typically available near the park office, at Tiger's Den and Sariska Palace (*see Where to Stay on page 257*). A Gypsy could cost around Rs 800 for 3 hrs. You can also hire vehicles from Alwar, and a day-trip from Alwar would cost Rs 1,000-1,500. As it's difficult to rent jeeps, rent your vehicle for the duration of your trip.

Monkeying around for water

Just past the Tehla Road, a 15-km long track branches off to the north to Kankwari. Passing through dense forest on the top of the Aravalli Ridge, this track leads to a point that gives an impressive view of **Kankwari**, a medieval fort standing on an isolated hill in the middle of a plateau. Kankwari has a *bund* with perennial water. It's believed that Aurangzeb imprisoned his brother Dara Shikoh here. Kankwari is worth a visit, with the splendid view it offers of the hilltop plateau. It also makes you realise that the Aravalli forest is retreating fast before the twin threats of grazing and encroachment. This plateau is also accessible by the metalled road running from Tehla and Neelkanth via Rajoregarh, an ancient settlement known for its 9th century Shiva temples.

Pandupol

Pandupol, to the south-east of RTDC's Tiger Den, is a lovely spot that has mythological significance: it's believed that the Pandavas spent part of their *Agyatvas* (exile) at this location. Pandupol is also the name of a 35-foot waterfall arising from near the crest of the Aravalli Ridge, where there's a deep fissure, said to have been created by Bhima. Near the waterfall, which is accessible by road, there is an old Hanuman temple. The road leading to the temple is full of langurs, peafowl, spurfowl, and ubiquitous tree pies. There is a large mela at Pandupol every year, attracting pilgrims from afar. Every Tuesday, pilgrims are permitted to drive through the park to visit this shrine. If you are interested only in seeing wildlife, it's best to avoid Tuesdays.

The temple trail

Neelkanth Mahadeva, a temple town near Tehla, houses the ruins of over 300 Hindu and Jain temples constructed between the 8th and 12th centuries. The carvings here resemble those of the Chandelas of Khajuraho, and probably date to that time (9th-10th centuries).

The **Naldeshwar shrine** nearby attracts several pilgrims. Located just off the main way to Sariska from Alwar, Naldeshwar is an old Mahadev temple. The approach to the temple, surrounded by dense forests, can be accessed only by a 2-km long walk from the main road.

Talvriksh, on the northern edge of the park, is another centre for pilgrimage in Rajasthan. It has a temple with hot and cold sources of water, and is close to the

---

FAUNA

- 28 mammal species, including leopard, wild boar, cheetal, sambar, nilgai, mongoose, porcupine, hyena, wild cats, civets and langur
- 355 bird species (a third of which are seasonal visitors between October and April) including the white-backed vulture, Pallas' fishing eagle, red and painted spurfowl, common sandgrouse, Indian pitta and the great horned owl

park on the Narayaniji Road. The **Bhartrihari Temple**, to the south of Kushalgarh in the sanctuary area, is famous all over Rajasthan for its fairs. The temple is located at the edge of the forest, though the throng of pilgrims undermine the pristine setting. It is named after the ancient ruler and sage, Bhartrihari of Ujjain, who renounced his kingdom to devote his time to prayer.

WHERE TO STAY

Sariska has only a few options, but it's still a better base than Alwar for those wishing to take an early morning ride through the park. (*For stay options in Alwar, see Alwar Where to Stay on pages 87-88 & 92*

Heritage

The **Sariska Palace** (Tel: 2841323/ 25; Tariff: Rs 5,777) is set in a large lawn. The construction of Sariska Palace (Connaught House) was started by Maharaja Mangal Singh, but was completed in 1894 by Maharaja Jai Singh of Alwar. During the latter's reign, arrangements were made for water harvesting in the forest. Wells were dug, streams dammed, and water channelised to suitable locations. Some of the shikar trophies and photographs of old shikars from this time can still be seen at the Sariska Palace. The hotel tariff includes all meals. Summer rates, starting March, are lower.

The hotel charges Rs 1,000 per jeep for a 3-hr safari in the sanctuary. You have to pay entry and video camera fee separately at the park entrance. It also offers a package (Rs 1,500 per person) that includes a picnic lunch and trips to the Neelkanth Temple and Kankwari Fort.

Others

The main accommodation at Sariska is RTDC's **Tiger's Den** (Tel: 0144-2841342, 2841344; Tariff: Rs 1,300-2,400), situated near the park's main gate. It's a convenient place to book jungle safaris. Its facilities include a restaurant, laundry

PUSHP JAIN

The medieval Kankwari Fort

and TV. Off-season rates are lower. Away from the park, at Village Thana Ghazi (7 km before Sariska), is the high-end **Hotel Amanbagh** (Tel: 01465-223333-34; Tariff: Rs 25,000-50,000) of Aman Resorts fame. It has a spa, arranges safaris and also offers indoor games besides much else. **Hotel Tiger Heaven** (Tel: 224815-17; Tariff: Rs 1,250-3,100), a WelcomHeritage property, is a more affordable option.

For more details, see Sariska Accommodation Listings on pages 488-489

WHERE TO EAT

Sariska offers little choice for those looking for a great meal. The fare at the hotels is plain. Those who want to sample authentic Rajasthani fare should drive down to Alwar to eat at the **Prem Pavitra Bhojanalaya** near the old bus stand. En route from Alwar to Sariska, you can find **milk cake** at roadside villages.

GIREESH GV

The impressive Sariska Palace, where shikar trophies and photos can be seen

AROUND SARISKA

Narayanpur Village (25 km NW)
To the west of Talvriksh, the village is home to **Narayani Mata Temple**. There is a small *kund* at the base of the marble slab near the temple.

Bhangarh-Ajaibgarh-Pratapgarh
Located within the bounds of Sariska are the remnants of three ancient settlements. Madho Singh, son of the Mughal general Man Singh of Amber, built

TOTAL CONTROL

→ GETTING THERE

Rail Nearest railhead: Alwar (35 km/ 1 hr). Connected to Delhi by Jaipur-Delhi Express. Taxi costs Rs 1,000 approx
Road Take NH8 to Shahpura via Kot Putli and Patwa; 1 km short of Shahpura, turn left before the toll gate for the 40-km run to Sariska. Bairat and Thana Gazi villages are your landmarks

Bhangarh Fort in the southern tip of the sanctuary, in 1613. It was abandoned soon after being built. From here, if you head north-west to Ajaibgarh, you will find a beautiful old fort situated along the forest edge between Bhangarh and Pratapgarh. The grandson of Madho Singh, Ajab Singh Rajawat, built the Ajaibgarh Fort. In good condition even today, it offers a lovely view of the eponymous walled town, the not-in-use Shri Raghunathji Temple, and old chhatris, all nearby. Heading westwards, you will reach Pratapgarh, a hill fort that dominates the region. Sariska Palace Hotel's package for all three costs about Rs 1,500 per person. The circuit can be done from within the sanctuary or from the main road outside it. Tiger Den charges Rs 2,500 for a full day's tour inclusive of lunch.

Jaisamand Bund (25 km N of Sariska, 8 km S of Alwar)
Close to Alwar, this large *bund* and its impounded waters are home to a multitude of water birds. The *bund* comprises a set of traditional chhatris, which make for a pleasant picnic destination. Maharaj Jai Singh constructed it in 1910. A taxi from Alwar costs about Rs 400 return. ◼

⳸ SARISKA ⳹
THE FORT VIEW CAMPS

A majestic location overlooking Shivalik foot hills and having Thanagazi fort as backdrop. An exclusive canvas accommodation combining warmth & comfort in the lap of nature.

Come and experience a life with a pace of its own, interact with nature, rediscover yourself and get nostalgic. Cultural evenings, folklores & dances would do the entertainment, and campfires are the way to mingle around.

For appointment with 'Nature', do call us...

Jitendra (9810726252), Email: jitendra@consortiumhotels.org
Rama (9818107473), Email: rama@theconsortiumhotels.com

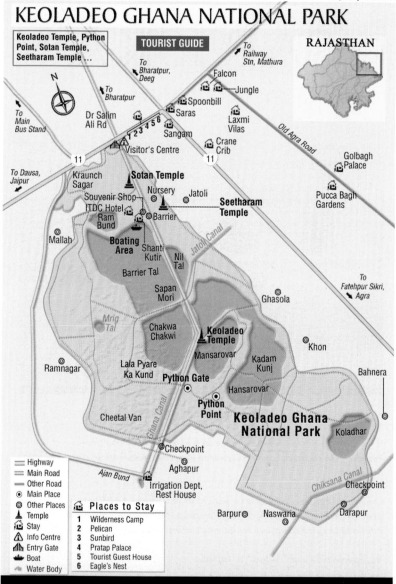

KEOLADEO GHANA NATIONAL PARK

Keoladeo Temple, Python Point, Sotan Temple, Seetharam Temple ...

TOURIST GUIDE

RAJASTHAN

To Railway Stn, Mathura

To Bharatpur, Deeg

To Bharatpur

Falcon

Jungle

Spoonbill

To Main Bus Stand

Dr Salim Ali Rd

Saras

Laxmi Vilas

Old Agra Road

Sangam

Crane Crib

Visitor's Centre

11   11

Golbagh Palace

To Dausa, Jaipur

Kraunch Sagar

Sotan Temple

Nursery   Jatoli

Seetharam Temple

Pucca Bagh Gardens

Souvenir Shop

ITDC Hotel

Ram Bund

Barrier

Jatoli Canal

Mallah

Boating Area

Shanti Kutir

Nil Tal

Barrier Tal

Sapan Mori

To Fatehpur Sikri, Agra

Mrig Tal

Ghasola

Chakwa Chakwi

Keoladeo Temple

Mansarovar

Kadam Kunj

Khon

Ramnagar

Lala Pyare Ka Kund

Python Gate

Hansarovar

Bahnera

Cheetal Van

Python Point

Keoladeo Ghana National Park

Ghana Canal

Koladhar

Checkpoint

Aghapur

Ajan Bund

Irrigation Dept, Rest House

Chiksana Canal

Checkpoint

Barpur   Naswaria

Darapur

═══ Highway
═══ Main Road
─── Other Road
◉ Main Place
◎ Other Places
⚓ Temple
🏠 Stay
⚠ Info Centre
⛩ Entry Gate
⚓ Boat
~ Water Body

🏠 **Places to Stay**

1 Wilderness Camp
2 Pelican
3 Sunbird
4 Pratap Palace
5 Tourist Guest House
6 Eagle's Nest

RECLAIM YOUR Life. Safari

Painted storks return to their homes at sunset at Keoladeo

KEOLADEO GHANA NATIONAL PARK

FLY AWAY HOME

District Bharatpur **Region** Mewat
Location In north-eastern Rajasthan, near the Uttar Pradesh border, within the golden triangle of Agra, Delhi and Jaipur, 38 km south-west of Mathura
Distances 38 km SW of Mathura, 64 km W of Agra, 185 km NE of Jaipur, 196 km SE of Delhi
Journey time *By road* 1 hr from Agra, 4 hrs from Jaipur, 4 hrs from Delhi
Route from Delhi NH2 to Mathura via Faridabad, Palwal, Hodal and Kosi Kalan; state road from Mathura to Bharatpur **Route from Jaipur** NH11 to Bharatpur via Balaji, Dausa Town and Mahua (*see route guide on page 62*)

■ BY GILLIAN WRIGHT

Keoladeo Ghana National Park is a gem in India's ecological crown despite being one of the smallest parks in the country. Declared a World Heritage Site in 1985, it has had to withstand devastating drought in recent years, which has caused lasting damage to its unique wetlands. It was like witnessing a miracle, therefore, to visit Keoladeo in the monsoon of 2005, when the area was seeing the wettest July in the past 20 years. Farmers had lost their crops and bridges had been washed away. But there was a glimmer of hope — perhaps Bharatpur could now regain its former glory.

Washed out or not, the monsoon is one of the times when maximum avian activity occurs in the park, a fact that

H SATISH

→ **FAST FACTS**

When to go The park is open all year. August to October are the peak months for breeding and October to late February for wintering migrants. However, whatever time of the year you go, there will always be interesting birds to see **Best sightings** November to March, when migratory birds flock to Bharatpur **Go there for** Birds **Wildlife/ Forest Dept office** ● Keoladeo Ghana NP Near Shanti Kunj (park area) Tel: 05644-222777 **STD code** 05644

often gets lost in all the attention that winter and the accompanying migratory birds receive. During the rains, some of India's most spectacular birds deck themselves out in their finest plumage, get together to court their mates and nest in huge colonies in the trees lining the paths of the sanctuary.

July marks the beginning of this season. I stood with water stretching as far as the eye could see on a muddy bank with one of the trained naturalists in the park and one of its cycle rickshaw-puller-cum-guides beside me. Above, long red legs extended to negotiate a tricky landing. An open-billed stork descended into a babul tree, only to be pecked by his neighbour; it fell out and flapped off to a nearby perch. As with humans, location is the primary thing when birds build houses — no self-respecting open-bill allows another to trespass on its prime few square feet of treetop.

There was a cracking sound across the road behind me and I turned to see another open-bill stork wrestling with a small branch it fancied as building material. Almost in slow motion, it grasped the branch in its heavy bill and wrenched it away before jumping into the air and solemnly flying to its nest. A pair of open-bills were arranging twigs together around the bowl of their new home, another pair were mating — a brief affair, and some, having got all the preliminaries over, were sitting on their eggs, eyes half-shut, looking profoundly content. I was sure that they would not look so happy once the chicks were born. They grow at a fast pace and demand food in loud voices. The colony of storks then dons a busy look, with parents flying in and out so fast that an Air Traffic Controller would have a heart attack.

The colony I saw was a multi-cultural avian metropolis. Amidst the black and white storks were snow-white large and intermediate egrets sporting delicate breeding plumes. Grey herons held their black head plumes erect as they interacted with their neighbours. Black-headed ibis on the uppermost branches raised their wings to reveal crimson armpits, and darters or snakebirds, each dark glossy feather outlined in pale shimmering colour, gulped fish down their long, elastic throats. Small cormorants, neat and dapper with streaks of white behind the ears, filled the empty branches.

The cacophony of painted storks with their yellow bills and pink and white behinds has to be heard to be believed. They are a hungry lot too. Studies estimate that the 2,000 painted storks in the colonies require 4 to 6 tonnes of food daily and, in the 30 to 40 days they breed, they consume 1,200 tonnes! And we are talking only about one species here.

Hopping along the road in front of us as we strolled towards the Keoladeo Temple in the centre of the park were some of the permanent residents, easy to dismiss as little brown jobs, or LBJs as they are called by birdwatchers. These were, in fact, the creatures responsible for Salim Ali, India's greatest ever ornithologist, first taking an interest in birds. As a child he had been given an air gun and had amused himself shooting some of the plentiful birds around him. One day he

shot what he assumed was a house sparrow. Then he noticed it had a yellow throat, was fascinated, and began to investigate what it could be. His observation of birds started here. However, these creatures are no longer called yellow-throated sparrows. They are now chestnut-shouldered petronias.

While rains bring their own glory, winter remains a splendid time to visit the park. When Keoladeo Ghana was made a World Heritage Site, its guests in the cold season included the Siberian cranes, with bills and faces as red as if dipped in blood, white plumage that was simply peerless and outstretched wingtips pitch black like a dark night. Sadly, the world proved too unfriendly a place for the flock that came to Bharatpur, which were driven away by consecutive years of drought. Siberian cranes are now on the verge of extinction because of habitat loss and hunting. The last documented sighting of Siberian cranes in India was during the winter of 2002. It would require a real miracle to bring these cranes back now,

A scene at the Deeg Fort (below); **Tourists enjoy a quiet walk** (top left)

GIREESH GV

H SATISH

Slow and steady wins the race: Turtles find their way on a tree stump

and one can only hope for one. The comforting factor is that although the vegetarian Siberian cranes are gone, there is still the chance of seeing delicate demoiselle cranes, common cranes, or our very own resident crane, the sarus, which now needs our protection so that in future years it will not meet the fate of its Siberian relative.

Despite the fact that the Keoladeo Ghana NP is surrounded by human habitation, it has maintained an atmosphere of the wild. On my most recent trip, I sat in the back of the rickshaw as the sun set. We stopped at regular intervals to see, not just the birds but the mammals. Mature nilgai, cheetal and sambar were grazing close to the road and from far off came the eerie wailing of countless jackals. A watersnake held its head aloft above the water, a turtle basked

on a branch, a monitor lizard — some excited young boys identified it as a crocodile — ambled across the road. A cormorant held out its wings to dry, silhouetted against the sky, and I felt the satisfaction and happiness that even a short visit to this park could bring.

ABOUT KEOLADEO GHANA NP

Keoladeo is actually a name of Lord Shiva and is the form in which he is worshipped at the small temple in the heart of the park, near a canteen that serves a welcome cup of hot tea. Ghana refers to the thick tree cover the area once had. This sanctuary is known by the name of the adjoining town of Bharatpur, which is also the name of the king who created the park in the late 19th century. He recognised the potential of this area of scrub woodland that formed a slight depression, a hollow where water could be collected to attract water birds until it dried up. By diverting water from an irrigation canal, building small dams and constructing a system of dykes and

KID TRIVIA One of the most famous residents of the Keoladeo NP are the big rock pythons that inhabit the 'Python Points' in the park and bask on rocks in winter

shooting butts, he succeeded in converting it into one of the richest wetland habitats in the world. Conservation was, however, a by-product of his main purpose — shikar. He entertained all the big guns of his time, including viceroys and princes (*see A shot in time on page 268*). Their bags are recorded on a sandstone inscription near the Keoladeo Temple.

In 1956, the hunting preserve was declared a sanctuary but the VIP shoots here continued until 1964; the royal family maintained their hunting rights until 1972. It is perhaps ironic that bird numbers seem to have decreased after hunting stopped. Other problems have hit the park, one of them being the decline in the number of migratory birds in their summer homes, drought, and buffalo and cattle straying into the park from nearby villages. Pesticide contamination in the water bodies is a cause for concern too. The huge number of tourists visiting the park has also contributed to the park's decline: many leave behind litter and plastic, adversely affecting the water quality in the swamps.

The shallow, freshwater lakes, which make up about a third of the park's 29 sq km, form just one part of this amazingly biodiverse area of the Gangetic Plain, where some 350 species of birds find refuge and some 120 species nest. Keoladeo Ghana also boasts an amazing variety of flora representing 181 genera.

ORIENTATION

The park is open from 6 am to 6 pm — excuse the pun, but it pays to be an early bird, as morning is a great time for birdwatching. The **main gate**, where entrance tickets are purchased, stands at one end of the tarred road that runs from the north to the eastern side of the park, through the largest area of wetland and along the line of the **Ghana Canal**. Either at the gate or the **ITDC Hotel**, you can

A tourist looks for birds

GIREESH GV

JAGDEEP RAJPUT

The Indian spoonbill strikes a pose

park and take a cycle rickshaw, some of whose pullers have been trained by the Bombay Natural History Society (BNHS) to recognise birdlife. At the main gate, you also have the option of hiring bicycles, or one of the tongas. You can go on walking trips too. Motor vehicles are not allowed inside the park. Binoculars are essential if you want to make the most of your visit, even though many of the birds are large and close to the road. Within the park, there are a number of well-maintained paths, which means you can make your visit as long or as diverse as you wish. The natural place to take a break is the **Keoladeo Temple** compound.

◆**Park entry fee** Indians Rs 25, foreigners Rs 200 **Guide fee** Rs 75 per hr **Video cameras** Rs 200 **Bicycle hire** Rs 30 per day **Cycle rickshaw** Rs 50-75 per hr

TIP Field guides and maps of the park are sold at the Tourist Reception Centre,

located at the place where you show your ticket to enter the park

THINGS TO SEE AND DO

The best way to see diverse species of birds and animals is to make trips at different times of the day. Wake up with the birds in the early mornings, see water birds in daylight and catch night birds such as owls after sunset. Birdwatching may mean long waits, so factor it in, and meanwhile, turn the pages of a good birdwatchers' guide such as Salim Ali's *Birds of Bharatpur — a Checklist*.

Birdwatching
There are many routes inside the park, but opt for the ones near the swamps for the maximum number of sightings. One route is to head to **Sapan Mori**, and then to turn right towards the **Keoladeo Temple**. If you head left (and it's best to do this in the afternoons), then you will reach the sunning ground of pythons. The **Mansarovar** and **Hansarovar marshes** and the swamps and lakes of Bharatpur form one of the most important heronries in the world.

If you are visiting it in winter, the sheer variety of birds will surprise you. With just a little application, you can see as many as 100 species of birds in 24 hrs. The wildfowl visitor I love the most is the

FAUNA

● 350 species of birds including openbill stork, egrets, grey herons, blackheaded ibis, cormorants, pipits, larks, waterfowl, ground-thrushes, rubythroats, sleeping nightjars, eagles, harriers, owls and migratory birds such as bar-headed geese, pied-crested cuckoo, garganey, Baikal teal, little grebe, northern shoveller, greylag goose
● Nilgai, sambar, spotted deer, jackal, wild boar, otter, hare, civet, porcupine, blackbuck and mongoose

Chandra Mahal Haveli

Chandra Mahal Haveli, *a heritage property*, reflects the magnificence of the Mughal architecture of that era having a courtyard with marble fountain and numerous balconies. The Haveli has 4 Terrace Rooms and 19 well-appointed Double Rooms with attached bath, running hot and cold water.

Built amidst a village untouched by modern life, the Haveli affords you a feel of the real India. Whether a camel ride, a village excursion or a cultural show – you can experience it all being at Chandra Mahal Haveli.

For reservation, kindly contact:
Chandra Mahal Haveli, Peharsar, Jaipur- Agra Road
Nadbai, Bharatpur – 321001, Rajasthan; Tel: +91-05643-264336

Gurgaon Central Reservation office:
C-892/B/B, Sushant Lok 1, M.G. Road, Gurgaon – 122002,
Haryana (India); Tel: +91-0124-2385184, Fax: +91-0124-4044657

www.chandramahalhaveli.com

A shot in time

The 29 sq km of the shallow jheels and marshes, scrub jungle, mature green woods and golden grass of the Keoladeo National Park play host to over 400 species of birds — about as many as in the entire UK! This World Heritage Site, however, did not start off as a sanctuary. It was conceived and designed by the Maharaja of Bharatpur for the single purpose of shooting birds. In fact, on one particular shoot held during the days of the Raj in the honour of the viceroy Lord Linlithgow, more than 4,000 feathered friends were shot down. The shooting records are etched on sandstone plaques near the Keoladeo Temple, in case you want to check yesteryear's 'score'.

In 1971, the guns fell silent thanks to the efforts of India's most famous ornithologist,

LOKESH ABROL

the late Salim Ali. Today the World Heritage Site is famous for its heronries and, of course, the sadly dwindling numbers of the great white (Siberian) cranes that visit during the balmy winters, along with thousands of other migrants — waterfowl, waders, passerines and raptors.

Ranjit Lal

blue-winged teal or garganey, but the most thrilling sight is a water surface full of birds, and the way they take off in swirling flocks when there is a slight disturbance. Waders from the godwit family, with over-sized bills, and tiny stints abound in shallow muddy areas. In low bushes and woodlands, you can test your spotting ability by looking out for orange-headed ground-thrushes, ruby-throats and sleeping nightjars. You'll spot eagles and harriers feeding on the wild-fowl, sometimes stealing each other's prey in mid-air.

Winter in the park is one of the best times to see the various birds of prey together and compare their size and plumage as, unlike leopards, they do change their spots. The largest and most impressive is the imperial eagle, while the smaller marsh harrier has an entertaining habit of gliding low over assembled ducks and putting them to flight. However, my favourites among the dozens of species of flesh-eaters are owls. If you're very quiet, and go with one of the trained guides, you might just be able to see the large

owls before they see you and, with a whoosh, set off for a further perch. The most visible ones are the magnificent dusky horned variety.

The scale of the journeys migratory birds undertake is breathtaking. Silvery-winged bar-headed geese return to remote parts of Ladakh to breed. Other species come from Central Asia and Siberia, and the pied-crested cuckoo, the monsoon bird, comes from East Africa with the monsoon winds. We still have a lot to learn about how they navigate.

The sanctuary is home to one of the rarest birds in the world, the sociable plover, which breeds on open steppes in Central Asia where its natural habitat has been destroyed to such an extent that it is on the brink of extinction. It's difficult to spot these plovers as they are much more modest in size and colour than the Siberian crane, and despite their name, are profoundly unsociable. They are not wetland birds and retreat, well camou-flaged, to the dry areas of the sanctuary where human disturbance is least, but if you are quiet and patient and don't try to

KADAMB KUNJ RESORT
B H A R A T P U R

For details please contact:
KADAMB KUNJ RESORT, Fatehpur Sikri Road , N H - 11 , Rajasthan.
Phone: 05644 - 220122
Delhi Sales: **The Consortium**, 011 - 41600150, 41601355
Email: info@theconsortiumhotels.com

PARVIN SINGH

Tourists enjoy a boat ride at the park

approach them closely, you can be rewarded with one of the hardest-sought sights in the world.

In drought years, Keoloadeo Ghana becomes a haven for the desert species of birds but a large area of the park is always dry land, home to pipits and larks. These are generally overlooked as the star attractions are waterfowl and waders. Among mammals, apart from the deer and antelope, you also have a chance of seeing otter, porcupine, wild boar, and fishing cats as well as palm civets.

Boat ride

At the Tourist Reception Centre, you can book boat rides if there's water in the lakes and it's boating season. Boats are available for hire from the boarding point near the ITDC Hotel (*see alongside for details*). These give you a peaceful way to get close to the birdlife and the otters.

♦**Boat ride** Rs 100 per person, per hr

Most places to stay are along Dr Salim Ali Road, which runs from Bharatpur Town to the entrance of the park.

Heritage

The pride of place is the **Laxmi Vilas Palace** (Tel: 05644-223523; Tariff: Rs 3,000-4,350), a fine heritage property run by members of the Bharatpur royal family. It's set amidst 50 acres in Kakaji-ki-Kothi on the old Agra-Jaipur Road. The palace is small and ornate, with a large courtyard. The staff is friendly, and the hotel offers jeep safaris and return transfers to the park and railway station.

The Bagh Resort (Tel: 228333, Reservations Tel: 011-27570446; Mobile: 09811200094; Tariff: Rs 3,500-4,500), located on the old Agra-Achnera Road, has a restaurant, bar and coffee shop; they arrange safaris. A popular option, despite being 23 km from the park, is **Hotel Chandra Mahal Haveli** (Tel: 05643-264336; Tariff: Rs 1,650-2,600), in Peharsar on Jaipur-Agra Road. The property has a restaurant.

Others

The ITDC **Bharatpur Forest Lodge** (Tel: 222760; Tariff: Rs 1,400-1,800) in the park has the best location, but is run down and needs renovation, although the staff is helpful. In-house facilities include a multi-cuisine restaurant and bar; they also help you hire forest guides. The hotel garden plays host to a number of birds. Its restaurant and bar is open to walk-ins.

The **Birder's Inn** (Tel: 227346; Mobile: 09414023340; Tariff: Rs 1,000-1,265) is near the sanctuary entrance. **Kadamb Kunj Resort** (Tel: 220122, 225067; Tariff: Rs 1,950-2,450) on Fatehpur Sikri Road, 3 km from the park, has a restaurant, a pool and organises cultural events in the evenings. **Hotel Sunbird** (Tel: 225701; Tariff: Rs 700-1,050), close to the park, offers clean rooms. RTDC's **Hotel Saras** (Tel: 223700; Tariff: Rs 350-900) has 28

rooms. At **Shanti Kutir**, 2 km inside the park, close to the Tourist Reception Centre, the Wildlife Warden's Office complex (Tel: 222777; Tariff: Rs 600) houses a **Forest Rest House** with five rooms for forest officials. Rooms are rented to tourists at the warden's discretion. The tariff includes meals.

For more hotels and details, see Keoladeo Ghana Accommodation Listings on pages 477-479

For more hotels and details, see Keoladeo Ghana Accommodation Listings on pages 477-479

WHERE TO EAT

Salim Ali Road is the best bet, as most of the restaurants in the hotels are open to non-residents. **Hotel Sunbird** has a good breakfast while **Nightingale** has tandoori options. ITDC is still the best place to head to for lunch — the food is not bad. The menu features Rajasthani, Mughlai and Continental fare.

AROUND KEOLADEO GHANA

Bharatpur Fort (3 km)
The central citadel of Bharatpur was built by the Jat ruler Suraj Mal in 1730. He was a ruler strong enough to take on Delhi and sack the Red Fort in Delhi. You can still see the mud walls of the fort he built here, with the occasional cannon in place on the bastions, surrounded by a moat. In the late 18th century, the fort was in the hands of the Raja of Bharatpur. The British stormed the fort in 1804, after which the bastions and walls were dismantled, which explains why these are in such a dilapidated state today. It is possible to visit the palaces, built as pleasure palaces on the island within the moat. There is a government museum in the fort, which has displays of arts and culture of the region, including inscriptions and sculptures dating to 2nd century CE.
◆**Timings** 10 am-4.30 pm; closed on Fridays and gazetted holidays

Deeg (36 km N)
Deeg was the second capital of Suraj Mal's kingdom in the 18th century. It was here that the king defeated a combined Mughal and Maratha army of 80,000 odd men. The fort here has massive walls that are nearly 30m high. Suraj Mal's palace, Gopal Bhavan and the gardens in the Mughal-Rajput style make the trip worthwhile. There is also an old Hanuman Mandir with a secret passage to the king's bedroom. Apparently, this was constructed so that the king could visit the temple before dressing up in his royal finery. There's an ancient water fountain system that works even now, but it's turned on only on special occasions.
◆**Palace entry fee** Rs 10 ∎

→ GETTING THERE

Air Nearest airport: Agra (64 km/ 1¹/₂ hrs). Taxi to Bharatpur Rs 1,500 approx
Rail Nearest railhead: Bharatpur Junction (4¹/₂ km/ 20 mins). A very convenient option if you are visiting from Delhi. The Frontier Mail and the Kota Janshatabdi are both good options from Delhi, especially in the monsoon when the Delhi-Agra Expressway can be in a bad shape. There are also rails links with Sawai Madhopur. Hotels will arrange to pick you up from the station; there are cycle-rickshaws at the station too. But beware of the local scooter rickshaws, which have zero suspension and are powered by noisy and polluting engines meant to be used for generators
Road Bharatpur is 186 km from Delhi on the Agra Highway via Mathura. It makes a natural extension to a trip to Agra and Fatehpur Sikri; there is also a good link road from Jaipur. Tour buses operate from these places to the park

RANTHAMBHORE NATIONAL PARK

IN AN ANTIQUE LAND

District Sawai Madhopur **Region**
Dhundhar
Location Ranthambhore is at the junction
of the Aravallis and the Vindhyas in the
south-eastern quarter of Rajasthan
Distances 15 km NE of Sawai Madhopur,
201 km SE of Jaipur, 457 km SW of Delhi
Journey time *By road* 8 hrs from Delhi,
$3^1/_2$ hrs from Jaipur, $^1/_2$ hr from
Sawai Madhopur
Route from Jaipur NH12 to Tonk via
Sanganer; state highway to Ranthambhore
via Uniara and Sawai Madhopur **Alter-
native route** NH11 to Dausa via Kanota;
state highway to Sawai Madhopur via
Lalsot **Route from Delhi** NH8 to Jaipur via
Dharuhera, Chandwaji and Amer; rest as
above (*see route guide on page 108*)

■ BY TARA SAHGAL

Antique rock crumbled under my
feet and bounced down the side of
Ranthambhore Fort to the sprawling dusty forest below. I walked into the
skeleton of a house broken into by the
roots of trees, and standing on a carpet of
grass, I looked out of a thousand-year-old
window. Really, Ranthambhore is magic.
The place is full of romance and intrigue
— tenth century ruins stand smothered
by roots, herons share lakes with holy
men and a million myths about Raja
Hamir and the glory days of the 'impreg-
nable' fort. The fort's fall, along with that
of the one at Chittaurgarh, is what is
unanimously credited with finally breaking the spirit of the legendarily resilient
Rajputs and the establishing of an undisputed Mughal empire in India. Locals still
visit a Ganesh temple here, as did their
ancestors. And like them, they must walk
through tiger forests to do so. I came here
on a longer pilgrimage.

Photographs by GIREESH GV

Leaving the madness, gloom and grime of Mumbai late in the evening, I arrived to the bright light, cold air and red brick of Sawai Madhopur Station the next morning. If all journeys are metaphors, this is an especially poetic one, the scene changing from Maharashtra's city slums at dusk to the benign open scrub and field of the Desert State at dawn. And as I moved out of mobile coverage area, I found myself shedding all urban angst, counting Indian rollers, blue jays, tree pies… and actually noticing three distinct shades of blue in the sky. Once at Sawai Madhopur, the short drive from the station to the park was equally un-creasing; apart from the busy market place at the start of the journey, it was all camel carts, heaps of guavas and that dazzling mirror work on the outfits of Rajasthani women sauntering by.

Once through the main gate, a canopy of trees provided leaf-dappled shade from the harsh desert sun and the air was at least a few degrees cooler. My open-top gypsy added whiplash wind to the experience, and at the ticket counter I was greeted by Ranthambhore's omniscient presence — a tree full of langurs. Scavenging on the left-overs from picnics, screeching for attention, somersaulting, showing-off, swinging from the vines, they landed with unnerving thuds on the tops of tourist buses, and in one case, even urinated to the disgusted delight of an open Canter full of school kids.

Ranthambhore is a popular holiday destination and in winter (the best season weather-wise) it is often chock-full of noisy tourists on an obsessive search for tigers, driving through the reserve talking noisily while waiting for an audience with The King. It is hard not to hope for tigers when you're in Ranthambhore, but there is something tainted about tracking them with walkie-talkies and harassing them with a constant barrage of gawkers. The trick to getting the most out of the

Graphic by ANIS KHAN

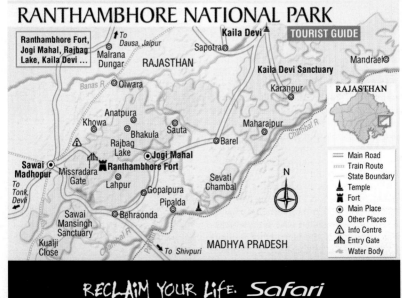

The painted walls of a house in a village near Ranthambhore

park is to distance yourself from the madding crowd and being satisfied just breathing tiger air. Suddenly then, everything about it becomes thrilling.

On my first day in the park, while watching cormorants dry their wings on a bare tree in the middle of Rajbag Lake, someone in the next vehicle swore they spotted a tiger peeping through the window of a ruin far on the other bank. Everything looked like a tiger when you were desperate to see one, I said, but around the bonfire at Ranthambhore Bagh (a lovely tented accommodation) that night, a photographer confirmed reports of a young tigress hiding her cubs there. The next day, back at the same spot, while a sambar stag foraged in the water, I watched with stripes on my brain. About a quarter of an hour later, for no apparent reason, the sambar stumbled out of the lake, antlers festooned with vegetation, and dashed off. The

mother tigress had begun her languid amble towards me long before I had noticed her. Making her way across a sliver of land in the water — literally a catwalk across the lake — she stopped a stone's throw from my parked vehicle, crouched down and began to drink. Close enough to see her whiskers quiver, the slapping of her flat pink tongue against the water was the only sound I heard for what seemed to be an eternity. Finally, she crossed the path in front of us and walked ahead, letting us follow her in our vehicle for at least 20 minutes down the road before disappearing into the foliage (leading us as far away from her cubs as she could). Tigers, my guide informed me, like walking on the un-tarred roads because these were soft on the paws. The road therefore made an unlikely place for incredible tiger sightings.

Slightly peeved with the six vehicles blocking the path in front of me the first

→ FAST FACTS

When to go The park is closed from July to September during the monsoons, and open from October to June. November to February is the best time. March, April and May are oppressively hot with the desert 'loo' — hot and dry winds that blow during the day — baking everything in its wake. On the up side, the dry summer months allow for some fantastic animal sightings through the bare vegetation

Go there for Tigers

Wildlife/ Forest Dept office
● Chief Conservator of Forests/ DFO Ranthambhore Tiger Reserve
Sawai Madhopur
Tel: 07462-220223

Tourist offices
● RTDC Tourist Information Centre ●
Hotel Vinayak, Sawai Madhopur
Tel: 221333
● Tourist Information Counter ●
Railway Station, Sawai Madhopur
Tel: 220808

Note All safaris into the park now are booked through the RTDC office at Hotel Vinayak. Book well in advance so as to avoid disappointment

STD code 07462

JAGDEEP RAJPUT

thing the next morning, I was forced to join the fray waiting for their promised tiger (a tip-off from a forest guard.). There was no way any wild animal was going to make an appearance with those many people around, I thought. I was wrong. Not only did the tiger make an appearance, he was on a hunt. Slipping silently into the tall grass just off the road, he crouched, waiting. There was no prey as far as anyone could see, but soon there was a wretched yelp, which was immediately thwarted. A few minutes later, out came the gorgeous predator awkwardly dragging along a cheetal (almost as big as himself) by the neck. There, right on the road, in full view of a few dozen awe-struck Homo sapiens, he sat down and half-hidden by the grass, began to feast.

Not all trips to tiger reserves are this rich. Even forest guards don't see a kill often — tigers are only successful once in 20 tries — and at the end, it's down to luck. Leaving the park a few days later, as I drove past Rajbag, past Jogi Mahal, past Gomukh, past the soaring cliff-face where eagles nest and leopards hide, past the last racket-tailed drongo and *dhok* tree, I turned around just in time to see the ancient fort looming like a vision borne of opiate excess. Leaving Ranthambhore is like leaving a vital organ behind. You have to come back for your heart.

ABOUT RANTHAMBHORE

Once the hunting grounds of the maharajas of Jaipur, and later the British, this area, spread over an expanse of 392.5 sq km, was declared the Sawai Madhopur Wildlife Sanctuary in 1955. In 1973, it was declared the Ranthambhore Tiger Reserve under Project Tiger. An area of 274.5 sq km from within the Tiger Reserve was notified the Ranthambhore National Park in 1980. With the launch of Project Tiger in 1973, the National Park began to be protected in earnest, and as the forest returned to health, aquifers in the area began to replenish, much to the

Forest vignettes: Deer lock horns (above); **Owls peep out of a tree** (bottom left)

benefit of surrounding villages. Even now, the difference in the ecology inside the park and out is staggering. The surrounding areas of Kaila Devi Sanctuary (674 sq km), the Sawai Mansingh Sanctuary (127 sq km) and the Kualji Close (7.58 sq km) were consolidated and added to the National Park in 1992, bringing the spread of the reserve to 1,174 sq km.

The current official count of tigers at Ranthambhore stands at 26. Yet tiger sightings are common as the animals have become fearless of humans. Even then, the tigers continue to fight a battle for survival as the problems of poaching and villagers grazing cattle in the park remain unresolved.

ORIENTATION

The **entry point** to the park falls on the **Ranthambhore Road**, about 10 km from the railway station at **Sawai Madhopur**. It passes through the **Missradara Gate** to the **Ranthambhore Fort**, which lies within the precincts of the park. The Ganesh Temple is within the fort, and the **Jogi Mahal** lies in the vicinity of the fort. The **Ranthambhore School of Art**,

where you can do a spot of shopping, is on the road that leads up to the park.

◆**Park entry fee** Indians Rs 25, foreigners Rs 200 **Vehicle fee** Gypsy/ Canter Rs 125 **Safari fee** Rs 1,350 **Guide fee** Rs 150 **Cameras** Still free, video Rs 200 **Park timings** 6.30-10 am, 1.30-5.30 pm (subject to change from time to time, so get an update when booking your trip)

THINGS TO SEE AND DO

Despite its popularity with tourists, there is something primal about being in and around Ranthambhore. While truckloads of visitors may seem annoying at first, it is, if you can yourself see it that way, what makes the park not an artefact, but rather a real place where ancient ruins, wild nature and contemporary village life make layers of history almost tangible. Don't miss the fort and wake up early to witness the forest at sunrise.

Tiger safaris
The highlight of your Ranthambhore experience is the $3^1/_2$-hr jungle jeep safari for tiger spotting. As no private vehicles are permitted into the park, book a tourist

FATEH SINGH RATHORE The tiger guru

Anyone who has been to Ranthambhore has heard something about the eccentricity, devotion and passion of Fateh Singh Rathore. He joined the Indian Forest Service in 1960 and spent many years as Field Director of Ranthambhore. He was one of the few hand-picked by Kailash Sankhala, the then director of Project Tiger, to be a part of the first Project Tiger team. Widely acknowledged as a 'tiger guru', his knowledge of the striped cat is legendary; he has an uncanny ability to predict where the tigers are and many have witnessed him 'talk' to them!

Needless to say, his single-minded drive towards protecting the park and its wildlife was not always popular. Once, infuriated at the bar on grazing cattle within the protected area, villagers ambushed Fateh Singh's vehicle, beat him terribly, and left him, bloody and unconscious, for dead. He was soon up and defending the reserve again of course, amidst plenty more threats to his life. In 1983, Fateh Singh was awarded the International Valour Award for bravery in the field.

Today, Fateh Singh has retired from the service, but not from his tigers. One of the best known warriors in the global effort to save the Indian tiger, he has been awarded the status of honorary warden of the park. He lives just about 10 minutes from the park's

gates at 'Maa Farms' where among other things he has started a school for local kids — not surprisingly with an emphasis on wildlife conservation. If during your visit you see a solitary figure standing upright in an open vehicle in khaki jodhpurs, aviator sunglasses, cowboy hat over a balding pate, twisting the ends of a huge Rajput moustache to a fine point, consider yourself lucky. You would have just spotted Ranthambhore's most exotic resident!

jeep safari well in advance (at least 60 days before), especially in the high season, with the RTDC office at Hotel Vinayak at Ranthambhore or through your travel agent. Bookings were earlier handled by the Forest Department but are now done by RTDC. Details such as these tend to change, so get an update when booking your tour. Two jungle safaris a day, which follow certain tourist trails (seven routes for Gypsys, five for Canters), are on offer currently. Jeep movement is monitored to ensure less interference to animal movement in the park.

Only 15 Gypsys and 20 Canters are allowed, per trip, on the routes.
♦**Safari fee** Rs 1,350 **Vehicle entry fee** Rs 125 **Guide fee** Rs 150 **Safari timings** 6.30-10 am, 1.30-5.30 pm **Bookings** RTDC Hotel Vinayak, Tel: 07462-221333, Ranthambhore Road, or through your travel agent

Ranthambhore Fort
This ancient citadel is situated almost exactly at the meeting point of the Vindhya and the Aravalli hill ranges. The fort, after which the National Park was

named, is thought to have been built in 944 CE. It was occupied by Raja Hamir for many years until the siege by Allauddin Khalji's army in 1301 forced the Rajput king to surrender. It can be tiring to walk up to the ramparts but the view of the park and its three lakes from the top is worth the effort. Locals believe that the mortar used in constructing the fort was mixed with the blood of brave warriors!

Ganesh Temple

Dedicated to Lord Ganesh, this temple is located inside the Ranthambhore Fort, within the park precincts. The Ganesh Chaturthi celebrations, wherein devotees join in the singing of devotional songs, draw large crowds. Entry to the fort itself is free to allow devotees easy access to the temple. They arrive on Wednesdays and on the *chauth* of every month.

TOTAL CONTROL

→ GETTING THERE

Rail Nearest railhead: Sawai Madhopur (15 km/ 1/2 hr) has good connections from the Delhi-Mumbai line. Most resorts will arrange pick-up/ drop from the railway station. Or hire a taxi (Rs 250) or an auto (Rs 60) to your hotel
Road The drive from Jaipur via Tonk and Sawai Madhopur to Ranthambhore is 10 km longer than an alternative route via Kanota, Dausa and Lalsot, which is a bad road. Since private vehicles aren't allowed in the park it might be better to go by train instead to Sawai Madhopur
TIP If you fly to Jaipur, you can hire a car and drive a couple of hours to Ranthambhore, but a direct train from Delhi or Mumbai is advisable. It's a lot cheaper and also less complicated and a much more interesting journey

Jogi Mahal

Located at the foot of the fort, Jogi Mahal is also home to the country's second largest **banyan tree**. The Forest Rest House (FRH) at Jogi Mahal offers stunning views of the Padam Talao, which is awash with water lilies. Tourists are not permitted to stay in this rest house.

Ranthambhore School of Art

Situated on the road that leads up to the park, the school is definitely worth a visit. Its wonderful wildlife paintings, many of which feature the tiger in its natural habitat, are created by local artists. The school contributes towards tiger conservation — a great reason to buy here rather than the slightly cheaper paintings you may find elsewhere around the park. Incidentally, close to the railway station is the **market place** from where you can buy traditional Rajasthani bangles made of glass and lac and knick knacks for the house.

WHERE TO STAY AND EAT

There are a plethora of hotels to choose from to fit every budget, most of them scattered on Ranthambhore Road, the long stretch that leads up to the park. Rates vary on and off-season, and it is best to book in advance. Many of the hotels include meals in the hotel package.

Run by the Oberoi chain, **Vanya Vilas** (Tel: 07462-223999; Tariff: Rs 26,750) on Ranthambhore Road is super lavish with prices to match. Coming back to Vanya Vilas from a drive through the forest is always a bit of a shock. Liveried staff welcomes you back with cold, scented towels and the temperature in the luxury tents is always right regardless of the desert outside. Get a massage or work out at the gym, and though you many flinch at their well-tended rolling greens and swimming pool in the midst of drought, the food here is heavenly. The **Aman-i-Khas Resort** (Tel: 252052, 252223; Tariff: Rs 34,000 approx), close to the park, has a spa and arranges safaris.

RANTHAMBHORE REGENCY
R A N T H A M B H O R E

For details please contact:
Ranthambhore Regency, Ranthanbhore Road, Sawai Madhopur, Rajasthan.
Phone: 07462 - 223456
Delhi Sales: **The Consortium**, 011 - 41600150, 41601355
Email: info@theconsortiumhotels.com

The Ranthambhore National Park spreads out under a clear blue sky

The **Sawai Madhopur Lodge** (Tel: 220541; Tariff: Rs 9,500-13,900) is run by the Taj Group of Hotels and has a restaurant, bar, swimming pool and travel desk. It also arranges safaris. **Sher Bagh** (Tel: 252119-20; Tariff: Rs 11,475-12,375) is 3 km from the gate in Village Sherpur. Run by polo player Jaisal Singh, this fancy establishment offers 5-star comforts.

Tiger Den Resort (Delhi Tel: 011-27570446, 09811200094; Tariff: Rs 4,000) is 2 km from the park on the Ranthambhore Road and has a restaurant, a pool

and a souvenir shop. It offers jeep safaris and nature walks. The price includes stay and meals. **Tiger Moon** (Telefax: 252042; Tariff: Rs 1,850-4,425), on Ranthambhore Road, has 32 cottages, a dining hall, wildlife library and a swimming pool.

The RTDC-run **Castle Jhoomar Baori** (Tel: 220495; Tariff: Rs 1,775-4,250), formerly a hunting lodge of the Maharaja of Jaipur, is located on top of a hill with a great view of the park. There are 12 rooms here with a multi-cuisine restaurant. Rates include two meals and taxes. **Ranthambhore Bagh** (Tel: 224251; Tariff: Rs 1,400-3,575) has a casual atmosphere with great food. Rooms with basic facilities are available, but the tented camp (each with electricity and attached bath) is highly recommended.

RTDC's **Hotel Vinayak** (Tel: 221333; Tariff: Rs 800-1,700), on Ranthambhore Road, near Vanya Vilas, has 14 rooms with attached baths. It also has a dining hall, arranges safaris and houses the RTDC Tourist Information Centre, functional in the tourist season.

For more hotels and details, see Ranthambhore Accommodation Listings on pages 487-488 ∎

FAUNA

● Mammals such as leopards, tigers, sloth bears, hyenas, jackals, sambar, cheetal, nilgai, langurs and wild boar
● Reptiles such as marsh crocodiles or muggers, turtles, monitor lizards, pythons and cobras
● Birds such as the paradise fly catcher, crested serpent eagle, pheasant tailed jacana, painted stork, Bonelli's eagle, great Indian horned owl, grey partridge, white-necked stork, spoonbill, king vulture, ring dove, coucal and golden-backed woodpecker

NAHARGARH RANTHAMBHORE

Located on the outskirts of the Ranthambhore National Park, Nahargarh is the ideal retreat after a hectic day in the jungle. Nahargarh is built like a traditional Rajput hunting Palace. With gardens, traditionally decorated rooms and a traditional chowk based design Nahargarh recreates the magical atmosphere of a royal hunting camp.

Rooms on the first floor have individual courtyards while the suites on the second floor have private terraces with stunning views of the National Park. All rooms are air conditioned and have attached bathrooms with running hot and cold water.

VISIT NAHARGARH WHEN YOU ARE IN RANTHAMBHORE

NAHARGARH
Village Khilchipur, Ranthambhore Road,District Sawai Madhopur,
Rajasthan, INDIA. Tel:+91-7462-252281/2/3.
www.nahargarhranthambore.com

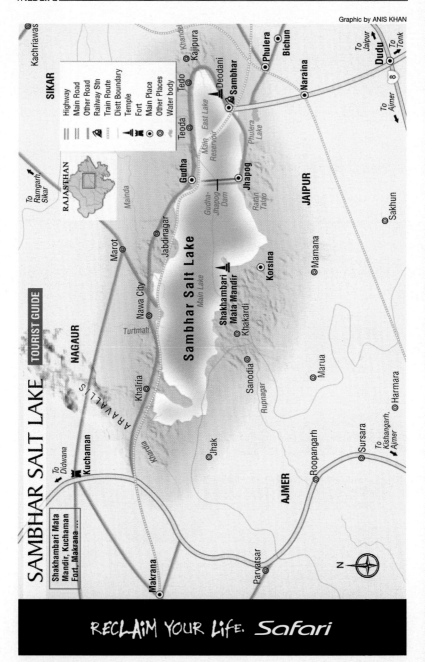

Graphic by ANIS KHAN

SAMBHAR SALT LAKE **TOURIST GUIDE**

Shakhambari Mata
Mandir, Kuchaman
Fort, Makrana .....

RECLAiM YOUR Life. *Safari*

Flight of fancy: Lesser flamingoes make a spectacular landing

SAMBHAR SALT LAKE

THE FLAMINGO DANCE

Districts Jaipur, Nagaur and Ajmer **Region** Dhundhar
Location Spread over an area of 190 sq km of the Sambhar Basin, with the Aravalli Hills skirting its north-western edge, the Sambhar Salt Lake lies at the junction of Jaipur, Ajmer and Nagaur districts
Distances 64 km SE of Kuchaman, 104 km W of Jaipur, 360 km SW of Delhi
Journey time By road $1^1/_2$ hrs from Kuchaman, 2 hrs from Jaipur, $6^1/_2$ hrs from Delhi
Route from Jaipur NH8 to Dudu via Bagru; state highway to Sambhar Salt Lake via Naraina (*see route guide on page 178*)

■ BY AKSHAI JAIN

It's five in the evening, and the searing heat of the day is giving way to a gentle breeze that murmurs over the dry bed of the Sambhar Salt Lake. There's little sign of water. Instead, a vast glacial sea of compacted mud spreads out for miles. The fading light frames the craggy Aravalli Hills that skirt the north-western edge of the lake. Small towns and villages that lie scattered along the distant shores of the lake flicker hesitantly to life. Strains of music drift by on the breeze. And then a vast flock of flamingoes flies by, the pink of their feathers catching the last rays of the sun. I stand gaping till their petulant honking is swallowed by the silence, and their lanky awkward shapes disappear over an embankment. I've been in Sambhar for three days, and I've seen many hundreds of flamingoes, but the odd and unlikely inhabitants of this muted landscape still come as a surprise.

The Sambhar Salt Lake is not so much a lake as a vast depression. A body of sand, saline and isolated pockets of water that straddles three districts (Nagaur, Jaipur and Ajmer) of Rajasthan, it spreads over an area of 190 sq km. For most of the year the lake remains dry. After the monsoons, a thin film of water covers the western reservoir, attracting thousands of local migrants like the greater and lesser flamingoes, painted storks and spot-billed pelicans. Huge colonies of birds congregate in the centre of the reservoir, shimmering in the haze that plays on the waters. By October the water recedes to a few small pools (the rest has either evaporated or been diverted to the salt pans in the eastern reservoir), leaving behind treacherously wet sand that is ideal terrain for waders such as pied avocets, Kentish plovers and black-winged stilts. It's also when the flamingoes breed, building their circular, 1-foot high nests in areas near Ratan Talao. During the day, a couple of hundred birds can be found feeding in the *kyars* (salt pans) and the freshwater ponds near the Jhapog Dam and in pools near Sambhar Town.

Come November, migratory birds start flying in. Shovellers, pochards, common teals and pintails gather in their hundreds in the less saline ponds, weaving between large groups of flamingoes that meander pensively through the waters. November to mid-March is also the best time to come to Sambhar — the cool sunny days allow for many hours of wandering. By this time, substantial areas of the lake would have dried out, making it easier to walk or drive (over certain areas) on its bed, and get closer to the birds. It's also less dusty, and the pockets of babul trees that emerge where the compacted mud of the lake bed gives way to looser desert sand are still green.

I visited Sambhar in late March, the fag end of the season, and I really didn't expect to find much. We took the road that skirts to the right of the Sambhar Lake Railway Station, and arrives a little beyond it at a railway crossing. A small bund there veered off from the tracks, flanking what appeared to be a small pool of water. A raucous group of children played cricket in the sand, and a few groups of men stood gossiping in small town intimacy. I walked for more than a kilometre, and had nearly given up hope

DINESH SHUKLA

Bharat Petroleum

→ **FAST FACTS**

When to go November to March is the best season to visit. Avoid the monsoons **Best sightings** October to February, when you have the most chances of seeing the migratory birds **Go there for** Flamingoes, pochards TIP No permits are required to visit Sambhar, and since it is not a protected area, there are no wildlife/ tourist offices here either **STD code** 01425

SANJOY GHOSH

The lake is a road at Sambhar (above); **A salt pan at the lake** (bottom left)

of spotting anything interesting when I noticed them — hundreds of dots gleaming in the afternoon sun: a flock of at least 400 lesser and greater flamingoes barely 300 ft from me.

It came as a shock — a field of white and pink birds poised on tall dainty legs, wandering cautiously through the stagnant waters in their ballerina tutus. Some preened themselves, others balanced nonchalantly on a single leg, while most stood still in the saline waters, long necks curved back towards their feet so that their broad pink and black bills disappeared under the water. They stood in a spot for a while, sifting the water for spirulina algae that flourishes in these saline waters. Then they took a few steps — a slight wiggle, followed by a little self-satisfied preening, and then a disdainful glance at us, down broken Roman noses, and upturned beaks. "The avian cousin of the camel," I thought to myself. Possibly a little more becoming, but every bit as crotchety as my old aunt Emma, a

duchess in the dirt, muttering 'must we, must we' to herself, grumbling and grunting at my unwanted intrusion.

I woke up early the next morning. Dawn was breaking, and from my perch on the verandah of the Circuit House, I could just about make out the outlines of the lake. A pair of little green bee-eaters flitted from one gnarled babul tree in the courtyard to another. Daulatji, the caretaker, brought me a cup of sweet tea, and as I rubbed the last bits of sleep from my eyes, a long dancing line of pink flamingoes wandered across my imagination. And they kept coming back — as I wandered through the dusty unremarkable lanes of Sambhar Town, past old havelis and kirana shops, and back to the comfort of the delightfully old-worldly circuit house, and as I made my way back to Delhi after three short days in Sambhar.

It starts getting hot in Sambhar towards the end of March. Dust-laden winds start blowing across the desert, the lake dries up and most of the birds leave.

Fantasy ride: Train passengers get a lovely view of lesser flamingoes

For the next three-and-a-half months, the lake retreats into itself — without its colourful inhabitants, the landscape turns a uniform, unmitigated shade of brown, while the still waters in the salt pans evaporate, leaving behind layer upon layer of the finest 'Sambhar' salt on the scorched earth.

ABOUT SAMBHAR

The ephemeral **Sambhar Salt Lake** is the largest lake in India (however, the last time the lake was full was in 1985). It's a shallow wetland with depths varying from 1.6-6.6 ft. Migratory birds such as pochards, waders and flamingoes are found here in large numbers. The lake is not a protected area, but it was designated a Ramsar Site in 1990 and was also identified as one of the sites for conservation action under the Indian Wetland Conservation Programme. The lake is owned by the state, but a large part of it is leased to Sambhar Salts Limited. Salt manufacturing units have been a cause of worry for conservationists, who say that

it has adversely affected the lake's ecosystem. Dams built on the rivers that feed the lake, and poor rainfall, have also resulted in a drop in water levels.

ORIENTATION

The Salt Lake lies at an altitude of 1,181 ft, and gets an average rainfall of 54 cm. In the best of years, the average depth of water in the lake is a few centimetres, with the maximum depth going up to 10 ft. The length of the lake basin is 22.5 km, while its width ranges from 3.2 km to 11.2 km. A 5-km long **stone dam** between the dusty villages of **Jhapog** to the south and **Gudha** to the north divides the lake into two unequal parts. The western part is an undisturbed reservoir that supplies water to the salt pans that dominate the eastern part. The Sambhar Lake in its eastern parts is more industrial area than lake — huge mounds of salt, salt pans and salt refining factories alternate with shrub-scattered patches of sand. There is a metalled road that connects all towns on the banks of the lake.

SANJOY GHOSH

The road from east of Sambhar to the **Shakhambari Mata Mandir** via Jhapog and Pipla ki Dhani is very rough in parts. There is a track that runs from the Shakhambari Mata Mandir to **Kuchaman** via Korsina, Badun and Manglana, but this is a dirt track that should only be travelled on during daylight.

Sambhar, a small dusty city on the south-eastern bank of the lake, is the only sizeable habitation in the area. The flats of the lake extend right up to the town, and you can often find flocks of flamingoes feeding in the rich, stagnant waters near the railway station. A series of roads branch out from the town — two of which skirt the boundaries of the lake while others lead to the salt pans. Salt production is the main occupation in Sambhar — the town has little else to offer. And while there are no professional guides in Sambhar, people (especially taxi drivers) in town will be able to give you the locations of some of the bird colonies.

THINGS TO SEE AND DO

Since Sambhar is not a Wildlife Sanctuary or a National Park, it has almost nothing by way of tourist infrastructure, and there are no marked trails around the lake. There is little else to see in this sleepy town — therefore a trip to Sambhar is essentially a birding trip. The lake is best

Flamingo facts

Flamingoes have been regular visitors to the Sambhar Salt Lake for decades. The lake is known for vast colonies of greater and lesser flamingoes, the former far outnumbering the latter. The birds can be found in most of the saline ponds that are scattered across the bed of the lake. A little known fact is that Sambhar is also a breeding ground for these birds (the Rann of Kutch is the only other known breeding ground in the country). If you're lucky, you might just come across a cluster of their small, foot-high mud nests on the bed of the lake. Sambhar is also probably the only lake you'll ever be able to drive across — and the experience of driving over endless salt flats littered with thousands of flamingo feathers can be quite surreal.

SANJOY GHOSH

Under the noonday sun: Workers at a salt pan at Sambhar Salt Lake

visited between October and February —
the time when most migratory birds can
be found. During the monsoons it is not
possible to drive across the lake, and
therefore, it's extremely difficult to get
close to the birds.

The drive
The best way to see the lake is to drive on
it. It's possible to drive on most parts of
the western reservoir. Two-wheelers
should stick to the well-trodden routes,
four-wheelers can venture off these, but
should proceed with caution as parts of
the lake can have extremely soft mud.

However, driving on the lake can be
confusing, and in case of problems, do
remember that there is little help available. So you might want to hire a jeep
from Sambhar Town for a day to roam
around the area. They are available for
hire at the New Bus Stand, and cost Rs
650 for 6-7 hrs. Sher Mohammed, who
took us around the area, can be contacted
at the local taxi stand.

Birdwatching
If you want to do some serious birding,
you should give yourself at least three to
four days in Sambhar. Given the size of
the lake, and the fact that pockets of
water can be extremely localised and far
apart, it will probably take you one day to
get the necessary information and orient
yourself. The sheer size of the lake can
often make it difficult to get close to the
birds; a good pair of binoculars is, therefore, absolutely essential. If you are going
to be driving around the lake, try to
obtain a detailed map of the lake from
Sambhar Salts Limited.

FAUNA

- Birds including oriental white-backed
vulture, long-billed vulture, painted stork,
lesser flamingo, greater flamingo,
northern shoveller, common pochard,
pied avocet, common teal
- Blue bull, golden jackal, saw-scaled
viper are also seen

Once you're done birding you might want to take a ride on the trolley run by Sambhar Salts Limited. It costs Rs 100 for a few hours, and can take you either to the new *kyars* or the Devyani *kyars*. A visit to the **Shakhambari Mata Mandir**, on the southern banks of the lake, is also worth it. From the hillock behind the mandir, you get a stunning view of mile upon mile of salt flats. The pujari of the Shakhambari Mata Temple here is a good person to talk to about the area — he will not only be able to tell you where bird colonies can be found, but will also be able to give you a history of the area. Alternatively, the manager of Sambhar Salts Limited might be able to provide you with some information.

→ GETTING THERE

Air Nearest airport: Jaipur 118 km/ 2 hrs. Connected by bus and train. Taxi fare to Sambhar is Rs 1,000 approx for a day-trip
Rail Nearest railhead: Sambhar Salt Lake Station. Many trains connect it from Jaipur. You can also take the local to Sambhar which leaves at 5.25 am, reaching around 6.45 am. Return local train to Jaipur leaves at 2.45 pm
TIP It's best to go by road to Sambhar from the Jaipur Sindhi Camp Bus Stand. Catch any one of the express buses heading to Nagaur or Kuchaman — Sambhar is the first main stop. At Sambhar you can take the trolley for local travel
Road From Delhi, take NH8 to Jaipur (256 km). Then take the Jaipur bypass (50 km out of the city) and continue on the same highway en route to Ajmer. At Dudu (77 km from Jaipur), take a right off the highway. There are few petrol pumps beyond this point, so make sure that you tank up before leaving the highway. The route from Dudu to Sambhar is via Naraina (13 km). The road can be bad in stretches but you will rarely encounter particularly bad patches. The total driving time to Sambhar from Delhi is about 6 1/2 hrs

WHERE TO STAY AND EAT

There are limited options in Sambhar and around, so be prepared for basic facilities. For a luxurious stay, head to the Kuchaman Fort. If you want to get to the lake early in the morning (which is when you'll spot most birds), you should definitely stay in Sambhar.

The **Circuit House** (Tel: 01425-224249/ 18; Tariff: Rs 300-700), run by Sambhar Salts Limited, is basic but very comfortable, and has lovely views of the lake. Meals are provided on request. For reservations, contact MS Rawat or BK Taneja of Sambhar Salts Limited. They are also the best people to contact for information on the lake. The only other stay option is the slightly grungy **Apna Hotel** near the New Bus Stand. There are no restaurants worth the name in Sambhar — just a few dhabas near the bus stand.

For more details, see Sambhar Salt Lake Accommodation Listings on page 488

AROUND SAMBHAR

Makrana (90 km NW)
The marble town of Makrana makes for an interesting side trip. Literally everything you get in the shops here is made from the marble that comes from the huge mines (also worth visiting) near the town. It takes about 1 1/2 hrs to drive from Sambhar to Makrana via Nawa, Mithri and Kuchaman. While most marble shops are located immediately outside town (on the Kuchaman-Makrana Road), the main market of the town also has a few (*also see Stories in stone on page 438*). ■

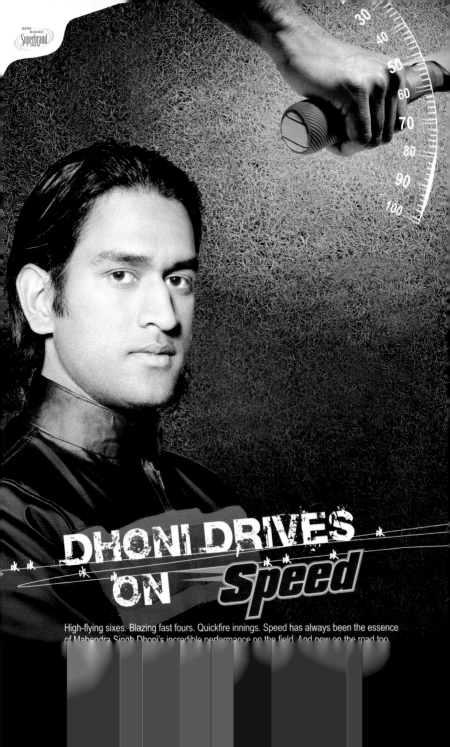

30
40
50
60
70
80
90
100

DHONI DRIVES ON Speed

High-flying sixes. Blazing fast fours. Quickfire innings. Speed has always been the essence of Mahendra Singh Dhoni's incredible performance on the field. And now on the road too.

BY KISHORE SINGH

Kuchaman Fort, set atop a steep hill along what was once an integral Central Asian trade route, was built by the Gurjara Pratihara dynasty as far back as 760 CE. From their strategic position near the Sambhar Salt Lake, the Pratiharas were able to control the salt trade, and did so for 200 years till they were overthrown by the Chauhans. The latter, in turn, were chased away by the Gaurs, later vanquished by the Rathores — who still rule the roost at Kuchaman. You can

Things to see and do
First on your itinerary is the fort itself. There are many sights near and around the fort as well.

Inside the fort
Visit the **Meera Mahal** for its paintings on the life and times of the poet-saint Meerabai, who was of the Rathore clan and married the son of the great Rajput hero of Chittaurgarh, Rana Sangha. Her nephew Ranjit Singh, who ruled Kuchaman, built this mahal in 1832. Ranjit Singh also built a unique temple within the

KUCHAMAN Thy kingdom come

SARVESH

relearn all this history at the fort itself, which is a luxury hotel today.

Kuchaman's ramparts, now no longer formidable, are studded with 32 bastions and 10 gateways, and the fort has a complex web of underground passages, hideouts, dungeons and water storage tanks, many of which are open to visitors. So, when you get bored of the luxury in your room, shake off your stupor and go exploring. Pay attention to the tanks, in particular. The genius who designed them was responsible for ensuring that Kuchaman never suffered the fate of Tughlaqabad and Fatehpur Sikri — magnificent in their time but vanquished by poor water management.

Meera Mahal that contains paintings of Lok Devatas, or the gurus of the masses, including sants Tejaji, Gogaji and Jambhoji, Kabir, Guru Nanak and Khwaja Moinuddin Chishti.

The temples in the fort are very interesting for the antiquity and origin of the idols of the presiding deities. The idol in the **Maa Kaali Mandir** is around 1,200 years old, and was brought to Kuchaman all the way from Karnataka by the Rathores after they won a campaign. The statue in the **Krishna Mandir** is older, around 2,000 years old. The Krishna statue was brought by the Rathores from Ahmedabad in 1741, and the temple was built later to house it.

Move on to the formal chambers of **Sabha Prakash**, with its polished walls that have an inlay of semi-precious stones and gilded paintings, and then to the extravagant court room, called the **Sunheri Burj** (Golden Palace) because of its frescoes of mating birds and animals framed lavishly in gold.

There are two swimming pools in the fort, of which the **Jal Mahal** stands out because of its historic significance and charm. This underground pool, similar to the Turkish hamams, was meant for royal women. The explicit yet tasteful frescoes of bathing women, and of Krishna playing with gopis on the ceiling,

GIREESH GV

The interiors of the Kuchaman Fort (above); **An aerial view of the fort** (left)

reflect on the water. Last on your tour is the **Sheesh Mahal**, where the maharajas played chess using real men as pawns.

Sightseeing far and near

The hotel takes you on a 4- to 5-hr long sightseeing tour of Kuchaman City, which includes visits to temples, havelis and the Old Market area where you see craftsmen at work. You can also go on a camel cart safari, a camelback safari and a horseback safari. The hotel also organises trips to **Sambhar Salt Lake** (64 km;

Rs 1,500 for six people for a half-day excursion without lunch), as well as longer ones to the **Tal Chhapar Blackbuck Sanctuary** (90 km; jeep tour costs Rs 250 per person without lunch).

Shopping

In Kuchaman's bazaar, you will find textiles and the *chura* or set of wedding bangles without which no marriage in Rajasthan is complete. For souvenirs, head to **Meena Bazaar**, the shopping arcade within the fort where artisans used to put up their wares for the royalty to purchase. Shop here for exquisite silver jewellery, lac bangles studded with coloured glass, Rajasthani puppets and mirror-work embroidery and the *bandhani* and *leheriya* fabric.

Where to stay and eat

Kuchaman Fort Hotel (Tel: 01586-220882/4; Mobile: 09313353431; Tariff: Rs 3,000-5,500) is both the destination and the only luxury accommodation here. The fort's **Diwan-i-Khas** serves Indian, Continental and Chinese cuisine. The fort also organises meals if you opt for its safari tours, which include live entertainment and folk performances. Should the fort be full, you can stay at **Roopangarh Fort Hotel** (*see Kishangarh Where to stay on page 185*), 80 km away.

For more details, see Kuchaman Accommodation Listings on page 480

Fast Facts

When to go October to February is pleasant
STD code 01586

Getting There

Kuchaman Fort is located up in the Aravallis at a height of 1,000 ft, in central Rajasthan, about 64 km/ 1$^1/_2$ hrs, from Sambhar Salt Lake. A taxi will cost about Rs 700-800. The closest airport is Jaipur's Sanganer Airport (196 km/ 3 hrs). Taxi costs Rs 1,500 for a drop. The closest railhead is Kuchaman City and the best connection from Delhi is the Mandore Express. It's 440 km SW of Delhi, a 7$^1/_2$-hr drive away. If travelling by road from Delhi, take NH8 up to Kishangarh. Take a right turn onto the state highway to Kuchaman via Roopangarh and Parbatsar. En route halts are Behror and Jaipur ■

Kumbhalgarh Fort, considered to be one of the most impressive forts in Mewar

KUMBHALGARH WILDLIFE SANCTUARY

PANTHER ON THE PROWL

Districts Spread across Rajsamand, Udaipur and Pali districts **Region** Mewar
Location In southern Rajasthan, near the formidable Kumbhalgarh Fort. The famous 15th-century Jain temples at Ranakpur lie to the west of the sanctuary
Distances 84 km N of Udaipur, 372 km SW of Jaipur
Journey time *By road* $2^{1}/_{2}$ hrs from Udaipur, $8^{1}/_{2}$ hrs from Jaipur
Route from Udaipur NH76 to Iswal; district roads to Kumbhalgarh WLS via Losingh Crossing, Auda and Kelwara **Route from Jaipur** NH8 to Gomti Crossing via Ajmer; state highway to Charbhuja; district road to Kumbhalgarh (*see route guide on page 134*)

■ BY DEVYANI ONIAL

It is six in the morning. The moon is still out and the road is a silvery ribbon. Indeed, ribbon is a fitting description in more ways than one, for the road spread out in front of us is just a narrow strip. Our driver Muhammad Hussain, however, negotiates it with remarkable ease. His experience of

GIREESH GV

Ghanerao, now a waterhole where animals and wildlife enthusiasts alike break journey. Along the way, a young sambar looks out anxiously, hidden partially by a rock. At Thandi Beri, we meet a French couple, with whom I compare notes about sightings. They have spotted only sambar, and our travel agent pitches in with an explanation: "This year, we have had good rain, and there's water all over the sanctuary, so animals don't necessarily come to these waterholes. Evening is a better time to spot animals." We make our way back from Thandi Beri, taking in the wild purple flowers brightening the forest. Grey jungle fowl run zigzag on the path for a while, and for no apparent reason dart off into the bushes. They add to the forest atmosphere with some spirited screeching. We return to the hotel, with the sounds and smells of the forest with us.

→ **FAST FACTS**

When to go Open through the year
Best sightings December to March is a good time to spot animals
Go there for Leopards, wolves, sloth bears, panthers
Wildlife/ Forest Dept offices
● Assistant Conservator of Forests
Kumbhalgarh WLS, Sadri
Tel: 02934-285529
● Deputy Chief Wildlife Warden
Gulab Bagh, Udaipur
Tel: 0294-2453686
Tourist office
● Rajasthan Tourism ℹ
Tourist Reception Centre
Fateh Memorial, Suraj Pol
Udaipur
Tel: 0294-2411535
STD code 02934

driving around Kumbhalgarh for four years has made him an expert.

As the sun begins its slow climb up the sky, the tall grass on the sides of the road glimmers in the first light of the day. The sanctuary is a field of gold but none of its residents are out basking in the sun. Then a crested hawk eagle comes into our view, its prominent crest bobbing up and down. The view is spectacular from the point where we are: at Mahuti Khet, which flaunts a dense cluster of mahua trees, clearly a favourite with langurs. We can see the Kumbhalgarh Fort, from which the sanctuary takes its name. The fort rises above the forest, a picture of formidable isolation. We get off the jeep, lingering in this patch of rustling trees, till the driver, eager to get on, woos us with promises of bigger and better sights.

We reach Choti Aodhi, once a hunting ground for the then rulers of

KUMBHALGARH WLS

Graphic by RAJESH KG

TOURIST GUIDE
Kumbhalgarh Fort, Ghanerao ...

● Main Place
◎ Other Places
♜ Fort
⟁ Temple

Safari

The following day, we visit the famous 15th century Jain temples at Ranakpur, located at one end of the sanctuary. We make our way back to Kumbhalgarh via Ghanerao and the Muchala Mahaveer Temple. In the twilight hour, as the candles inside the old Jain temple flicker hauntingly, darkness takes on another meaning. Heading back to Kumbhalgarh, we sit shivering slightly in the open jeep, the road again a ribbon of moonlight.

From somewhere in the darkness materialises the spotted-inky coat of a panther. It crosses the road in a lightening flash, disappearing from one dark patch of forest to another. "See," says our all-knowing travel agent, "I told you evening is a better time to come to the forest." For once, we can't help but agree.

ABOUT KUMBHALGARH

The Kumbhalgarh Sanctuary will come as a surprise to those who see Rajasthan only as a desert state. These green tracts form the dividing line between the former states of Mewar and Marwar. Once the hunting grounds of royals, this area was declared a wildlife sanctuary in 1971. The diverse topography of the sanctuary adds to its charms. In its eastern part are ranges that loom over 3,478 ft, as well as the source of the River Banas. The Marwar plains are to the north-west of the sanctuary. The rainwater on the western slopes flows as small rivers such as Sukdi, Mithdi, Sumer and Kot, all of which are the tributaries of River Luni that ultimately merges into the Arabian Sea. The sanctuary is known to be home to chausinghas (four-horned antelopes), leopards, panthers and sloth bears.

ORIENTATION

Kumbhalgarh spreads across 610 sq km of the Aravalli Ranges. If you are coming via NH76 from Udaipur, then you will pass through the **Ranakankar Forest House**, on the sanctuary's eastern boundary, 7 km south of the **Kumbhalgarh Fort**. Another way to enter the sanctuary is

JK TYRE
TOTAL CONTROL

→ GETTING THERE

Air Nearest airport: Maharana Pratap Airport, Udaipur (84 km/ 2$\frac{1}{2}$ hrs). Taxi to Kumbhalgarh costs Rs 1,000-1,200. Government and private buses run practically every hour from the Chetak Bus Stand

Rail Nearest railhead: Falna (80 km/ 2$\frac{1}{2}$ hrs). Taxi charges Rs 1,200 for a drop

Road From the north of Udaipur, take NH76 for about 25 km till Iswal; turn right to the main Losingh Crossing from where you turn left for Barwarha, Auda and Kelwara and on to Kumbhalgarh

Too sleepy to count my spots: A leopard gets set for a snooze

through the **Areth Gate**, from where the **Thandi Beri Forest Rest House** is 15 km away. **Ghanerao** lies on the western side of the sanctuary, north-west of Kumbhalgarh. **Falna**, the nearest railway station, lies 80 km west of the sanctuary. This is closer to the famous Jain temples of **Ranakpur**, which lie on the western boundary of the sanctuary. You can either stay at one of Ranakpur's many hotels or travel another 25 km to the **Roopanmata Rest House**. Thandi Beri is closer — it's just 10 km away. The **Sumer Forest Rest House**, close to the sanctuary's **Joba Wolf Point**, is 35 km from Ranakpur.

Since the Forest Department does not have its own vehicles, it's best to hire your vehicle from Kumbhalgarh or Kelwara (about 6 km before Kumbhalgarh). At Kelwara, you can contact Umaid Singh of **Ashapura Taxi Service** (Tel: 02954-242450), near the courts. The forest office (no phone here) is above his place. **Kumbhal Castle Hotel** (*see Where to Stay on page 301*) arranges jeeps to take their guests around the sanctuary. Ganpath

and Ajit Singh from Narlai (Mobile: 09414523037) arrange horse safaris around the sanctuary.

♦**Sanctuary entry fee** Indians Rs 10, foreigners Rs 80 **Vehicle entry fee** Two-wheelers Rs 10, jeeps, cars and mini-bus Rs 65, bus Rs 100 **Cameras** Still free, video Rs 200 **Sanctuary timings** Sunrise to sunset

THINGS TO SEE AND DO

Kumbhalgarh has many options for tourists — apart from jeep safaris, you can also go trekking here. There are points of historic interests in the sanctuary too.

Jeep jungle safari

The 15-km long drive from Kumbhalgarh to Thandi Beri is the most popular jeep journey in the sanctuary. In the roughly $3^1/_2$ hrs that will take you to get to Thandi Beri and back, you can see leopards, bears, sambar — if you are fortunate, that is. You can also visit the famous 15th century **Jain temples at Ranakpur**,

H SATISH

Fierce and furious: The hawk eagle

located at one end of the sanctuary (*also see Ranakpur on page 148*).

Horse safari
This is not a regular feature but the staff at the Kumbhal Castle Hotel might agree to arrange a horse safari in the sanctuary for you. Popular routes in the sanctuary include Kumbhalgarh to Ghanerao via Thandi Beri; Ranakpur to Thandi Beri; Thandi Beri to Sumer; and Roopanmata to Ranakpur.

Trekking
Trekking is allowed in the sanctuary, and the hilly terrain is ideal for it. You can either request a forest guard to accompany you (Rs 200 a day) or ask your travel agent to arrange a guide for you. Popular walking trails are Kumbhalgarh to Thandi Beri (14 km), Roopnagar to Sumer (98 km), Ranakpur to Ranakankar (15 km), Ranakpur to Kumbhalgarh (25 km), Malgarh to Magga (8 km), Roopanmata to Ranakpur (30 km) and Ranakpur to Thandi Beri (15 km). Your entry permit to the sanctuary is the only document required to go on treks.

Tirthankar nature trail
Located opposite the Ranakpur temples, this 3.7-km long trail is an ode to the Jain Tirthankaras and is also representative of an ideal Aravalli ecosystem. Along this trail are planted the species of various trees under which the 24 Jain Tirthankaras got enlightenment.

Joba Wolf Point
Situated about 7 km from Sadri near Joba Village, this is a wolf habitat. Set at the foothills near the Muchala Mahaveer Temple (*see below*), 500 hectares of the forest here are home to the Indian wolf.

Kumbhalgarh Fort
About 2 km from the sanctuary, the Kumbhalgarh Fort is considered the second most impressive fort in Mewar, after Chittaurgarh. Built in 1448 by King Rana Kumbha of Mewar (after whom the fort gets his name), at a height of 3,600 ft, it was also the birthplace of King Rana Pratap. There is a basti inside the fort, making it a 'living' monument. There are also two teashops on the fort premises.

Muchala Mahaveer Temple
This Jain temple near Ghanerao is devoted to Lord Mahaveer. The unique feature of this temple is that Lord Mahaveer sports a moustache — hence the name Muchala.

WHERE TO STAY

Tourists to Kumbhalgarh have the option of staying either within the sanctuary or outside. As people visit Kumbhalgarh for both the sanctuary and the fort, peak season is usually very busy — so do book in advance.

In the sanctuary

The **Forest Rest Houses** in the sanctuary are located at **Thandi Beri, Ranakankar, Sumer, Sadri** and **Roopanmata**. All have 2-3 rooms each at Rs 200-400 per night. For bookings, contact the Assistant Conservator of Forests, Kumbhalgarh WLS, Sadri or the Deputy Chief Wildlife Warden's office in Udaipur (*see Fast Facts on page 297*).

Remember to carry your own food and provisions as the forest guest houses don't provide food. However, in all the rest houses, the caretaker can arrange food on request. Occasionally, they may have a gas stove but don't take that as a given. Carry your own stove or packed meals. All the rooms have attached baths, but be warned that the facilities are delightfully rudimentary.

Outside the sanctuary

The Aodhi (Tel: 02954-242341-46; Tariff: Rs 5,000-6,500), situated near Kumbhalgarh Fort, is a top-end luxury hotel here with a multi-cuisine restaurant, a pool, a café and Internet. **Kumbhal Castle Hotel** (Tel: 242171; Tariff: Rs 1,200-1,500), about 2 km from the fort, has a pool, restaurant and AC rooms. The Kumbhalgarh Fort Hotel has been recently taken over by Club Mahindra; it was closed at the time of writing for renovation.

In Kelwara

About 6 km before Kumbhalgarh is Kelwara Village, where budget travellers can

TRIBHUVAN TIWARI

Tracking the elusive panther

find reasonably priced clean rooms. **Hotel Ratna Deep** (Tel: 02954-242217; Tariff: Rs 500-950) here has a restaurant, TV and parking facilities. **Karni Palace** (Tel: 242003; Tariff: Rs 750-2,000) has a vegetarian restaurant and a travel desk.

For more hotels and details, see Kumbhalgarh Accommodation Listings on pages 480-482

FAUNA

- Animals such as leopard, wolf, hyena, sloth bear, jackal, pangolin, wild pig, nilgai, chausingha and sambar
- Reptiles such as crocodile, starred tortoise, flap-shelled turtle; several snakes including cobra and python
- Over 200 species of birds including grey jungle fowl, partridge, changeable hawk eagle, parakeet and drongo

WHERE TO EAT

The hotels at Kumbhalgarh have restaurants that serve Rajasthani dishes such as **safed maas** (mutton in a curry of almonds, cashewnuts, coconut kernel paste, poppy seeds and white pepper) as well as pastas and fish and chips. One meal will cost you Rs 200 and above. The two hotels at Kelwara offer simpler and cheaper fare. It's best to stick to the traditional Rajasthani thali. ■

Photographs by NARENDRA BISHT

The rest of Rajasthan can keep their camels, but in Rawla, they love their horses

RAWLA NARLAI Saddle culture

BY MUNEEZA NAQVI

There are no gift shops in Narlai, no tie and dye fabrics in sight, and no restaurants serving dosas and veg chowmein. There is a little silver shop, but you have your work cut out trying to find it and the shop owners show very little interest in pushing you to buy anything. Is it possible that I've crossed some state boundary and left Rajasthan? Clearly not, because hurtling towards me in the wrong lane is a motorcycle and perched on it are three Rajput lads, and they prefer riding hats to crash helmets.

Tucked away between Jodhpur and Udaipur, this is the heart of equestrian Rajasthan, and Narlai Village is unlike anything you're likely to find in this most touristy of states. There is foreshadowing of a perfect holiday — beautiful Marwari horses and Rawla Narlai, an old palace that hasn't been completely given up to the gods of commerce. That's what I've been promised. The rest of

Rajasthan can keep their camels, but here in Marwar and neighbouring Mewar, they love their horses. It's been a long while since I've been in a saddle and I'm a teeny bit apprehensive. "It's like riding a bicycle," my brother says, "it'll all come back." Ganpat Singh, all of 15 and the owner of the horses I'm meant to ride, tells me, *"Hamare Marwar ke ghode rider pehchante hain."* (Our Marwar horses can identify riders.) Like almost everyone here, he's been riding since he was old enough to sit in a saddle. As with everything else here, the story of the Marwari horse is part history and part folklore. And looking at beautiful Kesar, it's very easy to believe that she can trace her history to the time when the gods churned the ocean for nectar and horses had wings.

Kesar is the baby of the family, only two years old, but clearly well aware of her beauty. She's all glossy black coat, limpid eyes and beautifully curled ears and not above being coy and frisky. We're all riding Marwari mares; the

At the rawla, or small palace, in Narlai

stallions, Ganpat tells me, are a bit useless for anything other than dressing pretty for wedding processions.

For the most part our little group walks gently — it's panchayat election time and there are large groups of men hanging around and discussing the event. This makes the horses a bit nervous. But once we're outside the village, the road opens out into the fields and this has a soothing effect on all of us.

Kesar is remarkably smooth to ride despite the tendency to canter ahead to lead the group. This is a problem initially because I'm not at all sure of what route we're going to take. My head is full of stories of the excellent homing instincts of the Marwari and after a while I give up the fight with Kesar. If her forefathers could bring back wounded soldiers from battlefields, surely Kesar can take me to Ganpat Singh's farm.

At the farm we meet the resident stallion Ali Baksh. He's quite the brat — kicking, rearing, snorting and generally acting up to impress the girls, but Kesar, Tejroop and Rajroop give him a chilly reception. They've had a long day and Ali Baksh will just have to wait.

So far Rawla Narlai has been everything I was told it would be. But there are some things that I wasn't told. Like the hot water bottle that is brought around after dinner. It brings back comforting memories of long ago winters — my grandmother quietly slipping her hot-water bottle to the favourite granddaughter, of matron handing out hot-water bottles (and salt water for gargles). After a day spent in the saddle, this is just what the sore limbs need. I allow myself to succumb completely to the Rawla's many charms. Primary among them is the feeling that you're visiting a very posh and proper relative and not a mere hotel.

A rawla is a smaller palace, often used as a hunting lodge. The rawla in Narlai took its current shape at some point in the early 18th century. It served as a hunting lodge for Jodhpur's last maharaja, Umaid Singh, who I'm told later, gifted it to his younger brother, Ajit Singh, after the latter saved his life during a shikar. Like some of the other family properties — Umaid Bhawan and Ajit Bhawan — descendants of the former Jodhpur royals now run it as a hotel. They have wisely chosen not to change too much of the old structure. This rawla is built around a small walled courtyard and the main rooms are located off a verandah that surrounds it. The largest and clearly the most 'royal' is the Maharaj Mahal.

This room and some of the others retain their original frescoes (in some disrepair) and stained glass windows. There are concessions to modern living — running hot water being one of them — but everything else seems frozen in time. Sepia-tinted family photographs from shikars, stiff family portraits, and photos of the family on horseback are scattered all over the lodge. If spending your days between riding and falling asleep on the *chaise lounges* is not sufficient excitement, there is enough in and around the village to keep you busy for several days. About 45 minutes by road (you can also ride across if you like) is the mighty **Kumbhalgarh Fort** (*see page 300*).

Back in Narlai, Bhanwar Singh, who by virtue of his retired-from-the-army status and impressively twirled moustache is an important person, decides to take me under his wing and show me around. The rawla itself is built at the

DISCOVER DELHI - THE MANY CITIES WITHIN THE CITY

DELHI & NCR CITY GUIDE

OUTLOOK
CITY LIMITS

ON NEWSSTANDS Rs.295/-

Speed

M EXIDE

EATING OUT ■ NIGHTLIFE ■ SHOPPING ■ WELLNESS ■ SIGHTSEEING...

A comprehensive guide on the capital of emerging superpower nation; that promises to make new discoveries and an enlightening companion to taste this vibrant city.

ORDER FORM

Name: Mr/Ms _____ DOB `D D M M Y Y`

Address: _____

_____ PIN ☐☐☐☐☐☐

Ph(Off): _____ (Res): _____ e-mail _____

Price per Delhi NCR Rs.295/-x_____ (qty required) = Rs. _____ /-. Please find

enclosed (✓) Cheque/DD No._____ dated _____ for Rs _____ favouring

OUTLOOK PUBLISHING (INDIA) PVT. LTD.

Please charge it to my (✓) Amex / Diners / Visa / Master card No. ☐☐☐☐☐☐☐☐☐☐☐☐☐☐☐☐ Card Expiry Date:

☐☐ ☐☐

Signature: _____ Date: _____ M M Y Y

Please fill in this order form and mail it with your remittance to: OUTLOOK TRAVELLER, AB 10, S J Enclave, New Delhi 110029 ● Rates and offer valid in India for a limited period ● Please allow 6-8 weeks for the delivery of the books ● For gift instructions or bulk orders please give recipient's name & address along with other details on a separate attached sheet ● There will be single point dispatch ● In case payment is through credit card, date of birth must be mentioned ● Credit card orders can be faxed to Delhi 011-26177416, Kolkata 033-22823593, Mumbai 022-30612233, Bangalore 080-25582810, Chennai 044-24662316, Hyderabad 040-23375676. For enquiries email: yourhelpline@outlooktraveller.com.

The pretty interiors of the rawla

foot of a huge rock (350 ft, I'm told) and right at the top sits the statue of a large and slightly out-of-place elephant. Looking out at a *kala pathar* was considered bad luck and so a local zamindar placed the white elephant to break the view. The walk all the way up isn't as daunting as it seems. Over the years, winding steps have been cut in and the path is dotted with tiny temples and stone Ganesh icons placed in crevices cut into the rock. I wake up at the crack of dawn to climb the rock and watch the sun rise over the village and hear the temple bells ring as the village wakes up. The village is split up between Rajputs, Rabaris and Jains and there is a temple at every corner. The most popular temple is the **Ai Mata ka Mandir**.

There is a 15-day festival here every Holi. Newly married couples come here to get blessed and later bring their first child here for its *mundan* ceremony. But the *pièce de résistance* in Narlai is the *baoli*. Outside, a board says that the stepwell is the private property of Maharaja Swaroop Singh. But if you're with Bhanwar Singh, all doors in Narlai open to you. There's no elaborately rich sculpting in stone

here. Just huge stone blocks placed with deceptive simplicity, nature's own air-conditioning and a small stone Saraswati idol placed in a niche at the top. What can I say? It really is perfect. I'm in Narlai, a little many-horse village in Rajasthan and all is well with the world.

Horse riding

Ganpat Singh (Tel: 02934-288371; Mobile: 09414523037) organises day-trips and safaris in and around the area. Costs start at Rs 500 depending on the level of expertise and duration. Previous riding experience is not required.

Where to stay
In Narlai
Rawla Narlai (Tel: 02934-260443; Tariff: Rs 4,500-5,500), surrounded by the Aravalli Hills, is the only hotel in the area. It has 20 rooms and five permanent luxury tents. It arranges horse and camel safaris as well as trekking and rock climbing. Reservations can also be made at the **Ajit Bhawan Palace Hotel** (Tel: 0291-2510410) in Jodhpur. Tourists can also stay in Jodhpur as Narlai is easily accessible from here (*see Jodhpur Where to Stay on page 225*).

For more details, see Rawla Narlai Accommodation Listings on page 488

Getting There
Air Udaipur (134 km/ 3 hrs) and Jodhpur (160 km/ 2^1/$_4$ hrs)
Rail Nearest railheads: Falna (69 km) is the nearest while Udaipur and Jodhpur are convenient railway junctions. One option is to come via Kumbhalgarh from Udaipur, but travelling via Jodhpur is faster because it's a highway. The most convenient trains are the Mandore Express (leaves Old Delhi Railway Station at 8.50 pm, arrives in Jodhpur at 8 am) and the Mewar Express (leaves Delhi's Hazrat Nizamuddin Station at 7 pm, arrives in Udaipur at 7 pm). For more details, log onto indianrail. gov.in
Road From Udaipur it will take 3 hrs to get to Narlai because it's a single carriageway. Taxi costs about Rs 1,500 one way. From Kumbhalgarh (50 km/ 1^1/$_2$ hrs) it costs about Rs 700 (one way) and from Jodhpur Rs 1,600 ∎

Photographs by AMRIT P SINGH/WILDPHOTOS

Demoiselle cranes, a species of birds commonly seen in Desert National Park

DESERT NATIONAL PARK

DESERT ROSE

Districts Jaisalmer and Barmer
Location In the Thar Desert in south-west Rajasthan, next to the border with Pakistan
Distances 42 km SW of Jaisalmer, 317 km NW of Jodhpur, 689 km W of Jaipur via Jodhpur
Journey time By road 1 hr from Jaisalmer, 6$^1/_2$ hrs from Jodhpur, 12 hrs from Jaipur
Route from Jaipur NH8 to Beawar via Ajmer; NH14 to Bar; state highway to Jodhpur via Bilara and Dangiawas; state highway to Pokaran via Balesar and Dechhu; NH15 to Jaisalmer via Odania and Chandan; district road to Sam Village (Desert NP) via Dedha (*see route guide on page 237*)

■ **BY AMIT MAHAJAN**

The drizzle has stopped. The wind picks up, and the sand joyously soars on it, gliding a few inches above the quavering surface of the dune. In a few dusty but dramatic moments, the dune changes its colour. The darkish brown wetness gives way to the lighter glow of the drier silica. But the skies are getting blacker and it starts to rain again; so much rain in the desert seems strange. The camels and their patrons have disappeared along with the sun, leaving us to gape wondrously at the desolate tract stretching to the horizon and beyond. It's wet and chilly in the Great Indian Desert! And then we notice the barrenness coming to life. A part of the desert moves, and then another. There are two of them or may be a herd, we are not sure. They are chinkara, light chestnut-coloured antelopes the colour of their surroundings. A while later, a rustle in the bushes behind makes us turn back, just in time to catch a fleeing apparition with a white-tipped bushy tail, a distinctive feature of the desert fox. Then, another fox crosses our path.

We are in the sand dunes close to Khuri Village on the edge of the Desert National Park. The drive from Jaisalmer till here had been hard and rocky. Yet, the first sight of the dunes is picture-perfect, like a painting with perfectly contoured shadows of ripples and undulating crests.

It is easy to see how deserts can be one of the most incredibly beautiful, thrilling, eerie, treacherous and inhospitable places on earth, all at the same time. And it's easy to see why people flock to gaze at them, to get their photographs clicked with camels in the foreground and sunset in the background. It is an out-of-the-world experience. We are so enchanted

with the sandy knolls that we don't even notice that because of the rain, the romantic 'sunset on the dune' experience hasn't even taken off.

The Wildlife Department officials tell us that the best way to see wildlife, especially the rare great Indian bustard, in the Desert National Park, is to go to Sudashri, about 55 km south-west of Jaisalmer. Early next morning, our jeep hurries on the deserted pebbly flats and the brownish piedmont plateau past the famous sand dunes near Sam, where we stop for just enough time to take in the red sun rising over the clean golden sand. Some dunes spill on to the road, the wilderness attempting to reclaim the tract. We turn off the road, which goes on to the Indo-Pak border and, in earlier times, would have led into Sindh.

Sudashri is a 2,000-acre area enclosed with barbed wire and, at first sight, the enclosure seems like an unlikely place to

Graphic by ANIS KHAN

DESERT NATIONAL PARK

Jaisalmer, Khuri, Sam, Akal Wood Fossil Park ...

TOURIST GUIDE

To Pokaran, Bikaner

Jaisalmer

Sam

Desert NP office

Akal Wood Fossil Park

Sudashri

Khuri

RAJASTHAN

Berisala

Myajlar

Girab

To Barmer, Jodhpur

To Barmer, Jodhpur

JAISALMER

BARMER

N

— Main Road
⊙ Main Place
◎ Other Places
🏠 Stay
⚠ Info Centre
⋯ Distt Boundary

Safari

A shepherd and his flock enjoy the esteemed company of demoiselle cranes

visit for a wildlife experience — patches of clumpy sewan grass, a few shrubs and, an occasional tree, mainly acacia. Plus six camels wandering around, grazing busily. We are offered a choice between walking and riding a camel cart to traverse the 4-km long trail. We choose the unknown entity — the camel cart — and immediately, the process of assembling it begins. One of the wandering camels, Babloo, is fetched, the cart — actually a wooden plank on two wheels — is hitched to it and a mattress placed on it as a favour to us city dwellers. We are to be accompanied by Uma Ram, our guide, who seems more excited than us about the prospect of spotting the Great Indian Bustard. He considers it a great privilege to be able to see this bird, which is nearing extinction.

As we make ourselves comfortable on the cart, we slowly become aware of our surroundings. That twig is, in fact, a pallid harrier; there is an Indian robin on that shrub; the flock above is sand grouse. There are a couple of chinkara behind that clump of bushes. Often we stop and the binoculars are passed around. The desert is teeming with life. We realise that the sparseness of the vegetation provides

an excellent wildlife viewing opportunity. There is far less occasion for the animals to disappear than there would be in a heavily wooded jungle. The possibilities to observe animals and birds are better, even when they have taken shelter.

And then we see our first Great Indian Bustard. There are two of them, tall birds, greyish in appearance, walking away from us slowly and elegantly. Females, we are informed. And another one, a female again. Occasionally, they pick something from the ground, maybe a berry or an insect and steadily keep moving from us. But Uma Ram is trying to draw our attention to a tree further away under which a chinkara is standing gazing at us. Realising that we have noticed it, the chinkara swiftly withdraws behind the tree, but is still visible. By the time we turn again, the bustards have covered quite a distance and disappeared behind shrubs. However, we are lucky. Uma Ram has spotted another bustard, this time a male (it's taller), and what fortune, there is not just one but two, three and why a fourth too. One of the big birds is fearless and stands its ground, giving us the opportunity to take a good look, while the rest start walking away. Now they are behind

The Great Indian Bustard story

VIVEK R SINHA/WILDERFILE

The bustard is related to the crane but has a rounder body, thicker neck, and a relatively short beak. They are found on the ground on open plains and fields. The term bustard simply means slow bird, and in reality, bustards are slow as a consequence of their heavy build. Although they are strong fliers, they usually do not leave the ground.

The Great Indian Bustard, or *Ardeotis nigriceps*, has a long, thick pale grey neck and long, yellow legs. Males grow up to 120 cm and females 92 cm. The two sexes are similar in appearance, although males have a larger black crown, long hind crown feathers and a black band across the breast.

Earlier, bustards were widespread and common across the Indian sub-continent, but today, this species has all but disappeared from Pakistan, and its population in India has reduced considerably. Now classified as endangered, the Great Indian Bustard has become extinct in almost 90 per cent of its former range, principally as a result of loss of habitat and poaching. At present, the number of birds is estimated to be 500; a continuation of the present trend will see the species get extinct in the next decade. The Desert NP was started primarily to save the bustard.

a tree but soon emerge on the other side. We are transfixed, but are suddenly alerted by the action in a nearby bush. A small and hairy creature darts away from us — a desert fox. We also spot the tawny eagle, the Eurasian owl, the common buzzard and the red-backed shrike. Of course, the bustards get most of our attention.

I learn that most visitors see three or four bustards. A sighting of seven or eight is considered very good. But we are moving well beyond all these benchmarks. Uma Ram is avidly counting, and by the thirteenth spotting he is excited beyond words — and more are still crossing our path. Once or twice, he even 'spots' bustards in places where we can only make out the vegetation.

By the time it's sunny and we end our excursion, Uma Ram has counted 21, and we have seen 17 or 18. This is a record of sorts. Nobody at Sudashri remembers anyone seeing so many Great Indian Bustards on a single day.

ABOUT DESERT NP

An area of 3,162 sq km in the desert was declared a sanctuary in 1980 to preserve its fascinating and fragile habitat. There are 72 villages within the park. Some enclosures of barbed wire, with water holes, have been created, to which the villagers and their cattle are denied access. This is meant to preserve the grasslands so that they can become wildlife enclaves. Sudashri is the most maintained of these enclaves, and the best place to see the fauna. The most outstanding of the fauna is the Great Indian Bustard, GIB to the initiated. Apart from the bustard, several others birds are also found here.

ORIENTATION

It's best to visit the park from Jaisalmer (*see page 236*). The park is to the south-west of the city. The villages of Sam and Khuri lie on the edge of the park and are

easily accessible from Jaisalmer. **Sam** is 45 km west of Jaisalmer and **Sudashri** is 10 km south-east of Sam. **Khuri** is 40 km south-west of Jaisalmer and Sudashri is about 8 km further on, heading north-west. To visit the park, you need a permit (get it a day in advance) from the office of the Deputy Director, Desert NP, Khuri Road, Jaisalmer (Tel: 02992-252489). Payments have to be made in advance.

◆**Permit fee** Indians Rs 10, foreigners Rs 80 **Park timings** 10 am-5 pm, interrupted by a lunch (usually 1.30-2 pm); Sundays closed **Vehicle fee** Rs 65 **Guide fee** Rs 200 **Cameras** Still free, video Rs 200

THINGS TO SEE AND DO

The two biggest draws at the park are the Great Indian Bustard and the chinkara, and the best place to see them and other birds and animals is Sudashri. From Jaisalmer, there are two, almost equidistant routes to Sudashri — via Sam or via Khuri. As this is a military area, the roads are well-maintained and generally free of traffic; you can make the journey in 1¹/₂ hrs. A jeep is the ideal vehicle to travel in and it costs about Rs 800 for a 4-hr long trip and Rs 1,500 for a day-trip.

Desert safari

There is a Forest Department post at Sudashri and the personnel stay in a few huts within the fencing. One of the gentlemen will act as your guide on the 3- to 4-km long circuit. You can either walk it or opt for a camel cart (Rs 300 for about 3 hrs). Morning is the ideal time and it's advisable to be there by sunrise. You can easily spend three to four hours on the walk, depending on how hot it gets. Alternatively, you can arrive in the afternoon, about three or four hours before sunset. Binoculars are a must; also remember to pack water and food.

Dunes and wildlife

A round of the sand dunes is not to be missed. The best places to see the dunes are the villages Sam and Khuri, located at the edge of the sanctuary. Take a jeep from Jaisalmer (Rs 700 to 1,000, depending upon the time you want to spend there) and arrive in time for the sunrise or the sunset. A short camel ride on the dunes costs about Rs 50.

Birds found here include sand grouses, partridges, bee-eaters, doves and bulbuls. Demoiselle cranes and common cranes arrive in winter. Among the mammals, the chinkara is easily spotted. Chinkara, or *Gazella Bennittii*, is the smallest Asiatic antelope. It grows to a height of 65 cm and weighs 25 kg. Most males have short horns, although some grow to a length of 25-30 cm. The other notable inhabitants of the Desert NP are the desert fox, desert cat, monitor lizard, spiny-tailed lizard, sandfish and saw-scaled viper. Jaipur-based naturalist and BNHS conservationist Manoj Kulshrestha arranges field tours in the park. His contact details are: Sneh Deep, B-33, Sethi Colony, Near Transport Nagar, Jaipur; Tel: 0141-2604570; Mobile: 09314880887.

→ **GETTING THERE**

Air Nearest airport: Jodhpur (322 km/ 6 hrs), well-connected to Khuri. Taxi costs about Rs 1,800
Rail Nearest railhead: Jaisalmer (42 km/ 1 hr). Taxi costs Rs 600 approx
Road As road journeys to Jaisalmer are very long, this option is best avoided

WHERE TO STAY

To visit the Desert NP, you should ideally base yourself at Jaisalmer, where there are plenty of hotels. There are a number of options at Khuri, but it's best to do a day-trip to Sudashri. It's also possible to spend

a night or two in Sam or Khuri during the high season, October to February. However, you will need to book a jeep from Jaisalmer itself. Many travel companies such as KK Travels (Tel: 02992-253087), located at Jaisalmer Fort, Sahara Travels (Tel: 252609) at Gopa Chowk and Thar Safari (Tel: 254295) offer an evening to morning package at the Sam dunes, comprising transport, camel ride, dance, dinner, night stay in a tent for two, sunrise and breakfast, all in the range of Rs 2,000-3,500 per head. The RTDC office (Tel: 252406) near Gadisagar arranges accommodation and can also help you find a reliable agent.

In Khuri

Khuri has a host of very basic staying options. Prices tend to vary according to the kind of stay option you choose. The **Gangaur Guest House** (Tel: 03014-274056; Mobile: 09414271035; Tariff: Rs 700-1,700) has eight mud and thatched huts and 10 fully furnished Swiss cottages with attached baths. You can opt for a night stay, which includes a Rajasthani dinner, cultural programmes, sand dune visits and breakfast the next day. If you want to return to Jaisalmer after the dinner, the charge is Rs 400. They also customise 3- to 4-day safaris at budget rates (for backpackers and students). The **Moonlight Safari Camp** (Tel: 274109; Mobile: 09829762275; Tariff: Rs 1,275 per person per night) is the new name of Moonlight Khuri Resort, and it has a new management too. It has eight mud huts

---

FAUNA

- Great Indian Bustard, Indian robin, tawny eagle, Eurasian owl, common buzzard, red-backed shrike, sand grouse, partridge, bee-eater, demoiselle crane and steppe eagle
- Chinkara, desert fox, desert cat, monitor lizard, spiny-tailed lizard, sandfish and saw-scaled viper

---

(four with attached baths, four with two common baths) and 15 Swiss tents. The tariff includes a night's stay, camel ride, dinner, entertainment and breakfast the next day. The camp is located between Khuri and Bharna villages in the dunes.

In Sam

Several desert camps are run here during high season. Amongst them is RTDC's **Sam Dhani** (Jaisalmer Tel: 02992-252392; Tariff: Rs 925-1,425), which has eight huts. The camp organises camel safaris and cultural events. **Oasis India Campsite** (Mobile: 09829311444; Tariff: Rs 5,000-5,500 per night), near Safe Parking, has 25 tents and their tariff includes dinner and breakfast the next day, 1 hr camel safari in the dunes, a cultural programme, camp fire and taxes. **Dune Safari Camp** (Mobile: 09829797807, 09414149807; Tariff: Rs 5,000-5,500) has 25 tents with attached toilets. The campsite has electricity and a permanent kitchen. Rates include two meals, a safari and a cultural programme.

In Jaisalmer
For details, see Jaisalmer Where to Stay on pages 244-246

For more hotels and details, see Desert NP Accommodation Listings on page 462

WHERE TO EAT

Sudashri has no food provisions. If you stay there, you can eat what the staff cooks for themselves. Travel agencies offer excursions to Sam and Khuri, with dinner, night stay and breakfast included. If you plan to visit Sudashri, take a picnic lunch with you or tie up with a travel agency to organise a meal at Sam or Khuri. *Also see Jaisalmer on pages 246-248.*

AROUND DESERT NP

Jaisalmer
See page 236 ■

Experience

A royal lifestyle at a heritage
hotel, the rigours of a camel
safari, the rustic pleasures of
a farm-stay and a cuisine
that's fiery and delicious

Scintillating Celebrations

 Rajasthan Tourism | Call: **Ahmedabad:** 079-26469580; **Chennai:** 044-25365554; **New Delhi:** 011-23389525, 23383837, 23381884; or

*R*ajasthan's Foundation

Day Celebrations

are an experience of a

lifetime. Come with your

family and friends and

partake in a non-stop

cultural extravaganza of

7 pulsating days and

evenings that just rock.

Don't miss it for the world. Be there!

RAJASTHAN DAY
C E L E B R A T I O N S
24-30 MARCH • JAIPUR

Highlights : • Run for Rajasthan and grand inaugural show on 24th March • Traditional rural sport competitions • Grand cultural evenings • Special prayers • Theatre festival• Classical & folk performances • Children film festival • Puppet festival • Golf tournament • Adventure sports • Polo tournament • Police Tattoo Show • Army show • Festival of Indian classical dances • Rajasthan food festival • Craft & Night bazaars • Dazzling fireworks • Procession of grand closing ceremony and Rajasthan Day evening on 30th March.

Jaipur: 0141-5110595, 2203531; **Kolkala:** 033-22132740; **Mumbai:** 022-22040417;
visit us at : **www.rajasthantourism.gov.in**

Neemrana Fort-Palace: Where the first chapter of restoration was written

And the rest is history

AMAN NATH recalls the stones and dreams that shaped Neemrana

Who hasn't heard of the pomp and splendour of the Indian maharajas? The minute we think of royalty, we can imagine their majesties, right down to their pearl-encrusted slippers and golden boots. And as one enters the palace of any of the erstwhile rulers, it is possible to recreate a royal past full of unapologetic opulence, glorious architecture, trophies of beheaded animals, gilded frescoes, stunning jewellery, shikar, polo matches and vintage cars.

Perhaps the question most likely to cross one's mind in the maze of rooms of a palace would be one about the queens: how many maharanis did a maharaja have? To this, one can safely say that there's no correct answer. It is said that Mandu's sultan had 5,000 wives, the Mughal Emperor Akbar about 500 women in his harem, while the Maharaja of Patiala had only half that number.

But where did they all live, the women who were guarded by eunuchs only because the latter were considered 'safe'? In Amber, one finds the ranis' quarters, fairly modest by today's standards, with little open spaces where women could dry their hair and paint their palms with henna. Maharaja Madho Singh of Jaipur forced his women to live huddled in hovel-like apartments when he left the City Palace to rest or hunt at Audhi. Here, there was just about space for a charpoy in one room, and worse, the loos were far from satisfactory. Orchha had more splendid spaces for royal women.

In opting to stay at a palace, these are the images of the past that tourists may find themselves recalling. Of course, what we visit today as heritage hotels are Westernised 'versions' of the real thing, palaces that the Indian royalty built after they had been considerably influenced by the West. And just as well, if you think about it, for what would a hotel be without attached bathrooms with hot and cold running water? It would have been difficult to spot luxury in a palace if water was carried on camel-back and then poured into brass or copper pots, as was done in less recent times for bathing.

We had our own set of challenges when we set about to restore, rebuild and raise the noble Neemrana Fort-Palace on the Delhi-Jaipur Highway, the origins of which date back to 1464. And ensuring that there were roofs over the mahals was just one of them! There was no plumbing or wiring and the labyrinthine layout made it difficult to chaise into the stone walls and the lime mortar floors. But there was much passion, so we were bound to hit upon a solution. We found inventive ways to hide water tanks and air conditioners and we pierced the turrets with small stone-grilled windows to make loos with views. We tried to be as minimalist as possible in our interventions.

Conservationists constantly tell you that all changes should be reversible. But who wanted the fort-palace to be a heap of rubble again? We were turning India's forgotten architectural heritage into an asset, an experience that guests would cherish and remember. Anything in that direction, we believed, was welcome.

We erected a tent on a rooftop and made an open-air bathroom. We fixed new mirrors in the ceiling of the Sheesh Mahal. The Rang Mahal had rafters in old mineral and vegetable colours and the striped, silken mushroom blinds we chose for the windows reflected these hues. The Surya Mahal or Sun Palace was decorated bright and yellow with a fabric that fashion designer Issey Miyake had designed in India, while the Chandra or Moon Palace was adorned in black, white, silver and grey.

We planted saplings in the rocky, sandy garden spaces we terraced to turn them into hanging gardens. We chose pomegranates and guavas for the gardens to the south, and bougainvilleas to clamber up all the walls we had raised. Tufts of grass kept the dusty sandgrains from flying into our guests' eyes.

'We turned India's forgotten architectural heritage into an asset, an experience that guests would cherish'

We opened in 1991 with just one wing restored. There were only 12 rooms, but the raw and rustic appeal of Neemrana won us many accolades. We knew then that every room we completed would be booked soon enough. August 2006 marked 20 years of our efforts in this field, efforts that most people called crazy. Today, there are 50 rooms/ suites and rampart gardens at Neemrana. An additional wing houses a pool and health spa, an amphitheatre, the hanging gardens with a salon, a restaurant with a rooftop garden and conference rooms and five special suites. Francis Wacziarg, my French-turned-Indian partner, could have very well said after Napoleon that "Impossible is not French", as we continue to make more and more things possible.

Today, when I look back, it is difficult for me to recreate or recall the ruins that stood where the Neemrana Fort-Palace now stands. It must be true that the human memory for unpleasant things is rather short. It is with this optimism that the Neemrana mission has spread across India in 12 more sites. The effort to resurrect more heritage buildings has its own rewards: each past speaks with a flavour that knows no equal in the history of personal and public experiences. (*Also see Neemrana: Holding Fort on page 90.*)

A passage at the Neemrana Fort

Courtesy NEEMRANA HOTELS

Royal holiday

RAJASTHAN IS SYNONYMOUS WITH romance. The very name conjures up images of costumes whose bright colours contrast with the state's parched landscape, of golden sands that stretch endlessly, of forts that are invincible and palaces and havelis that are majestic and exquisite. Indeed, it is in the latter that one can still glimpse the heydays of princely India and the sometimes eccentric charm of royal lifestyles, a scintillating leitmotif of those times just as much as the edifices they raised.

Most forts in Rajasthan were constructed between the 16th and the 18th centuries, with the Rajputs in the western desert of Thar being the most flamboyant. However, in 1947, a new tax law limited the extravagance of the royals. By the 1970s, their privy purses had also been withdrawn. It became a financial burden for the royal families that had two or three huge palaces to maintain these. Some sold their properties, some abandoned their forts, which were pillaged and pilfered, and some converted their properties into hotels.

It is in the ancient fortifications or residences that have been now converted into hotels that the tourist of today can enjoy a royal lifestyle marked by opulence and indulgence. Each hotel is a sanctuary from modernity in many ways, radiating a way of life that is now unfamiliar but nevertheless romantic. There is no question either of the guests forsaking any of the pleasures that come their way in other hotels — a heritage hotel also boasts of the same amenities, if not better ones.

We present in the following pages some of the top heritage hotels in Rajasthan, all of which were once forts, palaces or havelis.

20 Heritage hotel picks
Where the old and the new blend seamlessly

DEVI GARH, DELWARA

DEVI GARH is undoubtedly India's most elegant hotel in a heritage setting. The fort was built some time in the 1760s by the descendants of a certain Sajja Singh, who was awarded the principality of Delwara by Rana Pratap. When the present owners, the Poddars, acquired it in 1990, it was a series of small, dark interconnected chambers infested with bats and birds, and the edifice itself was falling apart. It took over six years of extensive restoration work by conservation organisations for the 200-room building to be converted into the 39 luxurious suites — built around five courtyards — that we see today. Each suite is spatially distinctive and individually composed of a separate bedroom, sitting area, patio or verandah, with an emphasis on detail accomplished using marble and semi-precious stones. The elegant interiors in pristine white were designed to highlight the contrast between tradition and a modern, minimalist design intervention. Today, Devi Garh successfully straddles two worlds like few hotels can: its façade remains traditional and ancient but the living areas are ultra modernistic (*also see page 410 for information on Devi Garh's spa*).
◆**Tariff** Rs 18,000-59,000 **Tel** 02953-289211 **Email** devigarh@deviresorts.com **Website** deviresorts.com

Courtesy ALSISAR HAVELI

ALSISAR HAVELI, JAIPUR

THE Alsisar Haveli, constructed in 1892 and in a delightful juggling of numbers, renovated in 1982, combines Rajput and Mughal architectural styles. Though today a modern-day hotel, it exudes an old-world charm, as is reflected most in its antique furniture. Surprisingly, the bustling city of Jaipur right outside its doors remains just there — the haveli is a haven of calm in itself. In the central area of the haveli is a platform that was once meant for men's get-togethers and is today a setting for puppet and dance shows. The lobby was once the women's space. The mansion's 47 rooms have frescoes and rug-covered floors while the common areas have crystal chandeliers and hunting trophies. The dining room has gold inlay work on the walls and the bar has, well, a number of drinks that you can enjoy.

♦ **Tariff** Rs 2,400-3,650 **Tel** 0141-2368290 **Email** alsisar@satyam.net.in **Website** alsisarhaveli.com

CASTLE MANDAWA, MANDAWA

TUCKED away in the dusty Shekhawati region of Rajasthan, Castle Mandawa, an amber-coloured fort, was built in 1755 by Thakur Nawal Singh to protect his principality, Mandawa. Today, Castle Mandawa is run by Nawal Singh's descendants as a heritage hotel and is an ideal base from which to explore Shekhawati. The turreted towers, winding staircases, terraces and canopied balconies of the castle are a throwback to its past. The spacious rooms here retain their old flavour, with period furniture and colourful local furnishings. Each of the 70 rooms is different, with beautiful frescoes, and some even boasting of tinkling fountains! The verandah, with comfortable, traditional wicker chairs, accommodates the bar and is an informal place where you can catch up with fellow travellers. But the best experience of the castle is on its ramparts, from where you can get a bird's eye-view of faraway temples and villages.

♦ **Tariff** Rs 2,500-12,000 **Tel** 01592-223124 **Email** castle@datainfosys.net **Website** mandawahotels.com

SANJOY GHOSH

DISCOVER THE EXQUISITE BEAUTY OF
MANDAWA

Castle Mandawa,
One of the oldest heritage hotels of India, Castle Mandawa is a curious mixture of the old and the new with medieval turreted and palanquin roofed balconies. With 75 rooms and

The Desert Resort, Mandawa
A pioneer in mud architecture, the resort has 75 rooms including luxury cottages and specious deluxe suites, each furnished in a distinct style.

Mandawa Haveli, Jaipur
Built in the Jaipur style of architecture with a view of the splendid Nahargarh Fort, Mandawa Haveli is synonymous with royal hospitality at

Jai Niwas Resort, Mandawa
Built in colonial style, the original clubrooms have been converted into 10 independent cottages. Ideal for a small group Jai Niwas

www.mandawahotels.com; e-mail: reservation@castlemandawa.com

BASSI FORT, **BASSI**

Courtesy BASSI FORT PALACE

CONSTRUCTED in the 16th century, the Bassi Fort, situated near Chittaurgarh, faced the onslaught of the Mughals and Marathas several times. Its inhabitants are believed to have laid down their lives defending the fort but none of that marauding history is today immediately visible in its peaceful and serene surroundings. It's a splendid fort, conveniently close to a wildlife sanctuary, and offering you, as the hotel's website promises, a chance to wake up to the calls of peacocks and humming birds every morning. It was renovated in 2000 and overlooks the town and has a pleasing setting amidst hills. Its domes, ramparts and its spacious rooms with jharokhas are stunning, and the old-world furniture adds to its charms. The hotel staff organises a lot of activities and the fort's setting is conducive for relaxing walks and exciting safaris.

♦**Tariff** Rs 1,500-2,500 **Tel** 01472-225321 **Email** resv@bassifortpalace.com **Website** bassifortpalace.com

KHIMSAR FORT, **KHIMSAR**

RAO KARAMSI constructed the Khimsar Fort in 1523 but it became the family's living quarters only in the mid-18th century when they added a new women's wing. As was the norm at that time, this section had finely carved windows and stone grills, the architectural equivalent of a veil. Now the fort has been converted into a hotel, but the royal family, including Rao Karamsi's 21st descendant, continues to live in a part of the fort. It's a beautiful place that offers guests a chance to go on camel and jeep safaris to the areas nearby and spot blackbucks and gazelles. It's best to take a break here if you are travelling from Jodhpur to Bikaner or vice versa. The fort is also an excellent stopover if you are looking for a relaxing holiday — it has gardens made for walks, games such as table tennis and kite-flying, and a telescope to facilitate birdwatching and star-gazing in equal measure.

♦**Tariff** Rs 4,000-5,000 **Tel** 01585-262345-49 **Email** khimsar_jp1@sancharnet.in **Website** khimsarfort.com

Courtesy WELCOMHERITAGE

Jagmandir, Udaipur
circa 1620s

In this 'garden of heaven on earth'
your dream-event becomes a reality.

The story begins just four centuries ago when a rebellious Mughal prince took refuge at Jagmandir on Lake Pichola in Udaipur. The world knows this rebel-prince as Emperor Shah Jehan who later built the Taj Mahal. Jagmandir, it is said, inspired him to build his eternal monument of love. Jagmandir continues to inspire.

An island-palace on a shimmering lake, it's an incomparable venue for glittering wedding ceremonies, glamour and corporate mega-events. Although a quiet dinner at the colonnaded Darikhana is bliss, say the lucky ones. *It's a spectacle that continues to unfold...*

Discover more on page 325

For Reservations and Enquiries contact: Central Reservations (Udaipur)
Toll Free: 1800 180 2933 & 1800 180 2944
Tel: (+91-294) 2528008, 2528016-19 Email: crs@udaipur.hrhindia.com

Eternal Mewat
*Custodianship unbroken
since 734 AD*

HRH Group of Hotels

LAKE PALACE, **UDAIPUR**

MANAGED by the Taj Group, the Lake Palace is inarguably one of the most romantic hotels in the world. Its location, on Udaipur's Lake Pichola, is as exquisite as the marble palace itself. The setting is even more breathtaking when the lake is full, as it was at the time of writing, and then all the clichés that harried travel writers trot out in its praise suddenly and magically seem appropriate. It was built in 1746 as a summer palace by Maharana Jagat Singh II, the 62nd king of the Mewar dynasty. Some people have criticised the Taj Group's renovation work, but luxury has a way of silencing such complaints. The hotel's 83 rooms and suites boast of stained-glass windows, balconies and ornate swings. The hotel offers heritage champagne walks and vintage car airport transfers, and its marvellous interiors combine tradition with modernity; after all, the ornate work in glass and paintings is set against Internet access and currency exchange facilities! The journey to the Lake Palace is beautiful too: take a boat from the Gangaur Ghat and soak in the play of blue and white of the water and the palace.

◆**Tariff** Rs 19,500-60,000 **Tel** 0294-2528800 **Email** lakepalace.udaipur @tajhotels.com **Website** tajhotels.com

MADHU KAPPARATH

GAJNER PALACE, **GAJNER**

BUILT in the early 20th century by Maharaja Ganga Singh, the Gajner Palace, near Bikaner, was once a stopover in the itinerary of visiting dignitaries. It was a private sandgrouse hunting reserve that attracted birds from as far away as Siberia. Now leased out to the HRH Group of Hotels, the palace, constructed in front of an artificial lake, is an excellent option if a quiet holiday is what you are looking for. The red sandstone palace is set in a ground sprawling across 6,000 acres, and boasts of its own wildlife sanctuary, perfect for those interested in birdwatching and animal spotting. That you can see sandgrouse, chinkara, gazelle and heron is, however, just one of the attractions here. The rooms are decidedly old-world, with brass beds and antique dressing tables. You can have your meals on the terrace overlooking the lake or try to dish up something yourself by taking part in the cooking classes at the hotel. The hotel also offers camel and jeep safaris, horse riding, cycling and Internet access.

◆**Tariff** Rs 2,900-3,600 **Tel** 01534-275061 **Email** crs@udaipur.hrhindia. com **Website** hrhhotels.com

SAMODE PALACE, **SAMODE**

LOCATED atop a hill, an hour's drive from Jaipur, the luxurious Samode Palace's USP is its magnificent Sheesh Mahal and the painted Durbar Hall; the beautiful frescoes, the elegant furnishings, the fountains and marble all add to the atmosphere of lavishness and indulgence. The expansion of the palace began under Rawal Berisal in the early 19th century and this work was continued by his descendant Rawal Sheo Singh, also the prime minister of Jaipur state in the mid-19th century. Samode was made a hotel in 1987, with 41 rooms, each opening into either a balcony or a patio. The look is traditional, with the furnishings and architecture showing clear-cut regional influences. A man-made lake — built in the 12th century — stands in front of the palace, which is surrounded by sprawling gardens. The hotel also has all modern amenities such as a health complex and a pool, and organises camel, jeep and horse safaris.

GIREESH GV

◆ **Tariff** Rs 7,700-19,350 **Tel** 01423-240014 **Email** reservations@samode.com **Website** samode.com

RAMBAGH PALACE, **JAIPUR**

IN its earliest form, which can be traced back to 1835, the palace was a more modest home for a favourite maid of the Jaipur royal family. It was later transformed into a hunting lodge and finally a palace in 1925. Converted into a hotel in 1957 by Maharaja Sawai Man Singh II, who lived here with his wife Gayatri Devi, it was leased out to the Taj Group of Hotels in 1972. The hotel assures guests of a luxurious stay, with four-poster beds, walk-in wardrobes and marble corridors, not to forget the landscaped gardens around it, which have given the palace its name. Those in the historical suites have personal butlers while the maharani suite has a bathroom full of mirrors and the princess suite its own fountains and a terrace garden. Though located in bustling Jaipur, not a single urban sound is likely to reach you, past the gardens and courtyards and fountains. The hotel can even arrange polo games on request at the Rambagh Polo grounds near the palace.

GIREESH GV

◆ **Tariff** Rs 20,300-1,76,000 **Tel** 0141-2211919 **Email** rambagh.jaipur@tajhotels.com **Website** tajhotels.com

SHIV NIWAS PALACE, **UDAIPUR**

A HERITAGE hotel with a Scottish band, this palace began its life as Maharana Fateh Singh's abode, and it's said that he entertained guests in the rooms around the courtyard. It's part of Udaipur's marvellous City Palace complex, and some of its rooms offer lovely lake views. The palace has suites with old-world furniture, chandeliers, private terraces and canopied beds. All imaginable luxuries are on offer here — you can pamper yourself by opting for an Ayurvedic massage, play squash or billiards, hire a limousine or enjoy rides on solar-powered boats on the lake. But most of all, you would probably want to spend time taking in the rich ornamentation in the walls in the interiors, the clever use of marble, the frescoes and the pavilions and the fountains. A royal high tea or a romantic dinner should feature in your list of must-do things at the hotel-palace. The service at the hotel can border on the obsequious, but if you are here looking for a fun-filled holiday, it's quite unlikely that you will be complaining about some extra attention!
◆ **Tariff** Rs 6,000-21,000 **Tel** 0294-2528016-19 **Email** crs@udaipur.hrh india.com **Website** hrhhotels.com

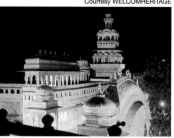

Courtesy WELCOMHERITAGE

MANDIR PALACE, **JAISALMER**

THE stone carvings of this two centuries old palace — whose name is derived from its proximity to temples — are breathtaking and deserve a visit on their own. That said, the palace is a wonderful place to stay as well. Its rooms flaunt antique furnishings while the regal touch in the suites is enhanced by the silver furniture here. The palace literally looms over the surrounding areas with its Badal Vilas, the over 50-m high tower. It boasts of all modern amenities, a multi-cuisine restaurant and a coffee shop. The Jawahir Vilas in the palace has lovely balconies and canopies while the glasshouse has latticework in glass and gold. The architecture follows the Indo-Saracenic style.
◆ **Tariff** Rs 2,200-4,200 **Tel** 02992-252788 **Email** welcom@ndf.vsnl.net. in **Website** welcomheritagehotels.com

Courtesy WELCOMHERITAGE

BAL SAMAND LAKE PALACE, **JODHPUR**

BUILT as the summer residence of the Jodhpur kings, the palace is a red sandstone structure overlooking a 13th century artificial lake. Each of the 10 suites in the palace has antique pieces of furniture, patios and lovely ornate windows. The arches in the rooms and the niches add to the old-world atmosphere. You can take a ride in a horse carriage, play golf or dine at the open-air garden restaurant. Its lounge and bar, overlooking the lake, are great places to relax. The palace promises a serene stay close to nature and the greenery around is a soothing sight. On the same grounds, sharing the same facilities, is the Bal Samand Garden Retreat, which has 26 rooms.
♦ **Tariff** Rs 4,100-11,000 **Tel** 0291-2572321-27 **Email** reservations@ jodhpurheritage.com **Website** wel comheritagehotels.com

DEOGARH MAHAL, **DEOGARH**

THIS 17th-century structure was converted into a hotel by the current owner, whose family still lives in a part of the hotel. The Rawats once ruled over the fourth largest principality in Rajputana, with their territory spreading across 210 villages. The Deogarh Mahal, however, isn't

Courtesy DEOGARH MAHAL

ostentatious — it somehow manages to be elegant and splendid without being opulent.

It bursts with turrets, domes and jharokhas, with an emphasis on stained glass, old portraits and photographs, and other objets d' art inside. One of the most interesting aspects of the palace is a wall that has a series of jharokhas, located in a wing meant for women, believed to have been inspired by Jaipur's Hawa Mahal. The hotel has friendly service and each of the 60 rooms here harks back to a particular era — the Ranjit Prakash room, for instance, is reminiscent of 1670 and the décor is Rajput-style. Lovely views of the surrounding ranges and lakes are on offer here.
♦ **Tariff** Rs 4,999-9,999 **Tel** 02904-252777 **Email** info@deogarhmahal. com **Website** deogarhmahal.com

UMAID BHAWAN PALACE
JODHPUR

FOR a structure constructed as part of a work-for-food programme in the time of famine, the palace's opulence is, well, striking. Work on it went on for 15 years and this 347-room palace was finally completed in 1943. Lutyens' friend Henry Lanchester designed the monument, named after and built by Maharaja Umaid Singh. It boasts of a 105-foot high cupola, towers inspired by Rajput traditions, a theatre, eight dining rooms plus a banquet hall that can accommodate 300 people, a ballroom, a smoking room, a wood-panelled library, private garages with vintage car collections... the list is endless. Not everything in the palace was a paean to the West, however. The room with the throne has murals from the

Courtesy TAJ UMAID BHAWAN PALACE

Ramayana. Apart from marvelling at the palace itself, guests can also enjoy themselves at the billiards room, at any of the four tennis courts or at one of the two marble-floored squash courts. There is also a spa and a 15-acre garden in this hotel-palace run by the Taj Group.
♦ **Tariff** Rs 19,300-1,76,000 **Tel** 0291-2510101 **Email** ubpresv.jodh@tajhotels.com **Website** tajhotels.com

UDAI BILAS PALACE
DUNGARPUR

RATHER quirky but nevertheless lovely is this palace located on the banks of the Gaibsagar Lake in

Courtesy UDAI BILAS PALACE

Dungarpur. A tourist attraction in itself, the palace is flanked by the lake and a small forest on two sides. Its construction was started in the mid-19th century, with the Ek Thambia Mahal (or the One-Pillared Palace) being the first edifice to be built. Made of bluish-grey *pareva* stone, the palace has sculpted pillars, ornate balconies, arches, turrets and balustrades. (The additions made in 1940 were all *art deco*.)

The combination of architectural styles does not take away from the palace's charm — if anything it enhances it. The palace has a swimming pool, jacuzzi, gym and offers boating facilities. It has 20 rooms altogether and as the hotel website charmingly declares, "No two rooms are alike as no two guests are alike." Amen to that.
♦ **Tariff** Rs 3,025-5,750 **Tel** 02964-230808 **Email** contact@udaibilaspalace.com **Website** udaibilaspalace.com

BHANWAR NIWAS, **BIKANER**

ONE of the most famous havelis in Bikaner, the Bhanwar Niwas was commissioned in 1927 by Bhanwar-lalji Rampuria, who had inherited a fortune by way of real estate and the textile industry. After his death in 1947, the haveli remained empty for decades till one of Rampuria's descendants converted it into a heritage hotel. The haveli has a Victorian ambience but that is only in the very beginning. You will spot the Indian influences soon enough (as in the case of the gold leaf work on the walls, done by artists from Bikaner) and the entire haveli showcases a delightful mix of Indian and European styles.

There are chandeliers from Belgium, antique items from France and England, and a 1927 Buick to boot. The intricately carved red sandstone front, the Belgian tiled bathrooms with huge tubs, the fountain in the courtyard, all add to the atmosphere. There are 26 rooms, which are, as is the case in most heritage hotels, different from each other. As the family is vegetarian, the cuisine is mostly Marwari vegetarian with a few European-style dishes thrown in as if in homage to the haveli's atmosphere. The food is excellent.

♦ **Tariff** Rs 2,800-3,600 **Tel** 0151-2529323 **Email** bhanwarniwas@rediffmail.com **Website** bhanwarniwas.com

Courtesy NEEMRANA HOTELS

PIRAMAL HAVELI, **BAGAR**

THIS haveli is worth a visit in itself only because of the unique frescoes on its walls: of flying angels, gods in motor cars, and flying machines, all of which make for a quaint and interesting sight. It makes you wonder what its owner Seth Piramal Chaturbhuj Makharia, who made his money from cotton and silver, had in mind when he had it built in 1928. The haveli is today run by the Neemrana group and has four courtyards, eight rooms, pillared corridors and huge

gardens. The activities at the haveli include card games, carrom and a treasure hunt to complete the picture. It's also a good place to base yourself to tour Shekhawati's havelis. You can have excellent Marwari food here, and for some added excitement, ask for dinner to be served in a sand dune setting, which also the hotel organises for a minimum of six guests at prior notice.

♦ **Tariff** Rs 1,500-2,000 **Tel** 01592-221220 **Email** sales@neemranahotels.com **Website** neemranahotels.com

Courtesy RAJ NIWAS PALACE

RAJ NIWAS PALACE, **DHOLPUR**

FULL of ancient fittings and furnishings that have clearly been preserved with affection and care, the Raj Niwas Palace is thought to date back to 1876, when it was apparently built to welcome the then Prince of Wales, Albert Edward. It has a maharaja suite (covered with ceramic tiles, with gilded plasterwork on the ceiling), a maharani suite, a Prince of Wales suite and four deluxe luxury suites. Most rooms are decorated with tiles. There is also a library and a movie theatre but a walk in the sprawling grounds may be the most ideal for relaxation. The staff is very friendly and make the stay wonderful. As a bonus, the palace is just 40 km from Agra.
◆ **Tariff** Rs 8,500-9,000 **Tel** 011-26436572-73, 41620674 **Email** info@dholpurpalace.com **Website** dholpurpalace.com

LAXMI NIWAS PALACE, **BIKANER**

The Lallgarh Palace was constructed in the 19th century by Maharaja Ganga Singh and today houses the Laxmi Niwas Palace, owned and run by a private hotelier. It is the most beautiful wing of the palace, with a number of hunting trophies in the bar and conference rooms. There may not be any old-world courtesies here but the 42 rooms here are regal. The dining room (and indeed several other rooms) has gold wall paintings and wooden ceilings. The king's old study is today a 24-hr coffee shop and the billiards room is a great place to relax.
◆ **Tariff** Rs 5,000-9,000 **Tel** 0151-2521188-89

CASTLE BIJAIPUR
CHITTAURGARH

CASTLE Bijaipur makes up in its serenity what it lacks in terms of ornamentation or ostentation. It's a world away from touristy Rajasthan, 40 km from the nearest tourist attraction of Chittaurgarh, and its charm is in the middle-of-nowhere feeling of peace that it offers. Built in the 16th century, when Bijaipur was an important bastion of the Mewar kingdom, the palace offers lovely views of the surrounding areas. You can spend some time in the pretty garden, go on a camel or horse safari, opt for birdwatching or go trekking. The food is organic, and yoga and meditation classes are on offer. What more could you ask for?
◆ **Tariff** Rs 2,640-7,500 **Tel** 01472-276222 **Email** castlebijaipur@rediffmail.com **Website** castlebijaipur.com

GIREESH GV

For more details on these heritage stay options, see Accommodation Listings on pages 455-494

Compiled by OTG Desk with ANURADHA KAPOOR

The camel ride guide

ABHILASH GAUR goes on a camel safari and lives to tell the tale

You can topple off a camel when it's rising on its hind legs or lowering itself on its forelegs. You can also fall when it turns sharply to one side, and, if you are not careful, you can even slip when it's walking briskly. If you have a lazy stomach, or have consumed something hard to digest, ride a camel. Its gait causes your back and stomach to trace a spiral trajectory, even as your bobbing head manages to nod back and forth. The anxiety of the first 15 minutes is also excellent for the heart, while forearms and wrists are exercised in the vital process of holding on to the saddle. If you are still anxious after the first 15 minutes, get off pronto in the interest of your cholesterol-choked urban arteries, otherwise roll on.

By now, you have figured out that the key to keeping your seat is to sit loose, rather than tight, and go with the flow of the beast. Also, by now, the turbaned Raika has led you far away from the fort, palace or desert camp where you are staying. As Rajasthani towns are small, you are probably in the countryside, with tall *kejdi* trees lining your path.

The camel will now insist on stopping and stripping a few *kejdi* branches of their thin, tender leaves, while the Raika will persuade it otherwise with a sharp knock to its knee. Regardless of the outcome of this debate, it's best to guard yourself against the outstretched thorny branches of the trees.

In the countryside, you will be made to feel like an elephant in a Gurgaon mall. Everybody, especially the kids, will stop to stare at you. Giggly voices will declare you a *gora*

SANJAY SHARMA

(white), notwithstanding your native colour. You will be asked "vaatij your nim" and showered with bye-byes. If you are attired in shorts, consider your foreigner status stamped and sealed. By the way, bare calves mean enduring the prickly camel hair pressing through the bright saddlecloth.

A camel's passage through the countryside has a charming effect on other beasts, at least in places where it is not too common a sight (contrary to belief, most of Rajasthan is like that). Cows and buffaloes that routinely defy pressure horns will run at the camel's approach. A buffalo running with its tail in the air is spectacular, to say the least.

Small talk

Out in the fields, and almost one with the camel by now, you might wonder what it is like to hold the reins. Don't be alarmed if the Raika now offers the black ropes to you on his own. You might fancy the beast making away with you at a trot. More so when it

In the countryside, the tourist on camelback may end up feeling like an elephant in a mall! But it's a small price to pay for the joys of a safari

casts its baleful eye upon the world, sensing the change in pressure on the reins. But it is a wise beast, accustomed to tourists. Running is hard work, so it will head for the fence of henna twigs instead, and steal a quick snack while you wonder whether to pull the reins or dig your heels in its sides, and weigh the possible outcomes of such violence.

You, who spin a big car out of jams everyday, have been humbled by a camel. And the Raika, with the

slightest superior air, will resume the 'safari', reins firmly in his hand. This is the time to get chatty with Nemji, or whatever his name is, about camels. If language is a barrier, let your hotel/ camp guide assist.

Ask Nemji where he bought the camel, and how much it cost. Also ask him how long it's likely to survive. Although common knowledge, you could still ask about and express amazement at the beast's eating and drinking habits. Chances are that your camel is not from the premium Jaisalmeri breed that costs at least Rs 35,000 each. Rather, the Raika would have picked up the Barmeri camel at Pushkar for under Rs 15,000. And though it will live to be 20-25, the Raika won't keep it more than a few years — they change their camels ever so often.

And back

You've been on the camel a couple of hours, and see no point in remaining there much longer. On the way back to your hotel/ camp, you no longer feel the animal's rolling gait, and are barely holding the saddle. Back in the town street, it's the camel's turn to be scared by the sounds of motorbikes and jeeps. The Raika does his best to shield the camel and calm it, but it still takes a few uncertain steps.

On this home run, you realise the change in perspective wrought by your perch. The shop signboards are below you. The shampoo sachets and packets of chips hung at lintel height are also below you. And that explains the high gateways of Rajputana's palaces and havelis: it's all about saving your head.

After two hours, you might fancy yourself as an accomplished camel rider, but now, as the beast dips on its forelegs, remember to hold on to the saddle. And then again, as it drops its rump. Finally, you are there! ∎

The camel and I

PRERNA SINGH falls for Diamond-Heera's sparkling charm

When the guide at Osian suggested we go on a camel safari, my first reaction was to yelp out a vehement 'no'. The camel was too tall for my comfort, its gait was rather ungainly, and its indifference a bit difficult to accept — or so I thought. Besides, what was there to see on camel-top that I couldn't see from the ground? And then I met Diamond-Heera.

To be sure, it wasn't love at first sight. Heck, it wasn't even camaraderie at first sight. The implausibly but endearingly named Diamond-Heera sauntered into our vision, his bulk massive, his swaying anything but reassuring. He seated himself on the sand, waiting for us — my friend and I, that is — to get going. We argued a little about who should sit in front but my friend had already decided that by virtue of being shorter, she would get to hold on to the saddle. So there I was, hanging in there by sheer willpower, muttering more than a prayer while watching with horror the camel's first three steps: getting up on his fore-knees, a move that almost threw me backwards; then raising his hind legs, which pushed me forward; and finally, on all four, much to my immediate relief.

All that dread soon proved pointless, however, for Diamond-Heera was an unbelievably gentle animal. My friend, nevertheless, started a monologue with the camel on what a rare beast he was, hoping to gain some brownie points (after all, we were $7^1/_2$ ft above the ground and at Diamond-Heera's mercy). I am proud to report that I was relaxed enough to take in the sights around us — the

PARVIN SINGH

cattle, the children shouting and waving — as we moved away from the little town of Osian on to the village where the camel owner stayed.

The camel owner broke my reverie by handing over the reins to us, a power trip we could very well do without. What if Diamond-Heera started running? Such worries were again unfounded — the thought of taking advantage of us novices, I am sure, did not even cross this wonderful animal's mind.

Soon, it started getting dark and we cut our safari short and headed back. We dismounted without incident (it must have helped that we were more confident by then), all the time feeling a surge of affection for Diamond-Heera, who had mitigated all our misgivings about him and his ilk. I patted him on his neck while my friend tipped the camel owner generously. Diamond-Heera shone against the desert sky like a true jewel. ∎

On a roll, in the Orient

AMIT MAHAJAN lives the royal life on board the Palace on Wheels

Photographs by SANJAY SHARMA

O ur group's guide is trying to enliven — or so he thinks — the experience of a remote past with crass comments about the kings' harems and their concubines. The other group has a woman guide, a rarity. Hopefully, she is different from the male of the species and does not rely on the 'men are all henpecked but large-hearted enough to laugh about it' variety of humour. Holly, sitting next to me, has no interest in either of the guides. Then she tells me why. She is waiting for the inevitable to happen: for The Body to turn up.

We are on a luxury train and Holly clearly knows her Agatha Christies well. So if you have a Luxury Train, a Murder has to happen. We are on board the Palace on Wheels, living the royal life — to put it mildly — across the length and breadth of that royal destination par excellence, Rajasthan. It's a worthy parallel to the Orient Express. Soon Holly and I have it all chalked out. A victim whom loads of fellow travellers are eager to bump off; a photographer who will inadvertently capture a vital clue in his camera; a couple who are obviously mismatched and a food scientist who knows much about poisons. The cast is all there waiting for their respective cues. But truth turns out to be stranger and stronger than fiction. Christie wanes as the Palace-on-Wheels journey takes over — it's like nothing we have ever experienced before.

The trip begins on a Wednesday afternoon, two hours before the 6.30 pm departure from the Safdarjung Railway Station. The reception includes shehnais, marigold garlands and Rajasthani turbans on tentative heads. We are escorted to our respective saloons by immaculately dressed captains in churidars, sherwanis and long-tailed *pagdis*. We're going to get used to such attention over the next few days.

The train has 14 air-conditioned deluxe saloons, each named after an erstwhile princely state of the Rajasthan region, and arranged alphabetically from Alwar to Udaipur. I am in Dungarpur. Each saloon has four twin-bedded chambers and a common sitting lounge with sofas, a television and a DVD player. The interior is done up tastefully in wood, and there is wall-to-wall carpeting. The chambers have two comfortable beds and there is a provision for a third pull-down sleeper (passengers can opt for single, double or triple occupancy). There is an attached bath with shower, hot and cold water and exhaust fan; the tiled floor and the wood panels are kept as clean as can be and there is a daily change of sparkling white linen. Each saloon car has a small pantry, where breakfast and small snacks are prepared. There is a captain and an attendant in each saloon, excellent in their work and ready to please. We have in our saloon the tall and graceful Siddhartha and the homely Prakash.

The first evening is for acclimatisation. Everyone tries to soak in the surrounding opulence and seeks to find familiarity with fellow travellers. The bar lounge is teeming with people who are busy with the initiation rites of such an occasion — nascent conversations and provisional friendships are being formed. Drinkers are keen to check what is on offer at the bar and, of course, the prices. The wine list is disappointing: the choice is only a couple of Indian wines and some not-so-great French

The staff (l) **roll out the red carpet for the passengers** (r)

stuff. However, spirits are high and make up for such inadequacies.

Of forts and palaces

Jaipur is our first halt. The wake-up call is at 6 am with a pot of Green Label, brewed just right (the previous afternoon, Prakash and Siddhartha figured out just how much brewing I like). Breakfast is at 7.30 am, and we are off to see Jaipur. Two beautifully decked elephants are there to welcome and amuse us. Right away, numerous cameras come out and every body part and gesture of the elephants is assiduously documented. Here the passengers on the train are divided into three groups, each on a different bus with a tour escort from the train and a local guide. This structure is adopted throughout the week, whenever we disembark the train and visit the sites.

We take short halts at the Albert Hall and the Hawa Mahal. As we alight at the Amber Fort, there are more elephants around than I have ever seen before. We are two persons to an elephant, and they ponderously walk up the ramp, occasionally prodded by the mahouts. The guide is eager and unrestrained in his attempts to populate the palaces and court-yards with names, characters and deeds of their famous inhabitants. In the afternoon we spend some time at the Jantar Mantar, marvelling at the play of light and shadow that can tell us the time of the day or the position of the sun vis-à-vis the equator. After a visit to an emporium, we are back on our hotel-on-wheels, moving on to the next destination.

> "Any journey is as good as the people you meet on the way. We had a wonderfully eclectic mix of people on board"

At daylight, **Jaisalmer** is the next port of call. It's cloudy and drizzling but that does not hamper the usual pomp and show at the station. It does dampen the glory of the Golden Fort, which is at its preening best when the sun's rays kiss it with their warmth. However, the Palace-on-Wheels group makes for a brilliant spectacle with scores of colourful parasols moving about in three separate gangs. In the fort now begins a charming two-way spectacle wherein two sets of dramatis personae simultaneously act and watch one another. There is the local populace — women in the streets, milkmen on motorcycles, peddlers in the square — and there are the tourists, mostly white, walking by. In this space both of them seem to be living with the sole purpose of looking at the other, with an enthusiastic search for comprehension, and an eagerness to engage.

We are glad Jaisalmer — the ramparts and the Jain temple in the fort and the havelis outside — is to be seen on foot. Living on the train, and being ferried by buses, means that walking gives us a sense of freedom and an opportunity to stretch our limbs. Lunch is back on the train. The food on the Palace on Wheels is not such a treat. All the meals are huge buffet affairs — a number of dishes, some Indian plus Continental or Chinese. The space does not permit self-service and people have strange combinations on the plate. Everybody has their share of bizarre mixes. You end up having, for example, pulao, rice, papad with steamed fish, or noodles with tandoori chicken and raita. The quality of cooking leaves much to be desired. Most passengers feel they need to focus on the quality rather than quantity.

Breakfasts are our best meal on board. It is a cozy affair between the six occupants of the coach who like

Luxury is assured both outside and inside the Palace on Wheels

each other's company and spend the morning hour with juices, coffees, eggs made to order and toasts. The conversation flows easily from Nicole's hot trauma of attending a sweaty, sari-clad wedding in Chennai to Maurice's intoxicating experiences involving saké in a Japanese port town. And Prakash handles the supply side with easy perfection.

The afternoon in Jaisalmer is on the train, doing nothing. After a day-and-a-half of hectic sightseeing, this is a welcome opportunity for most to get a siesta. A few adventurous types use the opportunity to venture out on their own — to get a local snack in the bazaars of Jaisalmer, or to walk the lanes without the pressure of being with a big group.

After the siesta is desert time, out in the **Sam sand dunes** close to the Indo-Pak border. The thrill of being on this uncommon territory is combined with the anxiety of riding the camel — the mammal is far too tall to feel

safe and secure. Still, everybody is on camel back, and soon most of us are enjoying the swaying walk. Dinner is at Hotel Gorbandh Palace, accompanied by Rajasthani music and dance. Most people have by now found their preferred companions and friendships are being formed. Many of the women are relaxed enough to join the professionals in their whirling and twirling. Men are more self-conscious.

The next day, we reach **Jodhpur** and the highlight of the day is the Jodhpur Fort. The weather is great — cloudy and breezy. As bonus, there is enough time to go through the royal enclave at an unhurried pace. This is not always the case, for, this journey is a conducted tour and the tour escorts and guides want their wards to be together and under observation. Mehrangarh Fort gives them an opportunity to relax as there is no real possibility that someone can get lost here. There is enough space for people to be on their own, to idle a while in a quiet courtyard or linger a wee bit more at a jharokha to gaze at the city below. The guide in Jodhpur is a big hit too; for a change, he knows his history.

Bollywood on wheels

We start early in the afternoon from Jodhpur, and this is the first time we have travelled in the daytime on the Palace on Wheels. We plan a 'living room experience' right on the train and watch a Hindi movie. It is just perfect but for the lack of popcorn. Nicole makes herself comfortable on the carpet, with a pillow propped against the sofa. Maurice has little interest in a film he is sure he won't understand, so he comes armed with a book. I am comfortably reclining on a sofa, and having seen the film before, I can watch it while reading my novel. Sanjay, the photographer traveling along with me, has also seen the film and he is appointed the interpreter. We are travelling on one of the 10 best train journeys in the world, and indeed it is a spoiled life.

It is too early in the season to visit the **Ranthambhore National Park**, famous for its tigers. The park is to open later, but they accommodate

View from the City Palace, Udaipur

the Palace-on-Wheels group. It is a nice crisp morning and the drive under the Ranthambhore Fort and past the lakes and woods in the open vehicle is stimulating. We hear some alarm calls by monkeys and deer and it is reported that there is a tigress with two cubs in the vicinity. We are, however, not lucky enough to spot the animal.

Back from the forest, we for once have a late and lazy breakfast. We are going south through the Aravallis towards **Chittaurgarh**. The signs of heavy rains in the previous months are all there. The area is lush green, lakes and ponds are full, and we can see flooding in some plains. We visit the Chittaurgarh Fort for a short while in the afternoon.

Now people have started missing an outing or two. A few are unwell, most with a case of the tummy capitulating under, I believe, a combination of factors — the stress of the packed schedule, holiday though it is supposed to be, a series of elaborate but similar buffet lunches and dinners and not too great food at that.

In the evening the bar lounge is packed. The chilled beers and the icy rum-colas are going down eager throats to increasingly heady heads. This is our fifth day on the train and the conversation has moved much ahead of the tentative "so what do you do?" of the initial evenings. Now it is either gossipy nuggets such as "what do you mean father and daughter! Are you mad?", or sincere discussions, many about 9/11, whose anniversary was the day before — there are people on the train who were affected by those events.

On board, there is already a sense that the best part of the week is over. The penultimate day is spent in **Udaipur**. Its lakes and palaces enchant most, even though tiredness can now be discerned in the air. The boat ride

The Ultra Edition 12.9
SAMSUNG SGH D-900

imagine doing more with less.
The Ultra Life.

Imagine always being in two places at once, doing two things at once. No office. No boundaries. No restrictions. With Samsung's new Ultra Edition it's not that hard to imagine.   www.samsung.com

Features: 3 Mega Pixel Camera with Auto-Focus • MP3 Player • Intelligent Display • Large 262K QVGA TFT Screen • Direct TV Out

Free accessories: Bluetooth™ Headset • 256 MB T Flash Memory Card • TV Out Cable • Battery Charger • Travel Adapter • Car Adapter • Straight Headset • Battery (2 Nos.) • Data Kit

The Ultra Edition 12.9
SAMSUNG SGH D-900

Leo Burnett D SMSCHLB-000013H

SAMSUNG

Fact File

7-NIGHT ITINERARY

Day 1 Wed: Check-in at the Safdarjung Railway Station, Delhi, at 4 pm **Day 2** Thu: Jaipur arrival 3 am, departure 7.30 pm **Day 3** Fri: Jaisalmer arrival 9 am, departure 11.45 pm **Day 4** Sat: Jodhpur arrival 7 am, departure 3.30 pm **Day 5** Sun: Sawai Madhopur arrival 4 am, departure 10.30 am; Chittaurgarh arrival 4 pm **Day 6** Mon: Chittaurgarh departure 5.30 am; Udaipur arrival 7.30 am, departure 5.30 pm **Day 7** Tue: Bharatpur arrival 6.30 am, departure 9 am; Agra arrival 12.15 pm, departure 9 pm **Day 8** Wed: Delhi arrival 6 am

FARES

◆ **Oct 2006-Mar 2007:** The fare is US$ 385 per night per person on double occupancy. Single and triple occupancy are US$ 535 and 315 respectively. A **7-night trip** costs US$ 2,695 on double occupancy. Single and triple occupancy fares are US$ 3,745 and 2,205 respectively.

The tariff includes the cost of travel, all meals, sightseeing, entrance fees for monuments, cultural entertainment at Jaipur and Jaisalmer and boat ride to Lake Palace Hotel at Udaipur, and elephant and camel rides. **Note** Tariff does not include liquor, laundry and other items of personal nature and video camera charges for entry into parks and monuments. Half fare for kids between 5 and 12 years

CONTACT

In Jaipur RTDC, Hotel Swagatam Campus, Near Railway Station, Jaipur Tel: 0141-5115777, 2203531/ 620 **In Delhi** Senior Manager, Palace on Wheels, Rajasthan Tourism Reception Centre, Bikaner House, New Delhi Tel: 011-23381884, 23386069 Website: palaceonwheels.net

in the afternoon in Lake Pichola and the fresh breeze on the Jagmandir Island restores many tired bodies and minds. The next morning, at dawn, we are out and about in cycle rickshaws in the Keoladeo Ghana Bird Sanctuary at Bharatpur. Water and, therefore, birds have sadly deserted the sanctuary but it is good to be out in the fresh coolness of the morning.

Now begins the unending streak of glorious adjectives — 'the last and the best', 'the icing on the cake' and many more. This is in preparation of seeing the Taj Mahal at Agra. But nothing can actually prepare you for the transcendental lustrousness of the white stone as it enters your eyes and pervades your senses. It's a fitting way to end a journey.

However, practical necessities of life remain. We still have to go back to the train. The organisers still want us to visit another emporium, where they offer drinks-on-the-house and wheedle us into making just one purchase. This is, in fact, a consistent pain on the tour. The regular visits to shops and emporia where zealous salesmen bombard us with 'just take a look, no charge for seeing, ok'. We endure all that and return.

Early Wednesday morning we are back in Delhi, and it's time for settling bills, exchanging contacts and many hugs and kisses. Any journey is as good as the people you meet on the way. On the Palace on Wheels there are many opportunities to get to know a lot of people. We had a wonderfully eclectic mix of people on board. On a table-for-four at lunch, there could have been a travel writer from Australia, an Indian couple settled in New Jersey and a retired professor from Germany. The train and its incredibly caring team will soon be ready, in fact, the same afternoon, to bring together another set of people and take them on a fantasy trip. ■

PHOTOS ARUN NANGLA

Vignettes of a journey on the new Heritage on Wheels train

New route to history

LAKSHMI INDRASIMHAN takes a ride on the Heritage on Wheels

The *kejdi* tree is shaved of leaves. At regular intervals through arid Shekhawati, the *kejdi*, with the primeval awkwardness of its form, stands stalwart, its branches above its head in a sort of writhing, stunted ambition. The landscape seems both quiet and restless, the geography "obscured by the wind blown over-burden". It is like watching a film with the sound off. The dogs here are slower, their reflexes unfit yet easily roused by motorbikes and strangers. There are camels and asses on the streets and peacocks in every mud-paved yard. Huge havelis emerge out of the dust, their green and silver shutters shut tight against the red sandstone of their façades. Where there is no water, wells stand on high platforms, and where there is irrigation, startlingly lush fields worry the eye now accustomed to dust. Everything else is twigs. There are few cars and the only horn comes from a van carrying that most precious of things: the heritage tourist.

Shekhawati has been romantically called the open-air art gallery of India. Today, the paintings are increasingly embattled, the exhausting forces of litter and open sewers and graffiti that have come with the dissipation of former powers. The gates are mostly shut, the paint peeling, the intricately carved doors pulled from their hinges to be made into tabletops for export.

The contrast between past opulence and present disintegration is all the more noticeable when you arrive as we did, amidst the pomp and bonhomie of RTDC's new venture, the Heritage on Wheels luxury train. Intended for those with more

The info

The Heritage on Wheels runs twice a week (Tuesdays and Sundays) from Jaipur. From Delhi, take the Ajmer Shatabdi (leaves New Delhi 6.10 am, arrives 10.40 am; Rs 465 on CC). Else, one of RTDC's deluxe buses which depart frequently from Bikaner House (Rs 436/ 5 hrs).

3-NIGHT ITINERARY

The train runs between September and April every year. It's a 3N/ 4D trip, Jaipur to Jaipur **Day 1** Depart for Bikaner from Jaipur 7.30 pm **Day 2** Arrive in Bikaner 6 am. Visit Junagarh Fort, Haat, Gajner (lunch, safari), Lallgarh Palace (tea). Leave for Tal Chhapar **Day 3** Day spent visiting Shekhawati's havelis: Mandawa Castle (lunch); Ramgarh and Nawalgarh. Leave for Jaipur 8 pm **Day 4** Arrive in Jaipur 6.30 am.

FACILITIES

The train features nine 'heritage' saloons, each of which accommodates eight persons in four bedrooms with two bathrooms shared. There are two restaurants and one bar-cum-lounge; both Continental and Rajasthani food is served.

FARES

The fare is Rs 8,500 per person per night, on double occupancy. Single and triple occupancy charges are Rs 12,500 and Rs 6,500 respectively. The charges are inclusive of accommodation, meals, transportation, entrance fees and guide services.

CONTACT
Rajasthan Tourism Development Corporation Ltd (Jaipur Tel: 0141-5115777, 2203531; Delhi Tel: 011-23381884/ 6069; Website: heritageonwheels.net.in)

'moderate' budgets, this new sibling of the Palace on Wheels attempts to reconstruct both the civilised past of rail travel and the Palace on Wheels' success. Luxury of this sort is mostly about privacy: the separation from the hordes, curtains to be drawn against curious noses, liveried staff to escort you, sliding cabin doors with locks, bathrooms that exhort you to cleanliness. It is about welcomes: fine lasses applying *tikas* and garlands, moustachioed guardsmen with flags and drumrolls, rose-strewn pathways and 'folk' musicians on the platform at Jaipur station. Each saloon is named after the different towns in the region: Ramgarh, Nawalgarh, Mandawa. This is all you will know of these places: their names and their faces. Tours like this promise pleasure amid an admittedly parvenu luxury.

The programme is still raw. On our journey there are only two tourists and the itinerary is a little muddy, but brightened by the accommodating hospitality of everyone working with the tour. The train is comfortable with all the amenities: bar, restaurants, hot water showers, beds (not berths), Biotique shampoo. The several courses of dinner come with almost endearing service.

Elevated by my associations: Delhi, *Outlook Traveller*, the Heritage on Wheels, I am a modern-day royal, and as a friend reminded me, the trip would be more digestible if I recognised that fact. So I add extra butter to my soup and try to consider it with the concerned furrow of do-gooder princesses like Angelina Jolie rather than the marauding joie de vivre of, say, Paris Hilton.

As it's billed as a heritage tour, one assumes that fellow travellers would have shared my fascination for the paintings that **Shekhawati** is famed. But RTDC knows the average tourist better than I do — we only stop at five

A fairy-tale trip

The **Fairy Queen** is the world's oldest running locomotive. It has a traditional steam engine and two bogeys, one of which is a chair car for its 60 passengers and the other a bogey for the train's attendants. This luxury train is only in operation from October to February and runs on the second and last weekend of each month. Passengers are required to be at the Delhi Cantonment Railway Station at 8.30 am on Saturday, from where the train leaves at 10 am. It reaches **Alwar** at 3 pm. An RTDC bus then takes passengers to the RTDC Siliserh Palace Hotel, where tea, a cultural evening and eventually dinner follows. The next morning, the guests are taken on a jeep safari inside the **Sariska Wildlife Sanctuary**, followed by breakfast at the hotel. After this, it's back to Alwar, from where the Fairy Queen leaves for Delhi at 1 pm. The train arrives at Delhi at 6.45 pm.
◆**Contact** ITB, National Rail Museum, Chanakyapuri, New Delhi-110021; Tel: 011-26881816 **Tariff** Adults Rs 7,500, children below 12 years Rs 3,500

GIREESH GV

or so sites, though I crane my neck for glimpses of the countless others we drove past. Instead, we spend an hour at a camel farm and another at a warehouse where Shekhawati's woodworkers now use circular saws to make bureaus and china cabinets for shops around the world. Instead of seeing traditions preserved, I feel we are seeing them as they have been interpreted for us. Rajasthan is not mine, but mine to use.

Our first stop is **Bikaner**, where we visit a Jain temple in the old town that is still covered with bright, intricate paintings: goddesses in saris and wings, fat rajas and consorts. Then a horse-drawn tonga ride to the amused curiosity of the locals, through the narrow streets to see the astounding, shut-up-and-out-of-reach havelis of Bikaner's migratory merchant classes. Junagarh Fort is the next stop. We are then whisked away to the Lallgarh Palace Hotel for tea and a quick look at its lovely indoor pool and the grisly stuffed tiger remnants of a lifetime of royal shikar.

For evening entertainment we are off to the Gajner Palace Hotel. Some take a quick camel ride (on Raja, the cigarette-smoking camel) amid the banyan trees. There is an evocative performance by a Langa troupe, the community whose voice has come to encompass and represent the desert. The hotel is all candlelit, tasteful loveliness with a sumptuous grand banquet room overlooking a lake.

The next morning we are awakened with tea at 6 am. The fog is thick and hangs to our ankles and the train stands confidently in its midst. We are going to **Tal Chhapar Sanctuary**, a pampas-like grassland for a jeep safari. We whiz quickly, guiltily past hitchhiking labourers and their steel-tiered tiffin boxes. We see black bucks, nilgai and the charmingly named demoiselles cranes, who, not surprisingly, rush away on our advance. We are only 12; how will they react to a trainloadful? Then it's back to the train for breakfast and a few hours' travel to **Ramgarh** where we are met by the town's entire population of males aged 5-13. As is common in Rajasthan, they ask for pens, failing that, candy, and then, attempts at scholarship and gluttony denied, shampoo. I notice there are no girls around and one of the stewards tells us how the entire town of Ramgarh organised a lovely welcome for the first trainload, only to be met by two bewildered passengers. Here we view one of the many cenotaphs and then onto the woodworking export factory where I spot, amid the pile of packed furniture, one with a label addressed to Urban Outfitters in my old home of Philadelphia.

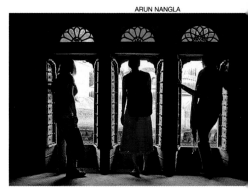

Inside a haveli at Nawalgarh

We move on to **Mandawa** and the Mandawa Castle for lunch but give its havelis a miss, and on to **Nawalgarh**, presumably for our last chance at some havelis. Then a quick stop at Roop Niwas Palace Hotel for tea in the waning light. Every leaf on every tree rustling in a rising cacophony of chirps and then like an untethered soloist, the welling shriek of a peacock. And there is something strangely satisfying about puncturing the royal pretensions of the guests we saw there with our loud chattiness.

We see many things cursorily. Like the great families who lock up their great homes and visit them but once a year, we contribute to this deadened, weekend gaze. It may seem ideal for those with limited time, who love a hands-free travel in an area not completely hustled and bound by tourism. I realise that if you were to gather your sense of humour and banish your guilt and empty yourself of too much curiosity, this trip is great. And the respite it offers from the difficulties of travel planning, meal hunting, guidebook poring over, is not at all unpleasant. Much of the amusement is in being outnumbered by our minders, the orchestrated drama that renders a royal life a babysat one. The least we have had to do is wave at the hordes of eager children. Some people couldn't even muster up the interest to do that. It seems not everyone is born a prince. ∎

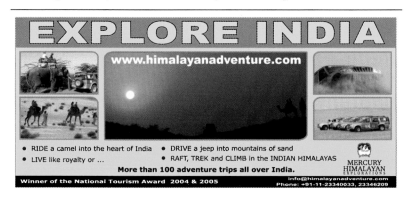

Down to earth

NIRAD GROVER on the many pleasures of an organic farm-stay

It's hard to decide who's more interesting: Binod Saharia or his farm. Basically, they complement each other. Both are big, for one — Binod in physical size and in business, and the farm, in acreage. Both are also down to earth. Binod has many opinions, espoused freely and unequivocally, and I listen to a lot of what he has to say during the course of my trip, which begins with a long, night drive from the Delhi airport to the farm, on the silky smooth, twinkling NH8. The farm is organic, its life rooted in an earth that's sandy but sans chemical fertilisers.

The gate outside proclaims 'Saharia Model Organic Farm'. Notice that the last part of the title does not say 'resort'. My ensuing interaction with Binod gave the impression that, on the balance, it was not his intention to promote it as such (though his website calls it one), and, anyway, the parts of his bucolic kingdom do not add up to the definition, as understood, of this touristy term. The fact that he welcomes paying visitors is a corollary to his main effort of

The Saharia Model Organic Farm's USP is that it is rooted in an earth that's sandy but sans chemical fertilisers

growing profitable plants on a fairly large scale without stuffing the soil with unnatural substances. But more on that later.

Both our nights there were spent on the terrace of Binod's house. He was excited about us doing that though I was skeptical. It was an unusually warm October but I knew from experience that nights in the semi-arid climate of Rajasthan could get chilly and dewy. Besides, I was tired the first day and wanted a good night's sleep. But what the heck, it was a starry night and the row of three charpoys canopied with old-fashioned mosquito meshes looked too charming to turn away from. Wrapped in a thick quilt, I determined to settle in, only to be unsettled immediately as my fumblings caused the netting to collapse on my face like a soft additional blanket.

It was too late to call for help, as adjacent snores indicated, and folding the defunct protection, I resigned myself to a cold, damp, sleepless night, with mosquitoes, thirsty for city-fostered inorganic human blood. I was right, it was a sleepless night. But that was because I rarely sleep well in a new bed the first night. About the rest, I was wrong. The temperature was divine, the cot pliant to perfection, and pests non-existent. (Binod was to reiterate during our stay there that mosquitoes find it tough to survive in organically disinfected environs.)

Standing at the rim of the swimming pool, one's low-angled line of sight skims over a carpet of lush treetops akin to an Amazonian rainforest. The trees are *amlas*, I discovered later, the flag species of the Saharia farm. On my early morning walk along a dusty track from the house, I also pleasantly concluded that the farm was indeed a farm. Tea was being prepared on a wood fire in an earthen stove tucked into a corner of the verandah. A stone wall seemed to have a random end. On the other

Photographs by SHASHWAT SAXENA

The grass is definitely greener on this side of the farm

side of it were some huts and the odd buffalo. A few semi-clothed boys bathed in the gushes of water spouted out by a pump. A lone woman, in colourful Rajasthani garb, absorbedly hacked away at the remainder of a half-harvested field of bajra. Sundry fragments of conversations that drifted from the distance, like the sounds from speakers turned at very low volume, gave a sense of reference to simple matters relating to the day's chores, which would unfold at an easy yet gainful pace. Though it was clear that I was an outsider in their area, and a guest of their master, there were no practised good mornings of the kind offered at country resorts by waiters and attendants — obviously, rural folk till recently engaged in simple farm tasks before being inducted into the lower ranks of the ever growing hospitality army. By the time I bumped into Binod out on his

morning round, I had decided I liked his place.

The formal guided tour began. The brown mud huts were probably the only visible testimony — unless the ruminative camel and its cart could be counted in that category — that the farm, after 14 years of growth and consolidation of a true identity, had taken a tentative step towards venturing into another area. Happily, they weren't trying very hard. Beyond keeping the layout airy and well-windowed, spacious and traditional, they stuck to the basics. One of my unimaginative suggestions to Binod that he hang a sickle or place a plough in a corner had already been considered and discarded. "We don't want to be pretentious." Agreed.

Strolling between *amla* trees laden with the sour fruit, Binod showed me a compost tank. It was filled with a black liquid that looked like coal tar

A cluster of amla beckons visitors

juice. The ingredients — dried leaves and other plant matter, cow urine, egg shells for calcium, and *gur* (jaggery) for fermenting the concoction — dumped together for their pesticidal and nourishing properties, were the essence of the organic practices followed at the farm. This mixture is eventually poured into the soil. "We encourage visitors to participate in our processes," Binod says. He handed me a long staff to stir the gruel. As we trudged further, he pointed out a wooden birdhouse nailed on trees, an invitation for owls to settle here and nail field rats.

Binod bought this land, all 18 hectares of it, as an investment for a rainy day. Today he calls it a home away from home. The time spent and the agricultural techniques used here are a labour of love, a vision aimed at reviving traditional practices and demonstrating their effectiveness, and thereby prodding a movement away from modern chemically enhanced farming. One of the things

he loves about his home is the swimming pool, which is the preferred and promoted option for frolicsome bathing. Embedded in an artificial hillock, it is actually an irrigation tank modified for the dual purpose of aquatic limbering and lolling. It is elevated to the height of the house's roof to disburse the stored water via gravity, besides offering a vantage point to survey the immediate domain. Yet it is a genuine swimming pool, tiled, with deep and shallow ends, equipped with inflated tyre tubes and water polo balls, but no nasty chlorine to irritate the eyes; pouches of neem leaves strung on the sides serve as natural cleaning agents.

The morning swim was followed by breakfast, a quintessentially hearty farm-fresh spread of hot bajra rotis rolled off the adjacent hearth, accompanied with dollops of white butter and ghee, vegetables, *chhaach* and milky tea. Brigadier Bhargava joined us at this point. He is the consultant-cum-administrator ("I'm just a passer-by," Binod says) of the farm, who'd come from Jaipur to educate us in the science of organics. His tour was focused and precise. The paste smeared on lower ends of tree trunks was termite repellent, applied in spring and just after the monsoon. Judging by the health of the trees, it worked. Most interesting was the vermiculture corner, a 20 ft x 30 ft patch layered with decaying biomass. Beneath it a fascinating process is constantly underway: deep burrowing worms are gorging on the gourmet fare, digesting, excreting and converting it to manure. Every two months some of this is skimmed off and fed to the soil around the plants, enriching it.

I was getting into a gluttonous mode myself and mowed into lunch, enriching vegetables, dal and everything else, with copious amounts of dairy distillates. We spent the middle part of the day exploring the deserted **Saharia havelis** in **Kala Dera** and picking up supplies from the bustling town of Chomu. On the way back, Binod veered off the tarmac road on to a maze of backcountry tracks. Destination: **the local potter's encampment**. Again, this was not an artisan, situated, sanitised, sartorialised and sensitised for tourists desiring to interact with obligatory exotica. He wore his curvaceous moustache for its own sake and, clearly, I was the first metrosexual ever to express admiration for his silver pendant. He and Saharia conducted their business and we wound back through the riddle of dirt trails to the farm.

As afternoon receded to evening, we tramped over furrowed land to an outlying tract. I revised my lesson in the flora of the Saharia sanctuary, confirming *roonj, shahtooth, sheesham, ber, babool, aldu,* tamarind, *kejdi,* all scattered amidst the endless groves of the shaggy green *amla.* One farm merged into another until we hit a small hamlet; with less than a dozen homes, it was amongst the smallest I have ever seen. Except for slops of cow dung, it was clean and quaint.

A house, fortified with thorn scrub and tall cacti, pricked Binod's fancy, "They can't afford barbed wire or cement walls but the means of protection are there in nature." Binod keeps good relations with his neighbours. His natural affability and fluency in the local Rajasthani dialect make for easy interaction. Smiles broke out on the faces of a conclave of villagers as they greeted him: "*Arre, sethji aaye* (the important man is here). Get a seat for him, quickly." Banter followed, and *sethji* displayed no discomfort fielding their tongue-in-cheek remarks. Soft peanuts, picked from a stack of freshly harvested stems, were organised with alacrity. The entourage followed us on our

The local potter's encampment

onward trek. By now we were once more on Binod's private territory and he was the critical observer whose eyes missed nothing. A water channel came up for assessment, and explanations were demanded for trees in decline. The halt provided the chance for a roasted upgradation of our munchies. On the walk back via the narrow metalled lane lined with reeds — this vegetation forms the roofing material for Binod's tourist block — a sweet perfume ghosted up from an unknown source. Perhaps it was that sparse tree by the roadside? Whereas we couldn't be sure, the rising moon was spotted through its slim branches. It was time for Binod's favourite pastoral pastime: a moonlit swim.

The swim gave way to a moonlit dinner of most delicious mutton curry, followed by informal folk dances by the sporting staff. Belly crammed shamelessly to maximum elasticity, I reclined on a chair-cum-cot designed by one of Binod's guests, and through half-closed eyes watched the amateur

And the info

Getting there

Air Nearest airport: Sanganer Airport, Jaipur (27 km/ 45 mins) is the nearest airport. Taxi fare is about Rs 250-300

Rail Nearest railhead: Jaipur is the most convenient railway station. Taxi Rs 250

Road The Saharia Model Organic Farm is located $2^1/_2$ km off the Jaipur-Chomu Highway (NH11). If approaching from Jaipur, turn left after $22^1/_2$ km at Maheshpura Village (Surya Vatika Road). If coming from Delhi, on NH8 to Jaipur, turn right at Chandwaji onto the Chomu Road. From Chandwaji it is approximately 45 km to Maheshpura. The farm can organise a car pick-up from Jaipur, and, for those interested, a camel cart on the final stretch of $2^1/_2$ km

Where to stay

One unit of four single and two double rooms with common bathrooms (the rooms are available separately). Extra beds can be provided. This unit has its own kitchen, with provisions from the farm. There are also three individual huts, with one room each, big enough for four beds. The huts have their own attached bathrooms which are walled on all sides but open on top. It's Rs 500 for a room with two beds. The rooms are pleasant with basic furniture. There is no air-conditioning or fans. Electricity is available but erratic. It is supplemented with solar power.

Where to eat

The staff prepares the food but you have the option of helping in the kitchen and in the cooking. Don't expect varieties of cuisines. The food is simple Indian (vegetarian unless requested) but wholesome and tasty. The charges are Rs 50 for breakfast, Rs 100 for lunch or dinner (per person).

Things to do

At the farm one can assist with various farm tasks and learn about organic methods of farming. The property is quite large and the leafy lanes are nice for walks, which can extend to the surrounding countryside. Away from the farm, one can visit the town of Chomu with its bazaars and old buildings.

Contact

◆Binod Saharia, Chottagola, AT Road, Dibrugarh-786001, Assam
Mobile 09435031097, 09435031101
Email info@sahariaorganicresort.com
Website sahariaorganicresort.com
◆Pushpendra Bhargava, 17 Shiva Marg, Bani Park, Jaipur-302016, Rajasthan
Mobile 09829013660 **Email** jaipurinn@ sancharnet.in

artistes swirl and trip to music belting out of a simple cassette recorder, all the time craving for the cot under the stars (with no disrespect to the performers who stepped and swayed in good rhythm). This time I slept well but awoke feeling somewhat delicate, a condition caused by careless consumption at the punchy poolside bar. I needed soothing and solitariness, and in retrospect, was surprised how naturally I knew I would find it in the set-apart interiors of the simple mud lodgings we had looked into yesterday. Sure enough, the retreat into one of the small earthen rooms smelling of wood furniture, with the open window ushering in a gentle breeze, faint farm sounds and unobtrusive daylight brushed by trees and crops was just the therapy I needed. For two hours I was out like a light on the jute. And when I awoke, it was with the thought of that big breakfast doused in all the goodness of organic cholesterol. ◼

Deogarh Mahal
Rajasthan, India
Abode of the Gods

For details please contact:
Deogarh Mahal, Madaria, District Rajsamand, Rajasthan.
Phone: 02904 - 252777
Delhi Sales:**The Consortium**, 011 - 41600150, 41601355
Email: info@theconsortiumhotels.com,

Indra Vilas
ALSISAR - SHEKHAWATI, RAJASTHAN

For details please contact:
Indra Vilas, Alsisar, Distt - Jhunjhunu, Shekhawati, Rajasthan.
Phone: 01595 - 2755600,
Delhi Sales: **The Consortium**, 011 - 41600150, 41601355
Email: info@theconsortiumhotels.com

GIREESH GV

Each arch, each door tells a story: A haveli in Shekhawati

To the mansion born

Rajasthan's havelis mirror the fortunes of families and towns

■ BY SHIKHA JAIN

Perhaps it's wise not to judge a book by its cover, but in the towns of Rajasthan, where glorious havelis often stand hidden amidst a maze of bylanes, it's possible to discern family histories and life stories by a mere look at the abodes of nobles and courtiers. For, unwittingly or otherwise, each haveli tells a tale about its owner, his family and, his relationships with the ruler. Why, some havelis even mirror the stories of the towns where they are set!

This remarkable feature was something I grasped over the 20-odd years I spent in Jaipur, savouring at leisure my treasured glimpses of old havelis. As an architect, I was fascinated by the beautiful mansions adorning the walled townscapes of Rajasthan, and my curiosity about the architecture and the lifestyles of those living in havelis led me to a four-year-long exploration of 40 towns in the state. I visited over 200 havelis; some were lying desolate, the locks echoing their despair; others were full of life, their rooms bursting with age-old tales of history and tradition that the residents were eager to narrate. Some havelis had transformed with time, assuming the colours of modernity, while others, resplendent in their ancient architectural glory, gave me the answers to questions that had bogged my mind for a long time. How were the rich architectural forms and variations seen in havelis linked to the diverse culture of Rajasthan? How was a Rajput haveli different from a Marwari or Brahmin haveli? Or more simply, how were the havelis in Jaipur different from those in Jodhpur, Udaipur or Jaisalmer? In my travels, I found the answers to all those questions and more.

The havelis, the mansions of the rich, reflected the colourful diversity of the land and its people. In response to the many geographic and cultural variations seen in Rajasthan, the havelis of each area exhibited a unique architectural style. The construction material was local and the architectural features respected the social customs of the place. The haveli catered to the requirements of its owners, and apart from accommodating the social structure inherent in joint families, aspired to achieve a grand image, competing with nothing less than the palaces of the maharajas.

Searching for the origin of the form, I discovered that it was the Rajput rulers of Rajasthan who started building havelis in the 16th century, to provide an ideal accommodation for their courtiers and nobles. By the end of the 18th century, havelis were being made by rich Hindu traders, the Marwaris. This trader class flourished during the British rule and built grand havelis in their hometowns in Rajasthan, a practice that continued till the beginning of the 20th century.

The stories behind the walls

Most havelis were mansions belonging to Rajput estate owners or thakurs of *thikanas* (estates), Marwaris or *banias*, Muslim nobles, ministers, royal doctors or hakims and a few Brahmin royal priests called rajpurohits. Those who managed royal departments, such as Kotharis (treasury in-charge), Dhabhais (nurses of the royal family), Bhandharis (store in-charge) and Dadu-Panthis (a religious sect), also owned havelis. Their mansions were symbols of their social status, next in hierarchy to the ruler's abode, and the kings even visited on special occasions. In a number of cases where the Rajput ruler married a thakur's daughter, the marriage ceremony took place in the haveli courtyard of the noble.

The havelis ranged from a house with a single courtyard to one with multiple courtyards. If the haveli owner was bestowed with a higher status, or if the number of family members went up, there was a commensurate increase in either the scale of the haveli or the number of courtyards. In the smaller towns or *thikanas*, the havelis had one or two courtyards while those in the royal capitals had as many as eight courtyards.

An intricate brass door at Karauli

GIREESH G V

Based on the patronage and the pattern of growth, havelis could be classified into two: the Rajput type, which was asymmetric, less ornate and sprawled out; and the Marwari type, with regular square and rectangular plots, symmetric and axial planning and a great emphasis on ornamentation. Beyond these two broad categories, the haveli as a dwelling held different meanings for those from different castes and professions. The change in the location and form of the havelis was based on the caste and occupation of the owner.

Brahmin havelis

The Brahmin havelis belonged mainly to the rajpurohits, the royal priests who were at the top of the social hierarchy and who performed the religious rituals of the rulers. The Rajput ruler consulted the royal priest about all his major decisions to assure himself of its auspiciousness. As the priests' services were required for

The Patwon-ki-Haveli in Jaisalmer

TRIBHUVAN TIWARI

ceremonies of all kinds, their havelis were usually located right next to the fort or palace, and sometimes within the fort complex, as in Jaisalmer.

Brahmin havelis often had a square courtyard with separate sections for men and women. However, as women did not have to wear purdah, most havelis had entrances that opened straight into the courtyard. The spaces inside such as *baithak* (the sitting space in the outer area) were not as elaborate as those found in the havelis of other castes; entertainment spaces were completely absent in the Brahmin havelis. The façade of Brahmin havelis was also less ornate as compared to the havelis of other castes. **Purohit's Haveli** in Ganesh Ghatti, Udaipur, is one of the grandest examples of a Brahmin haveli. The haveli has a magnificent entrance gate and a distinct chattri (dome) in the inner complex. Ganesh Ghatti, incidentally, is located at the highest point in Udaipur city. It was a rule in Udaipur that no haveli could be higher than the palace, but an exception was made for Purohit's Haveli, whose chattri stands at the same height as the palace.

Rajput havelis

The Rajput havelis belonged to the Rajput thakurs or to the military incharge and army officials. A Rajput thakur was the ruler of his *thikana* and on par with the king. These thakurs were younger brothers or cousins of the Rajput ruler, given land at a distance where they could rule independently. They had a palatial residence in the *thikana* (such as **Samode Palace** in Samode and **Begun Fort** at Begun) and a grand haveli in the capital (**Samode Haveli** in Jaipur or **Begun Haveli** in Udaipur). Their families lived in the *thikana*. These thakurs, while attending to the maharaja, lived in the havelis in the capital,

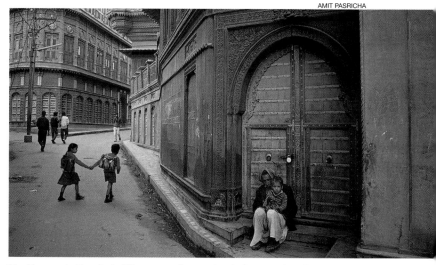

The Rampuria Havelis in Bikaner are known for their stone façades

located outside the walled city, at a distance from the palace. This was for security reasons as the ruler was at constant risk of being attacked by the thakurs. These havelis had at least three courtyards: the one outside for the servants and stables, the one in the middle or the **mardana** for the men to receive guests and the innermost one or the **zenana** for the women. The *baithak* was elaborate and was used for holding meetings as in a ruler's durbar (court). These havelis had lavish spaces comparable to the ones found in Mughal palaces such as Diwan-i-Aam (common court), Diwan-i-Khas (special court) and Rang Mahal (entertainment space). As the women had to follow a purdah system, the Rajput havelis had a direct entrance, opening into the mardana courtyard and an indirect entrance through a small enclosure to the zenana courtyard.

The Rajput havelis were designed with defence in mind, had fewer openings and were fortress-like. They catered to a family with its infrastructure of servants and stables. They had a bigger entrance gate than other havelis, called the 'Hathi Pol' (Elephant Gate), the kind that would allow an elephant to enter inside.

Just as the Rajput thakurs were the forerunners in making havelis, they were also the first ones to adapt to the British bungalow style. An interesting example of this transformation can be observed in the havelis of **Chaumoo Thakur** in Amber and Jaipur and the later 20th century **Chaumoo House** in Jaipur. The other kind of Rajput haveli, belonging to the military-in-charge, was usually a modest haveli close to the ruler's abode. Examples of these include the **Khurrewali Haveli** and the **Chauhan Haveli** in Alwar and the **Mammayon Ki Haveli** in Udaipur.

Marwari havelis

If the Rajputs were responsible for the origin of the haveli form, the Marwaris can be credited with ensuring the maximum evolution of this form. The term Marwari comes from the desert region of Marwar, as this trader class hailed from here. In Rajasthan, the maximum number of havelis were built and owned by this class.

The Marwaris were always on the move, depending on which Rajput ruler gave them a greater incentive to settle in his town. This wandering inclination of the Marwaris resulted in the number of havelis that are spread all over Rajasthan and also other parts of India. They were the richest class in the society and showed their affluence by building havelis. Their mansions were built on premium plots on the main commercial streets of towns. The Marwari havelis were most often present as clusters with a collection of single-courtyard havelis, each belonging to one brother, opening into a common forecourt. Since all the brothers of the family handled the family business together, it was a layout that worked well for them.

The *baithak* in the front portion of the haveli served as the work space, where the accountant would sit with

Each haveli catered to the requirements of its owners and accommodated the social structure of joint families

his *bahikhata* (accounts record). Though the purdah system was not as strict as in Rajput families, the Marwari havelis had both direct and indirect entrances, depending on the owner's wish. The havelis were richly decorated and their façades were full of ornamentation, be it in jaali (lattice) and stonework in Jaisalmer or paintings in Shekhawati.

One of the finest examples of a Marwari haveli is the intricately carved **Patwon ki Haveli** in Jaisalmer. This is a cluster of five havelis, each

with one courtyard, belonging to five brothers. The Patwas were one of the most affluent traders of Rajasthan in the early 19th century, dealing in zari and badla (silver and golden threads). Besides Jaisalmer, the Patwas also have havelis in Indore, Ratlam, Kota and Jhalarpatan. The Patwa Haveli in Jhalarpatan has an interesting façade with a central jharokha (a window opening with a screen) in Jaisalmer stone, carved and brought from Jaisalmer. This was supposed to serve as an example for the masons for producing similar jharokhas in local red sandstone on either side of the façade. Another interesting and lesser-known Patwa Haveli is in Ajmer. This is also a cluster of five havelis with one courtyard each, designed for the family of five brothers when they came to Ajmer for the wedding ceremony of one of the Patwa daughters. It is said that the haveli was built in one year purely for the purpose of this marriage.

Other havelis

Those belonging to castes such as Bhandharis, Kotharis and Dhabhais, named after the manner in which they served the ruler, also had a few impressive havelis. These were present as clusters of havelis with one or two courtyards, depending on the size of the family.

Muslim havelis in Rajasthan belonged to important Muslim ministers in the court and to Muslim hakims (royal doctors). These havelis were located on the main streets, like the **Nawab Sahib ki Haveli** at Chand Pol Bazaar in Jaipur and the **Bade Miya Haveli** in Jodhpur. Similar to the Rajput havelis, the complex had an outer courtyard for stables, another one for men and an inner one for women. There was often a masjid in the complex. Since the Muslim inhabitants of Rajasthan were Hindu

MALINI SHARMA

The window is the view: A haveli at Nawalgarh

converts, most of them observed Hindu customs as well.

Tonk has the maximum number of Muslim havelis in Rajasthan. **Mahmud Khan's Haveli** in Old Tonk, built in 1820, has three mosques and seven wells. Purdah was very important in these havelis and hence there were indirect entrances to the inner courts as in the Rajput havelis. The *baithak* was used as an assembly area or for performing professional duties, as was the case in the hakim's haveli in Tonk. These havelis were easily identifiable from their entrance gates, which had floral and not figural decorations. At times, they had Arabic inscriptions as seen today at the entrance of Tonk havelis.

The beauty is in the details

Across Rajasthan, the façades of havelis showed rich and diversified features. A variety of elements such as brackets and columns and decorative elements such as mouldings, parapets and jaalis adorned the façades. Each region had indigenous decorative

patterns for havelis. A frequently observed pattern for moulding plinths was of lotus petals. More complex stone carvings were seen in Jaisalmer and Pokaran. The stone parapets in the havelis also showed a rich variety in design, ranging from simple stone panels fixed in pillars to high walls with arched openings. In most cases, the columns in havelis were made of stone except in a few places like Salumbher and Udaipur, where timber columns were constructed. At times, they were decorated with mirror work as in **Dhabhai Haveli** in Udaipur. Sub-regional painting styles developed in Jaipur, Bundi, Udaipur, Kishangarh and the Shekhawati region while the Marwar region excelled in stone carving and jaalis.

The gates and doors of havelis were made of wood. The main gate in bigger havelis had a small opening called *mori*, as can be seen today in the gates in Shekhawati. The door lintels, in stone or wood, were often carved intricately. A lovely example is the **Bade Devta Haveli** in Kota, whose doors have ivory work. Great significance was attached to the entrances to the inner court of the haveli. The local term for the entrance gate was *pol* and the entrance lobby was called *poli*. The entrance was decorated with wall paintings, *bandanwars* (a row of mango leaves tied in a thread) and *mandanas* (patterns made on the floor with rice and colours) on all occasions. Besides being a physical access point, the entrance was also a source of communication with the outside society. It was like a notice board where events happening inside the haveli were broadcast — the joys and sorrows and festivities were all shared with the rest of the community through the symbols painted outside the entrance. In Rajput and Brahmin havelis, the niche at the top of the entrance was reserved for the *kul-devi* (clan-goddess), thus informing outsiders of the particular clan of the owner, serving the purpose of a nameplate. In the case of a Marwari haveli, the niche was occupied by an image of Lord Ganesh. In Muslim

The door to Rampuria Haveli

RAHUL SHARMA/INDIAPICTURE

havelis, the entrance doors were usually decorated in floral patterns.

A space for everything

The core of the havelis was always the inner zenana court. In havelis with many courtyards, with separate courts for men, the men rarely entered the female court. In the case of havelis with one courtyard, the men stayed outside during the day while the women remained in the courtyard and inner rooms. The courtyard was used for various household activities such as cooking and washing and drying of clothes and grains. The terrace spaces (*chhath*) were used by the women for drying clothes as well as spices and papad.

In those days, the men had more interaction with the outside world and the important obligation of hospitality gave rise to the necessity of spaces to receive guests, a function the *baithaks* fulfilled. The men spent most of their time outside the house or in the *baithak* and came into the courtyard only for specific purposes such as taking meals, or to sleep at night. *Baithaks* were also used for official purposes, for example as a durbar in a thakur's haveli or an accounts office in a Marwari haveli.

The mahal or *mol* was the most ornate space in the haveli, used for receiving special guests. The 'kanch mol' and 'hawa mol' in **Suraj Haveli** in Jaisalmer are specially decorated with mirror work and jharokhas. The **Dhabhai Haveli** in Udaipur has a *meena* mahal with intricate *meenakari* (ornamentation) work on the walls and pillars. Affluent Marwaris had lavish *baithaks* on the ground floor and a *mol* on the first floor, as observed in the gold-plated ceiling of the *mol* in **Patwa Haveli** in Jaisalmer. In more lavish havelis, the *baithak* and mahal were termed as the Diwan-i-Aam and Diwan-i-Khas.

SANJOY GHOSH

Nadine le Prince Haveli in Shekhawati, which has been lovingly restored

Spaces for entertainment were created in the more lavish havelis of Rajput thakurs and Muslim nobles. The rang mahal was used for evening entertainment; good examples of these can be seen in **Mathur Haveli** in Jodhpur and Dhabhai Haveli in Udaipur. Such spaces were not found in Marwari or Brahmin havelis as entertainment was not part of their social mores. The *baithaks* of Muslim havelis served as spaces for mushaira performances. Apart from rooms for domestic chores and entertainment, the owners of havelis also made space for storing their valuables. Gold and cash were hidden somewhere in the thick walls of the haveli and their location memorised by the owner and passed on verbally to the son. Most havelis also had secret places for stashing valuables, such as a basement room, accessed by removing a stone panel in a ground floor room. This is seen in **Saraf Haveli** in Jhalarpatan.

Winds of change

Despite their undisputed grandeur, the havelis of Rajasthan have suffered the ravages of time. Many have been neglected, though a large number of the havelis still remain with their original owners. Some havelis are lying locked while others are being used for commercial activities. It's heartbreaking to see Rajasthan's heritage being eroded by neglect.

The silver lining is that some of these havelis are today being used as centres of art. With Rajasthan witnessing a tourism boom, its owners are finding it lucrative to convert the havelis into heritage hotels. A few notable havelis that today function as heritage hotels include Chaumoo Haveli, now **The Raj Palace** in Jaipur, **Amet Haveli** in Udaipur, and **Alsisar Haveli** in Jaipur. It is in Shekhawati that one finds the most number of havelis, in towns such as Mandawa, Nawalgarh, Ramgarh, Bissau and Chiru, being used today as art centres and schools.

In whatever form it has taken today, the haveli is an integral part of Rajasthan's history and culture. And the bliss that one feels in discovering a lovely haveli while wandering in a forgotten bylane in a dusty town remains immeasurable. ∎

Step back in time

Get footloose and fancy-free with the dancers of Rajasthan

■ BY TRIPTI PANDEY

Rajasthani folk dance may largely be seen as the forte of women, but it has lured men from time immemorial. Even then, as if underlining the differences on account of gender, the styles of dancing of both the sexes are distinct. In keeping with the traditional, sometimes patriarchal, mores in which women were expected to behave in society, their dance has an inherent sensuous and graceful feel. Men, on the other hand, are more energetic on stage and their steps reflect vigour and dynamism.

Despite these pre-conditions and rules, I found dance liberating, even as a child. I rejoiced in the graceful movements, in the spontaneity of expression that dance afforded me as a little girl. It was fitting then that in my first stage show, I was part of a troupe that performed the **ghoomar** dance. The ceremonial dance of the Rajput community, ghoomar was part of all the celebrations in the women's quarters. The steps of the princesses and the queens were coordinated to the tunes sung by the female singers from the Dholi community, who also played the percussion. As they danced, they would cover their faces with a transparent veil, or the *odhani*, adding a romantic and mystic aura to the graceful and swift movements.

The ghoomar starts with slow movements but towards the end the dancers form circles to the tunes of a fast beat. If one were to watch the dance, it would appear to be deceptively simple. But the truth is that it is rather difficult to acquire the grace that the dance is known for. One sees a coordinated 'performance' on stage, as opposed to a more natural dance in the relaxed atmosphere of the women's quarters. Even then, as the veiled dancers, dressed in exotic *poshaks* — the traditional four-piece attire — perform, their gracefulness can take your breath away. The words of the song to which the dance is performed are worth mentioning here. "Oh my mother, it's time for ghoomar/ I wish to perform ghoomar/ The handsome headgear of the Rathore fascinates me/ Marry me into a family of Rathores," it goes. Of course, these lyrics are modified suitably when the dance is performed in a Rajput clan other than the Rathores.

If ghoomar emphasises grace, **terah tali**, performed by the women belonging to the Kamad community in Pali District, lays a premium on dexterity. The dancers sit on the floor but their body movements are astonishing. Terah tali started out as a devotional dance that symbolised an offering made to Baba Ramdeo, at his shrine near Pokaran, during the Ramdeoji Fair. This devotion is reflected in the dance: the men in the troupe sing devotional songs, playing the string instrument *chautara*, even as the women tie *manjeeras* or metallic discs on their arms and legs and strike them with the discs held in their hands. They also balance lamps on their heads, hold swords between their teeth and strike the discs, moving their hands over and under the swords! Today, the terah tali dance has moved beyond its religious precincts and is often performed on stage. One of the most senior performers in Rajasthan today is **Maangi Bai**, who made her debut with the late scholar of folk arts, **Komal Kothari**.

Kalbelia is another dance that has recently been rescued from anonymity. The dance of the snake-charmers, kalbelia has no form if one were to look at it technically. Yet, the dancers' suppleness, spontaneity, vigour and, not to forget, their black attire, all combine to make it an exciting performance to witness. I would like to recount here an interesting story about a star kalbelia performer, **Gulabi**. Her success has inspired many girls in her community to take to this dance and perform on stage. I saw her first during the Pushkar fair; Himmat Singh, a film director who is also a visualiser for shows, and I, were drawn to the place where she was performing because of the cheers of the large groups of people watching her. We were both mesmerised by her dancing skills. Indeed, everyone around showered coins on her as she spun clockwise and anti-clockwise. Enthralled, we persuaded her to be part of a show that we were presenting that evening. She came, she performed and she stole the show. From then on, there was no looking

Lost in dance (below and top left)

WAYNC AND MILRIAM CAEEVCLLA/INDIAPICTURE

back for Gulabi. She was invited to international festivals and even today, spreads the word about kalbelia on domestic and international arenas. With her tremendous stamina and stage presence, she has now become a brand ambassador for the kalbelia dance.

Like the snake-charmers, another group of people who have made their presence felt are the Kanjars of Kota region. Their ceremonial dance is referred to as **chakri**, and this name is derived from the fact that the dancer has to move fast in a circle or *chakkar*. The dancers dress in multi-panelled skirts of vibrant colours and spin to the beats of a drummer. The dance has an element of drama in it. At first, the dancers mock the drummer, refusing to dance when he plays. Finally, as the drummer gets annoyed, they try to make peace, begging him to play. When he is charged up, they dance their best, and it is almost as if the dancers and the drummer are competing with each other, instead of performing together.

The first step: Tying the ghungroo

AMIT PASRICHA

The dance that brings out all the earthy qualities of Rajasthan is the **chari**. Originally a dance of the Gujjar community living in the Kishangarh region, it is now performed by girls from other communities as well. However, the authentic form of the dance is preserved by the girls of Kishangarh. They dance to the music of *dhol* and *bankiya*, or the trumpet, even as they balance brass water pitchers topped with blazing cotton seeds on their head. Apart from the music created by the instruments, there is no song accompanying the dance. In the dance inspired by this form, dancers perform to the lyrics of a song called *chirmi*.

A fascinating dance form that also emphasises the art of balancing is the **charkula**. Hailing from the Brij region stretching from Bharatpur to Mathura and Vrindavan, the dance has a veiled woman performing with a multi-tiered lamp. Depicting the legends associated with Lord Krishna's life, such as those of him lifting a mountain on one finger, the dancer tosses a brass plate in the air, catches it and holds it on one finger. Also part of the *charkula* is a beautiful 'dance of the peacocks', in which the dancers perform wearing the exotic plumage of a peacock. This group of dancers also perform during Holi; their dance, called **lathmar Holi**, depicts the saga of Krishna's lovelorn *gopis*. A teasing group of male dancers are also part of the performance; the women dancers hit them with sticks even as the men defend themselves with shields.

The **bhawai** dance has its roots in neighbouring Gujarat. A form of folk theatre that was prevalent in Udaipur, it is thought to be associated with the Bhawai community of Gujarat, hence the name. Both men and women perform the dance, with each dancer honing their skills in balancing many things: some dance on glass tumblers

PP

Ghoomar, the ceremonial dance of the Rajput community

while carrying a heavy cartwheel; others balance water pitchers while dancing on a board of nails standing on pointed ends! It's a combination of jugglery and dance, and its effect on audiences is most pronounced: the viewers are always wonderstruck.

Amongst the tribal communities of Rajasthan, as it is in other groups, festive occasions are celebrated with dancing. An interesting dance form is the **wallar** of Garasias, in which the dancers move slowly in circles, clockwise and anti-clockwise. The dance of the Saharias of the Hadoti region includes movements such as that of a monkey. Some of them even dress up as monkeys and their renditions are simply incredible. Unfortunately, most of the dances can only be seen during a fair or a festival in the region as they do not perform otherwise.

In all the dances that I have described earlier, it is the women who dominate the proceedings. Dances in which the men play an important role include kacchi ghodi, ger, fire dance, dhap and deru.

In **kacchi ghodi** or the dummy mare dance, the men depict the moods of a pampered bridegroom. While many perform this dance today, some of the better performers belonged to the communities of Sargara and Mirasis in Marwar. **Ger** is also from the Marwar region and the

Like the desert storm, which often strikes without warning, the Rajasthani's desire to dance arrives without notice

deserts beyond. It was mainly performed by farmers and later adopted by the goldsmiths of Jodhpur. Today, however, the dance is seen across Rajasthan, with village after village organising ger nights that's comparable to Gujarat's dandiya sessions. The ger dancers dress in multi-panelled long attire, in white or red colours, and beat the long sticks they hold in their hands. They start with a slow beat and the music then rises to a

The black attire of the artistes adds to the beauty of the kalbelia dance

crescendo. Some villagers prefer wearing a short jacket or a *bandi* instead of a long robe. What is unique and lovely about this dance is that the school authorities in Marwar villages have had their students trained in ger. It is wonderful to see the children, wearing bright turbans and short jackets, performing the dance.

A mystical dance that's been raised to mythical proportions is the **fire dance** performed by the men of the Jasnathi sect, also known as Siddh. Performed as an offering to their mentor, Guru Sant Jasnath, who lived in the 15th-16th century, the men dance on burning coals. As the coal turns amber, they put it into their mouths in their devotional frenzy. The belief is that nothing can hurt them as they are protected by their mentor. This dance is performed in the villages near Bikaner.

Moving from Bikaner towards Shekhawati, one comes across two interesting dances: the **dhap** and the **deru**, both performed by dancers who also play their own drums. While dhap is commonly seen during Holi, deru is seen only when farmers have their own celebrations. Dhap has yet another interesting feature: one man dressed as a veiled woman dances in the centre while all the other men sing 'lift your veil' to him.

These are the dances that a traveller is likely to witness while travelling in Rajasthan. Of course, many of these dances are performed only during village ceremonies or festivals, and you would have to be very lucky indeed to see a dance in its traditional setting. But if that should happen, you can rest assured that it would be a wonderful experience. Just like the desert storm, which strikes often without warning, the villager's desire to dance to show his or her joy arrives without notice. A few seconds is all it takes for an impromptu dance session to begin, carrying within its rhythms and notes a hypnotic quality that will soon make you forget where you are, transporting you to a magical time when music and dance reigned over the desert. ■

Timeless melody

In the heart of the desert, folk music is in full bloom

■ BY TRIPTI PANDEY

Where did I hear it first? I often ask myself that question about Rajasthani folk music, which is as mellifluous as the wind whispering to the sand dunes, and as ethereal as the translucent, star-lit desert sky. But there is no one answer to that query. In trying to remember the moment when I was first enthralled by folk music, a swirl of images unfolds in my mind's eye: women construction workers humming as they toil in the sun; women singing as they rock themselves on swings during the Teej festival; and men hanging out of trucks, rushing to a fair, their joy mirrored in their faces and the melodies they sing along to. All these moments, in some way or the other, must have served as my introduction to Rajasthan's rich musical heritage.

I believe that Rajasthan's folk music is eternal, for its uniqueness has caught the attention of not just classical musicians but also the doyens of Hindi film music. Some of those catchy film numbers that have the entire nation foot-tapping owe more than a grudging acknowledgement to Rajasthani folk songs, many of which narrate the stories of heroes, love and devotion.

In Rajasthan, music is a way of life in more ways than one. It is not just an art form that exists for entertainment or as an expression of creativity — it is also a source of livelihood. For many communities, it is both a profession and a passion. In their families, music is a treasured inheritance that is passed down from one generation to another. Just as heart-warming is the fact that Rajasthan's music becomes richer as the landscapes turn more barren. Therefore, it is in the heart of the desert that folk music is in full bloom. To illustrate that fact, consider the two well-known musical clans of Langas and Manganiyars, who are desert-dwellers. The Langas live in and around Jodhpur, and the

Sound of music: The folk musicians of Rajasthan (left and above)

Manganiyars in Jaisalmer and Barmer. The Langas' main instrument is the stringed **sarangi** while **kamaycha**, a string instrument with a big resonator, played using a bow, is the exclusive domain of the Manganiyars. Langas even have two sub-castes created on the basis of the instruments they use. Those who play the *sarangi* are known as Sarangia Langas while those playing a wind instrument called **surnai** are referred to as Surnaia Langas. Today, one mostly sees Sarangia Langas on stage as the few Surnaia Langas who are in this field live in far-flung villages and prefer to perform for local patrons.

One of the main reasons why the Manganiyars and Langas have been able to uphold their tradition of folk music is because of a system called **jijmani**, or the patronage extended by Rajasthani families in a hereditary fashion — that is, one household supports the family of musicians attached to it for generations, with the musicians being part of all the rituals and ceremonies. Thanks to this, the artistes have a repertoire of songs to match the mood of the occasion at which they are called to perform, be it the birth of a child or a wedding.

The status of their patrons often decided the standing of the musicians as well. The Langas were supported by the rich Rathores of Jodhpur and the Sindhi Sepoys while the Manganiyars — traditionally patronised by the Bhati rulers — accepted help from weavers in times of dire need. Many make an incorrect assumption that the Manganiyars sought alms as the etymology of their name is thought to derive from the Hindi word *maang* or beg. This is incorrect as the term, in this particular case, denotes the obligatory relationship that the musicians share with their patrons.

Whatever be their differences, as the artistes come together on the performing arena, it becomes clear that music transcends all manmade boundaries. Though both Langas and

Music is not an art form that exists only for entertainment or creative expression. It is also a source of livelihood

Manganiyars are from the Muslim community, they sing the devotional songs of Hindus with such fervour that it reinforces the mystical power of music. Interestingly, for their part, the Manganiyars and Langas often sing the original *Nimbuda* song, made famous by the Hindi film *Hum Dil De Chuke Sanam*, claiming that it was hijacked by Bollywood! Of course, to the other extreme is the fact that their interactions with popular artistes have left a mark on their music as well. For instance, some even sing ghazals of the music maestro Ghulam Ali of Pakistan today.

Instruments common to both groups include the **morchang**, or the Jew's harp, held in the mouth by the teeth, and the double flute known as **satara** but also referred to as *algoja*, which is different from the *algoja* that is played by the farming communities around Jaipur. The main percussion instrument used by both the communities is **dholak**, a double-barrel, cylindrical drum. The accompanying instrument these days for their songs is the **harmonium**, chosen obviously for its convenience, as it doesn't have to be tuned like their traditional instruments sarangi or *kamaycha*.

An innovative introduction has been that of using earthen water pitchers or **matkas** for producing an array of fascinating rhythms. Unlike in the classical ensemble of percussion instruments in South India,

ANIL DEV/WILDPHOTOS

wherein they create rhythms with their nimble fingers on a *ghatam* (also a kind of water pitcher), here the musicians create rhythms by breathing into the pot as they throw it into the air. In between this, they manage to dance as well! Another special instrument that reflects the phenomenal skill of these musicians is **khartal**, which is akin to the Spanish castanets, comprised of four separate rectangular pieces of wood. Two of these are held in each hand and a rhythmic pattern is created by clashing one set against the other.

The Langas and Manganiyars share an unfortunate characteristic as well: there are no women performers amongst them. The only exception to this rule has been a Manganiyar woman performer named Rukma Devi, who went on to win the National Devi Ahilya Award in 2005 from the Indian Government.

Thankfully, there is no dearth of women performers in certain other communities, as in the case of **Dholis**, whose ancestors were singers in the zenana or the women's quarters of the Rajputs. These gifted singers were part of all the ceremonial occasions in the family. In the Muslim community, there is a group of singers called **Mirasis**, and one of the most well-known singers among them was the late Allah Jillai Bai of Bikaner, a Padmashri recipient. As a little girl, she sang in the court of her mentor Maharaja Ganga Singh when King George V visited Bikaner. The Dholis, however, are no longer taking up singing in large numbers as they used to earlier.

Another community for whom music is a source of livelihood is the **Mev** group, from the Mewat region. They sing devotional songs about Hindu gods, particularly Shiva, and their main instrument is **bhapang**. Over the years, they have also started

TRIBHUVAN TIWARI

 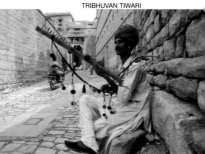

Playing along: Music transcends all manmade boundaries

playing it as a solo instrument. Though the *bhapang* has just one string, it is amazing to watch and listen to the variations the musicians are able to achieve by controlling the tension of the string and the pace of plucking it. The Mevs also use two rarely seen instruments — the **chikara**, which is akin to the *sarangi*, and the **mashak**, a bagpipe. Unlike the Langas and the Manganiyars, this community performs for the masses, as do the **Bhopas**.

The instrument **ravanhatta** that the Bhopas use is more famous than the community itself. *Ravanhatta* is a bowed instrument with two strings, one made of horse hair and the other from threads, with a coconut shell bowl. There is an interesting legend behind the *ravanhatta*. It is believed that its name is derived from the demon king Ravan, who created it with his hand. Apparently, when Ravan was performing a holy sacrifice, he clenched his fist so tightly that his veins emerged like strings. With the help of a bow, he created devotional sounds from his veins.

The Bhopas play the *ravanhatta* while singing ballads of the folk hero Pabuji, who is said to have used his divine powers to help people. Traditionally, they used a **phad** or a painted scroll of Pabuji, depicting various stories associated with his life. The player's wife would light a lamp, highlighting the relevant part of the story in the scroll even as it was musically narrated to the audience. In fact, the ballad would be sung for nights together on the request of Pabuji's

A musician creates a soulful melody

and the *shehnai* were an integral part of the royal lifestyle while the *dhol* was used during celebrations held in villages. The *dhol* was beaten to welcome and lead wedding processions and dances and it was played by both men and women. Men played it outdoors, often during processions, while the woman sat on the ground while playing it. In the case of the *shehnai* and the *nagada*, one can see an archway in several royal households and temples, where space is provided for these two instruments to be played. In royal families, it was customary to announce the arrival of important visitors and to welcome them with the music created by these two instruments.

Some of Rajasthan's other unique instruments include the flute used by snake charmers, called the **poongi** or **murli**. It has a bulge towards the middle, and varying pitches are created by using reeds of different lengths. They also use a single-barrel instrument called **dhapli**, and a percussion called **dhap** during Holi.

Farmers in Shekhawati play a small double-barrel drum called **deru**, also believed to have been the drum that Shiva used while performing his tandav dance.

To discover this rich tradition of music, the visitor to Rajasthan today may have to depend on the festivals organised throughout the year, across the state. There is a good chance that musicians will get together then and you may be lucky enough to be treated to one of their performances. Hotels do hold cultural shows but these often lack authenticity and the true local flavour and sounds. The best bet, of course, is to try and be part of a local ceremony, like a wedding. You can be assured that the sounds that enthral you have a history that's worth just as much as the jewels and paintings of yesteryear. ∎

devotees for making a wish come true or as an offering on the fulfilment of a request to the lord. Today, however, it would be rare to find Bhopas who can do so. They play Hindi and English songs, standing around major monuments or restaurants, to lure tourists. When they sing their own folk songs, they seldom perform the ballad in its entirety; only some of the old-timers in the community know the ballad fully and the children often learn only to play the instrument. Many Bhopas don't even own their own scroll of Pabuji as they have sold it off for money. Incidentally, the scroll is an artistic work that merits a mention in itself. Painted by the Joshis of Bhilwara, the *phad* is on par with an exquisite painting.

Despite the changes caused by modernity, it is clear to the visitor that Rajasthan has always had a strong tradition of using instruments such as the **shehnai**, **nagada** and **dhol**. The *nagada* consists of two drums of varying sizes while the *dhol* is a drum with stretched goat skin; it is played using a stick on one side and the hand on the other. The *nagada*

The Vintage and Classic Car Collection, Udaipur

Transporting you back to an era of royalty and magnificent machines.

For vintage car-lovers, this collection is priceless and a must-stopover. For lay visitors, it's a jaw-dropping collection of gleaming Rolls Royce, Mercedes and Cadillacs in perfect condition. The collection belongs to the House of Mewar; each car associated with different custodians of the House. Old photographs show these cars transporting royalty and heads of state in Udaipur.

Today the Vintage Car Crescent is a sought-after venue for special dinners and events. Your chance to raise a toast amidst this priceless collection…

Marvel as you holiday with the HRH Group.

More experiences await you on page 403

For Reservations and Enquiries contact: Central Reservations (Udaipur)
Toll Free: 1800 180 2933 & 1800 180 2944
Tel: (+91-294) 2528008, 2528016-19 Email: crs@udaipur.hrhindia.com

Eternal Mewar
*Custodianship unbroken
since 734 AD*

HRH Group of Hotels

Fit for a king

For a desert state with such a scarcity of ingredients, Rajasthan manages to cook up a veritable platter

■ BY PUSHPITA SINGH

Coming 'home' to Rajasthan every year from Kolkata, a culture shock always awaited me — the landscape looked bleak, the food tasted different, and home in itself seemed an intangible concept that I could not grasp. I didn't have grandparents on either side, and my visits to Rajasthan in summer, and sometimes blessedly in winter, were to the homes of relatives.

In Kolkata, where we saved money to buy cakes from Nahoum's and made sure we were invited to tea at Flury's by friends, home cooking was often a painful attempt. My mother was from the Shekhawati region, and more suited to be an entrepreneur than a homemaker. She combined in her cooking what she had learnt from her village as a child, with the tips she picked up from our neighbours in the eclectic neighbourhood of Park Street, where we lived. The result was sometimes dismaying, often adventurous, and never consistent.

I thought then — bitterly, I must confess — of the other mothers who would pack their children's school tiffins with such gourmet delights as soft idlis with thick coconut chutney and stuffed aloo-paranthas. Me, I carried the previous night's leftover mutton curry. It was social Siberia. The school I studied in had been set up by an industrialist-philanthropist from the Shekhawati belt. Most of the girl students there were Marwari, like the school's founder. And like him and the rest of the community, they were traditionally vegetarian. To meet their approval, I'd dump my tiffin in the trash and go hungry.

The good thing about being friends with the Marwari girls was that you got invited to their family events. We didn't go to Marwari weddings to *eat*; we went there to *drink*. Not alcohol — that hadn't become fashionable then — but an array of beverages such as the badam-flavoured milk and the sherbets that the hoi-polloi liked. My own favourite was the **thandai**, rich and creamy and laced with nuts and spices, though I loved the more commonplace **chhaach** and **jal jeera** as well.

Over the years, we also came to know Rajput families, descendants of royal lineage, some of who now held corporate jobs. The food at their parties was mostly cosmopolitan, a sort of pan-Indian dal and vegetables and rice, but there would always be

PHOTOS AGP PHOTOBANK/RAJEEV RASTOGI

SANJOY GHOSH

Khata curry is part of the lunch menu at a Rajasthani household (above);
Bajra rotis, lal maas and other dishes spice up the meal (bottom)

something Rajasthani on the menu, such as **curried green tomatoes, aam ki launj** (mango relish), or **ker-sangri**, or a variation of **lal maas.**

My father, like the Marwaris, had migrated from Rajasthan to Kolkata because of circumstances. He was born in a *thikana* of Jodhpur, but as he was part of the younger brother's family, primogeniture ensured that siblings enjoyed none of the feudal

SANJOY GHOSH

pomp and ceremony. My father studied in Delhi and Kolkata, and settled there, sufficiently far away from his roots for his immediate family to have little interest in him. As a result, we were robbed of what passed for gourmet food in the state. When we travelled to Rajasthan, it was to sneer at the scantiness of variety in the meals served there. Vegetables were scarce on the ground, and kitchens ran on extremely spartan produce, much of it stored in bins and consisting of dried beans, or made from chickpea flour, curds and whey. In the mornings, the tradition was to eat *baasi*, or leftovers from the previous night. It more often than not comprised either the **bajra** (millet) **rotis** or the **khichra** (a blend of millets and moth dal, a robust cousin of what passes for khichri in the rest of North

Picnic food

The British left us ideas of hampers packed with cucumber sandwiches, the North Indians have their aloo-paranthas, but it is only in Rajasthan that you have the concept of a menu that is particular to just picnics. Because rains are so rare in Rajasthan, the monsoons are picnic times. The **dal-baati-choorma** is a picnic meal that all of India associates with Rajasthan.

A variety of dals can be cooked though it is somewhat obligatory to make a *paanchmela dal*, which consists of five different kinds of lentils being cooked together without ginger, garlic or onions. Baatis, or balls of wheat and millet, would be cooked in either covered sandpits or, more easily, in open fires. When done, one simply brushed off the sand or the coal dust, and soaked them in ghee. These could then be had with the dal as well as with the choorma. The latter is essentially crushed baatis to which either sugar or jaggery powder has been added along with still more ghee, so that it keeps well and does not spoil any time fast.

There are seasons for some other foods as well. **Sattu** is made at the start of the monsoon with the flour of roasted gram. It is roasted in ghee to which powdered sugar is added at the last moment. Or *ghevar*, which is a lacy confection made of white flour and sugar, available only during the rainy season.

India) soaked in piping hot milk and sprinkled with sugar.

Rajput kitchens tend to be non-fussy. The spices, for all their fieriness, are basic. All you need is red chilli powder (make that a lot of red chilli powder), dhania or coriander powder, turmeric powder and salt. The cooking uses a considerable amount of garlic, and be prepared to peel and dice a lot of onions as well. With some curds or buttermilk, you're set for cooking almost anything in Rajasthan — at least in the most basic way. The Marwari kitchen might fuss with dry fruits and other garnishes that money can buy, but the Rajput kitchen needs little else. It does need a distinct cooking hand though.

It wasn't till my sister got married and went off to Jaipur that we discovered how much more there was to good Rajasthani cooking. Her mother-in-law was from Uttar Pradesh, but she had immersed herself in the ways of Rajasthani cooking and along with her Man Friday, Kakaji, she held sway over her kitchen like a matriarch. Sitting cross-legged in the courtyard surrounded by jars of pickles and relishes, pounded spices and condiments, she commanded every single thing that went into her kitchen and left it. And what delights she could conjure up! **Mangori ka pulao, macchi ki tikki** (in a state where fish was commonly considered inedible even

Dig into some delicious choorma

SANJOY GHOSH

TRIBHUVAN TIWARI

SANJOY GHOSH

Drink to your heart's content: A jal jeera vendor at Jaipur

though, thanks to the irrigation channels that brought water from Punjab, plenty of it was available), **besan ki hari mirch** or **makki ki subzi**.

As shikar had not been banned yet, this was the time I discovered what game gastronomy was about. I'd look out for any opportunity to spend my holidays with my sister and once there, would find one of her brothers-in-law deciding in the middle of the night that he wanted to cook himself a little something to satiate his pangs of hunger. So, in the courtyard vacated by his mother, he'd sit over the mortar and pestle, but only to contemplate briefly what he'd be cooking. At that time of night it was easiest to settle for just **junglee maas**, which is what the shikaris would have cooked on a night out. The recipe was so simple — all it called for was some form of game, oil, salt, red chilli powder and a little water. For that, the result was never less than divine.

That was okay for a quick bite. But meals could be much more ornate, like **khad khargosh**, for instance. It

was a complicated recipe, made all the more difficult because of the rarity of its chief ingredient — the wild hare. In the months when shooting was permitted, the rabbit would first be skinned, then split, washed, salted and, finally, stuffed with masalas. Now would come the complex part, since the recipe required that the rabbit be lowered into a freshly dug sandpit over which a lid would be placed, overlaid with a layer of red hot coals. This wasn't cooking in a hurry, but when the rabbit was removed from the pit, succulent and falling apart to the touch, it was to know gastronomic heaven.

Having grown up on Nizam's seekhs and kathi rolls in Kolkata, it was difficult to understand why Rajasthanis became excited about **soolas**, which I initially thought was just another kebab. But they weren't. Firstly, soolas were typically made of venison, so its availability was limited to the hunting period. Then, making it meant getting boneless chunks off the shank of a leg, marinating it in a

MADHU KAPPARATH   NARENDRA BISHT

No one can have just one bite: The truly sumptuous Rajasthani thali

paste of turmeric, red chilli powder, a hint of curd, crushed garlic and the powder of a sour desert vegetable called *kachri* (which, like most local produce, could be dried and stored for use round the year). This would be skewered and roasted over a bed of live coals until it was tender. Having once had it, Nizam's kathi was relegated to the mundane. There was no comparison with the soola — not even now, when venison is banned, and mutton used as a substitute.

Another fabulous dish is **soyta**, the Rajput equivalent of *haleem*, though it is no longer possible to cook it according to its original recipe as that requires the meat of a wild boar. Pork is a poor substitute, but a substitute nonetheless. I have never tasted the original, though my hus-

> **Many fear Rajasthani food for its fierce chillies, but the trick is to use Nagauri red chillies that are kinder on the palate**

band has, and my only attempt to cook it for a recipe book I was doing was a disaster. I followed the steps all the way — the pork was washed and diced, the millets soaked and cooked together with the masalas, then finally everything brought together and left to simmer-cook for hours and hours till it had become a thick

porridge. The taste wasn't bad, but in my haste I had forgotten to pick the bajra for stones (it had come from my village, not a convenience store) and so every bite ended in an enamel-erasing crunch that left my poor guinea pig neighbour wincing.

In all these decades, though, many things have changed. Foremost is the availability of fresh vegetables even in villages. No more are tomatoes the luxury they once were. Cauliflower and okra are as easily available as are bottle gourd, pumpkin and eggplant. Unfortunately, since these are all foreign to the Rajasthani palate, they are cooked in the same masalas in the same way, so there is little distinction between them and the more typical Rajasthani cuisine.

I often recall my bridal cooking debut. I was asked to cook **meethe chawal** or sweetened rice — something that has disappeared from the menus these days — and would have messed it all up, adding the sugar and saffron at the time of boiling the rice if the cook hadn't helped. Had that happened, the rice would have congealed into a squishy mess when what was required was for each grain to stand distinctly apart. I was allowed to add the ingredients, along with the pounded elaichi, only when the rice was almost done, so the fragrance and the taste were preserved.

My experiments with Rajasthani cooking thereafter were never disastrous, though not always successful. In most cases, I simply heeded the instructions.

The key thing in most Rajasthani dishes is to find the exact estimate of masalas to be used. Practicality might have been the basis for deciding how the masalas should be mixed — for instance, they were mixed in whey, not water. This technique helped in blending them well and in adding a hint of sourness. Because it was a wet paste, it did not singe when it was being fried with oil, thereby adding a better "cooked" taste to food than most other Indian recipes.

Many fear Rajasthani food for its fierce chillies, and there is no doubt it's hotter than most. But because garam masala is never used — it isn't a local produce — there is the whole issue of the blazing red chillies that spice up the curries. However, the trick is to get Nagauri red chillies, since these have a blistering colour

but are kinder on the palate. Naturally, there are as many recipes (even with those few basic ingredients) as there are households, but if there's one thing I've learned from my mother-in-law, it is to save the *baghaar* of crushed garlic till right at the end. It is that fragrance of hot spices and garlic that gets you salivating. It certainly works when I have to make the Rajasthani version of mangori, which makes even the Punjabi version appear bland. **Mangoris** are chickpea flour dumplings mixed with masalas that the women of joint family households put out to dry on rooftops (at about the same time that they roll out papads).

Or take **lal maas**. Here's how we do it in our home: marinate lamb pieces in red chilli powder, coriander powder, sliced onions, salt, turmeric and powdered *kachri* (or substitute with yoghurt) and keep aside for an hour. Heat oil in a pan and cook the

The Chokhi Dhani resort near Jaipur has a rural ambience

TRIBHUVAN TIWARI

lamb with all its masalas on a slow heat for 45 mins. Now add garlic and cook till the oil separates (this is known as **bhunav**). Finally, add water and bring to boil.

If *lal maas* is the public face of Rajasthani cooking (some would say Rajput cooking), then **safed maas** is its exotic makeover under the patronage of royal kitchens. Contrary to what you might think, *safed maas* is not cooked with chicken but with mutton that is first boiled in water to take out its red colour. All the masalas that are used in its cooking are white — yoghurt for marination, ghee (not oil) for cooking, khoya, blanched almonds, cashew nuts, the seeds of whole red chillies (ah, clever...) that are pounded into a powder, powdered coconut, poppy seeds or khuskhus, white peppercorns, sliced onions, lots

Don't cook up your anticipation

Here are a few pointers to what you should expect when you're invited over for a Rajasthan meal:

● The Rajputs eat, and serve, meat; the Marwaris don't. Many Marwaris may include onions and garlic in their cooking, but not everyone, and certainly the Maheshwari Jains, don't

● The staple sangri you eat at these three households will be completely different from each other. That should give you some idea of the difference in the way even simple produce will vary across households. My trick is to add the ker pickle to the sangri I'm cooking, so it adds the spicy *achari* quality of the Marwari dish to the more robust simplicity of our Rajput variaton

● Like their counterparts across India, the Rajputs fast during Navaratri, but with a difference. Not only do they consume liquor during this period (otherwise taboo for those keeping the fast in North India), they will also have meat as a part of their meal, especially if it has been sacrificed to Durga, the patron deity of the Rajputs, who worship Shakti, the goddess of war

● Even if you've been invited by a Marwari family to a hotel banquet, don't think you'll be getting your teeth into a juicy chicken. They may increasingly eat it outside their own homes, but they will never, ever serve it at a party

● And if you're in Rajasthan, don't count on getting the real lal maas or safed maas at hotel restaurants. Everything is muted to a pan-Indian sameness, alas. But for my money, I'd chance telling the chef or maharaj in a family-run heritage hotel to cook the real thing

● As for the specialities, you'll find the **mutton** best in Bikaner and Jodhpur — hot climates lead to lean mutton, as any Hyderabadi will know. Jaipur's **LMB** may be an institution, but it is **Rawat's onion kachoris** that are delicious. In Jodhpur, go looking for **mawa** (or sweet with syrup) **kachoris**, but have them right there and don't even think of getting them packed. Bikaner is best known for its spicy **moth bhujiya** though the rasmalai isn't too bad either. The **palangtor** (or blandly translated, milk cake) is best in Alwar. Again, get your **suparis** and **saunfs** and other mouth fresheners from the shops in **Johari Bazaar** in Jaipur, your **masalas** from Nagaur, and your **papads** and **mangori** and **sangri** from Bikaner. **Bajra** is best from the Shekhawati region. Remember, millet flour does not store well for long periods

AGP PHOTOBANK/RAJEEV RASTOGI

of garlic, sliced ginger, green carda-
moms, cloves and cinnamon. The
cooking is a bit complicated, so it's
best to follow a recipe book, though a
quick pointer is as follows: boil meat,
keep separate. In ghee, fry onions till
they are translucent with the rest of
the garam masala and ginger. Now
add meat and the remaining 'white'
masalas and cook for 45 mins. Add
poppy seeds and coconut powder and
simmer for 15 mins, then add khoya
and stir. Now add almonds and cashew nuts and, finally, the garlic paste.

The emphasis on meat should
explain why the cooking of the palaces never quite descended to most
Rajasthani homes. To begin with,
kitchens tended to be vegetarian, and
meat was not only cooked by the
menfolk, but it was also cooked over
rough and ready fires at makeshift
stoves outside the main house. If men
were going to do the cooking out in
the open, you didn't expect them to
go fancy with blanched almonds and
saffron water! Crushed garlic was
more their style. Nor should you forget that if it wasn't shikar meat that
was being cooked, it was a religious
sacrifice, the *chadawa* or offering usually being goat. As such cooking
tended to be undertaken for the
community, a certain simplicity and
robustness was what one could
expect from it. At its heart, Rajasthani

**Spicing it up: Some mirchi pakodas
to be had with sweet ghevar** (below);
Spices for sale at Jaipur (above)

cooking is about that simplicity,
because there was no local access to
food from outside. In desert villages,
all you had was bajra, presumably
milk, moth and dried *kachri*, or in
season *gwarphali* or cluster beans.

The labourers in the field got by
on more meagre meals. Their afternoon staple was a fistful of **bajra rotis**
taken with a searing **chutney** made
from red chillies and garlic pounded
and cooked together. To drink, there
would be **rabori**, which was millet
flour cooked with buttermilk and
cooled, an acquired taste, but useful
in fending off heatstroke.

Something I loved — and couldn't
understand why we never made at
home, seeing it was so simple — was
the **safed kande ka saag** or curry
made with white, not pink, onions.

Essentially, this was white onions quartered and cooked in a masala with *dhania* powder, a hint of asafoetida, and red chillies. The result was wonderful — onions never tasted sweeter, or better! Kadhi or, as it is called in Rajasthan, **khata**, is a part of every meal, made not from yoghurt but with *chhaach* or buttermilk.

The Marwari table boasted of a lot of dishes, and even though vegetables were rare (they were simply not available then, though now it's possible to find mushrooms and even baby corn in Bikaner), the lavish use of ghee, the limited use of chillies and the sprinkling of khoya and dry fruits into much of the cooking made the food prepared with the same ingredients taste vastly different. But it was the austere Maheshwaris whose cuisine was even more distinctive. For one,

A personal favourite: Bajre ka soyta

Historical records indicate that it originated during the time guerilla warfare was a technique adopted in the Mewar family, and the head of the Mewar clan, Shriji is as fond of it as anyone else I know. He even demonstrated a simpler version of it during a cook show recently. So, for what it's worth, here is my mother-in-law's recipe for **bajre ka soyta**. It's been likened to haleem, but is definitely more robust and has greater flavour. Typically, a soyta was made with wild boar, but pork can be used instead. But, my recipe uses mutton, as that is its most popular variation these days.

Ingredients
Mutton — $^1/_2$ kg
Bajra or whole millet grains— $^1/_2$ kg
Salt — to taste
Water — 6 cups
Ghee — $^1/_2$ cup
Red chilli powder — $^1/_4$ cup
Coriander powder — 6 tsps
Turmeric — 1 tsp
Onions, medium, sliced — 4
Ginger, ground, 3" piece — 1
Garlic pods, large, ground — 3
Green chillies — 15-20
Green coriander, chopped — 2 tbsps
Ginger, julienned — 1 tbsp
Red chillies, deseeded, fried — 4-5

Method
Sprinkle a little water on the millet grains and put aside for 30 mins. Pound slightly to split the grains. Pass through a sieve to remove the chaff. Boil the lamb with salt and one cup of water till it is half done. Heat the ghee in a pan, add all the dry spices along with the millet, and sauté. Add the onion, ginger, garlic, lamb and green chillies, stir together well. Add the remaining water, and cook on a low flame till the lamb is tender and the water is absorbed into a thick porridge. Garnish with chopped green coriander, ginger and red chilli seeds.

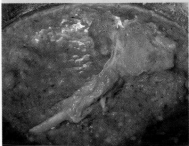

SANJOY GHOSH

GIREESH GV

Good food and great hospitality go together at this house in Jaipur

they abhorred garlic and onions; and, of course, they ate well, so the most appetising of their cooking could match the best anywhere else. Fabulous as their food and their desserts were, nothing could quite compete with the **shaadi ka laddoo**, as it were. It is a tradition of the business community that an invitation to a wedding in the family is never complete without a huge laddoo. These days, a box of sweets, or even chocolates, may accompany the invitation, but it's a poor substitute for the besan ki boondi and khoya that go into making this mammoth dessert.

As far as we were concerned, even the wedding sweets would be made at home. A few days before a wedding, the clan gathered for a wedding, *halwais* would get busy, taking up a free neighbouring plot, digging a pit in which to set the fire, bringing with them huge woks and *patilas* and *paraats*. The menu never varied — **boondi**, sugar-laced **shakkarparas**, **besan ki barfi**, **namakparas** and **matthi**, to be served after every meal, and also substituting as breakfast.

For years, I avoided a fierce and red-looking curry with diced green chillies (or so I thought) as the vegetable. Only recently did I discover what a treat I'd missed all these years, for what I mistook for green chillies were, in fact, **gwarphata** or aloe vera. While the rest of the world was busy applying it to their faces, we in Rajasthan had been packing it inside!

Much of Rajasthani cooking isn't too difficult. However, some things need to be adapted, such as the making of **baatis**, the round dumplings that are, in fact, breads. Typically, the recipe requires that the millet dough be cooked in sandpits (*see Picnic food on page 376*) but I have found a way of getting the temperature and time just right in my oven. Of course, what follows is what counts most — the baked baati has to be dunked, while still hot, in a bowl full of clarified butter. Crumble the baati on your plate, add lal maas, and you will know bliss. ∎

On a song and a dance

Rajasthan's festive spirit is not only colourful but also infectious

■ BY DHARMENDAR KANWAR

Some of the most vibrant and fondest memories of my growing-up years are those linked to festivals. Perhaps this is so for many Indians — our childhoods are captured in moments that refuse to grow sepia-tinted with years, preferring instead to don the shades of pinks, blues and greens of raucous Holi, or the golden hues of the lit lamps of Diwali, flickering even in the soft focus of a memory. This is all the more so, if like me, you have grown up in Rajasthan. For, in the arid landscape of the desert, the festivals were what imbued in us a sense of colour, adding to the parched terrain a vibrant beauty that nature herself did not bestow.

I remember that the preparations for festivals, big or small, were always elaborate. The house would be decorated with intricate *mandanas*, or flour patterns on the floor; the rooms

AMIT PASRICHA

BN KHAZHANCHI/INDIAPICTURE

SARVESH

It's a beautiful world: Glimpses of Rajasthan's many fairs

would be cleaned till they sparkled; the women would undertake fasts and we would all troop down to the temple to listen to a tale or sing bhajans and to marvel at the sights and sounds of the mela at the village square. Those are glorious memories, one that I am always willing to reflect on, and it is so for most Rajasthanis.

Hardly a month passes by without a festival being celebrated in one part of the state or the other. As in the rest of the country, the festivals have religious and mythological, seasonal or historical significance. Perhaps what's more unique to Rajasthan is the enormous number of traditional fairs that continue to be held today. These

double as photo-opportunities for tourists to see the 'real Rajasthan' touted in glossy brochures, but it remains at heart an opportunity for villagers to get together, do business and relax in the company of their brethren — just as it was decades ago.

If the fair is a religious one, then prayers and processions form an integral part of the celebrations. There are also fests associated with changing seasons — some to welcome the monsoon or spring, to seek the blessings of the rain gods for ensuring a plentiful harvest or to thank them if the yield is indeed good. It is worth mentioning here that the fairs are more than what they seem to be from the outside; apart from being an occasion for prayer or thanksgiving, these help in creating a sense of cohesion and solidarity among the community. Be that as it may, the joyous spirit of each and every festival remains the same, as is reflected in the colourful clothes of the people, in the bustling bazaars and in the enthusiasm with which cattle and grain are traded, or in the brisk haggling over handicrafts and clothes and household items. Here are some of the most popular fairs and festivals of Rajasthan.

Makar Sankranti

In the first quarter of the year, Jaipur and Jodhpur gear up to celebrate the annual **Kite Flying Festival** of Makar Sankranti, which falls on January 14. This marks the sun's entry into the Northern Hemisphere and also signals the end of winter. On this day, the sky is dotted with thousands of colourful paper kites as families gather on rooftops playing loud

Inspecting wares at Baneshwar Fair

AGP PHOTOBANK/RAJEEV RASTOGI

music and watching kite fights. People pray for a good harvest on this day and offerings of til and khichdi are made to the sun god.

Baneshwar Fair

Celebrated at the end of January or the first week of February in Dungarpur, the Baneshwar Fair sees a huge gathering of tribal communities. Baneshwar means the 'master of the delta', the local name that has been given to a Shivling at the Mahadeo Temple in Dungarpur. Tribal communities in the neighbouring states of Gujarat and Madhya Pradesh also hold Baneshwar sacred. On the occasion of the fair, thousands of devotees gather at the delta of Som and Mahi rivers, where the fair is held. They sing folk songs, sometimes around bonfires at night, and there are all the other ingredients of a mela: dances, acrobatics and some magic to boot.

Sheetla Mata Mela

In a small village called Chaksu, located close to Jaipur, crowds gather in March to honour the Goddess Sheetla Mata at her shrine. Food cooked the night before is offered to pacify the goddess, who is believed to have the power to prevent diseases. A small cattle fair is held at this time and a market is also set up for villagers to trade in utensils and tools. The different means of transport that the devotees use to reach the mela is a sight worth seeing: buses, jeeps, tractors, camel and bullock carts, cycles and scooters. In the open ground around the hilltop temple to the goddess, people keep themselves entertained by singing and dancing.

Kaila Devi Fair

The Kaila Devi Fair of Karauli, held in March-April, is dedicated to Goddess Mahalaxmi. This fair lasts 12 days and attracts devotees from all over

GIREESH GV

Cattle fairs

Rajasthan has several cattle and camel fairs in addition to its festivals. In some cases, cattle fairs are an integral part of the festivals themselves. We list below a handful of them:

Nagaur Fair
The second largest animal fair (the largest being the Pushkar Fair) in Rajasthan is held in January-February and is renowned for the trading of cows, bullocks, oxen, camel and horses. The animals are decorated colourfully and the owners dress up equally lavishly. One of the main attractions at the fair is a **chilli bazaar** — Nagaur is known for its red chillies in any case. The fair is full of contests such as camel races and bullock races and performances by a veritable list of entertainers ranging from jugglers to puppeteers. The colourful bazaars give the visitors ample opportunity to shop. Several activities such as music performances are also organised.

Bikaner Camel Festival
The year starts on a lively note with the Camel Festival in Bikaner held in January, organised by the Tourism Department. There are parades, races and dances by camels during the festival, which is spread over two days. Folk art performances, including fire dances, are also organised during this time.

Mallinath Fair
In March-April, the Mallinath Fair is held in Tilwara, Barmer, on the Luni river-bed. This is one of the bigger cattle fairs, lasting a fortnight. Bullock, camel and horse races are held as part of the fair.

Pushkar Fair
See page 392

the state. For days, the roads leading to this small temple town are jammed with busloads of pilgrims. Devotees cover the distance on foot or by lying prostrate and then pulling themselves ahead. The temple courtyard resounds with songs as religious processions from nearby towns come together here. There is also shopping for the visitors at the fair.

Mahavirji Fair
Held in honour of the 24th Tirthankara Mahavir in March-April, this fair is where thousands of pilgrims from West Bengal, Assam, Bihar and South India congregate to offer their salutations. The venue is the Mahavirji Shrine at Chandangaon in Sawai Madhopur District. A cobbler is believed to have discovered the lord's

image, now kept at the shrine, buried underground centuries ago. During the fair, the image is carried in a golden chariot drawn by two bullocks to the banks of the River Gambhiri. Pilgrims escort the chariot to the river and back, singing devotional songs. After the image is returned to the shrine, the festivity continues. Shops are set up during the fair, offering goods to visitors.

Gangaur

This is a festival celebrated by women across Rajasthan in March-April, on the day after Holi, and is spread over 18 days. The name Gangaur is a combination of the names of Lord Shiva — Gan being one of his names — and his consort Parvati, or Gauri. Many elaborate rituals are performed as part of the festival. In Nathdwara, near Udaipur, the entire township gathers at the Srinathji Temple for seven consecutive days to watch the idol of Gauri being taken in a procession. There are special pujas on this occasion. In Jaipur, the highlight of the festival is the colourful procession that is taken out from Tripolia Gate to Chaugan and then on to Talkatora. The images of Gauri and Isar (Shiva) are carried in palanquins, with decorated elephants, camels, horses and smartly dressed attendants for company. In the final ritual, the clay or wood images of the gods are immersed in a holy tank or lake.

Urs

Held in Ajmer in July, Urs falls on the first six days of Rajaab (the seventh month of the Islamic calendar). Thousands of devotees of Khwaja Moinuddin Chishti, popularly known as Gharib Nawaz, gather here and pay homage to this saint, whose mortal remains are buried here. Smaller gatherings are organised in Nagaur, Tala and Galiyakot. The pilgrims make offerings called *nazrana* to the saint, consisting of roses, jasmines and perfumes. Qawwali performances take place during this time and are a must-see. Kheer is distributed to devotees from two huge cauldrons or *degs*.

Gogaji

In a small village near Nohar in Hanumangarh District, a fair is held in August to honour a folk deity known as Gogaji Veer, popularly recognised as the God of Snakes. Revered by both Hindus and Muslims, the spot where Gogaji took samadhi is known as Goga Medi. Every year, thousands of

A boy seems to wonder what all the fuss is about (l); **The Baneshwar Fair** (r)

devotees gather here to pay homage to the saint. The fair lasts for three days and attracts visitors from neighbouring states as well. There is a belief among the devotees that Gogaji can cure diseases and many visitors come here to offer thanksgiving if their wishes are fulfilled.

Teej

This is a celebration that starts in the monsoon month of Shravan, as the desert region gets ready to welcome the first drops of rain that will bring a rush of green to the landscape. The third day, or Teej, of Shravan is celebrated in a big way in Rajasthan. The festival is dedicated to the union of Goddess Parvati and Lord Shiva. Women dress in green clothes, denoting the arrival of spring. In rural areas, the festivities begin weeks before the main day of Teej. New clothes are purchased, traditional sweetmeats are made and feasts organised.

Chandrabhaga Fair

Held in November in Jhalarpatan, close to Jhalawar, this annual fair takes place on the banks of the River Chandrabhaga. On the full moon night of Kartik Purnima, people converge here to take a dip in the river and to offer prayers at the temple known as Chandrawati. A cattle fair is

The dramatis personae of a fair

also held here, with cows, camels and bulls being sold, and traders from other states join in too.

Ramdeoji Fair

A folk deity revered in Runicha, a small village near Pokaran in Bhadra, Baba Ramdeoji or Ram Shah Pir was a 15th century saint who hailed from the Tomar Rajput clan. Believed to have been an incarnation of Lord Krishna by the Hindus, Ramdeoji is worshipped for having performed miracles to help the poor. In a fair that lasts for 10 days in August and

September, lakhs of devotees gather at Ramdeora to bathe in the Ramsar Tank, believed to have been constructed by the saint himself, and pay homage at his shrine-samadhi. In this religious fair, pilgrims spend most of their time singing devotional songs. The saint is said to have loved horses and to propitiate him today, devotees buy stuffed toy horses and offer these at the temple.

An attraction at the fair is the performance of terah tali by the members of the Kamod community. In this, two men relate the history of Ramdeoji to the accompaniment of the one-stringed *iktara*, and two women perform a dance. The performance can last through the night.

Kolayat

The full moon in the month of Kartik (October-November) has special religious significance and dozens of small religious fairs take place in villages all over the state during this time. One such is the **Kapil Muni Fair** at Kolayat near Bikaner, so called after the sage Kapil Muni, who is believed to have descended from Lord Brahma. He is said to have prayed at the lake here and while pilgrims visit Kolayat through the year, a dip during the full moon is considered especially sacred. It is thought that one day spent in Kolayat is equivalent to 10 years spent in other sacred places. A beautifully located temple dedicated to Kapil Muni and 52 shaded ghats add to the sanctity of the atmosphere. A cattle fair is also held at this time when prizes are given for the best breeders of camels, horses and cattle.

Tourist Festivals

Jaisalmer Desert Festival

The Desert Festival at Jaisalmer is held in January-February and culminates on Magh Purnima (full moon day). Meant to showcase Rajasthan's rich cultural heritage, the festival features folk dances and folk music performances, held on the gorgeous sand dunes of Sam, near Jaisalmer. Camel races are also part of the festival. The entire city is decorated to receive visitors from all over the country. The golden fort here is illuminated and is a sight to behold.

Hadoti Festival

A fairly new entrant to the festival scene is the Hadoti Festival meant to showcase the culture of the Hadoti Region, comprising Kota, Bundi and

The Teej procession at Jaipur (l); But is it fun for the elephant? At a fair (r)

PHOTOS BN KHAZHANCHI/INDIAPICTURE

Jhalawar. The festival itself is held in Bundi every year in February.

Mewar Festival
Coinciding with the Gangaur Festival, this festival in Udaipur in March-April is meant to welcome spring. Women carry images of gods to the Gangaur Ghat by the Lake Pichola. Soon after this, cultural performances are organised by the Rajasthan Tourism Department.

Elephant Festival
In Jaipur, the Elephant Festival held on the occasion of Holi attracts a lot of visitors who delight in watching the huge animals dressed in finery being led in a procession. There are elephant races and polo games (both favourites of Rajasthani royals at one time) as well.

Shekhawati Festival
The Shekhawati Festival is held in February and serves as a worthy introduction to this region. The festival is celebrated across a number of Shekhawati's painted towns such as Nawalgarh, Sikar, Jhunjhunu and Churu. Visitors are taken in jeeps and on camel safaris and cultural programmes are also held. They are also introduced to Shekhawati's heritage — the organisers hope that this move

SARVESH

Time to put the cart and the feet up

will work both ways and encourage the owners to preserve their havelis.

Marwar Festival
The Marwar Festival is held annually in Jodhpur in September-October in memory of the heroes of Marwar. The festival is held at the Umaid Bhawan Palace and the performances by folk dancers and singers provide a glimpse of the cultural heritage of Marwar. ■

Pushkar Fair

BY AMIT MAHAJAN

To understand the phenomenon called the Pushkar Fair, it's important to view it not as one fair but a conglomeration of two or even three fairs. There is the religious fair, which spans the last five days of the Hindu month of Kartik. This period, from the Ekadashi, or the 11th day, of the waxing phase of moon, to Purnima (full moon day) translates usually into five, but sometimes four days, in November. This is the most auspicious period to visit Pushkar. The cattle fair, which has acquired much international fame, has an amorphous beginning and starts taking shape about a week before Ekadashi. Once any animal arrives at the Pushkar Fair, there is a traditional taboo on its leaving before Ekadashi. From then on, the cattle fair wanes as the moon waxes; the rising full moon on Purnima evening, with the sun setting on the other side of the sand dunes, signals the closure of the cattle fair. In the interstices exists a rural trade and entertainment fair. It's a week-long, sometimes charming, often garish extravaganza, finishing on the night of the full moon.

The fair's origins can be traced to mythology. It's said that Lord Brahma made Pushkar the 'guru' of all tirthas. This dominating presence so disturbed the gods that they pleaded to Brahma for a correction in this lop-sided situation. Brahma agreed to send the Pushkar tirtha into the astral sphere, and to let it be present on earth only for five days. These were to be the last five days of the month of Kartik, from Ekadashi to Purnima. These are the days in which the fair is celebrated today.

Orientation
The spatial arrangement of the fair is best understood in terms of the three fairs described earlier. The cattle fair is held in the grounds and dunes to the north-west of Pushkar Town, beyond the Brahma

AJAY LAL/INDIAPICTURE

Temple. This area is next to the highway to Nagaur, on the northern boundary of the town. An enclosed stadium has been designated as the mela ground and it hosts the 'events' organised by the administration — races, games and fireworks.

To the west of the mela ground are the sand dunes, which function as the arena for camels, horses and cattle. Tucked in between the mela ground and the north-west edge of the town is the exhibition ground, the site for the rural trade and entertainment fair, with shops, giant wheels, a circus and eating stalls.

Two days before Purnima, the town is closed to all vehicular traffic. If arriving from Ajmer, you will have to park about half a kilometre ahead of the town. Only the outermost road through the east and the north (to the cattle fair ground) is accessible. From the afternoon before Purnima, the Bazaar Road is made one-way for pedestrians. This means that you can walk from the Varaha Ghat towards the Brahma Temple (east to west) through the bazaar. But on the way back, you will need to go through the bylanes to the north of Bazaar Road and can enter the bazaar only at two or three places. Travelling west to east, therefore, means taking long circuitous routes.

During the fair, for the devotee, two things are considered essential: to take a dip in the sarovar, and to visit the Brahma Temple. The offerings and their prices do not change during the fair. Many people take a dip and visit the Brahma Temple on all five days.

At the ghats

On the day of Purnima, people start to take a dip in the sarovar right after midnight (ie, the night before the full moon night). The rush will surprise you unless you have been part of a Kumbh Mela. The crowd often takes a life of its own, or is given one by administrative fiat. It will absorb you in itself, leaving you little choice in selecting your path. As you approach the Brahma Temple, the crowd can be crushing, especially till about noon.

Fair play

On the full moon day, after the Brahma Temple, the crowd will steer you north and then west towards the exhibition ground. On this path takes place the charming two-way spectacle wherein two sets of dramatis personae are simultaneously acting and watching one another. There are a few rooftop restaurants occupied mostly by foreigners; below, there is the enormous moving throng of mainly non-urbanite Rajasthanis. In this space, both of them seem to be living with the sole purpose of looking at the other, with an enthusiastic search for comprehension, and an eagerness to engage. This lane is lined with makeshift shops and the air filled with the sounds of the mela. As you come out of the town, the blaring music from the circus hits you, as does the visual of young boys doing a raunchy dance dressed in drag. The place is teeming with dhabas, offering very chilly bazaar food.

Past this village fair, you climb the sands of the modest dunes, and you are in the midst of the cattle fair. Horses just behind the circus, camels further ahead, and cows beyond them. There are the mendicant musicians — men and boys playing the ravanhatta, women and girls doing a dance. Most of them, across the gender divide, sing, and many in voices that one could travel miles to listen to.

The camels are undisputedly the stars of the show. There are camels of all sorts — old and young, female and male, very shabby-looking and enormously bedecked. If you are not satisfied with only looking at the camels, and desire a closer interaction, you have the choice between riding on camel back or on a camel cart. A camel cart is a basic wooden cart padded with a mattress and bolster and can accommodate five people; the charges are Rs 350-500 per hr. A ride on the camel back (Rs 250-350 per hr) is recommended only to those who are healthy in body and spirit.

The mela ground hosts a variety of events — camel race, camel decoration and horse dance. This is a week-long celebration and is well advertised. Information is readily available at the RTDC Tourist Information Centres at Hotel Sarovar and RTDC Tourist Village (see Pushkar on page 191). A part of this festivity is organised at the old Rangji Temple in Pushkar. End your day at the temple compound with folk and classical dance and singing. ■

One-stop shop

Your definitive guide to what to buy in Rajasthan and from where

Photographs by SANJOY GHOSH

■ BY DHARMENDAR KANWAR

The purposefulness disappears almost as soon you make your way through a maze of bylanes. You forget what you had set out to buy. Perhaps it was something as mundane as toothpaste, perhaps it was sunscreen. But right now you are hypnotised by the wares on offer: eye-catching puppets resting against a wall, an exquisite cloth painting that radiates serenity, a blue vase embossed with flowers, its simplicity as eloquent as its beauty.

Welcome to the shopaholic's delight that is Rajasthan. Here life is full of A-ha moments that make you stop on your tracks — no matter where you are headed, no matter what your plans — so that you can pick up a souvenir or two, perhaps even three. I should know. I am not a compulsive shopper, I live in Rajasthan and this has been my home for decades, yet all I can do is gaze at the shops full of goodies and try to convince myself that I should not indulge, not today at least, may be tomorrow?

It's true that shopping and Rajasthan are synonymous — and with good reason too. I personally feel that Rajasthan has preserved its craft heritage much better than several other states. And each souvenir that you pick up reflects not just the craftperson's skill but also a history spanning centuries, right from the time Rajput princes, influenced by the Mughals who were great patrons of art, invited skilled artisans from other parts to settle down in their principalities. This royal patronage was one of the main reasons why the artisans could work with single minded devotion towards enhancing the quality of their craft. The Rajputs commissioned goldsmiths, printers and dyers, painters, potters, stone carvers, weavers of cotton and silk to produce works of art for them and rewarded them handsomely when they excelled in their craft.

It is a legacy that lives on in Rajasthan. Each region has its own unique crafts, and every little town and village has its share of lanes where craftspersons hold fort. It is this treasure trove that tourists are privileged to discover, be it in a modern shopping centre in a big town or in a traditional bazaar in a small village. In the following pages, we look at some of the items that should figure in every tourist's shopping list.

Traditional paintings

Miniature paintings, portraits and paintings on cloth and furniture are to be found in Jaipur, Jodhpur, Nathdwara and Kishangarh. Not only are these attractive but also light and easy to carry back. The **phad**, or the scroll depicting the tales of folk hero Pabuji, which was used in the musical performances of the Bhopa community, is a more traditional form of painting that's seen in Rajasthan. Though it was initially done with vegetable and stone dyes in Chittaurgarh and Shahpura (Bhilwara), these are now sold all over Rajasthan. In Shahpura, there is only one family of painters pursuing this art form now.

Another painting form is the **pichhwai**, in which legends associated with Lord Krishna are illustrated. It was originally done on hand-spun fabric and hung behind (that is, *pichhe*) the deity's statue in temples. In its present-day avatar as a sought-after souvenir, the *pichhwai* painting is often a poor imitation of the real thing. You will find many being sold in the shops in Nathdwara (near

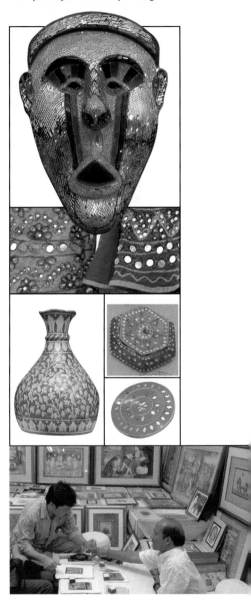

Below from top to bottom **A glass and lac mask**; **Mirrorwork on clothes**; **Blue pottery**; **Miniature paintings**

Udaipur), located on the lane leading from the bus stand to the temple. Several *pichhwais* are decorated with gold plating and precious stones. Depending on the design and the embellishment, the prices of *pichhwais* can go up to Rs 50,000 and more. On MI Road and Amber Road in Jaipur, you will find smaller replicas of *phads*.

Rajasthan is also known for its different schools of painting (*also see Small is beautiful on page 425*), each with its own distinctive style. The **Kishangarh School of Painting** — in which women in the paintings have sharp features and exaggerated eyes — is well known. Paintings in this style are now available in most Rajasthani towns. If you want to buy it in its home territory, head to the old quarter near the Kishangarh Fort. Here you will find families who make and sell replicas of old paintings. Jaipur is *the* place for miniatures of excellent

quality. In Bikaner, **Swami Art**, located en route to the Lallgarh Palace, has a superb collection of miniatures. In Udaipur, paintings are sold on Lake Palace Road and in the Jagdish Temple area, while in Jodhpur, Nai Sarak is a good place to scout around for the same. Their prices range from Rs 200 to 1,200 for the bigger ones. Wherever possible, do try and buy these from **Rajasthali** showrooms.

Leather items

Almost every town in Rajasthan has many items made of leather on sale. *Jootis*, in all sizes and colours, are obviously big favourites with tourists. Also sold are **bags**, pouches, **chair backrests**, lamp and lampshades, and **kopis**, all in leather, and water bottles made of camel leather. In places such as Bikaner and Jodhpur, camel hide is embellished with gold and stone colours to make it attractive.

The traditional centres where leather products are sold include Bikaner, Jaipur, Jodhpur and Jaisalmer. It is also possible to get good bargain deals at Ajmer, Bharatpur, Sikar and Sawai Madhopur. In Jaipur, the shops near Hawa Mahal stock a range of lovely *jootis*, as do the ones at Link Road and Ramganj Bazaar. You can also visit **Mojari** in Bhawani Villa at Chomu House, which has an excellent range of *jootis*. Other areas where you can pick up leather items include: Nai Sarak, Mochiwada and Sojati Gate area in Jodhpur, with **Juti Corner** opposite the railway station being a popular outlet; Station Road and Ganganagar Road in Bikaner; and Gandhi Chowk Bazaar in Jaisalmer. *Jootis* cost between Rs 120 and 500 depending on the embroidery on them. The plain leather ones are cheaper.

Blue pottery

This art form is thought to have originated in the first part of the 19th

Below Rajasthani jootis; Ceramic tiles; A woman buys bangles

SUMAN SARKAR

GIREESH GV

Outside Hawa Mahal at Jaipur are a number of shops stocking jootis

century, and came to India via Persia and Afghanistan. It remained neglected after the end of the Mughal era and was revived because of the efforts of Padmashri award winner Kirpal Singh Shekhawat. In 1962, while heading the Shilpa Kala Mandir in Jaipur, Kirpal Singh Shekhawat set up a kiln of his own and made blue pottery items that could be used in daily life.

Today, reasonably priced blue pottery items are to be easily found in most shops in Jaipur. Don't be confused if you find other colours in blue pottery items — pink, yellow, green, brown, mauve, grey and black are also integral colours for items that go under the very broad umbrella of blue pottery! Some of the interesting items that you may want to pick up include fruit bowls, glasses and plates, tiles with floral designs and flower vases. The prices can vary from Rs 25 for a small box to Rs 10,000 for large items.

Sanganer, Mahalan and Neota are also places from where you can pick up blue pottery. **Rajasthali** and other shops on MI Road and Amber Road in Jaipur have a wide range of goods.

Kripal Kumbh in Bani Park and **Neerja International** in C Scheme, both in Jaipur, are also good places to pick up these items.

Say it with lac

Always taken out for festive occasions, **lac bangles** come in a variety of designs and styles: plain, thin or floral. Some of the most beautiful bangles that you can pick up are those with cone-shaped rhinestone or crystal embedded in them. Small boxes, pens, paperweights and decorative joss stick holders made of lac are available in Bapu Bazaar, Link

Each souvenir that you pick up reflects not just the craftsperson's skill but also its history spanning centuries

Road, Jaipur. The bangles are priced at Rs 50 for a pair. Those with more work cost Rs 250. In Jodhpur, you can pick these up at the outlets in Lakhada Bazaar near Ghanta Ghar.

Of textiles and textures

Rajasthan's textile market spans across regions and fabrics — and that's putting it mildly. Be it the delicate floral motifs hand-block-printed in Sanganer or the earthy prints of Bagru, there is much for the shopper to look for. While traditionally Rajasthan's textiles came in vibrant colours, their look has been enriched by collaborations with designers from outside the state and across the country. It is, therefore, not surprising to find a contemporary look in the most traditional of clothes.

Perhaps the most heartening fact about the fabrics is the eco-friendly method used for its production. Wooden blocks are used for printing textiles while colours are added using vegetable dyes that have no chemicals. Some famous prints include Barmer's red and indigo geometric patterns called **ajraks**; Chittaurgarh's **jajam prints**; and Jaisalmer's **batik** and **embroidery work**. While **tie-and-dye** is popular in Sikar, Jodhpur and Jaipur, **mirror work**, **appliqué** and **embroidery** are done in Bikaner, Sikar and Jhunjhunu.

Kota doria, a lightweight fabric that is woven in the villages of Kaithoon, Siswali and Mangroal, is one of Rajasthan's most famous textiles. One remarkable feature about the makers of these fabrics is that the weavers are all women. You can get this fabric from markets in Kota such as **Gumanpura** and **Rampura Bazaar**. The saris made with powerlooms cost

between Rs 250 and 1,200, while hand-looms are priced between Rs 500 and 10,000 (depending on the workmanship). For genuine handlooms, it's better to take a trip to Kaithoon as it is only a half-an-hour's drive from Kota.

The **tie-and-dye technique** is an ancient art; the fabric is knotted in certain places, tied with thread and dipped in colour. When the threads are removed, it leaves behind patterns. Just like the tie-and-dye method, **mukaish** work is among the oldest styles of decorating fabrics, done with silver wire or *badla*. **Marori** work involves a kind of embroidery wherein gold threads are stitched on to the surface with a needle. In **gota** work, a gold border is woven into the cloth and the material is cut into various shapes, such as those of birds, animals and human figures, to create a variety of textures. Johari Bazaar in Jaipur, Nai Sarak in Jodhpur and Lake Palace Road in Udaipur are good places for buying fabrics with this kind of work. Prices range from Rs 250 for a cotton tie-and-dye sari to Rs 1,500 upwards for a chiffon, silk or georgette chiffon sari.

Tourists will do well to stop at the **Anokhi Museum of Hand Printing** at Anokhi Haveli near Jaipur's Kheri Gate, which has several exhibits worth mulling over. **Cottons, Ratan Textiles, Soma, Suvasa** and **Chippa Print N Craft** in the C Scheme area in Jaipur offer a fabulous range of home furnishings and accessories. **Naika** on MI Road and **Rashid** on Talkatora Road are also good options. Near Ramgarh Modh on Amber Road is **Arawali Textiles**, which exports hand-looms around the world and sells silk and cotton textiles as well as a range of home furnishings and handicrafts at reasonable rates. **Sikar House** on Jhotwada Road is a good option for inexpensive, export surplus items. **Ranas** in Ganapati Plaza in Jaipur stocks a superb collection of saris and bridal wear.

With OTG Desk

Clay and terracotta products

Each district of Rajasthan has its own distinct style of pottery. In Molela, near Udaipur, craftsmen are skilled at making terracotta idols of gods. This art form has been passed down from one generation to another. The women do the hard work of getting the clay ready while the men make the *murtis* and decorate them. The intricacy of the work involved and the size of the idol determine its price. Big ones can cost as much as Rs 1,000 while smaller ones sell for Rs 80. Roadside vendors sell the idols in Udaipur's markets but these are also available across the state. Alwar is known for paper-thin pottery known as **Kagzi pottery**, which is easily distinguishable because of the thin walls of the items. Pots made in this manner have double-walled surfaces cut into lovely patterns to augment airflow. The pots made in Pokaran on the other hand have geometrical etchings. Bikaner's **painted pottery** and the **terracotta products** of the Nohar Centre of Bikaner are equally famous. If you visit Jallore and Ahore, do pick up the **terracotta horses** that are made here as religious offerings. If visiting Nagaur and Merta during local fairs, you will find **terracotta toys** on sale.

Handmade paper

Sanganer is known for the wondrous and diverse range of items made of paper such as stationery, gift boxes, carry bags and photo frames. These items are not only beautiful but also eco-friendly, as these are made with recycled paper. **Salim's Paper** and **Kagzi Handmade Paper Industries** (both on Gramudyog Road) and **Kalpana Handmade Paper Industries** at Bawri ka Bas, Nashiyon ka Rasta, are the most popular outlets in Sanganer. **Chipa** on Bhawani Singh Road, **Khadi Ghar** and the

A range of handicrafts are on sale in Jaipur, including a ceramic door knob

Rajasthali showroom on MI Road in Jaipur also sell handmade paper.

Poetry in wood

While one may not traditionally associate a desert land with wood items, Rajasthan has a surprisingly large number of showpieces in wood that are incredibly beautiful. The only hitch is that it may not be possible to cart everything back home — not easily at least. You will find **doors** and **windows with beautiful carvings**, **beds**, **divans**, **chairs** and **swings** in Barmer, Bikaner, Shekhawati and Jodhpur. If you are looking for something that's smaller in size, there are plenty of options as well: **kavadhs**, which are wooden shrines that have seven panels, **wooden toys**, and **sindoor boxes** shaped like peacocks, all of which are available at Bassi, near

Chittaurgarh. For painted wooden furniture, shops in Jodhpur and Kishangarh are the best options. Other pieces of furniture that make for excellent souvenirs are the **leather-embroidered chairs** of Tilonia and the carved-back, **string-bottom chairs** of Shekhawati. Wooden furniture and antiques can also be purchased from **Lalji Handicrafts, Shekhawati Art Emporium, Rajasthan Art Emporium** and the **Heritage Art School** (near Circuit House) in Jodhpur.

Antiques

A word of caution is in order here first: what passes off as antique may not really be that old but skilled artisans can meet exacting standards and make something new look as good as old! Jodhpur, Shekhawati and Jaipur are the best places to look for

Below top to bottom **Marble pots and elephant; Antiques**

SANJAY SHARMA

antiques. The road at the foothill of Umaid Bhawan Palace, Jodhpur, has dozens of shops dealing in antiques. Fatehpur, Shekhawati and Jaipur have several dealers from whom you can buy antiques as well as replicas. On Jaipur's Tilak Marg, explore the fabulous variety of items on offer at **Saroj Handicrafts and Arts** (at Nandanam Apartments), where you'll find replicas of Venetian mirrors, lamps, lithographs, Raja Ravi Verma prints and period furniture. Prices begin at Rs 2,000. **Roopsi Handicrafts**, located at Saheli Marg, near Sahelion Ki Badi, is a good option in Udaipur.

Carved in stone

While stone carving is mostly seen in Jaipur, Makrana, Jodhpur and Jaisalmer, stone products are available in other cities as well. From functional domestic items that come in beautiful shapes to **elegantly carved pillars** and **doors ornamented with brass motifs**, you can find stone products of every conceivable nature across the state. Some of these may not feature in a typical souvenir hunt, but if you're looking at doing your house up and are all right with having some items shipped, then these are good options. Kishangarh is the best place to look for marble and stone items such as statues, fountains, table tops and lamp bases. You will find all these and more in the 50-odd shops lining NH8. A good place to pick up carved marble items is **Khajanewalon ka Raasta** in Jaipur. The prices start from Rs 250 for a small piece and go up to Rs 5,000, depending on the size and workmanship. The **Pandey Murti Kala Kendra** at Narain Bhawan here offers customised idols of all sizes and dimensions and for all budgets. **Shilpgram** in Udaipur has an attractive selection of marble, stone and pottery items. Other shops are to be found on the Jaipur-Agra and Jaipur-Ajmer highways. Bargaining is the norm in all these places.

Dhurries

Jodhpur, Bikaner and Jaisalmer are known for woollen and cotton dhurries. In most cases, villagers work with businesspersons from metros to boost their sales and to reach a wider market, and as a result, the weavers' work reflects a harmonious blend of traditional and contemporary designs. While dhurries are more reasonably priced and easy to maintain, **carpets** are also great buys. Jaipur and Bikaner have many carpet outlets. Incidentally, many of the looms for making carpets are operated by prisoners, a practice that was started by the Mughals. Bikaner, for instance, is known for carpets made in prisons, known popularly as **jail carpets**.

A floor covering that is used widely in Rajasthan is the **namdah** or the felted rug. It is available in mainly two styles: embroidered, or with appliqué work. Tonk is the main centre for this craft. Two places where the quality of carpets and rugs is assured are: **Salawas**, where **Pukhraj Prajapat Dhuree Udyog** sells dhurries; and **Ankur**, behind Anokhi on Tilak Marg in Jaipur.

Quilts

In Jaipur, do look out for light cotton quilts in the shops opposite Hawa Mahal. These are easy to carry and prove very useful. Some shops in **Chaura Raasta** as well as **Soma** and **Ratan Textiles** are also good places to pick up quilts. Prices start from Rs 200 and go up to Rs 2,000. Nagaur is not only famous for its chillies but is also known for light quilts. Bikaner, on the other hand, has bazaars selling cotton and camel-wool shawls. **Urmul outlets** are another option. Though their quilts may not be soft, they keep you warm.

TRIBHUVAN TIWARI

A historic backdrop for a carpet sale

Metalware

Everything from tabletops to picture frames is available in a range of metals in Rajasthan. Among the brass, iron or silver items that you can pick up are **pen cases**, **styluses** and **compasses**. Jodhpur is known for **brass toy** items — cannons, elephants, horses and camels — while Jaipur's speciality is its **brassware**. Lake Palace Road in Udaipur, Palace Road and Clock Tower Road in

Rajasthan has preserved its crafts heritage well, one reason why shopping is synonymous with the state

on a metal surface and later engravings of flowers, birds and fish are etched on to it. Nathdwara, Bikaner and Udaipur are famous for silver *meenakari* jewellery. Pratapgarh is known for **thewa** work, or **glass enamelling**, which involves fine gold work being carried out on the green enamel that is used as the base.

Before you splurge on jewellery, do keep two points in mind. One, it's best to buy from reputed shops or you may end up with suspect stuff from shops that may be promising you a steal; and two, be wary of touts who may pose as helpful guides.

Gopalji ka Raasta and **Haldiyon ka Raasta** in Johari Bazaar, Jaipur, have a formidable reputation for their *meenakari* and *kundan* work. MI Road, also in Jaipur, has a lot of showrooms with silver and precious stone jewellery. The **Gem Palace** here has been set up by a family whose ancestors were jewellers to Mughal emperors. They feature expensive stuff but it is still the finest collection in town.

Miss India on MI Road is famous for beautiful **silver jewellery** and **silverware**. **Saurashtra Jewels & Arts**, opposite the Ayurveda College inside Zoravar Singh Gate on Amber Road, sells gold and silver jewellery. They also stock miniature paintings and textiles made by tribal communities. Those looking for a personalised experience can contact Smita (Mobile: 09351793444), who stocks traditional gold and silver jewellery. **Silver Art Palace**, located past Holiday Inn, is a good place to shop for silver.

Nathdwara and Ghanta Ghar in Udaipur are good places to shop for jewellery with traditional designs. In Jodhpur, head to **Gems and Jewels** and **Gems and Art Plaza**, both located near the Circuit House, and the shops lining Sarafa Bazaar. Deogarh is the place to pick up some of the best silver jewellery in Rajasthan. ▪

Above top to bottom **Brass work**; **Wooden box**; **Jewellery**

Jodhpur, and MI Road, Amber Road and Tripolia Bazaar in Jaipur are good places to look for metalware.

Jewellery

Rajasthan is known for its jewellery, especially jewels made in the **kundan** (precious stone set in gold) style as also the **meenakari** variety. If Jaipur has sellers whose clients buy gems wholesale (*see Aladdin's cave on page 404*), Jodhpur has shops selling handmade silver jewellery and ornaments made with emeralds, diamonds, pearls and lapis lazuli.

Jaipur is the main centre of *meenakari*, or enamelling work, with the colours associated with the Mughals such as red, green and white dominating this art form. In enamelling, pieces of minerals are attached

Shine on you pretty diamond: Precious stones in various settings

Aladdin's cave

In Jaipur's jewellery markets, gems are sold in tonnes and kilos

■ BY PUSHPITA SINGH

Gerard — he's known as Jarot Sa'ab to the vendors in Chameli Bazaar — is surrounded by a haze of cigarette smoke. He's been staring at rows of semi-precious stones laid out on the counter for what seems like hours in meditative contemplation. Rajesh Bhai lets him be. Gerard arrives twice a year without fail, and his buying is more discreet than that of the backpacking tourists who buy bulk stones cheap to sell for profit when they get back home. You can feel his

mind tick as he visualises the ropes and strings of chalcedony and the lapis lazuli, the malachite and rose quartz, the amethysts and garnets, the onyx and crystal, the coral and turquoise, all of them to be set in elaborate pieces of jewellery. Sold here by their weight, often treated with heat to increase the density of their colour, sometimes synthetically constituted and passed off as the genuine thing, this is Jaipur's wholesale market for gemstones and semi-precious stones.

Alas, you're not welcome here as a retail buyer looking to put together a bit of amazonite with some citrine or carnelian. They can sniff out the retailer, shooing him or (mostly) her away like a pariah dog. This market caters only to bulk buyers, those looking to buy by the kilo tiger's eye and moonstone, smoky topaz and tourmaline in higgledy shop after piggledy shop. And the cuts — oh, the cuts! Polished to a fine glow, cut into amazing shapes, round like beads, plump like musk-melons, rectangular

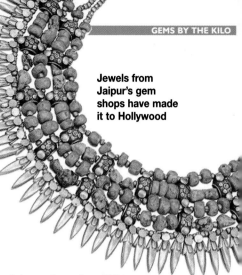

Jewels from Jaipur's gem shops have made it to Hollywood

like chewing gum, faceted, engraved, chiseled, either left rough in their natural state or smoothened like a baby's cheek, it is here that the world's gemstones come for cutting and polishing, imported for the purpose, then exported back to the country of origin (Afghanistan, Argentina, Thailand, Sri Lanka, Russia, South America and South Africa) or to world markets where they will be snapped up by jewellery designers.

In Benares and in Leh, in Chennai and in Goa, what's passed off as local stones are those that have been created in Jaipur. No wonder then that these are worn even to the Oscars. The brightest in Hollywood can in all probability be traced from here — Chameli Bazaar has the less expensive semi-precious strings and silver, and Johari Bazaar the more expensive rubies, emeralds and sapphires.

For pearls, don't bother going to Hyderabad just yet, because in a corner wholesaler's shop tucked in a labyrinthine street, then up some steep, unlit staircase, is Kishore Motiwallah, surrounded by sacks of pearls — the real stuff from the seas, the cultured variety, the dyed things that China has made so popular as mother-of-pearl, the expensive beads that come all the way from the South Pacific. He won't haggle over a string here or there. Kishore Bhai has consignments being couriered from the big cities of India to the big cities of the world. His scales are set to the finest milligram, but when it comes to selling, he certainly appreciates figures in tonnes over kilos.

No wonder Jaipurwallahs are so peeved. In *their city, their* traders will not sell to them at a discount, while designers from Delhi and Mumbai walk in to greet the traders like old friends and cart off bags-full of gems that is making the world sit up and take notice of a little town called Jaipur. But surely, you could get it a mite cheaper if you went shopping personally? That's unlikely — and people who're susceptible to bargains are likely to suffer the most.

At Jaipur's wholesale market for gems and semi-precious stones, they can sniff out the retailer a mile away

Yet, it would be churlish to deny the beauty of what the traders sell: brilliant Victorian settings in silver and gold and brass, zircon and crystal winking as sharply as diamonds. No wonder Gerard and his ilk spend days looking at the amazing spread — coiled, hung, suspended or packed before them like the treasures spilling out of Aladdin's cave. These come in all the colours and shapes and hues that you might want — a bright orange, an impeccable powder blue, black or poison green, a warm yellow — tantalisingly packed into impossibly tiny shops. And of course, gold too, in *kundan* settings, with uncut diamonds, emeralds and ruby cabochons, sold as is routine here, by the kilo! ■

From luxurious spas in old palaces to roadside head massages in Pushkar, Rajasthan offers much to cleanse the body and soul

Pushkar **Heady experiences**

JUHI SAKLANI

At home in the shop: Tourists come for regular massages

■ BY JUHI SAKLANI

Ajmer sees you off with a stall of *Bhayankar Soda*. For 15 minutes, self-effacing little Aravalli Hills, painted fresh and green, bow and courtesy you along to Pushkar. And on entering the lakeside town, you straightaway chance upon shops called 'Rasta-Roko Garments' and 'Same Same but Different'. Clearly, there is much room for relaxation in Pushkar. But, as it might have struck you by now, this is no aroma-therapeutic, music-laden, serene-chambered namby-pamby experience.

In keeping with hilly Manali and beachy Goa, religious Pushkar makes an unlikely but confirmed triangle for long-staying, long-haired backpacking tourists in India. The result of their search for 'India' is often *Boom Shiva* T-shirts, dhabas that give muesli, and the Indian Wellness

Experience. In Pushkar, much of the burden of the last is borne by barbers.

The 'Indian Head Massage' is the new treasure for European and American writers who need to spike their copy by letting readers in on a 'secret'. We gave up the humble *champi* with mustard oil some time back but they have just discovered it. But if you have to pay 10 pounds for it in London, here the local *nais* offer it for far fewer and highly negotiable rupees and, moreover, with what a tourist guide has called "turbo-charged hands".

Of these, the most venerable pair of hands belongs to Bihari Lal Sen. So sure was he of the healing powers of his massaging hands that he (a) wrote to a TV channel offering to demonstrate his prowess, and (b) wrote to the then Prime Minister Atal Behari Vajpayee to not go in for a knee replacement before trying him out. The *piece-de-resistance* of his ouvre is the traditional Chandra Massage. In Pushkar, **Chandra Massage** is the nomenclature for what the barbers say is a traditional Rajasthani massage, once given to weary kings after they had fought a good war. Now it means calling over the masseur to your hotel and having not just your body massaged but also your joints twisted, your muscles manipulated, your limbs rotated and your very essential self pushed and pulled.

Bihari Lal ji and his son Raju run a typical 'nai' shop called 'Shri Ram Janata Hair Dressers' in the bazaar, and their little place is full of photographs of satisfied tourists as well as quaint painted photographs of the old gent with female clients, looking like old issues of *Chandamama*. They give a wonderful, old-fashioned *champi* and a great head-neck-back massage with mustard oil.

◆**Raju, Shri Ram Janata Hairdressers**, main market; Mobile: 09414258351. The price is negotiable, depending on the length of the massage. Down the road, **Baba Hairdresser** offers similar services

Among other purveyors of the Chandra Massage, who claim that their forefathers used this technique on kings, is the Deepak Beauty Parlour. They offer massages: **Ayurvedic, chakra, herbal, Rajasthani, acupressure** and **shiatsu**. The boys are proud that female tourists feel safe in their hands, literally, and proudly show off glowing recommendations. They also give a lovely foot-and-leg massage, using instruments used by foot reflexology practitioners.

◆**Deepak Beauty Parlour**, on the way to Pushkar Palace Hotel; Mobile: 09829295612

But the **reflexology** available at NS Mathur's informal clinic is of another kind. An erstwhile medical representative, popularly called 'Dr Mathur', gives you the benefit of good reflexology (acupressure done for therapeutic purposes on the feet and hands), with some naturopathic dietary advice, yoga advice and supplementary instruments that aid the stern treatment. Not for immediate relaxation, this addresses specific problems of your body.

◆**NS Mathur's 'clinic'**, almost opposite the bus stand, before RTDC Hotel Sarovar; Timings: 10.30 am-6 pm; Rs 100 per session

And if wellness is here, can **yoga** be far behind? Yogi Sam, as the foreigners call him, is a young yoga teacher and ex-religious ascetic, who operates from the pleasant lawns of Sunset Restaurant at times fixed by appointment. But he also gives a mean massage: his Thai massage (with much twisting of the body) differs from his Ayurvedic (gentle rubbing) and Chinese (oriented to pressure points). For good measure, he also offers **laughter therapy** and **pranayam**. If you call him over to a big hotel such as Pushkar Palace or Jagat Palace, it could cost you Rs 1,000 for an hour, but at Sunset Restaurant the charge is halved.

◆**Yogi Sam**, Mobile: 09214842171

And finally, a word from the wise. "Good simple food, as close as

> There is room for relaxation in Pushkar but it is no aroma-therapeutic, music-laden namby-pamby experience

possible to its natural form, when sensibly consumed, has been known to heal…". After all your strenuous massages, settle down in the tiny **Honey and Spice** (Laxmi Market, Old Rangji Temple) and wallow in ginger cinnamon coffee, fresh juices, tofu on toast or spinach pineapple noodles.

Healing. Definitely healing.

Udaivilas Wellness by the waters

The king is not here anymore, looking out on the gentle lake and the hills beyond with power-weary eyes. The queen is not here either: she does not see the world through stone jaalis, there is no more confinement of a life to children and gods. The commoner goes on, though. She wraps her sari around her knees, sits on her haunches at the edge of Lake Pichola so full of water after so many parched years, and sighs out a statement of quotidian beauty and profundity under her breath: "From tomorrow, I'll bring the clothes here to wash."

Lake Pichola is the liquid foundation on which rests the idea of Udaipur. Palaces float on it, citadels stand by its side, hills surround it, and a heart that reaches its shore on a cloud-laden monsoon morning or a cold sunny winter sings like never before!

Udaivilas, the Oberoi Group's luxury resort by the Pichola, has taken the best of these palaces and citadels, these hills, clouds and waters, and made a thing of joy and beauty at the far shore of Lake Pichola. It's rather unthinkable that a new hotel would add to the skyline of a heritage site, but the planners and craftspersons of Udaivilas have managed it. A playful confection of light and wind and the sound of water, it is satisfyingly palatial yet delightfully light-footed, undulating down the sloping land, throwing up unexpected treats of architecture (like genuine *thekri* work and hand-crafted pillars), and making the most gratifying use of Lake Pichola at its doorstep.

Coming ashore from the jetty to the Udaivilas grounds, you are greeted by a magnificent banyan tree. This is felicitous because the **Banyan Tree Spa** at the resort is one of the most poetry-inducing spa and wellness experiences. The spa is run by Banyan Tree, the Thai Hotel and Spa chain, with awards from Conde Nast, Luxury Travel Gold List, National Geographic Readers' Choice and Pacific Asia Travel Association under their belt. They claim to, and do, combine a "high-touch, low-tech" approach that celebrates the healing energies of human touch combined with the most tasteful of surroundings.

The marriage of the foreign tourists' desire to undergo the Indian 'experience' and Banyan Tree's philosophy of using native ingredients results in a delightful situation. I, a UP-born Delhiite, greet my spa therapist from Thailand with a cheery "hello", while she folds her hands in a namaste and proceeds to give me an excellent Ayurvedic massage taught to her by a Malayali doctor. The world is a wonderful place!

Apart from the standard **Banyan Tree massages**, the spa now offers the constitutional analysis and advice of Dr Yogesh, trained at India's most respected Ayurvedic hospital, the Kottakkal Arya Vaidya Sala, as well as **yoga training** under the very pleasant Shri Vettri, a good teacher. An early-morning hour in the Bada Mahal (the erstwhile royal hunting lodge) by the lake, doing yoga tailored to your needs, seems, at that moment, to be the only possible way to start the day.

One of the best things about Udaivilas' Banyan Tree Spa is the view of the lake visible from wall-to-wall windows. Going through their signature **Oberoi Massage**, I soon find the desire to keep my eyes open to drink in the lake resisting the compulsion to close the eyes under the masseuse's soothing hands. The massage goes deep, ironing out knots and relaxing the muscles. In no time, I'm asleep. In a later session I have an **Ayurvedic Massage**, rhythmic and stroke-based with sesame oil. When the time comes for a *besan* scrub, I'm asleep again. Next, I undergo a profoundly soothing **Shirodhara treatment**: warm oil trickles from a pot overhead, onto my forehead as the masseuse moves the trickle across the forehead. That's it. No "massage" as we understand it and the body is left quite alone. Yet, this is a transformative hour, almost unnerving in its ability to drain restless thoughts away from a weary head. I, of course, fall asleep.

A last word. Luxury is for those who can afford it. But, even if you can't afford it, save money, borrow from friends and manage somehow to stay one day at the Udaivilas' deluxe room with a semi-private moat-like pool. It's an ambition worth putting on your 'I'll-do-this-one-day' list.

◆**Tel** 0294-2433300 **Email** reserva tions@oberoi-udaivilas.com **Website** oberoihotels.com **Spa tariffs** Rs 2,800 for 1-hr spa massage; Rs 2,000-4,250 for Ayurvedic massages; Rs 1,400-2,650 for scrubs **Room tariff** Rs 22,500-1,27,000

An aromatic experience and its essential ingredients (below); **Udaivilas** (left)

Devi Garh **Heaven on earth**

In the act of setting on the rest of the world, every evening, the sun pauses for an extra while at the hills surrounding Devi Garh Fort Palace and throws some special light-and-colour effects on it. It's the kind of light photographers would die for. But then it's the kind of resort aesthetes can live for. Welcome to the only heritage resort in Rajasthan that has had the imagination to eschew the route of colourful palatial sumptuousness. Mostly a palette of whites, off whites, creams, greys and silvers, elegantly arrayed in a romantically fading 18th-century fort-palace, Devi Garh is a soothing vision for overfed senses. The designers have, however, left the bright green of the Aravallis untouched. The only striking interior decoration in the rooms therefore is the exterior, brought in by wide windows, which turn into a cushioned bed for (a) the gazer, (b) the novel-reader, or (c) the purposeless muncher of the pistachios on offer.

In the morning, I try to do some pranayam seated on one such window. My first step, "close your eyes",

Devi Garh is the only heritage hotel in Rajasthan that has had the imagination to eschew palatial sumptuousness

is hard to follow. An inquisitive bird is quarrelling with her own reflection a foot away, a lake is shimmering with gentle consistency below, and the Aravallis are admiring their post-rain, freshly manicured fingernails. In the day-time I roam around, thrilled that the original 250-year-old parts of the palace have been left cleaned but otherwise untouched — remnants of

the Sheesh Mahal mirrors glittering dully from some past light, the frescoes fading and true. In between, I gorge on some sensational fusion cuisine: brilliant lemongrass coconut dal soup, palak pakora chaat, mango asparagus spring rolls. For dinner, a witty chef makes a bit of a joke of feeding me starters till I have to refuse the main course, and succeeds. At night, I return to a poem by Tagore and a vial of aromatherapy oil on my pillow. For a good night's sleep.

In the event, sleep has no choice. To make peace and happiness and general bliss completely inescapable, the resort has cunningly provided the services of **Serena Spa**. Serena is a spa chain that offers spa services to hotels and resorts, and runs its own in-house training academy. Their style incorporates aromatherapy, spa massages, acupressure-oriented stress relievers, special equipment such as ergonomically designed chairs for shoulder/ back massages, and interpretations of Ayurvedic massages.

The five rooms of the spa (plus one for couples, the massage in question being called Adam and Eve Serenity!) have glass walls that make good use of the surrounding hills. Steam and sauna rooms are attached. Rosemary and Ramita respectively give me a very competent **Serenity Full Body Massage** and an **Anti-Stress Head-Neck-Shoulder Massage**. Stress, poor thing, has little chance against their knowledge of acupressure points, sensitiveness to hard and soft pressure, and the rather scrumptious French essential oils being used. It entirely gives up the battle when, juice of choice in hand (watermelon, since you are curious), I settle down in the infinitely open poolside pavilion, under that

Like a dream: The sumptuous exterior is Devi Garh's most elaborate decoration

promising sunset, smelling of heaven come to life.

For those wanting to experience something out of the ordinary, the spa offers **Thai Yoga Massage** and **Soothing Hot Stone Massage**. Go for the former if you are a generally fit person but travel-weary and tired. Go for the latter if you are prone to general aches and pains. The Thai massage stretches, twists and turns you till you come to life; gentle strokes are not the norm in this one. The hot stones — riverbed stones that have gained the energy of the water that has smoothed them over the years — give deep muscle-relaxing heat and relief. Serena's interpretation of the Ayurvedic treatment **Shirodhara** — a steady trickle of oil poured on the forehead, concentrating on the 'third eye' point, while the reflex points on

hands and feet are massaged — is soothing. The spa also has a range of herbal body scrubs and polishes, of which the coffee/ orange/ cinnamon scrub is the most indulgent.

If you wish to feel you have earned all this delectation, the resort offers a range of activities from visits to the nearby Delwara Jain Temples to trekking in the Aravallis to camel/ horse safaris, mini-golf, bicycle tours, table-tennis and kite-flying. Don't be caught in the trap, though. Sit on your window-seat, and wait for the bird to come knocking.
◆**Tel** 02953-289211/ 09414170211 **Email** devigarh@deviresorts.com **Website** deviresorts.com **Spa tariffs** Full Body Massage: Rs 1,850; Anti-Stress Massage: Rs 1,100; Hot Stone Massage: Rs 3,000; Thai Yoga: Rs 1,850; Serena Dhara: Rs 2,600 **Room tariff** Rs 18,000-59,000 ■

Wellness Listings

Rajasthan has a fair number of places offering a range of 'wellness' activities — Ayurveda, yoga, naturopathy or meditation. Besides, the luxury hotels such as all the Oberoi Vilas brand of hotels and Taj hotels offer excellent spas, as do heritage hotels such as Jai Mahal, Ram Bagh Palace and Raj Palace in Jaipur. *For contact details, see Accommodatoin Listings on page 455*

NATUROPATHY/ ACUPRESSURE

Sunrise Naturopathy Health Resort, Jaipur
Village Sar, Bilochi, near Chandwaji, Delhi-Jaipur Bypass D Zone, Jaipur
Tel 01423-514166/ 01
sunrisenaturopathy.com
● Ayurveda, aromatherapy, hydro and mud therapy, massages, yoga, meditation
Tariff: Rs 1,600-2,500, Rs 3,450-4,950 (cottages). Packages available

Shanti Prasad Goenka Kayakalp & Research Centre, Sikar
'Tarakunj', Salasar Road, Lachmangarh, Dist Sikar
Tel 01570-264473-79
spgkayakalp.in
● 40 kinds of treatments such as hydrotherapy, acupressure, mud therapy, jet spinal bath, yoga
Tariff: Rs 1,300-2,500 (inclusive of stay, food, treatments, gym, swimming)

Acupressure Health Care System, Jodhpur
A-13 Kamla Nehru Nagar, Jodhpur
Tel 0291-2635852, 3098670
acupressureindia.com
● Acupressure, magnet therapy, sujok
Tariff: Rs 100-200. No provision for food, treatments free

Navneet Prakritik Yog Chikitsa Dham, Bassi
Bassi, Jaipur
Tel 01429-222352, 223007, 09414241227
navneetync.com
● Hydrotherapy, mud therapy, massage, sun and aero therapy, fasting, kalpa, electrotherapy, wheat grass, magnet, acupressure, yoga
Tariff: Rs 110-350 per person for stay and therapy

AYURVEDA

Kerala Ayurveda Kendra, Jaipur
F-30 Jamnalal Bajaj Marg, C-Scheme, Jaipur
Tel 0141-5106743-44
keralaayurvedakendra.com
● Ayurvedic treatments like shirodhara, abhyanga, patraswedan... and yoga. Online consultation

Maharishi Charak Ayurveda Clinic & Research Centre, Jaipur
'Saket' E-7, Kanti Chandra Road, Bani Park, Jaipur
Tel 0141-2205621/ 28, 09829107138
charakayurveda.com
● Ayurvedic treatments such as shirodhara, udavartana and pizhichil. Own manufacturing units for herbs and oils. Organise Ayurveda tours
Tariff: Rs 500-1,700

MEDITATION

Dhammathali Rajasthan Vipassana Centre, Jaipur
Via Sisodia Rani Bagh, Galtaji Road, Jaipur
Tel 0141-2680220, 2680311
dhamma.org
● Vipassana meditation courses observed in silence for 10 days. This is a residential course

WELLNESS TOUR PLANNERS

Health & Yoga
Ravi Tumuluri, B-36, Sector 31, Noida, UP
Tel 95120-2450146, 9818085707
info@healthandyoga.com
healthandyoga.com
● Planning yoga and Ayurveda treatments, with sightseeing in Jaipur

Indian Moments
Pankaj Sharma, S-207 Time Square, Central Spine, Vidyadhar Nagar, Jaipur
Tel 0141-2339668, 2336036, 09414064040
indianmoments.com
● Customised tours around Jaipur oriented towards yoga, meditation and Ayurvedic treatments

TIP *For stay options in the featured towns, see Accommodation Listings on pages 455-494*

SANJAY SHARMA

Specials

Cross deserts with nomadic
tribes, listen to the stories
that turbans tell or wait for
the skies to open up in a
parched desert

Chasing the monsoon

Would there be music if not for the patter of raindrops?

■ BY VIPUL MUDGAL

Every year, the women in Rajasthan eagerly wait for the first glimpse of *kurjan*, or the demoiselle crane, a migratory bird from Europe and Central Asia. The *kurjan* comes only after the skies have opened up and the showers have revived the dry lakes, after the seeds have been sown for the winter crop. Married women sing *Dhola Maru*, a timeless ballad about an even more timeless love story, pleading to the *kurjan* to bring back home their men who have stayed away all summer working in alien places.

The *kurjan* arrives around September to spend the next six months in Rajasthan and Gujarat. But if the lakes are not full, it will leave in a huff for other places — much like Rajasthan's migrant workers who come home and stay for the season only if there is hope of getting a crop. And without rains, the nomadic Gujjar community would also move on with their herds.

Little wonder then that much of the state's folk culture revolves around one sentiment: thirst. Without rain, the potter would not spin his wheel and the Langas and the Manganiyars, the mystical musicians of the desert, would not tune their drums or *iktaras*. Their words dry up without rain. But when the skies open up and the cosmic sounds give a cue, you could close your eyes and drench your senses in the divine cadence of desert ragas.

"*Paani ro barsa de mhara ram/ ubi ubi joun thari baat…,*" goes a Marwari ballad. It is about the women who are imploring their archangels to send rains. The lyrics have *neha* (eyes) raining with *megha* (clouds), words that bond hope with despair. The women nag, plead and beg, sometimes yearningly, sometimes in prayer and often in repentance, in the same lilting melody. When there is not a cloud in sight, they walk barefoot for miles to a *pir's* shrine or pull the ritual plough so that a miracle would rain down on them.

I have always been amazed by how little it takes to transform a dusty brown landscape into lush green in a matter of days. One decent splatter and all earthy colours spill out in the open. A good monsoon year would have medium to sparse showers spread over 10 to 15 days, and that's about it. Yet, these few showers set the tone for the whole year.

With rains come the festivals of Teej and Gangaur when women slip into their fineries for prayers and family outings. The flavour of the month is pink scarves with emerald bangles, and loads of jewellery. This is also when the peasant societies indulge in the curse of mass marriages of their underage, even infant, children. A good rain is, nevertheless, reflected in the scale of jubilations. The demon of drought, on the other hand, can suck the colour out of this vibrant milieu. A bad year means no harvest and yet another migration, often with children, pets and cattle in tow. Marriages get invariably postponed for the next season.

Sawan in early July coincides with the first sowing season and Bhadon follows with promises of good harvest. Rain gods willing, the crop is ripe before Dussehra. In between are dozens of Rajasthan's fabled *melas* or

SANJAY SHARMA

When the skies open up: A parched desert waits for the first rain

fairs: the Gogaji Pir Mela in Ganganagar, the Mata Jogania Mela in Mewar and the Ramdeo Pir ka Mela near Kawas, Barmer. Most fairs are thanksgiving rituals for good rains.

Rajasthanis have many expressions for rainfall. I love *rim-jhim, tip-tip* or *bauchhar*, meant for a drizzle's many hues but I am most fascinated by the term *jhamajham*, implying torrents. Another lyrical expression one hears in Rajasthan is *chadar chal gayee* (roughly translated as 'a bedspread afloat'). The phrase is used when a pond, lake or reservoir is brimming with a gentle overflow. *Chhappar phar ke* (roughly roof-breaching rain) symbolises generosity to a fault. In Bikaner, I once met a farmer whose seeds and sprouts had been washed away in the first, unusually heavy spell. To my surprise, he looked delighted because, in his own words, "Mother earth would be able to quench her thirst." It is as if in Rajasthan they prefer to

accept rain on its own terms. This equanimity extends to Rajasthan's lakes, marshlands and grasslands, all of which need very little water to sustain a variety of wildlife. In Ranthambhore and Kaila Devi sanctuaries, tigers and leopards start descending from the hills as soon as the first rains start to fill the jungle's watering holes. Just a few showers and the saltwater lakes around Sambhar and Pachpadra in Barmer become hospitable for flamingoes. Like *kurjan*, migratory as well as over 400 domestic birds come to the lakes in Jodhpur, Bhilwara and Udaipur. Even Jaisalmer and Barmer get their exotic visitors just after the rains.

Rajasthan's people value rain because they have learnt to treat drought as a season and famine as a way of life. They have seen 41 droughts in the past 50 years. That is why they consider rain as god's gift. And rightly so. ∎

Not just a pipedream

Indigenous water harvesting measures helped life bloom in a desert

■ BY DEEPAK MALIK

Rajasthan's rich heritage may be immediately apparent in its magnificent havelis and palaces but some of its loveliest treasures are those that were built with more utilitarian concerns at heart. For, it is in the state's stepwells, in its specially constructed wells and tanks, that the most eloquent tales of the resilience of the Rajasthani people are to be found. In the world's most densely populated desert — a sobriquet that the state has always held — these were the edifices around which life was built and sustained. Through their own indigenous modes of water storage and conservation, the people survived the hardships that came with living in a desert terrain, successfully fighting a perennial water crisis to cultivate land.

Today, Rajasthan struggles with recurrent droughts, marginal rainfall, low humidity and scorching heat. With the advancement of technology, there are now facilities such as borewells, and water is available in most cities in the state. However, this is not the case in many other areas, where water continues to be a scarce resource. In such a situation, the importance of traditional methods of water conservation, involving the use of water harvesting and storage structures such as the *taanka, beri* and *bavadi,* cannot be understated.

Amongst the various traditional water conservation measures, the **taanka,** found in the rural areas of Jodhpur, Jaisalmer, Barmer and Bikaner districts, is the most common. It is a manmade water harvesting and storage tank with a catchment area for collecting rainfall. Constructed outside the house, the *taanka* is an underground structure usually round in shape and lined with polished lime. When it rains, water is directed to the inlets of the *taanka* through its sloping catchment. If there is normal rainfall during the monsoons and light rains during winter, the *taanka* can cater to a family's needs for almost a year. When the rainfall is less, households get water from a nearby *nadi* (small pond) and fill up the *taanka.* This technology's effectiveness was recognised by kings who had such structures built in their forts. Many big *taankas* can be seen in forts such as Jaigarh in Jaipur and Mehrangarh in Jodhpur.

Beries, on the other hand, are shallow percolation wells that are broad at the base and narrow towards their upper ends, like long-necked earthen pots. These are constructed in areas where there is a subsurface layer of gypsum in the soil, which prevents the percolation of water deep down. The opening of a *beri* is small (5-6 ft in diameter), but below the surface, its diameter ranges from 5 to 15 ft. The depth of the *beries* is between 30 and 40 ft. When it rains, water trickles down through the layer of gravel and collects above the gypsum layer, remaining there for years, even during droughts. These structures can be seen in a Bikaneri village called Diyatra, which is on the way from Bikaner to Jaisalmer. It is said that a generation has to put in work to build a *beri,* though, of course, its benefits are to be enjoyed for decades to come.

While travelling in southern and western Rajasthan, particularly Udaipur, Rajsamand and Jodhpur, the visitor will see yet another kind of water conservation structure called **jhalara**. The lifeline of both urban and rural areas, the *jhalara* is a huge manmade tank, often rectangular in shape, with steps on three or four sides built on a series of levels. The *jhalaras* collect subterranean seepage of a *talaab* or a lake located upstream. The water from these *jhalaras* is not used for drinking but for baths and performing religious rites.

The more well-known of the water conservation structures in Rajasthan are the traditional stepwells called **baolis** or **bavadis**. Built by the nobility, usually for strategic or philanthropic reasons, these were structures from which everyone could draw water irrespective of their community. An interesting aspect of the stepwell was that their location suggested the way in which it was made use of. When a stepwell was located within or at the edge of a village, it was used for utilitarian purposes and also for social gatherings. When stepwells were located outside the village, on trade routes, these were frequented as resting places. Before borewells were invented, these structures also played an important role in irrigation. The sculptures and inscriptions seen in stepwells demonstrate their importance in the traditional, social and cultural lives of people.

Bundi District is well known for its stepwells, *kunds* and *taankas*, with a government survey pegging the number of *baolis* here at over 387. One of the most famous structures here is the **Nagar-Sagar Kund**, a pair of stepwells outside the Chougan Darwaza of the Old City (*also see Bundi on page 119*).

For the cultivation of fields in what is essentially a desert region, the Rajasthanis devised a technology called **khadin**. A half-moon shaped

Gadisagar Lake at Jaisalmer, built to store rainwater

MADHU KAPPARATH

SANJOY GHOSH

Chand Baoli at Abhaneri, a stepwell built for water conservation

earthen dam constructed on the lower end of a slope of land, its size was decided by the average rainfall in the region, the catchment area, the quality of the soil and the requirement of water. During the rains, water collected in the *khadin* and its quantity was usually sufficient for irrigating the field two times. Even during droughts, farmers were able to get some crop or fodder because of the moisture that remained in the soil thanks to the *khadin*. Studies have shown that *khadin* farmers were able to function better than those not using this system. *Khadin* structures can be found in the farms of Jodhpur, Jaisalmer, Barmer and Bikaner.

Unfortunately, just as with several other aspects of Rajasthan's heritage, most water conservation systems lie defunct now. One of the main reasons for this is the fact that agriculture is a more centralised activity today; besides, the space available for catchment areas itself has become less because of the pressure on land for both cultivation and construction. I would also say that insensitivity towards water conservation measures, and the lack of understanding of the need to conserve water, are also important factors that have contributed to this gradual decay.

The only beacon of hope is held by those like Shashi Tyagi, who have worked towards the rejuvenation of *taankas* and *khadins* in western Rajasthan. Thanks to her efforts over the past 21 years, thousands of destitute families have constructed traditional water conservation structures, which have reduced their dependence on tubewells and other government schemes. She has also combined technological advancements with traditional methods, thereby creating a unique model that's a fine blend of the past and the modern world. In some ways, what we see in the areas where Tyagi has worked is the realisation of Mahatma Gandhi's dream: self-reliant, decentralised villages where not a drop of water goes waste. It's a lesson that other parts of Rajasthan will do well to learn. ∎

A painted world

Rajasthan's historic murals are disappearing under coats of neglect

■ BY ILAY COOPER

The walls in Rajasthan have been embellished with decorations from the time rudimentary hunting scenes and patterns were painted inside pre-historic rock shelters in the Aravalli Hills. The painting enthusiast will notice that there's an absence of murals dating to the time between this early rock art and the 16th century. This, however, has more to do with the lack of surviving domestic buildings than a break in tradition. Before Islam came to India, the houses and palaces in the country were generally built of wood, none of which remain today. On the other hand, in the oldest masonry houses in Rajasthan, such as the 16th century havelis of Chittaurgarh, one can see faint traces of pictures.

Extant Rajasthani murals point to the influence of the Mughal school of art, itself a synthesis of indigenous and imported Persian styles, which evolved at Fatehpur Sikri, Akbar's

capital located to the east of Rajasthan. There, damaged wall paintings can be seen even today. The oldest discernible Rajasthani murals are in Amber, 200 km away, also the nearest Rajput principality to Fatehpur Sikri.

Man Singh, Amber's ruler from 1590 to 1614 and Akbar's foremost general, must have been inspired by the Mughal Emperor's freshly painted buildings. Between the brackets in the innermost section of the Amber Palace, which he built about 1600, are crude little pictures of animals and huntsmen. The chhatri raised in 1620 to his memory also contains murals, depicting Hindu deities, local folk tales such as Rajasthan's favourite Dhola-Maru and even Laila-Majnu, a West Asian story that has always been hugely popular in India. Red cinnabar and blue lapis lazuli dominate the colour scheme in the paintings.

Two other painted buildings, a Muslim tomb in the Hadipura sector of Amber and a domed hunting lodge 80 km north-east at Bairat, also date

Ride to glory: Frescoes on the walls of a haveli in Shekhawati

from the 1620s. The paintings in each are stylistically similar. The tomb, damaged by soot, contains flying birds, Persian-style angels, *simurghs* or Chinese pheasant-like birds that reached Mughal art via Persia, and a single European winged-head cherub. All these feature in, and were probably inspired by a painted pavilion 230 km away, built by Emperor Jehangir at Rambagh in Agra, circa 1618. The hunting lodge, much of it beautifully painted in burnished ochre, has a portrait of the current raja on the outer wall and, in a cupola, a panel showing Jehangir meeting Man Singh.

Jaipur, founded in 1727 to replace Amber as the capital of the surrounding kingdom, attracted craftsmen from Delhi, then the capital of a rapidly fading Mughal empire. It was soon famous for fine plasterwork, known as *arayish*, and for the mural painting that decorated the plaster. Teams of artists are known to have travelled from here to other parts of Rajasthan, including Jodhpur, Jaisalmer and Shekhawati.

In Jaipur, in the *fresco* (fresh or damp) style, a thick layer of pigment was applied onto wet plaster; this partially coalesced with the surface as it set. The paint was mixed with gum to strengthen its adherence. This technique was generally used while painting external walls, with the traditional pigments chosen being red, green, yellow, brown earth colours and lamp-black. It required skill and speed to produce figures and designs over an expanse of plaster before it set. The artist sketched outlines with a sharp stylus, correcting them as he applied the colour. Once painted, the surface was burnished with a piece of agate and then wiped over with coconut oil. Details such as jewellery were added later. Often, the painted plaster surface, once dry, was cut to create geometric patterns.

Most interior work was painted *secco*, or in a dry style, with the pigment being mixed with gum and then applied onto dry plaster. This allowed the artist to take his time in selecting a limited area of a wall, carefully sketching each subject and correcting his outlines before filling in the colours one by one. This technique is beautifully illustrated in a

1740s' temple in Parasrampura, Jhunjhunu District. The team must have stopped work overnight, leaving rough sketches, clearly corrected but only partially coloured, on a small part of the ceiling. They used stencils for repetitive work and also geometric devices such as compass arcs or ruled lines. Traces of both remain on the plaster surface in the temple today.

Shekhawati, comprising Jhunjhunu and Sikar districts, holds the richest collection of painted buildings in India. This area, long ruled by Muslim nawabs, fell to Hindu Rajput barons around 1730 and was absorbed into the Jaipur state. Mural paintings were already established there, but generally confined to decorative designs and poor figurative work. By the turn of the 18th century, fine *secco* murals appeared in several temples in the east of the area. Patronised by local rulers, the fashion of decorating forts and memorial chhatris soon spread. By the early 19th century, with the division of estates between sons, holdings diminished and the barons became impoverished. But a new set of patrons arose. A flourishing merchant community, drawn by caravan-borne trade, had concentrated in Shekhawati and neighbouring Churu District. This trade declined through the 19th century, so many young merchants shifted to Calcutta (now Kolkata) and other cities. There they made and repatriated huge fortunes.

In their desert hometown, each commissioned fine havelis, temples and chhatris, which, as a last touch, were covered with *fresco* paintings, largely in red and green ochres. After 1850, synthetic pigments flooded in from the German chemical industry and the dominant colours became blue ultramarine (artificial lapis lazuli) and red chrome. By the close of the century, many more colours arrived. These were often applied *secco*, as the process was less laborious and also because some new pigments responded badly to the *fresco* method.

The Shekhawati painters were mostly skilled masons, both Muslims and Hindus, drawn from the Jaipur region to service a new demand. Generally, they chose their subjects, though the patron could also suggest certain religious topics. The Hindu epics, particularly tales relating to Krishna and Rama, were most popular, as were folk tales. The artists used their freedom to depict battles, soldiers, princes, the merchant patron, animals, hunts, erotica and women giving birth. Sometimes there were map-pictures, accurate views of local towns or Jaipur. Later pictures included those created by carefully copying foreign prints or picture labels produced by British textile manufacturing companies. In the 1920s the demand for painted buildings declined as the merchants settled their families in their new city homes.

Although Shekhawati boasts of by far the richest concentration of murals in Rajasthan, they occur elsewhere too, generally in palaces or temples. Few predate 1800. Sometimes, as in Jodhpur, there is documentary evidence that the painters were summoned from Jaipur. Sometimes the suggestion comes from the pictures themselves, as with the map-pictures of Jaipur seen both in Jaisalmer's palace and one of its havelis.

Shrines in Bhilwara District contain pictures in the same folk idiom as those painted on long cloth screens, which depict the life of god and hero Pabuji. There are painted apartments in the palaces of Bundi and Kota, the early 19th century Chitrashala in Bundi being particularly fine. There are also interesting examples in the palaces of Amber, Banswara, Bikaner, Dungarpur, Jaipur, Jaisalmer, Jodhpur, Nagaur and Udaipur.

Most haveli murals in Jaipur succumbed in 1876, when Maharaja Ram Singh had the city painted pink, but fine interior paintings remain in the palace. Other painted buildings there include **Pundarik Haveli** (built in 1810), managed by the ASI, and **Saras Sadan**, now a jewellery shop, in Gangauri Bazaar. Late 18th-century murals at Galta, near Jaipur, were drastically repainted but there are some good, painted chhatris in and around Jaipur. There are also painted royal chhatris at Bikaner, Radhakund (near Bharatpur), and Rajgarh, south of Alwar. In Udaipur, there is still a tradition of painting bright *secco* murals to celebrate weddings. Important, though distinct from murals, are decorations on mud buildings by rural womenfolk. These include textural motifs, such as those on *bitodas* (cow-dung fuel stores) around Bharatpur and blocks of pastel colour on houses near Jaisalmer or fantastic white, stylised figures and flowers in Sawai Madhopur District.

India is astonishingly rich in fine monuments, but this heritage is in the danger of being forgotten. Since

Youngsters at a Shekhawati haveli

AMIT PASRICHA

the mid-1970s, when I first drew attention to Shekhawati's murals, each year has seen the disappearance of paintings. Some fade, some are whitewashed or painted over, sometimes plaster falls away, buildings are replaced or, each monsoon, collapse. In 1984, the then newly formed INTACH organised a seminar to discuss Shekhawati's painted buildings. As a result, aided by Ravindra Sharma of Churu, I spent two-and-a-half years documenting 2,260 buildings as a first step to conservation. We await the second step. Meanwhile, a new danger is that many murals are being repainted using bright acrylic: under the guise of restoration, old paintings are being destroyed. Murals draw many tourists to Shekhawati, yet their destruction and neglect are universal. There is no alternative to sensitive maintenance. Shekhawati is the heartland of the Marwaris, perhaps the richest community in India; its foremost clans could form a trust dedicated to preserving their heritage. It is impossible to save everything but, using our painstaking documentation, a selection of examples representative of particular periods and styles could be repaired. Initially, it would be enough to prevent further decay.

Murals are delicate and easily damaged. Recently, restorers in Orchha repainted black faces on figures in a small palace, unaware that they had only blackened it further as lead-based paint is bound to decay. At the INTACH Conservation Centre in Lucknow, students learn to restore sensitively; its graduates have much to do. The painted pavilions in Rambagh, Agra, fall under the ASI. It was discovered under whitewash in the 1970s, but the paintings have been neither conserved nor protected up till now. If these are not valued, what hope is there for the rest? ∎

Small is beautiful

The many colours of Rajasthan's miniature paintings

It's possible but difficult to find pre-Mughal Rajasthani miniature painting that has survived time and religious oppression. For instance, there was some sophisticated Jain work in Rajasthan, with figures in highly stylised positions, quirky with elongated eyes, both visible on one side of a sharp-profiled face. These miniatures illustrated 12th-16th century manuscripts, and formed the Western Indian school based in Gujarat and parts of Rajasthan. From this school emerged the surviving 16th century Hindu miniatures seen in the Delhi-Agra region. Interestingly, these paintings show a fascination with pattern rather than realism or movement.

But it was Mughal art that inspired a change to all this. Emperor Akbar (1556-1605), who enjoyed the services of Persian painters, set them to work with their Indian counterparts. The result was a distinct, vibrant school of art. Akbar, believing in god, not religion, had Hindu writings on Krishna and Rama as well as Islamic and other texts illustrated. At Fatehpur Sikri, which was for long his capital, the Rajput princes who were tributaries at his court were dazzled by the new painting method.

Miniatures were painted on paper prepared with chalk and mixed with a thin glue, rather like Italian *gesso*. As with murals, fine miniatures were often copied with stencils. The rich palette of colours used included ground lapis lazuli, Indian yellow made from the urine of cows fed with mango leaves, cinnabar for red, green copper chloride as well as gold and silver paints. The 19th century saw an increasing invasion of artificial pigments from Europe.

The Rajput schools of painting developed towards the close of the 16th century, drawing on native styles but strongly influenced by the Mughal school. The thriving Bhakti movement resulted in the popularity of Krishna amongst religious subjects in miniatures. A common, uniquely Indian subject was the *ragamala* (garland of musical modes), intended to reproduce visually the moods induced by music. These

are sometimes represented in stages of love (often illustrated by the deified lovers, Radha and Krishna), by seasons, times of day or even regions. The garland consists of six ragas, each having five or six subservient *raginis*.

The earliest known painting of the Rajasthan school is either a *ragamala* created for a Bundi ruler, doubtfully dated 1590, or another

Distance and division encouraged the evolution of a recognisably separate style at each major court. Bundi dominated neighbouring Kota, producing richly-coloured, red-bordered miniatures in which flowers and banana trees decorated the background. Then Kota eclipsed Bundi during the 18th century, and hunting, particularly of beautifully portrayed tigers and lions, became a favourite subject. In the paintings, horsemen emerge precariously from rich decorative jungles set amidst dramatic rocky landscapes. The Mewar genre advanced from highly stylised early work towards greater realism and more lifelike figures. There was a tendency towards making the pictures larger towards the late 18th century, and these paintings often portrayed court scenes, and boating on Pichola Lake. A strong green sometimes overwhelmed the palette.

Eighteenth and early 19th century Marwar (Jodhpur) art is characterised by horsemen with full sideburns and tall turbans, and a hill rising, nimbus-like, behind the principal figure. Amber/Jaipur painting was strongly influenced by the neighbouring Mughal school, but became overwhelmed by European idioms and pigments as the 19th century progressed. Jaipur's best creations were 18th century busts of women in profile, a common subject in nearby Kishangarh. This tiny state developed a characteristic style in the mid-18th century, under poet-ruler Sawant Singh. The women in the paintings have sharp features and grossly exaggerated, curving eyes, reflecting pre-Mughal Hindu styles. The courtly scenes are beautifully composed in gardens or architectural settings. Mughal art declined after the death of Jehangir in 1627, but the Rajasthani form, still in its infancy, continued to develop until the end of the 18th century. It produced a wonderful offshoot in the Pahari (Hill) schools of the Rajput-ruled states of the Himalayan foothills. Here, Sansad Chand, ruler of Kangra, encouraged the rise of a very elegant school of miniature painting. The 19th century marked a progressive decline. A flood of European prints and photographs profoundly influenced Indian painters. Attempts to integrate alien techniques for portraying light and shade helped in destroying the genre. ■

from Chawand, in Mewar (Udaipur) state, dated 1605. Bundi and Mewar both developed a style indebted to the Mughal forms, but retained the local love of blocks of strong colour, often reds and blues. In these paintings, plants are delicate items of composition, not living things, and figures appear posed, frozen in action.

Under Jehangir, Mughal art, strongly influenced by European work, reached its height. Realism was cherished and landscapes faded into the distance. These features passed onto Rajasthani work. Contrasting colours gave way to more gentle tones. Religious themes widened to include incidents from the Ramayana and Mahabharata, but Krishna's story remained the most popular. Non-religious subjects included hunting scenes, illustrations of folk tales and portraits of local rulers and nobles. Amongst the craftsmen in these kingdoms, there were Muslims as well as Hindus painting Hindu themes.

Explore a new highway. Search for a forgotten town. Find a new destination. Just hit the road with Speed, the high performance petrol and you will experience greater pick up, smoother drive and superior performance. Speed gives you the confidence to take on the road. Tank up, and head out. The whole of India is waiting for you.

Speed™
High Performance Petrol

INDIA
3.38 million Kms
Road Network

Bharat Petroleum

Take the first Road out.

To go places log on to www.speedfuels.com

With strings attached

A behind-the-scenes look at Rajasthani puppet performances

Rajasthani puppet performances mostly narrate the exploits of local heroes

■ BY ANURUPA ROY

The literal Hindi translation for the word 'puppet' is *kathputli*, but this can be misleading. All *kathputlis* are puppets but all puppets are not *kathputlis*, which is the name for the stylistically distinct, traditional string puppets of Rajasthan. *Kathputli* is a puppet made of *kath* or wood and the puppeteers are called Nats or Bhats, a wandering community from Rajasthan who perform their *khel* during the dry season and return to their villages to cultivate the fields after the rains. The puppeteers believe in the divine origin of their art and claim to have been the chief performers during the reign of the legendary king Vikramaditya, whose life and achievements they extol.

In Rajasthani puppet performances, the stories are mostly about the exploits of local heroes, unlike other Indian puppet traditions that revolve around the Ramayana and the Mahabharata. One hero who appeared often in the state's puppet performances was Amar Singh Rathore, the ruler of Nagaur in the 17th century, who was a great patron of the Bhat community and the *kathputli* tradition, which traces its origin to Nagaur.

Traditionally, the puppet performance comprised 52 puppets in the puppeteers' repertoire. Any less would be considered an incomplete puppet performance. The story of Amar Singh Rathore would be told to small groups in localities within the four walls of the *mohalla* or neighbourhood, ensuring the participation of the entire audience. The puppeteer would be an actor and also a puppet manipulator. Today, however, the puppet performance relegates Amar

Singh Rathore to the background and tricks and turns once performed for royal amusement take the centre-stage. There is the magician, the acrobat, the dancer Anarkali, the drummer Khabar Khan, a horse rider with lit torches in his hands, and a snake-charmer. Also among the cast of characters are the juggler and the Bahurupia, with two faces either carved back to back or so devised that with clever manipulation, one face is covered while the other is exposed.

The *kathputlis'* heads and head-gears are carved from mango wood with large, stylised eyes. They are up to 60 cm tall, wearing costumes made in the period Rajasthani style as seen in *phad* paintings. Their bodies are made of cloth and stuffed rags. With a few exceptions, *kathputlis* are made without legs, and from waist down wear a long pleated skirt of light material. Traditionally, *kathputlis* were carved by craftsmen in Sawai Madhopur, Bassi and Udaipur, but the Bhats now make their own puppets.

A *kathputli* performance is presented by placing two charpoys (string beds) vertically and tying bamboos across them. The front cloth curtain with scalloped arches is known as the *tibara* or Taj Mahal. It hides the manipulator's body and feet during the performance. The puppeteer often improvises his narrative on the spot to hold the attention of his audience, while his wit and comments enliven the performance. He speaks for the *kathputli* characters in a squeaky voice with a bamboo whistle known as *boli*, thereby creating a unique puppet language. The *dholak* player (drummer) converses with the *kathputlis* so that the audience can follow the course of the drama. This dialogue is cleverly coordinated with songs sung by the women of the family to the accompaniment of the *dholak*. *Kathputlis* are usually manipulated with

only a string, one end of which is attached to the *kathputli's* head and the other to its back. Most string puppet traditions around the world use a cross for manipulation; the weights in the puppet's torso, feet and hands help the puppeteer to create movement. The Rajasthani takes no help from gravity. It is the sheer skill in the manipulator's fingers that create the movements. The string is looped around the puppeteer's fingers and all movements are generated by a series of jerks on either end. A bracelet of bells, or *ghungrus*, is worn by the puppeteer on his wrists.

The dancing girl is a special type of *kathputli* — it has four strings and its limbs are sewn in such a manner that a range of movements such as the swinging of the hips and the arching backwards during a dance can be produced. The puppet has a needle concealed in its fingers that attaches itself to her *pallu* or her *ghagra*. Thanks to this device, the puppet can coquettishly cover and uncover her face.

For almost 400 years now, the *kathputli-wallahs* have travelled far and wide through India, performing with their puppets and leaving behind vivid memories of their dramatic performances. They may be the best known and the most remembered of the 20 or more traditional forms of puppetry. Today, there is a museum and Centre for Puppetry at the Lok Kala Mandal in Udaipur. In New Delhi, there is a large settlement of *kathputli* puppeteers at the Shadipur Depot, also called the Kathputli Colony. Five-star hotel guests and crowds at Surajkund Mela and Dilli Haat have replaced the *mohalla* audiences for puppet performances, which are in any case a watered down version of the past. Yet one can see the infusion of modern techniques and ideas in many, and it can be as heart-warming as it was centuries ago. ∎

SANJOY GHOSH

An artist's rendition of Dhola-Maru, Rajasthan's most beloved folk tale

Till death do us part

Where Romeo and Juliet ride into the sunset on camelback

■ BY KISHORE SINGH

If there was one thing the British residents taught the Rajasthani princes, it was the importance of keeping meticulous records of everything — every telegram received and sent, every invitation accepted or declined, correspondence over loans, waterworks or the railways, and even medical histories. But nowhere are they maintained as well as in Bikaner's Lallgarh Palace. The Anup Sanskrit Library at the palace is a treasure trove of manuscripts in Sanskrit, Urdu and other court languages, all of which found sanctuary here during the reign of Emperor Aurangzeb, when writers were persecuted and

their manuscripts burnt. Thankfully, Rajasthan's folktale tradition has always remained so irrevocably etched in the landscape and the minds of people that even authoritarian rulers could do little to obliterate it. Little wonder then that the state's oral tradition of storytelling and keeping its folk tales (and heroes) alive can be traced to ancient times.

If old-timers sit with their bottles of country liquor, reciting stirring tales of conquest from the *Prithviraj Raso*, and if their sophisticated counterparts turn to the *Annals and Antiquities of Rajasthan* by the state's well-loved travel writer (Col James Tod), you can be sure that there are many villagers who still gather to

listen to Pabuji's heroic exploits. **Pabuji** was a folk hero promoted to the status of a saint, even a god, someone who could battle everyone from evil marauders to demons. His tales are celebrated even today, when a scroll called the *phad* is unrolled before an audience, even as singers and dancers extol his valour and wisdom. Each episode in his life is highlighted by holding up a lantern to the scroll, and a corresponding story — usually of how Pabuji managed to tackle a particularly nasty spirit — is narrated.

Indeed, friendly demons, fierce spirits and witches with upside-down feet are the subjects of many a storyteller's craft. And sceptics need make just one trip to a witch temple to have their cynicism beaten out of them, quite literally sometimes! Perhaps an easier and more entertaining way of meeting a friendly spirit is to watch the Hindi film *Paheli*, based on a Rajasthani folk tale, which has actor Shah Rukh Khan essaying the role of a clever and endearing ghost.

A little known folk story deals with Prince Prithvi Singh of Bikaner, popularly known as Peethal, a poet who was one of the nine gems of Emperor Akbar's court. When the emperor received a letter of surrender from Rana Pratap of Mewar, who was probably tired of hiding and living like a refugee with the tribals of his kingdom, Peethal was quick to react. The Rana's letter was fake, he insisted, a trap for the emperor, and he would write to the Rana himself to ascertain the truth. Write he did, but in despair, asking the Rana whether he could no longer twirl his moustache in pride. He thus shamed the Rana (or "stirred his drooping spirits", as Col Tod notes). The Rana responded saying that he would never hail Akbar as his emperor. And even though Akbar recognised Peethal's duplicity in this

exchange, the two remained confidantes till Peethal's demise a few years later.

The most beloved of all the folk tales in the state are those about love, and for some reason, preferably about doomed love. Rajasthan has two parables that parallel the stories of Romeo and Juliet and Sohni and Mahiwal: **Dhola and Maru**, and **Moomal and Mahendra**. The characters are the same in both: star-crossed lovers who must remain apart because their families are opposed to their union. The story of Dhola and Maru approximates that of Sohni and Mehiwal to the extent that the fleeing lovers escape on a camel, are stoned to death, or are lost forever in a sandstorm, depending on who is telling you the story.

The tragic tale of Princess Moomal of Jaisalmer and Prince Mahendra of Amarkot (now in Pakistan) is more poignant. Mahendra would sneak into the princess' palace to spend nights of love with her. One night, wanting to spy on her sister's lover, Moomal's sister disguised herself as a man and waited in her chamber, only to fall asleep on her bed. Seeing his beloved in another man's arms, Mahendra took off, never to return. Moomal disguised herself as a bangle seller and set up a game of chess with the prince. Mahendra saw on his new friend's wrist a mark similar to the one on his beloved, and spoke to the stranger about how he had been betrayed by his love. Hearing this, Moomal took off her turban and the two lovers embraced.

Now the story deals us with the fatal blow: their hearts were so weakened by their separation that the two lovers died in each other's arms! And death, as the Hindi film industry has demonstrated time and again, has made them immortal in the Rajasthani mindscape. ∎

DHONI DRIVES ON *Speed*

High-flying sixes. Blazing fast fours. Quickfire innings. Speed has always been the essence of Mahendra Singh Dhoni's incredible performance on the field. And now on the road too.

Bharat Petroleum

Costumes tell a story

But Rajasthan's apparel code is not that easy to crack

■ BY KISHORE SINGH

In Rajasthan, layers of meanings and rituals are associated with each and every ceremony, as I discovered during the funeral of my paternal uncle. Outside the house was a gathering of men, and three of my cousins were seated amongst the members of their clan. In front of this group, their white turbans, worn as a symbol of mourning, were removed. The eldest was then given a turban that had belonged to his father, to indicate that he was now the head of the family. Then, the headgear of all three was replaced with pink turbans, marking the end of the period of mourning, and a return to a world of colour. This wasn't the case inside the house, where, at the same time, my aunt was being made to dispense her skirt and mantle, to be replaced forever by the pale colours of blue or green — the shades of widowhood in a state where bright is right. At one time, this would have been ochre brown, but this has changed over the years.

Bishnoi women wear gold nose rings

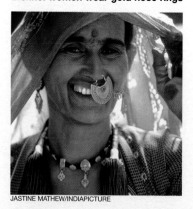

JASTINE MATHEW/INDIAPICTURE

It is on occasions such as weddings, births and funerals that one can still see the importance of clothes, colours and jewellery in Rajasthan. It's possible then to tell communities and moments apart, from the ornamentation and apparel that people don. But, as the state urbanises, these distinctions are being blurred — fortunately in several cases, as this does away with indicators of caste and community, and unfortunately in others, as when lovely traditions of making clothes are gobbled up by modern machinery. Colourful skirts are no longer of rich brocades and silks, or patterned with block prints from Sanganer or Bagru — why go through the inconvenience when the markets abound with silkscreen printed fabrics, Chinese imports and synthetic materials that do not fade?

But still, some traditions continue. The leheriya, or the tie-dye pattern of waves, is worn when the season changes and the rains descend, however sporadically, across the parched desert. The *peeliya*, the symbol of a married woman, can be worn only when she has given birth to a son (in this case, one can thankfully note that as these prints are available in the markets, the symbolism is no longer relevant). Rajasthan's beautiful silver jewellery is worn by women of the so-called 'lower' castes — the tribals, such as the Meenas and the Bhils, for whom it is as bankable as money. Worn on the head and forehead, around the neck and waist, on the wrist and arm, around the ankle and on the toes, it is exquisitely patterned. The Bishnoi women wear gold and elaborate nose rings while Rajput women wear gold on their feet

SARVESH

The colour of a turban can point to a person's region or community

and as a measure of their married status, gold toe rings.

Once, some men wore anklets too, also of gold. These were the *tazimi* sardars, those who attended court and enjoyed the privilege of remaining seated when the ruler walked into the durbar. They were usually trusted members of the clan who commanded the king's armies. Even today, men wear jewellery, and at weddings they offer stiff competition to women. There are gold buttons on their tunics, strings of rubies and emeralds tumbling down their collars, diamonds in their lobes, turban ornaments and glittering swords. And turbans — there are such a plethora of them! These are worn wound around the head peasant-style as protection against the sun, like a peaked hat in Mewar, or with a swagger and a long tail as in Jodhpur, which is also the style now preferred by most. Jodhpur, one must add, knew a thing or two about couture. The city made the

bandh-gala, the short tunic with a closed collar, a style statement. It also gave the world the riding breeches known as jodhpuris, to be worn on the saddle or at formal events.

In today's Rajasthan, where more of the same is what one sees, it is at fairs such as Pushkar that the clothes still point to the wearer's region or community. The woman with huge gathers at the skirt is a Jat, while the lady whose gathers rise above the ankle is a Bhil from the Aravallis. A black skirt trellised with silver embroidery is the mark of a kalbelia dancer. As for that man with the white turban, he is not in mourning — for, the men of a house in mourning are not allowed to step outside. Those wearing white — and that too from head to toe — are from the Bishnoi community. Considering these varied facets, there is only one thing you can be sure of about Rajasthan's canvas today: it's much more complicated that you can even begin to imagine! ∎

The original gypsies

Did Rajasthan's nomadic tribes wander all the way to Europe?

Photographs by AMIT PASRICHA

■ BY KISHORE SINGH

Children don't read Enid Blyton any more, at least not as much as we did, recreating our own version of an idyllic England with green meadows and hidden islands. But what even we didn't know while reading about the adventures of Barney in Blyton's *Circus Days Again* was that the colourful description of the circus hid a strong Indian connection: the gypsies.

For, it's widely believed that the gypsies can be traced to Indian nomadic tribes such as the Banjaras, Gadoliya Lohars and Rabaris of Rajasthan, and the Lambadis of Andhra Pradesh. No one has been able to figure out how and why they moved from India to Europe. What is certain is that the gypsies seen in Europe have much in common with certain Indian nomadic tribes: clothes, vestiges of the tongue, razor-sharp professional skills, and why, even a reputation — undeserved or otherwise — for thievery!

So did the Banjaras and the Rabaris simply wander off the map of India, driven away by severe drought, or did they seek to partner Alexander's residual army as it struggled to get back home after his conquest of North India? Researchers have many tales to tell, and in all probability the truth is a mélange of all their hypotheses, but what is known is that the nomadic tribal communities tended to serve in armies, sharpening the soldiers' swords and daggers, running errands, and even acting as listening outposts for the enemy.

Pre-eminent among these tribes were the Banjaras, who can only be described as itinerants on fixed itineraries. They travelled in large numbers, and were not entertainers, as is widely assumed, but transporters of grains on well-traversed trade routes across the Thar into Gujarat and Malwa. Some routes led as far away as Central Asia. The Banjaras' caravans carried thousands of people, and their ox-laden carts stretched for a kilometre or more. The people of the tribe have made a name for their good looks and no piece is ever written without mentioning this fact! Today, the Banjaras have settled down even as enthusiasts try to trace their erstwhile wanderings.

The Rabaris, or the wandering shepherds of the Thar, cross from the Kutch to Rajasthan and then back to Gujarat. Unlike the Banjaras, their travels are strictly governed by the season, as they go briskly by foot in search of fodder for their sheep.

The Gadoliya Lohars, or the blacksmiths with carts, perhaps lend the most colour to the legends built around the gypsies. Their carts are beautifully decorated, and they're always happy to travel from one place to another in search of work. They can be seen camping in the cities, by the roadside, with their tools of trade for company. According to the most popular version of the story, the Gaduliyas — as they are also referred to — hailed from Chittaurgarh, which they abandoned when the Mughals sacked it in the 16th century. At the time, according to popular re-telling, the Gaduliyas had taken a vow not to live in houses, sleep on beds or light a lamp till such time as the fort was freed. Those times have long gone, but the Gaduliyas still continue to keep a promise purportedly made centuries ago, moving slowly from town to town, repairing scissors and sharpening knives, their families small and their dogs fierce. The other wandering tribes of Rajasthan consist

The Rabaris, one of the nomadic tribes in Rajasthan (above and left)

of performers — the Nats and the Nayaks, who would hold audiences spellbound, the former with their renditions of the tales of the folk hero Pabuji, the latter with their acrobatics and ropewalking. Early British accounts refer to them as the sub-tribes of the Banjaras, but there is little to link the two apart from their peripatetic lifestyles.

The most popular of these performing gypsies today are the Kalbelias, or the snake dancers. Akin to the Nats (who as part of the Sansis, Kanjars and other vagrant tribes were once considered to be at the bottom of the caste ladder), their acceptance now seems complete with the grace and rhythm of their unique dance form winning worldwide acclaim.

Having seen the Kalbelia dance one evening, and the flamenco dance on another occasion, the romantic thought occurs while considering the common long skirts and gathers of the dancers, the similarity in their body movements and the tilt of their chins, that perhaps there is something linking the two. And after all, isn't Spain known for its gypsy caravans as well? Perhaps those caravans originated in Rajasthan, centuries ago. And thus begins another story. ■

Stories in stone

Mines have been the backbone of Rajasthan's economy

■ BY PRAKASH TYAGI

Every day, when dawn breaks over the small town of Makrana, thousands of mine workers walk towards the region's famed marble mines with chisels and hammers in their hands. In a few hours, dust fills the air as the workers give shape to the many pieces of marble stones, often squinting in the bright sunshine and braving the scorching heat. It's difficult to trace this toil and sweat to the milky white, shining pieces of marble that eventually find their way to posh homes. Known for its beauty and quality, the **marble** from **Makrana's mines** are to be seen in some of the most beautiful and historical monuments in India. Shahjahan's ode to love, the Taj Mahal, and the Victoria Memorial Palace in Kolkata, are two magnificent symbols of the elegance of the marble from Makrana.

Even a casual visitor to Makrana would be impressed by the number of shops in the town selling souvenirs and household items made of white marble, their prices starting as low as Rs 100. With 800 marble mines that employ between 14,000 and 16,000 people from the town, spreading across 100 sq km, Makrana stands as a reminder of Rajasthan's wealth in an arena that's not immediately apparent, unlike its rich cultural heritage. Endowed as it is with rich mineral and sandstone sources, Rajasthan is today considered as the second richest state in the country in terms of mineral wealth. The industry contributes over Rs 600 crore annually to the government exchequer.

The history of stone mining in Rajasthan goes back many centuries. As the state was often affected by drought, the traditional occupations of people such as agriculture and animal husbandry suffered in the

The salt of the earth

It is said that many centuries ago, several rivers criss-crossed the Thar Desert of Rajasthan, with their own well-integrated drainage systems. As geological changes took place over time, these water sources turned into lakes, as it happened in places such as Loonkarnsar, Didwana and Sambhar. Some of the lakes are extremely saline and have thus become a major source of salt production. The biggest salt lake in India, the **Sambhar Lake**, is a vast saline wetland with depths varying from a few centimetres to a few feet. Salt from this lake has been collected for centuries, under the Rajputs and Mughals and the

SANJOY GHOSH

British. Today, the salt pan industry is managed by Sambhar Salts Limited, a subsidiary company of the central government public sector undertaking Hindustan Salts Limited. The technology used here is a combination of modern and ancient, with some pumps installed by the British being active even now.

bargain. In such a situation, the mining industry turned to be an option that promised a constant source of livelihood, irrespective of rains or sunshine. Today, over 2 million people are estimated to be working in the mines in Rajasthan, digging out a number of minerals such as jasper, zinc, quartzite, copper, silver, gypsum and fluorite, among others.

Makrana is a microcosm of Rajasthan's mining industry, one that has seen tremendous growth thanks to the increasing demand for its beautiful marble. About 200 km west of Makrana, on the doorstep of the vast Thar Desert, are the **sandstone mines** of Rajasthan, spread over 250 sq km. Sandstone has a pleasing pink appearance and has been finding takers among architects from times immemorial. Most of the old palaces and forts of Rajasthan, including Jodhpur's **Mehrangarh Fort** and **Jaisalmer Fort**, have been constructed with sandstone. Though much of the sandstone was earlier used only locally, today it is even exported. But a more heartening feature is the fact that even now, in West Rajasthan, sandstone is used in most of the construction work.

Sandstone mines can be seen in Jodhpur, Barmer and Jaisalmer. Besides western Rajasthan, it is also seen in the Dholpur region. Similarly, while the Makrana marble is the most famous, the state has mines producing 10 different types of marble. Many of these mines are spread in the eastern and southern Rajasthan.

There is a flipside to the mining industry as well: the wondrous sandstone and marble that come out of the mines are also grave reminders of the poor working conditions of the miners. Till the recent past, mines made use of techniques that could only be described as primitive. Though new technology is utilised

DINODIA PHOTO LIBRARY

Where it all begins: A marble mine

now, there's tremendous scope for improvement in both the conditions and the terms of employment of miners. The working hours of miners are irregular, with no provision of holidays or weekly-offs. Many of the miners face serious health hazards such as silicosis, a fatal disease, and tuberculosis, because of the lack of protection onsite as well as inadequate healthcare. Considering the extent to which mining is contributing to Rajasthan's economic growth and development, it's clear the miners deserve a lot better. For, the state's mines cannot function on past glory alone. ■

AMIT PASRICHA

The Indira Gandhi Canal brings waters originating in the Himalaya to the Thar

Once there was a desert

How a canal transformed the desert into a sheath of green

■ BY DEEPAK MALIK

Perhaps not content with merely redrawing maps and boundaries, humankind has since time immemorial tried to reshape and redesign the environment into which it is born. We have devised ways to outwit the vagaries of weather, to ⸺ artificial rain, and to make ⸺ from the paths they have ⸺ nturies. Some of these ⸺ have had disastrous ⸺ have worked well, for ⸺ at least. In today's

Rajasthan, one can see the sleight of hand that has transformed parts of the arid desert into a verdant land.

Drive into north-western Rajasthan, past places such as Hanumangarh and Sriganganagar, and it would be difficult to imagine that this was once a desert, indeed part of the great Thar Desert. The sands have been replaced by trees, grazing lands and fields full of crops. There are no mirages here; instead, the water that gurgles in canals and distributaries is very much real and tangible. This idyllic transformation can be traced to

439

a project that was started well over 50 years ago, by the then chief engineer of Bikaner State, Kanwar Sain. In 1948, his efforts paved the way for one of the biggest irrigation projects in the country, called the Rajasthan Canal Project, now known as the Indira Gandhi Nahar Project. His idea took shape at a time when pre-Independence India had suffered several famines; the nation was being encouraged to grow more food to counter their recurrence.

But how could one do that in the sands of Rajasthan? Indeed, wasn't it ambitious to even consider putting to use the vast but hostile Thar Desert for cultivation? The answer to both questions came in the form of the canal, meant to tap the water from the Ravi and Beas rivers. This project, expected to provide drinking water to five districts of Rajasthan — namely Sriganganagar, Hanumangarh, Jaisalmer, Jodhpur and Bikaner — was started in the first five-year plan of the country. Work on this continues after several decades; by the eighth five-year plan (1992-97), 1,429 km of the canal had been completed.

The Indira Gandhi Canal represents an extraordinarily impressive endeavour to bring waters originating in the lofty heights of the Himalaya to the dune-covered Thar Desert. It is also one of the biggest such schemes in the world. Thanks to the irrigation and drinking water facilities that the canal has created, many people have settled down in the desert, which was once thinly populated. Already the most densely populated desert in the world, the Thar has seen an unprecedented rise in human population in recent years. This increase, especially in Sriganganagar and Bikaner districts, has been both due to natural growth and immigration. A study conducted by the National Council of Applied Economic Research (NCAER)

says in clear terms that the population has benefited both socially and economically from the canal. Just as interesting is the fact that thanks to the canal's irrigation facilities, afforestation has gone up considerably. As a result, soil erosion has decreased, while moisture, humidity and vegetation cover have all shown a marked increase. Instead of having to depend on crops that use the least amount of water, people are today able to grow wheat, rice, gram, sesame, mustard and cotton. Moreover, with the development of water bodies, many new animal and bird species that were not seen in the Thar earlier have been spotted.

The Thar Desert also has one of the largest livestock densities in the world. During the past 40 years, there has been a five-fold increase in livestock numbers, from 10.3 million in 1951 to 49.5 million in 1982. Given that water is available now, there is a lot of potential for modernisation, to introduce organised markets for meat, milk and food processing, and also for mechanising agriculture. If all this were to be done, it would open up tremendous growth opportunities for the region.

Before one gets carried away by the possibilities, however, a note of caution is necessary. Given that the rivers reined in by the canal originate in other states, inter-state water disputes have been common and often, unpleasant. In some parts through which the canal runs, water logging has become a problem while the accompanying change in biodiversity is a cause for both concern and study. Yet, despite all these worries, there is no doubt that the canal has succeeded in its original objective: to help people grow more food, and thus contribute towards making India a food-sufficient nation, where famines remain a distant memory. ■

Licence to kill

Taking aim was once both a sport and an act of diplomacy

■ BY KISHORE SINGH

It was an organised sport that they called pig sticking. It must have been legal till some time in the sixties because I remember my grandfather and his friends setting off on a trot on their horses. From the underbrush, their second force — a team of jawans — would set up a huge din, making the foraging wild boar charge across the open fields. And here, my grandfather and his fellow shikaris would fan into a circular flank of about 15 horsemen, from where they would charge down upon the grunting animals, reins in one hand and slender javelins raised to kill in the other. Pig sticking was a blood sport, and a dangerous one at that, because wild boar could be vicious and their tusks could cause a lot of damage — to the horses and to you, should you stumble from your saddle. Or should you be speared in the melee by one of the fellow shikaris!

By comparison, hunting with guns was a tame affair — almost. If it was deer you wanted, you outran the animal from an open jeep. Duck shoots required precise shots, though I suspect my cousins earned their spurs by peppering the sky with multiple shots as formations of migrant fowl, or 'imperials' (imperial sandgrouse), flew by. Partridge was easier if you knew their favourite watering spots — all you had to do was wait at dawn and then bang, you had game on the table.

Hunting was ultimately banned because of the wanton killing it resulted in, though it has not been successful in eliminating poaching. But before India became independent, when Rajasthan consisted of 22 kingdoms, each of them supported by a network of fiefdoms, shikar was very much legal. Princes (and sometimes princesses) were trained to go tiger hunting, often bagging their first kill as early as when they were in their teens. Tigers and leopards were mere trophies for their walls.

Winter was the time for shoots and elaborate arrangements were made for these. The hunting lodges that you see dotted across Rajasthan — now fortunately converted into heritage hotels — are enduring symbols of those days of shikar. Here, the royals would camp for a week or two or even longer. There were chinks (chinkaras) and blackbuck to be found, the possibility of hare for the pot and waterfowl for sure. Shoots in the forest were followed by revels at the hunting lodges, which were smaller versions of their palaces though often just as luxurious.

If the princes indulged in shikar as sport, they also guaranteed conservation as a practice. Shoots were not permitted in the rainy months, when the young are nurtured in the wilderness. Summer hunts were limited for the table and not for pleasure, since shooting at shrinking waterholes did not qualify as sport. And as forests and large water tracts belonged to the rulers, no one else was allowed to hunt, thereby ensuring a natural system of regeneration.

By the late 19th and early 20th centuries, the rulers had turned shikar into a diplomatic opportunity that enjoyed a position of prestige on pre-Independence India's social calendar. If the viceroy came to Maharaja Ganga Singh's elaborate duck shoots

A Royal Bengal tiger is a hapless victim of a royal shoot in 1930 in Rajasthan

at Gajner, visiting Ranthambhore for tigers, Jodhpur for wild boar and Bharatpur for its plethora of birds was par for the course for the noblest and bluest of British dignitaries.

True mayhem occurred in the fifties and sixties when anyone armed with a gun became a shikari. Vestiges of that still survive, as poaching continues to be rampant, sparing not even Rajasthan's designated wildlife sanctuaries. Yet the same state surprises you with its history of conservation as well. The members of the Bishnoi community, custodians of a way of life which considers the felling of trees as sacrilegious as the killing of animals, have ensured the protection of their environment. Therefore, as you drive between Jodhpur and Bikaner, it is not at all rare to see sambar, blackbuck, nilgai and chinkara lope elegantly across the undulating sands, and partridges scurrying ungainly from scrub to scrub. And as actor Salman Khan could very well vouch for, you would bring a gun here only at your peril. ■

TRANSPORT DIRECTORY

A ready reckoner to important numbers for your travel planning

■ AIR

Rajasthan is well connected by air, with three airports serving its many important tourist destinations. These are located at the capital city Jaipur, in eastern Rajasthan, Jodhpur, which lies in the central-west desert region and Udaipur, located in the south. Kota Airport is no longer used for commercial flights.

AIRPORT LINKS

Jaipur's Sanganer Airport offers onward road and rail connections to Sambhar Salt Lake Sanctuary, Kuchaman Fort, Ajmer, Pushkar, Ranthambhore, Kota, Bundi and Jhalawar.

Jodhpur Airport is the closest airport to Nimaj-Chhatra Sagar, Nagaur, Bikaner, Jaisalmer and Desert National Park, connected by road and/ or rail.

Udaipur's Dabok Airport serves a vast region including Mewar. Udaipur City is well connected by road/ rail with Chittaurgarh, Dungarpur, Kumbhalgarh, Ranakpur and Mount Abu.

NOTE Agra in Uttar Pradesh state is the airport link for Keoladeo Ghana National Park. The Shekhawati region is almost equidistant from **Jaipur** and **Delhi airports**, linked by both road and rail

CITY HELPLINES

JAIPUR

Sanganer Jaipur Airport, 10 km from the city, on NH8
Airport Director Tel: 0141-2550623 (O), 2722833 (R); Mobile: 09829059821
RTDC Counter Tel: 2722647
Website airportsindia.org.in

AIRLINES
Indian Airlines
International Counter/ Domestic Counter Tel: 0141-2721333 **Timings** 6 am-9 pm **Station Manager** Tel: 2743407 **Duty Manager** Tel: 2721519 **City Office** Reservation Centre, Nehru Palace, Lal Kothi (near Old Subzi Mandi), Tonk Road, Jaipur; Tel: 2743500, 2743324 **Timings** 10 am-5.25 pm **Website** indian-airlines.nic.in

Jet Airways
Domestic Counter Tel: 0141-2551352/ 54
Timings 5.30 am-10 am, 5 pm-8.30 pm
Airport Manager Tel: 2546230 **City Office** Reservation Centre, FF, Umaid Nagar House, Opp Ganpati Plaza, MI Road, Jaipur; Tel: 5112222-24 **Timings** 9 am-6 pm **Website** jetairways.com

Air Sahara
Airport Manager/ Domestic Counter Tel: 2546693-94 **Timings** 8 am-12 noon, 4 pm-6.30 pm **City Office** Reservation Office, 303 Luhadia Towers, Ashok Marg, C-Scheme, Jaipur; Tel: 5118050-52 **Timings** 10 am-6 pm **Website** airsahara.net

JODHPUR

Jodhpur Airport, 5 km from the city
Airport-in-Charge Tel: 0291-2512934
RTDC Counter Tel: 2545083
Website airportsindia.org.in

AIRLINES
Indian Airlines
Airport Counter Tel: 0291-2512615 **Timings** Open during flight time **City Office** Reservation Centre, 2 West Patel Nagar, Circuit House Road, Ratanada, Jodhpur; Tel: 2510757-58 **Timings** 10 am-4.30 pm **Website** indian-airlines.nic.in

Jet Airways
Airport Counter Tel: 2515551-52 **Timings** Open during flight time **City Office** Reservation Office, Osho Apartments, Residency Road (near Taj Hari Mahal), Jodhpur; Tel: 5102222/ 3333 **Timings** 9 am-6 pm **Website** jetairways.com

UDAIPUR

Maharana Pratap Airport, 22 km south of Udaipur City
Airport Director Tel: 0294-2655950 (O), 2656119 (R)
RTDC Counter Tel: 2655432
Website airportsindia.org.in

AIRLINES

Indian Airlines

Duty Manager/ Station Manager Tel: 0294-2410248 **Airport Manager** Tel: 2655453 **City Office** Reservation Office, LIC Building, Delhi Gate, Udaipur; Tel: 2410999 **Timings** 10 am-5 pm **Website** indian-airlines.nic.in

Jet Airways

Domestic Counter Tel: 0294-2656191/ 93 **Timings** Open during flight time **City Office** Reservation Centre, 56 Blue Circle Business Centre, Madhuban (near ICICI Bank), Udaipur; Tel: 5102222, 2561105 **Timings** 9.30 am-6 pm

METRO CITY HELPLINES

Website airportsindia.org.in
Direct metro flights to Rajasthan are only available from Mumbai and New Delhi.

MUMBAI

Chhatrapati Shivaji International Airport 26-30 km north of Mumbai
Enquiry Tel 022-26156600 (Terminal 1), 26829000 (Terminal 2)
Airport Director Tel 26156789, 28216801

NEW DELHI

Indira Gandhi International Airport, 15 km from Connaught Place
Enquiry Tel 011-1407 **Toll free No.** 18001801407
Airport Director Tel 26156789, 28216801
Duty Manager Tel 25675317 (Terminal 1); 25652173 (Terminal 2)

◼ RAIL

Contact information for all major railway stations in Rajasthan, and all stations that serve destinations and arounds in this book.

ONLINE RESERVATIONS

The easy-to-use and comprehensive official Indian Railways website provides information about reservations, schedules, fares, seat availability and current status and offers online ticket booking for all trains in the country. **Website** indianrail.gov.in

RAIL ENQUIRIES

For general rail enquiries anywhere in India call **1330** (Enquiry in English) or **1335** (Hindi). Excepting Bundi, Desert National Park, Dungarpur, Jhalawar, Kalakho, Karauli, Kumbhalgarh, Kuchaman, Mount Abu, Nimaj-Chhatra Sagar, Pushkar, Ranakpur, Rawla Narlai and Sariska National Park, our other destinations given in this guide are connected to Jaipur, Delhi and Mumbai by train.

◼ ROAD

Rajasthan has an exceptionally good network of national highways that criss-cross the state west to east and north to south, making highway driving a pleasure across smooth roads.

NATIONAL HIGHWAYS

The state is linked to both Delhi and Mumbai by NH8 via Jaipur, Ajmer, Udaipur and Ahmedabad. The highway is intersected at Jaipur by NH11, which connects Agra to Bikaner via Bharatpur, Dausa, Jaipur, Sikar and other important towns of the Shekhawati region.
♦ NH15 links Bikaner, Pokaran, Jaisalmer and Barmer to Pathankot in Punjab and Samkhyali in Gujarat
♦ Connecting Bikaner to Nagaur, Merta and Ajmer is NH89. Passing through Churu, Nagaur, Jodhpur, Pali and Sirohi is NH65
♦ NH12 originates at Jaipur, and passing through Tonk, Bundi, Kota and Jhalawar, goes into Madhya Pradesh, towards Bhopal
♦ NH79 starts at Ajmer and goes on to Indore via Bhilwara and Chittaurgarh
♦ NH76 connects Madhya Pradesh to most of Southern Rajasthan, intersecting NH12 at Kota, NH79 at Chittaurgarh, NH8 at Udaipur, and finally joining up with NH14 at Pindwara, north of Abu Road
♦ Track this network of national highways on *Outlook Traveller*'s Rajasthan pullout map

RAJASTHAN STATE ROAD TRANSPORT CORPORATION BUSES

Over 5,000 RSRTC buses offer over 13,000 services to major towns and cities in Rajasthan and the adjoining states of Gujarat, Haryana, Punjab, Delhi, Uttar Pradesh, Himachal Pradesh, Madhya Pradesh and Maharashtra. RSRTC operates regular AC and super deluxe coaches between Jaipur, Ajmer, Udaipur, Kota, Nagaur, Alwar and Delhi.

INFORMATION

Fares vary according to the services on offer and distances. From ISBT Kashmere Gate in Delhi, the Rajasthan Roadways/ RSRTC Delhi-Jaipur ordinary bus fare is Rs 145. Its AC Volvo service, operating from Bikaner House, costs Rs 460, and the non-AC Rs 270.

RESERVATIONS

Reservation facilities are available for RSRTC's express, super-deluxe and AC bus services at ISBT Kashmere Gate and Bikaner House in Delhi, Sindhi Camp Bus Stand in Jaipur and ST Bus Terminal in Ahmedabad (*see alongside*) and other bus depots in Rajasthan. You can also call individual bus terminal enquiry numbers (*see below*) or send an email to info@rajasthanroadways.com for details of express bus services. For more information on RSRTC bus services including schedules, fares and destinations, log on to rsrtc.gov.in

RSRTC HELPLINES

RSRTC Head Office, Jaipur
Location Parivahan Marg, Chomu House, Jaipur **Tel** 0141-2373043/ 44/ 51/ 54 **Email** mdrsrtc@datainfosys.net **Website** rsrtc.gov.in

RSRTC BUS DEPOTS IN RAJASTHAN
Abu Road Bus Depot **Tel** 02974-222323 **Chief Manager Tel** 222192 (O) **Location** $1/_2$ km from railway station
♦ Link for Mount Abu
Ajmer Bus Depot **Tel** 0145-2429398 **Chief Manager Tel** 2426798 (O) **Location** Jaipur Road, 3 km from railway station
♦ Link for Pushkar
Alwar Bus Depot **Tel** 0144-2334984 (Enquiry) **Chief Manager Tel** 2700019 (O), 2333360 (R) **Location** Kacheri Road, 2 km from railway station
♦ Link for Sariska Tiger Reserve
Bharatpur Bus Depot **Tel** 05644-260330, 2335285 **Chief Manager Tel** 260289 (O), 262252 (R) **Location** Hira Das Chauraha, Jaipur Road, 3 km from railway station
♦ Link for Keoladeo Ghana, Kalakho
Bikaner Bus Depot **Tel** 0151-2523800 **Chief Manager Tel** 2528143 (O), 2528967 (R) **Location** Lall Garh, Sri Ganganagar Road, 3 km from railway station
♦ Link to Jaisalmer, Jodhpur

Bundi Bus Depot **Tel** 0747-2445422 (Enquiry) **Chief Manager Tel** 2443482 (O), 2443568 (R) **Location** Kota Road, 2 km from railway station
♦ Link to Jhalawar
Chittaurgarh Bus Depot l **Tel** 01472-241177 **Chief Manager Tel** 241038 (O) **Location** Bundi Road, near police station at Gambhiri Puliya
Dungarpur Bus Depot **Tel** 02964-232260 **Chief Manager Tel** 232432 (O), 232406 (R) **Location** Near Government College, 2 km from railway station
Jaipur Central Bus Terminal **Tel** 0141-2364278 **Chief Manager Tel** 5116056, 2704902 **Location** Chandpol, Railway Station Road, $1^1/_2$ km from railway station
TIP Computerised reservation services available here
♦ Link for Sambhar Salt Lake, Nagaur and the rest of the state
Jodhpur Bus Depot **Tel** 0291-2544686 **Chief Manager Tel** 2544223 (O), 2514086 (R) **Location** Paota Chauraha, 3 km from railway station
Kota Bus Depot **Tel** 0744-2451020 **Chief Manager Tel** 2327910 (O), 2472873 (R) **Location** Nayapura, 7 km from railway station
♦ Link for Jhalawar
Sawai Madhopur/ Tonk Bus Depot **Chief Manager Mobile** 09414054909 **Location** 5 mins from Sawai Madhopur Railway Station
♦ Link for Ranthambhore, Karauli, Gangapur
Udaipur Bus Depot **Tel** 0294-2484191 **Chief Manager Mobile** 09414167175 **Location** Near Udai Pol, $1/_2$ km from railway station
♦ Link for Kumbhalgarh

RSRTC METRO HELPLINES

Ahmedabad
ST Bus Terminal **Tel** 079-25461264 **Location** Kalupur Road, No. 5 Bus Stand, 2 km from railway station
New Delhi
ISBT Kashmere Gate **Tel** 011-23864470 **Location** Ring Road, Near Tis Hazari Courts
Bikaner House Enquiry **Tel** 23383469 **Location** Near India Gate

PRIVATE COACH OPERATORS
Many private operators also run deluxe and super-deluxe coaches to Jaipur. *See Travel Agents Listings on pages 447-453*

TRAVEL AGENTS

AGENTS IN RAJASTHAN

AJMER

SONIA TRAVELS
Address Hotel Khadim, Ajmer
Tel 0145-2420025 **Email**
soniatravelsajmer@yahoo.com
Website soniatravels.com
Services Taxis, packages, air
and rail tickets, guides, hotel
bookings
Destinations Ajmer, Jaipur
Contact Nawal Kishore
Mobile 09828053225

SURYA TOURS & TRAVEL
Address Hotel Khadim, Ajmer
Tel 2631731 **Email**
suryatours@hotmail.com
Website suryatours.com
Services Packages, taxis, air
and rail tickets, guides, hotel
bookings
Destinations Chhatra Sagar-
Nimaj, Jaipur, Jodhpur,
Kishangarh, Kuchaman,
Pushkar, Roopangarh, Udaipur
Contact Bharat Yadav
Mobile 09414002831

*Also see Pushkar Listings on
page 450*

ALWAR

*See Jaipur and Metro Agents
Listings on pages 448, 450-453*

BIKANER

ARAVALI SAFARI TOURS
Address Junagarh Fort Road,
Bikaner **Tel** 0151-2201124,
5120690 **Email**
aravalibkn@sancharnet.in
Services Sightseeing, hotel
bookings, taxis, guides, air
and rail tickets, language
guides, safaris (camel and
jeep), transportation

Destinations Bikaner, Jaipur,
Jaisalmer, Jodhpur, Udaipur
Contact Tejvir Singh
Mobile 09829217217

BUBBLE'S DESERT SAFARI
Address Harasar House,
Dr Karni Singh Stadium Road,
Bikaner **Tel** 2209891 **Email**
harasar_haveli@yahoo.com
Services Camel and jeep
safaris, transportation
Destinations Bikaner,
Jaisalmer, Jodhpur
Contact Bilal
Mobile 09414142318

CAMEL MAN
Address Vijay Guest House,
Opp Sophia School, Jaipur
Road, Bikaner **Tel** 2231333
Email camelman_vijay@
rediffmail.com **Website**
camelman.com
Services Camel and jeep
safaris, transportation
Destinations Bikaner,
Jaisalmer, Jodhpur, Nagaur,
Pushkar
Contact Vijay Singh
Mobile 09829217331

FORTS AND PALACES TOURS
Address Jodhasar House,
Hanuman Hatha, Bikaner
Tel 2200561 **Email** sanjeev
singh_86@rediffmail.com
Website rajasthanunlimited.com
Services All travel related
services
Destinations All Rajasthan
Contact Sanjeev Singh
Chandrawat
Mobile 09414426553

FOUR SEASONS
Address Sardar Hall, Shop
No. 1, Junagadh Road,

Bikaner **Tel** 2523234 **Email**
fourseasonsbkn@sancharnet.in
Services Camel, jeep and
tonga safaris, hotel bookings
Destinations Bikaner,
Jaisalmer, Jodhpur, Udaipur
Contact Surinder Singh
Mobile 09829063446

RAJASTHAN TOURS PVT LTD
Address Kirti Stambh, Lall
Garh Palace, Bikaner
Tel 2543693 **Email** rajtours@
sancharnet.in **Website**
rajasthantouronline.com
Services All travel related
services; tented
accommodation at Pushkar;
offices in Bikaner, Jaisalmer,
Udaipur
Destinations All Rajasthan
Contact Arjun Singh

RAJPUTANA HOLIDAYMAKERS
Address 30, Kailash Puri,
Near Narendra Bhavan,
Bikaner **Tel** 2546311 **Fax**
2524806 **Email** rajputan@dil.in
Services All travel related
services
Destinations All Rajasthan
Contact Bhavani Singh Bhati

REGISTHAN TOURS
Address Siyana House,
Gangashehr Road, Bikaner
Tel 2540640 **Email**
regibkn@sancharnet.in
Services Camel safaris,
desert camps, hotel
bookings, language guides,
transport
Destinations Sam dunes,
Khuri dunes
Contact Bhawani Singh

*Also see Jaipur and Kota
Listings on pages 448-450*

INFORMATION

SHASHAWAT TOURS
Address Garh Palace, Bundi
Tel 0747-5120694 **Email**
stours@rediffmail.com
Services Sightseeing, hotel
bookings, taxis, guides, Chambal boat ride, air and rail tickets
Destinations Jhalawar, Kota
Contact JP Sharma
Mobile 09414175280

Also see Kota Listings on facing page

CHHATRA SAGAR-NIMAJ
*See Ajmer, Jaipur (below) and
Metro Agents Listings on
pages 447, 450-453*

CHITTAURGARH
*See Jaipur (below) and
Udaipur Listings on page 450*

DESERT NATIONAL PARK
*See Jaipur and Jaisalmer
Listings below and Jodhpur
Listings on facing page*

DUNGARPUR
See Jaipur Listings below

JAIPUR
ARAVALI SAFARI TOURS
Address Opp Rajputana
Palace Sheraton, Jaipur **Tel**
0141-2373124, 2365344
Email aravali2@eth.net
Services Sightseeing, hotel
bookings, guides, air and rail
tickets, language guides,
safaris (camel and jeep), transportation, office in Jaisalmer
Destinations All Rajasthan
Contact Bharat Singh
Mobile 09829065283

FORTS AND PALACES TOURS
Address S-1 Prabhakar
Apartments (Near Gandhi
Path), Vaishali Nagar, Jaipur

Tel 2354508, 2351117
Email jaipur@palaces-tours.com **Website**
rajasthanunlimited.com
Services All travel related
services, offices in Jaisalmer,
Jodhpur and Udaipur
Destinations All Rajasthan
Contact Bahadur S Rajavat
Mobile 09829065283

PARAMOUNT HOLIDAYS
Address 201, Amar Vijay
Tower, Lalpura House, Behind
Mansingh Tower, SC Road,
Jaipur **Tel** 3271350 **Email**
jpr@paramountholidays.com
Website dekhoindia.com
Services All travel related
services
Destinations All Rajasthan
Contact Chandra
Mobile 09352671350

RAJASTHAN TOURS PVT LTD
Address Rambagh Palace
Hotel, Jaipur **Tel** 2385141,
2385486 **Email** rajtours@
sancharnet.in **Website**
rajasthantouronline.com
Services All travel related services; tented accommodation
at Pushkar, offices in Jaisalmer,
Jodhpur and Udaipur
Destinations All Rajasthan
Contact Bhim Singh

RAJPUTANA HOLIDAYMAKERS
Address 207 Ganesham
Tower, Amrapali Marg, Vaishali
Nagar, Jaipur **Tel** 2353934,
2353956 **Email** rajputan@dil.in
Services All travel related
services
Destinations All Rajasthan
Contact Sanjay Kaushik
Mobile 09829008958

REGISTHAN TOURS
Address T-1 Jagan Sapphire,
4th Fl, Plot No. H-25, Tulsi

Marg, Bani Park, Jaipur
Tel 0141-2201796, 2207578
Email regijpr@sancharnet.in
Services Camel safaris, desert
camps, hotel bookings,
language guides, transport,
offices in Jaisalmer, Jodhpur
and Udaipur
Destinations Sam dunes,
Khuri dunes
Contact Jaydeep Singh,
Niranjan Singh
Mobile 09829015154

JAISALMER
DUNES SAFARI CAMP
Address Planet India Travels,
Kumarpara, Near Patwa
Haveli, Jaisalmer **Tel** 254463
Mobile 09414149807,
09829797807 **Email**
dunesafari@vsnl.net **Website**
rajasthanadventure.com
Services Deluxe tented camps,
safaris (jeep, camel and horse)
Destinations Ajmer, Bikaner,
Geej Garh near Sikandra,
Jaisalmer, Jodhpur,
Kumbhalgarh, Pushkar,
Samode, Shekhawati, Udaipur
Contact Ranjana Mudgal,
Delhi **Tel** 011-29521317/ 1476
Mobile 09810013634

GANESH TRAVELS
Address Near Jain Temple,
The Fort, Jaisalmer
Tel 250138, 253119 **Email**
ganeshtravel45@hotmail.com
Services Camel safari, open-air desert camp, tented
accommodation
Destination Jaisalmer
Contact Subhash Kumar
Mobile 09414319891

KK TRAVELS
Address Near Hawa Prol,
Jaisalmer **Tel** 253087 **Email**
kktravels_2000@yahoo.com.
Services Desert safaris, luxury

tented camps, guides, transportation, hotel bookings
Destinations Sam dunes, Khuri dunes
Contact KK Vyas
Mobile 0941220386

RAJPUTANA HOLIDAYMAKERS
Address Opp Hotel Rajdhani, Near Patwa Haveli, Jaisalmer
Telefax 250192 **Email** rholiday@sancharnet.in
Services All travel related services, office in Jodhpur
Destinations All Rajasthan
Contact Narendra Singh

ROYAL DESERT SAFARIS
Address Nachna Haveli, Gandhi Chowk, Jaisalmer
Tel 252538, 252733
Services Camel safaris, desert camps, hotel bookings, restaurant, guides, transport
Destinations Sam dunes, Khuri dunes
Contact Misra, BM Singh

JHALAWAR
See Bundi, Kota, Jaipur and Metro Agents Listings on pages 448-453

JODHPUR
ARAVALI SAFARI TOURS
Address 101, Osho Apartment, Residency Road, Jodhpur **Telefax** 0291-2643468-69 **Email** astjdh@sify.com
Services Sightseeing, hotel bookings, guides, air and rail tickets, language guides, safaris (camel and jeep), transportation
Destinations All Rajasthan
Contact Kusum Joshee

POLY TRAVELS
Address 10-D, Near State Bus Terminal, Paota, Jodhpur

Tel 2545210 **Email** contact@mandore.com
Website mandore.com
Services Jeep safaris, Bishnoi village tours, rural tours, voluntary work, hotel bookings, customized itineraries
Destinations Bikaner, Jaipur, Jaisalmer, Jodhpur, Mount Abu, Pushkar, Udaipur
Contact Surendra
Mobile 09829147470

REGISTHAN TOURS
Address FF, Palwa House, Airport Road, Jodhpur
Tel 2512787 **Email** regijdr@sancharnet.in
Services Camel safaris, desert camps, hotel bookings, language guides, transport
Destinations Sam dunes, Khuri dunes
Contact KS Solanki
Mobile 09414126591

ROYAL RAJASTHAN TOURS & TRAVELS
Address Opp Railway Station, Jodhpur **Tel** 2645006
Services Taxis, rail ticket, sightseeing
Destination Jodhpur
Contact Amit Arora
Mobile 09829022215

TRAVEL AID
Address Maruthar Tours & Travels, Umaid Bhawan Palace, Jodhpur **Tel** 5106661, 2511648 **Email** travel_aids@stayam.net.in
Services Air ticketing, transportation, hotel bookings, sightseeing, guides
Destination Jodhpur
Contact Dushyant Singh
Mobile 09829021943

Also see Jaipur and Kota Listings here

KALAKHO
CAMPS OF INDIA
Address 75 Sant Nagar, East of Kailash, New Delhi **Tel** 011-41659622 **Email** delhi@palacesofindia.com
Website campsofindia.com
Services Hotel bookings, transport, sightseeing, guide
Destinations Bikaner, Jaipur, Jaisalmer, Kalakho
Contact Ranjit Singh Parmar

FAR HORIZON TOURS
Address B-209 Chittaranjan Park, New Delhi **Tel** 011-46563600 **Website** farhorizonindia.com
Services Tour packages
Destinations All Rajasthan
Contact Rohit Ladsaria

KARAULI
See Karauli Accommodation Listings on page 477

KEOLADEO GHANA BIRD SANCTUARY
WILD WORLD INDIA
See Metro Agents Listings on page 452

KOTA
CYGNUS ADVENTURE TOURS
Address Opp 2nd R-A-C, Amar Niwas, Rawat Bhata Road, Kota **Tel** 0744-2502832 **Email** cygnuskota@yahoo.com
Services Chambal cruise, naturalist, hotel bookings, transport, guides, sightseeing, Udpuria (painted stork colony tour near Kota) and Jhalawar tours
Destinations Bundi, Jhalawar, Kota, Udpuria
Contact Ravinder Singh Tomar **Mobile** 09828079769

HADOTI TOURS
Address G-12 Vinayak Complex, Nayapur, Kota

INFORMATION

Tel 2326221, 2326224 **Email** hadotitours@yahoo.com **Services** Hotel bookings, transport, guides, sightseeing, Chambal cruise, safaris (camel and horse), bullock cart rides, Jhalawar tours
Destinations Bundi, Jhalawar, Kota
Contact Neeraj Bhatnagar

KUMBHALGARH
See Jaipur and Udaipur Listings here

MOUNT ABU
See Ajmer Listings on page 447

NAGAUR
See Jaipur and Jodhpur Listings on pages 448-449

PUSHKAR
EKTA TRAVELS
Address Near Ajmer Bus Stand, Pushkar **Tel** 0145-2772888 **Email** gopalanuj@yahoo.com
Services Sightseeing, puja arrangement, guides, traditional huts during Pushkar Mela and otherwise, safaris (camel, jeep, horse and camel cart)
Destinations Ajmer, Badnor, Fort Kharwa, Merta, Nagaur, Nathdwara, Pushkar, Roopangarh, Tilonia
Contact Gopal
Mobile 09828172131

RUKMANI TOURS & TRAVELS
Address Peacock Holiday Resort, Pushkar **Tel** 2772093 **Fax** 2772516 **Email** arajoria@ hotmail.com **Website** peacock-pushkar.com
Services All travel related services
Destinations All Rajasthan
Contact Rajindra P Rajoria
Mobile 09414006193

Also see Ajmer Listings on page 447

RANTHAMBHORE
FORTS AND PALACES TOURS
Address Dangwalon Ka Mohalla, Near RHED City Office, Sawai Madhopur
Email jaipurpalaces/tours.com
Website rajasthanunlimited.com
Services All travel related services; offices in Bikaner, Jaisalmer, Jodhpur, Udaipur
Destinations All Rajasthan
Contact Yadvendra S Rajawat
Mobile 09828755808

RAJPUTANA HOLIDAYMAKERS
Address 89, Raghuvansham, Jawahar Bhavan, Sawai Madhopur **Tel** 220871 **Email** rajputan@dil.in
Services All travel related services
Destinations All Rajasthan
Contact Pankaj Joshi
Mobile 09414297156

SAMBHAR SALT LAKE
See Jaipur Listings on page 448

SARISKA
See Jaipur and Metro Agents Listings here

SHEKHAWATI
See Jaipur and Metro Agents Listings here

UDAIPUR
ARAVALI SAFARI TOURS
Address 1, Sheetal Marg, Opp PWD Office, Lake Palace Road, Udaipur **Tel** 0294-2418324 **Fax** 2420121 **Email** astudn@maininfinity. com
Services Sightseeing, hotel bookings, taxis, guides, air and rail tickets, language guides, camel and jeep safaris, transportation

Destinations All Rajasthan
Contact Mukesh Tikku

HERITAGE HOLIDAYERS
Address 14/21 Oladar House, Lake Palace Road, Udaipur **Tel** 2423356
Email rediffmail.com
Services All travel related services; also horse safaris
Destinations All Rajasthan including Kumbhalgarh Wildlife Sanctuary
Contact Nagendra Mathur, Raghvendra Mathur
Mobile 09414152048/ 4844

RAJASTHAN TOURS PVT LTD
Address Lake Palace Road, Udaipur **Tel** 2525777
Email rajtours@sancharnet.in
Website rajasthantour online.com
Services All travel related services; tented accom-modation at Pushkar
Destinations All Rajasthan
Contact Virendra Singh

RAJPUTANA HOLIDAYMAKERS
Address 63-I-Block, Virat Nagar, Sector-14, Govardhan Vilas, Udaipur
Tel 2487099 **Email** rhmaker@datainfosys.net
Services All travel related services
Destinations All Rajasthan
Contact Jagpal Singh, Hemant Singh
Mobile 09829244592

Also see Jaipur Listings on page 448

AGENTS IN THE METROS

AHMEDABAD
ALL FOUR SEASONS HOLIDAYS
Address 51 Sardar Patel Nagar (Behind Navrangpura

Telephone Exchange),
Navrangpura, Ahmedabad
Tel 079-26440406, 40004800
Email 4season@amamail.net
Website 4seasononline.com
Services All travel related
services
Destinations All Rajasthan
Contact Darshan Shah

ARAVALI SAFARI TOURS
Address B-306, Fairdeal
House (Near Swastik
Chaurasta), Navrangpura,
Ahmedabad **Tel** 26440136
Fax 26444656 **Email**
crownamd@sancharnet.in
Services Sightseeing, hotel
bookings, taxis, guides, air
and rail tickets, language
guides, safaris (camel and
jeep), transportation
Destinations Bikaner, Jaipur,
Jaisalmer, Jodhpur, Udaipur
Contact Sunil Sharma
Mobile 09879770136

PARAMOUNT HOLIDAYS
Address 205, Anand Milan
Complex, Opp Jain Mandir,
Navrangpura, Ahmedabad
Tel 30985844 **Email** amd@
paramountholidays.com
Website dekhoindia.com
Services All travel related
services
Destinations All Rajasthan
Contact K Lalan, Ashok Patel
Mobile 09898325571,
09879523019

ROYAL HOLIDAY
Address F1-A, Sunder Gopal
Complex, Amabavari Circle,
Ahmedabad **Tel** 32945607
Email royal.ahmedabad@
gmail.com **Website**
colorsofgujarat.com
Services Packages, hotel
bookings, safaris (jeep and
camel)

Destinations Jaipur,
Jaisalmer, Jodhpur, Udaipur
Contact Liju Mathew
Mobile 09426070354

RAAG'S TOURS & TRAVELS
Address 110 Sarthee
Bungalows, Near Subhash
Chowk, Mem Nagar,
Ahmedabad **Tel** 27414301
Email raags@icenet.net
Website raags.net
Services All travel related
services except ticketing
Destinations All Rajasthan
Contact Abhay Goyal

BANGALORE
GREAT INDIA HOLIDAYS
Address 190 Pamadi
Chambers, Dr DVG Road,
Basavanagudi, Bangalore
Tel 080-41469036 **Email**
greatholidays@gmail.com
Website greatindiaholidays.
theindiancenter.com
Services Packages, car rental,
hotel bookings, air tickets
Destinations All Rajasthan
Contact Ashok **Mobile**
09342104499, 09845181507

INDIAN HOLIDAY PVT LTD
Address G-23-24, Bir Gate
Gardens, 19 Church Street,
Bangalore **Tel** 25582447,
25590429 **Email** bangalore@
indianholiday.com
Website indianholiday.com
Services Travel related
services
Destinations All Rajasthan
Contact Neel Kantha

PARAMOUNT HOLIDAYS
Address No. 10/ 5, Shop No.
G/ 4, Kuber Complex, Dinnur
Main Road, Opp Navodaya
Vidyaniketan School, RT Nagar
Post, Bangalore **Tel** 41244494
Telefax 41244495 **Email**

blr@para mountholidays.com
Website dekhoindia.com
Services All travel related
services
Destinations All Rajasthan
Contact Mohammad Ali,
Sumiya Nisar

SLS TOURIST
Address 120 Pamadi
Chambers, Basavangudi,
Bangalore **Tel** 41533745-48
Email info@slstourist.net
Website slstourist.net
Services Packages, car rental,
hotel bookings, air tickets
Destinations All Rajasthan
Contact R Madhu

CHENNAI
PARAMOUNT HOLIDAYS
Address 40/ 9 Kalathiappa
Street, Choolai, Chennai **Tel**
044-43539356 **Email** chennai
@paramountholidays.com
Website dekhoindia.com
Services All travel related
services
Destinations All Rajasthan
Contact Shobha, Sangeetha
Mobile 09382857700,
09941224800

SUGAL TOURISM DEV PVT LTD
Address 18 Veerapan Street,
Sowcar Peth, Chennai
Tel 26392345, 42162345
Email sugaltourism@yahoo.
com
Website sugaldimani.com
Services All travel related
services
Destinations All Rajasthan
Contact Lalit Jain

TRAVEL TIMES
Address 11 Clubhouse Road,
Mount Road, Chennai **Tel**
28461113, 28461131 **Email**
tourtimes@satyam.net.in
Website hillstations.com

INFORMATION

Services All travel related services
Destinations All Rajasthan
Contact Ganesh

TRAVEL ASSOCIATES
Address 107 Wallajah Road, Chennai **Tel** 55197083, 28526474 **Email** travel associates@vsnl.net
Services All travel related services
Destinations All Rajasthan
Contact Rajesh Nair
Mobile 09444002273

DELHI

COX & KINGS (I) PVT LTD
Address Indra Palace, H-Block, Connaught Circus, New Delhi **Tel** 011-41297900, 23738811 **Fax** 23317373
Website coxandkings.com
Services All travel related services except rail ticketing
Destinations All Rajasthan

IBEX EXPEDITIONS
Address G-66, East of Kailash, New Delhi **Tel** 26912641 **Fax** 26846403
Email mandipsinghsoin@hotmail.com **Website** ibexexpeditions.com
Services Soft adventures, luxury hotels and palaces, trekking
Destinations All Rajasthan
Contact Mandip Singh Soin
Mobile 09810087319

INDO ASIA TOURS
Address C-28, Housing Society, South Extension Part-1, New Delhi
Tel 24691733, 24691744
Fax 23742013 **Email** indoasia@vsnl.com
Website indoasia-tours.com
Services All travel related services

Destinations All Rajasthan
Contact Pramod Bhatnagar

MERCURY TRAVELS
Address Jeevan Tara Bldg, Parliament Street, New Delhi
Tel 23362008, 23742866
Fax 23742013 **Website** mercury-travels.com
Services All travel related services
Destinations All Rajasthan
Contact TN Bhat

NATURE SAFARI
Address 106-107, A-3, Sector 11, Rohini, New Delhi
Tel 27570446 **Fax** 27570833
Website naturesafariindia.com
Services Hotels, canter safari, boat rides
Destinations Bharatpur, Ranthambhore
Contact Sharad Vats
Mobile 09811200094

PARAMOUNT HOLIDAYS
Address S-465, Greater Kailash-II, New Delhi
Tel 29213779, 29214479
Fax 51639366 **Email** delhi@paramountholidays.com
Website dekhoindia.com
Services All travel related services
Destinations All Rajasthan
Contact Subhashish Chatterjee, Naveen Singh
Mobile 09313068400

SNOW LEOPARD
Address House No. 9174, Sector C, Vasant Kunj, New Delhi **Tel** 26134554, 26122775, 26898654
Fax 26898654 **Email** delhi@slapl.com **Website** snowleopardadventures.com
Services Hotel bookings, safaris (jeep, camel and horse) wildlife tours

Destinations Most of Rajasthan
Contact Ajeet Bajaj, Sophia

TCI (Travel Corporation of India)
Address 504-505, New Delhi House, 5th Floor, 27 Bara-khamba Road, New Delhi
Tel 23315834-38 **Fax** 23327468, 23376705
Email inbounddel@ tci.co.in
Website tcindia.com
Services All travel related services
Destinations All Rajasthan
Contact Homa Mistry

WILD WORLD INDIA
Address 21 Kailash Hills, New Delhi **Tel** 26914417 **Email** vikram@wildworldindia.com
Website wildworldindia.com
Services Safaris
Destinations Bharatpur, Jaipur, Jodhpur, Pushkar, Ranthambhore, Udaipur
Contact Dipin, Gaurav, Vikram
Mobile 09313772980

KOLKATA

HIMALCHURA TOURS AND TRAVELS
Address P263 CIT Road, Scheme 4M, Kolkata
Tel 033-23708004, 23633000
Email amal3000@tataone.in
Services All travel related services
Destinations All Rajasthan
Contact Amal Sarkar
Mobile 09433060007

LINK INDIA TOURS AND TRAVELS
Address 8/2 BBD Bagh (East), Kolkata **Tel** 22431435
Email linktrav@rediffmail.com
Services Packages, hotels, transport
Destinations All Rajasthan

Contact Umesh Khandelwal
Mobile 09830041024

PARAMOUNT HOLIDAYS
Address 439/1, Chatra
Bow Bazaar, Shree Rampur,
Hooghly, Kolkata
Tel 26320453, 31065545
Email kolkata@
paramountholidays.com
Website dekhoindia.com
Services All travel related
services
Destinations All Rajasthan
Contact Barun

POORVA TRAVELS
Address 183/2 Lenin
Sarani, Kolkata
Tel 22127301, 22128993
Email poorvatrvls@vsnl.net
Website poorvatravels.com
Services All travel related
services
Destinations All Rajasthan
Contact Minal Dey, Sujaya
Mobile 09831070828

MUMBAI

LOHANA TOURS AND TRAVELS
Address Brahmakrupa,
Kamla Nehru Road, Crossroad
No. 2, Kandivili (W), Mumbai
Tel 022-28052060 **Email**
sanjiv@lohanatoursindia.com
Website lohanatoursindia.com
Services All travel related
services, office in Ahmedabad
Destinations All Rajasthan
Contact Sanjiv Lohana **Mobile**
09820149200

MARWAR TRAVELS
Address SF, Printing
House, Police Court Lane,
DN Road, Fort, Mumbai
Tel 32535252 **Email**
marwartravels@mtnl.net.in
Services All travel related
services, luxury train tours,
Chambal River Cruise,

waterfall visit near Bundi
Destinations All Rajasthan
Contact Mahendra Jain
Mobile 09324087625

PARAMOUNT HOLIDAYS
Address 104, Siddhartha
Shopping Complex, Next to
Indraprastha Shopping Centre,
SV Road, Borivili (W), Mumbai
Tel 28636174, 28637253
Website dekhoindia.com
Services All travel related
services
Destinations All Rajasthan

Contact Pravin Singh,
Sanjay Thakkar
Mobile 09833934484-85/ 88

SUYASH TRAVELS
Address LJ Business
Centre, 364 NC Kelkar
Road, Dadar (W),
Mumbai **Tel** 24386104
Email suyashtours_nml
@rediff mail.com
Services All travel related
services
Destinations All Rajasthan
Contact Nitin Mahulkar

TOURIST OFFICES

IN RAJASTHAN

For travel-related queries including booking of rooms at RTDC
hotels, sightseeing tours, safaris and train journeys on Palace-
on-Wheels and Heritage-on-Wheels, call any of the official state
agencies listed below

INFORMATION ❶	**INFORMATION & BOOKING** ❶❷

**State tourist agencies and
website**
● Rajasthan Tourism Development Corporation (RTDC)
● Rajasthan Tourism
● www.rajasthantourism.gov.in

JAIPUR
RTDC ❶❷
Central Reservation Office
RTDC Hotel Swagatam
Near Railway Station, Jaipur
Tel 0141-2202586, 2203531
Fax 2204065, 2201045

Rajasthan Tourism ❶
Tourist Reception Office
Tourist Hotel (Govt Hostel)
MI Road, Jaipur
Tel 5110595, 5110597-98

RTDC ❶❷
Tourist Information Counter
Railway Station, Jaipur
Tel 2315714/ 2200778/ 1364

Rajasthan Tourism ❶
Tourist Information Counter
Sanganer Airport
Jaipur
Tel 2722647

RTDC ❶❷
Tourist Information Bureau
Near Deluxe Bus Depot
Platform No. 3, Jaipur
Tel 5064102

AJMER
Rajasthan Tourism ❶
Tourist Reception Centre
RTDC Hotel Khadim, Ajmer
Tel 0145-2627426/ 1364
Mobile 09829224354

ALWAR
Rajasthan Tourism ❶
Tourist Reception Centre
Opp Railway Station
Alwar
Tel 0144-2347348

INFORMATION

AMER

Rajasthan Tourism ℹ️
Tourist Office
Near Elephant Stand, Amer
Tel 0141-2530264

BHARATPUR

Rajasthan Tourism ℹ️
Tourist Reception Centre
Saras Circle, Agra Road
Bharatpur
Tel 05644-222542

BIKANER

Rajasthan Tourism ℹ️
Tourist Reception Centre
RTDC Hotel Dhola Maru
Bikaner
Tel 0151-2226701
Mobile 09414325608

BUNDI

Rajasthan Tourism ℹ️
Tourist Office
Collectorate Campus, Bundi
Tel 0747-2443697

CHITTAURGARH

Rajasthan Tourism ℹ️
Tourist Reception Office
Near Railway Station
Chittaurgarh
Tel 01472-241089

JAISALMER

Rajasthan Tourism ℹ️
Tourist Reception Centre
Station Road, Jaisalmer
Tel 02992-252406/ 1364

JHALAWAR

Rajasthan Tourism ℹ️
Tourist Information Centre
RTDC Hotel Chandravati
Jhalawar
Tel 07432-230081

JHUNJHUNU

Rajasthan Tourism ℹ️
Mandawa Circle
Churu Bypass Road

Jhunjhunu
Tel 01592-232909

JODHPUR

Rajasthan Tourism ℹ️
Tourist Reception Centre
RTDC Hotel Ghoomar
High Court Road, Jodhpur
Tel 0291-2545083

KOTA

Rajasthan Tourism ℹ️
Tourist Reception Centre
RTDC Hotel Chambal
Naipura, Kota
Tel 0744-2327695

MOUNT ABU

Rajasthan Tourism ℹ️
Tourist Reception Centre
Opp Bus Stand, Mount Abu
Tel 02974-235151

PUSHKAR

Rajasthan Tourism ℹ️
Tourist Office
Hotel Sarovar, Pushkar Lake
Pushkar
Tel 0145-2772040

SAWAI MADHOPUR

Rajasthan Tourism ℹ️
Tourist Reception Office
RTDC Hotel Vinayak
Ranthambhore Road
Sawai Madhopur
Tel 07462-220808

SIKAR

Rajasthan Tourism ℹ️
Tourist Office
Government Museum
Family Road, Sikar
Tel 01572-257473

UDAIPUR

Rajasthan Tourism ℹ️
Tourist Reception Centre
Fateh Memorial, Suraj Pol
Udaipur
Tel 0294-2411535, 2521971

RTDC ℹ️
Hotel Kajri, Shastri Circle
Udaipur
Tel 2410501-02

IN THE METROS

AHMEDABAD

RTDC, Reservation Office ℹ️
A-1, Divya Apartments
Near Mitha Khali Railway
Under Bridge, Navrangpura
Ahmedabad
Tel 079-26469580
Fax 26565187

CHENNAI

RTDC ℹ️
Tourist Office
FF, TTDC Complex
Wallajah Road
Chennai
Tel 044-25365554

KOLKATA

RTDC ℹ️
Tourist Office
2, Ganesh Chandra Avenue
FF, Commerce House
Kolkata
Tel 033-22132740
Mobile 09836010235

MUMBAI

RTDC ℹ️
Tourist Office
38-B, Kamer Bldg, GF
Cawasji Patel Street, Fort
Near Akbar Ali Furniture Shop
Mumbai
Tel 022-22040417, 22820683

NEW DELHI

Department of Tourism, Art &
Culture ℹ️
Government of Rajasthan
Tourist Reception Centre
Bikaner House, Pandara Road
New Delhi
Tel 011-23383837/ 9525
Telefax 23382823

METRO RESERVATIONS

To book any State Tourism hotel in your city, see the detailed listing of Tourist Offices on pages 453-454

Accommodation type?
Spot these flags
TENTS FRH
HOMESTAY

Special Hotel needs?
Spot these flags
HERITAGE ETHNIC
FARM-STAY SPA

Legend

ACF	Asst Conservator of Forests	Apts	Apartments	PB	Post Box
Dist	District	FRH	Forest Rest House	SF	Second Floor
FF	First Floor	NA	Not accepted	TE	Taxes extra
		Opp	Opposite	VPO	Village and Post

HOTELS EASY ACCESS

Note +All heritage hotels across Rajasthan are presented in boxes
++ Heritage hotels in destinations not covered in this guide are included in boxes titled 'Also near....'

Disclaimer Only a representative listing of hotels in each area has been given. The facilities listed may not be exhaustive. Tariff indicates the approx range (lowest to highest) of the rates prevailing at the time of going to press. The listings given here should not be construed as recommendations by the publisher

ACCOMMODATION LISTINGS

Hotel Aaram
Location Near bus stand
Address LIC Colony, Vaishali Nagar **Tel** 5120096, 2425250
Fax 2641992 **Rooms** 22 **Tariff** Rs 400-900 **Credit Cards** NA **Facilities** Laundry, room service, hot water, TV

Hotel Ajmeru
Location Near railway station
Address Khailand Market **Tel** 2431103 **Fax** 2429582 **Rooms** 15 **Tariff** Rs 350-1,100 **Credit Cards** NA **Facilities** Laundry, room service, hot water, TV

Hotel Ambassador
Location Nagina Bagh **Address** Ashok Marg, Lohagal Road **Tel** 2425095, 2428479 **Fax** 2633147 **Website** ambassadorajmer.com **Rooms** 27 **Tariff** Rs 600-2,950; TE **Credit Cards** Visa, Master **Facilities** Kitchen, travel desk, parking, laundry, doctor-on-call, room service, attached bath, TV

Hotel Delhi Durbar
Location Near Dargah Sharif
Address Dargah Bazaar **Tel** 2621597, 5100760 **Rooms** 18

HERITAGE EXPERIENCES: AJMER

Haveli Heritage Inn HOMESTAY
Location Near Khadi Bhandar
Address Phool Niwas, Kutchery Road **Tel** 2621607 **Rooms** 11 **Tariff** Rs 500-1,500 **Credit Cards** NA **Facilities** Home kitchen, sightseeing, laundry, room service, hot water, TV

Merwara Estate
Location Hilltop **Address** Near Daulat Bagh **Tel** 2420691 **Mobile** 09352009324 **Rooms** 46 **Tariff** Rs 2,200-5,500; TE **Credit Cards** NA **Facilities**

Tariff Rs 250-650; TE **Credit Cards** NA **Facilities** Restaurant, room service, attached bath, TV

Hotel Embassy
Location Opp City Power House
Address Jaipur Road **Tel** 2623859, 4100775 **Fax** 2630888 **Website** hotelembassyajmer.com **Rooms** 32 **Tariff** Rs 850-2,500; TE **Credit Cards** Visa, Master, Diners, BoB **Facilities** Restaurant, travel desk, guide, parking, laundry, doctor-on-call, room service, attached bath, TV

Hotel Khadim RTDC
Location Near Savitri College
Address Civil Lines **Tel** 2627490/536 **Telefax** 2431330 **Website** rajasthantourism.gov.in **Rooms** 55 **Tariff** Rs 400-2,000; TE **Credit Cards** AmEx, Visa, Master, Diners, BoB **Facilities** Restaurant, bar, travel desk, laundry, room service, attached bath, hot water, TV **Metro Reservations** See page 453

Hotel Malwa
Location Near railway station
Address Agra Gate, Sabzi Mandi Chauraha, Jaipur Road **Tel** Restaurant, sightseeing, laundry, doctor-on-call, room service, TV

IN BADNOR STD 0145
Jal Mahal
Location Lakeside **Address** Badnor, Dist Bhilwara **Tel** 2627579 **Rooms** 2 suites, 1 family room **Tariff** Rs 5,000 (2 nights for 2 adults & 2 children, inclusive of breakfast) **Credit Cards** NA **Facilities** Home kitchen, sightseeing, jeep safari, room service, attached bath

ALSO NEAR AJMER
IN JUNIA STD 01467
Amar Bagh, about 90 km from Ajmer, is the ancestral home of the Junia thakurs

Amar Bagh HERITAGE
Location Lakeside **Address** Village Junia, via Kekri, Ajmer **Tel** 285622 **Rooms** 4, suites 2, cottages 6 **Tariff** Rs 800-1,500; TE **Credit Cards** NA **Facilities** Dining hall, birdwatching, sightseeing, laundry, doctor-on-call, attached bath, hot water

2432343 **Rooms** 27 **Tariff** Rs 100-450 **Credit Cards** NA **Facilities** Restaurant, laundry, room service, hot water, TV

Hotel Mansingh Palace
Location Near Anasagar Lake
Address Vaishali Nagar **Tel** 2425857 **Mobile** 09414004694 **Website** mansinghhotels.com **Rooms** 50 **Tariff** Rs 3,000-7,500; TE **Credit Cards** AmEx, Visa, Master, Diners **Facilities** Restaurant, bar, travel desk, sightseeing, shopping arcade, health club, beauty parlour, laundry, room service, TV **Delhi Reservations** Indo-Continental Hotels & Resorts, Mansingh Group of Hotels, KCT Block, SF, 85A Panchkuian Road, New Delhi **Tel** 011-23450000

Hotel Sagar Palace
Location Opp Anand Music Gate **Address** Dargah Bazaar **Tel** 2432803 **Rooms** 58 **Tariff**

Rs 200-1,600; TE **Credit Cards** NA **Facilities** Restaurant, room service, attached bath, TV

Hotel Regency
Location Near Dargah Sharif **Address** Outside Delhi Gate **Tel** 2620296/ 2439 **Fax** 2621750 **Website** bahubaligroup.com **Rooms** 27 **Tariff** Rs 450-1,500 **Credit Cards** NA **Facilities** Restaurant, camel safari, laundry, room service, hot water, TV

Hotel Prithviraj
Location Opp Patel Stadium **Address** Jaipur Road **Tel** 2432297, 3295200 **Rooms** 27 **Tariff** Rs 250-1,000 **Credit Cards** NA **Facilities** Breakfast only, room service, hot water, TV

Hotel Sahil
Location Near Dargah Sharif **Address** Outside Delhi Gate **Tel** 2632994-95 **Website** hotelsahil ajmer.com **Rooms** 30 **Tariff** Rs 500-2,000; TE **Credit Cards** NA **Facilities** Restaurant, travel desk, laundry, room service, TV

Jannat Hotel & Restaurant
Location Near Nizam Gate **Address** Dargah Bazaar **Tel** 2432494, 5100774 **Fax** 2623823 **Website** ajmerhoteljannat.com

Rooms 36 **Tariff** Rs 480-1,560 **Credit Cards** Visa, Master **Facilities** Restaurant, travel desk, laundry, doctor-on-call, room service, attached bath, TV

ALWAR STD 0144

Alwar Bagh
Location 30 km from Sariska **Address** Village Dhawala, Dist Alwar **Tel** 288523 **Rooms** 7, tents 6 **Tariff** Rs 1,900-2,500, tents Rs 1,600-2,000; TE **Credit Cards** Visa, Master **Facilities** Restaurant, swimming pool, jeep safari, sightseeing, room service, hot water, TV **Delhi Reservations** Palaces of India, 75 GF, Sant Nagar, East of Kailash, New Delhi **Tel** 011-41659622, 26236610 **Website** palacesofindia.com

Alwar Guest House
Location Near bus stand **Address** 26, Manu Marg **Tel** 2700012, 2335754 **Fax** 2348757 **Website** hotelalwar.com **Rooms** 13 **Tariff** Rs 900-2,250; TE **Credit Cards** AmEx, Visa, Master **Facilities** Restaurant, room service, hot water, TV

Circuit House
Location Outskirts **Address** Near Bhawani Tope Circle, Alwar

Tel 2700650 **Rooms** 10 **Tariff** Rs 300-450 **Credit Cards** NA **Facilities** Dining hall, room service, attached bath, TV

Hotel Alwar
Location City centre **Address** 25, Manu Marg **Tel** 2700012, 3205251 **Mobile** 09829096328 **Fax** 2339501 **Website** hotel-alwar.com **Rooms** 16 **Tariff** Rs 900-2,200; TE **Credit Cards** Visa, Master, BoB **Facilities** Restaurant, safaris, travel desk, doctor-on-call, laundry, room service, attached bath, TV

Hotel Aravali
Address 1 CEB, Near railway station **Tel** 2332316/ 883 **Fax** 2332011 **Email** hotelaravali@ rediffmail.com **Website** aravali hotels.com **Rooms** 36 **Tariff** Rs 300-3,000; TE **Credit Cards** Visa, Master **Facilities** Restaurant, bar, swimming pool, laundry, room service, attached bath, hot water, TV

Hotel Arya
Location Near railway station **Address** 20, Tejmandi, Station Road **Tel** 2332985 **Rooms** 20 **Tariff** Rs 200-750 **Credit Cards** NA **Facilities** Restaurant, laundry, hot water, TV

ACCOMMODATION LISTINGS

Hotel Jhankar
Location Outskirts **Address** Delhi Road **Tel** 2372550 **Rooms** 17 **Tariff** Rs 300-600; TE **Credit Cards** NA **Facilities** Restaurant, laundry, room service, attached bath

HERITAGE EXPERIENCES: ALWAR

Hotel Burja Haveli
Location 7 km from Alwar **Address** Village Burja, Rajgarh Road **Tel** 5131288 **Mobile** 09829096285 **Rooms** 10 **Tariff** Rs 1,800-4,000; TE **Credit Cards** Visa, Master **Facilities** Restaurant, swimming pool, camel/ horse safari, sightseeing, pick-up/ transfer, laundry, doctor-on-call, room service, TV

IN KESROLI STD 01468
Hotel Hill Fort
Address Village Kesroli, via MIA **Telefax** 289352 **Mobile** 09829817465, 09811427198 **Website** neemranahotels.com **Rooms** 21 **Tariff** Rs 2,000-5,000; TE **Credit Cards** AmEx, Visa, Master, BoB **Facilities** Buffet dining, bar, camel cart trip, village safari, laundry **Delhi Reservations** Neemrana Hotels, A-58, Nizamuddin East, New Delhi **Tel** 011-24356145, 24358962 **Fax** 24351112

Hotel Meenal RTDC
Location Near Circuit House **Address** Bhawani Tope Circle **Tel** 2347352 **Rooms** 6 **Tariff** Rs 400-700 **Credit Cards** NA **Facilities** Restaurant, laundry, room service, attached bath, TV **Metro Reservations** *See page 453*

IN SILISERH STD 0144
Hotel Lake Palace RTDC
Location Near Siliserh Lake **Address** Siliserh Circle **Tel** 2886322 **Rooms** 10 **Tariff** Rs 2,350-3,425 **Credit Cards** NA **Facilities** Restaurant, boating, laundry, room service, TV **Metro Reservations** *See page 453*

BIKANER STD 0151

Dhola Maru RTDC
Location Central **Address** Sadul Ganj **Tel** 2529621 **Rooms** 32, dorm 1 **Tariff** Rs 400-700, dorm bed Rs 100 **Credit Cards** NA **Facilities** Bar, dining hall, attached bath, TV **Metro Reservations** *See page 454*

Harasar Haveli
Location Near Dr Karni Singh Stadium **Address** Harasar House, Dr Karni Singh Stadium Road **Tel** 2209891 **Fax** 2540044 **Rooms** 37 **Tariff** Rs 300-11,500 **Credit Cards** AmEx, Master, Visa **Facilities** Restaurant, travel desk, sightseeing, laundry,

ALSO NEAR BIKANER

IN RAISAR STD 0151
Balaji Resort, 6 km from Bikaner, offers its guests a desert experience

Balaji Resort
Location Amidst sand dunes on Bikaner-Jaipur Highway **Address** Village Raisar, Dist Bikaner **Tel** 2746902 **Website** balajiresort.com **Rooms** 2, huts 5 **Tariff** Rs 1,000-1,600 **Credit Cards** NA **Facilities** Unique rural huts, restaurant, swimming pools, safaris, Ayurvedic oil bath, sunbath treatment, reiki, hot iron fire dance, sand skiing, campfire, doctor in resort, room service **Reservations Mobile** 09351201616 **Contact** Brig NL Verma

doctor-on-call, attached bath, hot water, TV

Hotel City Palace
Location Near fort **Address** KEM Road, Daga Building **Tel** 2526320-21 **Fax** 2209180 **Rooms** 15 **Tariff** Rs 400-1,100 **Credit Cards** Master, Visa **Facilities** Restaurant, parking, laundry, doctor-on-call, attached bath, hot water

Hotel Gaj Kesari
Location Central **Address** Jodhpur-Jaipur Bypass Road **Tel** 2400372 **Rooms** 24 **Tariff** Rs 2,400-3,300; TE **Credit Cards** Visa, Master, AmEx **Facilities** Restaurant, travel desk, camel safari, sightseeing, doctor-on-call, laundry, room service, hot water, TV

Hotel Heritage Resort
Location 9 km milestone **Address** Bikaner-Jaipur Highway **Tel** 2752393-97 **Website**

Hotel Basant Vihar Palace
Location Near bus stand
Address NH15, Sri Ganganagar
Road **Tel** 2250675 **Fax** 2250676
Website basantviharpalace.com
Rooms 31 **Tariff** Rs 1,200-
2,150; TE **Credit Cards** Visa,
Master **Facilities** Restaurant,
travel desk, camel safari, folk
dances, parking, sightseeing,
laundry, room service, TV

Hotel Bhanwar Niwas
Location Near city kotwali
Address Rampuria Street **Tel**
2529323, 2201043 **Fax** 2200880
Website bhanwarniwas.com
Rooms 26 **Tariff** Rs 2,400-
3,300; TE **Credit Cards** AmEx,
Visa, Master **Facilities**
Restaurant, travel desk, camel
safari, sightseeing, doctor-on-
call, laundry, room service

Hotel Lallgarh Palace
Location Opp Central Bus
Stand **Address** Ganga Avenue
Road **Tel** 2540202-07 **Fax**
2522253 **Website** lallgarhpalace.
com **Rooms** 44 **Tariff** Rs 3,000-
4,800; TE **Credit Cards** Visa,
Master **Facilities** Restaurant,
swimming pool, tennis court,
billiards room, gift shop,
in-house museum, laundry,

doctor-on-call, room service,
hot water, TV

Hotel Laxmi Niwas Palace
Location Near bus stand
Address Main Lallgarh Palace
Complex, Karni Singh Road **Tel**
2521188-89, 2202777 **Fax**
2525219 **Website** laxminiwas
palace.com **Rooms** 42 **Tariff**
Rs 5,000-9,000; TE **Credit
Cards** AmEx, Visa, Master
Facilities Restaurant, bar,
coffee shop, doctor-on-call,
room service, attached bath, TV

Karni Bhawan Palace
Location Near Veterinary
College **Address** Gandhi
Colony **Tel** 2524701-06 **Fax**
2522408 **Rooms** 12 **Tariff**
Rs 2,000-4,000; TE **Credit
Cards** AmEx, Visa, Master
Facilities Restaurant, bar,
puppet shows, parking **Delhi
Reservations** HRH Group of
Hotels, C-41, Gulmohar Park,
New Delhi **Tel** 011-26611273-75
Website hrhindia.com

Maan Bilas Palace
Location Near Lallgarh Palace
Address Lallgarh Palace
Complex **Tel** 2540221-25 **Fax**
2522408 **Rooms** 10 **Tariff**

Karni Bhawan Palace

Rs 1,000-1,500; TE **Credit
Cards** Visa, Master **Facilities**
Restaurant, laundry, room
service, hot water, TV

IN GAJNER STD 01534
Gajner Palace
Location Lakeside **Address**
Tehsil Kolayat, Dist Bikaner **Tel**
275061, 255064-67 **Fax** 255060
Rooms 44 **Tariff** Rs 2,900-
3,600; TE **Credit Cards** Visa,
Master **Facilities** Restaurant,
travel desk, camel/ jeep safari,
horse riding, cycling, nature
walks, boating, solar boat
charters, billiards room, puppet
shows, laundry, room service
Delhi Reservations *See Karni
Bhawan Palace alongside*

carnivalhotels.com **Rooms** 36
Tariff Rs 2,500-4,000 **Credit
Cards** Visa, Master **Facilities**
Restaurant, bar, coffee shop,
swimming pool, camel safari,
Rajasthani and Kairali massage
parlour, puppet shows, travel
desk, laundry, doctor-on-call,
room service, attached bath,
hot water, TV **Gurgaon
Reservations** Carnival Hotels,
DLF, Plot No. 56, Sector 44,
Gurgaon **Tel** 0124-6452704
Email carnival@vsnl.net

Hotel Jaswant Bhawan
Location Near railway station
Address Daudsar House, Alakh
Sagar Road **Tel** 2548848 **Fax**
2521834 **Website** hoteljaswant
bhawan.com **Rooms** 15 **Tariff**
Rs 550-1,800; TE **Credit Cards**
NA **Facilities** Dining hall, lounge
bar, camel safari, folk music and
dance, laundry, travel desk, room
service, hot water, TV

Hotel Marudhar Heritage
Location Near railway station

Address Gangashehar Road **Tel**
2522524, 2205723 **Fax** 2523673
Email hmheritage2000@yahoo.
co.in **Rooms** 27 **Tariff** Rs 250-
999 **Credit Cards** NA **Facilities**
Restaurant, coffee shop, swimming pool, safaris, attached
bath, laundry, room service, TV

Hotel Maru Udyan
Location Near Bikaner Bypass
crossing **Address** Bikaner-Jaipur
Highway NH11 **Tel** 2400735
Mobile 09829477578 **Website**

ACCOMMODATION LISTINGS

Haveli Braj Bhushanjee
Location Below the palace **Address** Opp Ayurvedic Hospital **Tel** 2442322/ 509 **Fax** 2442142 **Website** kiplings bundi.com **Rooms** 24 **Tariff** Rs 950-2,450; TE **Credit Cards** AmEx, Visa, Master **Facilities** Restaurant, sightseeing, laundry, room service, TV

Ishwari Niwas Palace
Location Next to Collector's Bungalow **Address** 1 Civil Lines **Tel** 2442414 **Telefax** 2443541 **Mobile** 09414175851 **Website** ishwariniwas.com **Rooms** 20 **Tariff** Rs 3,000-4,000; TE **Credit Cards** NA **Facilities** Restaurant, horse/ jeep safari, laundry, sightseeing, doctor-on-call, room service, TV

Royal Retreat
Location Bundi Fort compound

marudyan.com **Rooms** 20 **Tariff** Rs 1,000-1,200 **Credit Cards** NA **Facilities** Restaurant, swimming pool, camel/ jeep safaris, parking, attached bath, hot water

Hotel Marudhar & Restaurant
Location Hospital Road **Address** Ambedkar Circle **Tel** 2546686-87 **Fax** 2526866 **Rooms** 32 **Tariff** Rs 300-800 **Credit Cards** Visa, Master, BoB **Facilities** Restaurant, travel

Address Garh Palace **Tel** 2444426 **Fax** 2443278 **Website** royalretreatbundi.com **Rooms** 5, tents 4 **Tariff** Rs 750-1,250, tent Rs 1,100; TE **Credit Cards** NA **Facilities** Restaurant, craft shop, sightseeing, doctor-on-call, laundry, room service, attached bath, hot water

IN SHAHPURA STD 01484
Shahpura Bagh
Location Lakeside **Address** Shahpura, Dist Bhilwara **Telefax** 222077 **Mobile** 09828122012-13 **Website** shahpurabagh.com **Rooms** 4, suites 5 **Tariff** Rs 5,400-7,000; TE (with breakfast and safari) **Credit Cards** NA **Facilities** Home kitchen, buffet meals, safari, sightseeing, boat ride, birdwatching, doctor-on-call, laundry, TV in lounge, room service, attached bath, hot water

desk, doctor-on-call, laundry, room service, attached bath, TV

Raj Vilas Palace
Location Near railway station **Address** Near Old RT Office, Public Park **Tel** 2525901-03 **Fax** 2525904 **Website** hotelrajvilas palace.com **Rooms** 55 **Tariff** Rs 1,950-5,000; TE **Credit Cards** Visa, Master **Facilities** Restaurant, bar, parking, pool, shopping arcade, laundry, TV

Vijay's Guest House
Location Opp Sophia School **Address** Jaipur Road **Tel** 2231244/ 333 **Mobile** 09829217331 **Website** camel man.com **Rooms** 8 **Tariff** Rs 300-500 **Credit Cards** NA **Facilities** Kitchen, home-cooked meals, camel safari, garden, laundry, doctor-on-call, campfire, folk dance, attached bath, TV

BUNDI STD 0747
Haveli Katkoun
Location Near Gopal Mandir **Address** Balchand Para **Tel** 2444679 **Mobile** 09414539146 **Website** havelikatkoun.com **Rooms** 6 **Tariff** Rs 350-600 **Credit Cards** NA **Facilities** Restaurant, home-cooked meals, sightseeing, travel assistance, laundry, room service, hot water

Hotel Vrindawati RTDC
Location Opp Jait Sagar **Address** Dablana Road **Tel** 2442473 **Rooms** 7 **Tariff** Rs 400-800 **Credit Cards** NA **Facilities** Restaurant, boating, room service, attached bath, TV **Metro Reservations** See page 454

Kasera Paradise
Location Below the palace **Address** Balchand Para **Tel** 2444679 **Mobile** 09829170982 **Website** kaseraparadise.com **Rooms** 17 **Tariff** Rs 500-2,500 **Credit Cards** Visa, Master **Facilities** Restaurant, sightseeing, travel assistance, laundry, room service, TV

CHHATRA SAGAR-NIMAJ STD 02939
Chhatra Sagar Nimaj TENTS
Location Lake view **Address** PO Nimaj, Dist Pali **Tel** 230118 **Mobile** 09414123118 **Website** chhatrasagar.com **Rooms** 11

Nimaj Palace

Location Off Ajmer-Jodhpur Highway NH112 **Address** Nimaj, Tehsil Jitaran, Dist Pali **Tel** 230022 **Mobile** 0941008787 **Website** nimaj palace.com **Rooms** 25 **Tariff** Rs 4,600-5,400 (with breakfast) **Credit Cards** NA **Facilities** Restaurant, special dinners, historical safari, village/ wildlife safari, camel/ horse rides, laundry

tents **Tariff** Rs 10,000-12,000 (inclusive of all meals, village safari, birdwatching tour and taxes) **Credit Cards** NA **Facilities** Dining tent, sightseeing, jeep safari, nature walks

Hotel Gaurav Palace

Location Central **Address** Near Apsara Talkies, Rana Sangha Bazaar **Tel** 246904/ 827 **Rooms** 20 **Tariff** Rs 300-550 **Credit Cards** NA **Facilities** Restaurant, laundry, room service, TV

Hotel Meera

Location Near bus stand **Address** Chittaurgarh **Tel** 250266, 241427 **Telefax** 240466 **Rooms** 26 **Tariff** Rs 800-3,000;

TE **Credit Cards** Visa, Master, BoB **Facilities** Restaurant, laundry, room service, TV

Hotel Padmini

Location Riverview **Address** Near Sainik School, Chanderia **Tel** 241711 **Telefax** 241718, 241997 **Website** hotelpadmini. com **Rooms** 47 **Tariff** Rs 500-1,700; TE **Credit Cards** Visa, Master **Facilities** Restaurant, laundry, swimming pool, room service, TV

Hotel Pratap Palace

Location Near Head Post Office **Address** Chittaurgarh **Tel** 243563, 240099 **Website** castle bijaipur.com **Rooms** 47 **Tariff** Rs 1,440-2,040; TE **Credit Cards** Visa, Master **Facilities** Restaurant, laundry, swimming pool, room service, TV

Hotel Vinayak Palace

Location Near railway station **Address** Vinayak Complex, Collectorate Circle **Tel** 245035, 240046 **Rooms** 12 **Tariff** Rs 350-1,000 **Credit Cards** NA **Facilities** Restaurant, laundry, room service, hot water, TV

Panna RTDC

Location Central **Address**

Bassi Fort Palace

Location Hillside **Address** PO Bassi, Dist Chittaurgarh **Tel** 225321, 225606/ 707 **Website** bassifortpalace.com **Rooms** 18 **Tariff** Rs 1,500-2,500; TE **Credit Cards** Master **Facilities** Restaurant, boating, cultural nights, travel desk, safaris **Delhi Reservations** WelcomHeritage, 31 FF, Siri Fort Road, New Delhi **Tel** 011-26266650-55 **Website** welcomheritagehotels.com

Castle Bijaipur

Location On a plateau **Address** Village Bijaipur, Dist Chittaurgarh **Tel** 276222, 240099 **Fax** 241042 **Website** castlebijaipur.com **Rooms** 24 **Tariff** Rs 2,640-7,500; TE **Credit Cards** Visa, Master **Facilities** Restaurant, folk dance, horse riding, jeep safari, swimming pool

Chittaurgarh **Tel** 241238 **Fax** 244024 **Rooms** 30 **Tariff** Rs 200-700 **Credit Cards** NA **Facilities** Restaurant, laundry, room service, attached bath, hot water, TV **Metro Reservations** *See page 454*

ACCOMMODATION LISTINGS

DESERT NATIONAL PARK

IN KHURI STD 03014

Gangaur Guest House **TENTS**
Location In the desert **Address**
Village Khuri, Jaisalmer **Tel**
274056 **Mobile** 09414271035
Rooms 8 huts, 10 Swiss tents
Tariff Rs 700-1,700 per person;
TE **Credit Cards** Visa, Master,
BoB **Facilities** Restaurant, camel
safari, cultural programmes,
doctor-on-call, room service

Moonlight Safari Camp **TENTS**
Location In the desert **Address**
Barana Village, Khuri, Jaisalmer
Tel 274109 **Mobile** 09829762275
Rooms 8 mud huts, 15 Swiss
tents **Tariff** Rs 1,275 per person
(including breakfast and dinner);
TE **Credit Cards** Visa, Master,
BoB **Facilities** Restaurant, camel
safari, cultural programmes,
laundry, room service

IN SAM STD 02992

Dune Safari Camp **TENTS**
Location Near Sam Dunes
Address Sam, Jaisalmer **Tel**
254463 **Mobile** 09829797807,
09414149807 **Website**
planetindiatravels.com **Rooms**
25 tents **Tariff** Rs 5,000-5,500
Credit Cards NA **Facilities**
Restaurant, camel/ jeep safari,
room service, attached bath
Delhi Reservations Tel 011-
29521317

Oasis India Campsite **TENTS**
Location Near Safe Parking
Address Sam, Jaisalmer **Tel**
09829311444 **Website** discovery
hospitality.com **Rooms** 25 tents
Tariff Rs 5,000-5,500 **Credit
Cards** NA **Facilities** Restaurant,
camel/ jeep safari, cultural
programmes, laundry, campfire,
room service, attached bath
Delhi Reservations Tel 011-
65646595 **Mobile** 09811552453

Royal Desert Safari Camp
Location Opp Sam dunes
Address Sam, Jaisalmer
Rooms 80 tents **Tariff** Rs 4,500-
6,000 **Credit Cards** Visa, Master
Facilities Dining tent, camel
safari, attached bath, hot water
**Jaisalmer Reservations
Mobile** 09414149636 **Contact**
BM Singh

Sam Dhani **RTDC** **TENTS**
Location Opp Sam Sand Dunes
Address C/o Hotel Moomal,
RTDC **Tel** 252392 **Rooms** 8
huts, 15 tents **Tariff** Rs 925-
1,425 **Credit Cards** NA
Facilities Dining room, camel
safari, cultural programmes,
laundry, room service **Metro
Reservations** *See page 454*

DEVI GARH STD 02953

HERITAGE EXPERIENCE

Devi Garh Resort
Location Amidst the Aravallis
Address NH8, Village
Delwara, Dist Rajsamand **Tel**
289211 **Fax** 289357 **Website**
deviresorts.com **Rooms** 39
suites **Tariff** Rs 18,000-
59,000; TE **Credit Cards** Visa,
Master **Facilities** Restaurants,
swimming pool, health club,
yoga, camel rides, laundry,
room service, hot water, TV
Delhi Reservations Boutique
Hotels India Ltd, UCO Bank
Bldg, 3rd Floor, Parliament
Street, New Delhi **Tel** 011-
23755540, 23354554

DUNGARPUR STD 02964

HERITAGE EXPERIENCE

Udai Bilas Palace
Location Near Gaibsagar
Lake **Address** Dungarpur **Tel**
230808 **Fax** 231008 **Website**
udaibilaspalace.com **Rooms**
22 **Tariff** Rs 3,025-5,750; TE
Credit Cards Visa, Master
Facilities Dining hall,
swimming pool, Jacuzzi,
birdwatching, boat ride,
sightseeing, laundry, doctor-
on-call, attached bath

JAIPUR STD 0141

Arya Niwas
Location Behind Amber Tower
Address Sansar Chandra Road
Tel 2372456/ 1773 **Fax** 2361871
Website aryaniwas.com **Rooms**
93 **Tariff** Rs 500-990 **Credit
Cards** AmEx, Visa, Master
Facilities Restaurant, travel desk,
sightseeing, library, gift shop,
laundry, room service (tea and
coffee only), attached bath, TV

Chokhi Dhani Resort **ETHNIC**
Location 5 km from airport
Address 12th Mile, Tonk road,
via Vatika **Tel** 2770555-57 **Fax**
2770558 **Website** chokhidhani.
com **Rooms** 65, suites 8 **Tariff**
Rs 5,000-8,000; TE **Credit
Cards** AmEx, Visa, Master
Facilities Restaurants, bar,
health club, swimming pool,
beauty parlour, parking, ethnic
village, room service, attached
bath, hot water, TV **Delhi
Reservations** 113 LGF, World
Trade Centre, Barakhamba Lane,
New Delhi **Tel** 011-41528602
Mobile 09811213585

Comfort Inn Hawa Mahal
Location Near Hawa Mahal
Address Civil Lines, Ajmer Road,

AMIT PASRICHA

Plot No. 40-41 **Tel** 2222402/ 3172 **Telefax** 2221982 **Email** bhatnagar@datainfosys.net **Rooms** 35 **Tariff** Rs 1,900-3,200; TE **Credit Cards** AmEx, Visa, Master, BoB **Facilities** Restaurant, laundry, travel desk, hot water, TV **Delhi Reservations** A-11, FF, Niti Bagh, New Delhi **Tel** 011-51642516 **Mobile** 09810068886 **Contact** Sodi

Chokhi Dhani Resort, on the outskirts of Jaipur

Country Inn & Suites SPA
Location Near Khasa Kothi Circle **Address** MI Road **Tel** 5103300 **Website** countryinns. com **Rooms** 84, suites 16 **Tariff** Rs 6,000-10,500; TE **Credit Cards** AmEx, Visa, Master **Facilities** Restaurant, bar, coffee shop, disco, spa gym, laundry, swimming pool, shopping arcade room service, TV **Delhi Reservations** Block E, No. 5, Masjid Moth, Greater Kailash II, New Delhi **Tel** 011-29223331

Govind Niwas HOMESTAY
Location Close to Raj Mahal Hotel **Address** Sardar Patel Road, Near Chomu House Circle **Tel** 2362977 **Email** govind niwas@hotmail.com **Rooms** 4 **Tariff** Rs 1,500 **Credit Cards** NA **Facilities** Home kitchen, garden, croquet, golf arranged, room service (breakfast and dinner only), TV, Internet

Harimahal Palace Hotel
Location City centre **Address** Jacob Road, Civil Lines **Tel** 2221399 **Telefax** 2226920 **Rooms** 11 **Tariff** Rs 2,800-4,000 **Credit Cards** AmEx, Visa, Master **Facilities** Restaurant, swimming pool, guided tours, room service, attached bath, hot water **Reservations Mobile** 09829051497 **Contact** Rajinder Singh

Harimahal Service Apartments
Location Adjoining Harimahal Palace Hotel **Address** Jacob Road, Civil Lines **Tel** 2221399 **Telefax** 2226920 **Rooms** 9 apts (3 bedrooms, lounge, kitchen each) **Tariff** Rs 2,000 (per bedroom) **Credit Cards** AmEx, Visa, Master **Facilities** Kitchen help available **Reservations** See *Harimahal Palace Hotel left*

Holiday Inn
Location Opp Ramgarh Modh Bus Stand **Address** Amer Road **Tel** 2672000 **Fax** 2672335 **Email** hijainn@sancharnet.in **Rooms** 72 **Tariff** Rs 4,000-6,000; TE **Credit Cards** Visa, Master **Facilities** Restaurant, coffee shop, swimming pool, table tennis, mini gym, travel desk, laundry, doctor-on-call, room service, TV

Holiday Resorts
Location City outskirts **Address** Khadmada Gati, Chomu Road **Tel** 2330294 **Fax** 2332852 **Email** support@hotelapnorajasthan. com **Rooms** 21 **Tariff** Rs 1,500-2,400; TE **Credit Cards** NA **Facilities** Restaurant, safaris, swimming pool, room service, TV

Hotel Aashish
Location Near Old Shalimar Cinema **Address** 298, Opp

Hathroi School, Ajmer Road **Tel** 2365005-06, 2375557 **Fax** 2365007 **Website** hotelashish. com **Rooms** 60 **Tariff** Rs 1,200-1,800; TE **Credit Cards**, Visa, Master **Facilities** Restaurant, travel desk, laundry, room service, hot water, TV

Hotel Clarks Amer
Location Opp Escorts Hospital **Address** PO Box 222, Jawahar Lal Nehru Marg **Tel** 2550616-19, 2549437-41 **Fax** 2550319 **Website** hotelclarks.com **Rooms** 211 **Tariff** Rs 5,000-17,500; TE **Credit Cards** AmEx, Visa, Master **Facilities** Restaurants, swimming pool, health club, travel desk, bank/ post office facilities, attached bath, TV

Hotel Diana Palace
Location Near railway station **Address** 12, Hathroi, Ajmer Road **Tel** 2375195-98 **Fax** 2375199 **Rooms** 27 **Tariff** Rs 1,800-2,100; TE **Credit Cards** Visa, Master **Facilities** Restaurant, laundry, room service, hot water, TV

Hotel Gangaur RTDC
Location Near AIR station **Address** Mirza Ismail Road **Tel** 2371642 **Rooms** 63 **Tariff** Rs 1,200; TE **Credit Cards** Visa,

ACCOMMODATION LISTINGS

The rich interiors at Narain Niwas Palace add to its royal ambience

Alsisar Haveli

Location Near Sindhi Camp Bus Stand **Address** Sansar Chandra Road **Tel** 2364685/ 8290, 5107167 **Website** alsisarhotels.com **Rooms** 47 **Tariff** Rs 2,400-3,650; TE **Credit Cards** AmEx, Visa, Master **Facilities** Restaurant, bar, swimming pool, travel desk, laundry, room service, TV

Bissau Palace

Location Near Saroj Cinema **Address** Outside Chandpole Gate **Tel** 2304371/ 628 **Website** bissaupalace.com **Rooms** 48 **Tariff** Rs 900-3,600; TE **Credit Cards** AmEx, Visa, Master **Facilities** Restaurants, bar, swimming pool, lawn tennis, library, folk dance and music, guided tours, laundry, gift shop, room service

Chirmi Palace Hotel

Location Near Kotak Mahindra Bank **Address** Dhuleshwar Garden, C-Scheme, Sardar Patel Marg **Tel** 2365063 **Telefax** 2364462 **Website** chirmi.com **Rooms** 23 **Tariff** Rs 850-1,700; TE **Credit Cards** AmEx, Visa, Master **Facilities** Dining hall, swimming pool, transport

assistance, sightseeing, laundry, room service, hot water, TV

Dera Rawatsar HOMESTAY

Location Behind Sindhi Camp Bus Stand **Address** D-194/C, Vijay Path, Bani Park **Tel** 2360717 **Mobile** 09314506391 **Fax** 2362556 **Rooms** 15 **Tariff** Rs 1,200-4,000; TE **Credit Cards** Visa, Master **Facilities** Restaurant, sightseeing, laundry, doctor-on-call, room service, attached bath, TV

Hotel Diggi Palace

Location Adjacent to Maharani College **Address** Diggi House, Shivaji Marg, SMS Hospital Road **Tel** 2373091, 2366120 **Fax** 2370359 **Website** hotel diggipalace.com **Rooms** 44 **Tariff** Rs 600-1,800 **Credit Cards** NA **Facilities** Restaurant, bar, safaris, yoga, horse riding, buggy ride, cultural events, laundry, travel desk, TV

Hotel Madhuban HOMESTAY

Location Near Collectorate Circle **Address** D-237 Behari Marg, Bani Park **Tel** 2200033/ 5427 **Fax** 2202344 **Website** madhuban.net **Rooms** 26 **Tariff** Rs 1,300-2,700; TE **Credit**

Cards Visa, Master **Facilities** Dining hall, swimming pool, puppet shows, folk dances, garden, free pick-up, TV

Jai Mahal Palace SPA

Location City centre **Address** Jacob Road, Civil Lines **Tel** 2223636 **Fax** 2223660 **Website** tajhotels.com **Rooms** 100 **Tariff** Rs 13,000-18,500; TE **Credit Cards** Visa, Master **Facilities** Restaurants, swimming pool, spa, health centre, beauty parlour, lawn tennis, putting green, travel desk, shopping arcade, laundry, doctor-on-call, room service, attached bath, TV **Taj Central Reservations** Toll free No. 1800111825

Khasa Kothi Hotel

Location Near railway station **Address** MI Road **Tel** 2375151-54 **Fax** 2374040 **Rooms** 36 **Tariff** Rs 1,475-3,000; TE **Credit Cards** BoB, Visa, Master **Facilities** Restaurant, swimming pool, beauty parlour, post office, laundry, doctor-on-call, room service, attached bath, TV

Mandawa Haveli

Location Near MI Road **Address** Sansar Chandra Road **Tel** 2374130/ 112, 5106081 **Fax** 2372084 **Website** mandawa hotels.com **Rooms** 41 **Tariff** Rs 2,000-3,000; TE **Credit Cards** AmEx, Visa, Master **Facilities** Dining hall, swimming pool, folk dances, music and puppet shows, laundry, doctor-on-call, room service, TV

Narain Niwas Palace

Location Central **Address** Kanota Bagh, Narain Singh Road **Tel** 2561291, 2563448

Fax 2561045 **Website** hotel
narainniwas.com **Rooms** 28,
suites 9 **Tariff** Rs 2,365-4,500;
TE **Credit Cards** AmEx, Visa,
Master **Facilities** Restaurant,
bar, health club, swimming pool,
snooker table, car rental,
laundry, doctor-on-call, parking,
room service, hot water, TV

Rambagh Palace
Location Near Rambagh Circle
Address Bhawani Singh Road
Tel 2211919 **Fax** 2385098
Website tajhotels.com **Rooms**
89 **Tariff** Rs 20,300-1,76,000;
TE **Credit Cards** AmEx, Visa,
Master, Diners **Facilities**
Restaurants, bar, health club,
room service, swimming pools,
beauty parlour, room service, TV
Taj Central Reservations Toll
free No.1800111825

Samode Haveli
Location City centre **Address**
Samode House, Gangapol
Tel 2632407, 2632370 **Website**
samode.com **Rooms** 29 **Tariff**
Rs 3,500-7,000; TE **Credit
Cards** AmEx, Visa, Master
Facilities Dining hall, pool bar,
swimming pool, Jacuzzi, puppet
shows, folk dance and music,
laundry, gift shop, room service,

TV **Reservations** Samode
House, Gangapol, Jaipur
Tel 0141-2632407, 2631942

Raj Mahal Palace Hotel
Location Near Civil Lines
Address Sardar Patel Marg,
C-Scheme **Tel** 5105665-67
Website royalfamilyjaipur.com
Rooms 29 **Tariff** Rs 2,500-
4,000; TE **Credit Cards** AmEx,
Visa, Master **Facilities** Restau-
rant, swimming pool, library,
laundry room service, TV

The Raj Palace **SPA**
Location On NH8 **Address**
Chomu Haveli, Outside Jorawar
Singh Gate, Amer Road
Tel 2634078-79 **Fax** 2630489
Website rajpalace.com **Rooms**
40 suites **Tariff** Rs 12,100-
1,70,0000; TE, **Credit Cards**
AmEx, Visa, Master **Facilities**
Restaurants, bar, Ayurvedic
massage, spa, camel/ elephant
safaris, gym, swimming pool,
travel desk, room service, TV

IN RAMGARH STD 01426
Lal Mahal Palace
Location Facing Aravalli Hills
Address Jamwu Ramgarh
Tel 0-9928012002-03 **Mobile**
09828225163 **Rooms** 10, luxury

tents 20 **Tariff** Rs 10,000
(inclusive of breakfast and
taxes) **Credit Cards** Visa,
Master **Facilities** Restaurant,
bar, dining hall, folk music and
dance, laundry, doctor-on-call,
room service, attached bath, TV

Ramgarh Lodge
Location Bank of Ramgarh
Lake **Address** Jamwu Ramgarh
Tel 252217, 252078 **Rooms** 11
Tariff Rs 4,400-7,000; TE **Credit
Cards** AmEx, Visa, Master
Facilities Restaurant, tennis,
swimming pool, laundry, doctor-
on-call, TV

IN SAMODE STD 01423
Samode Palace
Location On a hillock **Address**
Village Samode, Dist Chomu **Tel**
01423-240014/ 23 **Website**
samode.com **Rooms** 41 **Tariff**
Rs 7,700-19,350; TE **Credit
Cards** AmEx, Visa, Master
Facilities Restaurant, pool bar,
swimming pool, Jacuzzi, health
club, Kerala Ayurvedic centre,
camel/ jeep/ horse safaris,
puppet shows, folk dance and
music, laundry, gift shop, room
service, attached bath, hot water
Reservations See Samode
Haveli alongside

ACCOMMODATION LISTINGS

Master **Facilities** Restaurant, room service, hot water, TV **Metro Reservations** See page 453

Hotel Jaipur Ashok
Location Jai Singh Circle **Address** Bani Park **Tel** 2204491-94 **Website** the ashokgroup.com **Rooms** 97 **Tariff** Rs 1,600-3,000; TE **Credit Cards** AmEx, Visa, Master, Diners **Facilities** Restaurant, travel desk, laundry, swimming pool **Delhi Reservations** Ashok Reservations & Marketing Services, 3 Jeevan Vihar, Parliament Street, New Delhi **Tel** 011-23745557

Hotel Jaipur Palace
Location Near Laxmi Mandir Talkies **Address** Sahakar Marg, Tonk Road **Tel** 2743161-64 **Website** jaipurpalace. com **Rooms** 80 **Tariff** Rs 4,800-6,000; TE **Credit Cards** AmEx, Visa, Master **Facilities** Restaurant, health club, travel desk, swimming pool, room service, TV **Delhi Reservations** 5 DDA Complex,

Gulmohar Park, New Delhi **Tel** 011-26857849 **Telefax** 26511844

Hotel Kailrugji
Location Central **Address** 22-C, Gopal Vari, Hathroi Fort area **Tel** 2373426 **Fax** 2362556 **Email** kailrugji@india.com **Rooms** 22 **Tariff** Rs 1,300-2,200 (including breakfast); TE **Credit Cards** AmEx, Visa, Master, BoB, Diners **Facilities** Restaurant, laundry, parking, travel desk, room service, hot water, TV

Hotel Maharani Palace
Location Near Victory Cinema **Address** Station Road **Tel** 2204702 **Email** maharani@sancharnet.com **Rooms** 60 **Tariff** Rs 3,000-6,000; TE **Credit Cards** AmEx, Visa, Master, Diners **Facilities** Restaurant, health club, room service, travel desk, TV **Delhi Reservations** Maharani Hotels, D-57, Amar Bhavan, Hauz Khas Market, New Delhi **Tel** 011-26561547

Hotel Mansingh Palace
Location City centre **Address** Sansar Chandra Road **Tel** 2378771, 5118771 **Fax** 2377582 **Website** mansinghhotels.com **Rooms** 95 **Tariff** Rs 5,500-6,000; TE **Credit Cards** Visa, Master **Facilities** Restaurants, bar, coffee shop, swimming pool, health centre, shopping arcade, laundry, room service, TV **Delhi Reservations** Indo-Continental Hotels & Resorts, Mansingh Group of Hotels, KCT Block, SF, 85A Panchkuian Road, New Delhi **Tel** 011-23450000

Hotel Mansingh Towers
Location City centre **Address** Sansar Chandra Road **Tel** 2378771, 5118771 **Fax** 2360453 **Website** mansinghhotels.com

Rooms 45, suites 8 **Tariff** Rs 5,500-12,000; TE **Credit Cards** Visa, Master **Facilities** Restaurant, bar, laundry, doctor-on-call, room service, TV **Delhi Reservations** See Hotel Mansingh Palace left

Hotel Megh Niwas
Location Near Collectorate Circle **Address** C-9, Jai Singh Highway, Bani Park **Telefax** 2202034-36 **Website** megh niwas.com **Rooms** 27 **Tariff** Rs 1,400-2,600; TE **Credit Cards** AmEx, Visa, Master **Facilities** Restaurant, swimming pool, travel assistance, laundry, room service, TV

Hotel Meru Palace
Location Near SMS Hospital **Address** Ram Singh Road **Tel** 2371111-16 **Fax** 2378882 **Email** merupalace@hotmail.com **Rooms** 48 **Tariff** Rs 2,000-3,500; TE **Credit Cards** Visa, Master **Facilities** Restaurant, travel desk, room service, hot water

Hotel Sangam
Location Near railway station **Address** 17, Motilal Atal Road **Tel** 2371792-94 **Rooms** 28 **Tariff** Rs 800-2,000 **Credit Cards** Visa, Master **Facilities** Restaurant, bar, laundry, room service, TV

Hotel Sugandh Retreat
Location Near railway station **Address** 13, Bichun, SC Road **Tel** 2376303, 5118668 **Email** hotel_sugandhretreat@yahoo.com **Rooms** 15 **Tariff** Rs 400-1,500 **Credit Cards** NA **Facilities** Laundry, room service, hot water, TV

Jaipur Inn HOMESTAY
Location Collectorate Circle **Address** B-17, Shiv Marg, Bani

Park **Tel** 2201121 **Rooms** 25 **Tariff** Rs 750-1,250 **Facilities** Home-cooked meals, café, laundry, sightseeing, free pick-up, room service, TV **Reservations Mobile** 09829013660 **Contact** Pushpendra Bhargava

Jaipur Park Plaza
Location Near Statue Circle **Address** C-59, Prithviraj Road, C-Scheme **Tel** 2360202 **Fax** 2360707 **Website** sarovarhotels.com **Rooms** 83, suite 1 **Tariff** Rs 4,500-8,500; TE **Credit Cards** AmEx, Visa, Master **Facilities** Restaurants, pub, swimming pool, health club, travel desk, attached bath

Jas Vilas
Location Near Collectorate **Address** C-9, Sawai Jai Singh Highway, Bani Park **Tel** 2204638/902 **Website** jasvilas.com **Rooms** 11 **Tariff** Rs 2,000-4,000; TE **Credit Cards** Visa, Master **Facilities** Home kitchen, dining hall, swimming pool, laundry, doctor-on-call, attached bath, hot water, TV

Karauli House **HOMESTAY**
Location Near Sanjeevani Hospital **Address** New Sanganer Road **Tel** 2290763 **Mobile** 09414054257 **Fax** 2292633 **Rooms** 4 **Tariff** Rs 1,250-1,500; TE **Credit Cards** NA **Facilities** Dining hall, home-cooked meals, swimming pool, TV in lounge, laundry, doctor-on-call, room service, attached bath

Le Meridien **SPA**
Location NH8, Opp Sony Ericsson **Address** 1 RIICO, Kukas **Tel** 5114455-58 **Fax** 5114466 **Website** lemeridien jaipur.com **Rooms** 116 **Tariff** Rs 10,000-20,000; TE **Credit Cards**

ALSO NEAR JAIPUR

At Pachewar Garh outdoor activities are a major attraction

IN KANOTA STD 01429
Kanota is 15 km east of Jaipur

Royal Castle Kanota **HERITAGE**
Location Near Police Station **Address** VPO Kanota, Dist Jaipur **Tel** 234033 **Website** hotelnarainniwas.com **Rooms** 10 **Tariff** Rs 3,150; TE **Credit Cards** AmEx, Visa, Master **Facilities** Restaurant, sightseeing, village safari, elephant/ camel/ horse/ jeep safari, museum, library, garden, laundry, room service, TV **Jaipur Reservations** Narain Niwas Palace, Kanota Bagh, Narain Singh Road, Jaipur **Tel** 0141-2561291, 2563448

IN KUKAS STD 01426
The Gold Palace, close to Amer Fort and just 10 mins from Jaipur, offers horse riding

The Gold Palace and Resorts
Location Amidst Aravallis **Address** 8th Mile Amer Fort, Jaipur-Delhi Highway, Kukas **Tel** 241100 **Fax** 247188 **Website** hotelgoldpalace.com **Rooms** 70, 6 suites **Tariff** Rs 4,500-8,000; TE **Credit Cards** AmEx, Visa, Master **Facilities** Restaurants, bar, coffee shop, health club,

swimming pool, games centre, billiards room, meditation/ yoga room, room service, hot water, TV **Delhi Reservations** 38 LGF, World Trade Centre, Babar Road, New Delhi **Tel** 011-41528430 **Mobile** 09818590420

IN PACHEWAR STD 01437
90 km from Jaipur, Pachewar Garh offers 300 years of history, birding, fishing, horse safaris

Pachewar Garh **HERITAGE**
Location Near Pampa Sagar Lake **Address** Pachewar, Via Malpura, Dist Tonk **Tel** 228756 **Website** pachewargarh.com **Rooms** 20, suites 5 **Tariff** Rs 1,600-2,500; TE **Credit Cards** Visa, Master **Facilities** Restaurant, swimming pool, massage centre, camel/ horse/ jeep safaris, birdwatching, sightseeing, campfire **Jaipur Reservations** B-113, Pachewar House, Janta Colony, Jaipur **Tel** 0141-2601007 **Mobile** 09413340169 **Contact** Madhulika Singh **Delhi Reservations** Palaces of India, 75 GF, Sant Nagar, East of Kailash, New Delhi **Tel** 011-41659622, 26236610 **Website** palacesofindia.com

Rajvilas, voted 'most exotic resort in the world', redefines luxury

AmEx, Visa, Master **Facilities** Restaurants, bar, disco, theatre, swimming pool, spa gym, Jacuzzi, beauty parlour, yoga/ meditation room, children's club, games room, travel desk, laundry, doctor-on-call, room service, attached bath, TV

LMB Hotel

Location Central **Address** Johri Bazaar **Tel** 2565844/ 46-47 **Mobile** 09414073444 **Website** hotellmb.com **Rooms** 33 **Tariff** Rs 2,225-3,500; TE **Credit Cards** Visa, Master **Facilities** Restaurant, travel desk, laundry, doctor-on-call, room service, attached bath, TV

Rajvilas **SPA**

Location Outskirts, near Agra Road **Address** Babaji Ka Modh, Goner Road **Tel** 2680101 **Fax** 2680202 **Website** oberoihotels. com **Rooms** 54, luxury tents 14, villas 3 **Tariff** Rs 22,500-1,27,000; TE **Credit Cards** AmEx, Visa, Master, Diners **Facilities** Restaurants, bar, health club, laundry, shopping arcade, spa swimming pool, room service, TV **Delhi Reservations** Oberoi Hotels and Resorts, 7, Shamnath Marg, New Delhi **Tel** 011-23890606, Toll free No.1800112030

Rajputana Palace Sheraton

Location City centre **Address** Palace Road **Tel** 5100100 **Fax** 5102102 **Website** welcomgroup. com **Rooms** 216 **Tariff** Rs 8,000-50,000; TE **Credit Cards** AmEx, Visa, Master **Facilities** Restaurant, health centre, jogging track, beauty parlour, disco, shopping arcade, travel desk, laundry, home theatre, room service, TV **Reservations** Toll free No.1800111333

Shahpura House

Location Near Collectorate **Address** D-257, Devi Marg, Bani Park **Tel** 2202293, 2203069 **Fax** 2201494 **Website** shahpura house.com **Rooms** 32 **Tariff** Rs 2,500-3,500 **Credit Cards** Visa, Master **Facilities** Restaurant, travel desk, camel safari, buggy ride, cultural dance, doctor-on-call, laundry, room service, TV

Snehdeep **HOMESTAY**

Location Near Old City wall **Address** B-33, Sethi Colony, Govind Marg **Tel** 2604570, 3235743 **Mobile** 09314880887 **Website** snehdeep.com **Rooms** 8 **Tariff** Rs 400-850 **Credit Cards** NA **Facilities** Home-cooked meals by nutritionist hostess, birdwatching tours,

room service (for tea/ coffee only), attached bath, hot water

Sri Niwas Country Homes **HOMESTAY**

Location Opp Bhaironji Mandir **Address** Sirsi Nadia, Sirsi **Tel** 2240380 **Mobile** 09829239414 **Website** sriniwas.net **Rooms** 4 suites **Tariff** Rs 2,400 **Credit Cards** NA **Facilities** Dining hall, home-cooked meals, transport assistance, sightseeing, laundry

Suryavanshi Farms & Resorts

Location City outskirts **Address** Ramsagar ki Dhani, via Bindayaka Industrial Area, Sirsi Road **Email** suryavanshiresorts@ rediffmail.com **Rooms** 2, cottages 4 **Tariff** Rs 950 **Credit Cards** NA **Facilities** Restaurant, swimming pool, games, room service, attached bath, hot water **Reservations** 25 Lajpat Nagar, Khatipura Road, Jhotwara, Jaipur **Tel** 0141-2346413

Tara Niwas

Location Central **Address** B-22/ B, Shiv Marg, Babu Park **Tel** 2206823, 5107862 **Website** aryaniwas.com **Rooms** 25 **Tariff** Rs 750-950 **Credit Cards** Visa, Master **Facilities** Restaurant, parking, travel desk, room service, hot water, TV

Teej Hotel **RTDC**

Location Near Moti Mahal Cinema **Address** Collectorate Road **Tel** 2203199 **Rooms** 46 **Tariff** Rs 700-1000 **Credit Cards** Visa Master **Facilities** Dining hall, garden, hot water, TV **Metro Reservations** See page 453

The Farm **TENTS**

Location Near Green Belt **Address** Off Jaipur-Ajmer Highway **Tel** 2358770 **Website**

thefarmjaipur.com **Rooms** 6, tents 10 **Tariff** Rs 2,200-3,000 (inclusive of breakfast and taxes) **Credit Cards** NA **Facilities** Restaurant, swimming pool, horse riding, snooker **Reservations Mobile** 09828023030 **Contact** Suryapratap Singh

The General's Retreat

Location Opp BJP Office **Address** 9 Sardar Patel Marg **Tel** 2377134/ 539 **Website** generalsretreat.com **Rooms** 10 **Tariff** Rs 1,200-1,600; TE **Credit Cards** AmEx, Visa, Master **Facilities** Dining hall, sightseeing, car rental, laundry, room service (for tea/ coffee only), TV

Trident Hotel

Location Overlooking Mansagar Lake **Address** Amber Fort Road, Opp Jal Mahal **Tel** 2670101 **Rooms** 137 **Tariff** Rs 5,000-7,000 **Credit Cards** AmEx, Visa, Master **Facilities** Restaurant, bar, swimming pool, travel desk, gift shop, room service **Reservations Mobile** 09829051497 **Contact** Rajinder Singh

IN SAMODE STD 01423
Samode Bagh Garden Resort
TENTS
Location 4 km from Samode

Palace **Address** Village Fatehpura Bansa **Tel** 01423-240235-36 **Website** samode.com **Rooms** 44 tents **Tariff** Rs 3,500-3,750; TE **Credit Cards** AmEx, Visa, Master **Facilities** Dining hall, swimming pool, lawn tennis, croquet, handball, badminton, games and crafts for children, birdwatching, Ayurvedic massage, campfire, attached bath, hot water **Reservations** Samode House, Gangapol, Jaipur **Tel** 0141-2632407, 263194

IN VILLAGE MAHESHPURA
Saharia Organic Resort
FARM-STAY
Location Off NH11 (Sikar Road) **Address** Surya Vatika Road, On Jaipur-Chomu Road, Village Maheshpura **Mobile** 09314114027 **Website** sahariaorganicresort.com **Rooms** 9 **Tariff** Rs 500 **Credit Cards** NA **Facilities** Dining hall, serves organic farm food and organic tea from Assam, self-catering, organically maintained swimming pool, village safari, yoga classes on request, bicycles available, solar lights, interaction with volunteers from international voluntary organisations, attached bath, hot water

JAISALMER STD 02992
Desert Boys Guest House
Location Near Jain Mandir **Address** Fort, Vyasapada **Tel** 253091 **Rooms** 15 **Tariff** Rs 450-1,550 **Credit Cards** NA **Facilities** Restaurant, attached bath, hot water

Fort Rajwada
Location Overlooking Jaisalmer Fort **Address** No. 1, Hotel Complex, Jodhpur-Barmer Link Road **Tel** 253233/ 533, 254608 **Fax** 253733 **Website** fortrajwada.com **Rooms** 90, suites 4 **Tariff** Rs 4,100-12,000; TE **Credit Cards** Visa, Master **Facilities** Restaurant, bar, travel desk, camel/ jeep safari, swimming pool, Ayurvedic massage, tennis court, billiards room, laundry, room service, TV

Gorbandh Palace
Location Overlooking Jaisalmer Fort **Address** No. 1, Tourist Complex, Sam Road **Tel** 253801-07 **Rooms** 64, suites 3 **Tariff** Rs 5,000-7,000; TE **Credit Cards** AmEx, Visa, Master **Facilities** Restaurant, bar, coffee shop, travel desk, camel/ jeep safari, swimming pool, shopping arcade, laundry, room service, TV **Delhi Reservations** HRH

ACCOMMODATION LISTINGS

Hotel Jaisal Castle

Location Inside fort **Address** 186, Fort **Tel** 252362, 253755 **Fax** 252101 **Rooms** 11 **Tariff** Rs 1,500-2,000; TE **Credit Cards** NA **Facilities** Restaurant, camel safari, taxi arranged, laundry, doctor-on-call, attached bath, hot water

Hotel Jawahar Niwas Palace

Location Near Collectorate **Address** No. 1, Bada Bagh Road **Tel** 252288/ 08, 253540 **Fax** 250175 **Website** jawahar niwaspalace.com **Rooms** 22 **Tariff** Rs 2,400-4,200; TE **Credit Cards** AmEx, Visa, Master **Facilities** Restaurant, travel desk, camel safari, health club, fitness centre, horse riding, swimming pool, laundry, room service, attached bath, hot water, TV

Hotel Killa Bhawan

Location Fort rampart **Address** 445, Kothri Para, Fort **Tel** 251204 **Fax** 254518 **Website** killabhawan.com **Rooms** 7 **Tariff** Rs 2,700-5,500; TE **Credit Cards** AmEx, Visa, Master **Facilities** Camel safari, travel desk, laundry, room service, attached bath, hot water, TV

Hotel Nachana Haveli

Location Near Hanuman Chauraha **Address** Gandhi Chowk **Tel** 252110, 251910 **Fax** 252778 **Email** nachna_haveli@yahoo.com **Rooms** 14 **Tariff** Rs 1,950-2,750; TE **Credit Cards** Visa, Master **Facilities** Restaurant, Ayurvedic massage, travel desk, doctor-on-call, room service, hot water

MADHU KAPPARATH

Hotel Narayan Niwas Palace

Location Near Ramesh Talkies **Address** Malka Prol, Near Jain Bhawan **Tel** 252408, 251901-04 **Fax** 252101 **Website** narayan niwas.com **Rooms** 43 **Tariff** Rs 3,500-5,500; TE **Credit Cards** AmEx, Visa, Master, BoB, Diners **Facilities** Restaurant, tea lounge, camel safari, swimming pool, health club, cultural entertainment, laundry, room service, attached bath, TV **Gurgaon Reservations** Corporate Office, Q-6/7, SF, DLF Qutub Enclave, Phase-II, Gurgaon **Tel** 0124-2562047-48

Mandir Palace

Location Central **Address** Gandhi Chowk **Tel** 252788, 252951 **Rooms** 25 **Tariff** Rs 2,200-4,200; TE **Credit Cards** AmEx, Visa, Master **Facilities** Restaurant, bar, coffee shop, safaris, laundry, doctor-on-call, room service, **Delhi Reservations** Welcom-Heritage, 31 FF, Siri Fort Road, New Delhi **Tel** 011-26266650-55 **Fax** 26266656 **Website** welcomheritagehotels.com

Group of Hotels, C-41, Gulmohar Park, New Delhi **Tel** 011-26611273-75 **Website** hrhindia.com

Hotel Dhola Maru

Location Opp ITI **Address** PB No. 49, Jethwai Road **Tel** 252863 **Mobile** 09414149885 **Fax** 252761 **Website** hotel dholamaru.com **Rooms** 42 **Tariff** Rs 2,500-3,250; TE **Credit Cards** NA **Facilities** Restaurant, bar, swimming pool, desert safari, laundry, room service, TV **Delhi Reservations** Hotel Connections India, 11/27 West Patel Nagar, New Delhi **Tel** 011-65481693 **Mobile** 09811759245 **Contact** KB Mohanta **Website** hotelconnectionsindia.com

Hotel Gangaur

Location Near railway station **Address** Near Geeta Ashram **Tel** 251987 **Fax** 253591 **Rooms** 20 **Tariff** Rs 450-850; TE **Credit Cards** NA **Facilities** Restaurant, laundry, room service, attached bath, hot water, TV

Hotel Haveli

Location Near railway station **Address** Opp SBI, LIC Road **Tel** 252552 **Fax** 256021 **Email** haveli_hotel@yahoo.co.in **Rooms** 18 **Tariff** Rs 675-1,150; TE **Credit Cards** NA **Facilities** Restaurant, camel safari, laundry, room service, attached bath, TV

Hotel Himmatgarh Palace

Location Near ONGC Colony **Address** Ramgarh Road **Tel** 252002-04 **Fax** 252005 **Email** himmatgh@sancharnet.in **Rooms** 40 **Tariff** Rs 2,500-3,500; TE **Credit Cards** AmEx, Visa, Master **Facilities** Restaurant, bar, travel desk, swimming pool, camel safari, cultural programmes, laundry, room service, attached bath, hot water, TV **Delhi Reservations** Palaces of India, 75 GF, Sant Nagar, East of Kailash, New Delhi **Tel** 011-41659622, 41514120, 26236610 **Website** palacesofindia.com

Hotel Jaisal Palace

Location Central **Address** Gandhi Chowk, Talariya Pada **Tel** 252717, 251417 **Fax** 250257 **Website** hoteljaisalpalace.com **Rooms** 14 **Tariff** Rs 500-1,000; TE **Credit Cards** Visa, Master **Facilities** Restaurant, travel desk, laundry, room service, attached bath, hot water, TV

Hotel Moomal RTDC

Location Opp Sam Sand Dunes **Address** Sam Sand Dune Road **Tel** 252392 **Rooms** 60 **Tariff** Rs 700-1,500 **Credit Cards** NA **Facilities** Dining hall, lounge, camel safari, cultural prog-rammes, laundry, room service, attached bath, hot water **Metro Reservations** See page 454

Hotel Moonlight

Location Near Head Post Office **Address** Hanuman Circle **Tel** 250267, 254359 **Fax** 250257 **Website** moonlighthotelresort. com **Rooms** 5 **Tariff** Rs 1,050-1,250; TE **Credit Cards** Visa, Master, BoB **Facilities** Camel safari, travel desk, room service, attached bath, hot water, TV

Hotel Panihari

Location Opp Collector's Office **Address** 34, CV Singh Colony **Tel** 250173, 252836 **Fax** 252959 **Email** hpanihari@yahoo.co.in **Rooms** 16 **Tariff** Rs 750-2,200; TE **Credit Cards** NA **Facilities** Restaurant, camel safari, travel desk, laundry, room service, hot water, TV

Hotel Rang Mahal

Location Secluded **Address** 5, Hotel Complex, PB No. 50, Sam Road **Tel** 250907-09 **Fax** 251305 **Website** hotelrangmahal.com **Rooms** 55 **Tariff** Rs 3,000-3,500; TE **Credit Cards** AmEx, Visa, Master, Diners **Facilities** Poolside restaurant, coffee shop, desert safari, travel desk, swimming pool, Ayurvedic massage, laundry, room service, attached bath, hot water, TV

Hotel Rawal-Kot TENTS

Location Overlooking Jaisalmer Fort **Address** Jodhpur-Jaisalmer Road **Tel** 251874, 252638 **Fax** 250444 **Website** tajhotels.com **Rooms** 32 **Tariff** Rs 3,800-4,300 (inclusive of breakfast and taxes) **Credit Cards** AmEx, Visa, Master **Facilities** Restaurant, travel desk, swimming pool, Ayurvedic massage, camel/ jeep safari, folk music and dance, tented accommodation on sand dunes, laundry, room service, attached bath, hot water, TV **Jaipur Reservations** Taj Hotel Resorts & Palaces, Jai Mahal Palace Complex, Jacob Road, Civil Lines, Jaipur **Tel** 0141-2223636

Rajvansh Resorts SPA

Location Barabagh **Address** Ramgarh Road **Tel** 240210 **Website** rajvanshresorts.com **Rooms** 41 **Tariff** Rs 2,500-3,000; TE **Credit Cards** Visa, Master **Facilities** Restaurant, swimming pool, health club, spa camel safari, laundry, doctor-on-call, room service, attached bath, hot water **Jaipur Reservations** Jaisalmer Holiday, 36 Duleshwar Garden, C Scheme, Jaipur **Tel** 0141-3291111, 3292222 **Mobile** 09829066277 **Contact** Rakesh Baheti

IN KANOI STD 02992
Rawla Resort, 32 km from Jaisalmer, offers a romantic sand dunes experience

Rawla Resort TENTS

Location Surrounded by sand dunes **Address** After 15 km Sam Milestone, Village Kanoi, Jaisalmer **Tel** 251058, 253721 **Mobile** 09414149258, 09414149458 **Website** safaritoursindia.com **Rooms** 10 huts, 25 Swiss tents **Tariff** Rs 2,000-6,000 **Credit Cards** NA **Facilities** Dining hall, jeep/ camel/ camel cart safaris, birdwatching, sightseeing, cultural programmes, theme dinners, common toilets for huts, attached bath with tents, hot water

IN SODAKORE STD 02996
Mirvana Nature Resort is about 55 km from Jaisalmer

Mirvana Nature Resort ETHNIC TENTS

Location Jodhpur-Jaisalmer Highway **Address** RG Farms, Sodakore **Tel** 237487 **Mobile** 09414135861 **Website** mirvananatureresort.com **Rooms** 15 royal shikar huts, 4 luxury huts, 4 ethnic tents **Tariff** Rs 2,500-6,000 (inclusive of meals, cultural programmes, camel rides and taxes) **Credit Cards** Visa, Master **Facilities** Huts on a marble platform, restaurant, organic food, swimming pool, camel safari, birdwatching tours, cultural programmes, electricity **Delhi Reservations** Camps of India, 75 GF, Sant Nagar, East of Kailash, New Delhi **Tel** 011-41659622

ACCOMMODATION LISTINGS

HERITAGE EXPERIENCE

Prithvi Vilas Palace
Location Near SRG Hospital
Address Harish Chandra Civil
Lines **Tel** 231347/ 099 **Rooms**
16 **Tariff** Rs 1,250-3,000; TE
Credit Cards NA **Facilities**
Restaurant, guided tours,
library, room service, TV

Prithvi Vilas Guest House
Location Adjacent to Prithvi
Vilas Palace **Address** Harish
Chandra Civil Lines **Tel**
231347 **Rooms** 4 **Tariff** Rs
1,500-2,000; TE **Credit Cards**
NA **Facilities** Dining hall,
guided tours, room service

Hotel Chandrawati RTDC
Location On NH12 **Address**
Patan Road **Tel** 234023 **Rooms**
6 **Tariff** Rs 500-700 **Credit
Cards** NA **Facilities** Restaurant,
laundry, room service, attached
bath, hot water, TV **Metro
Reservations** See page 454

Hotel Dwarika
Location On NH12 **Address**
Hospital Road **Tel** 232626
Rooms 17 **Tariff** Rs 250-750
Credit Cards NA **Facilities**
Kitchen, dining room, parking,
room service, attached bath, hot
water, TV in some rooms only

Rain Basera
Location Lakeside **Address**
Kota Road **Rooms** 4 **Tariff**

Rs 250 **Credit Cards** NA
Facilities Basic accommodation
Jhalawar Reservations Jal
Sansadhan Vibhag, NH12, Patan
Road, Jhalawar **Tel** 07432-
232349 **Mobile** 09414310401
Contact Parnami

Abhay Days Inn
Location Near Rai-ka-Bagh
Railway Station **Address** Paota
Circle **Tel** 2542980-81/83-85 **Fax**
2542978 **Website** abhaydays.
com **Rooms** 72 **Tariff** Rs 2,700-
5,000; TE **Credit Cards** Visa,
Master **Facilities** Restaurant,
health club, laundry, shopping
arcade, swimming pool, travel
desk, Jacuzzi, room service, TV

Haveli Guest House
Location Opp Toorji-ka-Jhalra
Address Makrana Mohalla **Tel**
2614615 **Website** haveliguest
house.net **Rooms** 24 **Tariff**
Rs 300-2,000 **Credit Cards** NA
Facilities Restaurant, cultural
programmes, laundry, village
safari, attached bath, hot water

Hotel Chandra Inn
Location Near airport **Address**
Panchbatti Circle, Airport Road
Tel 2636583-84, 2433610/ 0765
Fax 5103791 **Website** chandra
inn.com **Rooms** 65 **Tariff**
Rs 1,295-2,495; TE **Credit
Cards** AmEx, Visa, Master
Facilities Restaurant, travel
desk, laundry, room service, TV

Hotel City Palace
Location Central **Address** 32,
Nai Sarak **Tel** 2431933, 2627130
Fax 2639033 **Email** hotel@
satyam.net.in **Rooms** 21 **Tariff**
Rs 990-1,190; TE **Credit Cards**
Visa, Master, BoB **Facilities**
Restaurant, laundry, travel desk,
room service, hot water, TV

Hotel Devi Bhawan
Location Next to Army Branch
Recruitment Office **Address**
1, Defence Laboratory Road,
Ratanada Circle **Tel** 2511067
Mobile 09828035359 **Telefax**
2512215 **Website** devibhawan.
com **Rooms** 14 **Tariff** Rs 850-
1,500 **Credit Cards** Visa, Master
Facilities Restaurant, swimming
pool, laundry, sightseeing, travel
desk, room service, TV

Hotel Durag Villas
Location Near Circuit House
Address House No. 1, Old
Public Park, Near KN Hall, Rai-
ka-Bagh **Tel** 2512298 **Website**
duragvillas.com **Rooms** 12 **Tariff**
Rs 300-1,250; TE **Credit Cards**
NA **Facilities** Restaurant, safaris,
Ayurvedic treatments, travel
desk, laundry, room service, TV

Hotel Ghoomar RTDC
Location Near Paota Circle
Address High Court Road **Tel**
2544010/ 8010/ 20 **Fax** 2545010
Rooms 75 **Tariff** Rs 550-1,200;
TE **Credit Cards** NA **Facilities**
Restaurant, laundry, room
service, hot water, TV **Metro
Reservations** See page 454

Hotel Rajputana Palace
Location Near airport **Address**
Panchbatti Circle, Airport Road
Tel 2431672/ 8059 **Fax** 2438672
Website hotelrajputana.com
Rooms 48, suites 2 **Tariff**
Rs 900-3,000 **Credit Cards**
AmEx, Visa, Master **Facilities**
Restaurants, bar, laundry, doctor-
on-call, room service, TV

Hotel Rajwara Palace
Location Opp Vet Hospital
Address Ratanada **Tel** 2515447/
3281 **Rooms** 18 **Tariff** Rs 995-
1,150; TE **Credit Cards** AmEx,
Master, BoB **Facilities**

Bal Samand Lake Palace/ Garden Retreat SPA
Location Outskirts, near BSF Camp **Address** Mandore Road **Tel** 2572321-27 **Fax** 2571240 **Website** jodhpurheritage.com **Rooms** 10, suites 26 **Tariff** Rs 4,100-11,000; TE **Credit Cards** AmEx, Visa, Master, BoB, Diners **Facilities** Restaurant, bar, coffee shop, horse-carriage ride, jogging trails, spa, swimming pool, travel desk, room service **Delhi Reservations** WelcomHeritage, 31 FF, Siri Fort Road, New Delhi **Tel** 011-26266650-55 **Fax** 26266656 **Website** welcom heritagehotels.com

Hotel Ajit Bhawan Palace SPA
Location Central **Address** Near Circuit House **Tel** 2510610/ 1410 **Fax** 2510674 **Website** ajitbhawan.com **Rooms** 72 **Tariff** Rs 4,500-7,000; TE **Credit Cards** AmEx, Visa, Master, Diners **Facilities** Restaurant, gym, laundry, spa, shopping arcade, swimming pool, travel desk, room service, TV

Hotel Karni Bhawan
Location Near Umaid Bhawan **Address** Palace Road,

Ratanada **Tel** 2512101-02 **Fax** 2512105 **Website** karnihotels. com **Rooms** 30 **Tariff** Rs 1,650-2,990; TE **Credit Cards** AmEx, Visa, Master **Facilities** Restaurant, swimming pool, travel desk, laundry, room service, hot water, TV

Hotel Ranbanka Palace SPA
Location Near airport **Address** Circuit House Road **Tel** 2512801-02 **Fax** 2510162 **Website** ranbankahotels.com **Rooms** 56 **Tariff** Rs 4,500-5,500; TE **Credit Cards** AmEx, Visa, Master **Facilities** Restaurants, indoor games, laundry, health spa, swimming pool, yoga, jeep/ camel safari, Meena Bazaar, folk music and dance, room service, TV **Delhi Reservations** WZ-272, G-Block, Hari Nagar, New Delhi **Mobile** 09811892683

Pal Haveli
Location Lakeside **Address** Gulab Sagar, Clock Tower **Tel** 3293328, 2638344 **Mobile** 09829243247 **Website** palhaveli.com **Rooms** 20 **Tariff** Rs 1,750-2,250; TE **Credit Cards** NA **Facilities** Restaurant, safari, sightseeing, travel desk,

museum, laundry, doctor-on-call, room service, attached bath, hot water, TV **Contact** Mahesh Karan

Taj Umaid Bhawan Palace SPA
Location On a hill **Address** Near Circuit House **Tel** 2510101 **Fax** 2510100 **Website** tajhotels.com **Rooms** 64 **Tariff** Rs 14,000-1,15,000; TE **Credit Cards** AmEx, Visa, Master, BoB, Diners **Facilities** Restaurant, bar, coffee shop, health club, spa, laundry, games, swimming pool, travel desk, room service, TV

IN JHALAMAND STD 0291
Jhalamand Garh
Location Udaipur-Ahmedabad Highway **Address** PO Jhalamand, Dist Jodhpur **Tel** 2720481 **Mobile** 09351514444 **Website** heritagehotelsindia. com **Rooms** 18 **Tariff** Rs 2,500-4,000; TE **Credit Cards** Visa, Master **Facilities**

ACCOMMODATION LISTINGS

Jeep safaris, birding at Lal Niwas

Home kitchen, village safari, TV lounge, garden, parking, travel assistance, folk music and dance, attached bath, hot water **Contact** Raghavendra Singh

IN LUNI STD 02931
Fort Chanwa
Location Around local Craft Centre **Address** Village Luni, Dist Jodhpur **Telefax** 284216 **Website** fortchanwa.com **Rooms** 31 **Tariff** Rs 2,500-4,500; TE **Credit Cards** Visa, Master **Facilities** Restaurant, bar, folk dance and music, jeep safaris, health club, swimming pool, laundry, massage, room service, hot water **Jodhpur Reservations** Dalip Bhawan, 1 PWD Road, Jodhpur **Tel** 0291-2432460 **Gurgaon Reservations** Carnival Hotels, DLF, Plot No. 56, Sector 44, Gurgaon **Tel** 0124-6452704 **Email** carnival @vsnl.net

IN PHALODI STD 02925
Lal Niwas
Location Dadha Haveli premises **Address** Dadha's Mohalla, Phalodi, Dist Jodhpur **Tel** 223813 **Fax** 224886

Website lalniwas.com **Rooms** 19 **Tariff** Rs 2,000-2,600; TE **Credit Cards** Visa, Master **Facilities** Restaurant, museum, swimming pool, birdwatching tour, camel/ jeep safari, folk music and dance, room service, TV **Delhi Reservations** WelcomHeritage, 31 FF, Siri Fort Road, New Delhi **Tel** 011-26266650-55 **Website** welcomheritagehotels.com

IN ROHET STD 02936
Rohet Garh
Location Opp Krishna Temple **Address** VPO Rohet, Dist Pali **Tel** 268231/ 531 **Website** rohetgarh.com **Rooms** 29 **Tariff** Rs 2,750-5,000 **Credit Cards** Visa, Master **Facilities** Restaurant, safaris, cultural programmes, laundry, massage, swimming pool **Jodhpur Reservations** Rohet House, PWD Road, Jodhpur **Tel** 0291-2431161 **Mobile** 09314711016 **Contact** Siddharth Singh **Delhi Reservations** Palaces of India, 75 GF, Sant Nagar, East of Kailash, New Delhi **Tel** 011-41659622, 26236610 **Website** palacesofindia.com

IN SARDAR SAMAND STD 02960
Sardar Samand Palace
Location Banks of Sardar Samand Lake **Address** Sardar Samand, Dist Pali **Tel** 245001-03 **Rooms** 19 **Tariff** Rs 3,300-4,400; TE **Credit Cards** Visa, Master **Facilities** Restaurant, travel desk, swimming pool, cultural shows, safaris, library, indoor games, laundry, room service, TV **Delhi Reservations** *See Lal Niwas left*

Restaurant, laundry, room service, hot water, TV

Hotel Ratnawali
Location City centre **Address** 149/ 150, Nai Sarak **Tel** 2555698-99 **Fax** 2547764 **Website** hotelratnawali.com **Rooms** 24 **Tariff** Rs 1,050-1,350; TE **Credit Cards** Master, Visa **Facilities** Kitchen, village safaris, travel desk, doctor-on-call, laundry, room service, attached bath, hot water, TV

Hotel Residency Palace
Location Near airport **Address** High Court Colony, Ratanada **Tel** 2639896, 2431747 **Telefax** 2640747 **Website** hotelresidency palace.com **Rooms** 26 **Tariff** Rs 849-1,999; TE **Credit Cards** AmEx, Visa, Master, Diners **Facilities** Restaurant, coffee shop, laundry, room service, TV

Indrashan Guest House
HOMESTAY
Location Central **Address** 593, High Court Colony **Tel** 2440665, 2438593 **Website** rajputana discovery.com **Rooms** 6 **Tariff** Rs 900-1200 (including breakfast) **Credit Cards** NA **Facilities** Paid lunch/ dinner with family, sightseeing and safaris arranged on request

Jodhpur Park Plaza
Location Near the airport **Address** Jhalamand House, Airport Road **Tel** 5105000, 5106000 **Rooms** 45 **Tariff** Rs 5,000-9,000; TE **Credit Cards** AmEx, Visa, Master **Facilities** Restaurants, coffee shop, health club, pool, laundry, room service, TV

Kalinga Hotel
Location Opp railway station **Address** Station Road

IN AUWA STD 02935
About 11 km from Marwar
junction in Pali District

Fortress Auwa HERITAGE
Address VPO Auwa, Via
Marwar Junction, Dist Pali **Tel**
264125 **Email** fortress_auwa@
rediffmail.com **Rooms** 15,
suites 3, tents 2 **Tariff**
Rs 4,000-6,000; TE **Credit
Cards** NA **Facilities** Restaurant,
bar, swimming pool, sightseeing, cycle/ horse/ jeep
safaris, gym, massage room,
cultural programmes, village
safari, lectures and battlefield
tours, room service, attached
bath **Jodhpur Reservations**
123 Golf Course, Jodhpur
Tel 0291-2440044

IN CHANDELAO STD 0291
Chandelao Fort is about 40 km
from Jodhpur

Chandelao Garh HERITAGE
Location Jodhpur-Ajmer
Highway **Address** Village
Chandelao, Dist Jodhpur **Tel**
6538004 **Mobile** 09414477694
Email chandelao@rediffmail.
com **Rooms** 16 **Tariff**
Rs 1,750-1,950; TE **Credit
Cards** NA **Facilities** Home
kitchen, dining hall, travel desk,
village walks, jeep safari, TV
lounge, attached bath, hot
water **Contact** Praduman Singh

IN DHAMLI STD 02935
Fort Dhamli Hotel in Pali District
is about 85 km from Jodhpur

Fort Dhamli HERITAGE
Location Surrounded by thick
forests **Address** Fort Dhamli,
Dist Pali **Tel** 267739 **Rooms** 12
Email ft_dhamli@hotmail.com

Tariff Rs 800-4,000 **Credit
Cards** NA **Facilities** Restaurant,
garden, horse riding, village
tour, laundry, room service, hot
water **Jaipur Reservations**
Thakur Inder Singh Rathore,
C-59B Siwar Area, Bapunagar,
Jaipur **Tel** 0141-2711468
Fax 356959

IN KHEJRALA STD 02930
Fort Khejrala Hotel is about 80
km from Jodhpur – good for
visits to stepwells and chhatris

Fort Khejrala HERITAGE
Location 80 km from Jodhpur
Address VPO Khejrala, Dist
Jodhpur **Tel** 25811 **Website**
campsofindia.com **Rooms** 25
Tariff Rs 2,500-3,000; TE **Credit
Cards** Visa, Master **Facilities**
Home kitchen, dining hall,
swimming pool, jeep safari,
indoor games, room service
Udaipur Reservations Ram
Pratap Palace, 5-B Alkapuri,
Fateh Sagar, Udaipur **Tel** 0294-
2431701 **Mobile** 09414159969
Contact Amit Vikram Singh

IN MANVAR STD 02928
Manvar Desert Resort, about
110 km from Jodhpur, offers
camel/ jeep safaris

Manvar Desert Resort
Location 10 km before Dechu
on Jodhpur-Jaisalmer Highway,
amidst sand dunes **Address**
NH114, PO Khiyansaria, Dist
Jodhpur **Tel** 268021, 268011
Mobile 09413323308 **Website**
manvar.com **Rooms** 21
cottages **Tariff** Rs 3,500-6,200
Credit Cards Visa, Master
Facilities Restaurant, bar,
swimming pool, desert and
village safari, birdwatching,

sightseeing, folk dance and
music, library, recreation room,
shopping arcade, traditional
massage, laundry, doctor-on-
call, room service, attached
bath, hot water **Jodhpur
Reservations** Manvar Resort &
Camp Pvt Ltd, 646, Hanuwant
Nagar 'A' (Opp Shiv Temple),
BJS Colony, Jodhpur-342001
Telefax 0291-2546188
Mobile 09414100424,
09414129767

Manvar Desert Camp TENTS
Location 7 km from Manvar
resort, surrounded by sand
dunes **Address** NH114, PO
Khiyansaria, Dist Jodhpur **Tel**
268021, 268011 **Mobile**
09413323308 **Website**
manvar.com **Rooms** 25 deluxe
tents **Tariff** Rs 4,500-7,500
Credit Cards Visa, Master
Facilities Dining tent, kitchen,
camel riding, desert/ village
safari, birdwatching, village
walks, campfire, folk dance and
music, attached bath, hot water
Jodhpur Reservations See
Manvar Desert Resort left

IN SODAWAS STD 02932
Karni Kot is 70 km from Jodhpur

Karni Kot HERITAGE
Address Village Sodawas, Near
Pali **Tel** 244928 **Website**
karnihotels.com **Rooms** 10
Tariff Rs 1,950-2,450 (including
breakfast); TE **Credit Cards** NA
Facilities Restaurant, horse
safari, sightseeing, laundry,
room service, attached bath,
hot water **Jodhpur
Reservations** Hotel Karni
Bhawan, Palace Road,
Ratanada, Jodhpur **Tel** 0291-
2512101-02 **Fax** 2512105

ACCOMMODATION LISTINGS

Tel 2627338, 2615871-72 **Fax** 2627314 **Website** kalingahotel. com **Rooms** 34 **Tariff** Rs 1,100-2,800; TE **Credit Cards** Visa, Master, BoB **Facilities** Restaurant, bar, room service, TV

Mandore Guest House
Location Near Mandore Garden **Address** Dadavari Lane, Mandore **Tel** 2571620 **Mobile** 09829147470 **Website** mandore. com **Rooms** 14 cottages **Tariff** Rs 500-950; TE **Credit Cards** Visa, Master **Facilities** Village safari, travel desk, laundry, TV

Raman Palace Guest House
Location Opp Kesar Bagh **Address** Shiv Road, Ratanada **Tel** 2516426/ 3980 **Rooms** 22 **Tariff** Rs 350-1,500 **Credit Cards** NA **Facilities** Restaurant, parking, sightseeing, room service, attached bath, TV

Ratan Vilas Haveli
Location Near Ratnada Circle **Address** Loco Shed Road, Ratanada **Tel** 2614418, 2613011 **Mobile** 09829127877 **Website** ratanvilas.com **Rooms** 21 **Tariff** Rs 1,400-1,650 **Credit Cards** Visa, Master **Facilities** Restaurant, village safari, sightseeing, pickup/ transfers, laundry, doctor-on-call, room service, TV

Shahi Guest House **HOMESTAY**
Location Opp Narsingh Temple **Address** City Police, Gandhi Street **Tel** 2623802 **Mobile** 09828252120 **Rooms** 4, suite 1 **Tariff** Rs 600-1,200 **Credit Cards** Visa, Master **Facilities** Restaurant, home-cooked meals, camel/ jeep safari, sightseeing, free pick-up, laundry, TV

Shivam Guest House
Location Near Clock Tower

Address Makrana Mohalla **Tel** 2610688 **Rooms** 10 **Tariff** Rs 450-650 **Credit Cards** NA **Facilities** Restaurant, doctor, laundry, ticket booking, room service, attached bath, TV

Taj Hari Mahal
Location City centre **Address** 5, Residency Road **Tel** 2439700 **Fax** 2614451 **Website** tajhotels. com **Rooms** 93 **Tariff** Rs 7,500-14,500; TE **Credit Cards** AmEx, Visa, Master, BoB, Diners **Facilities** Restaurant, bar, health club, laundry, swimming pool, travel desk, room service,TV **Delhi Reservations** Taj Reservations Network, 36 GF, Chandralok Building, 36 Janpath, New Delhi **Tel** 011-23322333/ 6901/ 9737

IN BISHNOI STD 0291
Bishnoi Village Camp & Resort
Location Near Guda Lake **Address** VPO Guda Bishnoiyan, Dist Jodhpur **Tel** 2868230 **Mobile** 09414129233 **Website** bishnoivillage.com **Rooms** 8 **Tariff** Rs 1,200-2,000; TE **Credit Cards** NA **Facilities** Restaurant, sightseeing, village walks, safaris, birdwatching, traditional massage, laundry, room service

IN OSIAN STD 0291
Camp Thar **TENTS**
Location In the dunes **Address** Osian **Website** campthar.com **Rooms** 20 tents **Tariff** Rs 7,000 (with all meals and camel safari) **Credit Cards** NA **Facilities** Dining hall, cultural programmes, safaris, attached bath, hot water **Jodhpur Reservations** Plot No. 33, Mandore Road, Jodhpur **Telefax** 0291-2573466 **Mobile** 09414128574 **Contact** Digvijay Singh **Delhi Reservations** Capt Sandeep Shekhawat **Mobile** 9891766996

Reggie's Camel Camp **TENTS**
Location In the dunes **Address** Osian **Website** camelcamposian. com **Rooms** 50 tents **Tariff** Rs 9,000 (inclusive of all meals and camel rides) **Credit Cards** Visa, Master **Facilities** Restaurant, safari, attached bath, hot water **Jodhpur Reservations** C/o The Jodhpur Safari Club, High Court Colony, Jodhpur **Tel** 0291-2437023, 2610192 **Mobile** 09828142012

IN PHALODI STD 02925
Dera Sand Dune Retreat **SPA**
Location Atop a high sand dune **Address** Village Jamba, Tehsil Phalodi, Dist Jodhpur **Tel** 290389 **Website** farhorizonindia.com **Rooms** 18 cottages **Tariff** Rs 3,800-4,400 (inclusive of meals and desert safari) **Credit Cards** Visa, Master **Facilities** Restaurant, bar, spa swimming pool, horse ride, camel trekking, safaris, room service, TV **Delhi Reservations** Far Horizon, B-209, CR Park, New Delhi **Tel** 011-41602100, 26277222

IN ROHET STD 02936
Rohet Wilderness Camp **TENTS**
Location Amidst sand dunes (16 km from Rohet Garh) **Address** VPO Rohet, Dist Pali **Rooms** 6 luxury tents **Tariff** Rs 7,500-8,500 (inclusive of all meals and safari); TE **Credit Cards** AmEx, Visa, Master **Facilities** Dining tent, safaris, cultural programmes, laundry, attached bath, hot water **Reservations** *See Rohet Garh on page 474*

KALAKHO

Dera Lakeview Retreat
Address Kalakho, Tehsil Sikrai, Dist Dausa **Tel** 01420-246088 **Mobile** 09414035871 **Website**

farhorizon.com **Rooms** 12 **Tariff** Rs 3,780-6,500; TE **Credit Cards** Visa, Master **Facilities** Restaurant, swimming pool, camel/ jeep safari, horse riding, village safaris, home visits, sightseeing, laundry, doctor-on-call, room service, TV **Delhi Reservations** *See Dera Sand Dune Retreat left*

Umaid Lake Palace
Location Lakeside, off Jaipur-Agra Highway **Address** PO

HERITAGE EXPERIENCES: KALAKHO

IN BHANDAREJ STD 01427
Bhadrawati Palace
Location Main market **Address** Village Bhandarej, Tehsil Dausa, Dist Jaipur **Tel** 283351 **Mobile** 09414043117 **Website** bhadrawatipalace. com **Rooms** 35 **Tariff** Rs 1,500; TE **Credit Cards** NA **Facilities** Restaurant, swimming pool, garden, camel safari, sightseeing **Jaipur Reservations** Karan's Guest House, Chomu House, Jaipur **Tel** 0141-2363262

IN MADHOGARH STD 01429
Fort Madhogarh
Location Off Jaipur-Agra Highway from Bassi **Address** Village Madhogarh, Tehsil Bassi, Dist Jaipur **Tel** 281141 **Mobile** 09829056676 **Website** fortmadhogarh.com **Rooms** 16 **Tariff** Rs 1,390-1,990; TE **Credit Cards** NA **Facilities** Dining hall, coffee shop, camel/ jeep safaris, sightseeing, laundry, doctor-on-call, TV **Jaipur Reservations** Madhogarh House, G-176 Udaipath, Shamnagar, Jaipur **Tel** 0141-2291409

KARAULI STD 07464

HERITAGE EXPERIENCES: KARAULI

Bhanwar Vilas Palace
Location Outskirts of Karauli city **Address** Agra-Jaipur Highway **Tel** 220024 **Mobile** 09414054257 **Website** karauli.com **Rooms** 20, cottages 5 **Tariff** Rs 1,400-3,000; TE **Credit Cards** NA **Facilities** Restaurant, camping, doctor-on-call, laundry, sightseeing, swimming pool, room service

Ramathra Fort
Location Surrounded by hills, overlooking Kalisil Lake **Address** PO Sapotra, Dist Karauli **Mobile** 09829013475 **Contact** Ravi Rajpal **Rooms** 6 tents **Tariff** Rs 9,200-10,350 (inclusive of all meals, taxes) **Credit Cards** NA **Facilities** Restaurant, bar, sightseeing,

Kalakho, Dist Dausa **Tel** 01427-283426 **Mobile** 09414035666 **Website** lakepalace.com **Rooms** 20 **Tariff** Rs 2,500-4,000; TE **Credit Cards** Visa, Master **Facilities** Restaurant, swimming pool, camel/ jeep safari, sight-seeing, yoga, games, laundry, room service, attached bath, hot water, TV **Delhi Reservations** Palaces of India, 75 GF, Sant Nagar, East of Kailash, New Delhi **Tel** 011-41659622 **Website** palacesofindia.com

KEOLADEO GHANA NP

IN BHARATPUR STD 05644
Birder's Inn
Location Park entrance **Address** Bird Sanctuary Road **Tel** 227346 **Mobile** 09414023340 **Telefax** 222830 **Website** birdersinn.com **Rooms** 12 **Tariff** Rs 1,000-1,265 **Credit Cards** NA **Facilities**

Bhanwar Vilas Palace

GIREESH GV

safaris, trekking, laundry, room service **Jaipur Reservations** C/o Ambika Exports, Naila House, Moti Doongri Road, Jaipur **Tel** 0141-2607665, 2615059 **Mobile** 09414057047 **Contact** Gitanjali Rajpal

Restaurant, resident naturalist, library, safari, laundry, room service, attached bath, hot water, TV **Delhi Reservations Tel** 011-26914417 **Contact** Dipin Gurung

Circuit House
Location Collectorate **Address** Agra Road **Tel** 223766 **Rooms** 7 **Tariff** Rs 300; TE **Credit Cards** NA **Facilities** Basic accom-modation, attached bath

Bharatpur Forest Lodge FRH
Location Inside the sanctuary **Address** Keoladeo NP, Bharatpur **Tel** 222760 **Fax** 222864 **Email** itdchba@sancharnet.in **Rooms** 17 **Tariff** Rs 1,400-1,800; TE **Credit Cards** AmEx, Visa, Master **Facilities** Restaurant, bar, guide, bicycles, laundry, room service, attached bath, hot water, TV **Delhi Reservations**

ACCOMMODATION LISTINGS

IN BHARATPUR STD 05644

Laxmi Vilas Palace
Location Near Circuit House **Address** Kakaji ki Kothi, Old Agra-Jaipur Road **Tel** 223523, 231199 **Fax** 225259 **Website** laxmivilas.com **Rooms** 30 **Tariff** Rs 3,000-4,350; TE **Credit Cards** NA **Facilities** Health club, restaurant, bar, swimming pool, laundry, room service, attached bath, TV

The Bagh Resort

Location Near Laxmi Vilas Palace **Address** Old Agra-Achmera Road **Tel** 228333, 225415 **Website** thebagh.com **Rooms** 21 **Tariff** Rs 3,500-4,500; TE **Credit Cards** Visa, Master **Facilities** Restaurant, bar, coffee shop, safari, gym, gift shop, laundry, room service,

ITDC, 3 Parliament Street, Jeevan Vihar Building, New Delhi **Tel** 011-23361607, 23365532

Hotel Eagle's Nest
Location Near railway station **Address** Bird Sanctuary Road **Tel** 225144 **Fax** 222310 **Email** hoteleaglesnest@indiatimes.com **Rooms** 12 **Tariff** Rs 400-1,050 **Credit Cards** NA **Facilities**

TV **Delhi Reservations** Nature Safari Pvt Ltd, 106-107, A-3, Sector-11, Rohini, New Delhi **Tel** 011-27570446

IN DHOLPUR STD 05642

Raj Niwas Palace
Location 35 km from Agra, near Collector's House **Address** Agra-Gwalior Highway, Dholpur **Tel** 220216 **Rooms** 9 **Tariff** Rs 8,500-9,000; TE **Credit Cards** NA **Facilities** Restaurant, bar, sightseeing, cycle safaris, pool table, laundry, doctor-on-call, room service, attached bath, hot water **Delhi Reservations** 141, SF, Sant Nagar, East of Kailash, New Delhi **Tel** 26436572-73, 41620674

IN PEHARSAR STD 05643

Hotel Chandra Mahal Haveli
Location 1 km off highway, 23 km from Bharatpur **Address** Village Peharsar, Jaipur-Agra Road, Nadbai Tehsil **Tel** 264336 **Website** chandra mahalhaveli. com **Rooms** 23 **Tariff** Rs 1,650-2,600; TE **Credit Cards** NA **Facilities** Restaurant, buffet dining, attached bath, hot water **Gurgaon Reservations** C-892, BB, Sushant Lok Phase-I, Gurgaon **Tel** 0124-2385184 **Fax** 4044657

Restaurant, bar, garden, laundry, room service, hot water, TV **Delhi Reservations Tel** 011-35224789

Hotel Park Palace
Location Kumher Gate Crossing **Address** Kumher Gate **Tel** 223783/ 222, 223051 **Rooms** 38 **Tariff** Rs 250-750 **Credit Cards** NA **Facilities** Restaurant, bar, garden, laundry, room service, TV

Hotel Park Regency
Location Saras Chauraha **Address** Bird Sanctuary Road **Tel** 224284/ 232 **Fax** 234325 **Email** hotelparkregency@yahoo.co.uk **Rooms** 8 **Tariff** Rs 850-1,050 **Credit Cards** NA **Facilities** Restaurant, bicycles, laundry, doctor-on-call, room service, attached bath, TV

Hotel Pratap Palace
Location Saras Chauraha **Address** Bird Sanctuary Road **Tel** 224245, 222211 **Fax** 224412 **Website** pratappalace.net **Rooms** 30 **Tariff** Rs 550-750 **Credit Cards** NA **Facilities** Restaurant, swimming pool, bicycles, laundry, room service, attached bath, hot water, TV

Hotel Saras RTDC
Location Park entrance **Address** Saras Chauraha, NH11 **Tel** 223700 **Fax** 222310 **Rooms** 28 **Tariff** Rs 350-900 **Credit Cards** NA **Facilities** Restaurant, laundry, room service, attached bath, hot water, TV **Metro Reservations** See page 454

Hotel Sunbird
Location 200m from sanctuary **Address** Agra-Jaipur Road **Tel** 221533, 225701 **Fax** 228344 **Website** hotelsunbird.com **Rooms** 12 **Tariff** Rs 700-1,050; TE **Credit Cards** NA **Facilities** Restaurant, laundry, hot water

Hotel Udai Vilas Palace
Location Near the sanctuary **Address** NH11, Fatehpur Sikri Road **Tel** 233161-62 **Fax** 229955 **Website** udaivilaspalace.com **Rooms** 48 **Tariff** Rs 3,500-9,600; TE **Credit Cards** NA **Facilities** Restaurant, bar, swimming pool, sauna, laundry, doctor-on-call, room service, attached bath, TV

KISHANGARH STD 01463

HERITAGE EXPERIENCES

Phool Mahal Palace
Location Near fort **Address** Old City **Tel** 247405 **Telefax** 247505 **Website** royal kishangarh.com **Rooms** 17 **Tariff** Rs 2,000-2,500; TE **Credit Cards** AmEx, Visa, Master **Facilities** Restaurant, sightseeing, swimming pool, library, yoga, folk music and dance, doctor-on-call, laundry, room service, attached bath, hot water, TV

IN ROOPANGARH STD 01497
Roopangarh Fort
Location Central **Address** Roopangarh, Dist Ajmer **Tel** 220444 **Telefax** 220217 **Website** royalkishangarh.com **Rooms** 22 **Tariff** Rs 2,000-3,600; TE **Credit Cards** NA **Facilities** Restaurant, camel safari, sightseeing, laundry, room service, terrace tennis court, doctor-on-call, room service, attached bath

Kadamb Kunj Resort
Location 3 km from Bharatpur **Address** NH11, Fatehpur Sikri Road **Tel** 220122, 225067 **Fax** 224241 **Website** kadambkunj.

com **Rooms** 16 **Tariff** Rs 1,950-2,450; TE **Credit Cards** NA **Facilities** Restaurant, bar, swimming pool, outdoor/ indoor games, cultural evenings, laundry, room service, TV

Shanti Kutir FRH
Location Inside the park **Address** WL Warden Office Complex **Tel** 222777 **Rooms** 5 **Tariff** Rs 600 **Credit Cards** NA **Facilities** Basic accommodation and meals, attached bath, hot water

KOTA STD 0744
Chambal Tourist Bungalow RTDC
Location Near Kishore Sagar Lake **Address** Sharbagh, Nayapura **Tel** 2326527 **Rooms** 12 **Tariff** Rs 500-800 **Credit Cards** NA **Facilities** Canteen, laundry, parking, room service, attached bath, hot water, TV **Metro Reservations** See page 454

Col Sudhir Farm FARM-STAY
Location Countryside **Address** Dhakerkheri, PO Kaithoon **Tel** 0744-2481841 **Mobile** 09829036384 **Email** victoria singh@hotmail.com **Website** colsudhirfarm.com **Rooms** 2 **Tariff** Rs 1,100-1,800 (all

inclusive) **Credit Cards** NA **Facilities** Experience of living in a traditional Rajasthani working farm, organic farming, DVD player, library, piano, laundry

Hotel Menaal Residency
Location Near bus stand **Address** Kilo-2, Bundi Road **Tel** 2371073-74 **Fax** 2371077 **Website** hotelmenaalkota.com **Rooms** 40 **Tariff** Rs 750-2,500; TE **Credit Cards** Visa, Master **Facilities** Restaurant, laundry, swimming pool, garden, room service, hot water, TV

Hotel Navrang
Location Near railway station **Address** Collectorate Circle, Civil Lines, Nayapura **Tel** 2323294, 2451253 **Telefax** 2450044 **Rooms** 25 **Tariff** Rs 385-2,400; TE **Credit Cards** Visa, Master **Facilities** Restaurant, laundry, room service, hot water, TV

Hotel Phul Plaza
Location Near GPO **Address** 6-D, Collectorate Circle, Civil Lines **Tel** 2329350-52 **Fax** 2322614 **Rooms** 20 **Tariff** Rs 550-1,200; TE **Credit Cards** Visa, Master **Facilities** Restaurant, laundry, room service, TV

ACCOMMODATION LISTINGS

Palkiya Haveli, beautiful period furniture and furnishings

Brijraj Bhawan Palace Hotel
Location Collectorate Circle
Address Civil Lines, Nayapura
Tel 2450529 **Fax** 2450057
Website indiaheritagehotel.com
Rooms 8 **Tel** Rs 1,740-2,900;
TE **Credit Cards** Visa, Master
Facilities Restaurant, laundry,
hot water, TV

Palkiya Haveli
Location Near Suraj Pole
Address Mokha Para **Tel**
2387497 **Telefax** 2387075
Mobile 09829747316 **Website**
alsisarhaveli.com **Rooms** 6
Tariff Rs 1,400-2,000 (with
breakfast); TE **Credit Cards** NA
Facilities Restaurant, travel
desk, transport arranged,
recreation area, folk dances and
puppet shows, jeep safari,
laundry, room service, hot water

Sukhdham Kothi
Location Near railway station
Address Civil Lines **Tel**
2320081, 2332661 **Fax**
2327781 **Email** sukhdham@
datainfosys.net **Rooms** 14
Tariff Rs 1,000-1,500; TE
Credit Cards Visa, Master
Facilities Restaurant, laundry,
swimming pool, room service,
attached bath, hot water

Umed Bhawan Palace
Location Near Kherli Phatak
Address Railway Station Road
Tel 2325262-65 **Fax** 2451110
Rooms 32 **Tariff** Rs 1,700-
3,500; TE **Credit Cards** AmEx,
Visa, Master, Diners **Facilities**
Restaurant, bar, games, indoor/
outdoor games, laundry, room
service, TV **Delhi Reservations**
WelcomHeritage, 31 FF,
Siri Fort Road, New Delhi
Tel 011-26266650-55 **Website**
welcomheritagehotels.com

Hotel Bhainsrorgarh Fort
Location Riverside **Address**
The Palace, PO Bhainsrorgarh,
via Kota, Dist Chittaurgarh **Tel**
232006 **Mobile** 09414186321
Website bhainsrorgarh.com
Rooms 5 suites **Tariff**
Rs 8,000-10,000 (all inclusive)
Credit Cards NA **Facilities**
Dining hall, village walks,
boating, birdwatching, laundry,
room service (tea/ coffee only)
Delhi Reservations Flat No.
2310, Green Glade Apartments,
Sector B-2, Vasant Kunj, New
Delhi **Contact** Hemendra Singh
Tel 011-32976879 **Mobile**
09350834515

Kuchaman Fort Hotel
Location Mountain top
Address Kuchaman City,
Dist Nagaur **Tel** 220882
Telefax 220884 **Website**
kuchamanfort.com **Rooms**
45 **Tariff** Rs 3,000-5,500; TE
Credit Cards Visa, Master
Facilities Restaurant, safari,
sightseeing, cultural
programmes, swimming pool,
room service, attached bath,
hot water, TV **Delhi Reserva-
tions** A-28, DDA Flats,
Vasant Vihar, New Delhi
Tel 011-42705271 **Telefax**
26155483 **Contact** Sebastian
Mobile 09313353431
Email kuchamanfort@
touchtelindia.net

Forest Rest House
(Ranakankar) **FRH**
Location Inside the sanctuary
Address Kumbhalgarh Wildlife
Sanctuary **Rooms** 3 **Tariff**
Rs 200 **Credit Cards** NA
Facilities Basic accommodation,
caretaker can arrange food,
attached bath **Kumbhalgarh
Reservations** ACF, Kumbhalgarh
Wildlife Sanctuary, Sadri **Tel**
02934-285529 **Udaipur Reser-
vations** Dy Chief Wildlife Warden,
Udaipur **Tel** 0294-2453686

Forest Rest House (Sadri) **FRH**
Location On the periphery
Address Kumbhalgarh Wildlife
Sanctuary **Rooms** 2 **Tariff**
Rs 200 **Facilities and Reserva-
tions** *See FRH Ranakankar
above*

Forest Rest House (Sumer) **FRH**
Location Inside the sanctuary
Address Kumbhalgarh Wildlife

Hotel Aodhi
Location Hillside, near
Kumbhalgarh Fort **Address**
PO Kelwara **Tel** 242341-46
Fax 242349 **Rooms** 23, suites
3 **Tariff** Rs 5,000-6,500; TE
Credit Cards AmEx, Visa,
Master **Facilities** Restaurant,
bar, swimming pool, café,
safaris, laundry, room service
Delhi Reservations HRH
Group of Hotels, C-41,
Gulmohar Park, New Delhi
Tel 011-26611273-75 **Website**
hrhindia.com

Sanctuary **Rooms** 3 **Tariff**
Rs 200 **Facilities and**
Reservations *See FRH*
Ranakankar left

Forest Rest House
(Thanchideri) **FRH**
Location Inside the sanctuary
Address Kumbhalgarh Wildlife
Sanctuary **Rooms** 2 **Tariff**
Rs 200 **Facilities and**

IN GHANERAO STD 02934
Ghanerao Royal Castle is 54
km from Kumbhalgarh Fort

Ghanerao Royal Castle
HERITAGE
Location Centre of town
Address VPO Ghanerao, Dist
Pali **Tel** 284035 **Website**
ghaneraoroyalcastle.com
Rooms 15, suites 2 **Tariff**
Rs 2,000-3,500; TE **Credit**
Cards NA **Facilities**
Restaurant, trekking, sight-
seeing, village walks, massage
parlour, laundry, room service

IN JOJAWAR STD 02935
Rawla Jojawar is 85 km from
Kumbhalgarh Fort

Rawla Jojawar **HERITAGE** **SPA**
Location Aravalli foothills

Reservations *See FRH*
Ranakankar left

Kumbhal Castle
Location Hillside **Address** Fort
Road, Kumbhalgarh, Dist
Rajsamand **Tel** 242171
Website kumbhalcastle.com
Rooms 12, dorm 1 **Tariff**
Rs 1,200-1,500, dorm bed
Rs 200; TE **Credit Cards** NA

Address VPO Jojawar,
via Manvar, Dist Pali
Tel 245011 **Website**
jojawar.com **Rooms** 35 **Tariff**
Rs 2,700-4,500; TE **Credit**
Cards Visa, Master **Facilities**
Home kitchen, dining hall,
swimming pool, spa, jeep
safari, Marwari horse safari,
train safari, trekking, TV in
lounge, room service,
attached bath, hot water
Udaipur Reservations
Ram Pratap Palace, 5-B
Alkapuri, Fateh Sagar Lake,
Udaipur **Tel** 0294-2431701
Contact Amit Vikram Singh
Mobile 09414159969
Reservations   Palaces of
India, 75 GF, Sant Nagar, East
of Kailash, New Delhi **Tel** 011-
41659622, 26236610 **Website**
palacesofindia.com

Facilities Restaurant, swimming
pool, travel desk, camel/ jeep
safari, cultural programmes,
laundry, room service, attached
bath, TV **Udaipur Reservations**
Heritage Holidayers, 14/21,
Oladar House, Lake Palace
Road, Udaipur **Tel** 0294-2423356
Fax 2423356 **Mobile**
09414162347 **Contact** Ekling
Singh Jhala

ACCOMMODATION LISTINGS

IN KELWARA STD 02954

Hotel Ratna Deep
Location 5 km from Kumbhalgarh Fort **Address** Kumbhalgarh, Kelwara, Dist Rajsamand **Tel** 242217/ 55, 242320 **Telefax** 242340 **Rooms** 14 **Tariff** Rs 500-950 **Facilities** Restaurant, parking, garden, attached bath, TV

Karni Palace Hotel
Location 6 km from sanctuary **Address** Bus Stand Road **Tel** 242003 **Rooms** 14, suites 3 **Tariff** Rs 750-2,000 **Credit Cards** Visa, Master **Facilities** Restaurant, travel desk, attached bath, TV

MOUNT ABU STD 02974

Hotel Aranya Village
Location En route to Delwara Temples **Address** Neelkanth Road **Tel** 238012-13 **Rooms** 52 **Tariff** Rs 1,950-4,500; TE **Credit Cards** Visa, Master **Facilities** Restaurant, bar, travel desk, sightseeing, games, swimming pool, laundry, room service, TV

Hotel Hillock
Location Opp petrol pump **Address** PB No. 40 **Tel** 238463-65 **Website** hotelhillock.com **Rooms** 40 **Tariff** Rs 2,990-5,590; TE **Credit Cards** AmEx, Visa, Master **Facilities** Restaurant, bar, coffee shop, travel desk, swimming pool, games, laundry, room service, TV

Hotel Lake Palace
Location 3 km from temple **Address** Opp Nakki Lake **Tel** 237154/ 254 **Website** savshanti.com **Rooms** 14 **Tariff** Rs 1,200-1,800; TE **Credit Cards** AmEx, Visa, Master **Facilities** Restaurant, travel desk, sightseeing, laundry, doctor-on-call, room service, TV

HERITAGE EXPERIENCES: MOUNT ABU

Cama Rajputana Club Resort
Location Near Circuit House **Address** Adhar Devi Road **Tel** 235171, 238205-06 **Website** camahotelsindia.com **Rooms** 42 **Tariff** Rs 3,200-4,950; TE **Credit Cards** Visa, Master **Facilities** Restaurant, travel desk, sightseeing, parking, swimming pool, health club, indoor games, laundry, doctor-on-call, room service, TV

Connaught House

Location City centre **Address** Rajendra Marg **Tel** 238560, 235439 **Rooms** 13 **Tariff** Rs 3,000-3,200; TE **Credit Cards** AmEx, Visa, Master, BoB **Facilities** Restaurant, travel desk, parking, laundry, room service, TV **Delhi Reservations** WelcomHeritage, 31 FF, Siri

Hotel Shikhar RTDC
Address Near petrol pump **Tel** 238944 **Rooms** 66 **Tariff** Rs 500-1,664 **Credit Cards** Visa **Facilities** Restaurant, garden, laundry, attached bath, hot water, TV **Metro Reservations** *See page 454*

Hotel Sunrise Palace
Location Opp petrol pump **Address** Old Bharatpur Kothi **Tel** 235573 **Website** sunrisepalace.co.in **Rooms** 14, suites 2 **Tariff** Rs 1,800-3,500; TE **Credit Cards** Visa, Master **Facilities** Restaurant, bar, travel desk, trekking, horse riding, Ayurvedic

Fort Road, New Delhi **Tel** 011-26266650-55 **Fax** 26266656 **Website** welcomheritagehotels.com

Kesar Bhawan Palace
Location Near the market **Address** Sunset Road **Tel** 235219, 238647 **Fax** 238551 **Website** kesarpalace.com **Rooms** 25 **Tariff** Rs 1,800-3,000; TE **Credit Cards** NA **Facilities** Restaurant, travel desk, sightseeing, guide, garden, laundry, doctor-on-call, room service, attached bath, hot water, TV

Palace Hotel
Location Near Delwara Temples **Address** Bikaner House, Delwara Road **Tel** 235121, 238673 **Website** palacehotelbikanerhouse.com **Rooms** 33 **Tariff** Rs 2,300-4,000; TE **Credit Cards** AmEx, Visa, Master **Facilities** Restaurant, bar, sightseeing, pool, indoor games, laundry, doctor-on-call, room service, attached bath, hot water, TV

massage, laundry, room service, attached bath, TV

Mushkil Aasaan Guest House
Location Near Telephone Exchange **Address** Global Hospital Road **Tel** 235150 **Mobile** 09824022565 **Rooms** 9 **Tariff** Rs 650-1,000 **Credit Cards** NA **Facilities** Restaurant, laundry, attached bath, TV

Rising Sun Retreat
Address Near Old Municipal Check Post **Tel** 238142, 235483 **Rooms** 12 **Tariff** Rs 1,000-1,200 **Credit Cards** Visa, Master **Facilities** Kitchen, travel desk,

sightseeing, car rental, nursery, folk dances, laundry, room service, TV **Udaipur Reservations** Heritage Holidayers, 14/ 21, Oladar House, Lake Palace Road, Udaipur **Tel** 0294-2423356 **Mobile** 09414162347 **Contact** Ekling Singh Jhala

Shri Ganesh Hotel
Location Near Sophia School **Address** Jaipur House Road **Tel** 237292, 235591 **Rooms** 17 **Tariff** Rs 150-500 **Credit Cards** NA **Facilities** Kitchen, travel desk, room service, attached bath, hot water, TV

The Jaipur House
Location Hilltop **Address** Near Nakki Lake **Tel** 235176 **Website** royalfamilyjaipur.com **Rooms** 23 **Tariff** Rs 2,500-4,900; TE **Credit Cards** AmEx, Visa, Master **Facilities** Restaurant, bar, laundry, room service, TV **Delhi Reservations** Palaces of India, 75 GF, Sant Nagar, East of Kailash, New Delhi **Tel** 011-41659622, 26236610 **Website** palacesofindia.com

NAGAUR STD 01582

Royal Camp `TENTS`
Location Inside the fort **Address** Nagaur Fort **Rooms** 10 tents, about 100 tents during the fair **Tariff** Rs 6,000-7,200; during Cattle Fair: Rs 11,000-12,100 (inclusive of all meals and taxes) **Credit Cards** AmEx, Visa, Master **Facilities** Restaurant, doctor-on-call, games, hot water **Jodhpur Reservations Tel**

HERITAGE EXPERIENCE: NAGAUR

IN KHIMSAR STD 01585
Khimsar Fort `SPA`
Location Edge of Thar Desert **Address** Bikaner Highway, Khimsar, Dist Nagaur **Tel** 262345-49 **Fax** 262228 **Website** khimsarfort.com **Rooms** 63 **Tariff** Rs 4,000-5,000; TE **Credit Cards** AmEx, Visa, Master **Facilities** Restaurant, museum, golf, handicrafts shop, star gazing, camel/ horse/ jeep safari, sightseeing, spa, swimming pool, yoga centre, room service, TV **Delhi Reservations** WelcomHeritage, 31 FF, Siri Fort Road, New Delhi **Tel** 011-26266650-55 **Fax** 26266656 **Website** welcomheritagehotels.com **Jaipur Reservations Tel** 0141-2229700

0291-2572321-27 **Fax** 2571240 **Delhi Reservations** See *Khimsar Fort above*

Shri Aditya Hotel
Location Ajmer Highway, near bus stand **Address** Near Laxmi Tara Cinema **Tel** 245438 **Rooms** 24 **Tariff** Rs 550-850 **Credit Cards** NA **Facilities** Restaurant, doctor-on-call, laundry, room service, hot water

Hotel Mahavir International
Location Vijay Vallabh Chowk

Address Deedwana Road **Tel** 243158 **Mobile** 09414729845 **Rooms** 30 **Tariff** Rs 350-1,050 **Credit Cards** NA **Facilities** Restaurant, bar, laundry, room service, hot water

Bhaskar Hotel
Location Opp Govt Hospital **Address** Bikaner Road **Tel** 420100 **Rooms** 16 **Tariff** Rs 250-800 **Credit Cards** NA **Facilities** Restaurant, bar, laundry, room service, hot water, TV

IN KHIMSAR STD 01585
Khimsar Sand Dunes Village
Location Heart of seven dunes of Akla **Address** Khimsar, District Nagaur **Tel** 262345-49 **Fax** 262228 **Rooms** 16 huts **Tariff** Rs 4,500-5,000; TE **Credit Cards** AmEx, Visa, Master **Facilities** Restaurant, cultural programmes, star gazing, yoga, massage, jeep safaris, camel rides, laundry, doctor-on-call, open-air showers with running hot and cold water **Reservations** *See Khimsar Fort left*

NEEMRANA STD 01494
HERITAGE EXPERIENCE
Neemrana Fort-Palace `SPA`
Location On a hillock off the Jaipur Highway **Address** Village Neemrana, Dist Alwar **Tel** 246006-08 **Fax** 246005 **Website** neemranahotels.com **Rooms** 44 **Tariff** Rs 1,500-15,000; TE **Credit Cards** Amex, Visa, Master **Facilities** Restaurant, bar, gym, health spa, Jacuzzi, indoor games, library, meditation, sight-seeing, swimming pool, yoga **Delhi Reservations** Neemrana Hotels, A-58, Nizamuddin East, New Delhi **Tel** 011-24356145/ 8962

ACCOMMODATION LISTINGS

HERITAGE EXPERIENCE

Fort Pokaran
Location Surrounded by five salt ranges **Address** PO Pokaran, Dist Jaisalmer **Tel** 222274 **Website** fortpokaran. com **Rooms** 19 **Tariff** Rs 1,700-4,999; TE **Credit Cards** NA **Facilities** Restaurant, swimming pool, travel desk, museum, library, village safari, wildlife safari, laundry, room service **Jodhpur Reservations** Pokaran House, PWD Road, Jodhpur **Tel** 0291-2432390 **Mobile** 09414469761 **Contact** Paramvijay Singh

Bharatpur Palace
Location Near Gau Ghat **Address** Yagna Ghat **Tel** 2772320 **Rooms** 20 **Tariff** Rs 500-1,000 **Credit Cards** NA **Facilities** Restaurant (breakfast, tea/ coffee only), travel desk, camel safari, laundry

Hotel Aroma
Location Near Brahma Chowk **Address** Kapaleshwar Road **Tel** 2772729 **Rooms** 9 **Tariff** Rs 200-450 **Credit Cards** NA **Facilities** Restaurant, travel desk, indoor games, laundry, room service, attached bath, hot water

Hotel Goyal Inn
Location Near gurudwara **Address** Gurudwara Road **Rooms** 56 **Tariff** Rs 1,250-2,250; TE **Credit Cards** Visa, Master **Facilities** Restaurant, room service, attached bath, TV **Delhi Reservations** Hotel Connections India, 11/27 FF, W Patel Nagar, New Delhi **Tel** 65481693-94 **Mobile** 9811759245, 9899767574 **Website** hotelconnectionsindia.com

Hotel Oasis
Address Near Ajmer Bus Stand **Tel** 2772100 **Mobile** 09828172102 **Email** karishparashar@yahoo.com **Rooms** 35 **Tariff** Rs 400-2,000; TE **Credit Cards** NA **Facilities** Restaurant, travel desk, jeep safari, swimming pool, laundry, room service, attached bath, TV

Hotel Peacock Holiday Resort
Location Near bus stand **Address** Panchkund Road **Tel** 2772093/ 414 **Fax** 2772516 **Email** arajouria@hotmail.com **Rooms** 32 **Tariff** Rs 800-900; TE **Credit Cards** AmEx, Visa, Master **Facilities** Restaurant, travel desk, safari, swimming pool, laundry, room service, TV

Hotel Pushkar Inn
Location Lakeside and Sunset Point **Address** Jaipur Ghat **Tel** 2772010/ 975 **Mobile** 09414006110 **Rooms** 18 **Tariff** Rs 150-1,000; TE **Credit Cards** NA **Facilities** Restaurant, travel desk, garden, laundry, room service, attached bath, hot water

Hotel Sarovar RTDC
Location Lakeside **Telefax** 2772040 **Rooms** 40, dorms 2 **Tariff** Rs 250-900, dorm bed Rs 50; TE **Credit Cards** NA **Facilities** Restaurant, travel desk, parking, indoor games, laundry, doctor-on-call, room service, attached bath, hot water, TV **Metro Reservations** See page 454

Hotel Sun Set
Location Near Pushkar Palace **Address** Jaipur Ghat **Tel** 2772382/ 725 **Rooms** 30 **Tariff** Rs 300-700 **Credit Cards** NA **Facilities** Restaurant, travel desk, laundry, room service, attached bath, hot water

Jodhpur Royal Tents TENTS
Location Fair grounds **Address** Mobile Camp **Rooms** 100 tents **Tariff** Rs 9,000-11,000 (inclusive of meals and taxes; rates vary year to year) **Credit Cards** AmEx, Visa, Master **Facilities** Dining hall, room service, safaris, hot water **Delhi Reservations** WelcomHeritage, 31 FF, Siri Fort Road, New Delhi **Tel** 011-26266651-54 **Jodhpur Reservations** Balsamand Palace, Mandore Road, Jodhpur **Tel** 0291-2572321-27

JP Tourist Village Resort
Location Outskirts, 1 km from fair ground **Address** Village Ganhera **Tel** 2772067/ 3366 **Mobile** 09829052326 **Website** pushkarhotel booking.com **Rooms** 35 **Tariff** Rs 850-1,500; TE **Credit Cards** AmEx, Visa, Master, BoB **Facilities** Restaurants, travel desk, parking, swimming pool, badminton, campfire, laundry, doctor-on-call, room service, TV **Jaipur Reservations** K-15, Keshav Path, Ashok Marg, Jaipur **Tel** 0141-3022000/ 3000 **Mobile** 09351510003

Oasis India Campsite `TENTS`

Location Near Mela Ground
Address Dev Nagar Road **Tel**
09829311444 **Website** discovery
hospitality.com **Rooms** 40 tents
Tariff Rs 5,000-5,500 (with all
meals and taxes) **Credit Cards**
NA **Facilities** Restaurant, camel/
jeep safari, laundry, room service
Delhi Reservations Tel 011-
65646595 **Mobile** 09811552453

Orchard `TENTS`

Location Near fair grounds
Address Ganehra **Website**
orchard.in **Rooms** 10 luxury
tents **Tariff** Rs 15,000-20,250
Credit Cards Visa, Master
Facilities World cuisine, dining
tent, aroma therapy, cultural
programme, room service **Delhi
Reservations** Eastbound, C-41
Gulmohar Park, New Delhi **Tel**
011-26531731 **Mobile**
09899478855

Pushkar Fort `ETHNIC` `TENTS`

Location Near Pushkar Resorts
Address Motisar Road, Village
Ganehra **Tel** 2772019
Telefax 2772644 **Mobile**
09829071817 **Website**
pushkarfort.com **Rooms** 36,
tents 40 (20 permanent) **Tariff**
Rs 3,000-3,500 (inclusive of
breakfast); TE; during the fair

Pushkar Palace, on the edge of the lake, has the best sunset views

Pushkar Palace

Location Lakeside **Address**
Chhoti Basti **Tel** 2773001-03
Fax 2772226/ 952 **Website**
pushkarpalace.com **Rooms** 53
Tariff Rs 2,200-6,000; TE
Credit Cards Visa, Master
Facilities Restaurant,
swimming pool, travel desk,
safaris, parking, laundry,
doctor-on-call, room service, TV

Rs 11,500, tents Rs 7,000 **Credit
Cards** Visa, Master **Facilities**
Restaurant, swimming pool,
travel desk, safaris, village tours,
laundry, room service
Reservations Tel 011-41659622,
26236610 **Website**
palacesofindia.com

Pushkar Resorts

Location 4 km from Pushkar

Jagat Palace

Location City outskirts **Address**
Ajmer Road **Tel** 2772953-54
Telefax 2772952 **Website**
pushkarpalace.com **Rooms** 36
Tariff Rs 2,200-2,700; TE **Credit
Cards** Visa, Master **Facilities**
Restaurant, swimming pool,
travel desk, safaris, health
club, parking, laundry, room
service, TV

Address Motisar Road, Village
Ganhera **Tel** 2772944, 2772945
Fax 2772946 **Website** pushkar
resorts.com **Rooms** 40 **Tariff**
Rs 3,195-3,495; TE **Credit
Cards** AmEx, Visa, Master,
Diners **Facilities** Restaurant, bar,
travel desk, swimming pool,
games, massage, laundry, room
service, TV **Delhi Reservations**
2, Karbala Lane, Jorbagh, New

ACCOMMODATION LISTINGS

Delhi **Tel** 011-24647370, 24644797-98 **Fax** 24604610 **Email** mail@pushkarresorts.com

Royal Desert Camp TENTS
Location Lakeside **Address** Near Sunset Point, Chhoti Basti **Tel** 2772001/ 401 **Fax** 2772226 **Website** pushkarpalace.com **Rooms** 400 **Tariff** Rs 6,750; TE **Credit Cards** Visa, Master **Facilities** Restaurant, coffee shop, travel desk, camel cart, camping, safaris, laundry, doctor-on-call, attached bath **Reservations** *See Pushkar Palace on previous page*

Sajjan Bagh Resort
Location Near Gurudwara **Address** Wamdev Road **Tel** 2773821 **Mobile** 09414006150 **Website** sajjanbagh.com **Rooms** 16, cottages 6 **Tariff** Rs 500-1,500; TE **Credit Cards** NA **Facilities** Restaurant, camel safari, laundry, room service, attached bath, hot water, TV

Thar Camps TENTS
Location Opp Fair Ground **Address** Ganhera Road **Website** campthar.com **Rooms** 100 tents **Tariff** Rs 9,200-14,720 (with all meals and taxes) **Credit Cards** NA **Facilities** Dining tent, cultural programmes, camel safari **Jodhpur Reservations** Plot No. 33, Mandore Road, Near Chamu House, Jodhpur **Telefax** 0291-2573466 **Mobile** 09414128574 **Contact** Digvijay Singh **Delhi Reservations Mobile** 9891766996 **Contact** Capt Sandeep Shekhawat

Tourist Village RTDC
Location Near Brahma Temple **Address** Cattle Fair ground, Ganhera Road **Tel** 2772074 **Rooms** 30 huts **Tariff** Rs 300-

400; during the fair Rs 4,000-7,000 (with all meals), dorm bed Rs 300 (without meals); TE **Credit Cards** NA **Facilities** Restaurant, parking, laundry, doctor-on-call, room service, attached bath **Metro Reservations** *See page 454*

White House
Location Lakeside **Address** Near Marwar Bus Station, Mali Mohalla, Chhoti Basti **Tel** 2772147 **Fax** 2773370 **Website** hotelwhitehouse.com **Rooms** 15 **Tariff** Rs 150-450; TE **Credit Cards** NA **Facilities** Restaurant, laundry, massage, yoga, room service, hot water, TV

IN MERTA STD 01582
Hotel Raj Palace
Address Merta City **Tel** 220202 **Rooms** 25 **Tariff** Rs 200-800 **Credit Cards** NA **Facilities** Kitchen, room service, hot water

RANAKPUR STD 02934
Sheth Sri Anandji Kalyanji Trust DHARAMSHALA
Location Jain Temple Complex **Address** Ranakpur **Tel** 285019 **Rooms** 75 **Tariff** Rs 100 **Credit Cards** NA **Facilities** Bhojanshala, basic accommodation, attached bath with 50 rooms

Hotel Shilpi RTDC
Location Near Jain Temple **Address** Sadri, Ranakpur, Dist Pali **Tel** 285074 **Rooms** 12 **Tariff** Rs 300-700; TE **Credit Cards** NA **Facilities** Dining hall, sightseeing, laundry, room service, attached bath, hot water, TV **Metro Reservations** *See page 453*

Shivika Lake Hotel
Location Lakeside **Address** Near Ranakpur Jain Temple, Ranakpur **Tel** 285078 **Website**

HERITAGE EXPERIENCES:
RANAKPUR

Maharani Bagh Orchard Retreat
Location Near Jain Temple **Address** Sadri, Ranakpur, Dist Pali **Tel** 285105 **Telefax** 285151 **Rooms** 15 cottages **Tariff** Rs 3,000-3,800; TE **Credit Cards** AmEx, Visa, Master **Facilities** Restaurant, swimming pool, travel desk, room service, hot water, TV **Delhi Reservations** WelcomHeritage, 31, FF, Siri Fort Road, New Delhi **Tel** 011-26266650-55 **Website** welcomheritage hotels.com

Fateh Bagh Hotel
Location Near River Sadri **Address** Ranakpur, Dist Pali **Telefax** 286186 **Rooms** 11, suites 7 **Tariff** Rs 5,000-6,500; TE **Credit Cards** NA **Facilities** Restaurant, bar, gym, health club, holistic massage, nature walks, spiritual recreation, yoga, swimming pool, room service, hot water, TV **Delhi Reservations** HRH Group of Hotels, C-41 Basement, Gulmohar Park, New Delhi **Tel** 011-26611273-75 **Website** hrhhotels.com

About 80 km from Ranakpur

IN JALORE STD 02978
Harji Fort **HERITAGE**
Location Surrounded by the
Aravallis **Address** VPO Harji,
Dist Jalore **Tel** 229131 **Rooms**
7 **Tariff** Rs 1,800-2,200; TE
Credit Cards NA **Facilities**
Home kitchen, dining hall,
sightseeing, village safaris,
laundry, doctor-on-call

shivikalakehotel.com **Rooms** 13,
tents 5 **Tariff** Rs 600-3,000; TE
Credit Cards Visa, Master
Facilities Restaurant, travel
desk, jeep safari, sightseeing,
nature walk, village safari, jungle
camps, laundry, room service,
attached bath

RANTHAMBHORE NP

IN SAWAI MADHOPUR
STD 07462
Aman-i-Khas **TENTS** **SPA**
Location Near the park **Address**
Sherpur Khiljipur **Tel** 252052,
252223-25 **Website** amanresorts.
com **Rooms** 10 tents **Tariff**
Rs 34,000; TE **Credit Cards**
AmEx, Visa, Master **Facilities**
Dining tent, stepwell, spa tent,
excursions, safari, attached bath
Singapore Reservations Aman
Resorts Corporate Office,
1, Orchard Spring Lane, 05-01,
Tourism Court, Singapore
Tel 00-65-68832555

Bhadrawati Safari Lodge
Location Riverside **Address**
Village Savati, Dharampuri, PO
Daulatpura **Rooms** 11 cottages
Tariff Rs 10,000 with meals
Credit Cards NA **Facilities**
Traditional tribal kevat boat rides,
fishing, rifle shooting and treks,
safaris, laundry, swimming pool
Jaipur Reservations Karan's

Guest House, D-76, Chomu
House, C-Scheme, Jaipur
Tel 0141-2363262 **Fax** 2372919

Castle Jhoomar Baori **RTDC**
Location Hilltop **Address**
Ranthambhore Road **Tel** 220495
Rooms 12 **Tariff** Rs 1,775-4,025
(with breakfast, dinner and taxes)
Credit Cards NA **Facilities**
Restaurant, travel desk, safari,
laundry, room service, TV **Metro**
Reservations See page 453

Dev Vilas
Location Near the helipad
Address Ranthambhore Road
Tel 252168/ 94 **Website**
devvilas.com **Rooms** 21 **Tariff**
Rs 6,700-10,000; TE **Credit**
Cards AmEx, Visa, Master, BoB
Facilities Restaurant, bar,
swimming pool, safari, laundry,
room service, TV **Delhi Reserva-**
tions Palaces of India, 75 GF,
Sant Nagar, East of Kailash, New
Delhi **Tel** 011-41659622
Website palacesofindia.com

Hammir Wildlife Resort
Location Near the park **Address**
Ranthambhore Road **Tel** 220562
Mobile 09414496566 **Website**
hammirwildliferesort.com
Rooms 30 **Tariff** Rs 900-2,000;
TE **Credit Cards** Visa, Master
Facilities Restaurant, travel
desk, swimming pool, safari,
cultural shows, laundry, room
service, attached bath, TV

Hotel Vinayak **RTDC**
Location 3 km from park
Address Tourist Complex,
Ranthambhore Road **Tel** 221333
Fax 222299 **Rooms** 14 **Tariff**
Rs 800-1,700; TE **Credit Cards**
NA **Facilities** Dining hall, safari,
laundry, room service, attached
bath, hot water, TV **Metro**
Reservations See page 453

Pugmark Resort
Location 4 km from the park,
Near Khiljipur **Address**
Ranthambhore Road **Tel**
252205 **Telefax** 252206
Website the pugmarkresort.com
Rooms 22, tents 6 **Tariff**
Rs 9,999-19,000 **Credit Cards**
Visa, Master **Facilities**
Restaurant, swimming pool,
massage, games, tennis court,
travel desk, laundry, room
service, attached bath, hot
water **Delhi Reservations** B-52,
FF, Amar Colony, Lajpat Nagar-
IV, New Delhi **Tel** 011-41644949,
Mobile 09873008468

Ranthambhore Safari Lodge
Location 5 km from the park
Address Ranthambhore Road
Tel 225083 **Rooms** 17, cottages
5 **Tariff** Rs 2,999-6,999 **Credit**
Cards Visa, Master **Facilities**
Restaurant, bar, safaris, cultural
evenings, swimming pool,
laundry, room service, attached
bath, hot water, TV **Delhi**
Reservations See Dev Vilas left

Sher Bagh
Location 3 km from park
Address Village Sherpur,
Khiljipur **Tel** 252119-20 **Website**

Sawai Madhopur Lodge
Location 14 km from park
Address Ranthambhore Road
Tel 220541, 220719/ 247,
223500 **Fax** 220718 **Email**
sawai.madhopur@tajhotels.
com **Rooms** 32, tents 6
Tariff Rs 9,500-13,900; TE
Credit Cards AmEx, Visa,
Master, Diners **Facilities**
Restaurant, bar, swimming
pool, indoor games, cultural
evenings, safaris, laundry, TV

sherbagh.com **Rooms** 12 **Tariff** Rs 11,475-12,375; TE **Credit Cards** Visa, Master **Facilities** Restaurant, bar, laundry, safaris, room service

The Ranthambhore Bagh

Location 12 km from park **Address** Ranthambhore Road **Tel** 224251 **Website** ranthambhorebagh.com **Rooms** 12 rooms, tents 12 **Tariff** Rs 1,400-3,575 **Facilities** Buffet dining, campfire, safaris, cultural evenings **Delhi Reservations** 21, Kailash Hills, SF, New Delhi **Tel** 26914417

Tiger Den Resort

Location 2 km from park **Address** Ranthambhore Road, Village Khiljipur **Tel** 252070 **Mobile** 09414045270 **Website** tigerdenresort.com **Rooms** 40 **Tariff** Rs 4,000; TE **Credit Cards** Visa, Master **Facilities** Restaurant, bar, safaris, nature walks, swimming pool, laundry, room service **Delhi Reservations** Nature Safari Pvt Ltd, 106-107, A-3, Sector 11, Rohini, New Delhi **Tel** 27570446, 27570581

Tiger Moon Resort

Location 2 km from park **Address** Sherpur-Khiljipur **Telefax** 252042 **Rooms** 32 cottages **Tariff** Rs 1,850-4,425; TE **Credit Cards** NA **Facilities** Dining hall, safari, nature walk, birdwatching, swimming pool, laundry, room service

Tiger Villa

Address Ranthambhore Road **Rooms** 18 **Tariff** Rs 4,000-4,500; TE **Credit Cards** AmEx, Visa, Master **Facilities** Restaurant, bar, safari, room service, attached bath, hot water **Delhi Reservations Tel** 65481693-94

Mobile 9811759245 **Website** hotelconnectionsindia.com

Vanya Vilas Wildlife Resort TENTS SPA

Address Ranthambhore Road, PO Sherpur **Tel** 223999 **Website** oberoihotels. com **Rooms** 25 luxury tents **Tariff** Rs 26,750 **Credit Cards** AmEx, Visa, Master, Diners **Facilities** Restaurant, pool, spa, fitness centre, observation tower, library-bar

RAWLA NARLAI STD 02934
HERITAGE EXPERIENCE

Rawla Narlai TENTS

Location Surrounded by the Aravallis **Address** PO Narlai, Near Jesuri, Dist Pali **Tel** 260443 **Website** narlai.com **Rooms** 20, luxury tents 5 (permanent) **Tariff** Rs 4,500-5,500; TE **Credit Cards** Visa, Master **Facilities** Kitchen, dining hall, horse riding, safaris, trekking, rock climbing, room service, TV **Jodhpur Reservations** Hotel Ajit Bhawan Palace, Jodhpur **Tel** 0291-2510410/ 610 **Fax** 2510674 **Contact** Lalit Singh Shishoria

SAMBHAR SALT LAKE
IN SAMBHAR STD 01425
Circuit House

Location Near bus stand **Address** Sambhar Salts Ltd, Sambhar **Tel** 224249/ 18 **Website** indiansalt.com **Rooms** 4 **Tariff** Rs 300-700 **Credit Cards** NA **Facilities** Kitchen, food on order, sightseeing, attached bath

SARISKA NATIONAL PARK
STD 0144

Tiger's Den RTDC

Location Near park main gate **Address** Sariska Road **Tel** 2841342/44 **Rooms** 30 **Tariff** Rs 975-3,100 with breakfast, dinner and taxes **Credit Cards** NA **Facilities** Restaurant, bar, lounge, safari, TV **Metro Reservations** See page 453

IN TEHSIL THANA GAZI STD 01465

Hotel Amanbagh SPA

Location Near Ajabgarh Dam **Address** Village Ajabgarh, Tehsil Thana Gazi **Tel** 223333-34 **Fax** 223335 **Website** amanresorts.com **Rooms** 40 **Tariff** Rs 25,000-50,000; TE **Credit Cards** AmEx, Visa, Master **Facilities** Restaurant, bar, lounge, library, board swimming pool, spa, safaris, sightseeing, room service **Singapore Reservations** Aman Resorts Corp Office, 1, Orchard Spring Lane, 05-01, Tourism Court, Singapore **Tel** 00-65-68832555

Hotel Tiger Heaven

Location Near Thank You Board **Address** Tehsil Thana Gazi **Tel** 224815-17 **Mobile** 09414016312 **Rooms** 10 **Tariff** Rs 1,250-3,100; TE **Credit Cards** NA **Facilities** Dining hall, excursions, laundry, doctor-on-call, TV **Delhi Reservations** WelcomHeritage, 31, FF, Siri Fort Road, New Delhi **Tel** 011-26266650-55 **Website** welcomheritagehotels.com

The Fort View Sariska

Location Facing Thana Gazi Fort **Address** Tehsil Thana Gazi **Website** theconsortium hotels.com **Rooms** 10 tents

GIREESH GV

Hotel Sariska Palace
Location Inside the reserve
Address Sariska **Tel** 2841322-25 **Email** sariska@del2.vsnl.net.in **Rooms** 111 **Tariff** Rs 6,666 (with meals and taxes) **Credit Cards** Master, Visa **Facilities** Buffet dining, bar, swimming pool, health club, safaris, hot water **Delhi Reservations** B-66, Hill View Apartments, Vasant Vihar, New Delhi **Tel** 011-32498570-75 **Mobile** 09350866151

Tariff Rs 3,000; TE **Credit Cards** NA **Facilities** Dining hall, sightseeing, village tour, cycling, attached bath, hot water **Delhi Reservations Mobile** 09810726252

SHEKHAWATI

IN CHURU STD 01562
Hotel Chirmi Churu **RTDC**
Location Near Panchayat
Address Behind Panchayat Samiti, Bhaleri Road Housing Board Colony, Churu **Tel** 256272 **Rooms** 4 **Tariff** Rs 300-400 **Credit Cards** NA **Facilities** Dining hall, kitchen, laundry, room service, hot water, TV **Metro Reservations** See page 454

IN FATEHPUR STD 01571
Hotel Haveli **RTDC**
Location NH11 **Address** Fatehpur **Tel** 230293 **Rooms** 8, dorm 1 **Tariff** Rs 300-700; Rs 75 **Credit Cards** NA **Facilities** Restaurant, sightseeing on request, room service, hot water, TV **Metro Reservations** See page 454

IN JHUNJHUNU STD 01592
Hotel Jamuna Resort
Location Opp Nathji ka Tila
Address Delhi-Pilani Road, Jhunjhunu **Tel** 232871 **Rooms** 14 **Tariff** Rs 800-1,500 **Credit Cards** AmEx, Visa, Master **Facilities** Restaurant, swimming pool, camel/ horse/ donkey rides (for Taiwanese tourists) can be arranged, room service, TV

Hotel Shiv Shekhawati
Location Near Muni Ashram
Address Khemisati Road, Jhunjhunu **Tel** 512695, 232651 **Rooms** 18 **Tariff** Rs 800-1,200 **Credit Cards** Visa, Master **Facilities** Restaurant, laundry, doctor-on-call, sightseeing, room service, hot water, TV

Tourist Bungalow **RTDC**
Location Mountainview
Address Mandawa Modh, Jhunjhunu **Tel** 238266 **Rooms** 6 **Tariff** Rs 300-400 **Credit Cards** NA **Facilities** Restaurant, room service, hot water **Metro Reservations** See page 454

IN MANDAWA STD 01592
Desert Resort
Location Near the town
Address Mandawa, Dist Jhunjhunu **Tel** 223245/ 514-15 **Fax** 223151 **Website** mandawahotels.com **Rooms** 70 **Tariff** Rs 2,500-12,000; TE **Credit Cards** AmEx, Visa, Master **Facilities** Restaurant, laundry, parking facility, room service, hot water, TV **Jaipur Reservations** Mandawa Haveli, Sansar Chandra Road, Jaipur **Tel** 0141-5101113, 5102510

ACCOMMODATION LISTINGS

HERITAGE EXPERIENCES: SHEKHAWATI

IN BAGAR STD 01592
The Piramal Haveli
Location Surrounded by other
havelis **Address** Village Bagar,
Dist Jhunjhunu **Tel** 221220
Rooms 8 **Tariff** Rs 1,500-2,000;
TE **Credit Cards** AmEx, Visa,
Master **Facilities** Restaurant,
hot water **Delhi Reservations**
Neemrana Hotels, A-58,
Nizamuddin East, New Delhi
Tel 011-24356145/ 8962
Fax 24351112 **Website**
neemranahotels.com

SANJOY GHOSH

Rooms 70 **Tariff** Rs 2,500-
12,000; TE **Credit Cards** AmEx,
Visa, Master **Facilities**
Restaurant, swimming pool,
laundry, parking, room service,
hot water, TV **Jaipur**
Reservations See Desert
Resort on previous page

IN DUNDLOD STD 01594
Dera Dundlod Fort
Location Central **Address**
Dundlod, Dist Jhunjhunu **Tel**
252199 **Telefax** 252519
Website dundlod.com **Rooms**
24 **Tariff** Rs 2,000-3,850; TE
Credit Cards AmEx, Visa,
Master, BoB **Facilities**
Restaurant, horse safari, puppet
shows, folk dances, laundry,
outdoor games, room service,
TV **Jaipur Reservations**
Dundlod House, Civil Lines,
Jaipur **Tel** 0141-221498/ 2537

IN MAHANSAR STD 01595
Narayan Niwas Palace
Location Adjoining the market
Address PO Mahansar, Dist
Jhunjhunu **Telefax** 264322
Rooms 16 **Tariff** Rs 800-1,200;
TE **Credit Cards** NA **Facilities**
Restaurant, bar, camel/ jeep/
horse safari, wildlife tours,
laundry, room service,
swimming pool, TV

IN MANDAWA STD 01592
Hotel Castle Mandawa
Location Central **Address**
Mandawa, Dist Jhunjhunu **Tel**
223124/ 480/ 432 **Fax** 223171
Website mandawahotels.com

IN MUKUNDGARH STD 01594
Mukundgarh Fort
Address Mukundgarh, Dist
Jhunjhunu **Tel** 252397-98
Rooms 49 **Tariff** Rs 1,500-
2,500; TE **Credit Cards** NA
Facilities Restaurant, camel
cart rides, garden, laundry,
swimming pool, room service,
TV **Delhi Reservations**
Pleasure Hotels Private Limited,
D-16, Phase I, Okhla Industrial
Area, New Delhi **Tel** 011-
26372565, 26372566 **Email**
pleasure hotels@rediffmail.com

IN NAWALGARH STD 01594
Roop Niwas Kothi
Address Nawalgarh, Dist
Jhunjhunu **Tel** 224152 **Fax**
220088 **Rooms** 37 **Tariff** Rs
1,700-3,000; TE **Credit Cards**
AmEx **Facilities** Restaurant,
billiards room, garden, horse
safari, swimming pool, room
service, TV

Hotel Mandawa Haveli
Location Near Sonthaliya
Gate **Address** Mandawa **Tel**
223088 **Fax** 224060 **Rooms** 20
Tariff Rs 1,550-2,700; TE
Credit Cards Visa **Facilities**
Restaurants, sightseeing, camel
safari, puppet show, folk
dances, Rajasthani, Ayurvedic
and Kairali massages, laundry,
room service, hot water

Hotel Shekhawati
Location Near Mukundgarh
Road **Address** Mandawa **Tel**
223036 **Mobile** 09314698079
Rooms 20 **Tariff** Rs 300-800
Credit Cards NA **Facilities**
Restaurant, camel safari, doctor-
on-call, laundry, room service,
hot water, TV

Jai Niwas Resort
Location Near Desert Resort
Address Mandawa, Dist
Jhunjhunu **Tel** 223245/ 514-15
Fax 223151 **Website** mandawa
hotels.com **Rooms** 10 **Tariff**
Rs 2,500-12,000; TE **Credit
Cards** AmEx, Visa, Master
Facilities Restaurant (only
breakfast), other meals
provided at Desert Resort,
laundry, parking, room service,
hot water, TV **Jaipur Reservations** See Desert Resort on
previous page

IN NAWALGARH STD 01594
Apani Dhani Lodge **FARM-STAY**
Location Near Nawalgarh
Address Jhunjhunu Road,
Nawalgarh **Tel** 222239 **Fax**
224061 **Website** apanidhani.com
Rooms 8 **Tariff** Rs 600-1,450
Credit Cards NA **Facilities**
Home made organic food,
guided visits to havelis of
Shekhawati, camel cart tours,
handicraft workshops with local
artisans, walk

IN ALSISAR STD 01595

Alsisar Mahal is about 23 km from Jhunjhunu

Alsisar Mahal HERITAGE

Location Old Fort **Address** Village Alsisar, Dist Jhunjhunu **Tel** 275271-72 **Website** alsisar haveli.com **Rooms** 35 **Tariff** Rs 2,400-3,650; TE **Credit Cards** AmEx, Visa, Master **Facilities** Restaurant, bar, pool, recreation area, guides, room service

IN PACHAR STD 01576

Golden Castle Resort is 105 km from Nawalgarh

Golden Castle Resort HERITAGE

Location Near Ganpat Jheel **Address** Village Pachar, Dist Sikar **Tel** 264611 **Website** castlepachar.com **Rooms** 7, suites 9 **Tariff** Rs 1,575-1,800 **Credit Cards** Visa, Master **Facilities** Dining hall, safaris, boating, fishing, village tour, room service **Jaipur Reservations** Malvea Apartments, Sardar Patel Marg, C-Scheme, Jaipur **Tel** 0141-2352127

IN SURAJGARH STD 01596

Surajgarh Fort is about 37 km from Jhunjhunu

Surajgarh Fort HERITAGE

Location Marketplace **Address** Village Surajgarh, Shekhawati, Dist Jhunjhunu **Tel** 238370 **Website** surajgarh.com **Rooms** 14 suites **Tariff** Rs 3,000-5,000; TE **Credit Cards** Visa, Master **Facilities** Dining hall, bar, pool, puppet shows, folk dance and music, TV **Delhi Reservations Tel** 011–25885709 **Mobile** 09810024711 **Contact** Manav

Hotel Anand Bhawan

Location Lake view **Address** Fateh Sagar Road **Tel** 2523018-19 **Fax** 2523247 **Rooms** 25 **Tariff** Rs 925-1,650; TE **Credit Cards** Visa, Master **Facilities** Restaurant, bar, laundry, room service, attached bath, hot water, TV

Hotel Hilltop Palace

Location Atop Ambavgarh Hill **Address** 5, Ambavgarh Gate, Fateh Sagar **Tel** 2432245-47 **Fax** 2432136 **Email** hilltop@bppl.net.in **Rooms** 58 **Tariff** Rs 3,250-4,000; TE **Credit Cards** Visa, Master **Facilities** Restaurant, bar, shopping arcade, swimming pool, recreation centre, puppet shows, laundry, room service, TV

Hotel Kajri RTDC

Location Hilltop **Address** Shastri Circle **Tel** 2410501-02 **Telefax** 2410503 **Rooms** 63 **Tariff** Rs 450-990 **Credit Cards** NA **Facilities** Restaurant, bar, sightseeing, travel desk, drivers' dorm, room service, TV **Metro Reservations** See page 454

Hotel Lake Pichola

Location Lakeside **Address** Outside Chandpole **Tel** 2430387/1197 **Fax** 2530575 **Website** lakepicholahotel.com **Rooms** 31 **Tariff** Rs 1,700-4,000; TE **Credit Cards** Visa, Master **Facilities** Restaurant, sightseeing, doctor-on-call, laundry, room service, TV

Hotel Lakend

Location Lakeside **Address** Alkapuri, Fateh Sagar Lake **Tel** 2431400-01 **Mobile** 09829044432 **Website** lakend.com **Rooms** 80 **Tariff** Rs 1,800-2,000; TE **Credit Cards** AmEx, Visa, Master **Facilities** Restaurant, bar, swimming pool, cultural

programmes, laundry, shopping arcade, room service, TV

Hotel Paras Mahal

Location Near Paras Cinema **Address** Hiran Magri, Sector 11 **Tel** 2483391-94 **Fax** 2584103 **Email** hotparas@datainfosys.net **Rooms** 60 **Tariff** Rs 2,500-3,600; TE **Credit Cards** AmEx, Visa, Master **Facilities** Restaurant, swimming pool, travel desk, room service, TV **Gurgaon Reservations** Carnival Hotels, DLF, Plot No. 56, Sector 44, Gurgaon **Tel** 0124-6452704

Hotel Sarovar

Location By Lake Pichola **Address** Outside Chandpole **Tel** 2432801-03 **Fax** 2431732 **Website** hotelsarovar.com **Rooms** 21 **Tariff** Rs 1,595-1,995; TE **Credit Cards** AmEx, Visa, Master **Facilities** Restaurant, laundry, room service, hot water, TV

Hotel Shambhu Vilas

Location Near Pichola Lake **Address** Lake Palace Road **Tel** 2421921 **Email** paratour95@hotmail.com **Rooms** 9 **Tariff** Rs 600-1,050; TE **Credit Cards** Visa, Master **Facilities** Restaurant, laundry, room service, hot water, TV

Hotel Trident

Location By Lake Pichola **Address** Haridasji Ki Magri **Tel** 2432200 **Website** hotelhilton.com **Rooms** 143 **Tariff** Rs 8,750-9,250; TE **Credit Cards** AmEx, Visa, Master, Diners **Facilities** Restaurant, book shop, pool, laundry, room service, TV **Reservations** Toll free No. 1800112122

Hotel Quality Inn Vishnupriya

Location Near Udaipur Hospital

ACCOMMODATION LISTINGS

Amet Haveli

Location Near Lake Pichola **Address** Outside Chandpole, Naga Nagri **Tel** 2431085 **Email** regiudr@datainfosys.net **Rooms** 11 **Tariff** Rs 2,500-3,000; TE **Credit Cards** Visa, Master **Facilities** Restaurant, bar, sightseeing, laundry, room service, TV

Fateh Prakash Palace

Location Near Lake Pichola **Address** City Palace Complex **Tel** 2528016-19 **Rooms** 30 **Tariff** Rs 15,700 **Credit Cards** AmEx, Visa, Master **Facilities** Restaurants, swimming pool, library, Crystal Gallery, squash courts, billiard room, Ayurvedic massage, beauty parlour, boat rides, museum, sound and light show, laundry, room service, TV **Delhi Reservations** HRH Group

Deogarh Mahal, a 17th-century heritage fort-palace hotel

MADHU KAPPARATH

of Hotels, C-41 Gulmohar Park, New Delhi **Tel** 011-26611273-75 **Website** hrhhotels.com

Hotel Caravan Serai

Location Old City **Address** 14, Lal Ghat, Jeevana House **Tel** 2521252 **Email** hotelcaravanserai @yahoo.com **Rooms** 24 **Tariff** Rs 900-1,500 **Credit Cards** Visa, Master **Facilities** Restaurant, sightseeing, room service

Jagat Niwas Palace

Location Behind Jagdish Temple **Address** 23-25, Lal Ghat **Tel** 2422860, 2415547 **Website** jagatniwaspalace.com **Rooms** 29 **Tariff** Rs 1,250-3,999; TE **Credit Cards** Visa, Master **Facilities** Restaurant, shopping arcade, travel desk, room service, TV

Kankarwa Haveli

Location Near Jagdish Temple **Address** 26 Lal Ghat **Tel** 2411457 **Rooms** 15 **Tariff** Rs 1,350-1,850; TE **Credit Cards** Visa, Master **Facilities** Home kitchen, dining hall, laundry, travel assistance, sightseeing, room service

Lake Palace Hotel

Location Jag Niwas Island **Address** PO Box 5, Lake Pichola **Tel** 2522990 **Website** tajhotels.com **Rooms** 83 **Tariff** Rs 19,500-60,000; TE **Credit Cards** AmEx, Visa, Master, Diners **Facilities** Restaurant, swimming pool, pool table, gym, room service, TV **Taj Central Reservations Tel** 55011825, Toll free No.1800111825

Rangniwas Palace Hotel

Location Near Gulab Bagh **Address** Lake Palace Road **Tel** 2523890-91 **Fax** 2427797 **Website** rangniwaspalace.com **Rooms** 20 **Tariff** Rs 880-3,000; TE **Credit Cards** NA **Facilities** Restaurant, swimming pool, sightseeing, games, laundry, TV lounge, room service

Shikarbadi Hotel

Location Amidst the Aravallis **Address** Govardhan Vihar, NH8 **Tel** 2583201-03 **Rooms** 21, suites 4 **Tariff** Rs 5,600-7,000; TE **Credit Cards** AmEx, Visa, Master **Facilities** Restaurant, helipad, laundry, room service, sanctuary, swimming pool, TV **Delhi Reservations** *See Fateh Prakash Palace left*

Shiv Niwas Palace

Location Lakeside **Address** City Palace Complex **Tel** 2528016-19 **Rooms** 36 **Tariff** Rs 6,000-21,000; TE **Credit Cards** AmEx, Visa, Master **Facilities** Restaurants, swimming pool, library, squash courts, billiards room, TV room, Ayurvedic massage, beauty parlour, museum, palace band, classical music, solar and motor boat rides, room service, TV **Delhi Reservations** *See Fateh Prakash Palace left*

IN BAMBORA STD 0294

Karni Fort

Location Outskirts of Udaipur **Address** Village Bambora, Tehsil Girwah, Dist Udaipur **Tel** 2398283-84/ 220 **Website** karni hotels.com **Rooms** 20, suites 10 **Tariff** Rs 2,800-5,000; TE **Credit Cards** AmEx, Visa, Master **Facilities** Restaurant, horse riding, swimming pool, indoor games, children's play area, village safari, drivers' dorm, complimentary food for drivers, laundry, room service **Jodhpur Reservations** Hotel Karni Bhawan, Palace Road, Ratanada, Jodhpur **Tel** 0291-2512101-02 **Fax** 2512105

IN DEOGARH STD 02904

Deogarh Mahal

Location On a hillock **Address** Deogarh Madaria, Dist Rajsamand **Tel** 252777, 253333 **Mobile** 09810726252 **Website** deogarhmahal.com **Rooms** 60 **Tariff** Rs 4,999-9,999; TE **Credit Cards** AmEx, Visa, Master **Facilities** Restaurants, bar, travel desk, Ayurvedic massage, games, swimming pool, Jacuzzi, health club, room service

Address 9, Garden Road, Gulabh Bagh Garden **Tel** 2421313/ 315-16 **Website** hotelvishnupriya.com **Rooms** 51 **Tariff** Rs 2,100-3,000; TE **Credit Cards** AmEx, Visa, Master **Facilities** Restaurant, coffee shop, swimming pool, beauty parlour, shopping arcade, games, laundry, room service, TV

Hotel Wonderview Palace

Location In front of Bada Ram Dwara **Address** Panch Diwari Marg, outside Chandpole **Tel** 2432494/ 317 **Website** wonder viewpalace.com **Rooms** 13 **Tariff** Rs 500-3,000; TE **Credit Cards** Visa, Master **Facilities** Restaurant, travel desk, puppet shows, car rental, laundry, room service, attached bath, TV

Oriental Palace Resort

Location Central **Address** Main Road, Subhash Nagar **Tel** 2412373/ 2360 **Mobile** 09352500408 **Website** oriental palaceresort.com **Rooms** 41, suites 9 **Tariff** Rs 1,600-3,000; TE **Credit Cards** AmEx, Visa, Master, BoB **Facilities** Restaurant, coffee shop, bar, swimming pool, laundry, room service, TV

Ram Pratap Palace

Location By Lake Fateh Sagar

Address 5, Alka Puri, Fateh Sagar Lake **Tel** 2431701 **Telefax** 2431700 **Email** rpp_udr@vsnl. com **Rooms** 25 **Tariff** Rs 2,485-2,885; TE **Credit Cards** AmEx, Visa, Master **Facilities** Restaurant, bar, laundry, room service, hot water, TV **Reservations** Palaces of India, New Delhi **Tel** 011-41659622, 26236610 **Website** palacesofindia.com

Sneh Resorts

Location NH8 **Address** Ahmedabad Road **Tel** 0294-3290302 **Website** snehresorts. com **Rooms** 27 **Tariff** Rs 2,300-3,300; TE **Credit Cards** Visa, Master **Facilities** Restaurant, swimming pool, lawn tennis, room service, attached bath, hot water, TV **Delhi Reservations Tel** 011-27120001 **Mobile** 09868230002

Udai Kothi

Location Lake view **Address** Outside Chandpole, Pichola Lake **Tel** 2432810-12 **Fax** 2430412 **Email** udaikothi@ yahoo.com **Rooms** 26 **Tariff** Rs 3,800-4,300; TE **Credit Cards** Visa, Master **Facilities** Restaurant, laundry, shopping arcade, swimming pool, room service, hot water, TV

ACCOMMODATION LISTINGS

ALSO NEAR UDAIPUR

IN DHARIYAWAD STD 02950
Fort Dhariyawad is about 120 km from Udaipur

Fort Dhariyawad HERITAGE
Location Village outskirts **Address** PO Dhariyawad, Dist Udaipur **Tel** 270050 **Fax** 270074 **Rooms** 13 **Tariff** Rs 1,400-2,200; TE **Credit Cards** NA **Facilities** Home kitchen, dining hall, safaris, games, laundry, room service, attached bath, hot water
Reservations Mobile 09414296746 **Contact** Bhanu Pratap Singh

IN KOTRI STD 0293
Kotri Raola HERITAGE HOMESTAY
Location Lake view **Address** VPO Kotri, Dist Pali **Tel** 240224 **Website** kotriraola.com **Rooms** 12 **Tariff** Rs 2,000-2,500 **Credit Cards** NA **Facilities** Restaurant, horseride

Udaivilas SPA
Location Near Lake Pichola **Address** Haridasji ki Magri **Tel** 2433300 **Website** oberoihotels.com **Rooms** 90 **Tariff** Rs 22,500-1,27,000; TE **Credit Cards** AmEx, Visa, Master, Diners **Facilities** Restaurant, bar, spa, yoga, fitness centre, library, swimming pools, TV **Central Reservations** Oberoi Hotels & Resorts, Corporate Marketing Division, 7, Sham Nath Marg, Delhi **Tel** 011-23890505

IN EKLINGJI STD 0294
Heritage Resort
Location Surrounded by Aravallis **Address** Lake Bagela, Nagda, Eklingji **Tel** 2441844 **Mobile** 09414162133 **Website** heritageresort.com **Rooms** 30

and safaris, village safari, trekking, cycling, sightseeing, lessons in traditional Rajasthan cuisine, laundry, room service
Udaipur Reservations Ghanerao Hotels Pvt Ltd, 2A New Fatehpura, Near Union Bank of India, Udaipur **Tel** 0294-2560822

IN SARDARGARH STD 02908
Sardargarh is about 94 km from Udaipur

Sardargarh Heritage Hotel
Location Near Manohar Sagar Lake **Address** Sardargarh, Dist Rajsamand **Tel** 254591-92 **Website** sardargarh.in **Rooms** 21 **Tariff** Rs 5,000-9,000; TE **Credit Cards** AmEx, Visa, Master **Facilities** Restaurant, swimming pool, safaris, sightseeing, laundry, room service, attached bath, hot water, TV **Mobile** 09928209594 **Contact** Mahipal Singh

Tariff Rs 3,865-4,520 (inclusive of breakfast, dinner and taxes) **Credit Cards** AmEx, Visa, Master **Facilities** Restaurant, bar, billiards, swimming pool, room service, walking track, TV

IN NATHDWARA STD 02953
Garden View Hotel
Location Near Nathdwara Bus Stand **Address** NH8, Opp Sihad Talab **Tel** 232285 **Website** gardenviewhotel.net **Rooms** 21 **Tariff** Rs 1,300-2,350 **Credit Cards** Visa, Master **Facilities** Restaurant, travel desk, kiddy play area, garden, laundry, room service, TV **Mumbai Reservations** KM & Co, Shop No. 9, GF, 26-A, Behind Jan Kalyan Bank, Mumba Devi Road, Mumbai **Tel** 022-22423830

Hotel Gokul RTDC
Location 3 km from temple **Address** Near Lal Bagh **Tel** 230917 **Rooms** 6, dorm 1 (8 beds) **Tariff** Rs 500-750, dorm bed Rs 50 **Credit Cards** NA **Facilities** Restaurant, beer bar, travel desk, puja arrangements, laundry, doctor-on-call, room service, attached bath, hot water, TV **Metro Reservations** See page 454

Hotel Vallabh Darshan
Location Close to the temple **Address** Choupati Bazaar **Tel** 234403, 230344/ 038 **Mobile** 09829041339, 0941470333 **Telefax** 234935 **Website** hotelvallabhdarshan.com **Rooms** 45 **Tariff** Rs 550-1,950; TE **Credit Cards** NA **Facilities** Dining hall, travel desk, puja arrangements, laundry, doctor-on-call, room service, attached bath, hot water, TV

Hotel Yatrika Mangala RTDC
Location 2 km from temple **Address** Nathuvas Temple Road **Tel** 231119 **Rooms** 7, dorms 1, family room 1 **Tariff** Rs 400-500, dorm bed Rs 50 **Credit Cards** NA **Facilities** Food from outside, attached bath, hot water **Metro Reservations** See page 454

IN JAISAMAND
Jaisamand Island Resort SPA
Location On the lake **Address** Jaisamand Lake, Udaipur **Tel** 0-9928098555 **Mobile** 098290 44432 **Website** jaisamand.com **Rooms** 20, suites 15 **Tariff** Rs 2,200-6,000; TE **Credit Cards** AmEx, Visa, Master **Facilities** Restaurant, swimming pool, spa, Ayurvedic massage, shopping arcade, health club, indoor games, parking, room service, attached bath, hot water, TV

GLOSSARY

aarti Hindu ritual of worship accompanied by the ringing of bells, offering of incense and fire, and chanting or singing; a welcome ritual to honoured visitors

arayish fine plasterwork or paintings on walls, done with lime, usually on religious or historical themes

ASI Archaeological Survey of India

attar, ittar oil made from flowers and used in perfumes

baithak sitting space of a haveli

bandh gala short tunic with a closed collar

bandhani tie-and-dye work done on textiles

baoli, baori stepwell

bhapang an instrument with just one string used by the Mer community

bhojanalaya eating house

burj tower, usually of a fort

chaadar sheet or bedspread; in this case, a ritual cloth offered at a dargah

chaitya prayer hall

charbagh in its canonical Mughal form, a walled garden divided into four quarters by walkways and canals

chhatri cenotaph to honour a person whose remains usually lie elsewhere; an umbrella-like structure

chinkara light chestnut-coloured antelope

dal-baati-choorma Rajasthani speciality of wheat and millet dough balls roasted over hot coals (baati) and served with lentils (dal); crumbled baati is called choorma

dargah saint's shrine, usually a place of pilgrimage

darwaza door, gate

deg cauldron, huge containers used to cook for devotees on a large scale

dhaba roadside eating and chai place, offering cheap, sometimes also wholesome, food

dhabai nurses of the royal family

diwan-i-aam hall of public audience

diwan-i-khas hall of private audience

doli palanquin

dwarpala doorkeeper

gaddi throne

gatte ki subzi gram flour nuggets cooked in a thick gravy

ghat steps leading to a river or any water body

guada cattle camp

gumbad dome on a mosque or tomb

gur jaggery

hamam bath complex; also, a building with corridors and halls closed on all sides except for the entrance and ventilators. The complex included a cooling device and was favoured by the Mughals during summer months

haveli multi-storeyed, decorated mansion

hindola large swing with space for four

jaali latticed or perforated stone (or sometimes wooden) screens used on windows and partitions. The screens are stylised and decorated with floral and decorative designs

jagir principality, or a grant of land and its revenue. In feudal India, this used to be bestowed by an emperor on a jagirdar

jal-durg water-protected fort

jauhar mass suicide by women and children, who immolated themselves on a pyre rather than face dishonour after their clan's defeat in battle

jhanki viewing, usually of a deity in a temple

jharokha covered balcony from which elite women watched social events in privacy

jijmani patronage extended by rich Rajasthani households to a family of musicians which continued in a hereditary fashion; the musicians would then perform in various family functions such as weddings

johara reservoir

jootis traditional handcrafted leather shoes

kachori savoury dumpling, stuffed with a spicy mixture and deep fried

kagzi form of pottery that is paper-thin, a speciality of Alwar District

kalakand milk cake

Kalbelias snake dancers, wandering performing gypsies

kara bangles; also, one of the five markers of Sikh faith, the others being kesh, kangha, kirpan and kachha

kathputli puppet, made of kath, or wood used by wandering communities from Rajasthan

keema baatis wheat balls stuffed with mince

ker sangri a popular Rajasthan dish made with berries (ker), desert beans (sangri), yoghurt, chillies, turmeric and other spices

RAJASTHAN

kesar saffron

khadim dargah official

khadin irrigation technology whereby a half-moon shaped earthen dam is constructed on the lower slope of land, its size decided by the volume of rainfall in the region, the catchment area, the quality of soil and of course the water requirement

kos minar milestone, placed every kos (3 km)

kothari official in charge of the royal treasury

kund lake

kundan jewellery style in which precious stones are set in gold

lal maas red meat cooked in traditional Rajasthani style

mahajanapada ancient kingdom of North India; there were 16 such kingdoms

mandana floor patterns made with flour during festivals

mandir temple

manjeera metallic discs worn by female dancers on their arms and legs

meenakari enamelling work done on jewellery

mela carnival

mirchi vada chillies deep-fried in a besan batter

mojari handcrafted leather foowear embellished with embroidery and sequin work

mol most ornate part of a Rajasthani haveli, used for receiving important guests

mori small opening in a haveli's main gate

nadi small pond

namda woollen rug

newri anklet

odhani transparent veil used by dancers

panchdhaatu an alloy of five metals

panchmela dal dish made of five pulses

pandas local priests

parody small, round sweet made of wheat flour, powdered dry fruits, sugar and ghee

phad scroll that depicts stories associated with Pabuji, a folk hero. The Bhopa community, who play the ravanhatta instrument, highlight different parts of the scroll while narrating the corresponding part of the tale

pichhwai a painting form in which legends associated with Lord Krishna are illustrated, originally done on hand-spun fabric and hung behind (*pichhe*) the deity; found in Nathdwara and Udaipur

pol gate, particularly of a fort or a city

qila fort

RSRTC Rajasthan State Roadways Transport Corporation

RTDC Rajasthan Tourism Development Corporation

ravanhatta bowed instrument with two strings

rawal feudal chieftan

rawla small palace, at times a hunting lodge

ret-ka-qila sand fort

safed maas mutton cooked in a curry of almonds, cashewnuts and coconut kernel paste, among other ingredients

saka a system of dating used by the Saka dynasty

sarovar lake

sati a woman immolating herself on the pyre of her dead husband, a horrific patriarchal practice that is sometimes seen even today

sattu flour of gram roasted in ghee with powdered sugar added

soolas kind of kebab made of boneless venison, marinated in a paste of turmeric, red chilli powder, curd, crushed garlic and the powder of a sour desert vegetable (kachri)

subah province of an erstwhile Rajput state

taanka manmade water harvesting and storage tank with a catchment area for collecting rainfall

tazimi sardars those members of the nobility who had the privilege of remaining seated in court while the ruler entered the durbar

thakur feudal lord owing allegiance to a king

thandai rich and creamy drink with milk, nuts and spices

thikana feudal principality; fiefdom; estate

tika anointment on the forehead, usually a mark of honoured welcome

Tirthankara one of 24 Jain sages born in each half cycle of time; Mahavira is considered the last in that line. Jains don't worship gods but venerate the Tirthankaras

toshakhana royal wardrobe

van-durg forest-protected fort

vav an elaborate stepwell, sometimes graced with intricate carvings such as the one at Bundi

yagna ritual in which ceremonial fire is worshipped

zenana section of a home or palace meant for women

GO THERE FOR ...

RAJASTHAN

ABOUT THE AUTHORS

abhilash gaur spent 15 months in Maharashtra looking up caves and stone temples. Back home in Chandigarh in 2004, he continued the pursuit, driven by a fondness for archaeology. He now works with the Outlook Group in Delhi

akshay jain did many degrees in Philosophy and didn't quite know what to do with himself after that. So in true philosophical style, he wandered. And one fine day, he wandered into the office of the *Outlook Traveller* magazine. He's glad that he's paid to do what he loves best

aman nath, a historian by education, has written several books on art, architecture and history. He is the founding co-chairperson of Neemrana Hotels

amit mahajan started his career as a journeyman engineer, making journeys on engineering pretexts. These days he practises reflexology. Travelling has persisted as a primary urge

anuradha kapoor (nee Seth) is a media consultant who has worked with *India Today*, *The Indian Express*, *Business Standard* and the Oberoi Group. It was while working for the latter that she acquired an interest in hotels, which took a tangible form in a book on heritage hotels

Twenty-eight-year-old **anurupa roy**, who has several diplomas in puppet theatre, was the WISCOMP (Women in Security, Conflict Management and Peace) Fellow of Peace for 2005. She worked on a project involving trauma therapy workshops using puppets with the young women of Beejbehara in Kashmir. She is the founder-director of Kat-Katha, an association of puppeteers and storytellers

A journalist for the past 15 years, **charu soni** has worked previously with *The Statesman*, *The Hindustan Times* and *Tehelka*. She has been a consulting editor with *Outlook Traveller Getaways* for the past two-and-a-half years

deepak malik is a development worker who has been working on human rights issues for the past seven years. He has worked in Rajasthan on drought, water management, unorganised labour and child rights. He is now working with HelpAge International in Indonesia on an advocacy project for the rights and welfare of the elderly affected by the tsunami of 2004

devyani onial is an Inlaks scholar and completed her education at Columbia University, New York. A journalist with *The Indian Express* in Delhi, she enjoys writing on travel

dharmendar kanwar has several books to her credit, including coffee-table books such as *Rajasthan*, *Palace on Wheels* and *Royal Cuisine*. She is also the author of *Jaipur 10 Easy Walks* and *Enduring Grace* (a biography of Rajmata Gayatri Devi). She has co-authored *The Living Traditions of Rajasthan* and edited *Gourmet's Gateway* with Gayatri Devi

dilbagh singh is a professor of medieval Indian history at the Centre for Historical Studies, Jawaharlal Nehru University. His published work includes the book *State, Landlords and Peasants: Rajasthan in the 18th Century*, as well as several research articles on Rajasthan's history. He was the former chairperson of the Centre for Historical Studies at JNU and president of the Rajasthan History Congress 2005

gillian wright is an author and journalist living in New Delhi. She is a keen birdwatcher and was one of the first people to see the bristled grassbird in Delhi after a long absence. She has written guides on Indian wildlife and hill stations, and on Sri Lanka. She is also co-author, with Mark Tully, of *India in Slow Motion*

himraj dang has worked in infrastructure finance and development. He is an advisor to various environmental projects and private equity investments

ilay cooper has spent much of his life in Rajasthan. In 1972, cycling across North India, he entered Churu and was impressed by its then-ignored murals. Based in Churu, he explored

Shekhawati's havelis, later documenting 2,260 local buildings for INTACH. He has published numerous articles and papers and given lectures on sub-continental murals. His books include *The Painted Towns of Shekhawati* (revised edition due 2006, Prakash Books, Delhi); *Arts and Crafts of India* (1996, Thames and Hudson, London); *Traditional Buildings of India* (1998, Thames and Hudson, London); and *Havelis of Rajasthan* (due 2006, Abhinav, New Delhi)

juhi saklani writes, researches, travels and practises acupressure

For someone who has packed in more visits to more places than most people in a few years, perhaps it is poetic justice that **kishore singh** now finds himself confined to his desk as an editor at *Business Standard*. But if you can't travel, it doesn't mean you can't write about it. Our armchair travel writer has done everything from books to films on Rajasthan

Former travel writer and naturalist **meenakshi pandey** now dons the role of Girl Friday at her husband's holiday resort in Corbett

Her idea of perfect happiness involves a comfy monthly salary cheque that isn't tied up to anything as mundane as work. In that quest, journalist **muneeza naqvi** is onto her third job in as many years. When she isn't travelling or shifting offices, she enjoys cooking and cleaning and doing the dishes. Honestly

nirad grover has been writing on travel for more than a decade. His work, which includes photography, has been published in magazines and newspapers in India and abroad. He has edited books on travel and history and runs his own book packaging firm in Delhi

prakash tyagi is the director of GRAVIS, a Rajasthan-based organisation that works for the empowerment of communities in the Thar Desert, with a focus on community healthcare, water management, human rights and education. He has an MD in Medicine and has also studied international health policies and public health issues in the US on a Fulbright Fellowship

A hobby historian who has followed royal life-styles, **pushpita singh** does not consider herself a writer. She enjoys cooking and lays a good table. Pushpita also designs jewellery. There's more money in it than in writing, she explains

rakesh kalshian is a journalist and is the head of environment programmes at Panos South Asia

sanjay singh badnor is a travel writer-cum-photographer based in Ajmer. His work has been published in numerous newspapers, travel magazines, websites and guidebooks. Sanjay worked as a stills photographer for an Australian Television documentary film on Indian royalty. He is also a stringer for *The Times of India*

shikha jain is the Director of Development and Research Organisation for Nature, Arts and Heritage and is currently working on conservation projects in Haryana and Rajasthan. She is the principal coordinator for the master planning of the City Palace Complex at Udaipur, funded by the Getty Foundation, USA. She is also the state co-convenor for INTACH's Haryana chapter

tara sahgal, herbivorous, crepuscular and often arboreal, lives and works in Mumbai. She is the editor of the *Sanctuary Cub* magazine, which is a wildlife bi-monthly for children

tripti pandey has a deep love for culture and her passion for Rajasthan's folk music and dance resulted in the book *Where Silence Sings*. She is a travel writer who likes highlighting features of various cultures. She was honoured with the Austrian President's Gold Medal in 2003

vipul mudgal has worked for over 20 years in the print and electronic media, with organisations such as *India Today* (Chandigarh), BBC World Service (London and New Delhi) and *Asia Times* (Bangkok). In 1991 he was awarded the Nehru Centenary British Fellowship to pursue his PhD at Leicester, UK, which he finished in 1995. He later joined *Hindustan Times* to launch its Jaipur edition as resident editor and is now based in New Delhi as associate editor. Vipul writes regularly on Rajasthan, particularly on issues of society, droughts and desert ecology

INFORMATION

INFORMATION

INFORMATION

PHOTO CREDITS

Back Cover
Above: Ferris wheel at the Pushkar Mela **DINODIA PHOTO LIBRARY**
Below: Camels at the Pushkar Cattle Fair **DINODIA PHOTO LIBRARY**

Inside the book

AMIT PASRICHA
Page 169 Water wheel in Mount Abu
Page 242 Women engaged in embroidery

DINESH SHUKLA
Page 119 Taragarh Fort, Bundi

DINODIA PHOTO LIBRARY
Pages 94-95 Golden green fields
around Kalakho

GIREESH GV
CONTENTS Page 4 Fresco on a haveli wall
in Shekhawati
Page 217 Nagaur Cattle Fair
SHOPPING *Page 399* Diyas

INDIAPICTURE
CONTENTS *Page 4* Desert Festival,
Jaisalmer **MD SHARMA**
Page 5 A Rajasthani woman
BN KHAZHANCHI

JAGDEEP RAJPUT
CONTENTS *Page 6* Owls at Ranthambhore
National Park

MADHU KAPPARATH
CONTENTS *Page 7* Haveli in Nawalgarh

MALINI SHARMA
CONTENTS *Page 5* Nachana Haveli in
Jaisalmer

SANJAY SHARMA
CONTENTS *Page 5* Palace-on-Wheels
Page 7 Camel safari
SHOPPING *Page 400* Marble elephant
Page 402 Jewellery

SANJEEV VERMA
Page 100 A woman dressed in traditional
Rajasthani attire

SHASHWAT SAXENA
SHOPPING *Page 402* Wooden inlay box

T NARAYAN
CONTENTS *Page 6* A Rajasthani man tries
on a new jacket

TRIBHUVAN TIWARI
CONTENTS *Page 7* At the Chokhi Dhani
kitchen

ACKNOWLEDGEMENTS

Outlook Traveller Getaways would like to thank Manoj Kulshrestha of Wildbrook in Rajaji National Park;
Sumita Saroch (Assistant Director) and RK Saini (Assistant Tourist Officer) of Rajasthan Tourism, Delhi; Sandip
Shrivastva of RTDC, Kota; Jai Vardhan and Harsh Vardhan of Sukhdham Kothi, Kota; Chandrajit Singh of Prithvi
Vilas Palace, Jhalawar; Kishore Singh, Delhi; Sanjay Badnor, Ajmer; Venkatesh of Devi Garh; BS Rajawat of Forts
& Palaces Tours, Jaipur; Deepak Malik, a development worker currently with HelpAge International, Indonesia;
Ishika Gems and Stones; and Silver Art Palace

RAJASTHAN STATE GUIDE

FEEDBACK FORM

We need your valuable suggestions to help us improve our guide and make it more user friendly. Mail this form to enable us to send you free updates on special packages, events and new destinations

PERSONAL INFORMATION

(BLOCK LETTERS PLEASE)

Name (Mr/ Ms) ....

Address..

....

....

PIN Code ....

Tel. ....

Email..

Age .... Gender: Male ☐ Female ☐

Occupation ....

Organisation ....

Single/ Married ....

No. of Children/ Ages ....

TRAVEL HISTORY

1. How often do you take a vacation?

Every 1-2 months ☐

Every 3-6 months ☐

Every 6-12 months ☐

Others (please specify) ☐

....

2. How long was your last vacation?

Weekend ☐

1-2 weeks ☐

2-4 weeks ☐

Others (please specify) ☐

....

3. Where did you stay?

Hotels/ Resorts ☐

Govt accommodation ☐

Friends/ Relatives ☐

4. How much did you spend on your vacation?

Less than Rs 5,000 ☐

Rs 5,000-Rs 10,000 ☐

Rs 10,000-Rs 20,000 ☐

Rs 20,000 and above ☐

5. Your idea of a holiday?

Adventure ☐

Leisure ☐

Pilgrimage ☐

Wildlife ☐

Others (please specify) ☐

....

6. Do you refer to a guide during your travels?

Yes ☐   No ☐

If yes, please specify ....

ABOUT US

1. Where did you hear about this book?

Advertising in the Outlook Group magazines ☐

Bookshop/ newsagent ☐

www.outlooktraveller.com ☐

Others (please specify) ☐

....

2. Rate us

Excellent (E)   Good (G)   Fair (F)   Average (A)

Content ☐   Design ☐

Destinations ☐   Facts ☐

Route guides ☐   Photographs ☐

YOUR RECOMMENDATIONS

I recommend for inclusion/ exclusion

Name of accommodation/ restaurant/ sights/ place

....

....

Address..

....

Tel. ....

Reason ....

....

....

....

Make as many recommendations as you like. Attach with this form and drop it in the mail.

Mail to

The Editor
OutlookTraveller.com
AB-10, Safdarjung Enclave
New Delhi-110029